D1595779

A Crisis
of the Weimar Republic:

A Study of the German Referendum
of 20 June 1926

A Crisis
of the Weimar Republic:

A Study of the German Referendum
of 20 June 1926

Franklin C. West

The American Philosophical Society
Independence Square Philadelphia
1985

MEMOIRS OF THE

AMERICAN PHILOSOPHICAL SOCIETY

Held at Philadelphia
For Promoting Useful Knowledge
Volume 164

Library of Congress Catalog Card No. 83-73277
International Standard Book No. 0-87169-164-7
US ISSN 0065-9738

For
M. U. W.

Contents

PREFACE

This work is a considerably revised version of my Ph.D. dissertation, "The Parties, the Princes, and the People: A Study of the German Referendum of June 20, 1926," completed at the University of California at Berkeley in 1970. The bulk of the research was undertaken some years earlier, in the early sixties, primarily in the collections of the University of California Library and the Hoover Library in Palo Alto, and then, thanks to the Class of 1883 Traveling Fellowship, in West Germany where I was able to make use of important documentary materials at the *Bundesarchiv* and the newspaper holdings of the *Institut für Zeitungsforschung* in Dortmund. Since that time I have attempted to keep up to date with the steady stream of publications relevant to the subject, but have not had the opportunity for further archival research.

The observant reader may note certain peculiarities in the citation of documents. These stem from the time and circumstances in which the basic research was completed. References to the records of the Reich cabinet meetings and related documents are to the microfilm collection of the "Kabinettsprotokolle" rather than to the documentary vol-

ix

umes now in the course of publication.[1] Likewise, I used the papers of the *Deutsche Demokratische Partei* in microfilm form, rather than the actual documents themselves now at the *Bundesarchiv* in Koblenz. An effort has been made to cite these documents clearly in terms of date and origin, as well as by microfilm reel and frame number, to facilitate reference to the actual documents, if that is desired. A number of important collections of personal papers have also become available since my trip to Germany in 1962–63 (most notably the *Nachlässe* of Erich Koch-Weser, Wilhelm Marx, Kuno Graf Westarp, and Otto Braun) but an examination of the recent monograph by Ulrich Schüren,[2] who has had access to these and other personal papers, suggests that while their use would have added further detail to this study, it would not have altered the main line of argumentation.

I am in the somewhat problematic situation of now publishing the results of my research after Dr. Schüren's more recent investigation has appeared in print. (He did not know of my dissertation until after the completion of his manuscript.) [3] Given these circumstances, some readers may question the need for two detailed historical studies concentrating on the same set of events. Although much has been written on the history of the Weimar Republic, scholarly attention has tended to concentrate on the revolutionary and immediately post-revolutionary period of 1918–23 or on the end phase culminating in the triumph of Hitler in 1933. Relatively little attention has been paid to the so-called "good years" between 1924 and the onset of the depression in 1929. In the following study I hope to elucidate prevalent attitudes which demonstratively affected the practice of politics in that rather understudied period.

Dr. Schüren has written a carefully researched account of the controversy over the property settlements made with Germany's former ruling families after 1918 and the ensuing *Fürstenenteignung* referendum in 1926. These subjects are clearly the main topic of the present volume as well; but I believe that the reader will recognize other themes of re-

---

[1] Germany. Reichskanzlei. *Akten der Reichskanzlei.* Weimarer Republik. *Die Kabinette Luther I und II.,* ed. Karl-Heinz Minuth, 2 vols. (Boppard am Rhein, 1977). The volume on the third Marx cabinet has not yet appeared. It has not been possible to include references to scholarly publications obtained after 1980.

[2] Ulrich Schüren, *Der Volksentscheid zur Fürstenenteignung 1926, Beiträge zur Geschichte des Parlamentarismus und der politischen Parteien,* 64 (Düsseldorf, 1978).

[3] Ibid., p. 16, note 17.

search interest which go beyond what Schüren has attempted, namely, the malfunctioning of both parliamentary and ple- biscitary forms of legislation when attempted *simultaneously,* the substantial difficulties impeding political cooperation (co- alitions) in a multiparty system, and the persistent recurrence of divisions *within* the various political parties which often affected the formulation of party tactics and policy.

The lengthy discussions of party history and factionalism which interrupt my account of the initiative and referendum campaign developed directly from an effort to understand why several important parties made a number of inconsistent policy decisions during the course of the year-long contro- versy in 1925–26. I have paid particular attention to the conduct of the Social Democratic Party, justified by the key role it played in the calculations of other parties. However, the behavior of other important parties has been examined as well, and one must conclude that mistaken judgments and the disavowal of expected commitments were not weaknesses peculiar to one party alone. Simply stated, no party's lead- ership could or would undertake actions which threatened its own party's unity. Commitments to other parties, policies which otherwise had arguable advantages, were abandoned at the threat of a party split.

Party leaders with good reason feared any disruption of party unity and effectiveness, as well as outspoken challenges to their own authority as leaders. The *Fürstenenteignung* ref- erendum campaign multiplied such challenges and, in a num- ber of cases, seriously disrupted party harmony. In part this was due to the exceptional nature of the issue itself, but fundamentally the threat to established party loyalties lay in the nature of initiative and referendum proceedings as such. There are only two sides in a referendum election; if voters participate, they must vote either "yes" or "no." The estab- lished patterns of German parliamentary life and election- eering were not well adapted to simple bipolar decisions. In a multiparty system each party consistently stressed its sep- arate and distinctive identity in matters of policy, doctrine, and organization. The pressures of a referendum campaign worked against the maintenance of separate positions; it forced some parties into awkward and unwanted associations. Furthermore, in accord with democratic theory but much to the surprise of some party leaders, the initiative and refer- endum encouraged many voters to decide for themselves how to vote, ignoring the instructions of their party officials. All these things created a mood of uncertainty, frustration, and, at times, alarm. The working of democracy, even in the relatively stable years of the mid-twenties, was not reassuring, as numerous quotations from contemporaries make clear.

Historians in the German Democratic Republic have devoted considerable attention to the *Fürstenenteignung* campaign. In their view it reveals the successful implementation of *Einheitsfront* tactics by the German Communist Party under the leadership of Ernst Thälmann.[4] Like Dr. Schüren, I think these writers overrate the actual successes of the United Front tactics and are hampered by the interpretive limitations of an official historiography.[5] Yet, some regional studies of the referendum campaign contain solid and enlightening information.[6] Historians and political scientists in the Federal Republic have tended to pass over the initiative and referendum campaigns of the Weimar Republic despite their strong interest in the history of the political parties and parliamentary elections. A few years ago, Reinhard Schiffers published a useful but rather dry study of the legal and political discussions of the plebiscitary elements in the Weimar constitution, in which he enumerated and briefly described the various efforts to carry out initiative and referendum proceedings on

---

[4] Heinz Karl, *Der deutsche Arbeiterklasse in Kampf um die Enteignung der Fürsten (1925/1926)*, Institut für Marxismus-Leninismus beim ZK der SED, *Beiträge zur Geschichte und Theorie der Arbeiterbewegung*, 20 (Berlin, 1957); Mirjam Kölling, "Der Kampf der Kommunistischen Partei Deutschlands unter der Führung Ernst Thälmanns für die Einheitsfront in den ersten Jahren der relativen Stabilisierung (1924 bis 1927)," *Zeitschrift für Geschichtswissenschaft*, 2 (Nr. 1, 1954): 3–36; Heinz Habedank, "Die Aktionseinheit der Arbeiterparteien gegen die Fürstenabfindung 1926 und die freien Gewerkschaften," *Die Arbeit. Theoretische Zeitschrift des FDGB* (Nr. 10, 1966), pp. 50–53. I have been unable to consult Ilse Kelbert-Girard, "Die grosse Volksbewegung für die entschädigungslose Fürstenenteignung. Volksbegehren und Volksentscheid 1926" (dissertation, Humboldt University, Berlin, 1960).

[5] Schüren, pp. 15–17.

[6] Erwin Könnemann, "Die Verhinderung der entschädingungslosen Enteignung der Fürsten 1925/26," *Wissenschaftliche Zeitschrift der Martin-Luther-Universität Halle-Wittenberg. Gesellschafts- und Sprachwissenschaftliche Reihe*, 7 (Nr. 3, 1957/58): 541–60; Gerhard Knoch, "Der Kampf der Magdeburger Bezirksorganisation der KPD gegen die Fürstenabfindung 1926," *Wissenschaftliche Zeitschrift der Technischen Hochschule Otto von Guericke Magdeburg*, 10 (Nr. 4, 1966): 417–24; Martin Kasper, "Oberlausitzer werktätige Bauern im Kampf gegen Fürstenabfindung, für den Reichskongress der Werktätigen," *Wissenschaftliche Zeitschrift der Universität Rostock. Gesellschafts- und Sprachwissenschaftliche Reihe*, 17 (Nr. 2/3, 1968): 173–80; and Werner Fritsch, "Die Massenbewegung der Werktätigen für die Enteignung der Fürsten 1925/26 in Thüringen," *Wissenschaftliche Zeitschrift der Friedrich-Schiller-Universität Jena. Gesellschafts- und Sprachwissenschaftliche Reihe*, 19 (Nr. 3, 1970): 375–93.

the state and national level.[7] I hope that other scholars will follow up on his work and that of Dr. Schüren. Certainly, the fuller investigation of the important initiative and referendum campaigns of the later twenties and early thirties is a desideratum.

I consider myself fortunate to have taken my Ph.D. at the University of California. My dissertation was completed under the direction of Professor Werner T. Angress, now at the State University of New York at Stony Brook. His insistence on clarity of expression and accuracy in detail have been coupled with patient understanding and friendship. In the preparation for my research or in the writing of the dissertation I have benefited from the aid and criticism of Professors Hans Rosenberg, the late Raymond J. Sontag, Carl Schorske, Wolfgang Sauer, and Paul Seabury. My colleagues at Portland State University have given me steady encouragement; I would particularly like to thank the former head of the department, Jesse L. Gilmore. My wife, Martha Ullman West, has given editorial advice, secretarial aid, and constant support, good humor and love. To her I dedicate this book.

I would like to acknowledge the aid of the archivists and staff at the *Bundesarchiv,* Koblenz, and the *Institut für Zeitungsforschung,* Dortmund, as well as the librarians at the University of California Library, the Hoover Library, the New York Public Library, the State University of New York at Stony Brook Library, the University of Oregon Library, the University of Washington Library, the Portland State University Library, and Reed College Library. Many of the items I wished to consult have not been easy to locate; the help of reference librarians and interlibrary loan services is especially appreciated.

The editorial staff at the American Philosophical Society has overseen the transformation of a lengthy, detailed manuscript into a finished book with great care and attention. I would also like to thank my graduate assistant, Robert Lanxon, for his help in reading the proofs. Any mistakes, of course, are the responsibility of the author.

Franklin C. West

---

[7] Reinhard Schiffers, *Elemente direkter Demokratie im Weimarer Regierungssystem, Beiträge zur Geschichte des Parlamentarismus und der politischen Parteien,* 40 (Düsseldorf, 1971).

I: Introduction

The mid-twenties marked a turning point in the history of the Weimar Republic in more than just a chronological sense. Between 1919 and 1924, the government of the nation was in the hands of parties which, notwithstanding certain reservations, had committed themselves to the support of the Republic. Cabinets changed frequently—there were twelve in the first six years of the Republic—and some use was already being made of *Fachminister,* supposedly non-partisan, expert administrators.[1] Nevertheless, the character of the different cabinets was set by the participation of leading members of the Social Democratic Party (SPD), the Catholic Center Party, the Democratic Party (DDP), and the German People's Party (DVP).[2] They joined together in varying pat-

[1] Karl Dietrich Bracher, *Die Auflösung der Weimarer Republik,* 3rd ed. (Villingen/ Schwarzwald, 1960), pp. 32–33; Otto Koellruetter, *Der deutschen Staat als Bundestaat und als Parteienstaat* (Tübingen, 1927), p. 32.

[2] Most DVP members hoped for an eventual return of the monarchy. The party therefore voted against the acceptance of the Weimar Constitution in 1919. However, after the 1920 elections it started participating in governments and following Stresemann's leadership—although not without occasional strong resistance—gradually adopted the *Vernunftrepublikaner* position of conditional acceptance of the Republic. Henry Ashby Turner, Jr., *Stresemann and the Politics of the Weimar Republic* (Princeton, 1963); Roland Thimme, *Stresemann und die deutsche Volkspartei, 1923–25, Historische Studien,* 382 (Lübeck and Hamburg, 1961); Lothar Albertin, *Liberalismus*

1

terns, sometimes combining two or all four of these parties, but usually involving three of them. The normal combination was the so-called "Weimar Coalition" of the SPD, Center, and DDP. However, after 1920 control of a strong majority in the Reichstag was possible only by including the DVP as well.[3] This four-party "Great Coalition" proved difficult to form and harder still to maintain because of many basic differences between the Social Democrats and the German People's Party. As a result, politicians frequently turned to the expedient of forming rather weak minority governments which were then tolerated, at least for a time, by parties not actually represented in the cabinet. Between 1923 and 1928 the Social Democratic Party preferred to allow other parties to bear the responsibility of governing the nation, while it made its influence felt more indirectly.

We know, of course, that in these years committed republicans failed to change the traditional attachments of the higher civil servants, the judiciary, and the army officers, or to replace them with men of a less conservative and authoritarian stamp. Nevertheless, up to 1924–25 the four main parties whose actions furthered the continuance of the Republic maintained a general dominance in the sphere of politics. Other parties persevered in "opposition on principle" on almost all great national issues, even though from time to time they acted opportunistically in state and local politics.[4] Dangerous restorative tendencies had been kept in check, without being eliminated. The Weimar Coalition (and for a time the Great Coalition) ruled in Prussia.[5] Friedrich Ebert, conscientious and active in fulfilling his responsibilities as president, symbolized the changes which the revolution of 1918–19 had accomplished despite all its limitations. It is important to remember that the parties we have been dis-

---

und Demokratie am Anfang der Weimarer Republik, Beiträge zur Geschichte des Parlamentarismus und der politischen Parteien, 45 (Düsseldorf, 1972).

[3] On the consequences of the loss of a republican majority in 1920, see the perceptive observations of Arnold Brecht, Aus nächster Nähe (Stuttgart, 1966), pp. 309–18.

[4] Sigmund Neumann's brief discussion of the DNVP centers around the problems such a party encountered in trying to maintain a policy of opposition. Die Parteien der Weimarer Republik (Stuttgart, 1965), pp. 61–65. This is a reprint of his Die politischen Parteien in Deutschland (Berlin, 1932). Also, Kuno Graf Westarp, Am Grabe der Parteiherrschaft (Berlin, 1932), pp. 68–69, and the valuable dissertation by Manfred Dörr, Die Deutschnationale Volkspartei 1925 bis 1928 (Marburg, 1964).

[5] Of basic importance is the recent biography by Hagen Schulze, Otto Braun oder Preussens demokratische Sendung (Frankfurt a. M., 1977).

cussing—in particular the Weimar parties—were all successors of parties that had never attained full social respectability during the period of the Empire and had been regarded, in varying degrees, as enemies of the established order.[6] The exercise of political power was, to a greater or lesser extent, new to them; their reaction to this responsibility was mixed with uncertainty as well as satisfaction.[7]

In the mid-twenties a shift took place in the relationship of political forces in Germany.[8] The right gained in strength and its leaders (for a time) developed policies of considerable political realism. The conservative German National People's Party (DNVP) made noteworthy gains in the elections of 1924. It obtained over a hundred seats in the Reichstag, second only to the SPD. It maintained this position until 1930 when it was bypassed by more dynamic rivals, the National Socialists. That a fifth of the German voters in the mid-1920s supported a party with a profile like that of the DNVP was significant. Monarchist, nationalist, authoritarian,

[6] To a limited extent this is true even of the DVP which represented big business and carried on the tradition of the old National Liberal Party. Throughout the Empire National Liberals had usually supported the government, but even so the dominant ruling groups, especially in Prussia, never quite accepted them. Few army officers or bureaucrats, especially after the 1880s, would have admitted this political affiliation. Brecht, pp. 20 and 256. Even Stresemann observed, "The times when just the naming of a National Liberal as a Prussian *Landrat* was considered a great concession to the middle classes (*Bürgertum*) we do not wish to see return again." Speech to the DVP party convention, 2 Oct. 1926. Stresemann *Nachlass*, reel 3147, frame H162624.

On the conservative orientation of the army and bureaucracy before 1918, Karl Demeter, *Das Deutsche Offizierkorps in Gesellschaft und Staat, 1650–1945* (Frankfurt a.M., 1964), pp. 151–57; Gerhard Ritter, *Staatskunst und Kriegshandwerk*, 2 (Munich, 1960): 123–31; Peter Molt, *Der Reichstag vor der improvisierten Revolution, Politische Forschungen*, 2 (Cologne and Opladen, 1963): 140–56; Eckart Kehr, "Das soziale System der Reaktion in Preussen unter dem Ministerium Puttkamer," in *Der Primat der Innenpolitik*, ed. Hans-Ulrich Wehler (Berlin, 1965), pp. 64–68; and Fritz Hartung, "Studien zur Geschichte des Beamtentums im 19. und 20. Jahrhundert," *Abhandlungen der Deutschen Akademie der Wissenschaften zu Berlin. Philosophisch-historische Klasse.* Jahrgang 1945/46, Nr. 8, pp. 34–38.

[7] This generalization fits the SPD best. In the course of time the Center party gained some notoriety for its persistent retention of ministerial office whatever the composition of the cabinets.

[8] For a concise, clear narrative: Helmut Heiber, *Die Republik von Weimar* (Munich, 1966), chapters 6 and 7. In much more detail, particularly about the problems of forming coalition governments, Peter Haungs, *Reichspräsident und parlamentarische Kabinettsregierung, Politische Forschungen*, 9 (Cologne and Opladen, 1968) and Michael Stürmer, *Koalition und Opposition in der Weimarer Republik, 1924–1928, Beiträge zur Geschichte des Parlamentarismus und der politischen Parteien*, 36 (Düsseldorf, 1967), summarized for English readers as "Parliamentary Government in Weimar Germany, 1924–1928," in Anthony Nicholls and Erich Matthias (eds.), *German Democracy and the Triumph of Hitler* (New York, 1971), pp. 59–77.

closely identified with the agrarian interests, predominantly orthodox Lutheran, it represented nearly everything sincere republicans had been trying to combat. The election of Field Marshal von Hindenburg as president in 1925 revealed that much of the public was in the process of reverting to older, more familiar attitudes. From the standpoint of our investigation, however, the strengthened parliamentary position of the German National People's Party is more significant than Hindenburg's election, especially since at first he observed his constitutional responsibilities rather more scrupulously than many of his conservative adherents had hoped he would.[9]

The increased strength of the DNVP after the 1924 elections opened the prospect for the formation of new political combinations. The middle parties, especially the Center Party and the People's Party, now had a feasible option to the right which had not been available earlier. However, before they would cooperate with the DNVP they insisted that it accept the "fulfillment" policy in foreign affairs. Many Nationalists found it difficult to abandon all-out opposition to the "traitorous" republican foreign policy.[10] The leaders of the DNVP, greatly interested in regaining influence on the everyday decisions of the government—a kind of influence which they had not had since the collapse of the Empire—attempted to convince their followers of the value of participating in a government coalition.[11] From the beginning of 1925 till the late fall they succeeded. The first Luther cabinet was in everything except in name a Right Coalition (DNVP, Center, DVP, BVP).[12] However, Stresemann's foreign policy proved more accommodating to the Western powers than the DNVP rank-and-file could bear. Pressure from below forced the Nation-

[9] See, for example, Stresemann's favorable comments regarding Hindenburg's strictly correct behavior on taking office. *Nachlass*, reel 3113, frames H147815–16, diary entry 12 May 1925; Brecht, p. 455; Dörr, pp. 131–33.

[10] Werner Liebe, *Die Deutschnationale Volkspartei, 1918–1924, Beiträge zur Geschichte des Parlamentarismus und der politischen Parteien*, 8 (Düsseldorf, 1956): 89–99; John W. Wheeler-Bennett, *Wooden Titan. Hindenburg in Twenty Years of German History, 1914–1936* (London, 1936, reprinted 1963), p. 275 and passim; Turner, pp. 167–77; and Annelise Thimme, *Flucht in den Mythos. Die Deutschnationale Volkspartei und die Niederlage von 1918* (Göttingen, 1969).

[11] Attila Chanaday, "The Disintegration of the German National Peoples' Party 1924–1930," *Journal of Modern History*, 39 (Nr. 1, March 1967): 71–76.

[12] Luther preferred to call it an "überparteiliche" government. Hans Luther, *Politiker ohne Partei. Erinnerungen* (Stuttgart, 1960), pp. 316–319, 323; Haungs, pp. 90–91.

alist ministers to resign from the cabinet shortly before the ratification of the Locarno Agreements.[13] The *Bürgerblock*, as this grouping was known, collapsed. Minority governments of the middle filled the interim of somewhat over a year before the combination of middle and right parties could be reestablished, but then (as the fourth Marx government) the reconstituted *Bürgerblock* lasted for almost a year and a half until the elections of 1928. Losses by the DNVP and large gains by the SPD in this election created a new balance in the Reichstag favorable to a return to a Great Coalition government, the last cabinet in the Weimar Republic to have any meaningful parliamentary support.

The active role of the DNVP in the years 1924–28 greatly affected the parties closest to it. On the one hand, as already mentioned, it gave the leaders of the middle parties greater freedom in interparty negotiations. "There was no clear, firm majority grouping which had to be recognized, but rather every combination was practically possible." [14] The middle parties were no longer forced to choose between cooperating with the SPD, or forming weak minority governments which in any case depended on hidden SPD support (toleration).[15] When the DNVP behaved "responsibly," the middle parties were happy to cooperate with it; even when it did not, the

[13] Mr. Addison, a member of the British Embassy in Berlin, sent a lengthy report on the reaction to the Locarno Treaty (and on German character!) to Foreign Minister Chamberlain, 10 Dec. 1925. *Documents on British Foreign Policy, 1919–1939.* Series IA, Vol. 1, Nr. 141. His observations on the DNVP leaders deserve quotation: "MM. Schiele, Neuhaus and von Schlieben are quiet sensible men and undoubtedly represent much that is good in German life. . . . The three . . . are the type of which thousands of examples are to be found in the country houses of England. Their thoughts run mainly on the prospects of the crops and the chances of a good shooting season. They represent thousands of individuals whose thoughts run in similar lines, and they are, as above mentioned, honest persons who are quite out of place in an electoral assembly and quite unversed in electoral tactics. . . . The Nationalist Minister appears to have been unable to explain anything except that he was very sorry that under a government of which he was a member, Germany should have attained to a position which was beyond the wildest dreams of any German at the time he took office." Ibid., pp. 239–40.
[14] *Frankfurter Zeitung*, 11 May 1926 (Nr. 348). Similarly, Joseph Joos, "Die Zentrumspartei in Koalitionen (1919–1927)," in Georg Schreiber (ed.), *Politisches Jahrbuch 1927/28* (M.-Gladbach, 1928), pp. 162–64.
[15] The SPD developed some liking for a situation where it could oppose in public measures which it allowed to become law. For example, the SPD Reichstag *Fraktion* voted for the *Ermächtigung* Act of December, 1923, which opened the way for the stabilization of the currency and reorganization of finances along conventionally conservative lines. The party then attacked many of the cutbacks in its propaganda for potential voters. Erich Eyck, *Geschichte der Weimarer Republik* (Erlenback-Zürich, 1956), 1:378–80, 396–97.

ever-open possibility of renewed cooperation gave them leverage when dealing with the left.

On the other hand, the existence of a serious option to the right intensified the friction of opposing tendencies *inside* all the *bürgerliche* parties. Groupings with a strong conservative orientation existed in the DVP and Center, and to some extent even in the DDP. Leading figures on the right in all these parties had always been able to make their views heard, but policy had generally been set by men who supported republican measures out of conviction or from a realistic awareness that other courses of action would have untenable consequences. The more conservative elements in the middle parties took encouragement from the strengthening of the DNVP. They urged concerted action with the Nationalists, especially in the fields of economic and social policy. Generally speaking, they achieved this aim while at the same time increasing their weight in party councils. Between 1924 and 1928, most domestic legislation was passed by the middle parties acting in conjunction with the right, although foreign policy continued to be made in association with the Social Democrats. Reacting to the increasing predominance of the right, the left wings in the various middle parties grew uneasy. For example, the former chancellor, Joseph Wirth, well-known for his pronounced republicanism, resigned from the Catholic Center Party's Reichstag *Fraktion* to protest against the party's increasingly close association with the right.[16] Thus, debates within the parties usually focused on the course of future party commitments, and the resulting tensions worried party leaders. The danger of party splits never left their minds. At times they had to work desperately to maintain party unity.

Although many observers believed the Republic had entered a new period of stabilization once the grave dangers of the year 1923 were overcome, dedicated republicans, whatever their party, still showed signs of nervousness and doubt. A disheartening tendency had been all too apparent in the elections of 1924. Voters had repudiated the parties which had previously borne responsibility and gave their votes in impressive numbers to "oppositional" parties. Although the Communists on the extreme left were an annoyance and to many an affront, they posed no serious danger after 1923.

[16] *Germania*, 24 Aug. (Nr. 393) and 1 Sept. 1925 (Nr. 406).

The various parties and movements on the right were more threatening. Virulent attacks on President Ebert, exaggerated reports of scandals and corruption, the unmistakable partiality of the courts, the continued activity of armed bands of rightists, not to speak of the Hindenburg election, were clear evidence that anti-republican values appealed to wide groups of the population. Leading republicans did not satisfy themselves with specific refutations or counter-charges; they often sought to extend their arguments beyond the controversies of the moment to more basic issues. In particular they wondered whether the further development of republican institutions would continue. Through rhetoric emphasizing the question, "The Republic or Monarchism?" speakers tried to create a greater public commitment in the defense of the republic.[17] In the early twenties the danger had been rather more obvious. When Joseph Wirth had said, *"dieser Feind steht rechts,"* political murder and *Putsche* were real threats.[18] Yet the pervasive growth of rightist strength which found its confirmation in the newly effective alliance of the DNVP with other parties also represented a serious, if less striking, danger for republican politicians. To be sure, a detached observer might have said that what appeared most in danger just then was not the existence of the Republic so much as the influence of republican politicians in their own party councils.

The realignment of political forces which we have been discussing kindled intense feelings. The realignment itself was a tentative, uneven process, subject to reversal or momentary collapse. It seems no coincidence, therefore, that issues of a highly symbolic nature came to the forefront at a time when so many parties were in the process of deciding

[17] The following references are only samples. On the presidential election of 1925, *Frankfurter Zeitung*, 13 March (Nr. 194) and 20 April 1925 (Nr. 290), Otto Braun, *Von Weimar zu Hitler* (2nd ed., New York, 1940), pp. 170–71; on the royal properties issue, *Frankfurter Zeitung*, 15 Jan. 1926 (Nr. 39), Dr. Kurt Rosenfeld, Reichstag. *Verhandlungen*, 390 (28 April 1926): p. 6900, Philipp Scheidemann, ibid. (6 May 1926), p. 7035; on the dismissal of General von Seeckt, Friedrich von Rabenau, *Seeckt: Aus seinem Leben, 1918–1936* (Leipzig, 1940), p. 558; on the Flag Decree, Julius Leber, *Ein Mann geht seinen Weg* (Berlin, 1952), p. 137. Friedrich Freiherr Hiller von Gaertringen has written an excellent article on the actual state of monarchist feelings and efforts toward a restoration, "Zur Beurteilung des 'Monarchismus' in der Weimarer Republik," in *Tradition und Reform in der deutschen Politik. Gedenkschrift für Waldemar Besson*, ed. Gotthard Jasper (Frankfurt a. M., 1976), 138–86.

[18] Eyck, 1: 292.

the future direction of their policies. The year and a quarter from the breakup of the Right Coalition under Luther at the end of 1925 until its formation again under Marx early in 1927 was especially rich in symbolic domestic issues: the prolonged dispute over the handling of the former royal properties, the crisis over the Flag Decree, the dismissal of General von Seeckt, the controversial *"Schund-und Schmutz"* [19] law, and the uproar over Social Democratic revelations concerning illegal Reichswehr activities. During this period when political combinations were more fluid than usual, debates which stressed fundamental principles served the needs of both right and left. By stressing basic ideological differences, party spokesmen hoped to strengthen their followers' commitments. In any case, as long as the basic political fronts remained unclear not much progress on the level of practical politics was likely.

The difficulties that hindered effective political action, particularly among republican politicians in the parties of the middle and left, stand out very clearly when one examines in some detail the most important of these quarrels over what might have been a relatively inconsequential issue. The dispute that arose over property claims advanced by the former ruling princes stimulated extraordinary public interest. The controversy was not only fought out among the various parties, but inside them as well. Some party leaders faced the danger of being repudiated by large numbers of their followers. Moreover, the dispute culminated in the first nationwide initiative and referendum in German history. The referendum proposal for the complete confiscation of the property of the princes failed to pass, certainly not to the surprise of any informed politician. Nevertheless, the kind of settlement finally reached was in fact the result of a political stalemate, rather than the conclusion of a well-functioning legislative process. It was a defeat for the left and as such had both immediate and more lasting consequences. Perhaps most disturbing was the fact that intensive political activity and strong public engagement ended with results that hardly justified the efforts which had been expended. Thus, it caused frustration and added to the growing sense of futility concerning the working of democratic institutions.

[19] A law to prohibit the sale of pornographic writings to young people, ibid., 2:123–25.

The dispute over the expropriation of the former royal properties developed because no general settlement was made during the 1918–19 revolution when it would have been appropriate. The leaders of the revolutionary government neglected, or avoided, making a general ruling concerning the property rights of the newly deposed German princes. They certainly did not copy their neighbors in Austria (or Russia!) and carry out a general expropriation of the royal properties. Instead, the provisional government left the responsibility for making a settlement up to each of the individual states. This was in accord with the federal structure of the German Reich, but the result was that those settlements which were concluded over the course of time showed little uniformity. Each state government determined for itself the terms of the overall settlement, the manner in which this was established, and the general guidelines used to decide whether disputed properties belonged to the state or to the former ruling family in their capacity as private citizens. Most of the states reached some kind of settlement with their former rulers during the early twenties, but some, most notably Prussia, still had not come to any final agreement by 1925.

As time went on, a number of national politicians recognized the irregularity of the situation, but knew very well that a general formula suitable for the entire nation would be difficult to devise and troublesome to enact. Thus over six years were allowed to pass without any consideration of the problem at the level of national politics. During 1924 and 1925, however, a series of court cases challenged some of the settlements which had been reached earlier. State governments found themselves faced with law suits, most of them almost certain to end unfavorably for the public interest. The general public, too, began to grow uneasy. This uneasiness turned into protest when, late in 1925, proposals were made for a national law to regularize the situation and block the excessive claims made by some former princes. From the start, it was apparent that serious differences concerning the most basic features of this legislation impeded agreement even among the members of the governing coalition in the Reichstag. The legal problems were complicated enough but increasing radicalization—affecting middle-class voters as well as workers—added many difficulties to the political parties' search for an acceptable solution. The possibility of the

Reichstag reaching a workable compromise diminished sharply in the early spring of 1926 as the initiative and referendum movement got under way. Its official backers, the Communist Party and the Social Democratic Party, proposed a drastic alternative to the idea of regulatory legislation, namely, total confiscation of all royal properties without examination of any legal claims and without compensation.

The call for an initiative and referendum directly increased public interest and involvement. At least one observer stated that not since the time of the revolution had the man-in-the-street been so aroused by any issue, while others commented on the unusually intense reactions among people normally not at all radical.[20] Even the Communists were amazed at the support they found during the circulation of petitions calling for the start of an initiative:

> Never before have the Red Front Fighters been received by the population of Neukölln as on last Sunday. They were invited into the houses, given chocolate, beer, cognac, wine, cigars and cigarettes out of joy because the insatiable muzzles of the Hohenzollerns, and their like, were finally going to be stopped. Time and again people emphasized, "We certainly are not supporters of the Communists, but on this question, we will go along with them completely." [21]

On that occasion they collected 30,000 signatures, where the goal had been 5,000.

The situation throughout the first half of 1926 was characterized by an overlapping debate on the two potential courses of action—Reichstag legislation or direct popular vote. The result was a political stalemate. Progress toward one solution obstructed the advancement of the other. Discussions among the various parties concerning the content of the desired regulatory legislation proceeded along a course shaped more by the pace of developments in the initiative and referendum movement than by any normal working out of differences of opinion. The grouping together of a combination of political parties large enough to ensure passage of the Reichstag bill was hindered by the possibility of a more

[20] Leber, pp. 46–47; the remarks of Erich Mader (Altenburg) at the Social Democratic Party convention in 1927, *Sozialdemokratischer Parteitag 1927 in Kiel. Protokoll* (Berlin, 1927), p. 67; and articles in the Catholic newspapers *Kölnische Volkszeitung,* 19 June 1926 (Nr. 446) and *Tremonia,* 25 Feb. and 24 June 1926.

[21] *Rote Fahne,* 19 Jan. 1926. This collection of signatures was a preliminary formality, not to be confused with the initiative itself.

far-reaching solution through the referendum. Yet at the same time, the extreme formulation of the referendum proposal (confiscation without compensation) prevented the coalescence of a political base sufficiently wide to bring a positive majority of the voters to the polls.

As the debate over the disposition of the royal properties progressed, the issues became drastically simplified. Moral and political principles were constantly intertwined. Each side invoked differing interpretations of justice. Social equity, particularly concern for those who had been ruined or maimed by the war, dominated the demands of the left; the right stressed the absolute, binding character of the legal order and professed to fear the overthrow of "law and morals" if existing property rights were challenged.[22] Above all, the conflict reduced itself to the formula: Republic *versus* Monarchy. While one side castigated all the deficiencies and past crimes of Germany's rulers, the other praised their immortal services, for which, they argued, a continuing debt of gratitude was due. The question of the responsibility for the war was drawn in as well. By the end the debate was little more than an exchange of worn slogans.

On 20 June 1926, the referendum took place. Only the Communist and Social Democratic parties openly supported the referendum, but many voters who normally followed the guidance of other parties voted for confiscation. Fourteen and a half million people voted "yes" (36 percent of the eligible voters) yet the referendum proposal failed.[23] According to the constitution, passage of such a law required a majority of all eligible voters (in this case, some twenty million affirmative votes), not merely a majority of those voting. In the days following the referendum the Reichstag resumed its consideration of the proposed regulatory legislation. However, for various reasons support from a combination of parties powerful enough to ensure its passage proved to be as elusive as it had been before the referendum. Early in July the government withdrew the bill rather than suffer a parliamentary defeat over it.

Seven months of intense debate ended without any constructive solution of the royal properties question at the na-

[22] The phrase comes from President Hindenburg's well-known letter to von Loebell of 22 May 1926. *Frankfurter Zeitung*, 8 June 1926 (Nr. 418), reprinted in Walther Hubatsch, *Hindenburg und der Staat* (Göttingen, 1966), pp. 237–39.

[23] *Wirtschaft und Statistik*, 6 (Nr. 12, July, 1926): 403–4.

tional level. When the Prussian government signed a
negotiated settlement with the Hohenzollern representatives
in October, 1926, the final agreement differed but little from
what would have been concluded a year earlier if the whole
controversy and public excitement had not intervened.[24] In
the process two different forms of democratic decision-making had been used. Both parliamentary action by the political
parties and direct consultation of the people through the
initiative and referendum had failed to produce concrete
results understandable and acceptable to the public at large.

The whole episode produced great annoyance among contemporaries, particularly among the men who had been actively engaged in the complex political and legal discussions.
They did not hesitate to blame specific parties or individuals.
The decision of the SPD Reichstag *Fraktion* not to aid in the
passage of regulatory legislation even after the referendum
had failed outraged many men in the Center and DDP who
had been expecting their eventual cooperation. The Democratic Party's Executive Board issued a statement that:

> The majority of the Social Democratic Reichstag *Fraktion* . . . has
> shown no regard for the necessity for the parties which support
> the constitution to work together. They bear the responsibility
> if today satisfaction and rejoicing prevail among the die-hard
> parties on the right. They also bear the responsibility if belief in
> the ability of parliamentarianism to accomplish anything is being
> shaken, and if today the gulf between the Social Democrats and
> the other republican parties threatens to deepen.[25]

The words of the distinguished elderly jurist, Dr. Wilhelm
Kahl, who was a member of the DVP and served as chairman
of the Reichstag Legal Committee (*Rechtsausschuss*), which
held numerous sessions trying to work out the details of the
proposed legislation, were more resigned than angry. A semi-
humorous formulation scarcely disguises a sense of considerable frustration:

> Drama provisionally in three acts: Compromise attempts, Ref-
> erendum, Fiasco in Reichstag.
> Time and Place of the Action: 44 sessions of the Legal Committee
> between January and June, 1926, along with innumerable special
> conferences; June 20 in thousands of voting places throughout
> Germany; a half dozen plenary sessions of the Reichstag with

[24] Schüren's assessment is less negative, pp. 252–60, 280–81.
[25] *Der Democrat*, 7 (Nr. 13/14, 15 July 1926): 262.

the final scene July 2, 1926: Surrender by the Government of its proposal after statements by the wing parties rejecting it.

Course and Result: In essence a purely legal question, notwithstanding its political wrappings, progressively degenerated into the angry plaything of the parties.[26]

Even Arthur Rosenberg, in 1926 a participant in the Reichstag debates as a member of the Communist Party and later one of the earliest historians of the Weimar Republic, thought, "The whole proceeding was a powerful republican demonstration that failed of any practical result. It was, therefore, a faithful reflection of the age." [27]

As such comments on the royal properties "fiasco" disclose, the malfunctioning of the existing political institutions had, well before the final crisis of the Republic, become a theme of editorial comment and a subject for recurrent thought and discussion among politicians. Nearly everyone saw signs of latent crisis; that genuinely effective political decisions were too rarely made; that too many difficult problems lingered on unresolved; and that improvement under existing conditions seemed increasingly unlikely. Many identified basic evils which they thought lay at the root of these troubles. The existence of too many political parties and the continuing tendency for more splinter parties to form; the unwillingness of enough parties to commit themselves to responsible, rather than demagogically motivated policies; the excessive power exercised by party hierarchies which no longer seemed to bother to keep in touch with the true state of mind of their followers—all were sharply criticized. Some of the recommended remedies tended to be highly specific, others were very vague. The revamping of the process by which parliamentary candidates were nominated, the abandonment of proportional representation and the return to single-member election districts, for instance, or the demands for greater "intra-party democracy" are examples.[28] Very sel-

[26] Wilhelm Kahl, "Das Fürstendrama," *Deutsche Juristen-Zeitung,* 31 (Nr. 15, Aug. 1926): 1057.

[27] *A History of the German Republic* (London, 1936), p. 267.

[28] Heinrich Teipel, *Wir müssen aus dem Turm heraus* (Berlin, 1925); Hermann Müller, "Vom Deutschen Parlamentarismus," *Die Gesellschaft* (1926: Part 1), pp. 239–305; Koellreutter, *Der deutsche Staat als Bundesstaat und als Parteienstaat,* p. 27; A. Mendelssohn-Bartholdy, "The Political Dilemma in Germany," *Foreign Affairs,* 8 (Nr. 4, July, 1930): 620–31; James K. Pollock, Jr., "The German Party System," *American Political Science Review,* 23 (Nr. 4, Nov. 1929): 859–91; and with many references to the contemporary discussion, Friedrich Schaefer, "Zur Frage des Wahlrechts in der

dom did such reform projects appear immediately practical. Indeed, "practicality" was not even an argument which was well received in defense of the expedients that from time to time had to be used to keep the system operating. The old hands in the Reichstag simply laughed when Chancellor Luther, impatient after a long cabinet crisis, declared, "But somehow Germany must be governed!" [29] Intelligent working politicians knew that further political changes were necessary in the mid-twenties, but considered the time not yet right for undertaking them.[30] Everyone kept working within the general structure of operating rules which had been established quite soon after the revolution and no one—no democratic politicians, at least—dared try to alter them.

During the past three decades, German historians and political scientists have devoted much attention to the identification of features of the Weimar system that impeded effective political action.[31] To be sure, their investigations have proceeded very largely from the basic standpoint articulated by Karl Dietrich Erdmann: "All research on the history of the Weimar Republic is by necessity (whether expressed or unstated) concerned with the causes of its collapse." [32] Great emphasis has therefore been placed on the study of

---

Weimarer Republik," in Ferdinand A. Hermans and Theodor Schieder (eds.), *Staat, Wirtschaft und Politik in der Weimarer Republik, Festschrift für Heinrich Brüning* (Berlin, 1967), 119–40; and Gerhard Leibholz, "Die Grundlagen des modernen Wahlrechts," in *Strukturprobleme der modernen Demokratie* (3rd ed., enlarged; Karlsruhe, 1967), pp. 9–40.

[29] Reichstag. *Verhandlungen* 188 (27 Jan. 1926): 5170.

[30] Both Stresemann and Koch-Weser considered the existence of two "liberal" parties in the long run undesirable, but neither of their parties was able to accept the practical consequences of merger. On 30 July 1926, Stresemann wrote Interior Minister Külz asking for a statistical calculation of what would have been the results of the last election if there had been single member districts in which the winner was decided by a simple majority instead of the existing system of proportional representation. He said, "I have the feeling that in such a system the German Democratic Party and the German People's Party would lose out completely." Stresemann *Nachlass*, reel 3146, frame H162171. Turner, pp. 166–67, 254–55; *Frankfurter Zeitung*, 2 Feb. 1926; DDP Papers (*Vorstand*) meetings 27 Nov. 1926 and 14–15 June 1928), reel 37, folder 730; Attila Chanady, "The Dissolution of the German Democratic Party in 1930," *American Historical Review*, 73 (Nr. 5, June, 1968): 1433–53; Bruce B. Frye, "The German Democratic Party, 1918–1930," *Western Political Quarterly*, 16 (Nr. 1, March, 1963): 167-79; Larry Eugene Jones, "Gustav Stresemann and the Crisis of German Liberalism," *European Studies Review*, 4 (Nr. 2, April, 1974): 141–63.

[31] The literature on this subject is very extensive. In the following footnotes, I have tried to mention only some of the more important contributions.

[32] "Die Geschichte der Weimarer Republik als Problem der Wissenschaft," *Vierteljahrshefte für Zeitgeschichte*, 5 (Nr. 1, Jan. 1955): 5.

the last years of the Republic. Nevertheless, it is more and more widely recognized that the collapse of parliamentary government was not due entirely to bad luck and the depression. The existence of an internal power vacuum caused by the breakdown of parliamentary institutions and the general discrediting of republican values permitted the easy triumph of a newly emergent totalitarian movement which worked together with, and took advantage of, a revival of more traditional authoritarianism in order to overthrow the little that was left of the republican order in 1933.[33] It is increasingly clear that the crisis at the end of the Republic was rooted in basic weaknesses which had existed throughout the entire period of the twenties and in some cases had originated much earlier.[34]

Some of the main problems were structural. One prime defect of the Weimar Constitution was that it contained elements which in operation tended to cancel each other out.[35] The attempt to graft a strong presidency onto what was basically a parliamentary system of government is the instance of this structural incongruity which has attracted most attention. Similarly problematic were the constitutional provisions allowing the use of nationwide initiative and referendum proceedings.[36] Although intended in theory to provide a kind of ultrademocratic alternative to decision-making by parliamentary bodies, the initiative and referendum were, in

[33] This is the thesis of Karl Dietrich Bracher's indispensable book, *Die Auflösung der Weimarer Republik.*

[34] Werner Conze, "Die Krise des Parteienstaates in Deutschland 1929/30," *Historische Zeitschrift,* 178 (1954): 47–83; Bracher, "Probleme der Wahlentwicklung in der Weimarer Republik," in *Deutschland zwischen Demokratie und Diktatur* (Bern and Munich, 1964), pp. 50–82; Josef Becker, "Heinrich Brüning in den Krisenjahren der Weimarer Republik," *Geschichte in Wissenschaft und Unterricht,* 17 (Nr. 4, April, 1966): 201–19; Erich Matthias und Rudolf Morsey (eds.), *Das Ende der Parteien 1933* (Düsseldorf, 1960); Theodor Eschenburg *et al., The Path to Dictatorship 1918–1933* (Garden City, N.Y., 1966); Alfred Milatz, *Wähler und Wahlen in der Weimarer Republik, Schriftenreihe der Bundeszentrale für politische Bildung,* 66 (Bonn, 1965); and Michael Stürmer, "Der unvollendete Parteienstaat—Zur Vorgeschichte des Präsidialregimes am Ende der Weimarer Republik," *Vierteljahrshefte für Zeitgeschichte,* 21 (Nr. 2, April, 1973): 119–26.

[35] Bracher, "Parteienstaat—Prasidialsystem—Notstand," in *Deutschland zwischen Demokratie und Diktatur,* pp. 33–49; Ernst Fraenkel, "Die repräsentative und die plebiszitäre Komponente im demokratischen Verfassungsstaat," in *Deutschland und die westlichen Demokratien* (Stuttgart, 1964), pp. 71–109; Reinhard Rürup, "Entwurf einer demokratischen Republik? Entstehung und Grundlagen der Weimarer Verfassung," in *Fünfzig Jahre deutsche Republik. Entstehung—Scheitern—Neubeginn,* ed. F. A. Krummacher (Frankfurt a. M., 1969), pp. 82–112.

[36] Reinhard Schiffers, *Elemente direkter Demokratie im Weimarer Regierungssystem, Beiträge zur Geschichte des Parlamentarismus und der politischen Parteien,* 40 (Düsseldorf, 1971).

fact, never successfully used in a constructive way.[37] Rather they were exploited by anti-republican parties for purposes of mass agitation through which the process of inter-party compromise inherent in the parliamentary system could be discredited, and the hold of the more responsible political parties on their followings shaken. Here, too, we see how the framers of the Weimar Constitution, by striving for "the greatest possible perfection" [38] in a constitutional document, ended in producing very different effects from those they had intended.[39]

It may be that they had not expected these particular innovations to be employed at all. (One thinks of the *Reichswirtschaftsrat*, which was also written into the Constitution but was never really allowed to function, or of numerous parts of the "Rights and Duties of the German Citizen" which lacked any precise juristic meaning.) [40] The original version of Hugo Preuss's draft constitution submitted to the National Assembly provided for only restricted use of referendum procedures.[41] During the course of the debates, further pro-

[37] "Henceforth direct voting by the people *(Volksabstimmung)* is just as important a foundation block of the Constitution as the president, the Reichstag, and the Reichsrat.... We are not of the opinion that parliament is the only form of expression [available in a] democracy; on the contrary we believe that the more pillars there are created in the democratic structure *(Aufbau)* of the state, so much more certainly is the will of the people established," Erich Koch-Weser in the *Verfassungs-Ausschuss* of the National Assembly. Germany. *Verhandlungen der versfassungsgebenden Deutschen Nationalversammlung,* 336: 307.

[38] Bracher, *Deutschland zwischen Demokratie und Diktatur,* p. 37.

[39] Koch-Weser acting as reporter *(Berichterstätter)* to the full Assembly presumably expressed the hopes of the dominant republican majority. "Precisely in excited times and in times when [there is] distrust of the government and of elected representatives it is desirable to be able to discover the mood *(Stimmung)* of the people concerning a proposed law." Far from encouraging radical demands, he said, "... [a] referendum has the great advantage over a general election because one is then able to speak to the people in detail on one single practical problem." With reference to the use of initiatives he returned to the idea "that in a time when there are many important signs that a certain distrust of representative democracy is present, it is desirable to create a [safety] valve for this distrust. (Very true, Left.)" *Verhandlungen der ... Nationalversammlung,* 327 (5 July 1919): 1345–46.

[40] The *"Grundrechte und Grundpflichten der Deutschen"* were exhaustively defined in Articles 109–165 of the Constitution; the *Reichswirtschaftsrat* was to be created according to Article 165. An English jurist in 1923 observed, "... [S]ome of the promises [in the list of rights] are ambiguous and, presumably of set purpose, vague; others give the impression of being made with mental reservations and with no serious intention of ultimate fulfillment." Heinrich Oppenheimer, *The Constitution of the German Republic* (London, 1923), pp. 179–80.

[41] Article 60 of the first published draft permitted the president to call for a referendum if the two houses of the legislature could not agree, and after five years would have required referenda on constitutional amendments (Art. 51). *Ursachen*

visions permitting fairly free use of the initiative, as well as greatly extending the list of circumstances in which referenda might be held, were added. Apparently these changes represented concessions to the Social Democrats which the middle-class republican parties were able to make at a minimum cost to their own principles. The Social Democratic Party's programs for half a century had called for extensive reliance on such methods of direct democracy.[42] Nevertheless, there is reason to suspect that the leaders of the majority in the National Assembly did not intend to encourage direct legislation in practice, however willing they were to support it in principle.[43] Certainly they made no use of these procedures during the first half of the Weimar Republic, and after 1926, they left them to be abused by radical parties of the right and left. Furthermore, the elaborate stipulations of the Constitution itself did not make the holding of an initiative or referendum easy.[44] Most cases where the use of the referendum was permitted were unlikely to occur at all frequently; the cases where its use was optional depended on the decision of either the president or the Reichstag itself; and in the case of a measure introduced by process of an initiative, acceptance by the Reichstag could serve in place of a vote by the populace at large. The procedures laid down for holding a valid initiative and referendum were complicated, and passage of any measure depended on participation of a high proportion of the active voters. Very largely for these reasons an expert writing in a basic reference work *in 1921* referred to the provisions establishing the initiative and referendum as "a democratic embellishment" and questioned whether they would have any practical significance.[45]

---

und Folgen, ed. Herbert Michaelis and Ernst Schraepler, 3 (Berlin, n.d.): 437–39; Schiffers, pp. 111–12.

[42] Fraenkel, pp. 99–100; Schiffers, pp. 17–27.

[43] Dr. Max Quarck (SPD) denied that any danger of over-frequent voting existed, ". . . direct voting by the people [will] come into consideration only as the last resort *(aüsserstes Mittel)* if sometime the parliamentary system fails." *Verhandlungen der . . . Nationalversammlung,* 326: 312.

[44] Gerhard Anschütz, *Die Verfassung des Deutschen Reiches vom 11. August 1919* (14th ed.; Berlin, 1933, reprint 1968), pp. 383–408, on Articles 73–76 of the Constitution. For a useful summary in English of the provisions for referenda in the constitutions of the individual states as well as the *Reich* by one of the leading German constitutional lawyers: Richard Thoma, "The Referendum in Germany," *Journal of Comparative Legislation and International Law,* 3rd Series, 10 (1928): 55–73.

[45] Hans Gmelin, "Referendum," *Handbuch der Politik,* 3 (3rd ed.; Berlin and Leipzig, 1921): 74–77; likewise, Oppenheimer, pp. 149–54; Schiffers, p. 263.

The effects of the failure of the writers of the Constitution to develop a set of institutions free of inherent contradictions were felt throughout the twenties, although they only became obvious during the terminal crisis after 1930. Even so, if Germany's political leaders had shown a wide-ranging determination to make the system work, many of these structural problems might have been overcome. The freedom of action of most politicians in the Weimar Republic was encumbered, however, by patterns of behavior and attitudes they had developed during the Empire.[46] As a whole, they showed little desire to accept responsibility or seek power. They prided themselves on their "experience," but overlooked the fact that most of that experience had been gained under an authoritarian, bureaucratic system which excluded representatives of the political parties from nearly all significant political and administrative decisions.[47]

The parties in Imperial Germany had more or less unconsciously accepted the limited roles allotted them; they were adept at criticizing legislation, negotiating special advantages for the interest groups most closely associated with them, and above all, expressing in determined, uncompromising form their basic ideological principles.[48] Party leaders, shut

[46] Conze, "Die deutschen Parteien in der Staatsverfassung vor 1933," in *Das Ende der Parteien,* pp. 3–28; Theodor Eschenburg, "Die improvisierte Demokratie," in a collection of his articles with the same title (Munich, 1963), pp. 11–60; Fraenkel, "Historische Vorbelastungen des deutschen Parlamentarismus," in *Deutschland und die westlichen Demokratien,* pp. 13–31; Bracher, "Entstehung der Weimarer Verfassung," in *Deutschland zwischen Demokratie und Diktatur,* pp. 11–32; and Gerhard A. Ritter, "Kontinuität und Umformung des deutschen Parteiensystems, 1918–1920," in *Entstehung und Wandel der modernen Gesellschaft: Festschrift für Hans Rosenberg zum 65. Geburtstag,* ed. Gerhard A. Ritter (Berlin, 1970), pp. 342–84 and "Entwicklungsprobleme des deutschen Parlamentarismus," in *Gesellschaft, Parlament, und Regierung,* ed. Gerhard A. Ritter (Düsseldorf, 1974), pp. 11–54.

[47] Molt, pp. 360–61, 363–64, 366–69. Almost anytime dissent within a party attracted general public attention, party leaders could be counted on to appeal to their followers to recognize party discipline and show greater trust in their judgment and knowledge of the situation. For example, Joseph Joos's article, "Zentrumswähler im Volksentscheid," *Germania,* 22 June 1926 (Nr. 282). Despite the fact that Joos belonged to the left wing of the Center Party, he stated that party followers should not have acted according to their own feelings. ". . . [O]ne must pay attention to the *authority of the party as a whole.* . . . The Center Party can not possibly permit the authority of its leadership *(Instanzen)* to be disregarded, otherwise it will cease to be a party. . . . The party must demand *obedience* and *subordination"* (emphasis in original).

[48] Fraenkel, "Parlament und öffentliche Meinung," in *Deutschland und die westlichen Demokratien,* pp. 110–30; Eberhard Pikart, "Die Rolle der Parteien im deutschen konstitutionellen System vor 1914," *Zeitschrift für Politik,* 9 (N.F.) (Nr. 1, March, 1962): 12–32; Theodor Schieder, "Die Theorie der Partei im alteren deutschen

off from any possibility of advancement to high governmental office, concentrated their attention on internal party affairs. They strove to maintain the intense loyalty of those population groups normally identified with their parties, rather than building the widest possible popular support. Correspondingly, they tried to conciliate divergent elements within their parties in order to present the strongest possible appearance of unity to the eyes of other parties and the public at large. For most politicians these attitudes did not change in the 1920s, even though the working of the Constitution now imposed new responsibilities upon the parties to form cabinets, determine policy, and oversee its execution.[49] With a few exceptions—Braun and Severing in Prussia, Erzberger, Stresemann, and Ebert—most of the Weimar Republic's leading party politicians conceived of their role in narrow terms no longer appropriate for their true duties. Moreover, their followers did not have a proper conception of political action either.

> The true meaning *(Sinn)* of coalitions is to form a majority to insure that the government can fulfill its tasks. . . . The psychology of German party life poses the sharpest [possible] resistance against a natural, politically realistic assessment of [the need for] the formation of coalitions. In the up-and-down of coalitions since Weimar we witness the conflict of an unpolitical attitude with the requirements of politics.[50]

In fact, most cabinet crises developed out of this "psychology," from the refusal of key parties to share responsibility for an unpopular decision, a wide-spread preference for the freedom of "opposition," the unwillingness to accept the necessity of compromise, and very frequently, the repudiation

Liberalismus," and "Die geschichtlichen Grundlagen und Epochen des deutschen Parteiwesens," in *Staat und Gesellschaft im Wandel unserer Zeit* (Munich, 1958), pp. 110–32 and 133–71; James J. Sheehan, "Political Leadership in the German *Reichstag, 1871–1918*," *American Historical Review,* 74 (Nr. 2, Dec., 1968): 511–28, and his book, *German Liberalism in the Nineteenth Century* (Chicago, 1978); Thomas Nipperdey, *Die Organisation der deutschen Parteien vor 1918, Beiträge zur Geschichte des Parlamentarismus und der politischen Parteien,* 18 (Düsseldorf, 1961); and the two important articles by Max Weber, "Wahlrecht und Demokratie in Deutschland," and "Parlament und Regierung im neugeordneten Deutschland," *Gesammelte politische Schriften,* ed. Johannes Wickelmann (2nd ed.; Tübingen, 1958), pp. 232–79 and 292–431.
[49] This point was particularly stressed by Klaus Epstein in his review article, "The Zentrum Party in the Weimar Republic," *Journal of Modern History,* 39 (Nr. 2, June, 1967): 160–63.
[50] Joos, *Politisches Jahrbuch 1927/28,* p. 155.

by their own party followers of decisions taken by cabinet ministers.[51]

With these considerations in mind, the story of the handling of the dispute over the former royal properties seems worth a detailed examination.[52] The episode may serve as a case study in political ineffectiveness. Political and economic conditions in Germany during 1925–26 were reasonably normal, at any rate better than they had been earlier and would be later. At that time, the moderate parties faced no really dangerous competition from the radical parties on the extreme right and left (the NSDAP and KPD). Their freedom of action was not restricted by the need to cope with any overwhelming emergencies such as the inflation, the Ruhr occupation, or the depression. The question of how the former royal properties should be handled was not an issue which produced direct clashes among strongly organized interest groups as did the problem of unemployment insurance a few years later.[53] Nevertheless, it proved impossible to bring about political agreement and thus achieve recognizably meaningful results. The reasons for such a failure need to be explored.

The wide range of types of property involved in the various settlements and the diversity of legal forms which had governed the ownership of princely estates added to the difficulty of the attempt to work out a single general piece of legislation. Certainly the legal and historical evidence necessary for an impartial evaluation of the many disputed claims was very complicated and not easily understood by laymen. However, it must be emphasized that technical difficulties of this nature were not what blocked a satisfactory solution. The basic failure was a political one.

Some political leaders, particularly those of the republican parties, reacted with considerable uncertainty to the first use of the initiative and referendum. Various prominent leaders in the Democratic and Social Democratic parties, for example, were seriously in error when they expected that the referendum movement would have "helpful" effects, even if it

[51] Bracher, *Die Auflösung*, p. 34; Haungs, pp. 280–85.
[52] See the preface, above, p. xii, for discussion of other publications on this subject.
[53] The large landowners, of course, feared that the confiscation of the estates belonging to royalty might serve as a precedent for further confiscations, but on the whole their opposition seems to have been stimulated more by general principles rather than immediate self-interest.

failed.[54] Here too, it would be wrong to infer that the clumsiness of decision-making resulted simply from novel and unforeseeable complexities. Several of the most crucial decisions were made in accord with basic habits of thought well-established among party leaders. As the controversy reached its high-point, they concentrated their attention on the immediate political consequences of the choices available to them. Under these circumstances, considerations only indirectly related to the issue itself played a determining part— especially the fear of losing control of one's own followers, or the possibility of an intra-party split. The statement reportedly made by a Social Democratic Reichstag member, "If the SPD doesn't go along with [the Communist-backed confiscation proposal], then their people will run away not by battalions, but in whole armies," [55] reminds one of Ledru-Rollin's classic remark during the revolution of 1848, "I am their leader, I have to follow them." [56]

[54] The idea was quite widely held that heavy voter participation in the initiative and referendum movement would put pressure on the Reichstag to pass a strong regulative law. *Frankfurter Zeitung,* 4 March (Nr. 169), 7 March (Nr. 177), 11 June 1926 (Nr. 482); *Vorwärts,* 27 Feb. (Nr. 98), 21 June 1926 (Nr. 286a). No one, to my knowledge, foresaw that a highly aroused public opinion would make compromise among the key left and middle parties in the Reichstag impossible.

[55] *Rote Fahne,* 19 Jan. 1926. One of the prominent left socialists, Heinrich Ströbel, was identified as the author of this statement.

[56] Quoted in the *New Cambridge Modern History,* 10 (Cambridge, 1960): 598.

II: The Uncompleted Work of the Revolution and the Origins of the Dispute over the Princes' Properties

During October, 1918, Germany's ruling classes made last-ditch efforts to avert the consequences of military defeat by introducing the full practice of parliamentary government within the system of constitutional monarchy. By the end of the month the various federal states, following the lead of the national government, had made or were in the process of making these basic changes. However, the transformation came too late. Early in November revolutionary unrest spread throughout Germany, and immediately it seemed evident that the twenty-odd ruling houses must vanish. Even before the abdication of the kaiser was announced, the duke of Brunswick renounced his throne and the king of Bavaria fled from his capital.[1] None of the old authorities offered any serious resistance to the revolution. Within a few days all the princes were deposed, or voluntarily gave up their thrones, and withdrew from the public eye. Only a few felt the need to go into exile. As one constitutional lawyer said, the transition was characterized by "a genteel moderation."[2]

[1] For a chronology of the various abdications see *Ursachen und Folgen*, 3: 83, note 1.
[2] Walter Jellinek, "Revolution und Reichsverfassung," *Jahrbuch des öffentlichen Rechts*, 1 (1920): 82. In tiny Schwarzburg-Rudolstadt the prince and the *Landtag* conveniently agreed on a property settlement *before* the prince formally renounced

From the moment of abdication the former rulers became private persons. In addition to the obvious political consequences, such a step had important legal ramifications. Once a ruler lost his special position as a sovereign in public law, nothing distinguished him in private law from any ordinary citizen. Indeed, much weight was later given the legal argument that the rights of the former rulers were entirely the same as those of all other citizens. From this premise it was argued that any attempt to pass special legislation regarding their property rights would violate both the constitution and basic concepts of an equitable legal system.[3] Nonetheless certain rights, properties, and sources of income which a former ruler possessed, or might claim, clearly derived from his one-time status as sovereign prince. How were these to be distinguished from his purely private property rights as an individual or as head of a family?[4] None of the German states or the national government adopted the simple, common revolutionary expedient of ignoring the distinction and confiscating all the properties the former rulers had either possessed or traditionally enjoyed the use of.[5] Neighboring Austria and the other successor states seized the Habsburg properties, but Germany left its former princes relatively unharmed in their wealth and possessions.[6]

---

his throne. Ibid., p. 227. Friedrich Stampfer, *Die vierzehn Jahre der ersten Deutschen Republik* (Karlsbad, 1936), p. 443, states "that one must remember that the revolution of 1918 by no means took place in an atmosphere of hate against the princely houses!" Similarly, Scheidemann, Reichstag. *Verhandlungen*, 388 (2 Dec 1925): 4728.

[3] For example, Dr. Wilhelm Kahl, "Recht und Volksentscheid," *Kölnische Zeitung*, 19 June 1926 (Nr. 450). Such legal arguments were widely used by spokesmen for parties on the right and center: Hans-Erdmann von Lindeiner-Wildau (DNVP), Reichstag. *Verhandlungen*, 388 (2 Dec. 1925): 4735–39; Dr. Johannes Wunderlich (DVP), ibid., 390 (28 April 1926): 6906–07; Karl Anton Schulte (Center), ibid., 6918–20; and of course the famous Hindenburg letter to von Loebell.

[4] Quite naturally writers unsympathetic to the princes' claims tried to argue that much of their so-called "private" wealth derived from their exercise of public functions. For instance, Wilhelm Kiefer, "Das Problem der Fürstenabfindung. I. Historische Entwicklung," *Frankfurter Zeitung*, 17 March 1926 (Nr. 202). However, even some scholars who tried hard to be impartial argued that the assumption that one could clearly distinguish between *privatrechtlich* and *öffentlich-rechtlich* titles to the disputed properties was invalid. Professor Ottmar Bühler, "Grundsätzliches zur Frage der Hohenzollernabfindung," *Kölnische Zeitung*, 4 Jan. (Nr. 8) and 6 Jan. 1926 (Nr. 14); Otto Koellreutter, "Die Auseinandersetzung mit den ehemaligen Fürstenhäusern," *Deutsche Juristen-Zeitung*, 21 (15 Jan. 1926, Nr. 2): 114; Theodor Günther, *Das Problem der Vermögensauseinandersetzung mit den ehemaligen Fürstenhäusern* (dissertation, University of Leipzig, 1928), pp. 11–12, 24–25, 113–14, 132.

[5] With the exceptions discussed below, pp. 26–28.

[6] By a law 3 April 1919, the Austrian republic took possession of the properties that had been devoted to the maintenance of the court and also the entailed estates

When in 1925–26 the royal properties issue became highly controversial, the right liked to use the argument that while changes in property relationships might have been permissible as revolutionary acts, the failure to undertake a revolutionary transfer of properties could not be remedied retroactively without violating the Constitution.[7] The Communists, too, liked to jeer at the Social Democrats for this and other failures in 1918–19.[8] In one of the last debates on the issue a speaker for the Social Democrats admitted, ". . . I say openly and honestly: in the question of the confiscation of the princes' properties and in the question of the treatment of the princes the Revolution neglected many things and did not do many things."[9] However, representative Alwin Saenger was not one of his party's principal leaders. Sensitive on this point, most republican spokesmen in 1926–27 did not spend much time trying to explain why no clear and unequivocal general settlement had been made at the proper moment.

Occasionally one does encounter a brief explanation or two. A "Confidential Memorandum" in the files of the German Democratic Party states that a national law regulating this set of problems was not considered necessary in 1919, because it was thought that the individual states would be able to reach satisfactory agreements with their former rulers without much difficulty.[10] An information leaflet distributed for the use of Social Democratic speakers suggests a similar reason: the Council of People's Representatives left the decision to the various states "due to the complexity of the different relationships."[11] It goes on to add that had either

---

of the Habsburgs. The strictly private property of individual members of the family was not seized. Ernst C. Hellbling, *Oesterreichische Verfassungs- und Verwaltungsgeschichte* (Vienna, 1956), pp. 424–25; Reinhold Lorenz, *Kaiser Karl und der Untergang der Donaumonarchie* (Graz, 1959), pp. 579, 583–85.

[7] Dr. Kahl, cited above, note 3; Dr. Wunderlich, "Volksentscheid und Regierungsvorlage," *Kölnische Zeitung,* 15 June 1926 (Nr. 438); Paul Schröder (Mecklenburg) (Deutschvölkische Freiheitspartei), Reichstag. *Verhandlungen,* 388 (3 Dec. 1925):4754.

[8] Theodor Neubauer, Reichstag. *Verhandlungen,* 388 (2 Dec. 1925): 4719–27; Ernst Schneller, ibid., 390 (30 April 1926): 6946–51.

[9] Ibid., 391 (9 Nov. 1926): 7977.

[10] DDP Papers, reel 38, folder 759, p.1. This memorandum is a valuable source concerning the first stages of the interparty discussions over possible regulatory legislation. There is no indication of author. It was perhaps composed by Baron von Richthofen, who served as the party's chief spokesman on these matters.

[11] Vorstand der Sozialdemokratischen Partei Deutschlands, *Referentenmaterial zur Fürstenabfindung* (n.p., n.d.), p. 2.

the Reich or the Prussian government attempted to confiscate the royal properties, action would have been blocked by the non-Socialist (*bürgerliche*) majority in the National Assembly or the Prussian Constitutional Assembly. This may perhaps be correct for the period after the elections for the National Assembly (19 January 1919), but does not explain why nothing was done immediately after the overthrow of the monarchy.[12] In 1927 Kurt Rosenfeld, a former Independent Social Democrat and for a short time during the revolution Prussian minister of justice, claimed he had discussed the seizure of the princes' properties with Hugo Haase late in 1918. He said Haase had stated that Prussia should go ahead on its own because the Council of People's Representatives was too busy with other matters to undertake any such action.[13]

Although there is some truth in the statement that the national government did not act because other business seemed more urgent and because it thought that the state governments could handle the problem satisfactorily, the basic reason no general confiscation occurred at the time of the revolution appears to have been rather different: "In the year 1919," Erich Koch-Weser stated, "the problem was to protect the princes from having their property confiscated without compensation, especially since this was attempted several times by Workers' and Soldiers' Councils." [14] Even though this statement was made several years after the event, Koch-Weser's remark is characteristic of attitudes then prevalent in "responsible" republican circles. Throughout this period the leaders of most of the parties, including the Majority Social Democrats, were constantly worried that the direction of affairs might slip from their hands. Eberhard Kolb has given abundant evidence of the republican leaders'

[12] Stampfer, pp. 443–44, describes the reasoning of the Council of People's Representatives as follows: ". . . [A]n ordinance by the Council of People's Representatives could have led to highly disagreeable consequences since one could foresee that under [certain] circumstances the ordinance [might be] revoked by means of regular [parliamentary] legislation. If they had decided on confiscation measures, the question would have at once turned to whom the confiscation applied: only the dynasties that had until then ruled and whose properties consisted mostly of agricultural holdings (*Grossgrundbesitz*), or large agricultural holdings in general, or all sizable property holdings [of whatever kind]? The Council of People's Representatives hesitated to make a decision on this complicated question." It is not clear whether Stampfer based this statement on definite information or simply described apparent reasons for the Council's inaction.

[13] *Sozialdemokratischer Parteitag 1927*, pp. 94–98.

[14] Reichstag. *Verhandlungen*, 388 (2 Dec. 1925): 4740, 4741.

26   CRISIS OF THE WEIMAR REPUBLIC

distrust of independent action on the part of Workers' and Soldiers' Councils.[15]

The agitation of the two parties on the extreme left likewise made republican leaders uneasy. The Spartacus League had proposed confiscation of all dynastic properties as well as the expropriation of the great landed estates and capitalistic industries, demands later continued by the Communists.[16] During the first months of the revolution the Independent Socialists appear to have assumed that the bulk of the former royal properties would pass into public ownership as a matter of course; they concentrated their attention on wider-ranging plans for socialization.[17] Later on, when the KPD began to threaten the Independents' role as spokesmen for many of the more radical workers, the USPD's parliamentary representatives made their demands for total confiscation of the princes' properties explicit.[18] Under the circumstances, when the appeal of socialization was great, it appears that moderate republican leaders simply did not dare consider any general confiscation of royal properties. The example would have been too dangerous.[19]

The Workers' and Soldiers' Council in Lippe-Detmold wanted to seize the properties of that small territory's former ruling family. When, early in December 1918, the Council

[15] *Die Arbeiterräte in der deutschen Innenpolitik 1918–1919, Beiträge zur Geschichte des Parlamentarismus und der politischen Parteien,* 23 (Düsseldorf, 1962): 121–22, 129–33, 183–96, 256–61, 292–302, 404–9. Unfortunately he does not discuss any conflicts arising out of the mishandling of royal properties. However, his treatment of the professional party leaders' fears of "disorder" in response to some councils' attempts to begin socialization is pertinent. In the same connection, see Richard N. Hunt, "Friedrich Ebert and the German Revolution of 1918," in Leonard Krieger and Fritz Stern (eds.), *The Responsibility of Power. Historical Essays in Honor of Hajo Holborn* (Garden City, 1967), pp. 315–34 and D.K. Buse, "Ebert and the German Crisis, 1917–1920," *Central European History,* 5 (Sept., 1972, Nr. 3): 234–55.

[16] Ossip K. Flechtheim, *Die Kommunistische Partei Deutschlands in der Weimarer Republik* (Offenbach a.M., 1948), p. 243; Eric Waldman, *The Spartacist Uprising of 1919* (Milwaukee, 1958), pp. 75–76, 104–5.

[17] See Hilferding's speech to the Congress of Workers' and Soldiers' Councils, *Die Freiheit* 20 Dec. 1918 (Nr. 66); Karl Kautsky, "Richtlinien für ein sozialistisches Aktions-Programm," ibid., 28 Jan. 1919 (Nr. 48); and the statement of party aims, ibid., 8 March 1919 (Nr. 113).

[18] For example, Drucksache (Nr. 1909), *Sitzungsberichte der verfassunggebend Preussischen Landesversammlung 1919/1921,* 8: col. 10285 and the related debate 2 March 1920.

[19] Ebert said in another context, "Socialism excludes everything arbitrary, it is order on the highest level; disorder, personal caprice and violence are mortal enemies of socialism" (quoted by A.J. Ryder, *The German Revolution of 1918,* Cambridge, 1967, p. 169). Könnemann, *Wissenschaftliche Zeitschrift der Universität Halle-Wittenberg,* 7: 543–45.

requested the opinion of the Provisional Government in Berlin, Ebert replied that "the question is a legal one, the decision of which must be reserved for the appropriate courts" and, about a month later, he repeated that "attacks on private property are not to be permitted." [20] In July 1919, the state's *Landtag* declared that all the former ruler's properties belonged to the state; however, this appears to have been enacted for tactical reasons in order to encourage the former ruler to discuss the terms of a reasonable settlement. At any rate, a legal settlement agreed to by both sides was concluded toward the end of December 1919.[21]

A handful of similar incidents happened elsewhere. In Brunswick the Workers' and Soldiers' Council tried to confiscate the duke's estates but their efforts were not lasting.[22] The *Volksrat* in Reuss considered seizure without compensation, but abandoned the idea when Eduard David, the national minister of interior, informed them that such an action would not be in accord with the principles of the new Constitution very soon to go into effect.[23]

The government of one small state was not deterred by such words of caution. In Saxe-Coburg-Gotha the ducal properties comprised nearly one-seventh of the territory of the state. The new state government, controlled by left-wing Independent Socialists, was determined to acquire these valuable properties.[24] When the duke rejected a very nominal cash offer, the government whipped a bill through the *Landtag* in a single day, 31 July 1919, dispossessing him of all his wealth.[25] Actually, the confiscation was of short duration. Within a few months, the national government felt obliged to intervene in the affairs of Gotha because of some very controversial school reforms. The Independent ministers

[20] Quoted by von Lindeiner-Wildau, Reichstag. *Verhandlungen*, 388 (2 Dec. 1925): 4736; Günther, p. 27.

[21] *Schulthess' Europäischer Geschichtskalender. 1919*, p. 307.

[22] Waldman, p. 98, note 61.

[23] Von Lindeiner-Wildau, Reichstag. *Verhandlungen*, 388 (2 Dec. 1925): 4737; Günther, pp. 27–28.

[24] Georg Witzmann, *Thüringen von 1918–1933. Erinnerungen eines Politikers* (Meisenheim am Glan, 1958), pp. 20–21, 182–84; Dr. Hermann Anders Krüger, "Das Reichsgerichtsurteil im Gothaer Herzogsprozess," *Frankfurter Zeitung*, 4 Dec. 1925 (Nr. 902). The fact that Duke Carl Eduard was by birth an English prince did not add to his popularity. *Vossische Zeitung*, 13 Jan. 1926 (Nr. 11).

[25] The need to enact such legislation before the new national constitution with its guarantee of private property rights came into effect was the reason for this haste.

were removed.[26] When a much less radical government was formed, it returned some of the seized properties to the duke and attempted to start discussions with him hoping to find the basis for a mutually satisfactory settlement. The duke, however, adopted a very stiff attitude. He preferred to win recognition of all his "legal" rights through the courts. A lengthy lawsuit followed, and ultimately the Supreme Court (*Reichsgericht*) voided the *Landtag*'s action.[27]

The national government's failure to confiscate the princes' properties (or regulate the situation in some other way) meant that the solution of the problem was transferred to the level of the state governments. The consequences of this policy became clear in a few years' time. With each state acting on its own, the terms according to which property settlements (*Abfindungen*) were made varied considerably.[28] In some cases, most notably that of Prussia, temporary measures taken during the revolution remained in effect seven years later, since no acceptable settlement had in the meantime been reached. Moreover, during the mid-twenties, lawsuits began to challenge the validity of many apparently settled arrangements. Out of this unclear situation came the highly excited, complex, but basically unnecessary, controversy of 1925–26.

It was hardly surprising that the various settlements showed considerable diversity. The arrangements made for the support of the ruling families before the revolution had also been complicated. Many different types of property were involved, and individual holdings had been acquired in a variety of ways. The existing laws distinguishing state property from that of the ruling houses represented the accumulated result of several centuries of princely decrees, family compacts, administrative orders, and parliamentary legislation. Accordingly, the exact legal status of a particular piece of property was sometimes very difficult to determine, even by experts.[29]

The negotiators entrusted with working out the settlements in the early twenties (and the legislators in the Reichstag in

[26] Günther, pp. 28–31; the exchange among representatives Neubauer, Bell, and Koch-Weser, Reichstag. *Verhandlungen*, 388 (2 Dec. 1925), 4725–26, 4739, 4740–41.

[27] Günther, p. 31.

[28] Schüren has assembled information on the various settlements, pp. 283–98; also see *Schulthess' Europäischer Geschichtskalender. 1919* ff.

[29] Günther, p. 109.

1926) had to try to ascertain the status of all kinds of possessions. The variety was endless: great agricultural estates, extensive forests, hunting preserves, urban real estate of all kinds, palaces and their furnishings, museums and art collections, theaters along with the props and costumes, family archives, manuscripts, coin collections, the crown jewels and regalia, castles, historical ruins, parks and gardens, spas, various business investments, government bonds, savings accounts and some large sums of cash, numerous endowments and charitable foundations, pensions, civil list payments, etc. A list itemizing the Hohenzollern property holdings filled seventeen large pages.[30]

These extensive properties had been acquired by correspondingly diverse means. If one searched far enough into historical records, certain estates proved to be allodial properties that had always been in the private possession of the princely families; others were originally fiefs acquired and transmitted according to the principles of feudal law, and still others had been obtained in recent times according to the forms of modern private law.[31] In part the ruling families had increased their wealth in the same manner as rich people everywhere. Some of them had made substantial savings from their annual income through efficient management of their estates or by personal economies.[32] Easy access to well-informed advice facilitated the discovery of remunerative investment possibilities—especially, but by no means exclusively, in real estate. Family estates were entailed, but personal inheritances, sometimes from outside the circle of close

---

[30] *Denkschrift zur Frage der Vermögensauseinandersetzung zwischen dem Preussischen Staat und dem vormals regierenden Königshause.* Prussia. Landtag. *Drucksache* (Nr. 8043), pp. 9032–48.

[31] The articles on "Domänen" by Rintelen, Praetorius, and J. Conrad in *Handwörterbuch der Staatswissenschaften* (3rd ed.; Jena, 1909–1911) provide a comprehensive survey of the legal, historical, financial, and administrative arrangements in the different German states before the revolution. The treatment of the subject in the 4th ed. (Jena, 1923–28) is less full. Also useful are the entries "Civilliste" and "Domänen" in *Wörterbuch des Deutschen Staats-und Verwaltungsrechts* (2nd ed.; Tübingen, 1911–14), 1: 537–44, 585–602; "Domänen," "Fürstenabfindung," and "Hofkammer der kgl. Familiengüter," in Bitter, *Handwörterbuch der Preussischen Verwaltung,* ed. Bill Drews and Franz Hoffmann (3rd ed.; Berlin and Leipzig, 1928), 1: 388–93, 597, 820; and Fritz Stier-Somlo, "Domänen" in *Handwörterbuch der Rechtswissenschaft,* ed. Fritz Stier-Somlo and Alexander Elster (Berlin and Leipzig, 1926–37), 2: 86–92.

[32] For instance, the very large fortune accumulated by the last grand duke of Mecklenburg-Strelitz. *Jahrbuch des öffentlichen Rechts,* 9: (1920): 223.

relatives, helped establish the fortunes of individual members of a ruling house.

However, it was undeniable that princes had had advantages for enriching themselves unavailable to private citizens. Their income had been tax exempt. The state treasuries had provided for the upkeep of the palaces, civil list payments, and other expenses required to maintain a dignity suitable for their rank. More importantly, much property had come to them in the past through political acts. Church properties in Protestant states had been secularized during the Reformation, and to a large degree suffered the same fate in Catholic territories later. Wars had resulted in the transfer of new properties into the hands of successful princes. As recently as 1866, conquest had given the Hohenzollerns title to properties in Hanover, Electoral Hesse, and Nassau where the legitimate rulers were deposed.[33] King William had even presented the Schmalkaldic Forest, taken from the elector of Hesse, to the duke of Saxe-Gotha as a reward for his services as an ally.[34] Critics on the left never forgot to cite the sale of mercenaries in the eighteenth century as the source of some princely fortunes, no doubt emphasizing the importance of these examples because they so clearly illustrated the basic disparity between the interests of princes and the interests of the people.[35]

After the revolution when officials of the state governments attempted to determine what properties belonged to the state, they accepted the general framework of laws and administrative practices as they had existed before 1918. Thus, in most cases, title was established at least preliminarily by reference to fixed pre-revolutionary legal categories. Here, too, the subject was very complicated. Basically these laws distinguished between property belonging to the state, en-

[33] Bismarck commented on 17 Aug. 1866, "It is perhaps true this makes an impression of injustice . . . however we have to do what is necessary for the Prussian state, and therefore we have not let ourselves be guided by any dynastic sympathy" (Die gesammelten Werke, 10, Berlin, 1928: 276). The princes of Hesse and Nassau obtained generous property settlements but Bismarck never released the funds intended for the settlement with the king of Hanover. This was the origin of the notorious Welfenfonds. Erich Eyck, Bismarck, Leben und Werk (Erlenbach-Zürich, 1941–44), 2: 369–78. Leftist speakers liked to remind conservatives of Bismarck's example. For instance the speech given by Scheidemann at a Reichsbanner meeting in Königsberg. Frankfurter Zeitung, 2 Feb. 1926 (Nr. 86).

[34] Handwörterbuch der Staatswissenschaften, 3rd ed., 3: 519.

[35] Berliner Tageblatt (Wochen-Ausgabe), 18 Feb. 1926; Frankfurter Zeitung, 23 Feb. 1926 (Nr. 144) and 27 Feb. 1926 (Nr. 156).

tailed possessions which were the private property of the
ruling family, and the personal property of individual members of the ruling family. Intermediate or debatable cases of
course existed. For example, the title to certain lands might
belong to the ruler although the income from them regularly
went to the state,[36] or, vice versa, palaces could be state
property to which, however, the ruling family had a recognized right of use.[37] How the ownership of specific types of
property had been defined in detail varied according to the
historical evolution of the individual states. Notwithstanding
certain general similarities, each state's laws were separate
and distinct.

Until early modern times no systematic division was made
between a ruler's private wealth and the income drawn from
the lands he ruled, just as no conceptual distinction was made
between the person of the ruler and his position as sovereign.[38] The *Kammer* or *Hofrentei* officials, who supervised the
collection and expenditure of revenues coming from the domainal properties and regalian rights, served the prince; the
formation of a *state* bureaucracy with its distinct areas of
responsibility was still in the future.[39] With the transition from
the old patriarchal system to the modern state the ideas and
practices of administration altered.[40] As early as the sixteenth
century in Brandenburg certain revenues had been ear-
marked for the regularly occurring expenses of the court.
Other specified revenues were assigned to the elector's privy
purse *(Schatulle)*, where they were available for the ruler to
use as he saw fit.[41] The separate management of the *Schatulle*

[36] In Baden, for example, domainal lands were recognized in 1818 as the property
of the grand duke but the *Land* had usufructuary rights (*Nutzniessung*). Köhler, p.
109.

[37] In Württemberg palaces and other property necessary for the maintenance of
the royal dignity constituted the *Krondotation* with legal rights divided between the
state and the royal family. *Handwörterbuch der Staatswissenschaften*, 3rd ed., 3: 517–18.

[38] Otto Hintze, "Geist und Epochen der preussischen Geschichte,"*Regierung und
Verwaltung* (2nd ed.; Göttingen, 1967), p. 6, and "Hof- und Landesverwaltung in
der Mark Brandenburg unter Joachim II.," ibid., p. 204; Gustav Schmoller, "Die
Epochen der Preussischen Finanzpolitik bis zur Gründung des deutschen Reiches,"
Umrisse und Untersuchungen zur Verfassungs-, Verwaltungs- und Wirtschaftsgeschichte
(Leipzig, 1898), pp. 114–19.

[39] Tax revenues were managed separately, usually under the control of territorial
Estates.

[40] In addition to the important articles by Hintze on this subject see Hans Haussherr, *Verwaltungseinheit und Ressorttrennung vom Ende des 17. bis zum Beginn des 19.
Jahrhunderts* (Berlin, 1953).

[41] Schmoller, pp. 124–26; Wilhelm Kiefer, "Das Problem der Fürstenabfindung.
I. Historische Entwicklung," *Frankfurter Zeitung*, 17 March 1926 (Nr. 202).

was terminated by Frederick William I, but later kings maintained a special *Dispositionsfonds,* which they spent for private or public purposes without accounting to anyone.[42] During the eighteenth century steps were taken in both Prussia and Austria to define the state properties and separate them from purely family possessions. Older forms lingered on in the small and middle-sized German states; ultimately the changes of the Napoleonic period necessitated a clarification. The task was gradually completed in the early nineteenth century. The process was not necessarily accomplished by one clean act. In Prussia, for example, King Frederick William I reorganized and unified the administration of the domains shortly after his accession in 1713. At the same time he proclaimed the rule that henceforth no part of them should be alienated. In itself this new regulation merely established the unity and indivisibility of all the dynastic properties,[43] however, the *Allgemeine Landrecht* (1794) proceeded further and recognized the domains as property of the state. The burden of debts incurred during the Napoleonic wars forced certain further changes; many domains had to be sold or mortgaged. In 1820 a new permanent arrangement was established. A fixed sum, the *Kronfideikommissfonds,* was drawn from the domainal revenues for the expenses of the royal house, the maintenance of palaces, and the like.[44] The remainder of the income from the domains was devoted to the payment of state debts.

Whereas during the early nineteenth century the middle-sized states followed the pattern of the larger powers in declaring the domains state property, the smaller states generally recognized their ruling families' title to the domains; not, however, without disputes. Since a prince's holdings often constituted a substantial portion of the territory, most state governments had insisted on the establishment of fixed rules regarding the management of the domains and specifying the share of revenues they could expect for the state budget. Sometimes, but not always, the states participated in the administration in the domains. Mecklenburg, with its *landständische* constitution, remained something of an anomaly

[42] Reinhold Koser, *Geschichte Friedrichs des Grossen* (Darmstadt, 1963; reprint of the 1925 edition), 2: 110–12.

[43] Cf. the significant comment of Otto Hintze, "Der österreichische und der preussische Beamtenstaat im 17. and 18. Jahrhundert," *Staat und Verfassung* (2nd ed.; Göttingen, 1962), p. 325, note 1.

[44] It amounted to 2.5 million thaler (7.5 million marks).

and never progressed even this far.[45] Forty-two and a half percent of the land in Mecklenburg-Schwerin belonged to the grand duke. For reasons of administrative convenience his officials distinguished between the domains proper and the domains of the household, but no legal separation was ever made.

Domains, to be sure, constituted only one source of income for princely families before 1918. Individual members of the ruling families sometimes built up private fortunes which they managed themselves. Property acquired by a ruler before his accession was considered strictly personal and he could dispose of it as he saw fit; property acquired later became part of the entailed family estates. These entailed possessions (the *Hausfideikommiss,* for instance) consisted of properties that had been kept apart from the domains when they were transferred to the state, or had been obtained later. In Prussia a special department of the royal household, the *Hofkammer,* was established in 1843 to manage the entailed properties of the ruling family and certain side branches, while the domains were administered by the Prussian *Ministerium für Landwirtschaft, Domänen und Forsten.*[46] The *Hofkammer* also was responsible for upkeep of the palaces and other royal buildings. Its officials were not part of the state bureaucracy.

Given such complexity of historical facts and laws, after the revolution most state governments tried to reach settlements by means of private negotiations with the legal and financial representatives of the former ruling house.[47] Agreements reached in this manner were normally ratified in due course by the state legislatures. Under the circumstances there were many occasions when divergent views over the actual facts had to be unwillingly reconciled. The final settlements therefore reflected advantages gained by one party or the other in the course of bargaining. Obviously, too, the political coloration of the cabinet responsible for the final compact affected the terms of the settlement.

Although each settlement differed from settlements concluded in other states, generally speaking the sorting out of private from state properties proceeded along broadly similar lines. Wherever the domains had not already been recognized as state property, the transfer was now made, sometimes, but

[45] *Handwörterbuch der Staatswissenschaften,* 3rd ed., 3: 544.
[46] Bitter, p. 830.
[47] Günther, pp. 37–41.

not always, with compensation allowed to the former ruling house. Likewise, the state governments gained title and possession of the most noteworthy palaces, museums, and other public buildings. On the other hand, nearly all entailed family possessions, as well as properties in the hands of individual members of the ruling family, all personal belongings and many furnishings, savings accounts, etc., were regarded as the uncontestably private property of the deposed royalty. There remained, however, in nearly all cases a large mass of various kinds of property for which both sides could present plausible claims. Former princes might argue that palaces which had been used primarily for residential purposes rather than for ceremonial functions were really their private dwellings, or they might insist that certain gardens and parks that had been improved through the expenditure of their private funds should not be transferred to the public without appropriate compensation. If private holdings adjacent to unquestioned state properties were transferred to the state to avoid administratively impractical parceling, suitable compensation, or perhaps the exchange of properties of equivalent worth, had to be determined. Most difficulties arose over valuable, income-producing properties, where with understandable zeal, each side showed particular persistence in trying to establish a clear title. Other kinds of problems also had to be worked out; for instance, who was to assume responsibility for the employment of former court servants and see that their pensions were paid. Many difficult hours were spent determining how much compensation, if any, was to be paid for the cessation of civil list payments which the states had formerly been obligated to make. Sometimes in order to avoid a deadlock over disputed claims, the negotiators resorted to barter.[48]

By 1925 the process of negotiations had, in most cases, been completed and the state governments believed that they had concluded permanent legal settlements with their former ruling families. In Baden, Württemberg, Saxony and Bavaria, for instance, the final agreements satisfied both sides on all essential points.[49] However, serious problems arose for a number of other states when the former rulers began to

[48] *Denkschrift*, p. 9023.
[49] See the statements made to the Legal Committee of the Reichstag, *Frankfurter Zeitung*, 13 Jan. (Nr. 31), 14 Jan. (Nr. 34), 15 Jan. (Nr. 37), 20 Jan. (Nr. 51), and 22 Jan. 1926 (Nr. 57).

contest the settlements they had accepted earlier. Some princes felt that they had been unfairly treated. Their lawyers argued that the state governments had obtained properties which did not rightfully belong to them. The situation in Thuringia was especially uncertain.[50] The state itself had been formed after the revolution by combining eight minor principalities. The former rulers advanced twenty-three different suits for compensation or the return of property. Chief among these claimants was the duke of Saxe-Coburg-Gotha, who adamantly rejected any talk of a negotiated settlement.[51] In June 1925, the Supreme Court ordered the state to return all the property claimed by the Saxe-Coburg-Gotha line.[52] The loss of these valuable properties and the threat of further adverse decisions in the courts left the Thuringian government with the prospect of hopelessly ruined finances. Only a few princes made such claims at first, but their example was speedily followed by members of other former ruling houses. It began to appear to many people that the princes and their legal advisers were seizing any pretext for demanding revision of the property settlements. "One cannot avoid the impression that these formerly ruling families presently have designs to draw as much land, money and [other] things of value as possible out of the states they earlier ruled in order to ensure themselves a highly luxurious and agreeable existence forever." [53] Often, too, it appeared that the more insignificant the prince, the more extreme were the demands made in his name.[54]

During the years 1924–25 the princely houses turned ever more frequently to the courts for redress. The preferred tactic was to challenge the state's title to a particular piece of property rather than to contest the validity of any settlement as a whole.[55] In the course of such a lawsuit the court was

[50] *Frankfurter Zeitung,* 25 Nov. 1925 (Nr. 877), 16 Feb. 1926 (Nr. 123).

[51] Ibid., 25 July (Nr. 548), 4 Dec. 1925 (Nr. 902).

[52] Ibid., 27 June 1925 (Nr. 472). The decision was based on a technicality regarding the drafting of the law. Neubauer, Reichstag, *Verhandlungen,* 388 (2 Dec. 1925): 4726.

[53] The "confidential" memorandum in the DDP Papers, cited above, note 10.

[54] The most scandalous case revolved around claims of two former mistresses of the last grand duke of Mecklenburg-Strelitz that the state was obligated to pay pensions which the duke had settled upon them. *Frankfurter Zeitung,* 9 and 10 Jan. 1926 (Nrs. 23–25). Even the descendants of princes who had lost their position as rulers of minor territories during the nineteenth century demanded *Aufwertung* of their "fixed" pensions. *Berliner Tageblatt* (*Wochen-Ausgabe*), 18 Feb. 1926.

[55] *Denkschrift,* p. 9023; Martin Schumacher (ed.), *Erinnerungen und Dokumente von Joh. Victor Bredt, 1914 bis 1933. Quellen zur Geschichte des Parlamentarismus und der politischen Parteien.* Dritte Reihe, Band 1 (Düsseldorf, 1970): 199–201.

presented with detailed historical and legal evidence that the contested piece of property was "private" in nature or origin. Since the courts usually decided in favor of the royal plaintiffs, some former rulers seemed to be regaining bit by bit most of the property they had previously ceded to the state.

The lawsuits the public found most irritating, and which even moderate politicians thought were unwarranted, concerned problems of *Aufwertung*, that is, the adjustment of the nominal worth of capital sums in old marks to a realistic, but necessarily much lower amount in the newly stabilized currency.[56] Like everyone else the princes had felt the full effect of the inflation on their fixed capital assets, on their wealth tied up in government bonds, savings accounts, the lump sum compensations some of them had received, and on the pensions or other fixed annual payments due them.[57] Once the inflation was curbed, the princes, again like everyone else, wanted to obtain restitution of the wealth they had lost and to have those assets they had managed to preserve recognized at full gold value. However, in 1924 the national government limited *Aufwertung* to 15 percent. (Later the Reichstag raised it to 25 percent for certain types of holdings.)[58] The judges reluctantly accepted this law in its application to ordinary citizens but they soon were hearing and accepting arguments that the normal restrictions of the *Auf-*

[56] "Whoever now has a law-suit with the state is certain of winning his case. Look at the settlements with the princes. I said the princes ought to receive the standard *Aufwertung*, nothing more. Stresemann vigorously agreed." Harry Graf Kessler, *Tagebücher 1918-1937* (Frankfurt/M., 1961), p. 444, diary entry for 16 Dec. 1925; Kohler, pp. 109–10; Günther, p. 58.

[57] The effects of the inflation are bitterly registered in the correspondence of the former duke of Saxe-Meiningen with his old friend General von Gossler. For example, the letters of 7 October, 26 Nov. and 27 Dec. 1923 and 5 March 1924. Bundesarchiv. H 08-34/7. At one point he apologized for not writing sooner, but he had not been able to afford a postage stamp until a relative in Italy sent him a small sum in lira. He also complained that his household no longer had any wine. In this letter (26 Nov. 1923) he wrote, "Truly it is an axiom: Any nation that submits itself to Social Democrats and lets them govern commits suicide, harakiri, and unquestionably must go to ruin. That is a natural law." On some—relatively minor—difficulties felt by members of the Hohenzollern family, see Sigurd von Ilsemann, *Der Kaiser in Holland* (2 vols.; Munich, 1967-68), 1: 112–14, 193–94, 228–29.

[58] Constantino Bresciani-Turroni, *The Economics of Inflation* (London, 1937), pp. 322–23; the dissertation by Otto Pirlet, *Der politische Kampf um die Aufwertungsgesetzgebung nach dem I. Weltkrieg* (University of Cologne, 1959); David B. Southern, "The Revaluation Question in the Weimar Republic," *Journal of Modern History.* On-Demand Supplement to Vol. 51, Nr. 1 (March, 1979): D1029–53; and Larry Eugene Jones, "Inflation, Revaluation and the Crisis of Middle-Class Politics: A Study of the Dissolution of the German Party System, 1923–28," *Central European History,* 12 (Nr. 2, June, 1979): 143–68.

wertung law did not apply to princely settlements.[59] For example, an arbitration court *(Schiedsgericht)* awarded the former grand duke of Mecklenburg-Schwerin a yearly income *(Rente)* of 230,000 marks plus a substantial lump sum payment in place of the *Rente* agreed upon in 1919. The award amounted to a revaluation at 65 percent. When the state government appealed, higher courts sustained the award.[60]

By the second half of 1925 a pattern of court decisions nearly always favorable to the princely families was only too visible. Monarchist sentiments and scarcely concealed anti-republicanism predominated in the courts and in much of the legal profession.[61] Once the controversy broke out into the open, the left stressed the evil results caused by obsequious jurists honoring nearly any financial claims their former masters made.

> Even more absurd—is the playing [around] with different property classifications in order to confuse the picture completely. [They] deal in Crown properties, public properties, entailed properties, with Crown estates, allodial estates, privy purse estates, etc., etc.; everything mixed helter-skelter. The net result, however, is always the same. The monarchistic judges come up with gold for the princes by the basketful, at the cost of the poor, suffering people.[62]

Without a doubt the courts were generous in their decisions, but the problem was more complex than the left often pretended, or the ordinary man in the street believed. The judges

---

[59] Eyck, 1: 381–84.

[60] *Frankfurter Zeitung,* 21 Dec. 1925 (Nr. 948).

[61] Bracher, *Die Auflösung,* pp. 191–98; Ernst Fraenkel, *Zur Soziologie der Klassenjustiz* (Berlin, 1927). The following exchange in the Reichstag was characteristic: Dr. Rosenfeld (SPD) attacked the greedy princes "and, secondly, our German justice which has helped them in their avarice. (Denials, Right.—Very true! Left)—I will give you the particulars. (Representative Dr. Schaeffer, Breslau: I can't understand how a jurist can say such a thing!)—Precisely as a jurist I have to say that, because I am obliged to state what I am able to criticize on the basis of my training *(Kenntnisse).* (Very true! Left—Representative Dr. Schaeffer, Breslau: No, you shouldn't do it because you are biased!)—Do you maintain that you personify neutrality? (Representative Dr. Schaeffer, Breslau: More than you!)" Reichstag. *Verhandlungen,* 390 (28 April 1926): 6897–98.

[62] Scheidemann (SPD), ibid. 388 (2 Dec. 1925): 4731. Alfred Brodauf (DDP) declared that the legal decisions against the states could be explained "essentially only by the anti-republican attitude [present] among German jurists today." *Frankfurter Zeitung,* 7 Feb. 1926 (Nr. 100); Wolfgang Heine, "Politik statt Judikatur," *Vossische Zeitung,* 17 Feb. 1926 (Nr. 41); Hellmut von Gerlach in *Welt am Montag* (22 Feb. 1926), quoted by Ruth Greuner, *Wandlungen eines Aufrechten. Lebensbild Hellmut von Gerlachs* (Berlin [East], 1965), p. 173.

were bound by existing law when rendering any decision. Since the Weimar government had never enacted appropriate legislation, the only relevant existing law dated from before the revolution and was, therefore, intrinsically favorable to the royal families. In form, most settlements were private agreements *(Vergleiche)* which, while legally binding, did not preclude either party from turning to the courts to judge conditions of fact or resolve differences of interpretation. And the courts did not hesitate to pass judgment. The decisions they reached, their defenders argued, were based on juridical considerations alone, uninfluenced by partisan attitudes.[63] Nevertheless, the tendency of the courts to ignore the interests of the states and the people was only too apparent.

It was the threat of numerous, long, expensive lawsuits, most of which were likely to be decided against the state, that finally induced the Prussian government to renew its efforts to work out a final settlement with the Hohenzollerns in mid-1925.[64] All earlier attempts to reach a settlement had failed. The views of the Prussian Ministry of Finance and legal representatives for the former royal family diverged on many important particulars. Division of the mass of contested property was difficult. Some critics claimed that the royal family wanted to rid itself of various palaces and museums which were white-elephants to maintain, while retaining the greatest part of the valuable income-producing properties.[65] But however important differences of this kind were, the chief impediment was the sensitivity of the political issues which were involved. Relatively few Germans were willing to accept the determination of the Hohenzollern claims by private negotiations or by "impartial" expert judgment. Large segments of the public interpreted a favorable assessment of the Hohenzollerns' legal rights as the moral and political equivalent of approval of their role in modern German history and, correspondingly, translated a denial of their property

[63] "One should not attack the courts because [their decisions] were not to the taste of a [particular political] party." Dr. Kahl (DVP), Reichstag. *Verhandlungen,* 388 (3 Dec. 1926): 4751. In a similar tenor, an article by Dr. Wilhelm Kisky in the *Kölnische Volkszeitung,* 8 Dec. 1925 (Nr. 935)—the paper's editors indicated that they did not agree with him on all points—and an editorial in the *Kölnische Zeitung,* 11 March 1926 (Nr. 186).

[64] Dr. Hermann Höpker-Aschoff (Finance Minister), Prussia. Landtag. *Sitzungsberichte,* 5 (2. Wahlperiode, 9 Dec. 1925): 7118–23; Günther, p. 110.

[65] See the pamphlet, *Verdienste der Hohenzollern* (Berlin, [1920]), p. 18. *Vossische Zeitung,* 23 June 1926 (Nr. 149); and Günther's relevant comments, pp. 52 and 105.

claims into a rejection of their claims to greatness. Scarcely any other issue divided the left and the right more distinctly than the debate over the historical merits of the Hohenzollerns. Above all, this bitter argument centered on the responsibility of William II for the war and Germany's eventual defeat.[66] His resounding promises were all too easily remembered and held against him, e.g., Paul Loebe's quasi-citation, "I see no parties any more, I will take money from them all." [67] Moreover, fears—for some, hopes—regarding the future of monarchism in Germany were on the minds of many people.[68]

The story of the handling of the Prussian royal properties after the revolution is quite complicated.[69] The kaiser's abdication was announced without his knowledge or consent in Berlin on 9 November 1918. Right up to the last minute he had tried to evade the necessary decision; he even considered renouncing the imperial dignity, while retaining the crown of Prussia. On 13 November, the Prussian provisional government sequestered all properties belonging to the entailed royal estates (*Kronfideikommissvermogen*),[70] apparently to preclude irregular seizures by unauthorized revolutionary

[66] "He and the . . . princes led the German people into the World War and, in doing so, into the greatest disaster and into the greatest economic chaos . . . . If the well-being (*Heil*) of the people is credited to the princes then the ruin of the people must be debited against the princes." Arnold Freymuth, *Fürstenenteignung—Volksrecht* (Berlin, 1926), pp. 19–20. The *Frankfurter Zeitung* stated, ". . . Germany owes its misfortune to the present head [of the Hohenzollern family]." 11 March 1926 (Nr. 188).

[67] *Frankfurter Zeitung*, 11 Jan. 1926 (Nr. 26). Likewise the speech by representative Saenger (SPD), Reichstag. *Verhandlungen*, 390 (29 April 1926): 6935–41. Ruth Fischer reports that Communist women's groups made yard-long garlands of the worthless currency from the inflation and carried them with placards saying, "This is Wilhelm's compensation." *Stalin and German Communism* (Cambridge, Mass., 1948), p. 608. Also the cartoons in *Rote Fahne*, 25 Dec. 1925 and 2 Feb. 1926.

[68] Some republicans proposed that the government be empowered to oversee the use of the funds which the former princes obtained as the result of the property settlements. For instance, the suggestion of Dr. Krüger, member of the Thuringian *Landtag*, "that all princes be paid annuities which could be withdrawn for counter-revolutionary acts (*bei staatsfeindlichem Gebaren*)." *Frankfurter Zeitung*, 4 Dec. 1925 (Nr. 902). The final compromise bill, which never passed the Reichstag, contained a section (Nr. 18) that provoked lively debate, establishing supervision and restrictions on how the former ruling families might use their money. Von Richthofen (DDP) approved controls on the grounds that "the state ought not supply the means for promoting a political tendency or supporting newspapers which continuously try to attack the government." In the *Rechtsausschuss* meeting of 25 June 1926, *Frankfurter Zeitung*, 26 June 1926 (Nr. 567); also, Reichstag. *Verhandlungen*, 390 (30 June 1926): 7720–24.

[69] Compare Schüren, pp. 26–46.

[70] *Preussische Gesetzsammlung*, 1918, Nr. 38.

bodies, and to establish its claim to properties which in its view now properly belonged to the state.[71] The Prussian minister of finance was entrusted with the responsibility for administering these properties. Actually, as so often happened in this quasi-revolution, the old officials (in this case, *court* officials, not even Prussian bureaucrats) remained in charge of the day-to-day management.[72] The Finance Ministry, we are told, "was not itself at once in the position to take over full administrative responsibilities [for properties] so widely distributed and difficult to supervise." [73]

The Decree of 13 November excepted the personal property *(Sondereigentum)* of the king and royal family from sequestration. However, the complex structure of property relationships did not permit such a simple division. In order to gain time for a more careful determination of ownership in doubtful cases, a supplementary decree (30 November 1918) ordered the "preliminary" sequestration of "all objects which belong to the personal property—whether part of the private property or part of the entailed possessions—of the former king of Prussia, of the royal house, and its members, and [which] are located in Prussia." [74] The general expectation seems to have been that the separation would take a little time; no one appears to have foreseen the difficulties which would ensue. The Prussian government explicitly assured the Hohenzollern family that the sequestration was only "a preliminary security measure." [75] Thus in November 1918, the official policy of the new revolutionary government in Prussia was temporary sequestration coupled with *de facto* recognition of extensive private rights of the Hohenzollern family. Confiscation was not on the agenda.[76]

[71] The "Begründung" to the 1920 proposed settlement. "Entwurf eines Gesetzes über die Vermögensauseinandersetzung zwischen dem Preussischen Staate und dem Preussischen Königshause." *Drucksache,* Nr. 1722. *Sammlung der Drucksachen der verfassunggebenden Preussischen Landesversammlung 1919/21.* 5: 2389; Günther, p. 26.

[72] *Denkschrift,* p. 9020.

[73] Ibid.

[74] *Preussische Gesetzsammlung, 1918,* Nr. 39.

[75] Fritz Schönbeck, "Zur Vermögenauseinandersetzung zwischen dem preussischen Staat und dem Hause Hohenzollern," *Die Justiz,* 1 (Nr. 2, Dec. 1925): 150. William II's formal renunciation of the throne was accompanied by a note (28 Nov. 1918), in which he urged the government to keep its promise to "free my property and that of my family and, also to ensure the unrestricted protection of life, honor, and property for the entire royal family." Otto Braun, *Von Weimar zu Hitler* (2nd ed.; New York, 1940), p. 211; Ilsemann, 1: 61.

[76] See Dr. Südekum's subsequent defense of the sequestration order. Prussia. *Sitzungsberichte der verfassunggebenden Preussischen Landesversammlung,* 4: 4808–11.

It appears to have been discussed, however. In 1927 Kurt Rosenfeld criticized the leaders of the SPD for their half-hearted policies during the royal properties' controversy the preceding year and, in defending his own conduct as Prussian minister of justice in 1918, said he had proposed confiscating the Hohenzollern properties at a meeting of the Prussian provisional government late in November.[77] The Majority Socialists argued against it, he said, on the grounds that they could not seize private property. His motion failed due to a 3 to 3 vote, with the Majority Socialists dividing against the Independents. Otto Braun hotly denied that any such vote had occurred; it was all Rosenfeld's imagination, he said.[78] On the other hand, Adolf Hoffmann, another former Independent minister, confirmed Rosenfeld's memory of the events.[79] Despite the sharpness of Braun's reply to Rosenfeld at the 1927 Party Convention, he himself admitted in his memoirs that the Prussian cabinet discussed the subject. From the start, he said, he had never wanted to treat the problem as a strictly legal matter. He had recommended "that the entire property of the Hohenzollerns be declared state property by a legally binding ordinance, and to settle a suitable *(angemessenen)* income on the royal house, which, if they wished, could be capitalized and paid at once." [80] According to Braun the Independent ministers excitedly rejected the idea. "How could I dare to demand that the hungering masses out there [give] the Hohenzollerns . . . a present [worth] millions." [81] He acknowledged that it would have been hard to do, given the revolutionary mood of the time. His memoirs do not say if the Independents made counterproposals, yet it hardly seems likely that they did not.

The brief period of cooperation between the two Social Democratic parties ended shortly after Christmas 1918. The Independents withdrew their ministers from both the national and the Prussian provisional governments. The Majority Social Democrats briefly carried the responsibility of governing alone, but soon the Democrats and the Center Party joined with them to form the first of the Weimar Co-

---

[77] *Sozialdemokratischer Parteitag 1927*, pp. 94–98.
[78] Ibid., pp. 98–100; Schulze, p. 236 and note 57, supports Braun's view.
[79] *Sozialdemokratischer Parteitag 1927*, p. 101.
[80] Braun, p. 212.
[81] Idem.

alitions.[82] In January, the Prussian government ordered the
establishment of a special commission of experts *(Immediat-
kommission)* which was to report on the legal problems relating
to the division of the royal properties, and to decide on the
proper classification (state or private) of the various individual pieces of property in question.[83] Once the commission
set to work, however, it showed a decided tendency to favor
the claims of the Hohenzollerns over those of the state.[84]
The members of the commission whose knowledge was most
expert were without question the old administrators; other
members of the commission tended to defer to their expertise, not at first suspecting that in numerous cases fuller
investigation might have disclosed reasons to question the
"private" character of some of the properties.

Before the commission had completed its work, representatives for the Hohenzollern family and the Prussian government initiated discussions with the hope of reaching a
mutually acceptable settlement *(Vergleich)*. The proposed settlement, under consideration throughout most of 1919 and
1920, followed most of the commission's recommendations,
and was, therefore, very generous to the former royal family.
Nonetheless, Dr. Albert Südekum, the finance minister,
placed great weight on the acceptance of the *Vergleich,* particularly after the new Weimar Constitution with its strong
guarantees of property rights came into effect in August
1919.[85] Otto Braun, then Prussian minister of agriculture,[86]
argued against the suggested settlement in the cabinet but
was not able to block it there. However, he did manage to
persuade the cabinet to submit any such settlement to the
Prussian Assembly for ratification, knowing that the members
of the Assembly were unlikely to approve a settlement unduly
favoring the Hohenzollerns. The representatives for the former royal house and the Prussian ministries of finance and
justice concluded their negotiations on 22 January 1920, with

[82] The new Reich cabinet headed by Scheidemann was formed 13 Feb.; the same
political combination took shape in Prussia a few weeks later (25 March) with Paul
Hirsch as minister-president.
[83] Schönbeck, *Die Justiz,* 1: 152; *Denkschrift,* p. 9022.
[84] Braun, pp. 212–13; Schüren, p. 32.
[85] Braun accused his colleague Südekum of wanting to be thought of as "a polite
obliging gentleman" by the representatives of the Hohenzollerns. Braun, p. 213.
Schulze, pp. 245–47.
[86] He became minister-president only after the Kapp *Putsch.* Schulze, pp. 290–
309.

the acceptance of the final text of a settlement which was to "regulate definitively" the property question.[87]

The terms of the settlement were, in Braun's words, "most unfavorable for the state." [88] It is unnecessary to describe the details of the proposed settlement; the all too obvious fact that the Hohenzollerns would obtain the bulk of the income-producing properties and, at the same time, receive a very large cash payment from the Prussian state in compensation for various rights which they were relinquishing aroused much protest. Moreover, serious critics found fault with the basic principles that had been applied in reaching the agreement, in particular, the handling of disputed issues entirely from a juristic point of view. The official commentary to the *Vergleich* itself emphasized that it "was limited to defining and regulating the relations of the state *(fiscus)* and the royal house [according to] civil law." [89] As a consequence, justifiable political or economic interests of the state were often disregarded, because its representatives were not in a position to make strong arguments for the retention of a particular piece of property solely on legal grounds while the agents for the royal family usually could do so. One of the general guidelines *(Richtlinien)* used in reaching the settlement worked especially to the advantage of the royal family. Ownership was determined first and foremost "on the basis of the existing legal situation," [90] that is, while some consideration was given to how a particular piece of property had originally been acquired, as well as to any changes in the form of ownership that had taken place in the course of time, decisive weight was given to the legal relationship operative "at the end of the development" (i.e., 1918).[91] In the past some important properties had been transferred from the domains to the entailed holdings of the royal family; the state's claim to them on the basis of the "existing law" was weak, but might have been much stronger if a different set of guidelines had been used.

The Prussian cabinet voted to submit the settlement to the Assembly despite the opposition of three Social Democrats (Braun, Hirsch, Haenisch). Two Social Democrats, Dr. Sü-

[87] *Drucksache,* Nr. 1722, p. 2389.
[88] Braun, p. 213.
[89] *Drucksache,* Nr. 1722, p. 2389.
[90] Ibid., p. 2391.
[91] Ibid., p. 2396.

dekum and Wolfgang Heine, the minister of interior, helped to make the majority. (Later, a speaker for the SPD excused their action on the grounds that they had been misled by a false memorandum on the subject.) [92] In fact, both men belonged to the right wing of the SPD; after the Kapp *Putsch* they fell into discredit and lost their cabinet posts.

The Prussian Assembly's first full debate on the proposed settlement took place on 2 March 1920. Within two weeks the Kapp *Putsch* supervened. Criticism of the Hohenzollern settlement had been voiced earlier, but with the experience of a monarchist *coup* vividly in mind, opposition to the *Vergleich* grew mightily during the spring and summer of 1920. The press and members of the Assembly's Legal Committee discovered many unsatisfactory features in the proposed agreement. The bill was tied up in committee until the end of the year. After some further debate, the house recommended that the government reexamine the settlement and the basis on which it had been drawn up—a face-saving formula to spare the cabinet and the governing parties the necessity of withdrawing the bill, or worse yet, proceeding to a vote on which the ruling coalition would have split.[93] Thus the 1920 agreement between the Prussian government and the Hohenzollern family came to naught; it was several years before any really significant progress toward a new agreement was made.

Most of the basic themes and arguments that were later used in the active controversy over the princely properties in 1925–26 were present in the 1920 debates. The supporters of a generous settlement for the Hohenzollerns argued that the question must be decided by legal criteria alone; that any intrusion of political considerations would be unjust; and, more generally, that the sanctity of property must be preserved (i.e., no dangerous precedents should be set in the handling of the royal properties).[94] The opponents of the settlement argued that the interests of the state and the people should be taken into account, not merely the, in part

---

[92] Ernst Heilmann (Charlottenburg), Prussia, Landtag. *Sitzungsberichte*, 11 (30 Nov. 1920): 14309.

[93] The motion is printed as *Drucksache*, Nr. 3654. It was debated 17 Dec. 1920. Günther, p. 30.

[94] Joseph Oppenhoff (Z), Prussia. Landtag. *Sitzungsberichte*, 8 (2 March 1920): 10305–8; Oskar Hergt (DVNP), ibid., 10315–26; Paul v. Krause (Ostpreussen) (DVP), ibid., 10368–72; Dr. Franz Alexander Kaufmann (DVNP), ibid., 11, (30 Nov. 1920): 14281–86; Ernst v. Richter (DVP), ibid., 14301–5.

outmoded, legal rights of the old ruling family.[95] They also held that the resources in question should be used to alleviate the general suffering, in particular to aid those wounded or otherwise hurt by the war.[96] The radical left (Independent Socialists and Communists) wanted to see complete confiscation.[97] The Social Democrats proposed a less drastic alternative: action by the Reichstag to permit legal expropriation in return for a "suitable" compensation.[98] None of the middle-class parties, including the DDP and Center, would consider either of these proposals. As mentioned, the general arguments pro and con and views regarding the form which a final settlement should take did not differ in any important respect between 1920 and 1925–26. What did change in the later period were the positions held by a number of significant parties. The Social Democrats, at least outwardly, went over to the radical idea of total confiscation. The Democrats and the Catholic Center moved away from the strict *Rechtsstandpunkt.* Indeed, some of their members entirely abandoned it. Even among the parties on the right qualifications crept into previously unequivocal statements. The inconclusive debate over the Prussian settlement in 1920 is, for our purposes, significant mostly as the basis from which debate would resume five years later on the national level.

Throughout these years the contested properties remained in sequestration. However, the officials of the Prussian ministry of finance treated the interests of the Hohenzollern family with great consideration.[99] Their legal and financial advisers were regularly consulted regarding normal management decisions affecting these properties. The ministry released some properties that were judged unquestionably private in character, as well as personal belongings and furnishings. For example, the former kaiser purchased his residence in Doorn with money obtained from the sale of a piece of property on the Wilhelmstrasse regarded as the private

[95] Eduard Gräf (SPD), ibid., 8 (2 March 1920): 10286–395; Heilmann (SPD), ibid., 11, (30 Nov. 1920): 14237–61.
[96] The remarks of Adolf Hoffmann (USPD) were typical, "I say time and again: Children's homes, homes for veterans, for the blind and crippled, homes for illegitimate children, orphanages, convalescent homes for the suffering [men] who have returned from the field—these are needed. . . . The splendidly situated palaces and castles should be used for them." Ibid. 8 (2 March 1920): 10342.
[97] *Drucksache,* Nr. 1909.
[98] *Drucksache,* Nr. 2043, Nr. 3415.
[99] *Denkschrift,* p. 9021.

possession of the royal family.[100] For his personal expenses he received substantial sums from the "private" *Königlichen Hausschatz* and from the income of the *Hofkammer* administration. Beginning in 1924 the former royal house received for its support a monthly payment of 50,000 marks derived from *Hofkammer* revenues. Although the revolution had reduced the royal family to the status of private citizens obliged to pay taxes, they had, in fact, been exempted from taxes until 1922.[101]

Between 1920 and 1925 efforts were made intermittently to work out a new agreement between the Prussian government and the Hohenzollern family.[102] On the basis of information discovered by thorough legal and historical investigations the Prussian government claimed some properties which it had earlier conceded to the former royal family. Moreover, the state put great weight on obtaining entire property complexes including the furnishings and equipment needed to maintain them, whereas a strictly legalistic division would have resulted in scattered parcels of land or buildings with few appurtenances. In order to obtain a single definitive settlement the negotiators for the Prussian government offered to submit all disputed claims to a special arbitration court *(Schiedsgericht)* to be made up of trained jurists. On the other hand, the legal advisers of the former royal family apparently felt no urgency to reach a final settlement. They insisted on the full recognition of the "legal" rights of the Hohenzollerns and would consider any variance from them only if suitable compensation was offered. They even argued that it would be a considerable renunciation of legitimate rights for the Hohenzollerns to accept arbitration procedures and that the state should match this concession by lowering its demands!

Therefore, very little progress was made until the winter of 1923–24. Dr. Ernst von Richter, Prussian finance minister since the end of 1921, submitted a new draft agreement to the representatives of the Hohenzollerns on 28 February 1924.[103] In this proposal were listed certain properties that

[100] Ibid., p. 9022.

[101] See the reports of the Reichstag *Rechtsausschuss* meetings on 21 Jan. and 4 Feb. 1926. *Frankfurter Zeitung,* 22 Jan. (Nr. 56) and 5 Feb. 1926 (Nr. 94).

[102] *Denkschrift,* p. 9023.

[103] Ibid. Von Richter was a member of the German People's Party (DVP). Schüren, pp. 39–41.

would go to the state and others which would definitely be turned over to the former ruling family, but the bulk of the disputed properties were to be submitted to the specially constituted court of arbitration. In addition, irrespective of legal rights, the state offered to turn over to the main line of the Hohenzollern family sufficient agricultural land and forest properties to permit them to maintain a "satisfactory" standard of living.[104] The Hohenzollerns were to renounce claims to certain specified palaces, parks, art works, the *Kronfideikommissrente,* and the like. Despite the fact that this proposal had been formulated in consultation with the Hohenzollern representatives, the response of their chief negotiator, Friedrich von Berg, was unfavorable, although not a complete rejection.[105] Further negotiations continued throughout the spring, but von Berg tenaciously maintained that the proposed settlement was insufficient—his hard line undoubtedly encouraged by the marked swing of public opinion to the right during the first half of 1924. The finance minister soon came to doubt that agreement was possible, and the negotiations once again languished.

During the course of these unproductive discussions, the representatives of the royal family began a series of lawsuits in an effort to obtain a clear title to some of the disputed properties and, very probably, to pressure the Prussian government into improving its terms. Until then the main line of the Hohenzollern family had not sought to gain recognition of its claims through the law courts although the head of a side branch of the family, Prince Friedrich Leopold, had started a suit in 1920 which was finally decided in 1924.[106] The Prussian government countered by introducing some legal proceedings of its own. Litigation, however, was both time-consuming and expensive and, as we have already pointed out, seldom resulted in decisions favorable to the state. During 1924–25 the courts decided a number of important cases. The Flatow-Krojanke properties claimed by Prince Friedrich Leopold;[107] the *Thronlehen* Oels, the chief

---

[104] The normal income from those properties was valued at one and a quarter million gold marks.

[105] Several letters between von Berg and Finance Minister von Richter are printed in the *Denkschrift,* pp. 9024–9. On von Berg's close ties to William II and the royal family see Heinrich Potthoff's introduction to *Freidrich v. Berg als Chef des Geheimen Zivilkabinetts 1918: Erinnerungen aus seinem Nachlass, Quellen zur Geschichte des Parlamentarismus und der politischen Parteien,* Series I, Vol. 7 (Düsseldorf, 1971): 37–73.

[106] *Denkschrift,* p. 9030.

[107] Ibid., p. 9075; Schönbeck, *Die Justiz,* 1: 156–58.

48   CRISIS OF THE WEIMAR REPUBLIC

holding and residence of the former crown prince; [108] and
the estate, Theurow, part of the *Hausfideikommiss*, [109] were all
declared private properties to which the Prussian state had
no claim.

Braun claims in his memoirs that because of monarchistic
sympathies Finance Minister von Richter showed too little
energy in fighting for the state's interests, but considering
the record of the German courts in judging other cases
Braun's criticism seems somewhat unfair.[110] In any case, von
Richter left the cabinet very early in 1925 as a result of the
break-up of the Great Coalition in Prussia. His replacement
was a member of the DDP, Dr. Hermann Hoepker-Aschoff,
under whose direction negotiations with the former royal
house were concluded. By the spring of 1925 it was apparent
that the Prussian state would gain nothing by waiting any
longer for a definitive settlement.[111] The prospect of further
unfavorable lawsuits was all too clear. Moreover, doubts had
been expressed whether the sequestration "temporarily" established in 1918 was still valid.[112] Confidential discussions
with the legal representatives for the Hohenzollern family
were therefore resumed, good progress was made, and on
12 October 1925 a new *Vergleich* was formally signed. The
agreement, of course, still had to be ratified by the *Landtag*,
but for the time being the terms of the settlement were kept
secret.[113]

The main portion of the *Vergleich* of October 1925 listed
the separate properties to be returned to the Hohenzollerns,
and those to be transferred to the state.[114] The Prussian
government estimated the value of the properties the Hohenzollerns would receive at just under 185 million marks and
those that the state would receive at 686 million.[115] In addition the Prussian state promised to pay 30 million marks
in compensation for the abandonment of its former obliga-

[108] *Denkschrift*, pp. 9088–89; Schönbeck, *Die Justiz*, 1: 158–160.
[109] *Frankfurter Zeitung*, 27 June 1925 (Nr. 472); Schumacher, *Bredt*, p. 208.
[110] Braun, p. 214.
[111] Schüren, p. 42, note 89, on the legal costs of the law suits.
[112] Schönbeck, *Die Justiz*, 1: 163.
[113] A deadline for ratification by 1 April 1926, was written into the agreement.
[114] The *Vergleich* along with later amendments is printed in *Preussische Gesetz-sammlung 1926*, Nr. 42.
[115] *Frankfurter Zeitung*, 3 Dec. 1925 (Nr. 900) and 9 Jan. 1926 (Nr. 21). These
estimates were challenged from various sides. Herr von Berg gave rather lower
figures, ibid., 10 Dec. 1925 (Nr. 920), while the Communists claimed that about
2,600 million was involved. Ibid., 3 Feb. 1926 (Nr. 89).

tions to provide the royal family a regular subsidy (the *Kronfideikommissrente*). Detailed arrangements were made regarding the administration and public use of the House Archives, the Royal Library, and a number of art collections.[116] Provisions were made for the employment or pensioning of former court servants and, finally, it was agreed to establish arbitration proceedings if any differences arose in the execution of the settlement. Dr. Hoepker-Aschoff later revealed—it was really no secret—that the Prussian Government had accepted the terms of the *Vergleich* somewhat unwillingly.[117]

By early November 1925, vague reports regarding the conclusion of the settlement began to circulate, even though the Prussian officials did not release any information until the first of December. The lack of definite facts encouraged rumors and speculation over the size of the settlement. The conjunction of the impending Hohenzollern settlement and the recent court decisions so favorable to the former princes, caused fear in republican circles that justifiable interests of the people (and the states) were being neglected. The conclusion of the negotiated agreement between the Prussian government and its former ruling house boded ill for some of the smaller states still facing difficult settlements. The finance minister of Thuringia announced that he had suggested to his counterparts in Prussia that they cooperate in seeking appropriate national legislation, but found them uninterested because of the near prospect of a settlement.[118] Under these circumstances the DDP, which, like so many parties, had long preferred not to involve itself with this "in all respects so complicated problem," [119] now decided to introduce a bill into the Reichstag in order to establish a new legal basis for all further settlements.

---

[116] A number of specified art objects were transferred into the private possession of the former royal family.

[117] To a meeting of the Rechtsausschuss, 24 April 1926. *Frankfurter Zeitung,* 25 April 1926 (Nr. 305) and his comments at the DDP *Parteiausschuss* meeting 10 March 1926. DDP Papers, reel 37, folder 731, pp. 8–10. He complained that the SPD was especially at fault for not taking action immediately after the revolution because the courts would not have challenged any ruling made by the Council of People's Representatives.

[118] *Frankfurter Zeitung,* 7 Nov. 1925 (Nr. 833).

[119] The *Vertraulich* memorandum, p. 3. DDP Papers, reel 38, folder 759.

III: The First Stages of the Controversy, November 1925 to January 1926: The Communists Set the Pace

The members of the Democratic Party's Reichstag delegation introduced their "Draft of a Law Concerning the Conflict with the Earlier Ruling Princely Houses over Property Rights" on 23 November 1925.[1] They acted in response to a formal request from their colleagues in the Prussian *Landtag* and less formal urgings from members of the Thuringian *Landtag*.[2] The concern they expressed was genuine, but it is hardly likely that the leaders of the DDP would have proposed this bill had they foreseen the difficulties which soon developed.[3] Clearly, they hoped for rapid action; this was essential if the bill was to aid the Prussian government.[4] The provisions of the bill were deliberately kept brief. The proposal would

[1] Reichstag. 3. Wahlperiode. *Drucksache*, Nr. 1527. *Frankfurter Zeitung*, 22 Nov. 1925 (Nr. 871); letter from the DDP *Reichsgeschäftsstelle*, "Die Arbeit der Deutschen Demokratischen Landtagsfraktion," dated 26 July 1926. DDP Papers, reel 30, folder 760.

[2] Hermann Dietrich (DDP), Reichstag. *Verhandlungen*, 388 (2 Dec. 1925): 4716; *Frankfurter Zeitung*, 7 Nov. 1925 (Nr. 833).

[3] Werner Stephan, *Aufstieg und Verfall des Linksliberalismus, 1918–1933* (Göttingen, 1973), pp. 318–22.

[4] The "Vertraulich" memorandum, DDP Papers, reel 38, folder 759, p. 3. A letter from the national party office to party workers in the election districts, 28 Dec. 1925, mentioned the princes' property settlements as a good subject for publicity. There was no indication that the issue might cause controversy within the party. DDP Papers, reel 38, folder 758.

have empowered each state to make a definitive settlement with its former ruling family through the passage of appropriate legislation in the state legislature. Significantly, no appeal to the courts would have been allowed (*Ausschluss des Rechtsweges*).[5] In addition to these main features, the bill stipulated that no compensation was to be made for payments or for other rights to which the princes had been entitled in their capacity as heads of state, and that revaluation of previously concluded settlements (*Aufwertung*) must be according to the same rules affecting ordinary citizens.

The bill's sponsors obviously expected it to receive considerable support from other parties. Given the relatively small size of the Democratic Party—it controlled only 32 seats out of 493 in the Reichstag[6]—such a bill would have been hardly more than a gesture unless there existed reasonably good prospects of gaining support from other parties.[7] It is not certain whether representatives for the DDP sounded out other parties before they introduced their bill.[8] One thing is clear; the text of the bill itself indicates one political party from which they expected to get substantial cooperation. The DDP proposal was simply a revised and slightly expanded version of a bill which had been submitted to the Reichstag in 1923 by the Social Democratic Party and had never been acted upon.[9] As recently as September, the SPD Party Convention had accepted and referred to the Reichstag delegation a resolution which recommended:

Property settlements with the former princely (*landesfürstlichen*) families are to be regulated for all the states by a national law.

[5] *Drucksache*, Nr. 1527.
[6] Statistisches Reichsamt, *Statistisches Jahrbuch für das Deutsche Reich*, 45: 446–49. Useful on the problems caused by the party's relatively small size: Werner Schneider, *Die Deutsche Demokratische Partei in der Weimarer Republik, 1924–1930* (Munich, 1978).
[7] One of the DDP members who was most active in the long legislative discussions subsequently wrote that the DDP's proposal had had no real chance of success because it involved a constitutional issue and thus required a two-thirds vote to pass. But this statement may have been influenced by hindsight. Hartmann Freiherr von Richthofen, "Aufwertung und Fürstenabfindung," in *Zehn Jahre Deutsche Republik*, ed. Anton Erkelenz (Berlin, 1928), pp. 295–98.
[8] It seems very likely that there was contact among members of the DDP Reichstag delegation and some of their colleagues in the SPD and probably also the Center Party; however, I did not find any conclusive evidence of such discussions. It is also not clear to what degree the Prussian finance minister Hermann Hoepker-Aschoff, who was a member of the DDP, was drawn into the discussion of the proposed bill. He very promptly stated that the Prussian government hoped it would succeed. *Frankfurter Zeitung*, 6 Dec. 1925 (Nr. 909).
[9] Reichstag. 1. Wahlperiode. *Drucksache*, Nr. 5778; *Vorwärts*, 4 May 1923 (Nr. 208).

The real property of these families (i.e. palaces, museums, estates, forests) is to be declared, in principle, public property. Manner and extent of the compensation [to be] granted will be determined by law, excluding appeal to the courts.[10]

The origin of the DDP proposal did not go unobserved. Dr. Kahl, speaking for the DVP, pointed out, ". . .the Democrats have only borrowed this bill, if I may say so." [11]

It is possible that the DDP's decision to sponsor a new version of an old SPD bill was simply designed to increase the chances of getting appropriate legislation passed promptly; more likely, it may have been intended as part of a wider strategy, a gesture of accommodation toward the Social Democrats. Ever since October, when the German Nationalists left the first Luther cabinet, leaders of all the parties had been preparing the ground for the formation of a new governing coalition. The chairman of the DDP, Erich Koch-Weser, believed that the time had come for the creation of a Great Coalition government.[12] At a meeting of the party's Advisory Committee (Parteiausschuss) 4 December, he stated,

> Intrinsically no one can blame them [the Social Democrats] for not having any great desire for this coalition and that they demand guarantees. However, if the Social Democrats refuse on principle [to join] the Great Coalition, then that signifies a disavowal of our policies. We will attempt to bring the Social Democrats onto the straight middle [path].[13]

He did not explicitly mention the bill regarding the princes' property settlements, or, indeed, any other specific issues except the Locarno agreements, but it is plausible to consider the DDP bill as part of a bid for generally closer cooperation with the SPD.[14]

On the second and third of December, the first reading of the DDP bill took place in the Reichstag. Its reception was

[10] *Sozialdemokratischer Parteitag 1925*, p. 316.
[11] Reichstag. *Verhandlungen*, 388 (3 Dec. 1925): 4749.
[12] For example, his remarks to the party Executive Board (*Vorstand*), 3 Nov. 1925. DDP Papers, reel 36, folder 729; also the letter from the national office to party officials throughout the country, 10 Nov. 1925. DDP Papers, reel 38, folder 758.
[13] DDP Papers, reel 38, folder 749, p. 1. His support of the Great Coalition was based primarily on considerations of expediency: "Our policies must aim . . . at the creation of a Great Coalition so that the Social Democrats protect us from the unreliability of the right, and the Center Party and the German People's Party protect us from the Social Democrats pursuing a one-sided policy of socialization." Idem. A little later, however, he said that the Great Coalition was necessary to keep parliamentarism from faltering. Ibid., p. 3.
[14] So, too, Schüren, pp. 49–51.

mixed. Generally speaking, the parties of the right and right center opposed it, some preferring not to interfere with the conclusion of the settlement between Prussia and the Hohenzollerns.[15] They raised a number of legal and constitutional objections, particularly against any suspension of normal recourse to the courts.[16] Furthermore, the bill was criticized because it would turn the state governments into judges of cases in which they were themselves interested parties.[17] Only the Social Democrats expressed general approval of the bill, but without making a strong early commitment that might have been expected, considering the derivation of the DDP proposal.[18] Even they suggested that it required further improvement.[19] The Center Party expressed its desire to work for a solution "which combines the defense of private rights that truly need protection with the required consideration of the state's welfare," but indicated a number of serious reservations concerning the formulation of the DDP bill.[20] The Communist Party rejected the proposal outright.[21]

At best, the DDP proposal was accepted only "as a useful basis for further discussions." [22] Even Hermann Dietrich, who

[15] *Berliner Lokal-Anzeiger*, 2 Dec. 1925; Eduard Heilfron, "Die Abfindung der Fürstenhäuser," *Deutsche Allgemeine Zeitung*, 1 Dec. 1925.

[16] "It is clear to me that this law not only [involves] a constitutional change but is directly contrary to the constitution." Von Lindeiner-Wildau (DNVP), Reichstag. *Verhandlungen*, 388 (2 Dec. 1925): 4737; August Hampe (WV), ibid., (3 Dec. 1925), pp. 4745–48; "I am of the opinion that the exclusion of recourse to legal proceedings is absolutely incompatible with democratic principles." Dr. Kahl (DVP), ibid., p. 4739.

[17] Dr. Pfleger (BVP), ibid., pp. 4752–54; Karl Anton Schulte, "Die vermögensrechtliche Auseinandersetzung mit den Fürsten," *Germania*, 30 Jan. 1926 (Nr. 49); like Schulte, Otto Koellreutter recognized the need for legislation but considered the DDP bill poorly written. "Die Auseinandersetzung mit den ehemaligen Fürstenhäusern," *Deutsche Juristen-Zeitung*, 31; (Nr. 2, 15 Jan. 1926): 111–12.

[18] Scheidemann (SPD), Reichstag. *Verhandlungen*, 388 (2 Dec. 1925): 4734. Social Democratic sources contented themselves with merely noting the similarity between the two bills. *Vorwärts*, 1 Dec. 1925 (Nr. 566); Vorstand der Sozialdemokratische Partei Deutschlands, *Referentenmaterial zur Fürstenabfindung*, p. 2; *Jahrbuch der Deutschen Sozialdemokratie für das Jahr 1926* (Berlin, 1927), p. 112.

[19] One of the points the Social Democrats were to insist most strongly upon was the possibility of revising previously settled arrangements (*Rückwirkung*). Scheidemann, Reichstag. *Verhandlungen*, 388 (2 Dec. 1925): 4734.

[20] Dr. Bell, ibid., pp. 4739–40. *Germania*, the party's official paper, reported the latest developments but at first avoided any expression of opinion, cf. 29 Nov. (Nr. 558), 3 Dec. (Nr. 564) and 4 Dec. 1925 (Nr. 566); the *Kölnische Volkszeitung*, however, printed differing viewpoints at an early date, 5 Dec. (Nr. 902), 8 Dec. (Nr. 909) and 18 Dec. 1925 (Nr. 935).

[21] Neubauer, Reichstag. *Verhandlungen*, 388 (2 Dec. 1925): 4719–27; Schneller, ibid. (3 Dec. 1925), pp. 4759–61; *Rote Fahne*, 2 Dec. 1925.

[22] Scheidemann, ibid., p. 4734. Dr. Bell's statement for the Center Party was even more guarded, ibid., p. 4740.

introduced the bill for the Democrats, conceded that it was not the only possible solution; he said he would define merely "the core" of the proposal and leave the details to be improved or modified in committee.[23] By and large only general principles were touched upon in the debate. Nevertheless, it was clear that most of the parties recognized the need— however qualified—for some kind of legislation, and were preparing for the usual process of argumentation, bargaining, and compromise. At this point, none of them wished to be tied down too closely. Rather typically, the speaker for the Center Party ended his statement of principles by quoting two imposing, but not very specific, Latin maxims: *justitia est fundamentum regnorum* and *salus publica suprema lex esto.*[24]

The Communist Party (KPD) submitted an alternative proposal, which was debated along with the bill submitted by the Democrats.[25] The Communists wanted national legislation to confiscate all royal properties without compensation and then to use the proceeds for the relief of the needy.[26] No other party took the KPD bill seriously, although they all denounced it. Even the chief Social Democratic speaker said, "The Communist bill is introduced entirely for [purposes of] agitation. It will get nowhere in parliament." [27] The spokesman for the KPD himself admitted that the bill had no chance in the Reichstag.[28] In a more constructive vein, the Communists very soon introduced a bill to suspend all lawsuits until a *Reich* law was passed, the so-called *Sperrgesetz.*[29] After

[23] Ibid., p. 4716.
[24] Ibid., p. 4740. The *Vossiche Zeitung* declared that the Center Party would probably decide the fate of the DDP's bill, 2 Dec. 1925 (Nr. 288).
[25] Reichstag. 3. Wahlperiode. *Drucksache,* Nr. 1539.
[26] They specified in some detail how each type of property was to be used for the relief of wounded veterans, orphans, landless peasants, etc. Similar proposals were submitted to, and rejected by, the Prussian *Landtag. Sitzungsberichte,* 5 (14 Nov. 1925); 6516, 6820; ibid. (9 Dec. 1925), pp. 6958–59, 7493.
[27] Scheidemann, Reichstag. *Verhandlungen,* 388 (2 Dec. 1925): 4734; *Vorwärts,* 3 Dec. 1925 (Nr. 570). Dr. Kahl (DVP), whose views otherwise had little in common with those of Scheidemann, held, "The Reichstag would stand in danger of losing its authority if it seriously thought to occupy itself with a motion of this sort." Ibid. (3 Dec. 1925), p. 4738.
[28] Neubauer, ibid. (2 Dec. 1925), p. 4721.
[29] Ibid. (11 Dec. 1925), p. 4811. The *Sperrgesetz* received speedy and generally favorable handling by the Legal Committee. The proposal received some modifications—in particular a time limit for the suspension of legal proceedings. *Frankfurter Zeitung,* 27 Jan. (Nr. 69), 29 Jan. (Nr. 76), and 3 Feb. 1926 (Nr. 89). The Reichstag then passed the bill with a minimum of debate. *Verhandlungen,* 388 (4 Feb. 1926): 5299–300. The period of the law's validity was later extended several times, but it finally expired 30 July 1927. *Jahrbuch der Deutschen Sozialdemokratie für das Jahr 1927*

the completion of the first round of debate all three bills were referred to the Legal Committee for a detailed examination.

The first mention of the possible organization of a referendum occurred while the DDP and KPD bills were being discussed. On 1 December, one of the Berlin tabloids, *Berliner Zeitung*, broke in a sensational way the story that some Social Democrats were discussing the possibility of a referendum.[30] The next day, Scheidemann ended a speech he delivered in the Reichstag with a warning to his fellow legislators:

> The land owes the princes nothing, the princes [owe] the land everything. . . . There is inflammable material enough outside. Let us prevent sparks spreading which could cause great harm. Imagine how upset the people must be by a referendum. . . . I have no doubt what answer they would give.[31]

The Communists immediately pursued the idea. On 3 December, Ernst Schneller turned to Scheidemann: "We will not make it so easy for you to pose here as [a party] that fights monarchist designs and compensation for the princes. We know full well that somewhere off in the committees you will still vote guardedly for the settlements." He continued,

> Gentlemen of the Social Democratic Party, if you truly think that the princes owe the land everything, then you should ask the majority of the working people outside. You will have the millions of unemployed and part-time workers, victims of the war and of working [conditions], . . . the millions of mortgage holders and the small savers, the millions and millions of workers, white collar people and public employees behind you. However, . . . you fear the mobilization of the masses because your politics can only be a politics [directed] against the masses. You feed the masses with fine phrases here in parliament but don't want to take even a single practical step really to help them. We shall utilize the occasion in order to show all the victims of the capitalistic system how your politics look, and call upon them to protest this crying scandal by which millions [are being] thrown to the princes.[32]

(Berlin, 1928), pp. 21–22; August Wegmann, "Rechtspflege," in *Politisches Jahrbuch 1927/28*, pp. 619–20.

[30] Vorstand der Sozialdemokratischen Partei Deutschlands [ed.], *Sozialdemokratische Parteikorrespondenz für die Jahre 1923 bis 1928 (Ergänzungsband)* (Berlin, 1930), p. 303; *Vorwärts*, 1 Dec. 1925 (Nr. 567).

[31] Reichstag. *Verhandlungen*, 388 (2 Dec. 1925): 4735. This speech was later reprinted as a pamphlet for use in the referendum campaign, *Fürsten-Habgier; Die Forderungen der Fürsten an das notleidende Volk* (Cassel, 1926).

[32] Reichstag. *Verhandlungen*, 388 (3 Dec. 1925): 4761.

Two of the chief Communist goals that would be maintained for the duration of the controversy were apparent in this statement: to embarrass the leaders of the SPD as much as possible by trying to make them appear insincere in their commitment to the interests of the working classes and to suggest that any action instituted through parliamentary channels was *ipso facto* suspect.

Simultaneously, the KPD Central Committee sent an open letter to the leaders of the SPD, the Free Trade Unions,[33] the *Reichsbanner,* and the Red Front Fighters League.[34] The letter stressed the mass dissatisfaction with the property settlements, the plight of millions of working people, and the great wealth of the former rulers which would undoubtedly be used to finance anti-republican activities. "It would be a crime for the workers to watch this plundering expedition [directed] against the laboring population without taking action." In order to stop the princes, the Communist leaders recommended the use of "the small means which the Weimar Constitution offers." Mentioning the news item that some Social Democratic circles were considering a referendum, they indicated that the KPD Central Committee had also discussed the subject in a recent meeting and urged that it was important to take "unified steps in order to start a referendum" on the basis of confiscation without compensation. They expressed confidence that the millions of needed votes could be assured by decisive joint action, and suggested as a first step that all the organizations participate in a planning session within the next few days. Except for the Red Front Fighters, none of the organizations addressed considered the letter worth formal reply. They treated it simply as a "maneuver" which it would be best to ignore.[35]

Later, the Social Democrats claimed that the Communists stole the idea of a referendum.[36] According to Social Dem-

[33] The *Allgemeiner Deutscher Gewerkschaftsbund* (ADGB), the *Allgemeiner freier Angestelltenbund* (AfA), and the *Allgemeiner Deutscher Beamtenbund* (ADB).

[34] Dated 2 Dec., published by *Rote Fahne,* 4 Dec. 1925. The main slogan of the referendum campaign, "Keinen Pfenning den Fürsten!" served already as a headline. Idem.

[35] This was also the judgment of the *Frankfurter Zeitung,* 4 Dec. 1925 (Nr. 904). Heinz Habedank, *Der Feind steht rechts* (Berlin, 1965), pp. 24–26. Cf. the statement of the *Reichsbanner* leaders: "The Executive Board of the *Reichsbanner* has . . . still not answered. And it will *not* answer! . . . Allies like the Communists who want to fight against the princes' robberies only in order to serve their partisan aims and not for the sake of the cause itself would be enemies inside our camp." Reprinted from *Volkstimme* (Magdeburg), 22 Dec. 1925, by *Rote Fahne,* 23 Dec. 1925.

[36] *Vorwärts,* 20 Jan. (Nr. 31) and 9 Feb. 1926 (Nr. 65); *Sozialdemokratische Partei-*

ocratic sources, their party leaders had been discussing the possibility of a referendum in the fall of 1925 even before the public at large became concerned.[37] However, they had then been impressed by the difficulties of organizing and, especially, financing a nationwide initiative and referendum movement and, therefore, decided against it. Also, certain unspecified "tactical questions which were no less weighty had to be taken into account," [38] no doubt, the far-ranging implications involved in the choice of parties with which the SPD would cooperate in such a venture. By early December, to judge by the Scheidemann speech, the party leadership had presumably decided to hold the announcement of a referendum in reserve, but to use the recurrent mention of this possibility as a means of putting pressure on the Reichstag for speedy passage of effective legislation.[39]

Lacking definitive evidence when and how the KPD Central Committee made its decisions, it is impossible to judge whether the Social Democrats were correct in their assertion that the Communists appropriated the project for a referendum for their own partisan purposes without concern for "genuine results." [40] The Communist Party certainly used the campaign against the princely settlements to identify themselves very successfully with a popular mass issue and to create as many difficulties as possible for rival parties. However, it is not impossible that the Communists developed the idea of proposing a referendum on their own. After all, the idea of using the Weimar Constitution's provisions for direct popular legislation was no monopoly of the SPD. Various plans regarding referenda were circulating among a number of different groups in 1924–25. Middle-class people ruined by the inflation were discussing initiative and referendum proceedings to revise the *Aufwertung* law,[41] while a

---

korrespondenz... 1923 bis 1928, p. 303; so, too, Carl Landauer, *European Socialism* (Berkeley, 1959), 2: 1280–81.

[37] *Jahrbuch der Deutschen Sozialdemokratie... 1926*, p. 6; Stampfer, p. 445.

[38] From the report by Prussian *Landtag* representative Ernst Heilmann to a conference of Berlin party functionaries, "Unsere Stellung zur Fürstenabfindung," *Vorwärts*, 27 Oct. 1926 (Nr. 506).

[39] In addition to the speech in the Reichstag quoted above, Scheidemann made similar remarks at a large meeting in Berlin on 8 Dec., *Frankfurter Zeitung*, 10 Dec. 1925 (Nr. 918); see also *Vorwärts*'s comments 2 Dec. 1925 (Nr. 569) and Heilmann's statement. Prussia, Landtag, *Sitzungsberichte* 5 (12 Dec. 1925): 7174–75.

[40] *Sozialdemokratische Parteikorrespondenz... 1923 bis 1928*, p. 303.

[41] Mentioned by Wilhelm Keil in a report to the SPD convention September 1925. *Sozialdemokratischer Parteitag 1925 in Heidelberg* (Berlin, 1925), p. 199. The success of

group concerned over land settlement problems had actually taken the first steps, but had then dropped the project.[42] In 1924, the *Deutsch-Hannoveranische Partei* sponsored a plebiscite to separate Hanover from Prussia and thus undo the results of the war of 1866.[43] The British ambassador reported persistent rumors that the government would submit the Locarno pact to the people through a referendum.[44] Some trade union groups urged the reestablishment of the eight-hour day by popular vote.[45] Several resolutions calling for the use of referendum proceedings were submitted to the SPD's national party convention in 1925. The Breslau party organization, for example, proposed a series of radical social and economic measures (including the confiscation of the Hohenzollern properties in return for moderate pensions for the living members of the family) as a kind of "general accounting" with profiteers of the war and inflation.[46] The Communists themselves had advocated mass demonstrations and a referendum against the new tariff legislation passed earlier in 1925; [47] they had even undertaken to collect signatures for the start of an initiative and referendum to give full amnesty to political prisoners.[48] With so much talk of referenda for different purposes in the wind, it is not too important whether

---

the SPD-KPD sponsored initiative over the' princes' properties encouraged the inflation victims actually to try to start their own initiative. The government was highly alarmed and blocked further developments. Schiffers, pp. 206–10, 224–26; Southern, *Journal of Modern History,* On-Demand Supplement to Vol. 51, Nr. 1: D1047–48.

[42] Anschütz, p. 390; Schiffers, pp. 223–24.

[43] Carl Severing, *Mein Lebensweg* (Cologne, 1950), 2: 14–16; Schulz, 1: 319.

[44] Lord D'Abernon to Foreign Minister Chamberlain, 1 Nov. 1925. *Documents on British Foreign Policy, 1919–1939.* Series 1A, Vol. 1, Nr. 43. The preceding year *Vorwärts* had suggested that the Dawes Plan be submitted to the people in a referendum. Stürmer, p. 47.

[45] Dissman and Schafer, both representatives of the Metal Workers Union, argued for this course of action at the 1925 ADGB convention. Allgemeiner Deutscher Gewerkschaftsbund, *Protokoll der Verhandlungen des 12. Kongresses der Gewerkschaften Deutschlands* (Berlin, 1925), pp. 137–42, 150. However, Schleicher, for the Wood Workers in Berlin, expressed the more dominant view: "In my opinion the referendum can only be one of the many weapons that one uses in the fight for the shorter working day. . . . I am of the conviction that one must treat this weapon very cautiously, that much depends on when it is employed. (Very true!) To ask a people [to make] a decision over the 8-hour day through the ballot box, who just a half-year ago elected a Hindenburg to the Presidency, I hold far out of place. (Very true!)" ibid., p. 167.

[46] *Sozialdemokratischer Parteitag 1925,* pp. 313–15.

[47] According to a report in the *Frankfurter Zeitung,* 22 June 1925 (Nr. 456).

[48] The confidential "Lagebericht! Im August 1925," German Foreign Office Records, reel 2281, frame E137158.

the KPD picked up the idea of a referendum on the properties issue from the SPD; much more significant is the fact that it set about putting the idea into action.

The KPD had always advocated confiscation of the princes' properties. Nevertheless, it is not entirely certain that the Communist leaders had actually committed themselves to sponsor an initiative and referendum when they sent their open letter to the SPD and the other organizations.[49] The letter probably was intended to sound out rank-and-file Social Democrats and trade unionists as much as the leaders to whom it was addressed.[50] One suspects that perhaps the crucial decision was made somewhat later (mid-December?) when it had become quite plain that a great many people would welcome a simple, drastic law. The official East German history of this period states that the Central Committee decided on 11 November 1925 to have the KPD Reichstag delegation submit a bill proposing total confiscation of the princes' properties and to make preparations for an initiative and referendum in case the Reichstag rejected this confiscation proposal.[51] However, it does not say when the actual decision to go ahead with the plans for a referendum was made.[52] The Communist Party's leaders in the fall of 1925 were realistic men. They knew the limits of their party's strength, and surely would have avoided any highly publicized undertaking that ran any great risk of turning into a damaging failure.[53]

[49] Communist accounts, of course, credit the party's leaders with seeing at once the opportunities which the royal properties issue offered and rapidly adopting the proper tactics. For example, Thälmann's analysis in *Rote Fahne*, 20 June 1926; *Bericht der Bezirksleitung der KPD Berlin-Brandenburg-Lausitz über die Tätigkeit der Organisation von 15. November 1925 bis 31. Mai 1926* (Berlin, 1926), pp. 13–14; and Karl, pp. 11–15, 53–57. Without denying that the Communist leaders recognized the possibilities which could be made out of the issue much more rapidly than republican politicans did, crediting them with discerning these possibilities immediately seems a little too pat.

[50] *Bericht der Bezirksleitung der KPD Berlin-Brandenburg-Lausitz*, p. 15.

[51] Institut für Marxismus-Leninismus beim Zentralkomitee der SED, *Geschichte der deutschen Arbeiterbewegung*, Vol. 4: *Von 1924 bis Januar 1933* (Berlin, 1966): 109.

[52] A supplementary publication to the above mentioned work lists a meeting of the Central Committee on 10 December 1925, at which the party's tactics for exploiting the problems of unemployment and the confiscation of the former rulers' properties were discussed, without however describing the content of the discussion. Institut für Marxismus-Leninismus beim Zentralkomitee der SED, *Geschichte der deutschen Arbeiterbewegung. Chronik* (Berlin, 1966), 2: 190.

[53] They never worried that the referendum proposal might fail—they expected that it would—as long as the KPD's participation was creditable and helped the party in other respects.

Evidence for the conjecture that the Communists were only sounding out the possibility of action and had not yet committed themselves to sponsoring a referendum at the beginning of December is nearly all circumstantial. Social Democratic sources charged that the KPD was too weak to carry out the organizational effort necessary to mount an initiative and referendum by itself and therefore had been forced to seek Social Democratic cooperation.[54] There are some grounds for this belief. Throughout the campaign *Rote Fahne* printed very detailed instructions concerning organizational preparations and methods for reaching previously unreceptive social groups.[55] It followed the instructions regularly with systematic evaluations of the work accomplished.[56] A recurrent insistence on the need for "perfecting" the organization leads one to suspect it was not in an altogether strong condition in 1925.[57] *Agitprop* informed the local and regional units that only a limited amount of propaganda material could be supplied free of charge and the local units should collect money to pay for the materials they distributed.[58]

Very few figures are available to serve as a basis for comparison of the efforts of the KPD and SPD during the campaign. *Rote Fahne* reported that Communist activists *sold* 30,000 copies of the leaflet, *Keinen Pfennig den Fürsten,* during the period of the initiative proceedings in Berlin, and another 59,000 immediately before the referendum.[59] A fair comparison is not really possible, but the SPD *distributed* 108 million leaflets and similar materials throughout the nation during the entire campaign.[60] Similarly, while the SPD spent over two million marks, the few KPD references available name

[54] *Vorwärts,* 5 Jan. 1926 (Nr. 6). So, too, Eyck, 2: 88.
[55] *Rote Fahne,* 23 Feb., 1 May, 20 May, 1 and 4 June 1926.
[56] Ibid., 19 March and 13 July 1926.
[57] Knoch, *Wissenschaftliche Zeitschrift der Technischen Hochschule ... Magdeburg,* 10: 417–24, contains a number of enlightening details regarding the KPD's activities on a local level. He states that leaders of the KPD in the Magdeburg region recognized from the start that "the very numerous burdens of the referendum" could not be borne by the Communists alone and that the other working class organizations had to share the responsibility. Ibid., p. 419.
[58] *Rote Fahne,* 20 May 1926; the head of the Social Democrats in Berlin wrote that some Red Front Fighters distributed leaflets they had obtained from the SPD. *Vorwärts,* 24 June 1926 (Nr. 293).
[59] *Rote Fahne,* 16 June 1926.
[60] *Jahrbuch der Deutschen Sozialdemokratie ... 1926,* p. 20.

sums of a much smaller order.[61] Contrast, too, the 855 meetings or demonstrations held by the regional KPD organization in Berlin, with the 32,920 public meetings sponsored by the SPD nationwide.[62] If one estimates that the Communists devoted one-tenth of their effort to the residents of Berlin, they may have held only about a quarter of the number of meetings the Social Democrats did throughout Germany as a whole.[63]

In April 1926, a spokesman for the KPD reminded critics within the party that the referendum campaign helped to reestablish contact with the masses, lost since 1923, and that for some time party activities had been restricted to purely parliamentary opposition, because of the lack of mass backing.[64] Confidential reports from government files indicate the party's failure earlier in 1925 to organize successful mass demonstrations.[65] Finally, important as an indication of how restricted the KPD's strength was during the second half of the 1920s was the disappointing outcome of its attempt to sponsor an initiative against the construction of the battle cruiser "A" in 1928.[66] The Communists obtained only 1,216,968 signatures (less than 3 percent of the qualified voters instead of the necessary 10), so that the campaign failed without proceeding to the stage of a referendum. Yet, over 12 million signatures were collected in 1926 when the Social Democrats and many middle-class voters joined with them favoring confiscation of the property of the former ruling houses.

[61] Idem; the KPD in the Berlin area collected 34,489 marks in their "Sammlung Volksbegehren," *Bericht der Bezirksleitung der KPD Berlin-Brandenburg-Lausitz . . .*, p. 161; on two other occasions goals of 10,000 and 30,000 marks were set for party collection activities in Berlin. *Rote Fahne*, 4 and 12 May 1926. The Comintern contributed 120,000 marks for the referendum. Hermann Weber, *Die Wandlung des deutschen Kommunismus* (Frankfurt a. M., 1969), 1: 309; Schüren, pp. 120–21, 201.

[62] *Bericht der Bezirksleitung der KPD Berlin-Brandenburg-Lausitz*, pp. 128–30; *Jahrbuch der Deutschen Sozialdemokratie . . . 1926*, p. 20.

[63] This is no more than a rough guess. Berlin with 3,900,000 qualified voters contained almost exactly 1/10 of all voters in the nation (39,700,000). However, surely more Communist efforts were concentrated in urban areas like Berlin than in small towns and the countryside.

[64] Schmidt in *Rote Fahne*, 15–16 April 1926.

[65] German Foreign Office Records, reel 2281, frames E136850-51 and E137156.

[66] *Sozialdemokratische Parteikorrespondenz . . . 1923 bis 1928*, pp. 361–63; Wolfgang Wacker, *Der Bau des Panzerschiffes "A" und der Reichstag*, Tübingen Studien zur Geschichte und Politik, 2 (Tübingen, 1959): 104–107; *Geschichte der deutschen Arbeiterbewegung*, 4: 172–81.

Rote Fahne's handling of this question during the first stage
of the controversy in November and December, 1925, also
suggests that it took the party leadership some time to exploit
the full potentiality of the issue as a popular cause. The first
reports of the princes' claims and of the proposals for legislative action, including the KPD's own recommendation for
confiscation, were interwoven with a number of other issues,
particularly the problem of unemployment. On 3 December,
for instance, *Rote Fahne* wrote:

> An invalid, wounded in the war, who lost his lower leg receives
> a monthly pension of 24.50 marks for a family of four. However,
> the deserter in Amerongen who has the lives of 2 million dead
> and the blood of 1⅓ million maimed on his conscience receives
> from the Prussian government 50,000 marks a month. . . .

> An unemployed person draws payments of 8 marks a week, but
> the duke of Mecklenburg-Schwerin receives an annual pension
> of 389,000 marks.[67]

The Central Committee's letter to the leaders of the SPD
and the other organizations used a similar conjunction:

> Millions of German workers, white collar people, government
> employees, small peasants, and members of the middle class are
> unable to earn even a minimum existence. *A million workers are
> out of jobs.* Innumerable people on pensions—victims of the war
> in a wider sense of the word—lead a starvation existence. No
> means of support are available for the unemployed. There is no
> money for raising the salaries of the lower and middle grades of
> government employees. However, *a billion (Milliarde) is going to
> be thrown into the mouths of the Hohenzollerns and the other princely
> houses.* . . .[68]

Never during the subsequent course of the referendum did
the *Rote Fahne* fail to connect the princely settlements with
other, far-ranging social issues,[69] but only from January 1926
on did prominent coverage in the party organ establish beyond doubt that this was a question of more than incidental

---

[67] *Rote Fahne*, 3 Dec. 1925.
[68] Ibid., 4 Dec. 1925, emphasis in original; also the articles of 25 Nov., 2 and 6
Dec. 1925.
[69] Non-Communist writers and speakers (mostly from the SPD, DDP, and Center
Party) also utilized the plight of the unemployed and especially the sufferers from
the war and inflation to give added pathos to their appeals; however, they did not
tie their suggested goals into a comprehensive set of social and economic demands
the way the Communists did.

interest.[70] The party leaders had found a perfect opportunity for putting "united front" policies into effect.

*   *   *   *

The chances for the KPD to win partisan victories in the mid-twenties were very limited.[71] The stabilization of economic and political conditions in 1924–25 and the accompanying swing of public opinion to the right made it difficult for the party to influence, even indirectly, the course of events, and left it isolated from the masses that it wanted to lead. Moreover, the weakness of the party itself, the result of a combination of its diminished appeal to the voters and

---

[70] This is difficult to document but the attentive reader cannot help noticing a change in emphasis—more space given the subject, more articles on the front page, conspicuous headlines, etc.

[71] For this section I have relied heavily on Ossip K. Flechtheim, *Die Kommunistische Partei Deutschlands in der Weimarer Republik* (Offenbach a. M., 1948) and Hermann Weber, *Die Wandlung des deutschen Kommunismus. Die Stalinisierung der KPD in der Weimarer Republik* (2 vols.; Frankfurt a. M., 1969). Important, but to be used with caution, is Ruth Fischer, *Stalin and German Communism* (Cambridge, Mass., 1948). Very valuable on earlier conflicts within the party is Werner T. Angress, *Stillborn Revolution: The Communist Bid for Power 1921–23* (Princeton, 1963); and on some of the later deviations Siegfried Bahne, "Zwischen 'Luxemburgismus' und 'Stalinismus'. Die 'ultralinke' Opposition in der KPD," *Vierteljahrshefte für Zeitgeschichte*, 9 (Nr. 4, Oct. 1961): 359–83.

On the complicated story of the relations between the German Communist Party and the Comintern I have used the relevant portions of Jane Degras (ed.), *The Communist International, 1919–1943. Documents*, Vol. 1: *1919–1922* and Vol. 2: *1923–1928* (London, 1956–60) as well as Edward Hallett Carr, *The Interregnum 1923–1924* (London, 1954) and *Socialism in One Country 1924–1926*. Vol. 3, Part 1 (London, 1964); Günther Nollau, *International Communism and World Revolution* (New York, 1961); Julius Braunthal, *History of the International*, Vol. 2: *1914–1943* (New York, 1967); and Hermann Weber, "Zu den Beziehungen zwischen der KPD und der Kommunistischen Internationale," *Vierteljahrshefte für Zeitgeschichte*, 16 (Nr. 2, April, 1968): 177–208.

Some East German contributions have been of limited value, for example, Willi Bredel, *Ernst Thälmann. Ein Beitrag zu einem politischen Lebensbild* (Berlin, 1958) or the inadequate documentary volume, Marx-Engels-Lenin-Stalin-Institut beim Zentralkomitee der SED, ed., *Zur Geschichte der Kommunistischen Partei Deutschlands* (Berlin, 1954). The official *Geschichte der deutschen Arbeiterbewegung*, Vol. 4 (cited above, note 51) presents a retouched picture of the KPD in the mid-twenties but must be consulted, as does Siegfried Vietzke and Heinz Wohlgemuth, *Deutschland und die deutsche Arbeiterbewegung in der Zeit der Weimarer Republik, 1919–1933* (Berlin, 1966). See, too, the articles by Mirjam Kölling, "Der Kampf der Kommunistischen Partei Deutschlands unter der Führung Ernst Thälmanns für die Einheitsfront in den ersten Jahren der relativen Stabilisierung (1924 bis 1927)," *Zeitschrift für Geschichtswissenschaft*, 2 (Nr. 1, 1954): 3–36; Hans-Joachim Fieber, "Die Bedeutung der Zentralausschusstagung der KPD vom 9. und 10. Mai 1925 für die Herausbildung einer marxistische-leninistischen Führung," ibid., 15 (Nr. 7, 1967): 1212–26; and Wilhelm Ersil and Ernst Laboor, "Die Parteidiskussion im September/Oktober 1925 und ihre Bedeutung für die marxistisch-leninistische Entwicklung der KPD," *Beiträge zur Geschichte der deutschen Arbeiterbewegung*, 8 (Nr. 4, 1966): 595–617.

very serious internal divisions, prompted the leaders of the Comintern to increase their efforts to control the German party organization, and thus placed further constraints on the policies of the KPD. The achievement, or really even the consideration of revolutionary action was out of the question.[72] Prevailing conditions dictated a defensive strategy: the husbanding of strength, recruitment of new forces, elimination of internal dissension, the discrediting of its more successful Social Democratic rival; in short, much slow, hard, unspectacular work at the organizational level. The attainment of these aims required an elastic response as situations changed, but at the same time demanded undeviating awareness of long-run objectives in order to avoid mere "opportunism." This was not an easy task.

The weakness of the party was at least partly its own fault. The adoption of consistent, workable, and theoretically defensible policies troubled the German Communist party throughout the entire period of the Weimar republic.[73] Although the party changed its leaders time and again during the first years of its history, they all failed to assess realistically the true political conditions in Germany and to develop policies which received sustained approval from the leaders of the Comintern. They proved incapable of reconciling the divergent and often hostile tendencies which existed within the party. Most important, the party leadership had never been able to control activist elements who pressed for, and in 1919, 1921, and 1923, actually attempted armed uprisings. Long afterward, the "lessons" of these years remained alive in the minds of both the Communists and their opponents in the SPD and trade unions.

During the mid-twenties, the KPD still had to master the heritage of the troubled year, 1923. The disordered internal conditions resulting from the occupation of the Ruhr and the final stage of the great inflation had seemed to offer exceptionally good chances for the KPD to put itself at the head of the working people in Germany.[74] The policy established by the leader of the party, Heinrich Brandler, in close consultation with agents of the Comintern, stressed pushing the party's influence far beyond the relatively small base of de-

---

[72] Weber, *Die Wandlung*, 1: 319–20.
[73] One expert has called the KPD "the party of turns and changes par excellence." Flechtheim, pp. xiii–xiv. See, too, Bracher, *Die Auflösung*, pp. 100–105.
[74] Angress, pp. 281–94, 327–38, 369–75, 391–406.

pendable party members and sympathizers. For some time, Brandler had identified himself with the active pursuit of the "united front" *(Einheitsfront)* policy.[75] Insofar as this policy was not simply a tactic designed to expose the half-heartedness or "treason" of Social Democratic Party leaders, it emphasized the need for the Communists to establish close ties with non-Communist workers and other potentially sympathetic population groups. This could be done either "from below," i.e., by means of various forms of propaganda and, especially, through close contact with individual workers or small groups in the factories, trade unions, residential quarters, etc., or more rarely and with great caution, "from the top," by formal cooperation for specific purposes arranged by negotiating with the leaders of the rival organizations. The general policy had much to recommend it, particularly in the light of the strained, or at best ambivalent, feelings toward the KPD held by the bulk of the German working population. However, the united front policy was difficult to execute, especially when as in 1923 the desire for revolutionary action was strong within the party.

In the fall of 1923, after much discussion and a few preparations, the party acted; but it acted ineffectively, followed misapplied theories of revolution, and showed much ignorance of the real mood of the German people. Everywhere, the party's leaders seemed to misjudge the situation. ". . . The Communists were an insufficiently organized group of panic-stricken people, torn by factional quarrels, unable to come to a decision, and unclear about their own aims."[76] Both the united front policy of tactical cooperation with the SPD[77] and the alternative course of a Communist-led armed uprising[78] failed, to say nothing of the short-lived attempt at an alliance between the Communist and extreme Nationalists, the so-called "Schlageter" policy.[79] The failure pre-

[75] Flechtheim, pp. 79–80, 85–86; Angress, pp. 223–53; Weber, *Die Wandlung,* 1: 44.

[76] Fischer, p. 338.

[77] In Saxony and Thuringia the KPD went so far as to participate in coalition governments with the Social Democrats. Angress, pp. 381–87, 400–405, 429–39.

[78] The party had encouraged the organization of armed bands of proletarians, the "Red Hundreds," and at times seemed to believe the moment for a revolution had come. However, its call for a general strike after the national government ordered the military occupation of Saxony went unheeded and only a mistaken and futile uprising in Hamburg took place. Angress, pp. 290–91, 406–14, 420–25, 440–56.

[79] Ibid., pp. 332–56.

cluded any possibility of apologetic disguise.[80] The German Communist Party simply had not had enough popular support for a confrontation with the established forces of the German state and society. Hopes of soon accomplishing a genuine proletarian revolution had remained alive in party circles despite all earlier setbacks;[81] in the years after 1923 those hopes had to be subordinated to much more limited objectives although revolution always remained the ultimate goal. The October retreat of 1923 and the stabilization of the German economy in 1924 had a shattering effect on the party.[82] Ruth Fischer claims that membership dropped from 267,000 in September 1923, to 121,294 in April 1924.[83] The party's popularity with the voters suffered as well, although the effects were not quite so rapidly evident. In the May elections of 1924, the KPD, like the other parties of extreme opposition (the DNVP and NSDAP), benefited from the emotional aftereffects of the disordered conditions that had existed during the preceding year. The Communists received nearly 3,700,000 votes (12.6 percent) and thus obtained 62 seats in the Reichstag.[84] However, when new elections were held again in December 1924, over a quarter of the KPD's previous support had melted away. This time the Communists obtained only 2,700,000 votes (9.0 percent) while their Reichstag delegation shrank to 45.[85] This drop in popular support alarmed the watchful leaders of the Comintern; Moscow became more insistent than ever that the leaders of the German party follow its advice.[86] Another consequence was the revival of bitter factional disputes.

Reasons for the failure had to be analyzed. Broad lines of policy, the tactics used in specific situations, individual decisions, and the outcome of the events themselves all underwent close scrutiny in order to learn how to avoid such mistakes in the future.[87] Each faction within the party interpreted the facts differently, in accord with the complex the-

[80] Radek's comment was, "We missed a great historic opportunity, a favorable situation the like of which one seldom sees . . . ," quoted by Braunthal, 2: 284.

[81] Carr, *The Interregnum*, pp. 213–14.

[82] Flechtheim, pp. 92–118; Weber, *Die Wandlung*, 1: 101–4.

[83] Fischer, p. 392; cf. Weber, *Die Wandlung*, 1: 362–63.

[84] It became the fourth largest party in the Reichstag, nearly equal in size to the Catholic Center Party (62 seats to 65).

[85] It fell to fifth place behind the German People's Party and the Center Party in addition to the much larger Nationalists and Social Democrats.

[86] Fischer, pp. 410–11.

[87] Flechtheim, pp. 100–135.

oretical arguments that the customary style of intra-party disputes required. The "Left Opposition," which had been playing an increasingly significant role in intra-party disputes since 1921, had disagreed with Brandler's policies even when he was trying to put them into operation.[88] These "Left" critics immediately revived their attacks as events "proved" how mistaken Brandler's policies had been.[89] Heinrich Brandler himself immediately became the scapegoat for all the party's mistakes; he was removed from office and a party convention, meeting in April 1924, supported left-wing charges against the "Brandlerites." Spokesmen for the "Left" gained control of the leading positions in the party.[90] Zinoviev and other leading figures in the Comintern played an important role in this change of leadership within the KPD. Indeed, the power struggle among Lenin's successors in Russia added much to the complexity of the KPD's intra-party conflicts in the years 1924–25.

The rejection of "Brandlerism" meant that the party turned its back on any course of action that smacked of reformism.[91] The united front policy, the base of most of Brandler's plans, fell into discredit, except for its safest form, agitation among the workers "from below." The mood of the party encouraged a return to purely revolutionary slogans. The "Left" argued that fighting for limited demands which could satisfy only the temporary day-to-day needs of the workers was self-defeating. Limited demands, they said, weakened revolutionary sentiments and distracted the party's adherents from their true objectives:

> The task of the KPD is that of the proletarian revolution in Germany. . . . It is both possible and very probable that the decisive struggles will develop much more quickly than many believe. . . . The party for its part must so orient its members that they are ready for the final battle in the very shortest time.[92]

In line with this renewed militancy, the party formally denounced any further cooperation with Social Democratic Party leaders. One resolution stated that ". . . the complete

---

[88] Angress, pp. 254–78, 303–10, 367–68, 375–76, 398–99.
[89] Ibid., pp. 463–71; Carr, *The Interregnum*, pp. 241–42; Degras, 2: 16–18, 62–65, 84–86.
[90] Angress, pp. 470–73; Weber, *Die Wandlung*, 1: 62–73.
[91] *Geschichte der deutschen Arbeiterbewegung*, 4: 25–27.
[92] From a resolution passed by the Frankfurt party convention, Flechtheim, p. 106.

liquidation of the SPD is recognized as the central task." [93]
The KPD now identified the Social Democrats as the prime
enemies of the party and classified them as a branch of German Fascism.[94]

Ruth Fischer and Arkadi Maslow, the chief spokesmen for
the "Left," guided the KPD from the spring of 1924 until
the late summer of 1925.[95] At first they seemed quite successful in forcing recognition of their authority as party leaders.[96] But as time went on they found that they had to defend
their own policies while trying to mediate among increasingly
antagonistic factions. During 1924–25 the "Right" grouping
within the KPD dwindled to virtual insignificance, but the
"Left" and "Middle" factions in the Brandlerite dispute now
split and regrouped.[97] A new "Ultra-left" argued for a firmer
commitment to undiluted revolutionary goals; even more
important, this group resisted the organizational reforms demanded by the Comintern, i.e., the "bolshevization" of the
German party.[98] On the other hand many important German
Communists, including Maslow and Fischer's earlier ally,
Ernst Thälmann, insisted that the party accept completely
the Comintern's policies.[99]

The Comintern formulated its specific recommendations
on the basis of a general assessment of the Communist movement as a whole. According to its analysis, capitalism had
entered a period of "relative stabilization" in 1924, making
conditions temporarily unsuitable for revolution.[100] This was

[93] Ibid., p. 104.
[94] ". . . [T]he leading levels of German Social Democracy are at the present moment
nothing other than a branch (*Fraktion*) of German Fascism wearing socialistic masks.
There are shades [of difference] between Ebert, Seeckt and Ludendorff. However
. . . the German Communists should never forget that it is most important to bring
the working class to a clear awareness of the truth of the matter: that in the battle
between Capital and Labor, the leaders of the SPD are fast united with the White
generals." Ibid., p. 107; Weber, *Die Wandlung*, 1: 101–2.
[95] Bahne, *Vierteljahrshefte für Zeitgeschichte*, 9: 360–61. Maslow was held in prison
throughout most of this period but the confinement did not prevent him from
carrying out his duties as party leader. Fischer, pp. 433, 454. Initially Maslow and
Fischer were able to rely somewhat on the support of Zinoviev in the Comintern,
but when Stalin moved to displace this rival their position became highly precarious.
Angress, pp. 467–71, 473–74.
[96] Weber, *Die Wandlung*, 1: 74–81.
[97] Bahne, *Vierteljahrshefte für Zeitgeschichte*, 9: 362–63.
[98] Ibid., p. 360; Weber, *Die Wandlung*, 1: 107–12.
[99] Flechtheim, pp. 125–29, 132–35; Kölling, *Zeitschrift für Geschichtswissenschaft*, 2:
13–18; and the sympathetic biography by the West German Hannes Heer, *Ernst
Thälmann in Selbstzeugnissen und Bilddokumenten* (Reinbek, 1975), pp. 82–88.
[100] The formulation of the Comintern's policies in the mid-twenties can be followed in Degras, 2: 68–82, 84–89, 113–17, 142–56, 188–200, 223–32.

a period in which to build up strength, to recruit new members, to improve the organizational basis of the party, and to win sympathy whenever possible from non-party supporters. In particular, the Comintern directed attention to work in the trade unions and the factory cells.[101] In the political arena, the party was to propose and fight for a carefully chosen set of specific demands and not simply restrict itself to general criticism and promises. Housing, unemployment, and the eight-hour day, were to provide some of the suitable issues. In other words, the leaders of the Comintern urged the resumption of united front tactics as the appropriate policy for a situation that required a "temporary" defensive posture. They also saw such tactics as the best means to discredit the Social Democratic Party and a way to reach the workers who still did not identify their interests with those of the KPD.

Stalin, whose influence in the Comintern was becoming decisive by 1925, had been expressing the same views.[102] His followers in Germany wasted no time adopting these arguments and policy recommendations. Relying on Stalin's support, they claimed to be the sole representatives of true Marxist-Leninism when debating with other factions in the KPD.[103] Some of Maslow's and Fischer's policies were attacked by the "Ultra-left." [104] More serious opposition to their leadership, however, developed from the Thälmann group, when it became clear that they would not follow Stalin unreservedly.[105]

Maslow and Fischer were unable to prevent their own per-

[101] Thälmann's *Referat* at the KPD's tenth party convention embodied the Comintern's resolutions on the trade union question and applied them to the situation in Germany. *Bericht über die Verhandlungen des X. Parteitages der Kommunistischen Partei Deutschlands* (Berlin, 1926), pp. 519–44; Degras, 2: 127–34, 192–93.

[102] J. V. Stalin, *Works* (Moscow, 1954), in particular: "The Prospects of the Communist Party of Germany and the Question of Bolshevisation," 7 (3 Feb. 1925): 34–41; "The International Situation and the Tasks of the Communist Parties," 7 (22 March 1925), pp. 51–57; "The Results of the Work of the Fourteenth Conference of the R.C.P. (B.)," 7 (9 May 1925), pp. 102–7; "The Fight Against Right and 'Ultra-Left' Deviations," 8 (22 Jan. 1926): pp. 1–10; "Speech Delivered in the German Commission of the Sixth Enlarged Plenum of the E.C.C.I." 8 (8 March 1926), pp. 115–22.

[103] Bredel, pp. 70–71.

[104] Flechtheim, pp. 126–27.

[105] Ibid., pp. 132–34; Bahne, *Vierteljahrshefte für Zeitgeschichte,* 9: 363, identifies the group which opposed Maslow and Fischer as former members of the "Left," some representatives from the moderate "Right," and party bureaucrats. Fischer, pp. 503–5, particularly castigated the party functionaries who saved their jobs by supporting Stalin.

formance as leaders from being criticized. The situation in which the party found itself in 1924–25 hardly suited the independent radical action and uncompromising purity they had so strongly professed. Indeed, by the spring of 1925, Maslow offered parliamentary aid (toleration) to the hard-pressed Weimar Coalition in Prussia.[106] Nothing came of the offer, but its resemblance to the policy that Brandler had followed, and Maslow and Fischer themselves had sharply criticized, is striking.[107] In any case, cooperation was hardly possible since the Social Democratic leaders still held to the policy of refusing any kind of joint activity with the KPD, a policy which they had adopted immediately after the disastrous experiments in Saxony and Thuringia in 1923.[108] Nor had Maslow and Fischer been able to stop an unwise shift in Communist trade-union policy.[109] Throughout 1924, Communist workers broke away from the old unions dominated by Social Democratic functionaries and formed competing Communist unions. This maneuver produced great bitterness among workers who otherwise might have been receptive to Communist appeals.[110] Moscow, recognizing a failure, soon insisted on a new slogan: "[Back] into the unions." [111] Fur-

[106] Flechtheim, pp. 119–20; Fischer, pp. 415–17. Maslow offered this "toleration" in return for a commitment from the republican parties to enact a series of measures which the Communists considered rather moderate: the elimination of the Reichswehr and the monarchistic associations, the demilitarization of the special police squads (*Schutzpolizei*), amnesty for political prisoners, *confiscation of the dynastic properties* [my italics], exile of the members of the earlier ruling families, dissolution of the Supreme Court (*Staatsgerichtshof*), the eight-hour day, and the ending of the heavy taxes borne by the masses. *Frankfurter Zeitung*, 6 May 1925 (Nr. 335). Similar "goals" had been emphasized in the KPD's propaganda for the presidential election, *Zur Geschichte der Kommunistischen Partei Deutschlands*, pp. 165–71; Fieber, *Zeitschrift für Geschichtswissenschaft*, 15: 1217.

[107] The "Ultra-left" accused Maslow of offering a "Brandlerite" program. Fischer, p. 419. Maslow himself defended the decision he had made, arguing that it was impossible to determine in advance, irrespective of circumstances, what policies would be successful. Many a middle-class party leader might have agreed with his statement, "If only it were possible to prepare a kind of catalog, such as the catalogs of plants in botany, with an index of [all] possible, necessary, reliable compromises, maneuvers, and tactical turns, then politics would be a very simple matter." "Ueber einige neuartige Umstände der Lage und über einige dementsprechend neuartige Aufgaben," *Die Internationale* (Berlin), 8 (Nr. 7, July 1925): 408.

[108] See the order issued by the SPD *Parteiausschuss*, 27 Nov. 1923. *Ursachen und Folgen*, 5: 504.

[109] Flechtheim, pp. 112–17.

[110] Kölling, *Zeitschrift für Geschichtswissenschaft*, 2: 12, reports that the Communists regularly received 30–35% of the vote in factory council elections up to 1923 but in 1925 could get the support of only 10% of the union members. See, too, Flechtheim, pp. 114–15; Weber, *Vierteljahrshefte für Zeitgeschichte*, 16: 190–91, 201.

[111] Carr, *Socialism in One Country*, 3, part 1: 554–58, 560–62, 574–76.

thermore, although Maslow and Fischer had wholeheartedly
accepted the Comintern's instructions for "bolshevising" the
party organization, their achievements in this respect were
ultimately denounced as insufficient.[112] While the Communist
party retained a considerable body of determined followers
despite all setbacks,[113] most ordinary German workers
thought Communist radicalism irresponsible and risky.[114]
Rightly or wrongly, Maslow and Fischer were blamed for the
party's diminished popularity, visible in nearly all spheres of
its activity after early 1924.[115]

The intra-party dispute reached a turning point in the late
summer of 1925. In mid-July, when the party convention met
in Berlin, the delegates reaffirmed their support for the
course Maslow and Fischer were taking.[116] The meeting was
dubbed—quite inappropriately as it turned out—the "Convention of internal cohesion" (Parteitag der inneren Sammlung).[117] The most openly expressed criticism, such as it was,
came from the "Ultra-left," but there were also some indications that more dangerous opposition was developing.
Ernst Thälmann delivered a major address on the trade-union
question. While he did not at this time attack Maslow and
Fischer directly, he did enumerate the party's persistent failures in handling this vital question. He stated that the KPD
must recognize that "union work stands at the center of the
political work of the party as a whole." [118] Within a few weeks
Maslow and Fischer were to be held responsible for all the
failures Thälmann had described. Furthermore, a rather surprising incident occurred at the party convention. The Com-

[112] Weber, Die Wandlung, 1: 85–97; Rote Fahne, 18 and 20 Sept. 1925.

[113] Particularly among the unemployed and unskilled, but certainly not exclusively
so. Fischer, p. 520. An official of the KPD in Berlin reported to the Bezirksparteitag
in July 1926, that only 52% of the district's party members were fully employed,
10% were partially employed or rural laborers, 38% unemployed. Rote Fahne, 6
July 1926.

[114] Rosenberg said that in this period even the Communist workers "wanted peace
and quiet and did not think of revolution," p. 449.

[115] Geschichte der deutschen Arbeiterbewegung, 4: 58, 80.

[116] Ibid., 4: 80–84; Flechtheim, pp. 126–29; Weber, Die Wandlung, 1: 112–19.

[117] German Foreign Office Records, reel 2281, frame E137152. Thälmann wrote,
"the convention must link the party together still more than has happened since
Frankfurt, still more unify it, still more energetically make all factions and groups
impossible" (emphasis in original). "Zum 10. Parteitag," Die Internationale (Berlin),
8 (special number, 12 July 1925): 4.

[118] Bericht . . . des X. Parteitages, p. 519. The convention approved Thälmann's
recommendations unanimously, ibid., p. 651. Many of the same points were also
made by August Enderle, "Die Partei und die Lage in den Gewerkschaften," Die
Internationale (Berlin), 8 (Special number, 12 July 1925): 42–47.

intern's representative there, Manuilsky, interpreted a ruling of the convention chairman as a personal affront. He then used the incident as an occasion for castigating anti-Bolshevik attitudes current among many German Communists and tried, unsuccessfully, to influence the election of the Central Committee.[119]

After the German party convention was over, the leaders of the Comintern decided to remove Maslow and Fischer. In August, the KPD Central Committee was summoned to Moscow where its members were told that the unsatisfactory leadership must be replaced.[120] Meanwhile, the Executive Committee of the Communist International composed a lengthy "Open Letter" to the German party itemizing the case against Maslow and Fischer.[121] The ECCI's analysis of the current situation indicated that many possibilities existed for increasing the power and influence of Communism, but mistakes made by the German party leadership had prevented the KPD from exploiting favorable opportunities. "The most important question . . . is . . . the problem of increasing the *recruiting power* of our party, the problem of capturing the masses and especially the masses of Social Democratic workers." [122] This could not be done with Maslow and Fischer at the head of the party. They had discouraged inner-party democracy, they did not understand the ordinary worker, they were too intellectual.[123] They had shown themselves extraordinarily indifferent to the proper conduct of trade union work and had neglected necessary organizational changes in the party's structure.[124] They had even tried to foster opposition to the Comintern's policies among other European Communist parties.[125] They had followed a suspect

[119] Fischer, pp. 443–44; reportedly there were yells for him to go back to Moscow, Nollau, p. 91.
[120] Fischer, p. 447; Flechtheim, p. 133; Weber, *Die Wandlung,* 1: 121–23.
[121] *Rote Fahne,* 1 Sept. 1925. All the following accusations can be found in the "Open Letter"; however, I have also given some references to charges which were more fully elaborated in the subsequent controversy.
[122] Ibid., emphasis in the original. About the same time, *Pravda* commented on the ECCI letter and the situation in the KPD. It exhorted: "[Go] to the masses! Nearer to the Social Democratic workers. Real performance of the united front tactic, not [just] in words, but in action; energetic strengthening of trade union work. . . . The main task is to enlarge the influence of the party on the masses." Ibid., 12 Sept. 1925.
[123] "Liquidierung der Ultralinken in der KPD," *Die Kommunistische Internationale,* 7: 239.
[124] *Rote Fahne,* 18 Sept. 1925.
[125] Fischer, p. 432.

political program which put too much weight on parliamentary achievements. In sum, they were not truly loyal to the party.[126]

Moreover, their attitude toward the "Ultra-left" had been suspect. The ECCI blamed the extreme views of this group for most of the difficulties the party encountered in trying to expand its influence. The "pseudo-revolutionary" phraseology of the "Ultra-left," and the intransigent trade union policy of its adherents, frightened away potential followers.[127] Furthermore, the "Ultra-left" harbored anti-Bolshevik views. Maslow and Fischer had done far too little to combat these ideas.

Indeed, it appears that Maslow and Fischer sympathized more with the "Ultra-left," despite some differences over tactics, than they did with the Stalinist group around Thälmann. Maslow had wanted to preserve the "Ultra-left" within the KPD, rather than force the expulsion of its leading figures, which is what the Russian leaders demanded and the German party later carried out.[128] Ruth Fischer stressed in her memoirs how she had fought to keep Stalin from gaining complete control over the Communist movement.[129] Yet while she was in Moscow with the other members of the KPD Central Committee, she did sign the "Open Letter," presumably under pressure. It is perhaps not necessary to judge whether she acted from a mistaken sense of obedience to party discipline, as she later said, or simply in the hope of staying in power, as her opponents asserted.[130] There is no doubt that she associated herself closely with the "Ultra-left" after her removal from the leadership of the KPD. Stalin charged her

---

[126] Maslow was even attacked for exposing party differences to the public in his defense during his trial in Leipzig. Kommunistische Partei Deutschlands. Zentralkomitee, *Zum Fall Maslow* (Berlin, 1926), pp. 18–19, 29; Fischer, pp. 453–54.

[127] These charges were repeated in the resolution on the German situation passed by the sixth plenum of the ECCI (March, 1926), *Rote Fahne*, 2 April 1926.

[128] Fischer, p. 433.

[129] Specific references seem unnecessary. Fischer's outspoken hostility toward Stalin and his supporters is an essential element of her entire book. Stalin returned the dislike. He said of the Fischer group, ". . . of all the undesirable and objectionable groups in the German Communist Party, this group is the most undesirable and the most objectionable." He attacked its "double-dealing in politics, its habit of saying one thing and doing another." *Works*, 8: 120.

[130] Her explanation is that she "still had too high a regard for the value of Communist discipline" and that Zinoviev asked her not to make his own position more difficult; but she herself implies that in accepting the letter she and Zinoviev were playing for time to get it rescinded. Fischer, pp. 451–52.

with "keeping two sets of books." [131] Fischer's opponents
argued that she had accepted the criticism of the "Open
Letter" insincerely, with numerous mental reservations, and
that she then helped oppositional groups within the party to
organize resistance to the letter.[132]

The leaders of the Comintern did not hesitate to spell out
"recommendations" for the future work of the German party.

> In every locality and on every political question we must seek
> platforms from which the party [can] speak to the working masses
> in the unions and the Social Democratic Party in order to bring
> them over to the side of the class struggle. We must set forth
> the issues of the guarantee pact, the League of Nations, the trade
> treaties, credit, tariffs, taxes, housing policies, etc. in this light.

> At the same time the battle against the monarchist danger, against
> biased justice, for full amnesty, etc. must be tied in with the
> everyday economic struggles of the proletariat [regarding] wages
> and working [conditions]. . . . It must find new formulas, a new
> tone, a new content for its agitation among the Social Democratic
> working masses who are turning toward the left. The Social
> Democratic workers . . . must have the feeling that "the Com-
> munist Party is really a party of the workers, a party which is
> determined to fight for our interests, our political demands, [and]
> our daily needs; that it considers us not just as objects for prop-
> aganda, but as class brothers; [that] it honestly wants the creation
> of a proletarian united front for the class struggle." [133]

The ECCI said that brawling between Communists and Socialists had to cease. The Communist press was to learn how
to expose the "criminal policies" of the leaders of the SPD
so that ordinary Social Democratic workers would feel closer
to their Communist fellow workers than to "the 'Barmat'
leaders who sell the workers in parliament whenever they
can." The KPD was instructed to concentrate its efforts on
work within the free trade unions and in the factory cells.
". . . The chief mistake the German Communists recently
committed was that they devoted all too much attention to
'serious' parliamentary questions and all too little attention
to the work in the factories."

The ECCI's "Open Letter" immediately gave a decisive
turn to the factional dispute within the KPD. *Rote Fahne* pub-

[131] Quoted by Kölling, *Zeitschrift für Geschichtswissenschaft*, 2: 14.
[132] The ECCI resolution of March, 1926. *Rote Fahne*, 2 April 1926; Fischer,
p. 453.
[133] *Rote Fahne*, 1 Sept. 1925.

lished the "Open Letter" on 1 September 1925, but the text
had been circulated among party officials earlier. In an accompanying statement, the newly reshuffled KPD Central
Committee announced that it accepted the letter "without
reservation." [134] Other efforts were made to explain to a surprised rank-and-file why the sudden attack on the former
party chairmen was necessary. When some district organizations at first rejected the ECCI letter out of loyalty to
Maslow and Fischer, other district organizations urged their
comrades "not to be led by sentimental, purely personal,
feelings." [135]

The first task of the new Thälmann-led Central Committee
was to set its house in order and to insist that the policies
laid down by the Executive Committee of the Communist
International were accepted by the party at large. It made
full use of its control of the party press to discredit both the
ousted leaders and the policies of the "Ultra-left." Only rarely
were statements by opposition figures permitted to appear
in the *Rote Fahne,* while abundant space was available for
attacks on them.[136] However, the Central Committee did not
content itself with issuing statements and writing articles. Its
power was not yet established firmly enough for it to issue
a set of directives and find automatic compliance.[137] It is
particularly significant that the executive council *(Zentralvor-
stand)* of the Berlin organization, passed a resolution refusing
to accept the recommendations of the ECCI.[138] The Central
Committee responded at once by denouncing this action and
then arranging for other local districts to pass resolutions in
its behalf.[139] This was followed by small meetings of the
organized party members in Berlin, convened by members
of the Central Committee in such a way that oppositional
functionaries who sat on the district *Vorstand* were by-passed.
Such membership meetings nearly always supported the Central Committee and, within a short time, the Berlin organi-

[134] Ibid. The Central Committee had approved the "Open Letter" and suspended
Maslow and Fischer on 20 August. *Geschichte der deutschen Arbeiterbewegung. Chronik,*
2: 183.

[135] *Rote Fahne,* 9 Sept. 1925.

[136] See *Rote Fahne* especially during Sept. and Oct. 1925 and again in April 1926.

[137] Ruth Fischer wrote, "In spite of both Comintern discipline and the interfac-
tional quarrels, the party as a whole was inclined to reject the Open Letter and the
Russian domination it denoted" (p. 453). The "as a whole" is rather exaggerated,
but there can be no doubt that some strong resistance existed.

[138] *Rote Fahne,* 4 Sept. 1925.

[139] Ibid., 9–12 Sept., 1925; Weber, *Die Wandlung,* 1: 127–30.

zation repudiated its earlier opposition to the ECCI letter.[140] A report on these events by an important Comintern official pointed out how organizational reforms served to curb factional dissent.

> Numerous factory cells in the industrial regions of Germany have thoroughly discussed the "Open Letter" of the ECCI (September 1925) and passed specific resolutions on the questions which it contained. Previously . . . such questions would have been discussed only by the functionaries; only the functionaries would have passed resolutions on them. The difference between the former and the present resolutions strikes the eye. . . . In Berlin, as laid down in the statute, only members of factory and street cells participated in the voting—[a fact] which necessarily affected the resolutions of that conference. The organization in Berlin-Brandenburg, which was one of the strong-holds of the "Ultra-left" faction and the Maslow-Fischer group because of the aid [given] by functionaries from the former organizational units in residential areas . . . has now, after the formation of cells and their participation in the discussion, become an organization whose members, in the majority, have declared themselves as followers of the ECCI and the new KPD leadership.[141]

As the debate in the party progressed, the Central Committee successfully isolated most of the leaders of the opposition. Ordinary workingmen who had supported the "Ultra-left" were to be shown how they had been misled in order to win back their loyal support but all "Ultra-left" ideas must be eliminated from the party.[142] Despite their radical talk, the spokesmen of the "Ultra-left" were accused of acting like Social Democrats or Mensheviks who had to be treated accordingly—i.e. expelled.[143] In a few areas dissident local leaders continued to retain control over their followings, at least temporarily.[144] In most cases, however, the "resumption

---

[140] *Rote Fahne*, 22–29 Oct. 1925. Once the organization in Berlin was brought into line, a conference of party leaders from throughout the country was held. Only 30 oppositional votes were cast against a resolution proposed by the Central Committee; 227 supported it. Ibid., 1 and 3 Nov. 1925; *Geschichte der deutschen Arbeiterbewegung, Chronik*, 2: 188; Weber, *Die Wandlung*, 1: 133–37.

[141] Ossip Piatnitzki, "Zur Zweiten ORG-Beratung der KI-Sektionen," *Die Kommunistische Internationale*, 7 (Nr. 2, Feb. 1926, "issued in March"): 124.

[142] Resolution of the 6th Enlarged Executive of the Communist International concerning Germany, *Rote Fahne*, 2 April 1926.

[143] Ibid., 30 March 1926.

[144] Bahne, *Vierteljahrshefte für Zeitgeschichte*, 9: 366–81, traces the short histories of the "Ultra-left" groups which eventually broke away from the KPD in the mid-1920s.

of intra-party democracy" greatly strengthened the control of the Central Committee.

As the elimination of its most serious rivals progressed and oppositional viewpoints were gradually reduced to sectarian insignificance, the Thälmann-led Central Committee faced the problem of demonstrating its qualities of leadership in some more positive way. Unfortunately, very little evidence is available revealing the thoughts of the leading party figures as they made day-to-day decisions regarding the party's activities. Official announcements of purpose are abundant, but they generally conceal the political considerations that shaped any given decision. Nevertheless, attentive reading of the party press and other publications does provide some basis for reconstructing, at least approximately, the grounds on which decisions were made. The new Central Committee, by its full acceptance of the ECCI letter, had committed itself to the execution of a definite set of policies. A routine application of these policies to German affairs would not have satisfied the Comintern—this had been one of the chief complaints against Maslow and Fischer. It is reasonable to assume that the Central Committee looked for a field of action where it could demonstrate that its reliability in theoretical matters was paired with effectiveness in practice.[145] Furthermore, it must have been aware of undercurrents of distrust and the persistence of old habits among rank-and-file party members. We know from an official report that party membership dropped "during the reorientation *(Umstellung)* of the party."[146] Here, too, a success was needed to reinforce the authority of members of the Committee as leaders. An East German historian refers to the initiative and referendum cam-

---

[145] For example, Heinz Neumann, who at this time closely identified himself with Stalin and was given an important role in the new leadership, defined the correct attitude toward united front campaigns: "People say, 'United front tactics, sure— but in no case through arrangements with the leaders, only from below—only for [the purpose] of exposing [the SPD leaders], etc.' . . . On the contrary, in particular situations the united front policy 'from above' with the simultaneous mobilization of the masses is not only admissable, but *unqualifiedly necessary.* . . .

"The purpose of united front tactics is not maneuvering and exposure, but the true, absolutely honest formation of a common fighting front with the Social Democratic and free trade union workers, without any reservations. The revelation of the tricks and betrayals of the Social Democratic leaders is only one of the means to accelerate the true development of the united front." "Der neue Kurs der KPD," *Die Internationale* (Berlin), 8 (Nr. 9, "End of Sept. 1925"): 532 (emphasis in original).

[146] Reported by an official (Gohlke) at the *Bezirksparteitag* in early July 1926. *Rote Fahne,* 6 July 1926.

paign as the new Central Committee's "political baptism under fire." [147]

From the start, the party leadership pushed on with the organizational changes desired by the Comintern.[148] We have seen how changing the emphasis from basic organizational units in residential areas to factory cells helped to suppress the intra-party opposition. The elimination of trouble spots was one thing, but the transformation of the entire party structure, starting with its smallest units, took time. Spectacular results were not possible. Orders were issued that the center of each member's party activities should be the cell in the factory where he worked, and that more efforts were to be made to gain members in the biggest plants (*Grossbetriebe*) and key industries.[149] Slogans such as "seventy-five percent of the party's work must be in the trade unions" [150] were easily formulated, but the actual accomplishment of these objectives was more difficult.[151] The repeated insistence on further progress suggests that actual compliance was not fully satisfactory. Even with the best of will, loyal Communists could not always do rapidly some of the things required of them. A Communist worker often found it hard to get himself elected to even a minor union post or to establish cells in a large factory. In retrospect, the transformation of the KPD organizationally, as well as ideologically, into a fully "bolshevik" party has been regarded as one of the major achievements of the Thälmann-led Central Committee.[152] But at the time when it was just beginning to feel its way, little immediate credit could be gained from results which would only be realized in the future, if at all.[153]

---

[147] Könnemann, *Wissenschaftliche Zeitschrift der Universität Halle-Wittenberg,* 7: 550.

[148] *Geschichte der deutschen Arbeiterbewegung,* 4: 92–93.

[149] *Rote Fahne,* 18 and 20 Sept. 1925, 6 June 1926. In fact, the reorganization of the party on the basis of factory cells was never entirely successful. Weber, *Die Wandlung,* 1: 268–71.

[150] *Rote Fahne,* 16 Oct. 1925, 1 April 1926.

[151] Knoch, *Wissenschaftliche Zeitschrift der Technischen Hochschule Magdeburg,* 10: 419. These efforts were not entirely unavailing, however. The Free Trade Unions noticed increased Communist activity after the removal of Maslow and Fischer. Allgemeiner Deutscher Gewerkschaftsbund, *Jahrbuch 1925* (Berlin, 1926), pp. 190–91.

[152] For example, the official East German historical outline, "Grundriss der Geschichte der deutschen Arbeiterbewegung," *Zeitschrift für Geschichtswissenschaft,* 10 (Nr. 6, 1962): 1424–25.

[153] See the article "Locarno, die Regierungskrise und unsere Partei," *Die Internationale* (Berlin), 8 (Nr. 12, 15 Dec. 1925): 715–16, where the writer emphasized that passing appropriate resolutions was fine, but carrying them out was much more important.

While they devoted much attention to organizational problems, the new leaders did not neglect the political issues of the day. The change in leadership had little effect on the publicly announced aims and objectives of the German Communist Party. No new formulation of ideas was expected from, or attempted by, the Thälmann Central Committee. The party's basic position was well established. Any important change in policy, or reinterpretation of the current political situation had to come from the Comintern. The German party leaders had the more narrow responsibility of deciding on the timing and emphasis of issues which would yield the greatest possible political return in the near future. With the presidential campaigns just over and no general election in sight for the next three years, the chief gains that could be hoped for were not votes, but a greater degree of sympathy from the masses, the encouragement of oppositional tendencies in the Social Democratic Party and the free trade unions, and the recruitment of new members.

During the fall of 1925 the editors of *Rote Fahne* were apparently probing for a viable issue—or set of issues—which would truly arouse public concern.[154] The paper regularly attacked a variety of political and social evils that ranged from inadequate working class housing and the reactionary bias of the courts to the "enslavement" of the German people by the Dawes Plan and the Locarno Agreements. It sought, following authoritative statements from Moscow, to identify the KPD with the satisfaction of many of the German workers' needs.[155] Nevertheless, few of these issues seemed to produce much resonance. The party needed a cause around which various wider-ranging demands and issues could center, a cause sufficiently vital to sustain popular agitation for a reasonably prolonged period of time.

At some point in the fall of 1925, the KPD leadership

[154] *Rote Fahne's* style of presenting issues was always that of insistent urgency, nevertheless the handling of many issues in the fall of 1925 seems more than usually forced. For example, the attempt to connect the intensified trade union activities of the party with the fight against the Locarno Treaties. "Locarno must be the point of departure for the mass mobilization of the German proletariat against the new dangers of imperialistic war. In every *factory*, in every *trade union*, in every town, we must assemble the working masses. . . ." 18 Oct. 1925.

[155] "Social-Democracy can be exposed and reduced to an insignificant minority in the working class only in the course of the day-to-day struggle for the concrete aims of the working class. . . [I]n this, questions concerning wages, hours, housing conditions, insurance, taxation, unemployment, high cost of living, and so forth, must play a most important if not the decisive role. . . ." Stalin, *Works*, 7: 37.

decided to concentrate its attention on problems of unemployment.[156] Unlike the "dangers" that were said to be lurking in the Locarno Agreements, the effects of unemployment were clear and well-known to the workers. Any discussion of its most immediate or technical aspects could easily be expanded into a full-scale critique of the existing social and economic order. In this sphere, attention directed to specific problems of the day-to-day existence of the workers was not likely to produce any diminution of ideological vigor, a potential danger which the party leaders well understood they had to avoid.[157] Although employment conditions had been generally good during most of 1924 and 1925, it was widely recognized that the ranks of the unemployed would grow considerably during the winter of 1925–26. Not only did this expected unemployment develop, but it remained at quite a high level during the ensuing spring and summer, when unemployment usually dropped sharply.[158] Moreover, the highest rates of unemployment occurred in the largest cities where the KPD was most strongly based.[159] The possibilities of finding mass support for a sustained campaign against unemployment could hardly have escaped the leaders of the KPD, nor did the possibility of trouble escape the attention of official governmental circles.[160]

[156] This statement is made primarily on the basis of the large amount of space the party paper devoted to the topic in the fall of 1925, but see the later official statements: Zentralkomitee der KPD. Sekretariat. Rundschreiben Nr. 1/26. *Anweisungen für die Kampagne zur Fürstenenteignung, gegen die Erwerblosigkeit* (Berlin, 5 Feb. 1926) and the "Resolution of the Sixth ECCI Plenum on the German Question," *Rote Fahne,* 2 April 1926, partially translated by Degras, 2: 285–91.

[157] ". . . [S]uch a policy [of fighting for limited aims] can be conducted only by a party which is headed by cadres of leaders sufficiently experienced to be able to take advantage of every single blunder of Social-Democracy in order to strengthen the Party, and possessing sufficient theoretical training not to lose sight of the prospects of revolutionary development because of partial successes." Stalin, *Works,* 7: 37. The danger of succumbing to partial successes by actually curing the unemployment problem in Germany was surely rather slight.

[158] See Table I. A valuable monograph on the short, but sharp slump is Fritz Blaich, *Die Wirtschaftskrise 1925/26 und die Reichsregierung* (Kallmünz, 1977).

[159] See Table II.

[160] A secret informant to the foreign office on Communist Party affairs commented in August 1925: "The KPD is definitely counting on the coming fall and winter to bring especially hard conflict in the economic sphere and is eagerly at work in the factories forming action committees as battle units for the expected conflicts, particularly stressing the tariff and tax questions. . . ." "Lagebericht! Im August 1925," German Foreign Office Records, reel 2281, frame E137151.

Stresemann apparently took this, or some similar report, seriously enough to discuss with Hindenburg what to do "if because of great unemployment in the autumn or winter the Communists think the time is come for them to proceed

TABLE I

Per cent of Trade Union members unemployed or working part-time 1925–26.

	Jan.	Feb.	Mar.	Apr.	May	June	July	Aug.	Sept.	Oct.	Nov.	Dec.
1925												
unemployed	8.1	7.3	5.8	4.3	3.6	3.5	3.7	4.3	4.5	5.8	10.7	19.4
part-time	5.5	5.3	5.1	4.9	5.0	5.2	5.8	6.9	8.5	12.4	16.0	19.8
1926												
unemployed	22.6	22.0	21.4	18.6	18.1	18.1	17.7	16.7	15.2	14.2	14.2	16.7
part-time	22.6	21.6	21.7	19.1	18.2	17.2	16.6	15.0	12.7	10.2	8.3	7.3

Statistisches Reichsamt, *Statistisches Jahrbuch für das Deutsche Reich 1927* (Berlin, 1927), 336–37.

TABLE II

The Statistics Office published figures for the number of recipients of unemployment payments; however, not all the jobless were qualified for support and others had exhausted their coverage. Workers on relief (*Notstandsarbeiter*) were not included in these figures. Furthermore, the Statistics Office made a distinction between heads of families (*Hauptunter-stützungsempfänger*) and other family members who received payments (*Zuschlagsempfänger*) and used only the first category in its main calculations. The trend can be seen in the number of *Hauptunterstützungsempfänger* receiving unemployment benefits:

	1 July 1925	1 Oct. 1925	1 Jan. 1926	1 Apr. 1926	1 July 1926	1 Oct. 1926	1 Jan. 1927
In the German Reich as a whole	195,099	266,078	1,498,681	1,942,011	1,740,754	1,394,062	1,748,597
Per 1,000 inhabitants	3.1	4.3	24.0	31.1	27.9	22.4	28.0
Average for cities with over 100,000 population	1,996	2,832	10,721	15,356	16,116	14,075	14,311
Per 1,000 inhabitants	5.4	7.7	29.0	41.4	43.4	37.9	38.6
Average for cities between 50,000 and 100,000 in population	350	499	1922	2531	2553	2133	2427
Per 1,000 inhabitants	4.9	6.9	27.9	36.4	35.8	29.9	34.0

Statistisches Reichsamt, *Statistisches Jahrbuch für das Deutsche Reich 1926* (Berlin, 1926), 307–310 and *1927*, 339–42.

Unemployment, moreover, could be tied in with other economic problems. The Communists perceived signs of increasing exploitation in such factors as inadequate unemployment insurance, the new tariff, the refusal of the industrialists to restore the eight-hour day, and the introduction of more modern and efficient production techniques ("Taylorism"). Everything, they said, pointed to the unashamed greed of the employers who callously used their power in the factories and their political influence to pass the costs resulting from hard competition in the world market on to the helpless poorer classes in Germany.[161]

As was pointed out earlier, the KPD's campaign to confiscate the royal properties developed in close association with its campaign against unemployment. It will be instructive to compare how the leadership of the Communist Party handled these issues and to observe the different results. Party leaders chose both issues for intensive propaganda campaigns and made a conscious effort to tie them into a comprehensive sequence of Communist objectives. The support and cooperation of non-Communists was seriously courted. Yet, although the unemployment situation troubled other parties and the unions, they never considered joining with the KPD to publicize such an issue, or to force any kind of legislative action.[162] The question arises, therefore, why were the Communists' united front appeals in this period genuinely successful only in the case of the royal properties question? The answer to this question will require the examination of crucial policy decisions undertaken by several other political parties, especially the Social Democrats.

*   *   *   *

For a month after the first parliamentary discussion of the DDP and KDP bills, few new developments relating to the royal properties question occurred. The resignation of the Luther government on 5 December 1925, set off a cabinet

---

against the state." Stresemann *Nachlass,* 11 Aug. 1925, reel 3113, frame H147951; also 16 Dec. 1925, a mention of plans made by the Prussian government to counter Communist-led disturbances. Ibid., frame H148102.

[161] *Rote Fahne,* 11, 18, 23 Dec. 1925, and 1 Jan., 18 Feb., and 1 April 1926.

[162] The SPD simply ignored the KPD's demands for common action against unemployment and for the dissolution of the Reichstag after the conclusion of the agreement to sponsor the referendum together. *Rote Fahne,* 19, 21 and 22 Jan. 1926; Karl, p. 21.

crisis that lasted a full six weeks.[163] The Reichstag was recessed part of this time for the Christmas holidays, while the major parties concentrated their attention on negotiations to form a viable new coalition government. There were only two coalition possibilities that could command at least potentially firm majorities in the Reichstag—either the *Bürgerblock* combination including the German Nationalists, or a Great Coalition of the Democratic, Catholic Center, and the People's Parties, in alliance with the Social Democrats.[164] The recently proven unreliability of the Nationalists on foreign policy made the first combination impossible.[165] Therefore, the Great Coalition seemed the obvious and necessary solution, particularly to the leaders of the DDP and Center.[166] On the other hand, neither the DVP nor the SPD saw any great attraction in this marriage of convenience.[167]

Alternatively, there existed the possibility of some kind of minority government, which would have been easier for the parties to form, but would have been weaker in its relation to the Reichstag, and probably unable to give the strong

[163] *Schulthess' Europäischer Geschichtskalender, 1926*, pp. 507; Georg Schreiber, "Innenpolitik des Reiches," *Politisches Jahrbuch 1926*, pp. 52–54; Eyck, 2: 71–75; Conze, *Historische Zeitschrift*, 77: 52–53; Haungs, pp. 94–109.

[164] Koch-Weser's report to the DDP's *Parteiausschuss*, 24 Jan. 1926. DDP Papers, reel 37, folder 731, p. 3.

[165] A letter from the DDP party office, 10 Nov. 1925, stated that the DNVP had shown themselves *"für regierungsunfähig."* DDP Papers, reel 38, folder 758, p. 4; Stresemann's letter to Dr. Walter von Keudell, 27 Nov. 1925, explaining why further cooperation between the DVP and DNVP was impossible, Stresemann, *Vermächtnis*, 2 (Berlin, 1932): 246; report from Lord D'Abernon to Foreign Minister Chamberlain, 3 Nov. 1925, *Documents on British Foreign Policy, 1919–1939*. Series 1A. Vol. 1, Nr. 49.

[166] For DDP views see above, notes 12 and 13, *Vossische Zeitung*, 27 Oct. (Nr. 257) and 20 Dec. 1925 (Nr. 304); for the Center Party, *Germania*, 30 Nov. 1925, the declaration by the Center's *Parteivorstand* and *Fraktionvorstand*, printed in *Vorwärts*, 11 Jan. 1926 (Nr. 16), and the remarks of *Arbeitsminister* Brauns at a meeting of cabinet ministers 5 Dec. 1925: "Only a government with an entirely firm majority will be able to get through the coming hard winter." *Kabinettsprotokolle*, reel 1836, frames D766841–42.

[167] Stresemann indicated at the meeting on 5 Dec. that while the DVP would not do anything to oppose the formation of a Great Coalition, the question of personnel would be of great importance. "Statesman-like heads" such as Braun or Severing would be acceptable but figures such as the former ministers Robert Schmidt and Wilhelm Sollmann would not do. Ibid., frame D766842. More generally on the elements in the DVP which opposed political cooperation with the SPD, see Turner, pp. 155–63, 220–29. On the attitude of the Social Democrats, *Vorwärts*, 7 Dec. (Nr. 577), 14 Dec. (Nr. 589) and 15 Dec. 1925 (Nr. 591); resolutions against the creation of a Great Coalition government were passed by SPD organizations in Berlin, Stuttgart, and Breslau, ibid., 5 Jan. (Nr. 6) and 11 Jan. 1926 (Nr. 16); *Rote Fahne*, 10 Dec. 1925; Carl Severing, *Mein Lebensweg*, 2 (Cologne, 1950): 79–80.

direction required by affairs of the nation.[168] Theoretically, a Weimar Coalition of the DDP, Center, and SPD might have been formed as a minority government. It worked in Prussia.[169] At the level of national politics, however, the two middle-class parties disliked the demands which the Social Democrats, conscious of their weight in such a grouping, were apt to insist on.[170] In any case, the formation of a Weimar

[168] Koch-Weser's report cited above, note 164; *Germania* insisted that a stable government supported by a majority in the Reichstag was necessary. "Any other solution is no solution." 23 Dec. 1925 (Nr. 598). The Social Democrats tended to play down the urgency of forming a broadly based coalition government. *Vorwärts* contrasted the deteriorating economic situation with the cabinet crisis, terming the latter a *"gemütliche Regierungskrise."* 13 Dec. 1925 (Nr. 588). Hermann Müller, speaking on the occasion of the presentation of the newly formed second Luther government to the Reichstag, insisted, ". . . I must protest against [thinking] that the existence of a minority government has anything to do with the first stages of or the conditions [leading to] a crisis in our nation *(Staatskrise)."* Reichstag. *Verhandlungen*, 388 (27 Jan. 1926): 5160. The seriousness of the parliamentary crisis and the possibility of a dictatorship were mentioned by a number of speakers in the Reichstag debate. Representative excerpts are given in *Ursachen und Folgen*, 7: 224–29.

Certain heavy industrialists at a meeting of the *Verein deutscher Eisen- und Stahlwaren Industrieller*, 16 Dec. 1925, considered the situation critical. Dr. Reichert, head of this important association and a DNVP member of the Reichstag, expressed the opinion that a Great Coalition would not be formed and a government of the middle would lack both a majority and any great authority. He argued, therefore, "That there is nothing else to do except govern on the basis of Art. 48 and convene the Reichstag when hell freezes over *(wenn das Jahr 13 Monate habe)."* Ernst von Borsig, owner of the famous industrial works and chairman of the *Vereinigung deutscher Arbeitgeberverbände*, and a Herr Gröbler agreed. There was further discussion how to win President von Hindenburg over to this idea. Stresemann *Nachlass*, reel 3113, folder H148101. Interestingly enough, Alfred Hugenberg wrote against nebulous talk of a dictatorship; he urged instead the creation of a broadly based "national" party. "Parteien und Parlamentarismus," *Eiserne Blätter. Wochenschrift für deutsche Politik und Kultur*, 7 (Nr. 3, 17 Jan. 1926): 45–48.

[169] From April 1925 until the new elections in 1928 the Weimar Coalition Cabinet under Braun's leadership survived despite the fact it lacked a majority. He said, "I had a majority minus four plus [the] fear of the opposition and that sufficed." Braun, p. 175; Bracher, *Die Auflösung*, p. 574; Schulze, pp. 475–538.

[170] Rudolf Morsey abundantly documents the tendencies in the Center Party which opposed close cooperation with the Social Democrats in the early twenties, *Die Deutsche Zentrumspartei 1919–1923, Beiträge zur Geschichte des Parlamentarismus und der politischen Parteien*, 32 (Düsseldorf, 1966): 311–13, 409–30, 457–75, 613–14. While normally willing to cooperate with the SPD, the Democratic Party consistently tried to keep the SPD from becoming too strong. For example: "A strong growth of the Social Democrats, however, will . . . radicalize the Social Democratic party and lead to all kinds of political experiments. . . ." Deutsche Demokratische Partei, *Schriftenreihe für politische Werbung. Nr. 1: Der Wahlkampf 1928* (Berlin, 1928), p. 5. This had been the view of the DDP since the first elections for the Weimar National Assembly. Otto Nuschke, "Wie die Deutsche Demokratische Partei wurde, was sie leistete und was sie ist," in *Zehn Jahre Deutsche Republik*, pp. 32, 41. Koch-Weser reported that a Weimar Coalition would have been a poor solution of the crisis in the winter of 1925–26 because it would have driven the DVP into the arms of the DNVP. Despite

Coalition in the winter of 1925–26 would have meant dropping Luther as chancellor and Stresemann as foreign minister—scarcely realistic possibilities at that time.[171] Practically, therefore, a minority coalition of the relatively small parties of the middle (DDP, Center, BVP, DVP) was the only real possibility and ultimately this combination of parties did in fact form the second Luther government. Although not a very strong combination, the coalition of middle parties was able to seek support from different parties in the Reichstag, changing from the SPD on the left to the DNVP on the right, depending on the particular issue under consideration.[172]

Before the public would accept a minority government of the middle parties as a tolerable solution of the cabinet crisis, it was necessary "to run through the exercise [book]."[173] In particular, this involved sustained efforts by Konstantin Fehrenbach, head of the Center Party's Reichstag delegation, and Erich Koch-Weser, chairman of the Democratic Party, to form a cabinet on the basis of the Great Coalition.[174] Once before and once again after Christmas, they undertook to bring the four parties together, in part by trying to work out a program for future parliamentary cooperation. On both occasions the Social Democratic Reichstag delegation found

---

reservations, he said, the DDP would have joined such a government, but the resistance of the Center Party prevented such a cabinet from being formed. DDP Papers, reel 37, folder 731, p. 3. Hartmut Schustereit, *Linksliberalismus und Sozialdemokratie in der Weimarer Republik* (Düsseldorf, 1975), pp. 194–96, 250–63.

[171] Koch-Weser's comments at the meeting of the DDP *Parteiausschuss*, 4 Dec. 1925. DDP Papers, reel 38, folder 749, p. 3; *Germania*, 6 Dec. 1925 (Nr. 570); report of Lord D'Abernon to Foreign Minister Chamberlain, 1 Nov. 1925. *Documents on British Foreign Policy, 1919–1939.* Series 1A, Vol. 1, Nr. 43.

[172] The current phrase was that the second Luther government could govern "mit wechselnden Mehrheiten." *Germania*, 18 Jan. 1926 (Nr. 28) and, critically, the *Frankfurter Zeitung*, 11 May 1926 (Nr. 348).

[173] Chancellor Luther in a 5 Dec. meeting of Cabinet ministers. *Kabinettsprotokolle*, reel 1836, frame D766844. Realistic politicians saw in advance that the Great Coalition had little chance. Otto Gessler wrote in his memoirs that when the governmental crisis first developed Hindenburg wanted to keep Luther on as chancellor. Gessler advised him to keep Luther in reserve, to let Koch-Weser and others prove their inability to form a government, and then name Luther. The whole sequence of events, Gessler wrote, went "according to [this] program." *Reichswehrpolitik in der Weimarer Zeit* (Stuttgart, 1958), pp. 348–49. He also reported that Hindenburg was "visibly depressed" by his first experience with the lengthy interparty negotiations. Ibid., p. 423. Stresemann predicted a similar outcome to the British ambassador, diary entry, 22 Dec. 1925. *Vermächtnis*, 2: 382. Stürmer's account of the 1925–26 "Christmas crisis" confirms this interpretation (pp. 134–40, 288–91).

[174] The principal efforts were made by Koch-Weser; Fehrenbach's involvement was more in the nature of a courteous formality.

reasons for rejecting the Great Coalition.[175] The ostensible reasons the SPD leaders gave for breaking off further negotiations deceived no one; it was all too clear that the bulk of the Social Democrats wanted to avoid governmental responsibility at what they thought was an unfavorable time.[176] One of the obstacles over which the negotiations faltered was the considerable variance between the views of the SPD and DVP concerning the handling of the royal properties question. The Social Democrats wanted acceptance of the DDP bill with some modifications, but the much more conservative People's Party wanted to establish the final settlements in another fashion, through a specially constituted arbitration court to be composed of trained jurists.[177] This disagreement was certainly not the decisive reason the formation of a Great Coalition government in the winter of 1925–26 failed;[178] but the emergence of the properties issue, with its heavily weighted symbolic overtones, converged with other forces to prompt the SPD to reject cooperation with the middle-class parties.

[175] *Vorwärts*, 17 Dec. 1925 (Nrs. 594 and 595), 13 Jan. 1926 (Nr. 19). Lord D'Abernon wrote Sir W. Tyrrell in the foreign office that "Dr. Stresemann attributed the failure of the attempt to form a Great Coalition to the absence of Herr Ebert's influence. If the late President had been alive, even if he had not remained President, his strong common sense would have prevailed against petty party considerations which had prevented the Socialists from showing courage. The fact was that the Socialists had no great leader. Dr. Braun . . . was an extremely able man but he was also very lazy and if an opportunity offered to shoot stags he left the Socialist party to take care of itself and went after the stags for six weeks. Modern politics required greater energy and concentration. Severing was also very able but he was a sick man." 23 Dec. 1925. *Documents on British Foreign Policy, 1919–1939*, Series 1A, Vol. 1, Nr. 158.

[176] *Germania* stated that the negotiations "shattered because fear of responsibility coupled with doctrinaire prejudices once again killed sound common sense *(Menschenverstand)*." 17 Dec. 1925 (Nr. 588), also 13 Jan. 1926 (Nr. 19); and a resolution passed by the DDP *Parteiausschuss, Frankfurter Zeitung,* 25 Jan. 1926 (Nr. 64). Luther at the beginning of the crisis foresaw that the SPD would try to blame the DVP for the breakdown of the negotiations. *Kabinettsprotokolle,* reel 1836, frame D766843. Eyck's criticism of the Social Democratic decision is very strong (2: 72–75).

[177] On 10 Dec., the Social Democratic Reichstag *Fraktion* set forth a series of program points which it insisted the other parties would have to accept if they were to join a Great Coalition. Among these points were "clear adherence to the Republic, Defense against all attempts at monarchist restoration. . . . Regulation of the princely settlements by national legislation with revisionary force." *Vorwärts,* 11 Dec. 1925 (Nr. 584); *Frankfurter Zeitung,* 11 Dec. 1925 (Nr. 598). Koch-Weser's own program of action included "creation of a law for the establishment of a just settlement with the former princes compatible with the state's prosperity." *Frankfurter Zeitung,* 18 Dec. 1925 (Nr. 940). *Vossische Zeitung,* 18 Dec. 1925 (Nr. 302).

[178] Differences over social and economic policies (eight-hour day, unemployment insurance, etc.) played an important role. We shall discuss the deeper grounds for the SPD's rejection of participation in the Great Coalition in the next chapter.

Public interest in the properties issue continued to mount
throughout the holiday season. A variety of groups held meetings and passed resolutions attacking the settlements.[179] A
Reichsbanner meeting in Cassel favored "the suspension of the
princely settlements . . . as long as there are citizens in Germany who have nothing to eat."[180] Individual citizens also
reacted strongly. A non-Communist worker, who had served
in the Navy wrote to *Rote Fahne:*

> During the war something was always taken out of our clothing
> allowance, i.e. we simply were not paid all [that was due], and
> in exchange we sailors were credited with war bonds. The total
> that was deducted from my [pay] was 300 gold marks. Now, like
> so many others, I find myself in dire need. Where is my settle-
> ment? William the Second who disgracefully abandoned the army
> in 1918 can surely make no claim for *Aufwertung.*[181]

He hoped for a referendum to put a stop to the princely
settlements so that perhaps then there would be "money for
old people on pensions and the rest of us from whom money
was, so to speak, stolen during the war."[182]

During the lengthy process of forming a new cabinet, the
Communist Party was restricted to the role of malicious outsider as there was no chance that it would be included in any
coalition. The party leadership was not idle, however. By
mid-December it had made contact with certain middle-class
intellectuals sharing strong leftist sympathies, and encouraged them to undertake the formation of a non-partisan committee to organize a referendum.[183] A distinguished

[179] Resolutions by the *Republikanischer Reichsbund* and *Republikanischer Anwaltsbund,*
Frankfurter Zeitung, 3 Dec. (Nr. 899) and 9 Dec. 1925 (Nr. 916); *Vorwärts,* 9 Dec. (Nr.
580), 16 Dec. (Nr. 593) and, reporting a resolution passed by a Center Party meeting
in Gelsenkirchen, 20 Dec. 1925 (Nr. 600); *Rote Fahne,* 10, 22, and 24 Dec. 1925, a
number of these reporting actions by SPD or ADGB locals.
[180] The resolution was then submitted to the town council where through the
combined votes of the SPD, DDP, and Center it passed against the opposition of
the right. *Das Reichsbanner,* 1 Jan. 1926.
[181] *Rote Fahne,* 13 Dec. 1925.
[182] Idem. *Rote Fahne* and the *Vossische Zeitung* made a regular practice of printing
such letters.
[183] Karl, pp. 16–17. According to Babette Gross, Willi Münzenberg recommended
the formation of such a committee even before the KPD itself was ready to join in
the undertaking. He also wrote the widely distributed pamphlet, "Keinen Pfennig
den Fürsten." *Willi Münzenberg, Schriftenreihe der Vierteljahrshefte für Zeitgeschichte,* 14/
15 (Stuttgart, 1967): 172. Her article, "The German Communists' United Front
and Popular Front Ventures," in Milorad M. Drachkovitch and Branko Lazich, eds.,
The Comintern: Historical Highlights (New York, 1966), pp. 111–138, concentrates on
the 1930s; also unrewarding for our purposes is Helmut Gruber, "Willi Münzen-

economist and statistician, Robert René Kuczynski, undertook the chief responsibility for forming the committee, relying in the first instance on his contacts in the *Liga für Menschenrechte*.[184] In conjunction with Ludwig Quidde, the well-known pacifist, and Helene Stöcker, who was active in various feminist causes, Kuczynski invited a number of "politically neutral" organizations to participate in a preliminary non-binding discussion on 17 December. "We should consider if and how the popular movement [which is] developing against [the princes' settlements] can and ought to be channeled into a referendum, and what goal is to be set for this movement."[185] The participants at this first planning session generally agreed that a referendum was desirable, but felt that further discussion, including contact with the parties on the left, was necessary.[186]

On 6 January 1926, one day before the Reichstag's Legal Committee began its discussion of the property settlements, the *Ausschuss zur Durchführung des Volksentscheids für entschädigungslose Enteignung der Fürsten* established itself formally.[187] The Kuczynski Committee, as it was generally known, obtained support from a number of organizations.[188] Many of

---

berg's German Communist Propaganda Empire 1921–1933," *Journal of Modern History*, 38 (Nr. 3, September 1966): 278–97.

[184] Jürgen Kuczynski, *René Kuczynski, ein fortschrittlicher Wissenschaftler in der ersten Häfte des 20. Jahrhunderts* (Berlin, 1957), p. 85; Habedank, p. 32; Schüren, pp. 70–75.

[185] Kuczynski, pp. 85, 115–20.

[186] Ibid., p. 86.

[187] On the organizational meeting of 6 Jan. 1926, see Kuczynski, pp. 86–87, and especially, pp. 155–57, where he prints the protocol of the meeting. Regrettably he gives the protocols for only two of the Committee's meetings, 6 and 21 Jan. 1926.

[188] According to Heinz Karl (p. 16), the following organizations joined the Committee: "*KPD, RFB, USPD, Sozialistischer Bund, Internationale Arbeiter-hilfe, Deutsche Liga für Menschenrechte, Internationaler Bund der Opfer des Krieges und der Arbeit, Internationale Frauenliga für Frieden und Freiheit—deutscher Zweig, Reichsbund deutscher Kleinbauern, Gemeinschaft der proletarischen Freidenker, Pazifistischer Studentenbund, Freie aktivistische Jugend, Bund für radikale Ethik, Republikanischer Anwaltsbund, Arbeitsgemeinschaft freigeistiger Verbände, Verein sozialistischer Ärzte, Volksbund für Geistesfreiheit, Arbeiter-Wanderbund "Der Naturfreunde," Internationaler Sozialistischer Kampfbund, Arbeiterverein für Biochemie und Lebensreform, Physiokratischer Kampfbund, Arbeitsgemeinschaft entscheidener Republikaner, Verband der ausgeschlossenen Bauarbeiter, Arbeiter Ido-Bund, Kartell der selbstständigen Verbände, Berlin;* [and later], *Bund für Mütterschutz, Deutscher Industrieverband, Deutscher Monistenbund, Reichsbund für Siedlung und Pachtung, Roter Frauen- und Mädchenbund, Rote Hilfe Deutschlands, Schriftstellervereinigung 1925, Verband Volksgesundheit, Verein linksgerichteter Verleger, Vereinigte Rechtsschutzverbände.*" At the first meeting at least one organization, the *Zentralkommission für Arbeiter-Sport und Körperpflege*, reported it could not participate because its member parties failed to view the problem from the same

these groups were small and often closely associated with the Communist Party, but nevertheless, the Kuczynski Committee also enlisted the aid of several left-liberal and "proletarian" groups which had never previously cooperated.[189] The draft of a law on which the public would be asked to vote was accepted. Like the KPD's Reichstag bill, the Committee's proposal detailed the uses to which the confiscated properties would be put in an obvious effort to appeal to many disadvantaged groups.[190] The Communist representatives at the meeting insisted that there could be no watering down of the principle of total confiscation without compensation, and obtained acceptance of this view.[191]

During the first half of January, attempts to persuade the SPD and ADGB to participate in the Committee were unsuccessful. Newspapers such as the *Berliner Tageblatt* and the *Frankfurter Zeitung* carried more information about the activities of the Kuczynski Committee than did *Vorwärts*.[192] On 16 January, Dr. Kuczynski reported that the leaders of the SPD still refused to send representatives to the Committee's meetings.[193] However, informal contacts had been established, and

---

perspective and it did not want to give them cause for "unpleasant discussions." Kuczynski, p. 155. Theodor Heuss reports a bitter fight with Kuczynski at a meeting of the *Schutzverband Deutscher Schriftsteller* and that he prevented the passage of a resolution favoring confiscation only by threatening to resign as chairman. *Erinnerungen, 1905–1933* (Tübingen, 1965), pp. 341–42; Kuczynski on this meeting, pp. 101–4.

[189] Fischer, p. 522; Kuczynski, p. 89.

[190] "1. Capital wealth will be applied to raising [the level] of support for those requiring help, especially for war invalids and dependents [of men killed in the] war.

2. The rural estates will be used to alleviate the scarcity of land for small peasants, leaseholders, and rural laborers.

3. The palaces, dwelling houses, and other structures will be used for purposes of general welfare and education, in particular for the establishment of nursing and old-age homes for war invalids, dependents [of men killed in the] war, people [living on] small pensions or insurance, as well as for orphanages and educational institutions." *Rote Fahne*, 17 Jan. 1926.

[191] Kuczynski, p. 155. The role played by the KPD in encouraging this Committee was even more clearly revealed in the meeting on 21 January. By that time the Social Democrats were expressing willingness to support a referendum. Dr. Kuczynski suggested that if the SPD's support was assured the Committee would be unnecessary; however, the KPD representative, Schneller, clearly indicated that the party did not want to see the Committee dissolved. Ibid., pp. 161–62.

[192] For example, see the very brief notice of the formation of the Kuczynski Committee in *Vorwärts*, 7 Jan. 1926 (Nr. 9). *Rote Fahne* published a letter 25 Feb. 1926, from a SPD functionary complaining against *Vorwärts*'s virtual blackout of news regarding the activities of the Kuczynski Committee.

[193] Kuczynski, p. 91.

it was known that some leading union and party officials were sympathetic to the idea of a referendum.[194] Moreover, the organizers of the referendum were aware that rank-and-file Social Democrats and trade unionists had few reservations about cooperating with the Communists and other groups against the princes. The increasing number of resolutions passed by local organizations made that very clear.[195] In the meantime, the Kuczynski Committee began the first legal steps toward starting an initiative and referendum. Kuczynski and Thälmann submitted their proposed law to the ministry of interior 18 January 1926, along with the request that an early date be set for the circulation of initiative petitions.[196]

In their association with the Kuczynski Committee, the spokesmen for the KPD took some pains to avoid creating "the appearance [that it was] a Communist Committee."[197] In part, this was done to permit contact with segments of the middle-class population which normally would have rejected any association with the KPD. The financial and organizational resources of the groups participating in the Committee were not great, but they sufficed to make it serve as an effective center for the publication and distribution of pamphlets, posters, and information for campaign workers.[198] One important consideration on the mind of the KPD leadership surely must have been the tactical convenience of permitting an ostensibly non-Communist Committee to undertake the formal preparations for an initiative and referendum. If the effort to arouse a strong public response had failed—and one must remember that it was the first time a nationwide referendum had been attempted—the Communist party could have easily disclaimed responsibility. Even as it was, the KPD argued that confiscation of the royal prop-

[194] At the meeting on 6 Jan., Otto Lehmann-Russbuldt reported on talks with Albert Falkenberg of the ADBG and Wilhelm Dittmann. Both men expressed, in a cautious way, personally favorable attitudes. Ibid., p. 156.
[195] For example, a local united front committee with unusually wide support was formed in Opladen. Rote Fahne, 19 Jan. 1926; Geschichte der deutschen Arbeiterbewegung, Chronik, 2: 191–92.
[196] Kuczynski, p. 91, Frankfurter Zeitung, 17 Jan. 1926 (Nr. 44).
[197] Kuczynski, p. 162.
[198] Later in the month, Social Democratic leaders were unfavorably impressed by the small amount (3,000 marks) the Kuczynski Committee reported it could contribute toward the official costs of the referendum. Jahrbuch der Deutschen Sozialdemokratie . . . 1926, p. 7. The costs of financing an initiative and referendum campaign had played a part in the SPD's initial reluctance to start such proceedings. See Rote Fahne's sharp attack on such hesitations, 8 Dec. 1925.

erties was "a democratic demand,"[199] which did not directly involve Communist principles. The formation of the Kuczynski Committee saved the KPD from risking any further damage to its depleted stock of prestige, but at the same time, enabled the Communists to probe the extent of public discontent.

In mid-January the leaders of the KPD, aware of mounting pressures inside the SPD, renewed their appeal for the two parties to work together as sponsors of the initiative and referendum movement.[200] At the same time, they urged common action on the problem of unemployment and joint steps to force the dissolution of the Reichstag and thus bring about new elections. The timing of the appeal is significant: on 12 January, the Social-Democratic Reichstag delegation refused for the second time participation in a Great Coalition government. As long as the possibility of Social Democratic cooperation with the middle-class parties had existed, neither the KPD nor the SPD would have considered joint political action on even a single issue. However, once the Social Democrats had for their own reasons decided to remain in what they liked to call "opposition," they began to consider a limited alliance with the KPD even though it meant a break with the policy of non-association with Communists the SPD had followed since the end of 1923. Neither party trusted the other, and the Social Democratic leaders knew full well that the Communists would attempt to discredit them in the eyes of their followers, regardless of whether or not the two parties cooperated in supporting the referendum.[201]

On 19 January, the SPD's Advisory Committee (*Parteiausschuss*) was convened to discuss the question of a referendum on the royal properties issue.[202] It considered sponsoring a

[199] Ibid., 22 June 1926; Karl, p. 56.

[200] Statement by the *Polbüro des Zentralkomitees* issued just before the meeting of the SPD *Parteiausschuss*. *Rote Fahne*, 19 Jan. 1926; also 21 Jan. 1926.

[201] *Jahrbuch der Deutschen Sozialdemokratie . . . 1926*, p. 7. Recognition of the general untrustworthiness of the KPD was widespread. See the editorial comments of Julius Leber, 17 Oct. 1925: "For years the Communists have supported all efforts by the parties of the right against the Republic and Social Democracy. For them, it was the highest 'proletarian duty.' Now they suddenly declare that proletarian feelings of duty require the opposite. And tomorrow?

"Only political fools could still have confidence in a party which makes such . . . verbal gymnastics." *Ein Mann Geht seinen Weg*, pp. 116–17.

[202] The party Executive Board (*Vorstand*) had already discussed the possibility. *Vorwärts*, 5 Jan. 1926 (Nr. 6); and on 16 Jan. called for a meeting of the *Parteiausschuss*, ibid., 16 Jan. 1926 (Nr. 26); *Jahrbuch der Deutschen Sozialdemokratie . . . 1926*, p. 6. Further reports on these discussions in *Vorwärts*, 20 Jan. (Nr. 31) and 9 Feb. 1926 (Nr. 65).

separate referendum in the event that the Reichstag failed
to act, but recognized the infeasibility of two competing appeals to the voters. Consequently it authorized discussions
with the Kuczynski Committee and the Communists.[203] The
Free Trade Union organization (ADGB) was called upon to
serve as mediator: "The *Allgemeine Deutsche Gewerkschaftsbund*
is suited for this [role as] intermediary because [the discussion] concerns important questions of social policy, and all
the political views [which must be] taken into consideration
are represented in the trade unions." [204] On 22 and 23 January 1926—that is, after the second Luther government had
been formed—representatives of the SPD, ADGB, KPD and
the Kuczynski Committee met in the Reichstag building and
worked out their differences.[205] The SPD insisted on certain

[203] The text of the resolution of the SPD *Parteiausschuss* is printed in the *Frankfurter
Zeitung*, 20 Jan. 1926 (Nr. 51); also see the discussions in the Kuczynski Committee
regarding these developments, Kuczynski, pp. 161–62.

[204] From the resolution cited above, note 203. It is clear the union assumed the
role of mediator only because the SPD wanted it to. A letter was sent by the ADGB
Vorstand to the KPD on 21 Jan. accepting the undertaking. *Rote Fahne*, 22 Jan. 1926.
A few days earlier the union's leaders had issued a statement declaring that the
properties question was a political matter and that any decision must be left to the
parties. *Vorwärts*, 18 Jan. 1926 (Nr. 28); also the letter of Clemens Nörpel, secretary
of the ADGB *Vorstand*, replying to attacks on an earlier statement, *Rote Fahne*, 19
Jan. 1926. The AfA likewise had declared it a matter for the parties, *Frankfurter
Zeitung*, 20 Jan. 1926 (Nr. 52). It is true, however, that some local union organizations
were putting pressure on the national leadership to support the confiscation proposal, just as there was similar pressure on the SPD leaders, *Rote Fahne*, 20 Jan.
1926.
Despite the normal hostility between the Free Trade Union leaders and the
Communist Party, this decision to function as mediator among the parties of the
left was not without precedent. After the Kapp *Putsch*, Karl Legien tried to bring
about the formation of a "working class government" based on the support of the
two Socialist parties and the trade unions (both Christian and Free). The project
failed due to the opposition of some left Independents. Braunthal, 2: 219–20;
Rosenberg, pp. 367–68; Hunt, *German Social Democracy*, pp. 181–85; and Hans H.
Biegert, "Gewerkschaftspolitik in der Phase des Kapp-Lüttwitz-Putsches," in Hans
Mommsen, Dietmar Petzina and Bernd Weisbrod, eds., *Industrielles System und politische
Entwicklung in der Weimarer Republik* (Düsseldorf, 1974), pp. 190–205. Again after
the Rathenau murder in 1922, the union leaders tried to arrange for the Communists
and the Social Democrats to follow a common line of policies. The Communists,
however, refused to abandon their own aims or give up attacks on their allies. Three
years later, Leipart remarked, "Unfortunately, the distressing experiences that we
had to undergo a repeated number of times ... have led all the members of the
National Executive Board to the conviction that this was the last attempt [we could
make] to form a United Front with the Communist Party." Allgemeiner Deutscher
Gewerkschaftsbund, *Protokoll der Verhandlungen des 12. Kongresses der Gewerkschaften
Deutschlands* (Berlin, 1925), pp. 110, 124–29. The unions' negative reaction to the
behavior of the Communists in 1922 can be seen in the pamphlet, *Ist ein Einheitsfront
mit den Kommunisten möglich? Denkschrift über die Verhandlungen der Gewerkschaften mit den
Arbeiterparteien über den Schutz der Republik* (Berlin, 1922).

[205] *Vorwärts*, 23 Jan. 1926 (Nr. 37); *Frankfurter Zeitung*, 23 Jan. 1926 (Nr. 60).

modifications of the Kuczynski Committee's proposal, limited, however, to specific improvements in wording.[206] The basic text remained in all essentials as the Communists had drafted it.[207] On 25 January, Otto Wels and Konrad Ludwig for the SPD, Ernst Thälmann for the KPD, and Dr. Kuczynski submitted the formal request for the start of initiative proceedings to the national Ministry of Interior.[208] Thälmann and Kuczynski withdrew their earlier request in order to clear the way for the new joint proposal. To no one's surprise, the Communist press was already proclaiming, "The Communists lead!" [209]

[206] The Social Democrats protested that sufferers from the inflation were omitted from the list of those to be aided by the confiscated wealth, and wanted some changes in wording in order to ensure that the courts could not void the law on technicalities. *Vorwärts*, 16 Jan. 1926 (Nr. 26); *Frankfurter Zeitung*, 20 Jan. 1926 (Nr. 51). The Communists refused the SPD's suggestion that a modest compensation be permitted. Stampfer, p. 445. René Kuczynski said that the SPD's amendments were accepted "not because we regard them as improvements on our draft, but because we consider them of no importance *(belanglos)*." Kuczynski, pp. 96–97. See, too, Philipp Dengel's comments, quoted by Karl, p. 21.

[207] The full text is given by Karl, pp. 66–67. The main provisions were:

"Article 1
All the property of the princes who ruled . . . the German states until the revolution of 1918 as well as the entire property of the princely houses, their families, and the [individual] members of the families is to be confiscated without compensation for [purposes relating] to the general welfare.

The confiscated property is to become the property of the state in which each princely house ruled until its abdication or deposition.

Article 2
The confiscated property is to be utilized in favor of:
   (a) the unemployed;
   (b) war invalids, widows and orphans;
   (c) people on pensions *(Sozial- und Kleinrentner)*;
   (d) needy victims of the inflation;
   (e) rural laborers, small tenant farmers and peasants through the creation of [new] settlements from the confiscated agricultural land.

The palaces, dwellings, and other buildings are to be employed for purposes relating to the general welfare, cultural or educational uses, and in particular for the establishment of hospitals and rest homes . . . as well as for children's homes and educational institutions.

Article 3
Any conditions . . . regarding [the disposition] of the properties confiscated by this law . . . [established] by [judicial] decision, mutual agreement, contract, or in any other way, are invalid.

Article 4
[details regarding the implementation of the law]."

[208] *Frankfurter Zeitung*, 26 Jan. 1926 (Nr. 67).

[209] *Rote Fahne*, 22 Jan. 1926. "Thanks to the initiative and action of the KPD even the leaders of the SPD now have to capitulate before the mass movement for the referendum." Ibid., 21 Jan. 1926. Habedank, pp. 34–35.

IV: The Social Democratic Party Astride Two Horses: The SPD's Decision to Support the Referendum, January 1926.

Whereas the remarkable shifts in the KPD's policies during the 1920s resulted in large part from Moscow's periodic interference in the affairs of the German Communist Party, the less erratic but by no means steady course of Social Democratic policy was shaped by two forces of a different kind: the persistent efforts of its leaders to maintain party strength and unity, sometimes at the expense of otherwise sensible political aims, and the necessity to accept commitments which grew unavoidably out of the party's size, its relationship to other parties, and the role it had played in the creation of the Republic.[1] Despite the loss of most of its left wing during

[1] The following works are essential for an understanding of the basic problems faced by the German Social Democratic Party: Bracher, *Die Auflösung*, pp. 70–83 and passim; Neumann, *Die Parteien der Weimarer Republik*, pp. 28–41; and Hans Mommsen, ed., *Sozialdemokratie zwischen Klassenbewegung und Volkspartei* (Frankfurt a. M., 1974). Erich Matthias is one of the most prominent West German scholars working on the history of the SPD. He has edited a number of important documentary collections (not used in this volume) and summarized his interpretation of the party's political development in several articles, "The Social Democratic Party and Government Power," in *The Path to Dictatorship*, pp. 50–67; "Die Sozialdemokratische Partei Deutschlands," in *Das Ende der Parteien 1933*, pp. 101–278; "Der sozialistische Einfluss in der Weimarer Republik," in Oswald Hauser, ed., *Politische Parteien in Deutschland und Frankreich, 1918–1939* (Wiesbaden, 1969), pp. 116–27, the substance of which appeared in English as "German Social Democracy in the Weimar Republic," in Nicholls and Matthias, eds., *German Democracy and the Triumph of Hitler*,

the war and immediately thereafter, SPD remained the largest and best organized of all the German parties.[2] Election setbacks during the early twenties do not seem to have affected the confidence felt at all levels of the party that it would ultimately win and keep the votes of the majority of the

---

pp. 47–57. A West German Marxist has criticized his work, Bärbel Kunze, "Erich Matthias' Apologie der SPD-Entwicklung," *Das Argument,* Issue 63, 13 (Nr. 1/2, March, 1971): 54–78.

Surveys of the party's history for the general reader are offered by Helga Grebing, *Geschichte der deutschen Arbeiterbewegung* (Munich, 1966) and by Heinrich Potthoff, *Die Sozialdemokratie von den Anfänge bis 1945,* Vol. 1 of *Kleine Geschichte der SPD* (Bonn and Bad Godesberg, 1974). For left socialist views of the nature of the party, Siegfried Marck, *Sozialdemokratie* (Berlin, 1931) and, more recently, Wolfgang Abendroth, *Aufstieg und Krise der deutschen Sozialdemokratie* (Frankfurt A. M., 1964) or Georg Fülberth and Jürgen Harrer, *Die deutsche Sozialdemokratie, 1890–1933,* Vol. 1 of *Arbeiterbewegung und SPD* (Darmstadt, 1974).

On the ties between the SPD and the Free Trade Unions: Gerard Braunthal's dissertation, "The Politics of the German Free Trade Unions during the Weimar Period" (Columbia University, 1954); Wolfgang Hirsch-Weber, *Gewerkschaften in der Politik: Von der Massenstreikdebatte zum Kampf um das Mitbestimmungsrecht* (Cologne, 1959); Walter Pahl, "Gewerkschaften und Sozialdemokratie vor 1933," *Gewerkschaftliche Monatshefte,* 4 (1953): 720–24; and Hilga Timm, *Die deutsche Sozialpolitik und der Bruch der Grossen Koalition im März 1930, Beiträge zur Geschichte des Parlamentarismus und der politischen Parteien,* 1 (Düsseldorf, 1952). On the role of the Social Democratic press, Kurt Koszyk, *Zwischen Kaiserreich und Diktatur. Die sozialdemokratische Presse von 1914 bis 1933,* Deutsche Presseforschung, 1 (Heidelberg, 1958), as well as his more comprehensive *Geschichte der deutschen Presse,* 3: *Deutsche Presse, 1914–1945* (Berlin, 1972).

For a long time the part played by the Social Democrats in the government of the state of Prussia lacked adequate scholarly investigation. Hajo Holborn offered some observations on this topic, "Prussia and the Weimar Republic," *Social Research,* 23 (Nr. 3, Autumn, 1956): 333–42. Since then three major works have appeared: Enno Eimers, *Das Verhältnis von Preussen und Reich in den ersten Jahren der Weimarer Republik, 1918–1923* (Berlin, 1969); Hans-Peter Ehni, *Bollwerk Preussen? Preussen-Regierung, Reich-Länder-Problem und Sozialdemokratie, 1928–1932,* Schriftenreihe des Forschungsinstituts der Friedrich-Ebert-Stiftung, 3 (Bonn and Bad Godesberg, 1975); and Hagen Schulze's biography of Otto Braun, cited above, Chapter I, note 5. Useful articles on the coalition governments in Prussia are Hans-Peter Ehni, "Zum Parteienverhältnis in Preussen 1918–32. Ein Beitrag zur Funktion und Arbeitsweise der Weimarer Koalitionsparteien," *Archiv für Sozialgeschichte,* 11 (1971): 241–88, and Hagen Schulze, "Stabilität und Instabilität in der politischen Ordnung von Weimar," *Vierteljahrshefte für Zeitgeschichte,* 26 (Nr. 3, July, 1978): 419–32.

Clarifying the main lines of development of the party before 1918 are: Carl Schorske, *German Social Democracy, 1905–1917* (Cambridge, Mass., 1955) and Gerhard A. Ritter, *Die Arbeiterbewegung im Wilhelminischen Reich* (Berlin, 1959). See, also, Peter Nettl, "The German Social Democratic Party 1890–1914 as a Political Model," *Past and Present* (Nr. 30, April, 1965): 65–95; Guenther Roth, *The Social Democrats in Imperial Germany* (Totowa, 1963); and Vernon Lidtke, *The Outlawed Party, 1878–1890* (Princeton, 1966). The monograph by A. Joseph Berlau, *The German Social Democratic Party, 1914–1921,* Columbia University, Faculty of Political Science. *Studies in History, Economics and Public Law,* 557 (New York, 1949) is now outdated. Preferred are the authoritative volumes by Susanne Miller, *Burgfrieden und Klassenkampf. Die deutsche Sozialdemokratie im Ersten Weltkrieg, Beiträge zur Geschichte des Parlamentarismus und der*

German electorate [3]—a confidence which had been fostered by widespread acceptance of vulgarized Marxian doctrines of historical inevitability and proudly remembered successes from before the war.[4] Consequently, a strong temptation existed for the SPD to concentrate on strengthening its internal cohesiveness in order to emphasize its character as a working class movement, rather than appear merely as another political party.[5] Oppositional postures were widely regarded as the best means of increasing the party's attractiveness in the eyes of potential voters and active members alike. Such "opposition on principle" involved constant criticism of the existing social and economic order; the rejection of compromises which, it was claimed, diluted the purity and profound appeal of the party's basic commitment to trans-

---

politischen Parteien, 53 (Düsseldorf, 1974) and *Die Bürde der Macht. Die deutsche Sozialdemokratie, 1918–1920, Beiträge zur Geschichte des Parlamentarismus und der politischen Parteien,* 63 (Düsseldorf, 1978).

Among the memoirs of leading party figures I have found most useful: Otto Braun, *Von Weimar zu Hitler* (2nd ed.; New York, 1940); Wilhelm Keil, *Erlebnisse eines Sozialdemokraten,* 2 (Stuttgart, 1948); Julius Leber, *Ein Mann geht seinen Weg* (Berlin, 1952); and Carl Severing, *Mein Lebensweg* (2 vols.; Cologne, 1950). Friedrich Stampfer's *Erfahrungen und Erkenntnisse* (Cologne, 1957) is somewhat disappointing but his historical account, *Die vierzehn Jahre der ersten Deutschen Republik* reveals the background for some important decisions. Paul Löbe's *Erinnerungen eines Reichstagspräsidenten* (Berlin, 1949), revised edition under the title *Der Weg war lang* (Berlin, 1954), reports little of interest. The biography by Hans J. L. Adolph, *Otto Wels und die Politik der Deutschen Sozialdemokratie, 1894–1939, Veröffentlichungen der Historischen Kommission zu Berlin,* 33 (Berlin, 1971), describes Wels's role in the intra-party controversies of his time, but is not a fully satisfactory study.

[2] According to Franz Osterroth and Dieter Schuster, *Chronik der deutschen Sozialdemokratie* (Hanover, 1963), p. 313, membership on 1 Jan. 1926, was 654,457. Hunt, *German Social Democracy,* pp. 99–130; Neumann, p. 120, note 8.

[3] "The Social Democrats are the only great party which is still capable of growth, it is the only party which in a foreseeable time . . . can succeed in rallying a *majority of the people* to its banner." Friedrich Stampfer, "Die Partei der Zukunft," *Vorwärts,* 13 Sept. 1925 (Nr. 433); *Jahrbuch der Deutschen Sozialdemokratie . . . 1927,* pp. 315–17; and Georg Decker's regular political analyses in *Die Gesellschaft,* especially "Krise des deutschen Parteisystems?" (1926, Nr. 1), pp. 1–16; "Die Reichstagswahlen" (1928, Nr. 1), pp. 481–84; and "Wahlrechtsreform oder Reform der Politik" (1928, Nr. 2), pp. 385–99.

[4] Matthias in *The Path to Dictatorship,* p. 66. One of the advocates of a stronger policy of opposition at the 1925 *Parteitag,* Paul Prien (Dessau), complained that the recent tariff legislation should have been fought more resolutely. "Certainly the Reichstag *Fraktion* did diligent work, but I miss the great energy *(Schwung)* which we saw for example in 1902. Even though the situation undoubtedly has changed, still a closer contact between actions in parliament and the masses outside must be created. Regrettably we have seen that this close contact was lacking, otherwise the streets would have been black with people." *Sozialdemokratischer Parteitag 1925,* pp. 202–3.

[5] Neumann, pp. 105–7; Bracher, *Die Auflösung,* pp. 78–83.

form society; and, above all, the refusal to share power with other parties under conditions unfavorable to the realization of socialist aims.[6] Rival parties, particularly those that from time to time had to associate with the SPD, denounced these "party-egotistic" tendencies.[7] Yet, in fact, what they disliked was basically only the continuation of Social Democratic parliamentary and electioneering practices formed during the Empire.[8]

Many Social Democrats criticized the insufficiencies of the Weimar Republic, but generally they accepted it as an improvement over the old regime.[9] Formerly, the party had been able, at most, to influence the content of some legislation, now it could share in the administration as well as the formulation of laws, and, in conjunction with other parties, exercise power at the highest levels of government.[10] Risks were involved in the acceptance of such responsibilities. The necessity for frequent tenuous compromises, the impossibility of obtaining many desirable objectives—often because of the unfavorable conditions caused by Germany's military defeat—and exposure to unsparing criticism from their Communist rivals inevitably resulted from taking office.[11] Nevertheless, many of the party's leaders considered the exercise of political power necessary and desirable. Otto Braun,

[6] The line between tactical and "pure" opposition was sometimes rather indistinct, particularly when it came to guarding the integrity of the party. Wilhelm Sollmann, a former cabinet minister, opposed the formation of a Great Coalition government in 1926 on the grounds that "the party ought not to endanger its great future for small momentary successes.... The strength of our party ... is and remains its supporters throughout the country and the great masses which stand true to us." Quoted with adverse comments by the *Kölnische Volkszeitung,* 19 Oct. 1926 (Nr. 774).

[7] See above, Chapter III, note 176. Stresemann, who had had occasion to observe Social Democratic behavior well, could be quite cutting. "The SPD is an opposition party—one has to accustom oneself to this thought. It is also entirely understandable if the Social Democrats vote against a proposed law because of their fundamental opposition although they fundamentally have nothing against the proposal." *Kabinettsprotokolle* (30 June 1925), reel 1834, frame D765137.

[8] Bracher, *Die Auflösung,* pp. 33, 72; Hans Mommsen, "Die Sozialdemokratie in der Defensive: Der Immobilismus der SPD und der Aufstieg des Nationalsozialismus," in Mommsen, ed., *Sozialdemokratie zwischen Klassenbewegung und Volkspartei,* pp. 107–33.

[9] Hunt, *German Social Democracy,* pp. 222–23.

[10] Nettl, pp. 65–68, 85–86; *Vorwärts,* 11 June 1924 (Nr. 270), quoted by Stürmer, p. 255.

[11] Hans Luther mentions a revealing incident that occurred at one of the cabinet meetings of the Great Coalition government in 1923, "... the Social Democratic Minister for Reconstruction, Robert Schmidt, ... broke out into tears because the harsh facts [forced him] to give up political goals for which he ... had sat for years in prison." *Politiker ohne Partei* (Stuttgart, 1960), p. 110. Otto Braun accepted such limitations with more composure. Braun, p. 164.

for example, called upon his party comrades in January 1926, to have "confidence in their own strength" and "the courage [to accept] responsibility." [12]

Many members of the party leadership recognized that the alternatives to participation in governments were likely to be even less attractive than the difficulties encountered in joining a coalition. Wilhelm Keil, a powerful figure in the party's Württemberg organization, argued against a resolution at the 1925 party convention that called for the forthright defense of the interests of the proletariat without any consideration for the views of the middle-class parties:

> The consequence would be: withdrawal from the Prussian government, renunciation of any increase of the party's power within the present state, surrender of any direct influence, while letting the middle-class parties do whatever they like.... [13]

Two years later in a major speech the distinguished theoretician, Rudolf Hilferding, devoted much attention to the same theme:

> If we declare that under no circumstances [will] we share in the government, under no circumstances support a government, then a government will be formed by the opponents of Social Democracy. (Agreement.) ... It will just mean making it easy for the Center Party if we declare: under no circumstances a coalition government in the Reich! (Agreement.) We would at the same time be declaring that the German Nationals must under all circumstances remain in the government. (Renewed agreement.) [14]

[12] *Vorwärts*, 12 Jan. 1926, quoted by Stürmer, p. 141. Carl Severing wrote, "The best [form of] criticism is to make things better.... To have power among the people requires power in the state. That means cooperation. Then, cooperation in bettering the state will create and maintain power among the people." "Die beste Kritik," *Sozialistische Monatshefte*, 65 (19 Sept. 1927): 701. The spokesman for the SPD in Hesse, Wilhelm Widmann, declared that "coalitions are not so bad" and went on to ask, "Why is the Center Party the most powerful party today in the German *Reich* and in many of the states? Because it never says, 'I will leave the government,' but rather always declares 'I won't be forced out.' " *Sozialdemokratischer Parteitag 1925*, p. 171. The SPD's *Fraktion* leader in the Baden *Landtag*, Ludwig Marum, announced, "If the Social Democrats in Baden leave the government, they won't remain permanently in opposition but do all [in their power] to get back into the government again." *Jahrbuch der Deutschen Sozialdemokratie . . . 1926*, p. 421. These last two statements are especially significant since Baden and Hesse were the only states in which the SPD was continuously in office between 1918 and 1926.

[13] *Sozialdemokratischer Parteitag 1925*, p. 229. The resolution he opposed was sponsored by Max Seydewitz and others. The convention rejected it by a vote of 285 to 81. Ibid., pp. 316–17.

[14] From Hilferding's *Referate*, "Die Aufgaben der Sozialdemokratie in der Republik," at the 1927 Party Convention. *Sozialdemokratischer Parteitag 1927 in Kiel* (Berlin,

Practical considerations of the advantages to be gained from taking an active role in coalition governments weighed heavily with the SPD's leaders. It must be stressed, however, that such considerations were not their sole concern.

Unlike the Communist leadership, the Social Democratic leaders rarely changed. Most of them had worked their way into positions of influence before the First World War and had little reason to believe that their authority would be challenged by anyone who had not made his way up within the organization.[15] The striking career of Matthias Erzberger in the Center Party had no real counterpart in the SPD. On the other hand, Social Democratic leaders had no reason to fear the fate of Paul Levi, Heinrich Brandler, or Arkadi Maslow.[16] Observers commented on the unusual loyalty of the rank-and-file to their chosen leaders.[17]

Since the death of Bebel in 1913, no single dominating figure stood at the head of the party; his successors, Friedrich Ebert, Hermann Müller, and Otto Wels, lacked his forceful personality and charismatic qualities.[18] Critics found it easy to caricature them as routine organizational hacks.

> Herr Party Chairman Müller has presided over our revolution-factory since 1918 with skill, pot-belly and eye glasses. Herr Müller, whose party membership book is always in order, has in this time signed 54,674 letters, 5,463 postcards, 303 election proclamations and about one appeal for political prisoners. Müller naturally couldn't be troubled too much about the German working class movement since he has been held up by important discussions in the Reichstag. What Müller has accomplished in the past years through clever surrender and wise retreats cannot be expressed.[19]

1927), p. 181. He complained that one could think from reading some of the resolutions that "the most important object of the proletarian class struggle in Germany was the overthrow of the Prussian government." Idem.

[15] Bracher, *Die Auflösung*, pp. 75–76; Hunt, *German Social Democracy*, pp. 70–72, 242–47. Robert Michels was the first to call attention to this tendency. His classic study, *Political Parties: A Sociological Study of the Oligarchical Tendencies of Modern Democracy* (Glencoe, Ill., 1949) appeared originally in 1911.

[16] Gustav Noske, perhaps, is the exception that proves the rule.

[17] Hunt, *German Social Democracy*, pp. 68–69.

[18] Hunt, in *The Responsibility of Power*, p. 318; and the pointed criticism early in 1919 by the later German Democratic Party chairman, Erich Koch-Weser, Günter Arns, ed., "Erich Koch-Wesers Aufzeichnungen vom 13. Februar 1919," *Vierteljahrshefte für Zeitgeschichte*, 17 (Nr. 1, Jan. 1969): 105–7.

[19] Kaspar Hauser [i.e., Kurt Tucholsky], "Dienstzeugnisse," *Weltbühne*, 21 (Nr. 23, 9 June 1925): 856–57.

Kurt Tucholsky, of course, was not trying to be fair. These party officials did indeed lack the color, the revolutionary *élan*, much valued by intellectuals influenced by the Expressionist movement.[20] Their good qualities, in particular a generally open, pragmatic attitude toward politics, were little appreciated in the Weimar era.[21]

The power of decision-making was distributed among a relatively small number of men in high party posts,[22] although decisions were sometimes subject to revision because of pressure from the middle and lower ranks of the party. As with other German parties, the practice was to distribute leading positions in the party organization, the parliamentary *Fraktionen*, and the cabinet (if the party was participating in a government) among different individuals.[23] This necessitated time-consuming negotiations within the party before its spokesmen could present the party's views to the other parties. Differences among the various party *Instanzen* occasionally forced embarrassing reversals of policy.[24] The most important leaders were normally members of the party Executive Board *(Parteivorstand)* or that of the Reichstag delegation *(Fraktionsvorstand)*, but not all *Vorstand* members appear to have been equally involved in the day-to-day discussion of tactics.[25]

[20] See Gordon A. Craig, "Engagement and Neutrality in Weimar Germany," *Journal of Contemporary History,* 2 (Nr. 2, April, 1967): 49–63, esp. pp. 57–59 on Tucholsky; and more generally, Peter Gay, *Weimar Culture: The Outsider as Insider* (New York, 1968) and Istvan Deak, *Weimar Germany's Left-Wing Intellectuals. A Political History of the Weltbühne and Its Circle* (Berkeley and Los Angeles, 1968).

[21] Leading German political scientists and sociologists have subjected traditional German attitudes toward politics and politicians to sharp criticism, urging positive acceptance of pluralistic conflict and the pragmatic adjustment of social and economic differences. Bracher, *Die Auflösung,* pp. 30–31, 37–44; Fraenkel, "Deutschland und die westlichen Demokratien," and "Parlament und öffentliche Meinung," in *Deutschland und die westlichen Demokratien,* pp. 32–47, 110–30; and Ralf Dahrendorf, *Society and Democracy in Germany* (Garden City, 1967).

[22] Adolph, pp. 105–18, 345–53.

[23] Friedrich Glum, *Das parlamentarische Regierungssystem in Deutschland, Grossbritannien und Frankreich* (Munich and Berlin, 1950), p. 216. Similarly, Bracher, *Die Auflösung,* pp. 76, 80. For comparative purposes consult Rudolf von Albertini, "Parteiorganisation und Parteibegriff in Frankreich 1789–1940," *Historische Zeitschrift,* 193 (Nr. 3, Dec., 1961): 529–600, esp. pp. 590–593.

[24] Wacker, pp. 109–10; Werner Conze, "Brünings Politik unter dem Druck der grossen Krise," *Historische Zeitschrift,* 199 (1964): 536–37.

[25] Or at least did not pay attention to all details. Leber relates that a high point in the debate over the battle cruiser "A" a prominent member of both the party and *Fraktion* Executive Boards remarked, "For the first time today I learned that it was only a question of building a replacement foreseen in the Versailles Treaty. If I had known that earlier, my position would have been entirely different." He did

Perhaps to compensate for the diffuseness of policy-making authority, prominent Social Democrats generally tapped a variety of channels of support and maintained extensive personal influence by overlapping membership in one or more parliamentary bodies, high office in a trade union or cooperative, close ties with an important regional or local party organization.[26] To be sure, such ties were sometimes only nominal, merely part of every successful politician's duties.[27] However, each man had a carefully cultivated body of support and contacts—this is what gave weight in party councils, not merely length of service, or organizational reliability in the narrow sense of the word.[28] Although the SPD and the Center Party differed greatly in overall organizational structure, they resembled each other in the oligarchic composition of their leadership.[29] The two "liberal" parties (the DDP and DVP) retained the older form of leadership by a single dominant figure.[30]

---

not identify the individual but his bitter comment is significant. "Over the accumulation of capital and expropriation of the expropriators these expositors could write whole books, before the basic (wirkenden) facts of every day politics they often stood fully innocent." Leber, p. 229.

[26] Consider Wilhelm Keil's description of his own activities: "My name was placed at the head of the list of candidates for both national and state elections. . . . Naturally I was in demand as a speaker by party units in all parts of the state. I had to stake out the directions at the speakers' conferences, I had to compose the general guidelines for the party speakers and do whatever other similar jobs there were. In addition, I was a member of the state Executive Board. Since the direction of the leading party paper in the state also lay in my hands, the uniformity of our policies was to some degree [!] ensured." Keil, 2: 128. Elsewhere he clearly suggests that the retention of such a position with real powers and secure tenure was much more attractive than the acceptance of a post in either the national or state government that inevitably would be of limited duration. Ibid., pp. 173, 242–43. On the importance of at least a period of journalistic activity in the career of a rising Social Democratic politician, see Walther G. Oschilewski's Nachwort to Paul Löbe, Der Weg war lang, p. 306.

[27] Löbe, pp. 186–7.

[28] An investigation which clearly identified the regional ties of major party figures, their close association with specific unions, newspapers, etc., in addition to their formal careers in the party itself might be more rewarding than the rather bare statistical tabulations of age, social origin, and occupation such as Professor Hunt and others have made. Such an investigation should distinguish if possible between the more or less nominal and the truly "working" members of the party's Vorstand and Fraktionen. It might also identify those men who were valued for their contacts with men in other parties, for expertise on some technical subject, or for other abilities, in distinction from those who won importance solely through work in the party organization or trade unions.

[29] After the death of Windthorst and Lieber the Center Party was guided by a kind of directory of prominent older party leaders. Morsey, pp. 580–81, 617–21; Neumann, pp. 47–48.

[30] Was this symptomatic of the general tendency of the "liberal" parties to lag

The existence of different factions had been a prime feature in the development of the Social Democratic Party since the turn of the century.[31] The generation active in the party during the 1920s had lived through a series of bitter disputes over basic policies and proposals to change the character of the party itself. The arguments had shifted from the debate over reformist policies before 1914 to the painful question whether to support the war and then to what course should be followed during the revolution of 1918/19. Despite the different subjects, the quarrel steadily returned to the basic alternative: would the Social Democratic Party accept a place in and assume responsibilities for the existing German society, however much it might insist on further changes, or would it intensify its traditional opposition to the German state and society by using new methods such as the general strike or workers' councils to pursue radical goals, even at the risk of unforeseeable consequences.[32] It had been impossible for individuals to avoid taking sides. The Independents split away in 1917 and further defections occurred in the early twenties. The choices men had made were never entirely forgotten, and even though some efforts at reconciliation succeeded, fissures remained.[33] This is not to say that the lines of division in the different disputes were identical. Some Revisionists became Independents; some radical Independents returned to the SPD rather than join the KPD, and by no means all the former Independents supported the new opposition which began to develop after 1923.[34]

Like the Communists, many Social Democrats were left gravely dissatisfied by their experiences in the year 1923. For the next five years 1923 was depicted as a low watermark in

behind the mass parties organizationally? Cf. Schieder, *Staat und Gesellschaft im Wandel unserer Zeit*, pp. 133–71, and Thomas Nipperdey, "Die Organisation der bürgerlichen Parteien in Deutschland vor 1918," *Historische Zeitschrift*, 185 (June, 1958): 550–602. Or was it possible only because these parties were relatively small?

[31] Even then such conflicts were not totally new. The problem of reconciling the differences between the followers of Lassalle and of Marx dominated much of the early history of the party. However, the years of persecution under the Anti-Socialist Law drove the disputing segments of the party together and, because the party prospered under the attacks of a hostile state, left a much honored tradition of opposition. Lidtke, *The Outlawed Party*, has shown that important conflicts existed even during the "heroic age" of the SPD, but the generation after 1890 tended to forget them, pp. 129–54, 176–212 and passim.

[32] Cf. Bracher's section, "Das Dilemma der SPD," in *Die Auflösung*, pp. 70–77.

[33] Hunt, *German Social Democracy*, pp. 204–10; Adolph, pp. 110–11, 127–30.

[34] Hunt, *German Social Democracy*, pp. 195, 203, 225.

the party's history, the source of bad examples to be avoided thereafter.[35] Many SPD members felt that their leaders had sacrificed the interests of the working classes, especially when they allowed the national government to send the army into Saxony which was governed by a coalition of Socialists and Communists, but failed to require it to take equivalent measures against the unquestionably disloyal and reactionary regime in Bavaria.[36] They thought that the concessions the middle-class parties in the Great Coalition had demanded and obtained from the SPD were too great, while the SPD had gained nothing in return. The most generally accepted rule of thumb in Weimar politics, namely, that a party lost strength by accepting governmental responsibilities,[37] seemed abundantly confirmed when the voters turned against the SPD in the elections of 1924 after the SPD's participation in the Stresemann cabinets in 1923.[38] Simul-

[35] The failings of 1923 were of course abundantly discussed at the 1924 *Parteitag* but references persistently cropped up at the 1925 and 1927 sessions as well. When Friedrich Bartels, the party treasurer, stated in 1925 that the economic distress of recent years had caused political indifference among the workers and thus produced a drop in party membership, Oskar Edel (Dresden) countered that the loss of over 100,000 members couldn't be explained away by the inflation, etc., but was due to "a mistaken policy of weakness and compromise." *Sozialdemokratischer Parteitag 1925*, pp. 108, 153–55. Shortly after the 1927 Convention, Severing wrote an article directed against those who had argued that 1923 had shown that a Great Coalition was impossible. He stated that the conditions that year had been so unusual it could not be treated as a generally valid example. "For a government party to obtain brilliant . . . successes was then impossible. That should be considered especially by those comrades who constantly remind us that we are only so strong or so weak in government as are our organizations and the strength *(Bedeutung)* of our voting support in the country. And that *they* were especially imposing in the autumn months of 1923, no one will try to maintain." Carl Severing, "Kiel: Ein Nachwort zum Parteitag," *Die Gesellschaft* (1927, Nr. 2), p. 4.

[36] This incident also gave rise to the very complicated dispute between the national party leadership and the bulk of the party in Saxony. On the *Sachsenkonflikt*, see Hunt, *German Social Democracy*, pp. 210–21; Hanno Drechsler, *Die Sozialistische Arbeiterpartei Deutschlands (SAPD), Marburger Abhandlungen zur Politischen Wissenschaft*, 2 (Meisenheim am Glan, 1964): 6–10. Though the "Saxon Conflict" may have involved problems of intra-party democracy, readers should bear in mind that the dispute formally centered around interpretations of the authority of *different party policy-making bodies*, namely, the *Landtag* delegation, the national Executive Board, the regional party convention, and the regional organizations.

[37] Schreiber, *Politisches Jahrbuch 1926*, p. 76; Hugo Preuss, *Um die Reichsverfassung von Weimar* (Berlin, 1924), pp. 71–72; the comments of Anton Erkelenz at the DDP *Vorstand* meeting, 6 Nov. 1926, DDP Papers, reel 37, folder 730, p. 2.

[38] Despite the unification with the rump USPD in 1922 the party obtained fewer votes in the May 1924 Reichstag election than the Majority Socialists alone in 1920: 6,008,900 (20.5%) compared to the earlier 6,104,400 (21.6%). The Communist vote was nearly two-thirds that of the SPD: 3,693,300 (12.6%). Moreover, the DNVP with 95 Reichstag seats came very close to challenging the Social Democrats' position

taneously large numbers of workers left the party and the trade unions which had been forced to curtail many of their functions because of the crippling effect of inflation.[39]

As a result of these setbacks, some local organizations and a number of moderately prominent individuals took the opportunity to attack the national party leaders.[40] From 1924 onwards these left-wing socialists sponsored bluntly worded resolutions and ran their own candidates at the party convention, built up support wherever possible among the rank-and-file, particularly in the youth organization, and in 1927 established their own journal, *Klassenkampf*,[41] because of difficulties encountered in getting their views printed in the official party organs.[42] This left opposition grew in significance throughout the late twenties, achieving their greatest success in 1929. At the party convention that year they obtained support from between one-third and two-fifths of the delegates on certain key tests of strength.[43] At no time, however, was the left wing able to break the official leadership's control over the party, or even place representatives of their viewpoint on the party's Executive Board.[44] Later, in 1931, the intensity of their opposition and some tactical mistakes caused the expulsion of some of the key left spokesmen, who then established a new splinter party, the SAPD *(Sozialistische Arbeiterpartei Deutschlands).*[45]

---

as largest party in the Reichstag (100 delegates). The new election on Dec. 1924 brought some improvements for the SPD. Its vote rose to 7,881,000 (26%) while the Communists lost heavily. (See above, Chapter III, p. 66). Despite further Nationalist gains which gave the party a total of 103 seats, the SPD won 31 new seats to give it a somewhat larger lead as the biggest party in the Reichstag.

[39] Rosenberg, p. 406; Hunt, *German Social Democracy*, pp. 168–69; Severing, *Die Gesellschaft* (1927, Nr. 2), p. 1.

[40] Hunt, *German Social Democracy*, pp. 221–30; Drechsler, pp. 3–63; Conze, *Historische Zeitschrift*, 178: 60–63; Adolph, pp. 121–45.

[41] On *Klassenkampf*, Drechsler, pp. 21–24.

[42] Drechsler points out that they called themselves the *Mahner, Warner,* and *Gewissen* of the party, p. 4. In 1931 a *Mahnruf an die Partei*, issued by the editors of the *Klassenkampf*, became the occasion for their expulsion from the SPD. Ibid., pp. 82–87. The deliberate use of such words surely expresses symbolically the kind of relationship they wished to establish for themselves in the party, i.e., not necessarily to control it outright, but to prevent others from following wrong paths.

[43] Ibid., pp. 40–50; Hunt, *German Social Democracy*, pp. 228–29. The increased strength of the left opposition reflected widespread disapproval of the reversal of the party's earlier opposition to the construction of the battle cruiser "A". In the 1928 election the Social Democrats had campaigned on the slogan "Rather food for children than a battleship." Drechsler, pp. 32–39.

[44] Hunt, *German Social Democracy*, p. 229.

[45] Ibid., pp. 230–38; Drechsler, pp. 64–202.

The improper influence of the party's *Bonzen,* the routine-minded functionaries who held fast to their offices, come what may, was a favorite theme of critics inside and outside the SPD. The party bosses were accused of sticking together, advancing the careers of men like themselves while short-sightedly keeping men of ability from trying out new ideas.[46] It was said they discouraged dissent by using official control of the party press to prevent the expression of unwanted views,[47] that they made crucial decisions on their own and then expected the party "loyally" to ratify these policies with hardly any discussion.[48] They were blamed for undemocratic behavior in their personal lives as well as in the conduct of party affairs. Once a party functionary became accustomed to a permanent job with a secure income and associated regularly with middle-class people in town councils, parliamentary bodies, etc., it was claimed he lost contact with the common workers and ceased to understand their wishes and basic needs.[49] Supposedly infected with bourgeois values, he

[46] "Only those were let in [the party elite] who offered security that they would keep discipline faithfully and honestly, and who would push neither those above nor those below. Good intellectual mediocrity and drill in routine commanded the field, and the powers of the leaders ensured that the road to the top opened only through this gate." Julius Leber, quoted by Hunt, *German Social Democracy,* p. 71.

[47] For example the comments of Max Leuteritz (Hamburg), Hermann Liebmann (Leipzig), and Hermann Wilke (Stettin) at the 1927 Party Convention. *Sozialdemokratischer Parteitag 1927,* pp. 63–65, 72–74, 79–80. There were also demands that a special paper for the Berlin party organization, separate from *Vorwärts,* be established because many Berlin Social Democrats felt that their own views were not given sufficient space or were watered down by the editors of the national party paper. Koszyk, *Zwischen Kaiserreich und Diktatur,* p. 179.

[48] Hunt, *German Social Democracy,* pp. 67–68, 75–78.

[49] The Frankfurt a. M. delegation submitted a resolution at the 1925 convention that the national Executive Board *(Vorstand)* be chosen from men who had the confidence of the working masses and who had kept in touch with them, even going so far as to say, "This is no longer the case with the majority of the previous *Vorstand* members." Professor Erik Nölting spoke in favor of the resolution: "It is not . . . exclusively a question of this *Vorstand,* but of any *Vorstand* at all. We fear that everywhere in the party the tendency for the leadership to cut itself off is becoming ever stronger, that our meetings are constantly becoming more and more company exercises where importance is put on having no one step out of line. And that should not be. . . . Sociology knows [that] all governing causes [growing] conservatism. In addition, there are [strong] pressures to prize the organization too highly and to value living meaning *(Sinn)* too little. We want, however, a leadership behind whom we can stand like a living wind behind the sail. We want a *Vorstand* that is the living crown of our party and not a bare institution [depending on the] paragraphs [of the party statutes]." *Sozialdemokratischer Parteitag 1925,* p. 153. Johannes Stelling, pp. 98–107, and Herman Müller, p. 172, defended the *Vorstand.* Müller's comment was, "When I read in resolution 209 that we had lost contact with the masses, I said with Maruschka, 'That doesn't mean me.' The other members of the *Vorstand* thought the same thing." He then went on to accuse the leaders of

was charged with forgetting how to speak the language of the masses, abandoning revolutionary concerns, and pursuing his own personal ambitions at the expense of the party's true line of development.[50]

It was not difficult to uncover evidence which made these assertions plausible. The Social Democratic leaders were undoubtedly guilty of some of the failings described above.[51] But one should not overlook the fact that most of these attacks came from men who fundamentally disapproved of *the policies* the party was following. It might be wise, therefore, not to take the particular charges entirely at face value.[52] In many ways only the reversal of everything the party had done since 1914 would have satisfied the left opposition within the SPD. These critics, many of them former Independents, favored policies such as socialization, radical educational and religious policies, etc., for which in the mid-twenties no realistic chances of accomplishment existed.[53] In their desire to make the party's political practice consistent with its Marxian theories, they tended to overlook the realities of Germany's current situation. The scarcely diminished strength of the

---

the Frankfurt delegation of failing in their comradely duties. He rejected their excuse that the resolution originated in a purely proletarian section of the city. The leaders, he said, should have seen that "truth" was served.

Criticism of the party leaders for losing touch with the masses remained a persistent theme until the end of the Republic. Cf. Leo Lania, "Eberts Erbe", *Weltbühne*, 21 (Nr. 18, 5 May 1925): 649; Siegfried Marck, pp. 34–36; Henning Duderstadt, *Vom Reichsbanner zum Hakenkreuz* (Stuttgart, 1933), pp. 13, 114. The tendency had already been criticized before the war, see Schorske, p. 128.

[50] Cf. the quotation from Gustav Mayer's memoirs in Hunt, *German Social Democracy*, p. 75.

[51] For example, there can be no question that the party press was relatively closely controlled. On the other hand, Professor Hunt's appropriation of three basic concepts used by the contemporary critics of the party leadership, i.e., *Verbonzung, Verkalkung,* and *Verbürgerlichung (German Social Democracy*, p. 241 and passim) fails, in my estimation, due to the assumption that these concepts conformed more or less directly with reality, rather than seeing them as assertions that originated in the course of a prolonged controversy and basically expressed moral and political values rather than empirically verifiable "truth."

[52] Drechsler, pp. 115–16, points out that the dissident left socialists who founded the SAPD in 1931 avoided instituting a number of the democratic organizational changes they had demanded while still members of the SPD!

[53] This is not to say the Social Democratic leaders could not have accomplished more in the way of fundamental changes than they did, particularly in the first years of the Republic. Hilferding wrote Karl Kautsky on 23 Sept. 1933: "Certainly our policy in Germany after 1923 was on the whole forced by the situation and could not have been much different. In this period a different policy would scarcely have had a different result. However in the time before 1914 and all the more from 1918 until the Kapp *Putsch*, politics were fluid *(plastisch)*, and in this time the worst mistakes were made" (quoted by Kolb, p. 7).

elements defending a bourgeois order and the trend of public opinion toward the right, the precarious economic situation and the attitudes of foreign powers, made drastic changes in existing conditions according to a left-socialist but non-Communist line most unlikely. One of the most prominent practitioners of reformist politics in the SPD commented:

> If Comrade Rosenfeld thinks [that] we must attain power according to the methods of scientific socialism, then I have to say: if we wanted to content ourselves with this comfortable expression during the everyday struggles of politics, we wouldn't get one step ahead.[54]

To justify giving Otto Braun the final word, it must be said that those who criticized his kind of politics did not pretend to value the forms of bourgeois democracy. The left-wing Social Democrats regarded themselves as the true defenders of the interests of the working classes and were convinced that the class struggle continued unabated despite the transition to a republic. "A true democracy is realizable only in a different state from that which is ruled by the bourgeoisie." [55] They apparently did not see, or at least did not let it worry them, that a number of their most frequent complaints shared certain themes popular among the antidemocratic publicists on the right. Despite differences in values and vocabulary, the writers of the nascent "Conservative Revolution" also enjoyed denouncing party politics, measuring parliamentary behavior by an idealized standard of perfection,[56] rejecting bureaucratic routine in favor of an immediate intuitive relationship between leaders and led, condemning the pervasive hold of bourgeois values, and demanding that the parties be brought more in touch with youth.[57]

[54] Braun, *Sozialdemokratischer Parteitag 1927*, p. 75.

[55] Paul Levi at the 1925 Party Convention (quoted by Drechsler, p. 16). A motion at the 1924 Convention read: "The bourgeoisie have proven that they carry on their fight internally within the Republic with no less brutality than in any other form of government and that, therefore, the degree of responsibility Social Democrats [bear] for this state can go no farther than [the degree to which] the working classes actually have power in the state." Ibid., p. 13.

[56] Carl Schmitt set the pattern for making devastating contrasts between parliamentary practice and theory in his essay, *Die geistgeschichtliche Lage des heutigen Parlamentarismus* (2nd ed.; Munich, 1926).

[57] Kurt Sontheimer, *Antidemokratisches Denken in der Weimarer Republik* (Munich, 1962), pp. 189–211, 269–70, 278–79. The limits of Sontheimer's study prevented him from doing more than mention the acceptance of some of the current antidemocratic ideas by defenders of the Republic, and he did not try to discuss the radical left.

None the less, some of the harsh criticism was justified. It cannot be denied, particularly in light of our knowledge of the way the party failed in the years 1930–33, that the Social Democratic leaders were rather smug and complacent.[58] Julius Leber's perceptive "Gedanken zum Verbot der deutschen Sozialdemokratie" has influenced the thinking of many recent scholars.[59] The circumstances of its composition—he wrote his notes in a Nazi jail—make comprehensible his sharp criticism of the leaders of the party and their great faith in the organization. However, one must also remember that in the 1920s it was precisely the highly developed organization of the SPD that was generally credited with the party's strength and effectiveness.[60] Leber himself knew of the relatively recent emergence of the functionaries to a dominant position within the party; he saw that the perfecting of the organization was a consequence of the disastrous "Hottentot" elections of 1907.[61] In the twenties the SPD was still a model imitated by other parties interested in building up their strength with the voters.[62] The Social Democratic leaders during the Weimar Republic had reason to be proud of their party organization even if we know now that it was already old-fashioned. In this respect, they can be compared to battleship admirals a few years before Pearl Harbor and Midway.

When Professor Richard Hunt states that the left opposition was "unable to influence the national policy of the SPD to any appreciable extent,"[63] he restricts the meaning of "influence" to the ability to force the official leadership to adopt left-socialist policies. It is true that the left opposition never obtained enough backing to have its resolutions substituted for those favored by the party leaders. But, if one

[58] Matthias, in *The Path to Dictatorship*, pp. 65–67; similarly, Hunt, *German Social Democracy*, pp. 74–75.

[59] Leber, pp. 185–247.

[60] An American political scientist wrote, "The party is in every respect truly imposing, and without any doubt is the greatest political influence in the new Germany." James K. Pollock, Jr., "The German Party System," *American Political Science Review*, 23 (Nr. 4, Nov., 1929): 863.

[61] Leber, pp. 194–95; see, too, Schorske, pp. 116–45.

[62] Both the DDP and Center Party tried to adopt some of its organizational features. On the Center Party's rather weak organization, Morsey, pp. 583–90, 599–602. On the DDP, A. A. Chanady, "Anton Erkelenz and Erich Koch-Weser," *Historical Studies, Australia and New Zealand*, 12 (Nr. 48, April, 1967), 491–505, and Ernst Portner, "Der Ansatz zur demokratischen Massenpartei im deutschen Linksliberalismus," *Vierteljahrshefte für Zeitgeschichte*, 12 (Nr. 2, April, 1965): 150–61.

[63] *German Social Democracy*, p. 299. He also speaks of their "impotence," p. 230, and "permanent and ineffectual opposition," p. 237.

understands "influence" in a broader sense as the ability to
prevent the party leaders from doing certain things that they
wanted to do,[64] or to compel them to fight hard to win acceptance of their policies,[65] then one must disagree with Professor Hunt's conclusion.

The power of the left-wing socialists did not depend altogether on the number of members of the Reichstag delegation who openly sided with them, or on the handful of
local organizations and newspapers in their control.[66] Their
influence rested on their capacity to mobilize latent discontent among the active party members who under normal
conditions accepted the directions of the party leadership.
From time to time, and on particular issues, if the party
leadership failed to explain its decisions intelligibly to the
rank-and-file, the left opposition gave voice to the general
dissatisfaction, and was able to organize short-term resistance. The party leaders usually felt obliged to institute further
intra-party discussions or alter their course of action in order
to stem the discontent. Contemporary observers attributed
the doctrinaire and sometimes unpolitic actions of the reunified SPD to the influence of the former Independents.[67]
Joseph Joos wrote, "The union with the Independents . . .
lay like a 'lead weight' on the Majority Socialists and took
their courage away on decisive questions. . . ." [68] The identification of the oppositional grouping active in the mid-
twenties with the old Independents was an oversimplification,

[64] Such as joining a Great Coalition government in 1925–26.
[65] Otto Braun had to threaten to resign in order to prevent the SPD Prussian
Landtag delegation from voting against the Hohenzollern settlement late in 1926.
See below, Chapter VIII, p. 307.
[66] Hunt, *German Social Democracy*, pp. 81, 226–29; Drechsler, pp. 24, 49–50, 87–
108, 161–62. It is perhaps unfair to complain that Drechsler's very detailed monograph on the SAPD does not investigate the role of the left opposition before the
split in 1931 as thoroughly as one might desire. In his introductory chapters he
concentrates on the debates at party conventions. Neither he nor Hunt examines
the activities of the opposition *between* conventions.
[67] Ernst Troeltsch saw this trend developing even before the reunification of the
two parties occurred. "The Social Democrats were a middle party in the beginning
of the German Republic, in truth its founder and savior. Today they strive after
greater strength through a community somehow formed with the Independents,
desire to go back into a posture of opposition, and from their very torn ideology
emphasize again . . . the idea of the class struggle in order to hold their people
together through an idea." *Spektator-Briefe* (5 July 1921), p. 199; Keil, 2: 269–70;
Severing, 1: 358–59; Brecht, p. 407.
[68] *Politisches Jahrbuch 1927/28*, p. 161.

although an understandable one.[69] The prevalence of this opinion surely supports our interpretation that the opposition within the SPD knew how to make its weight felt.

In any case, there are a number of signs that views inside the party were to some degree fluid, even among "organization men." [70] As prominent a figure as Paul Löbe, the Reichstag president, spoke out against the policy of joining coalitions at the national level.[71] The party organization in Berlin, headed by Franz Künstler, played a major role in opposing the coalition policy favored by the party leaders in 1925–26 and in blocking SPD support of moderate regulatory legislation after the 1926 referendum failed.[72] Resort to a radical uncompromising tone was undoubtedly popular with most Social Democrats. *Vorwärts* commented at the time of the formation of the first Luther government, "The Social Democratic Party grew large in opposition." [73] Sometimes actions by Social Democrats as well as their words possessed an unmistakable "oppositional" character, e.g. Scheidemann's sensational revelations concerning illegal Reichswehr activities in December 1926.[74] Moreover, a strong desire to

[69] On the divergent backgrounds of members of the left opposition, see Drechsler, pp. 1–3 and passim. He speaks (p. 3) of "Luxemburgianer, Kautskyaner, Revisionisten und Sozialpazifisten" joining to oppose the policies of the party leadership after 1923. One former leader of the opposition, Fritz Bieligk, told Drechsler the left in the SPD was "never an organized group. Therefore it never was possible to say precisely who belonged to it or who did not. In their informal meetings, attended mostly by *editors, party secretaries, Landtag* and *Reichstag delegates,* strongly differing opinions on actual problems [of the day] and political decisions were almost always expressed." Ibid., p. 23, note 18 (italics added). Certainly many former Independents were among them however. Hunt observes that leading right Independents such as Hilferding, Crispien, and Breitscheid found places made for them in the reunified party's leadership in a way that the former left Independents did not. *German Social Democracy,* pp. 206–10, 225. Günter Arns, "Die Linke in der SPD-Reichstagsfraktion in Herbst 1923," *Vierteljahrshefte für Zeitgeschichte,* 22 (Nr. 2, April, 1974): 191–203.
[70] Professor Hunt uses this term, p. 74.
[71] *Sozialdemokratischer Parteitag 1927,* pp. 196–98; Severing, 2: 139–140. Löbe had close ties with the Breslau party organization. Its head, Ernst Eckstein, was a leading figure in the left opposition. Wilhelm Marx noted the contrast between Löbe's conciliatory behavior as presiding officer of the Reichstag and radical vocabulary as a party politician. Stehkämper, 3: 308–9. Among other prominent individuals, Siegfried Aufhäuser, head of the white collar worker's union (AfA), and Robert Dissmann, head of the metal workers' union (DMV) until his early death in Oct. 1926, played notable roles as critics of the party leadership.
[72] See below, pp. 130–31 and Chapter VIII, pp. 296, 307.
[73] Quoted by Stürmer, p. 91.
[74] Eyck, 2: 126–35; Haungs, pp. 121–22.

avoid the divisive factionalism that had caused so much trouble in the past prevailed in most circles of the party. Thus, the party leadership was encouraged to find slogans and follow tactics which were as accommodating as possible. In April 1927, for instance, the Reichstag *Fraktion* voted against the budget for the first time since the Republic was established.[75]

However comforting the security of tenure enjoyed by the Social Democratic leaders may have been, the responsibilities required of them were not always pleasant, nor were they always able to follow their own best judgment. Indeed, like their counterparts at the head of the Center Party,[76] they attempted to soften criticism of their unpopular actions by insisting on their own sense of responsibility and the need to act contrary to their basic inclinations.

> After the lost war neither we nor the Nationalists can . . . conduct German politics as we would like. We stand . . . unavoidably under the influence of foreign affairs. It could easily occur in the near future . . . that we have to share responsibility [for governing Germany], whether we want to or not. In such a complicated situation the Social Democratic Party can . . . do nothing but [try to] orient itself according to the facts.[77]

These statements often mingled the invocation of duty and self-sacrifice with the necessity of choosing the "lesser evil." [78] Whatever the element of self-justification in such statements, it is clear that Social Democratic leaders did not freely make policy according to their own desires. Over and above the limited range of options permitted by the existing balance of political forces in Germany, any important policy decision which the leaders of the SPD reached had to take into account the likely response of party members. A strong, genuine current of feeling within the party easily sufficed to halt an otherwise viable choice of tactics. Above all else, the party leaders wanted to preserve the unity of the party. The adoption of an "oppositional" stance was, at least tempo-

---

[75] "It [the SPD] wanted thereby to clearly express that the *Besitzbürgerblock alone bears responsibility for the present politics." Jahrbuch der Deutschen Sozialdemokratie . . . 1927*, p. 11 (emphasis in original).

[76] Morsey, *Die Deutsche Zentrumspartei, 1917–1923*, pp. 163–76, 378–86, and passim.

[77] Müller, *Sozialdemokratischer Parteitag 1925*, p. 176. "We will do our duty and [fulfill] our obligations." Scheidemann, ibid., p. 159.

[78] Braun, pp. 113–14; *Vorwärts*, 13 June 1924 (Nr. 284), quoted by Stürmer, p. 258.

rarily, always the easiest way to maintain intra-party harmony.[79] In such circumstances, the leaders of the SPD were prone to reverse previous decisions or break off promising negotiations with other parties, at times letting the SPD's line of policy fluctuate embarrassingly.

The leaders of the SPD prided themselves on trying to keep meaningful practical results in sight as they determined policy, rather than just repeating slogans or talking principles.[80] Like the leaders of other parties the Social Democrats found that the proper, i.e. most successful, response to pressing questions of the day could not always be determined by the application of general principles.[81] Decisions of timing and other tactics, the judgment of priorities within a limited context required a sensitivity for what was parliamentarily possible, not what was given by any fixed theoretical axiom. Basically, the establishment of a line of policy that corresponded faithfully to the SPD's *Weltanschauung* would have been possible only if the party obtained and kept the backing of a sufficiently large number of voters to permit it to act without considering other political groupings or powerful existing institutions. But to wait long years with pure hands until that millennium occurred was not actually possible. Whether the SPD acted positively by cooperating in a government or indirectly by refusing to do so, as the largest party it always shared some responsibility for the outcome of events.[82]

The established party leadership saw the integration of the Social Democratic Party into the political life of the Republic as a reality, not as a hypothetical or contingent option.

Never forget it. We have indestructible rights in this Republic. Seven years ago German Social Democracy was the state! (Lively cheers!) When the country was quiet once more . . . they came out of their holes again, out of their nooks and crannies, the Junkers, the factory barons, the greedy merchants *(Pfeffersäcke)*

[79] See Adolph's discussion of Otto Wels's role in opposing the construction of the battle cruiser "A," pp. 162–69.

[80] Cf. the statements by Stelling, Müller, and Breitscheid, *Sozialdemokratischer Parteitag 1925*, pp. 99–100, 219, 222–24.

[81] Stresemann once remarked, "Statecraft in a fragmented nation cannot be anything else than the politics of compromise, the bringing together of all forces which at any given time are in the situation to move things ahead" (quoted by Stürmer, pp. 42–43).

[82] Severing, 2: 79; Conze, *Historische Zeitschrift*, 178: 62–63.

and their agents, and they polluted the political atmosphere with the stench of their lies and crudities.[83]

In such a situation words alone would not suffice. Responsible acts were necessary, and "No republican party ought to content itself forever [by] standing outside the door and criticizing. Now it is simply a matter of not [just] speaking but acting like republicans." [84] To those within the party who did not consider the preservation of democracy a major concern for socialists, they said: "If you have not [yet] understood that the preservation of democracy and the Republic is the most important interest of the party, you have not learned the ABC's of political thinking. (Bravo! and applause.)" [85]

As these quotations suggest, the party leaders often adopted a rather schoolmasterish tone when addressing their own followers.[86] They regarded themselves as experts, as masters of political skills acquired through long training and experience.[87] To a large extent they were justified in this conception of themselves; however much various critics assailed their limitations, no one accused them of being political amateurs.[88] Well-versed in the intricacies of German domestic politics and skilled in negotiation, they attempted to establish a course of policy which fit their informed analyses of the situation.[89] They clearly believed that ordinary party mem-

[83] From Otto Wels's speech honoring Ebert, *Sozialdemokratischer Parteitag 1925*, pp. 84–85; Adolph, pp. 216–19.

[84] Scheidemann at a national meeting of the *Reichsbanner* at Magdeburg 13 May 1926. *Frankfurter Zeitung*, 14 May 1926 (Nr. 354).

[85] Hilferding, *Sozialdemokratischer Parteitag 1927*, p. 173.

[86] The tone was most apparent in official reprimands of "improper" left-wing activities among the party youth. The following quotation is taken from a somewhat later period (1931) than we are discussing, but it is worth quoting because of the obvious self-assurance of the speaker. "Nothing is easier today than to encourage the young people in a youth group to vote for radical resolutions. (Agreement.) Not the slightest pedagogical ability is required for it. Party comrades who fulfill their assignments in this way are not conscious of their pedagogical responsibility. We must recognize anew that in this time of crisis the responsibility of pedagogues is especially great." Erich Ollenhauer at the 1931 *Parteitag* (quoted by Drechsler, p. 165).

[87] Bracher, *Die Auflösung*, p. 75; but see Miller's comments on their lack of experience in political decision-making and administration prior to 1918, *Die Bürde der Macht*, pp. 445–51.

[88] The most prevalent line of criticism emphasized the SPD leaders' lack of imagination. Cf. Ernst Troeltsch at the beginning of the Republic: "They are not entirely certain of the art and technique of governing. They rule the state like an awkward trade union." *Spektator-Briefe* (30 Dec. 1918), p. 28 and Julius Leber, p. 242, at the end: "For they [Braun and Severing] had become . . . the bureaucrats of politics."

[89] "We live in a time when one must have the courage [to face] unpopularity in order to carry out *what one has recognized as correct*" (italics added), Hermann Müller to the Reichstag, 9 Oct. 1923, as quoted by Luther, *Politiker ohne Partei*, p. 124.

bers did not understand many of the tactical considerations that they knew must be taken into account.[90] The Social Democratic leaders regarded the mass of their supporters with a certain distrust.[91] They considered them likely to demand illusionary goals, and hence feared their susceptibility to demagogic appeals.[92] The party's leaders persistently called for discipline, unity, and trust.[93] Questioning of their judgment was generally treated as a challenge to their authority. (In fact, it sometimes was.) When, on occasion, the leaders demanded the acceptance of their decisions by the rank-and-file, they not merely insisted that a specific policy be approved but expected to be reconfirmed as leaders as well.[94] The party membership, acting through the appropriate bodies, normally ratified the decisions of their "proven" leadership, but at times with a show of resistance. In response to criticism the leadership sometimes modified its chosen policies even as those policies were being put into effect, or worse, from a historian's standpoint, revised the reports of previous actions to convey an impression of unswerving correctness and consistency in the judgments it had made.[95]

Because the party leaders exercised wide-ranging powers, yet never could feel entirely certain that their followers would

[90] Müller once remarked while defending the policy of coalitions, "You have spoken so much of the cleverness *(Schlauheit)* and wile of the Center Party. Many a time I have wished that this cleverness could be found everywhere in our [midst]." *Sozialdemokratischer Parteitag 1925,* p. 175; *Vorwärts,* 9 March 1924 (Nr. 117; quoted by Stürmer, p. 40).

[91] Scheidemann, *Sozialdemokratischer Parteitag 1925,* pp. 157, 159, and the report by Johannes Stelling, who observed that criticism of the leadership did not "serve" the party. "The right course is that of close comradeship combined with a clear sense of responsibility for that which benefits [*frommt*] the party." Ibid., p. 101.

[92] Professor Nölting's remarks on Hilferding's speech, *Sozialdemokratischer Parteitag 1927,* pp. 194–96. See, too, the remarks of the Free Trade Union leaders, Fritz Tarnow and Hermann Müller. *Protokoll der Verhandlungen des 12. Kongresses der Gewerkschaften Deutschlands* (Berlin, 1925), pp. 230–31, 267.

[93] Ebert's warning remarks on 18 Nov. 1918, are significant as an expression of a general attitude, not merely as his personal reaction to a particular crisis. He said all would be ruined "in a week's time" if order were not maintained, particularly if the *Räte* and other groups continued to act on their own authority. ". . . [A]n organization functions only if it has an undivided *(einheitliche)* leadership and if a single [set of] basic principles exist for the unrolling [of every step]" (quoted by Schulz, *Zwischen Demokratie und Diktatur,* 1: 52).

[94] This practice was by no means limited to German Social Democratic leaders. See R. T. McKenzie, *British Political Parties* (2nd ed.; New York and London, 1963), pp. 100–1, 131–40, 310–15, 381–82, 638, 642.

[95] Anyone using the official published reports of the party's activities must compare the statements made later with those which appeared in the press at the time in question. Even *Vorwärts* cannot be relied on uncritically. The tendentiousness of such reports consists primarily of omission of information which did not fit the official view, rather than outright falsification.

comprehend or accept the reasons that determined their own decisions, they reacted with particular sensitivity to charges that they were "untrue" to the cause of the workers. Exposing the "halfheartedness" and "deceits" of the Social Democratic leadership was, it scarcely needs saying, a regular practice of the Communists. At times oppositional voices within the SPD were almost equally strident.[96] Even though the Communist *Entlarvenstaktik* did not actually succeed in destroying the trust of most of the rank-and-file in their leaders, it did work well as a persistent harassment and kept the SPD leaders on the defensive. The Social Democratic position was particularly vulnerable to this kind of attack. The bulk of the SPD's policies was defined by a process of compromise, often worked out "behind the scenes" for reasons that were not clear to the public. In retrospect we must say that many of these compromises were intelligent and reasonable ones. However, most German politicians, not merely those on the left, found it hard to convince their followers that compromise was a respectable part of politics.[97] All too often Social Democratic leaders committed to a reasonable compromise felt compelled to put it into effect by methods which were scarcely straightforward.

Without question the leaders of the SPD usually acted in good faith.[98] Nevertheless, they were caught in a situation where much that they did, given the expectations of their followers, was bound to be unpopular. Yet the rhetoric of daily party politics required partisan victories. As a result, the Social Democratic leadership became notably adept at assuming complex political postures.[99] These took various

[96] Otto Wels protested sharply against the nature of such attacks, Drechsler, pp. 11 and 77.

[97] "To be sure the compulsion to work together has in many respects reduced the frictions between the parties that bore common responsibility for a time. . . . [T]he compulsion however has now brought difficulties *into* the parties since . . . ideological *(weltanschauliche)* views and positions of principle are no longer discussed so exclusively as they once were, while now tactical questions have to be fought out. The fall of Wirth in November 1922 and Luther's resignation after Locarno resulted not from battles among the [different] party delegations, but were due to majorities *inside* the Social Democratic and German National delegations, respectively, opposed to the current tactics." Theodor Heuss, "Demokratie und Parlamentarismus, ihre Geschichte, ihre Gegner und ihre Zukunft," in *Zehn Jahre Deutsche Republik*, p. 110 (emphasis in original).

[98] Brecht, p. 214.

[99] It goes without saying that leaders of other parties did so, too. However, I believe that the tactics used by the SPD, particularly its policy of tolerating minority governments while maintaining the formal appearance of being in opposition, were rather more complex than the policies followed by other parties.

forms. Frequently the party officials offered verbal concessions to those who wanted a different or stronger policy.
Thus, they might adopt somewhat more determined language
in resolutions or speeches without necessarily altering their
course of action in any significant way, or substitute one of
their own resolutions for proposals that were considered
dangerous because they came from the intra-party opposition.[100] The distinct difference between the theoretical portion of the 1925 Heidelberg Program, written with an eye
toward the Independents who had rejoined the party, and
the more openly reformist Görlitz Program of 1921 is a major
case in point.[101]

Similarly, spokesmen for the SPD nearly always established
what they insisted was a firm and clear position in accordance
with relevant party principles when they announced the party's stand on a given issue in the Reichstag or in the party
press. But even as this initial position was being declared,
key members of the party were probably engaged in confidential discussions with representatives of other parties working out legislative action along rather different lines. Later
on, the leaders of the SPD might well announce their support
for a proposal that they had previously rejected, of course,
now emphasizing "major concessions" that the other parties
had made. The adoption of an initially strong stand is part
and parcel of all bargaining; however, for the SPD this technique was more than a method of negotiating with other
parties: it played an important part in maintaining the support
of the rank-and-file membership. The party leaders felt
obliged to act out their "resolute conviction" before asking
the party to accept a compromise. The Social Democratic
Party's participation in the initiative and referendum of 1926
had much of this demonstrative character, and was intended
to precede realistic accommodation of the other parties'
views. The same process of first satisfying the party's supporters and then turning to practical politics is clearly apparent in the behavior of the SPD during the presidential
elections of 1925.

---

[100] Drechsler, pp. 76–77.

[101] Ibid., pp. 14–16; Ludwig Bergstraesser, *Geschichte der politischen Parteien in Deutschland* (11th ed.; Munich, 1965), p. 208. Criticism of these programs from a DDR standpoint: Heinz Niemann, "Das Görlitzer Programm der SPD von 1921," *Zeitschrift für Geschichtswissenschaft*, 23 (Nr. 8, 1975): 908–19, and "Das Heidelberger Programm der SPD von 1925," ibid., 24 (Nr. 7, 1976): 786–94.

New presidential elections were due in 1925, but the sudden death of Friedrich Ebert caught everyone by surprise.[102] Even before Ebert's death several high-ranking Social Democrats had discussed the possibility of supporting a joint republican candidate in the first round of the upcoming election, since they foresaw that no Social Democrat would win.[103] The Democrats would have agreed to a joint candidacy and hoped that the man chosen would come from their ranks.[104] The Center Party would probably have made some difficulties, but in the end would very likely have endorsed a suitable candidate.[105] But as it happened, the parties of the former Weimar Coalition had still not reached any definite agreement when the date for the first of the presidential elections was set. The SPD Executive Board consulted with the Advisory Council, but since opinion in that body was almost evenly divided, the party leaders decided to run a separate candidate.[106] Otto Braun reluctantly consented to be his party's nominee.[107] Nearly all the other parties also put up candidates of their own. There were seven altogether; none had any chance of winning.[108] Since victory in the run-off election required only a plurality rather than a clear majority as in the first round, this time most of the parties tried seriously to find a winning candidate.[109] The republican parties agreed

[102] He died 28 Feb. 1925; his term as president would have expired 1 July. Eyck, 1: 440–42.

[103] Hermann Müller, *Sozialdemokratischer Parteitag 1925,* p. 174.

[104] Stephan, pp. 286–88; Schneider, pp. 108–113.

[105] According to Koch-Weser at a meeting of the DDP's Advisory Committee 1 March 1925. DDP Papers, reel 38, folder 749, pp. 9–10. He called the presidential election "the greatest test which the Republic has yet had to undergo . . ." and said that he would be sorry to see "the Social Democrats once again . . . forced into opposition." He recognized that it would be difficult to unite the three republican parties behind one candidate. Particularly, he said, because "also on this eminently important question the Center Party continues in [a state of] sorry *(träger)* indecision." Idem.

[106] Johannes Stelling, *Sozialdemokratischer Parteitag 1925,* p. 106.

[107] Braun, p. 169; Schulze, pp. 471–72. The Democratic editor, Theodor Wolff, called the SPD's decision to run a separate candidate a mistake. "It is thought clever tactics in Social Democratic circles to give the masses a party candidate during the first round of the election. . . . Too much [concern about] tactics has often brought harm, and too much cleverness usually saps energy." *Berliner Tageblatt* (Wochen-Ausgabe), 12 March 1926.

[108] The Center Party ran Wilhelm Marx; the Democrats, Willy Hellpach; the DVP and DNVP, Karl Jarres; the Bavarian People's Party, Heinrich Held; the Communists, Ernst Thälmann; and the National Socialists, General Ludendorff. Milatz, pp. 118–20.

[109] Marx and Hindenburg were the only serious candidates, although the Communists insisted on running Thälmann again. Bracher, *Deutschland zwischen Demokratie und Diktatur,* pp. 69–71; Rosenberg, pp. 450–53.

upon a joint candidate, the prominent though rather colorless Center Party leader, Wilhelm Marx. Although Marx would have had a good chance against Karl Jarres, the mayor of Duisburg, who had been the candidate for the DVP and DNVP during the first election, he was hopelessly outmatched by Field Marshal von Hindenburg, whose name was substituted for that of Jarres in the second round. The results are well known. A few months later Hermann Müller, chairman of the Social Democratic Party, commented on the opportunity which had been missed by failing to name a joint republican candidate at the start: "I wonder if, within even the next [few] years, many of us will not ask ourselves would it not have been better, perhaps, if a republican and democrat stood at the head of this Republic rather than Hindenburg?"[110]

The Social Democrats had quarreled over the wisdom of supporting a joint candidate. Some argued that the party should have run its own man in both elections,[111] that it confused Social Democratic voters to ask them to support the Catholic Marx.

> In the presidential elections the Executive Board allowed itself to be guided by the idea of a joint republican candidate and thought of furthering the consolidation of the Republic. . . . However, I represent the contrary view that German Social Democracy has the great historical task of solidifying and consolidating the Socialist workers' movement. Under these banners a Social Democratic candidate in the second round of the elections would have reduced the Communist Party . . . to insignificance.[112]

Men who held this view clearly wanted to avoid any regular cooperation with the Center Party and the Democrats.[113] Speakers for the *Vorstand* defended the decision to support Marx: to have entered a separate Social Democratic candidate a second time would have made Hindenburg's election absolutely certain.[114] But, even they evidently agreed that a

[110] *Sozialdemokratischer Parteitag 1925*, p. 174.

[111] See the speeches of Hermann Fleissner (Dresden), Franz Künstler (Berlin), Hermann Liebmann (Leipzig), ibid., pp. 145–46, 146–48, 149.

[112] Emil Theil (Bremen), ibid., p. 170.

[113] Especially the comments of Hoffmann (Berlin), ibid., p. 151–52.

[114] In addition to Stelling and Müller cited above notes 103 and 106, the delegates Heilmann (Berlin), Riedmiller (Cologne) and Widmann (Offenbach a.M.) defended the course taken by the party Executive. Ibid., pp. 159–61, 161–62, 170–71. Also see Severing's article, "Der 2. Wahlgang," *Sozialistische Monatshefte*, 62 (14 April 1925): 197–99. "In these confusing times a party that does not stand firmly behind its leadership is not going to be able to find allies *(nicht bündnisfähig)* and must sooner or later collapse" (p. 199).

partisan candidate in the first election had been necessary:

> After we had confirmed our powerful strength in the first election and astonished the middle-class parties, we concentrated all our efforts on the defeat of the monarchistic-nationalistic parties.
>
> Our party offered the greatest sacrifice for the Republic when it . . . campaigned for Marx . . . as president.[115]

Alas, the SPD did not make this sacrifice in time! Hermann Müller sensed the mistake, but even he saw the lesson in too narrow terms. Next time, he said, the republican parties must concentrate their forces—presidential elections were not the same as Reichstag or *Landtag* elections where the parties competed with each other directly.[116] The Social Democratic leaders do not seem to have understood a few months later that this basic truth applied to an initiative and referendum as well.

We have already discussed how adept the Social Democratic leaders were at altering a position they had been maintaining if dissatisfaction inside the party became strong enough. The decision to force the collapse of the Stresemann government in 1923 despite continued approval of his foreign policy is a well-known example.[117] Nevertheless, it should be noted that if political conditions were grave enough, the SPD's policy makers were capable of abrupt reversals despite strong reactions within the party. Thus, the Social Democratic Party voted for the acceptance of the Treaty of Versailles even though most party members had shared the initial patriotic reaction of Chancellor Scheidemann who had exclaimed that "the hand would wither" which laid such burdens on the German nation.[118]

Rapid changes in policy, even if they were only temporary, opened the door to charges of opportunism and inconsist-

[115] From the "Bericht des Parteivorstandes," *Sozialdemokratischer Parteitag 1925*, p. 23. Severing reports in his memoirs that he combated the views of those "who looked on every election only as [an exercise in] mustering one's own supporters." He said he tried to make clear "that such a mustering *that was useful or even necessary in the first election* would be political folly in the second election." Severing, 2: 53 (italics added).

[116] *Sozialdemokratischer Parteitag 1925*, p. 174.

[117] Eyck, 1: 375–76. On this occasion Ebert said, "What caused you to overthrow the chancellor will be forgotten in six weeks. But you will still feel the consequences of your foolishness ten years from now."

[118] Eyck, 1: 136, 143. The sudden adoption of a "toleration" policy toward the Brüning government after the catastrophic 1930 election is a later example of the same sort of reversal. Ibid., 2: 362–68; Bracher, *Die Auflösung*, pp. 370–71, 391–93; Severing, 2: 272.

ency. The SPD spokesmen usually knew how to defend their conduct satisfactorily when attacked by opponents who were themselves politically sophisticated men. They answered some charges, ignored others, and replied with counter-charges of their own. They seem to have encountered more difficulty, however, in explaining their maneuvers to the public at large. As experienced politicians they were aware of growing public cynicism about political horsetrading *(Kuhhandel)*.[119] But their normal response on such occasions was to sing their own praises and demand that party followers continue to respect their authority.[120] Such exhortations retained a certain effectiveness with the older generation of voters who remembered the past achievements of the party. But, the old appeals, and especially the inevitable reference to party discipline, did not greatly attract younger men and women.[121] Inadequate communication between the party leaders and the mass of their followers, or for that matter, with the public at large, was a genuine problem. The forms, the language, the style normally used became more and more outdated.[122] It may well be that this problem of communication lay at the heart of the persistent complaints about "lack of contact" or "too little real understanding" between party leaders and followers, rather than—as many people then thought—an insufficiently democratic organizational structure or social changes in the composition of the party leadership. However the complaints were phrased, all stressed the need for clearer policies.[123] The party leaders

[119] The Communists loved to denounce the negotiations of the SPD with other parties in these terms. For instance, *Rote Fahne*, 23 June 1926. This kind of distrust was widespread, however, Heiber, p. 177.

[120] Otto Wels's words are typical: ". . .[T]his gas war of lies and defamation can become dangerous for us, comrades, only if we lose faith in ourselves (Very true!), faith in the purity and the greatness of our movement, as well as faith in the spotlessness of the leadership and the party. (Bravo!)" *Sozialdemokratischer Parteitag 1925*, p. 85.

[121] Hunt, *German Social Democracy*, pp. 106–11; Neumann, pp. 35–36. The methods used by the party leadership to curb the radicalism of the party youth groups were crudely disciplinary, i.e. curtailing their freedom to elect their own leaders, restricting the age of members, etc. Drechsler, pp. 24–28, 74–75, 164–66.

[122] Matthias in *The Path to Dictatorship*, pp. 65–67; Leber, pp. 208–10.

[123] Leber, who was by no means part of the left opposition (p. 253), said of the handling of the battle cruiser affair: ". . .[T]he manner of the public handling of this prickly question was an absolute catastrophe. Everywhere in meetings and in the press there still raged the deepest aversion toward this poor ship and then without any preparation, without any explanation, [came] the surprise. No one knew how to come to terms with the public for this sudden blow, least of all Hermann Müller and his colleagues. Their true reasons they could not state, neither did they

also failed to find modern, effective methods of communicating their views through meaningful actions.[124] They were handicapped by their unwitting acceptance of the traditional separation of the sphere of practical politics, largely reserved for trained experts on the one hand, from old-fashioned mass politics, with its fine but often ineffectual principles and demonstrative gestures on the other.

The spokesmen for the middle-class parties, who from time to time cooperated with the Social Democrats, regarded the SPD's sudden shifts of policy with a mixture of annoyance and condescension. They complained about the SPD's "irresponsibility," but knew that the Social Democrats' bark was worse than their bite.[125] They rightly appraised many official statements at less than face value, and learned to wait patiently until the SPD leaders offered a modified position. By tacit consent a number of complicated arrangements were worked out by which the SPD kept in close touch with the governing parties and enjoyed some of the advantages normally associated with participation in a government even when the party insisted that it was in opposition.[126] These arrangements, which permitted the SPD to exercise considerable influence without having to accept unwanted governmental responsibilities, originated in the so-called "toleration" policy.[127]

Between the Reichstag elections of 1920 and 1928, the Social Democratic Party avoided the conspicuous obligations which acceptance of the chancellorship by one of its leaders would have involved. Moreover, of the twelve cabinets formed in that interval, Social Democrats sat as ministers in only four—the two Wirth cabinets, 1921–22, and the two

---

want simply to confess [that they approved of] the building [of the ship]; thus arose that unhealthy mixture of bad conscience and lame excuses." Leber, p. 229, also p. 188.

[124] An exception might be their support of the *Reichsbanner*.

[125] Gessler reports that one of the Social Democratic members of the Great Coalition government of 1923 told him, "Let us out of the government; it makes no sense if we wear ourselves out here uselessly. It is better if we leave, [we will] bark outside and not bite." *Reichswehrpolitik in der Weimarer Zeit*, p. 272.

[126] These comments apply to national politics. The situation in Prussia was a different matter; indeed, the virtually uninterrupted exercise of power in the Prussian government ensured that the SPD's refusal to accept national responsibilities did not have too many immediately dangerous consequences. Carl Landauer suggests that it was only fear that the Center Party might be provoked into breaking the coalition in Prussia that kept the SPD from following a more aggressive policy nationally. *European Socialism*, 2: 1282; Braun, pp. 184–86.

[127] Gessler, p. 357; Stürmer, pp. 47–48, 110, 137–42, 254–60.

Stresemann cabinets of 1923.[128] The remainder of the time the party was formally in opposition. Most of the cabinets during this period could govern only as long as the various opposition parties, normally the KPD, SPD, DNVP, and NSDAP, did not cooperate in opposing the same legislative proposals or vote together on motions of no confidence.[129] On matters of foreign policy the SPD was considered virtually a governmental party.[130] On domestic issues, however, toleration meant that while the party felt perfectly free to oppose governmental measures not to its liking, it nonetheless ensured the existence of a minority cabinet by abstaining during votes of confidence and, thereby, permitting the governmental parties to outvote the remaining opposition parties.[131] The practice of toleration was no exclusive tactic of the SPD—the DDP tolerated the right-of-center Luther cabinet in 1925 and even the KPD toyed with the idea at times.[132] For the Social Democrats, however, the toleration policy became virtually the be-all and end-all of their political practice throughout much of the Weimar era.[133]

[128] Party publications took some pride in pointing out *how seldom* the party had taken office nationally. "The Social Democratic Party, which has not been represented in the national government since November, 1923 [and] thus *bears no political responsibility for the politics of these legislative periods. . . ." Jahrbuch der Deutschen Sozialdemokratie . . . 1927*, p. 12 (emphasis in original); *Jahrbuch . . . 1926*, p. 80. The same sort of disclaimer based on a calculation of the number of months SPD men sat in the national cabinet (37 months in 14 years!) was still made after the war. Löbe, pp. 123–25.

[129] On the problem of minority governments: Becker, *Geschichte in Wissenschaft und Unterricht*, 17: 217; Glum, p. 244; Preuss, pp. 52–53; Haungs, pp. 49–51, 67–71, and passim.

[130] Former Chancellor Luther wrote that as long as Stresemann was alive "we always had the so-called Great Coalition in the Reichstag, no matter how the cabinets as such were composed." Hans Luther, *Weimar und Bonn* (Munich, 1951), p. 22; Braun, pp. 184–85.

[131] See Count Westarp's bitter comments, *Am Grabe der Parteiherrschaft*, pp. 78–79. One test which shows how much more apparent than real the SPD's opposition in these years was is the failure of efforts to bring about an early dissolution of the Reichstag. During the legislative period 1924–28 the Social Democrats repeatedly called for dissolution and new elections, claiming they had nothing to fear from the voters. Nevertheless the SPD did nothing which would have forced a dissolution (for example, by voting against the confirmation of the second Luther government) and the Reichstag lived out virtually its full four years. For some occasions when the SPD claimed it wanted a dissolution, see *Vorwärts*, 27 Oct. 1925 (Nr. 508), 20 May (Nr. 233), 2 July (Nr. 307) and 2 Sept. 1926 (Nr. 412); *Jahrbuch . . . 1927*, p. 12.

[132] Haungs, p. 91; Weber, *Die Wandlung*, 1: 336.

[133] Bracher, *Deutschland zwischen Demokratie und Diktatur*, pp. 62–66; Heiber, p. 88. Hermann Müller justified this policy in an article, "Vom deutschen Parlamentarismus," *Die Gesellschaft* (1926, Nr. 1), pp. 299–300.

Obviously, the SPD demanded a price for its toleration policy. By skillful negotiation the leaders of the SPD were sometimes able to demand more concessions on matters that strongly interested them (details of social legislation, questions of personnel, etc.) than they would have obtained as partners in a governing coalition. A letter issued by the Democratic Party's business office, 10 November 1925, gave as an argument for the formation of a Great Coalition "the pressure of the Social Democrats . . . would presumably be weaker inside a government than [if they] promise support from case to case but remain outside the government." [134] Furthermore, toleration could be rescinded at any time, permitting the Social Democrats to force (or threaten to force) a government to resign if that suited their own partisan purposes. Many Social Democrats favored this course of parliamentary action because it enabled the party to avoid bearing public responsibility for necessary but unpopular laws.[135] The SPD left it to the other parties to formulate and defend most of the rather stringent economic and social welfare measures, but took credit for any improvements obtained through their pressure.[136] Keeping the middle parties in office and dependent on the SPD also helped prevent the sharp reorientation toward the right which some elements in the Center and DVP decidedly wanted.

In time, the toleration policy acquired new refinements. The custom of *Tuchfühlung* developed, whereby leading members of the government, or of the parties supporting the government, discussed important legislation and other matters with a small circle of Social Democratic leaders *before* the cabinet made its final decisions or presented its proposals to the Reichstag.[137] The practice was intended to iron out differences and establish preliminary commitments before any of the parties adopted a stance in public that might make subsequent compromise difficult. Thus, the Social Democratic Party managed to obtain some of the important rights of governmental participation—prior communication of important information and a privileged hearing for its own views—without necessarily having to defend the policies

[134] DDP Papers, reel 38, folder 758, p. 6.
[135] Leber, however, spoke out against such parliamentary tactics, p. 49.
[136] See, for instance, the unsigned *Vorwärts* article, "Sozialdemokratie und Reichstag," 7 July 1926 (Nr. 314).
[137] *Jahrbuch der Deutschen Sozialdemokratie . . . 1926*, pp. 90–93.

which it helped to formulate, a key duty of any governing party. The KPD repeatedly denounced the SPD for being secretly part of the government, an assertion that was only an exaggeration, not a falsehood.[138] By the time of the third Marx government, during the second half of 1926, the leaders of the SPD's Reichstag *Fraktion* moved to have the previous informal arrangements confirmed by a binding statement from the governing parties.[139]

The key Social Democratic parliamentarians who maintained the *Tuchfühlung* rather too easily accustomed themselves to this bad habit. Satisfied with an arrangement by which they could combine both opposition and participation, they neglected opportunities in the mid-twenties to put German domestic politics on a clearer, more stable basis.[140] The inherent arbitrariness of such covert arrangements apparently did not worry them. Given their other concerns as party leaders, they were content to exercise indirect influence on political decisions without necessarily desiring power for its own sake.[141] They followed a path—as Gerhard Schulz observed of Ebert's course in 1918–19—"against the relatively least resistance." [142]

Despite the fact that the Social Democrats did not participate in any of the national cabinets between 1923 and 1928, the question of coalitions was the most disputed issue within the party during these years.[143] All the important differences between the left opposition and the official party leadership were revealed as the debate progressed year after year. Both sides wanted to serve the best interests of the party, but they did not agree on the definition of that interest or on their assessments of the current political situation.

The language used by both sides in the debate did not

[138] For example, *Rote Fahne*, 1 and 20 May 1926.

[139] *Vorwärts*, 13 Nov. (Nr. 536), and 16 Nov. 1926 (Nr. 540); *Frankfurter Zeitung*, 12 Nov. (Nrs. 845 and 846) and 13 Nov. 1926 (Nr. 848); Haungs, pp. 118–19.

[140] A few voices such as Wilhelm Keil's opposed the ambiguity of the political commitments that toleration involved. Keil, 2: 206–7, 330. Scheidemann, too, favored either participation in the government or clear opposition. *Vorwärts*, 8 Dec. 1926 (Nr. 577).

[141] The reversion to patterns of behavior more characteristic of a well-organized pressure group than a properly functioning political party has been observed by a number of scholars. See above Chapter I, pp. 18–19.

[142] Schulz, 1: 49.

[143] Neumann, pp. 37–39; Hunt, *German Social Democracy*, pp. 222–23. Critical, from an East German standpoint: Roswitha Berndt, "Rechtssozialdemokratische Koalitionspolitik in der Weimarer Republik," *Wissenschaftliche Zeitschrift der Universität Halle-Wittenberg. Gesellschafts- und sprachwissenschaftliche Reihe.* 26 (Nr. 1, 1977): 43–52.

always convey the full extent to which the opposing views diverged. Those who favored coalitions never claimed that a general commitment to share power with certain other parties was a matter of fundamental principle; they argued that decisions regarding coalitions were tactical in nature and conceded that under certain circumstances, outright and explicit opposition was necessary.[144] But, they also believed that the party should not restrict its freedom of action by enunciating a policy which defined once and for all what types of coalitions were acceptable or which set down other fixed conditions largely on the basis of theoretical considerations.

> Participation by the Social Democrats in the national government depends on whether [its] strength among the people and in the Reichstag can assure the attainment of its objectives, [which are in turn] determined by its share [of responsibility] in the government in a given situation and in accord with the interests of the labor movement, or [it may participate as a] defense against reactionary dangers. The decision [how much of] a share to take in the government is a tactical question, the answer for which cannot be laid down once and for all by definite formulas.[145]

The opponents of coalitions admitted at least as a debating point that joint action with other parties was sometimes desirable, yet they usually raised objections to the timing, the terms of partnership, and the inherent frailties of any actual or proposed coalition.[146] These men persistently attacked what they viewed as the mistaken policies of the past.

The left socialists stressed the unique value of the Social Democratic Party as a workers' movement and did not want to see its character destroyed through a series of ill-advised compromises.[147] Toni Sender stated in 1927:

> . . . [I]t is much easier for parties which represent the existing order to gain successes in a coalition because these coalitions by necessity are formed on the basis of the existing system. Already

---

[144] Cf. the comments of Severing, Breitscheid, and Hilferding, *Sozialdemokratischer Parteitag 1927*, pp. 200–204, 206–9, 217–23.

[145] The resolution submitted by Hilferding and passed by the 1927 *Parteitag*, as quoted by Drechsler, p. 19.

[146] Künstler and Prien, *Sozialdemokratischer Parteitag 1925*, pp. 147–48, 203; Siegfried Aufhäuser and Georg Dietrich (Erfurt), *Sozialdemokratischer Parteitag 1927*, pp. 198–200, 213–15.

[147] Levi, *Sozialdemokratischer Parteitag 1925*, pp. 215–17. He said among other things, "If we have previously attacked coalitions so sharply [it was] because in coalitions our appeal to the masses echoes in a void, and we cannot obtain our goal without the masses" (p. 217).

in this sense as partners in a coalition the Social Democrats have
to be the party that makes the sacrifices first.

She continued: "We do not fear to undertake responsibility
for *our policies,* but we shy away from having to bear responsibility for policies heavily influenced by the middle-class half
of the government."[148] The appeal and strength of the movement, they thought, lay in its dedication and in actions that
aroused the enthusiasm of the masses. *"Every policy is harmful
which is not effective as agitation."*[149] In order to obtain their
goals, they preferred to wait until the party was able to secure
an uncontestable majority. They set a low value on parliamentary work.[150] On occasion they reminded the leadership
of the party officials whose contacts were far removed from
the centers of government:

> Are the functionaries in the factories able to defend what the
> political leadership has done? Are they able to influence the
> indifferent and outraged masses in the factories . . . ? Only if the
> policy of the party permits this is it a policy that will be buoyed
> up by the great confidence of the working functionaries through-
> out the nation.[151]

The proponents of coalitions, on the other hand, refused to
ignore the already existing strength of the party. These re-
formists thought that it was possible for the party to achieve
many immediate, if limited, aims and believed they could do
so without losing sight of ultimate goals. They accepted the
validity of parliamentary processes, scorning agitation for
agitation's sake. ". . . [O]ur party has a different task from
simply beating the drum. . . . When we work for the parliament, we also work for ourselves."[152] Although many of the
party leaders reacted ambiguously to the exercise of power,
thinking that the party lost strength through the acceptance
of unpopular responsibilities, some of them—for example,
Severing—were aware that the steady exercise of political

---

[148] *Sozialdemokratischer Parteitag 1927,* pp. 184–88 (emphasis in original).

[149] Eckstein (Breslau), ibid., p. 190 (emphasis in original).

[150] Antiparliamentary attitudes or rather what Lidtke properly calls "ambivalent
parliamentarism" had a long history among the Social Democrats. Lidtke, *The Outlawed Party,* pp. 149–54, 232–40, 305–19, 326–29; Michels, p. 83.

[151] Dietrich, *Sozialdemokratischer Parteitag 1927,* p. 215. However, Gustav Ferl
(Magdeburg) argued that functionaries found their work more difficult when the
SPD was not in office (pp. 188–89); Drechsler, p. 60.

[152] Breitscheid, *Sozialdemokratischer Parteitag 1925,* p. 224.

power, particularly through the control of the administration, could be very important.[153]

Both sides differed in their appraisals of the current political situation as it affected the party's future. The leaders of the party tended to emphasize the unfavorable aspects of the political climate and the precariousness of Germany's economic situation.[154] According to their estimate the SPD had relatively few viable options. "If it is possible to prevent something worse [from happening] by being in a coalition and to produce good even to a modest extent, then we have the duty to work positively within such a coalition in the interest of the laboring population." [155] If a radical course of opposition drove the Center Party into the arms of the right, they feared not only conservative national governments, but the break-up of the Weimar Coalition in Prussia.[156] They also foresaw that if the SPD once lost contact with its coalition partners, a long time might elapse before it would be able to regain a position of power even if it decided to seek a new coalition.[157]

The critics of the coalition policy were less pessimistic. They argued that the adoption of out-and-out opposition was not only feasible but the surest way to success.[158] A truly forceful policy of opposition would dispel indifference among workers and rally them in growing numbers to the party. Cautious deference to the views of the other parties, necessitated by cooperation with them, had the opposite effect. The whole party strategy should be directed toward winning voters on the left. They saw the Communists as the party's chief rivals although they recommended cooperation with the

[153] "With [any] lengthy abstinence from the business of governing one finally loses . . . close contact with the politics of the Reich and influence on the administration altogether. *Administration is often just as important as passing laws.*" Severing, 2: 80 (emphasis in original). Cf. the similar observations by Schulz, 1: 53.

[154] Hilferding, *Sozialdemokratischer Parteitag 1927*, pp. 179–82; Severing, 2: 79.

[155] Fritz Ulrich (Heilbronn), *Sozialdemokratischer Parteitag 1927*, p. 210; also Heilmann's remarks, pp. 216–17.

[156] Breitscheid, ibid., pp. 208–9. Löbe favored a vigorous opposition policy in the Reich but did not share the opinion that the coalition government in Prussia should be abandoned. Ibid., pp. 196–98.

[157] Ulrich, cited above, note 155, used the example of what happened in Württemberg as a warning. In 1920 the SPD resigned from a position of power in the hope that a period in opposition would enable it to win back some lost voters. However, the SPD's abandonment of governmental responsibilities led to a regrouping of the middle parties and ultimately the entrance of the DNVP into office. The SPD never again held power in Württemberg. Likewise, Keil, 2: 208–10.

[158] Eckstein, *Sozialdemokratischer Parteitag 1927*, pp. 189–90.

Communists on occasion. The drift of the masses toward the KPD could be stopped, they believed, by altering the general thrust of the SPD's appeal.[159]

The leaders of the party, on the other hand, argued that few gains were to be made in that direction. At least in public they tried to suggest that the Communists were not a genuine threat. In 1925, Otto Wels said:

> For us today, the position of the Communist Party is of rather secondary significance . . . That party is in the process of full dissolution . . . Now it is adopting new tricks. They know that the Communist strength is not able to pull their upset cart out of the mud. That's why they are trying to get Social Democratic help *(Vorspanndienst)*.[160]

The most fertile ground for finding new supporters, these Social Democrats thought, was among the white and blue collar followers of the middle-class parties.[161] Radical phrases would not win their support, but a positive *(sachliche)* handling of politics coupled with tangible results would.[162] "We will lead the class struggle that much better as soon as the working masses that still stand aside from us find their way to us." [163]

The debate over coalition policy was never resolved; the basic positions of those who most actively participated in the controversy could not be reconciled. Ultimately the topic lost all immediate relevance when, after 1931, the most determined left-wing socialists split away from the SPD in the face of increasingly serious tests for the party and the Republic.[164] During the mid-twenties, however, the idea of active opposition found a sympathetic hearing with many of the party members.

*   *   *   *

[159] See the remarks by Hermann Liebmann, Adolf Hoffmann, and Emil Theil, *Sozialdemokratischer Parteitag 1925,* pp. 149, 151, 170.

[160] Ibid., pp. 81–82; Scheidemann claimed that Communism was like measles and the German workers would outgrow this "children's disease." Ibid., p. 159. In 1927 Hilferding said that the KPD was losing out, that it may have picked up some votes from people driven to despair by the inflation, "but [as for] a significance for the socialist movement the Communist Party has absolutely none, it is lost!" *Sozialdemokratischer Parteitag 1927,* p. 184.

[161] Müller, ibid., pp. 9–10. Wels used this as a reason to attack the activities of the left opposition, "Don't destroy the beginnings for good, for the growth of the party and of our views by heretic hunting, by petty tattling, and by policies which would be all right for a sect but do not serve [the needs of] a party that wants to embrace the masses of the people." Ibid., p. 41.

[162] Müller, *Sozialdemokratischer Parteitag 1925,* p. 218–19.

[163] Müller, *Sozialdemokratischer Parteitag 1927,* p. 10.

[164] Hunt, *German Social Democracy,* pp. 230–37.

During the "Christmas crisis" of 1925–26, there was sufficient resistance to prevent the party leaders from concluding the coalition arrangements they themselves advocated. At the end of the last chapter we mentioned how the Social Democratic Reichstag *Fraktion* twice considered bids to form a Great Coalition government. The DDP leader, Erich Koch-Weser, observed then that "at no [previous] instance in German parliamentary history" had the Great Coalition been so achievable, yet the Social Democrats rejected it. A number of prominent figures spoke or wrote articles favoring the coalition.[165] Nevertheless, many party members refused to take notice of these well-reasoned arguments. The party's spokesmen gave various reasons to justify the decision.[166] None publicly confessed the degree of resistance which welled up inside the party at the idea of sharing power with the DVP. The basic attitudes described above, combined with a vivid memory of the bad experiences of 1923, aroused a degree of feeling the party's parliamentary leaders did not care to challenge.[167]

Early in January 1926 a meeting of Berlin party and trade union officials passed a resolution commending the *Fraktion* for refusing to form a Great Coalition and stated that they expected it to refuse its consent again if there was a new attempt to form such a government.[168] This resolution was carried despite the fact that party chairman Müller argued against it in person. From the start of the meeting Müller and his supporters had been forced to bend with the wind; [169]

[165] At the meeting of the *Parteiausschuss*, 24 Jan. 1926. DPP Papers, reel 37, folder 731, p. 3. Among those who actively argued for a Great Coalition were Braun, Severing, Scheidemann, David, and Keil.

[166] They emphasized the inadequacy of the concessions other parties were willing to make to the SPD and found fault especially with the posture taken by the DVP. For example, *Vorwärts*, 17 Dec. 1925 (Nrs. 594 and 595); Müller, *Die Gesellschaft* (1926, Nr. 1), p. 298.

[167] At the beginning of the crisis President Hindenburg met with the different party leaders. Müller and Dittmann informed him that "very strong reservations" against the Great Coalition existed among the Social Democrats because of the experience of 1923. *Vorwärts*, 7 Dec. 1925 (Nr. 577). An article in *Vorwärts*, entitled "Lessons of the Past" stated: "The Social Democrats have never forced [their way] into a government. They have only participated in it if the extreme need of the people ... demanded this sacrifice of them. They have conjured up many inner conflicts in the party by their temporary participation in the national government and many times made life truly difficult for their *functionaries* who had to defend their politics in the factories." 6 Dec. 1925 (Nr. 576; emphasis in the original).

[168] *Vorwärts*, 5 Jan. 1926 (Nr. 5).

[169] In his discussion of the current political situation he admitted that the party was right to be very cautious in undertaking the experiment of a Great Coalition.

nonetheless, the Berlin functionaries followed the recommendations of speakers closely associated with the left opposition, among others Dr. Kurt Rosenfeld and Dr. Walter Fabian.[170] The mood of the men attending the meeting was undoubtedly influenced by the question of the royal property settlements which also came up for debate.[171] Participation in the Great Coalition was debated by party organizations throughout Germany and some of them likewise passed resolutions similar to that of the Berlin meeting.[172] The significance of party regulars passing resolutions contrary to the advice of the party leadership surely must have influenced the Reichstag *Fraktion* when it rejected the Great Coalition for a second time on 12 January.[173] Paul Löbe reportedly remarked about this time, "One has to determine policy against a minority of the party; one may dare to make it against a majority of the party; one cannot do so against the entire party." [174]

The preceding discussion of the conflicting visions which the Social Democrats had of their proper role in the Republic, and the methods which the party leadership used to evade too direct a confrontation with dissident followers, should help us understand the course followed by the SPD throughout the referendum campaign of 1926. The party's policy makers could no more ignore the state of mind of the rank-and-file Social Democrats and the openly expressed views of the left opposition regarding the royal properties question, than risk affronting their prejudices against the Great Coalition. When unmistakable evidence developed during December 1925 and early January 1926 that many Social

---

"We have to guard ourselves against running into difficulties . . . such as we have already once experienced." Idem.

[170] In addition to Rosenfeld and Fabian, Künstler, Schulze, and Georg Maderholz are reported to have spoken for the resolution. Müller's views were supported by Hermes and Karl Hildenbrand. *Vorwärts*, 5 Jan. 1926 (Nr. 6).

[171] Support of a referendum was strongly advocated by Rosenfeld, Künstler, and Hoffmann. Idem. Hoffmann argued that even if the referendum failed, there would be no reason to be ashamed.

[172] For example, Stuttgart, Breslau, Greater-Leipzig, and Magdeburg. Social Democratic papers in Dresden, Frankfurt a.M., and Zwickau reportedly commended the resolution passed by the Berlin functionaries. *Geschichte der deutschen Arbeiterbewegung. Chronik*, 2: 192; Karl, p. 17.

[173] In reporting the final rejection of the Great Coalition, *Vorwärts* wrote, "In a word, we are free and will wait and see what comes." 13 Jan. 1926 (Nr. 19).

[174] Theodor Heuss (DDP), who remarked he had heard it from a number of SPD members. Reichstag. *Verhandlungen*, 388 (27 Jan. 1926): 5182.

Democrats favored confiscation, the party leaders were forced
to re-examine their earlier refusal to consider the Communist
appeal for a jointly sponsored referendum.

It is clear that the Social Democratic leaders had not taken
the initial KPD proposal seriously. The circumstances suggested a rather ordinary Communist propaganda maneuver:
the bid was timed to coincide with the first Reichstag debates
on a much more moderate legislative proposal and was publicized immediately, without any exploration of the SPD's
views beforehand. It seemed just another effort to "unmask"
the SPD leaders. *Vorwärts* remembered past experiences:
"They [the KPD] took over the command. Social Democrats,
trade unions and *Reichsbanner* had nothing to say thereafter;
[their job was] to march along behind." The newspaper continued: "It appears they imagine a joint action in which they
supply the good advice while the other partners have to give
the money and, in addition, take a beating if the undertaking
falls flat." [175]

During the first stages of the controversy when popular
concern was beginning to manifest itself but no one knew
how extensive it would become, the leaders of the SPD seem
to have believed that reminders about the well-known untrustworthiness of the Communists would keep their own
followers from being overly attracted by the radical suggestion of an initiative to confiscate the royal properties. They
certainly understood that the Communists hoped to use the
issue to build up support for strictly partisan goals of the
KPD.[176]

Members of the SPD Executive Board examined the fea-
sibility of organizing a referendum quite early in order, as a
party publication later said, "to come before the public with
a well-prepared action that promised success." [177] More truth-
fully, the party leaders were reluctant to undertake the organizational demands which a referendum campaign would
require and were also deterred by the uncertain prospect of
finding a sufficiently large base of support to ensure success.[178] On 8 December the *Vorstand* heard reports by Ernst
Heilmann on the Prussian settlement and by Wilhelm Ditt-

[175] 8 Dec. 1925 (Nr. 579).
[176] *Rote Fahne* openly admitted it, 4 Dec. 1925 and 6 Jan. 1926.
[177] *Sozialdemokratische Parteikorrespondenz . . . 1923 bis 1928*, p. 303; also, *Jahrbuch der Deutschen Sozialdemokratie . . . 1926*, pp. 6–7.
[178] *Vorwärts*, 5 Jan. (Nr. 6) and 27 Oct. 1926 (Nr. 506).

mann on the legal and financial requirements for a referendum.[179] Then, on 4 January, aware that the Kuczynski Committee was about to be formed, the *Vorstand* discussed the matter again.[180] The Executive Board decided to delay any decision concerning a referendum until the positions of the other parties regarding the Reichstag bills became clearer. It did recognize the importance of such a decision, however, by announcing that it would consult the Advisory Committee before determining party policy.

Simultaneously, Dittmann published an explanatory article in *Vorwärts* which struck a very cautious note:

> The referendum [following upon a popular] initiative is the *greatest exertion of political effort* that the Constitution knows. It requires far more expenditure in time, work, and money than a Reichstag election. Whoever wants a referendum must be able to see to it that the question which is to be decided totally occupies public attention *for two or three months*. During this period steadily increasing propagandistic activities (*Agitation*) must . . . manage [to] arouse and carry along the whole nation. Questions for which this is not possible are not suited for a referendum.[181]

Only if normal legislative methods failed to protect the people's interests, he concluded, might an appeal to the people become necessary. The article was clearly intended to cool the enthusiasm for a referendum spreading among the Social Democrats. About the same time Hermann Müller said, "With feelings and with resolutions alone nothing on this matter will be accomplished." [182]

Nonetheless, within two weeks' time the party leaders hurriedly decided to support a referendum.[183] They called a meeting of the Advisory Committee on the 19th of January even though the parties in the Reichstag had not yet completely defined their positions.[184] After much discussion, the Advisory Committee authorized the Executive Board to engage in discussions with the Communist Party and the

---

[179] According to an unsigned article "Volksbegehren—Volksentscheid. Selbständiger Kampf der Sozialdemokratie," *Vorwärts*, 9 Feb. 1926 (Nr. 65).

[180] Ibid., 5 Jan. 1926 (Nr. 6).

[181] Idem (emphasis in original).

[182] Ibid., 5 Jan. 1926 (Nr. 5). On pressures within the party for support of the initiative and referendum campaign, Heer, p. 90.

[183] *Jahrbuch . . . 1926*, p. 6.

[184] *Vorwärts*, 16 Jan. 1926 (Nr. 26). The heads of the Reichstag delegation knew very well that the representatives of the middle parties were trying to agree on a compromise bill. See below, Chapter V, p. 156.

Kuczynski Committee. A few days later the SPD announced its support of a jointly sponsored referendum, reversing the initial position it had taken only six weeks before and, even more noteworthy, abandoning a policy of no cooperation with the Communists which had been in effect since the end of 1923. These reversals were only superficially surprising, however. The Social Democratic policy-makers were acting in accordance with their customary precept: first mollify their party followers and then, if possible, try to adopt a more responsible solution.

The considerations that induced the leaders of the SPD to revise their party's position can be described reasonably accurately even though this reconstruction must be based primarily on an examination of the timing and character of the actions they took, supplemented to some extent by later explanations of their conduct. The bulk of the most reliable source materials—the records of the *Vorstand, Parteiausschuss* and Reichstag *Fraktion*—were either destroyed to prevent them from falling into the hands of the Nazis, or lost during the war.[185]

The leaders of the SPD did not want to permit the KPD to benefit by being the only party which took a strong, determined stand against the claims of the princes. They particularly did not want to leave their own followers exposed to Communist appeals at a time when the Communists were making renewed efforts to establish contact with the Social Democratic workers. Since no major elections were due in the near future—barring the dissolution of the Reichstag or the Prussian *Landtag,* which did not, in fact, occur—the heads of the SPD did not need to fear any direct loss of voters. Naturally, they wanted to guard against the KPD establishing temporary contacts with rank-and-file Social Democrats for fear it would find ways to make its influence stronger thereafter. A more immediate risk was that regular party members might transfer to the Communist Party, or at any rate cooperate with the Communists in ways the party and trade union leadership considered dangerous (united front committees in factories, friendship trips to Russia, etc.).[186] The

---

[185] See the preface by Hagen Schulze (ed.), *Anpassung oder Widerstand? Aus den Akten des Parteivorstands der deutschen Sozialdemokratie, 1932/33, Archiv für Sozialgeschichte,* Beiheft 4 (Bonn and Bad Godesberg, 1975): vii.

[186] On the visits to Russia see the comments of Wels and Stelling, *Sozialdemokratischer Parteitag 1925,* pp. 82, 107, and of Wels, *Sozialdemokratischer Parteitag 1927,*

left wing of the SPD would have been attracted to the KPD's line of approach, in part because of the idea of confiscation, but also because it utilized direct popular action. (The opposition of the Independent Social Democrats to the speedy establishment of parliamentary forms in 1919 must be remembered.)[187]

If the SPD had not co-sponsored the referendum the party might have been threatened with a new split,[188] something its leaders obviously would not allow to happen if they could prevent it. Otto Wels, speaking at the 1927 party convention, acknowledged that the leadership's decisions had been attacked from various sides. But, he went on,

> ... if they [the critics] had been in our situation they could not have acted any differently than we did. We would otherwise have had only much greater disunity (*Zersplitterung*) and the split would have gone right through the middle of the Social Democratic Party.[189]

And that was exactly what the Communists had wanted, he said. Whether or not major defections occurred, support of a more moderate course than full confiscation would have added to the already well-established body of charges which the left opposition used to damn the party leadership. Moreover, the openly avowed activity of a substantial number of party followers along lines opposed by the party leaders would have severely discredited the existing leadership both within the party and in the estimation of other parties.

By the third week of January, the leaders of the SPD were, to all intents and purposes, forced to accept the KPD's renewed proposal for joint action.[190] The Communists appeared entirely willing to undertake initiative and referendum proceedings with the aid of the Kuczynski Committee if the

---

pp. 40–41; *Geschichte der deutschen Arbeiterbewegung. Chronik*, 2: 181–82, 199. On the activities of the *Internationale Arbeiter Hilfe* (IAH) see Gruber, *Journal of Modern History*, 38: 284–87.

[187] Ryder, pp. 156–59, 167–71, 220–23.

[188] See the comments of *Germania* with particular reference to the Saxon Conflict as precedent, 15 April 1926 (Nr. 173).

[189] *Sozialdemokratischer Parteitag 1927*, p. 29.

[190] In this case, the statement of the regional organization of the KPD in Berlin may be accepted as generally correct: "The Social Democratic Party functionaries and members took, on the other hand, a substantially different position from that of the leadership and favored the referendum promoted by the Communists. The opposition inside the SPD was increased even more by the openly expressed inclination of the SPD leaders to enter the government again on the basis of a Great Coalition." *Bericht der Bezirksleitung der KPD Berlin-Brandenburg-Lausitz . . .* , p. 15.

Social Democrats persisted in rejecting all collaboration.[191] By formally applying to the ministry of interior on 18 January for authorization to start the initiative process, the Communists showed that they were now serious and did not intend to satisfy themselves with a cheap propaganda victory. This is surely the reason the SPD Advisory Committee was hastily convened. No one dared to ignore the prospect of severe difficulties if the party officially continued to stay aloof from the referendum movement. The Social Democratic leaders knew that the best way to control their followers in such situations was to lead them the way they wanted to go. (The participation of Ebert and others in the great January strike of 1918 set an example, if one were needed.)[192] In any case, it would have played into the Communists' hands to have refused to consider their proposition a second time. *Vorwärts* later wrote that they would have been "able to propagandize against the SPD for years to come" if the Social Democrats had not surprised them by accepting.[193]

It appears very likely that the Social Democratic leaders, being well-informed politicians, never expected that the referendum would succeed.[194] The combined KPD-SPD vote in the last Reichstag election had been a little over ten and one-half million, while passage of the measure required some twenty million "yes" votes. The Social Democratic leadership briefly considered starting a separate initiative and referendum movement on a less radical measure that would have confiscated the former rulers' properties but allowed them some compensation.[195] Such a proposal would have been in accord with numerous previous statements made by Social Democrats and probably could have also been backed by the Center Party and the Democrats.[196] Nevertheless, the leaders

[191] *Rote Fahne,* 21 Jan. 1926.
[192] Ryder, pp. 116–19.
[193] *Vorwärts,* 15 Oct. 1926 (Nr. 487).
[194] "Today it should and must be said that this referendum was no practical means to produce a real solution." Idem.
[195] Ibid., 16 Jan. 1926 (Nr. 26); Stampfer, p. 445.
[196] Prussia. *Sitzungsberichte der verfassunggebend Preussischen Landesversammlung 1919–1921,* 8: 10285 (Drucksache 2048); ibid., 11: 14237 (Drucksache 3415). On this occasion, 30 Nov. 1920, the Social Democratic spokesman, Heilmann, stated, "We do not envisage treating the question [of the compensation for] the Hohenzollerns in a petty or spiteful manner." Ibid., p. 14242. Also *Sozialdemokratischer Parteitag 1925,* p. 316, and *Rote Fahne,* 13 Feb. 1926, reporting a comment by a SPD member of the Reichstag's Legal Committee. *Frankfurter Zeitung,* 21 June 1926 (Nr. 454); *Germania,* 27 Jan. 1926 (Nr. 43); Braun, p. 215.

foresaw that two rival referendum measures would have destroyed any chance for the passage of either, and made their position vis-à-vis their own more radical followers uncomfortable, to say the least.[197]

The Social Democratic leaders felt obliged to join in backing the Communist-formulated referendum project in order to satisfy their own supporters, just as they had thought it necessary to run a separate candidate in the first presidential election. No doubt they also expected to derive some residual profit from the expenditure of great efforts in a campaign doomed to fail. If the state of aroused and angry public opinion were heightened by the campaign, they believed the parties of the middle and right would be compelled to pass stronger legislation than they otherwise might have sanctioned.[198] The Social Democratic leaders, having already made the decision not to become a governing party, wanted to use their strong position outside the government together with the organized weight of public opinion to force the weak, newly-formed minority coalition to make as many concessions as possible. From the point of view of the SPD's leaders, there were no compelling reasons by mid-January why they should continue to reject co-sponsorship of the referendum while there were many apparent advantages in supporting it, especially since the decision to favor the referendum's confiscation proposal *did not* involve abandonment of efforts to influence the outcome of more moderate Reichstag legislation.[199] Thus the SPD became the only party supporting both the referendum and some kind of legislative solution.

Neither did the commitment bind the party to numerous close and unwanted associations with the Communists. The negotiators for the SPD insisted on a precisely worded agreement defining the extent of joint responsibilities and actions as a condition for the acceptance of the referendum pro-

---

[197] *Sozialdemokratische Parteikorrespondenz . . . 1923 bis 1928,* p. 304.

[198] Even before the final decision to support the referendum was made, *Vorwärts* headlined the report of a large public meeting against the princes' claims, "A Warning for the Reichstag" *Vorwärts,* 18 Jan. 1926 (Nr. 28). Also, Kurt Rosenfeld's article, "Die Fürsten und die Reichstag," ibid., 27 Feb. 1926 (Nr. 98).

[199] The party leadership, in an obvious effort to answer current criticism, explained that even though the SPD was fighting with all its might for the referendum, there were sound reasons for seeking improvements in the Reichstag bill—that there was no point in leaving the parliamentary work in the hands of agents of the former rulers. Vorstand der Sozialdemokratische Partei, *Referentenmaterial zur Fürstenabfindung,* p. 7.

posal.[200] The terms of partnership could scarcely have been
more restricted: the parties were to split the costs of the
necessary petitions and formal notices for the initiative and
referendum; they would make arrangements for the proper
distribution of the required material and attempt to avoid
duplicating each other's work, but "all propaganda, meetings,
demonstrations and other arrangements . . . [were] to be
carried out independently by the single corpora-
tions. . . ." [201] Throughout the campaign the SPD leadership
constantly reiterated warnings to local party organizations or
members not to let themselves be tempted by the KPD's
United Front appeals.

Despite the many pressures upon them, the leaders of the
SPD must have thought that they had set a relatively open
course of action which would permit them to make appropriate adjustments to circumstances as the debate over the
properties question advanced over the next few months. It
did, in fact, enable them to avoid major dissension within
the party until after the referendum was over. The Center
and Democratic press, however, expressed nervous concern
over the way the SPD had considered only its own interest.[202]
Both of these republican parties had wanted to cooperate
with the SPD, but through its refusal to join the Great Coalition and by its abrupt acceptance of the Communists' suggestion for a referendum they were left quite isolated. Yet
they were burdened with the major responsibility for leading
the forthcoming legislative battles with the right, battles in
whose outcome the SPD was as much interested as they. A
strong tone of warning crept into editorial statements.[203] *Germania* wrote in mid-January that ". . . the concessions that

[200] The text of the agreement was printed by *Rote Fahne*, 27 Jan. 1926. See, too,
the resolution passed by the SPD *Parteiausschuss* on 19 Jan. *Frankfurter Zeitung*, 20
Jan. 1926 (Nr. 51).

[201] *Rote Fahne*, 27 Jan. 1926. For explanations why such limited cooperation was
necessary, *Vorwärts*, 9 Feb. 1926 (Nr. 65) and *Jahrbuch . . . 1926*, pp. 7–8.

[202] *Germania*, 11 Dec. (Nr. 578), and 17 Dec. 1925 (Nr. 588), 13 Jan. (Nr. 19), 27
Jan. (Nr. 43), and 6 Feb. 1926 (Nr. 62); *Rhein-Mainische Volkszeitung*, 4 Feb. 1926;
Frankfurter Zeitung, 9 Feb. 1926 (Nr. 106), reporting views expressed at the DDP's
provincial convention in Pomerania. Even the *Deutsche Allgemeine Zeitung*, which had
DVP connections, commented, "This is the second serious mistake the Social Dem-
ocratic Party has made in a short time." 26 Jan. 1926 (Nr. 39/40).

[203] Already at the beginning of the "Christmas crisis" Koch-Weser had warned:
"If the Social Democratic Party wants to hold itself in reserve until it has a majority
by itself, then the middle parties will have to set up resistance to such a change of
course." Protocol of the *Parteitag* in Breslau, 5 Dec. 1925. DDP Papers, reel 37,
folder 739, p. 70.

the middle parties were unable to make if the Social Democrats shared [power] responsibly *can be considered less than ever* if the Social Democrats stand outside." It went on to observe that *Vorwärts* had written that the SPD was not opposed to coalitions on principle. "It will now depend upon . . . the Social Democrats not assuming a posture outside the government that would make them finally unsuited for coalitions *(koalitionsunfähig)*." [204] Two days later it returned to the same theme: the Center Party supported the new minority coalition of the middle parties out of a sense of responsibility for the nation. In doing so, however, it had not "issued to the wing parties outside the coalition a *license for an unrestrained policy of agitation.*" [205] The tensions between the SPD and its sometime Weimar Coalition partners were thus fated to increase, particularly as spreading enthusiasm for the referendum campaign began to set important groups within these two parties against the policies of their leaders.

[204] *Germania,* 18 Jan. 1926 (Nr. 28; emphasis in original).

[205] Ibid., 20 Jan. 1926 (Nr. 31; emphasis in original). Koch-Weser's observations to the DDP *Parteiausschuss* were remarkably similar: he commented on how the resistance of the SPD had blocked the formation of a Great Coalition. "And yet [the Social Democrats] would have been able to obtain economic and financial advantages which would have been much greater than the discomforts *(Unbequemlichkeiten)* of the Great Coalition. . . . The Social Democrats would have played an extraordinarily significant role in it. They have not wanted it and explained their aversion in various different ways. Their great failing has been that they did not have the courage to step into responsibility at this time." He added that the Social Democrats were now coming to rather like being in opposition, since it allowed them to make sensational propagandistic gestures. Koch admitted that such displays might be nice, but termed them politically "meaningless." "So it stands with the princely settlements. . . . If the Social Democrats were in the government then a compromise on this question could be made within the government that was even more unfavorable for the princes than now where the provisions have to be traded about among the middle parties." DDP Papers, reel 37, folder 731, pp. 3–4.

V: The Dilemma of the Middle Parties: Could the Reichstag Find an Alternative to the Initiative Proposal? January–March, 1926

The following chapters will describe the response of the various parties to the initiative and referendum campaign and simultaneously trace the developments in the battle for parliamentary regulation of the royal property claims. Although the initiative and referendum were carried on altogether separately from the parliamentary discussions, actually the temporarily successful progress of the one directly influenced the pace and content of the other. It is possible to distinguish three periods in which intensive attempts were made to resolve party differences in order to permit passage of Reichstag legislation *before June 20,* the date of the referendum. In each period negotiations reached a peak of activity (and then broke down) *just preceding* a key stage in the progress of the initiative and referendum campaign.

The first series of interparty negotiations was concentrated around the first of March, just before the official dates for the signing of the initiative petitions (4–17 March). The second build-up of compromise efforts occurred in mid-April, just before the Reichstag was to debate the confiscation proposal submitted to it as a result of the successful initiative campaign. A third set of interparty negotiations took place just prior to the referendum itself; but since by then only negligible prospects for rapid Reichstag action existed, the

140

efforts made to reach a generally acceptable agreement were less intense than on the two previous occasions. For two weeks after 20 June, a fourth and final set of efforts was made to reach legislative agreement, but, although the referendum had failed, the very strength of the "yes" vote made parliamentary compromise impossible. Whatever opportunity for a legislative solution by the Reichstag that may have existed earlier had now been lost.

Admirers of initiative and referendum proceedings once argued that this form of legislation was superior to law-making through a representative body, because it permitted the direct expression of the will of the people, eliminating the distortion always possible through the use of intermediaries.[1] More recently, it has been recognized that such arguments rest on rather too simplified a view of how the popular will is formed.[2] The more "direct" methods of a referendum do not necessarily guarantee that the popular will will be accurately expressed. Like any other institution of government a referendum can be subject to abuse; it can be manipulated to suit the purposes of a particular party or the desires of special interest groups. Even if these dangers are avoided, certain difficulties peculiar to the initiative and referendum restrict their overall usefulness. Any proposal submitted to the entire voting public must be reasonably simple and deal with a matter of general interest, otherwise the voters are unlikely to respond in sufficient numbers to produce a valid result.[3] Moreover, the initial formulation of a referendum proposal has crucial importance not necessarily present in

[1] Agnes Headlam-Morley, *The New Democratic Constitutions of Europe* (London, 1928), pp. 132–47, and A. L. Lowell, *Public Opinion and Popular Government* (New York, 1926), pp. 152–235, provide informative introductions to the theory and practice of direct democracy as it was understood in the 1920s. William B. Munro, "Initiative and Referendum," *Encyclopedia of the Social Sciences* (New York, 1932), 8: 51–52, concentrates its attention on developments in the United States. All three have bibliographies listing the older literature.

[2] Hermann Finer, *Theory and Practice of Modern Government* (revised ed.; New York, 1949), pp. 560–68. His rather critical appraisal of the usefulness of initiatives and referenda stems in large part from an examination of how they were misused during the Weimar Republic. Carl J. Friedrich, *Constitutional Government and Democracy* (revised ed.; Boston, 1950), pp. 555–57, 570–71, takes a somewhat more favorable view.

Since the 1950s political scientists have turned their attention in other directions and the discussion of the problems of direct legislation has virtually disappeared from current surveys of political science. The *International Encyclopedia of the Social Sciences* (17 vols.; New York, 1968) has no entry for Initiative and Referendum.

[3] Richard Thoma, "Sinn und Gestaltung des deutschen Parlamentarismus," in Bernhard Harms, ed., *Recht und Staat im Neuen Deutschland* (Berlin, 1929),1: 114.

parliamentary legislation.[4] The first draft of a normal legislative bill can be amended as it progresses through the various
stages of parliamentary discussion. Political compromise, the
accommodation of initially divergent views, is thus constantly
possible. Once a referendum measure has been submitted to
the public, however, the voters can only accept or reject the
measure offered them. There is no way for them to modify
the proposal to their greater liking. Compromises, if any, are
possible only among the sponsors of the referendum before
they announce their intentions. In effect, the first draft of a
referendum proposal must also be its final draft.[5]

The slower and more complicated forms of parliamentary
negotiation are clearly advantageous in dealing with intricate
legislative problems.[6] They also permit changes responsive
to public opinion if it alters during the course of a prolonged
controversy; a referendum vote simply reflects the weight of
greater or fewer numbers. Moreover, parliamentary practice
takes into account the existence of political parties, whereas
referenda in principle ignore or even attempt to supplant
them.[7] Realistically, of course, no referendum is organized
by "the people" themselves. Parties or important interest
groups are bound to be involved in the sponsorship of major
initiative and referendum campaigns.

The difficulties inherent in the functioning of any referendum become particularly conspicuous when these forms
of direct democracy are combined with an established multi-
party system. With seven or eight major parties in existence
in the Weimar Republic, political activity was shaped to a
large degree by the parties' determination to maintain their
distinct identities. A referendum, by its very formulation compelling a "yes" or "no" answer, unavoidably disrupted the

[4] Weber, *Gesammelte Politische Schriften*, pp. 386–87; Lowell, pp. 219–20.

[5] The Weimar Constitution foresaw that the Reichstag might choose to amend a
proposed measure submitted to it as a result of a popular initiative. If it did so,
however, both the original and amended versions must be submitted to the people
in a referendum. In fact this never occurred. Thomas, *Journal of Comparative Legislation
and International Law*, 10: 57.

[6] Weber, *Gesammelte Politische Schriften*, pp. 278–79; Lowell, pp. 159–61.

[7] Even an expert such as Richard Thoma, writing in 1929, thought this a particular
virtue of referenda. "Perhaps nowhere so much as in Germany do the parties and
the *Fraktionen* incline toward a certain rigidity in their organization, their leadership
and their party doctrines. An initiative which freely stemmed from the body of
citizens (*der Gesellschaft*), a referendum which presented the citizen with a single yes
or no [decision] uninfluenced by his party ties, might be very healthy from time to
time." In *Recht und Staat im Neuen Deutschland*, 1: 114.

normal balance of party relationships. It forced the parties into unwanted associations and produced sharply felt strains inside those parties whose followers were not all of one mind. At first, a clear division between the "middle-class" and the "proletarian" parties seemed to exist concerning the initiative and referendum proposal. Only the KPD and SPD directed their voters to sign the initiative petitions; all the other significant parties (the DNVP, DVP, BVP, the *Wirtschaftliche Vereinigung,* the Center, and the DDP) issued statements officially opposing the initiative. However, some of the parties, particularly the Center and DDP, found to their dismay that many of their followers were dissatisfied with this order and would not obey it. By the time the referendum occurred, the Democrats tried to avoid grave party disunity by not issuing an official statement of policy. They left each member free to choose for himself how to vote. The Center, too, was troubled by dissidents, but the leaders of the party held steadfastly to the position that confiscation without compensation constituted an unacceptable violation of legal and moral principles. Nevertheless, as time went on, they found it necessary to distinguish the grounds for the Center Party's opposition to the referendum from the too openly reactionary line adopted by the parties of the right. The KPD and SPD gained the support of numerous middle-class voters for the referendum, but no new formal allies. On the other hand, the right's hope of creating a solid middle-class front against "Bolshevism" failed.

The referendum had very little chance of success. The procedures established for the use of the initiative *(Volksbegehren)* and referendum *(Volksentscheid)* had been made complicated in order to discourage irresponsible misuse.[8] Individuals or organizations wishing to start initiative proceedings were required to notify the ministry of interior and submit a proposal suitably worded for enactment.[9] If the proponents satisfied certain general requirements, the minister of interior then officially set a two-week period for the signing of the initiative petitions. German procedure did not allow the free circulation of petitions by the sponsoring or-

[8] Oppenheimer, p. 149; Schiffers, pp. 200–203; Milatz, pp. 53–57; Stehkämper, 2: 308.

[9] Thoma, *Journal of Comparative Legislation and International Law,* 10: 56; Anschütz, p. 389.

ganizations with which we are familiar in American states.[10]
Specially designated registration offices under proper governmental supervision must be established in each locality.
Citizens were required to go to one of these offices in order
to sign the initiative petitions. During the 1926 campaign
there were numerous complaints that there were not enough
offices, that they were sometimes hard to find, or that they
were open only at hours inconvenient for working people.[11]
A much more serious problem developed in rural areas and
in small towns. Voters who may have wanted to participate
in the initiative and referendum hesitated to go to the registration or voting places out of fear of being identified and
then suffering reprisals from their employers or important
customers.[12]

For an initiative measure to succeed, one-tenth of the qualified voters (approximately four million) must sign the lists.[13]
If this total was obtained the measure then must be submitted
to the Reichstag. If the Reichstag passed the measure, no
further consultation of the popular will was necessary; however, if the Reichstag rejected it, the proposal still must be
submitted to the people in a referendum.[14] In cases where
the proposal under consideration involved a constitutional
change, as the confiscation proposal did, one-half of all qualified voters, not simply a majority of those voting, must approve it.[15] This requirement was itself a major hindrance for
any sponsoring group. In 1926 there were roughly forty million qualified voters in Germany; therefore at least twenty

[10] Oppenheimer, p. 150; Anschütz, p. 393, note 1.
[11] During the course of the initiative, speakers for the SPD and KPD in the
Reichstag cited many cases of negligence or deliberate obstruction. After some
debate the Reichstag passed a resolution calling upon the government to ensure
that the initiative was carried out without any official hindrance. Reichstag. *Verhandlungen*, 339 (6 March 1926), 6017ff. The minister of interior then issued orders
against any administrative chicanery. *Frankfurter Zeitung*, 9 March 1926 (Nr. 181).
[12] The press reported cases where influential landowners and conservative local
officials attempted to prevent voters from participating in the initiative process. For
example, Graf Schack, a member of the DNVP, issued a statement in his locality
(*Kreis* Strehlen in Central Silesia) that "through inspection of the lists it will be
possible to determine who participated in this 'crude robbery' and 'plundering of
private property.'" *Frankfurter Zeitung*, 6 March 1926 (Nr. 173). Schüren, pp. 114–
20.
[13] Thoma, *Journal of Comparative Legislation and International Law*, 10: 56; Anschütz,
p. 388.
[14] Anschütz, pp. 389, 393.
[15] Thoma, *Journal of Comparative Legislation and International Law*, 10: 57; Anschütz,
p. 388.

million "yes" votes were necessary for such a referendum to pass. Normal voter participation in regular elections during the Weimar period ran between 70 and 80 percent; half the total participation in the last Reichstag election would have been approximately fifteen million. The extra five million were in effect a built-in cushion for the opponents of the referendum movement. Furthermore, the parties which opposed the referendum proposal did not have to run the risk that some of their supporters might cast "yes" votes in the privacy of the polling place. By ordering their followers to abstain from voting, they accomplished the same result as voting against the measure, and at the same time, especially in smaller localities, created an opportunity for intimidating yet other voters. Finally, even if sufficient votes were cast in the referendum, the proposal would have become law only when promulgated by the president. Normally this would have been a simple formality, but given Hindenburg's views it is quite likely he would have preferred to provoke a constitutional crisis rather than sign into law a bill dispossessing his former sovereign.[16]

However clearly realistic observers may have foreseen that the referendum campaign would not succeed, once it had started party leaders found that they could neither ignore it, nor treat it as a matter of secondary importance.[17] As sponsors of the confiscation proposal the Communists and Social Democrats were obliged to devote the bulk of their activities to its support. The other parties would have preferred to reject confiscation by a few neat references to the sanctity of property rights or similar slogans, but discovered all too often

[16] In March 1926, he refused to sign a law amending the rules of military justice (*Gesetz zur Vereinfachung des Militarstrafrechts*) because he disapproved of the way it punished duelling. *Vossische Zeitung*, 10 April (Nr. 86) and 13 April 1926 (Nr. 88). He claimed it violated the Constitution by imposing special penalties on one class of citizens, in this case, army officers. The government ultimately amended the bill to meet his objections. Hubatsch, pp. 234–35.

Other possible consequences in addition to the resignation of the president were foreseen by the writer of the confidential memorandum in the DDP Papers (reel 38, folder 759, p. 8). Some state governments (Bavaria, for instance) quite probably would have refused to permit the execution of such a law in their territories or some state legislatures might have circumvented the law by returning the confiscated properties to their former rulers.

[17] *Kölnische Zeitung*, 26 Jan. 1926 (Nr. 67); *Deutsche Allgemeine Zeitung*, 26 Jan. 1926 (Nr. 39/40); *Frankfurter Zeitung*, reporting comments by DDP representatives Hermann Dietrich, 9 March (Nr. 180), and its own editorial comments, 28 April 1926 (Nr. 313); Hoepker-Aschoff at the DDP *Parteiausschuss* meeting, 10 March 1926. DDP Papers, reel 37, folder 731, p. 9.

that their own followers took the referendum very seriously indeed. The totally unexpected degree of mass support for confiscation without compensation, even among "respectable" social groups that usually voted for middle-class parties, became a prime factor in German domestic politics during the spring of 1926. Politicians grew more and more preoccupied with the question of how they could cope with a public response that threatened to rupture the normal allegiances of many voters and discredit their own authority as party spokesmen. Increasingly the tactics of some key parties were oriented toward minimizing the harm the controversy was doing. Other considerations, even important ones, had to be pushed aside. In the following chapters much of the narrative will deal with the progress (or rather lack of it!) of the parliamentary legislation; however, the reader should not lose sight of the way the initiative and referendum movement acted as both the prime stimulator and a major impediment to developments in the parliamentary sphere.

Constitutional lawyers have usually considered the use of the initiative and referendum as an *alternative* to parliamentary processes.[18] Undoubtedly there are times when the consultation of the popular will by a direct vote is appropriate. However, the German referendum of 1926 was conducted *simultaneously* with efforts to reach a parliamentary solution. The result was that neither of these legitimate channels of decision-making could function properly, because the political combinations necessary to produce a legislative solution were blocked by the conflicting demands of the referendum. The referendum proposal, for all its popular backing, was too radical to attract enough support to be certain of passing. It was, therefore, regarded by all the parties as a demonstrative gesture, whatever they said publicly. Some parties hoped that popular feeling aroused by the referendum campaign would force the Reichstag to act more stringently than it otherwise would have done. This proved to be an illusionary expectation. Several parties wanted to avoid putting their voters' reliability to too great a test, and tried hard to find a parliamentary solution which would render the popular vote unnecessary. Other parties, foreseeing that the referendum

[18] Speakers for the republican majority in the Weimar National Assembly justified the processes of direct democracy on these grounds. Germany. *Verhandlungen der verfassungsgebenden Deutschen Nationalversammlung.* Koch (DDP), 327: 1345–46; Dr. Quarck (SPD), ibid., pp. 1357–58 and 336: 312.

would not pass, preferred to delay making any legislative compromise until the tide of popular agitation had subsided. Thus the best opportunities for reaching a generally acceptable law through parliamentary action were neglected, because the various parties were not only pursuing different aims, but were following different strategies for realizing those aims.[19]

The parties' views regarding regulatory legislation showed much greater variety than the policies they adopted concerning the initiative and referendum. The Communists regarded any solution other than confiscation with no compensation as a betrayal of the people's interests and therefore rejected all the suggested legislative proposals. Monarchist sentiments were strong in the DNVP and BVP. Basically neither party wanted to see any regulatory controls placed on the property settlements, but for tactical reasons their representatives in the Reichstag sometimes suggested that they might approve restrictions on some of the more extreme claims that had not yet been adjudicated.[20] The two chief middle parties, the Center and the People's Party, started from a relatively conservative point of view, trying to treat the question primarily as a legal one. When it became obvious how strong public discontent was, their parliamentary spokesmen admitted that not all of the princes' old "legal" rights were still justifiable and showed some willingness to consider certain other restrictions on the settlements. However, these parties, especially the DVP, refused to accept the contention that the problem was essentially a political one. There was a clear limit to how far they would go in order to win the support of the SPD. We have already described how the Democratic Party was the first to advocate national legislation. When it became apparent that most of the parties would not accept their proposal, representatives of the DDP joined with members of the other middle parties in lengthy negotiations and tried to convince them that they should write rigorous controls into the "Compromise" legislation. The Social Democrats indicated that they were will-

[19] Baron Hartmann von Richthofen, the DDP's chief representative on the Reichstag Legal Committee, later commented on how the initiative and referendum movement undercut parliamentary work on regulatory legislation. *Zehn Jahre Deutsche Republik*, pp. 295–98.
[20] On the DNVP's preference for the tactics of delay and abstention rather than out-and-out opposition, see Dorr, p. 241.

ing to "improve" the parliamentary proposals. Accordingly they made a large number of far-reaching demands, even though they still continued to back the referendum. Experienced politicians expected the SPD to support a suitable Reichstag bill; whether they would do so before the referendum, or wait until after, remained unclear for some time.

It was hard to reconcile such divergent views, particularly since even informed opinion within many of the parties varied over details of the legislation. Groups that did not accept the positions adopted by their party's Reichstag representatives tried to gain new modifications more to their liking. The policy followed by Chancellor Luther and his cabinet did nothing to give order to the welter of opinions in the parties. Indeed, quite clearly Luther's intention was to allow the parties in the Reichstag to wear themselves out and then intervene with an authoritative decision.

Clear partisan positions were difficult to maintain. Each party was compelled to formulate and defend two quite different positions concerning the royal properties issue, one regarding the referendum, the other on the proposed Reichstag legislation. The application of basic principles in a situation that abounded in conflicting moral and legal claims required considerable dexterity. Moreover, since in some cases very different viewpoints existed in one and the same party, the practical difficulty of reconciling these views in a single harmonious statement of goals slowed the articulation of clear party positions. The longer a major party delayed issuing a definitive statement of policy the more likely individual party members were to follow their own judgment. Under pressure some party leaders ended by issuing policy guidelines which were palpable compromises. Others pursued rather complex policies, the purpose of which escaped the understanding of unsophisticated party members. Confronted by protests, party leaders repeated their set explanations but saw less and less automatic acceptance of their "official" views; a crisis of confidence between party leaders and their followers was clearly developing.

In summary, the positions adopted by the various parties, 1) regarding the referendum campaign and, 2) regarding the parliamentary regulation of the matter can be schematized as follows:

1) Official positions taken on the initiative and referendum:

Supported both	Opposed both	Opposed the initiative but in the referendum left the decision up to each individual member
KPD, SPD	DVP, DNVP BVP, WV, Center	DDP

2) Positions adopted concerning Reichstag legislation:

Opposed to anything except confiscation without compensation	Favored legislation "if strong enough" but without making any express commitments	Most interested in passage of regulatory legislation; favored relatively rigorous treatment of princes' claims
KPD	SPD	DDP, the Center (after the initiative)

Interested to some extent in passage of moderate legislation		Not really interested in any Reich legislation, but adopted bargaining positions during legislative discussions
DVP, WV, the Center (before the initiative)		DNVP, BVP

Given a sharp variance in attitudes toward the property rights of the princes, it would have been difficult to reach a workable legislative compromise even if the referendum campaign had not been in progress. The necessity of obtaining a two-thirds majority, mandatory for legislation involving a constitutional change, created intractable problems for any parliamentary solution.[21] Even if the SPD joined with the middle parties in voting for regulatory legislation, the cooperation of at least some Nationalists would still have been necessary for the measure to pass. Finding a compromise acceptable to such a large portion of the party spectrum would have been a parliamentary achievement of some mag-

[21] Political calculations for somehow finding a two-thirds majority were discussed very frequently. For example, the "Vertraulich" memorandum, DDP Papers, reel 38, folder 759, pp. 5–7; *Frankfurter Zeitung,* 22 and 24 June 1926 (Nrs. 456 and 462); Karl Anton Schulte, "Die Auseinandersetzung mit den ehemals regierenden Fürsten," *Politisches Jahrbuch 1926,* p. 527; and a report from Undersecretary of Interior Zweigert to the Reich chancellor's office, 5 Feb. 1926. Reichskanzlei. "Akten betreffend ver-mögensrechtliche Auseinandersetzung mit den früher regierenden Fürstenhäusern. Alte Reichskanzlei. *Kais. Haus* 2." Band 1, RK507, now at the *Bundesarchiv* in Koblenz. Items in this set of documents will hereafter be identified by the short title reference: Bundesarchiv, "Auseinandersetzung."

nitude. Nevertheless, it seems likely that some sort of legislation would have been accepted because of the great scandal caused by the more outrageous princely claims.[22] However, since the SPD persevered in its decision to cosponsor the referendum with the KPD, its relations with the other parties became more tenuous and a situation developed in which no sufficiently wide area of agreement could be found.

Once the SPD decided to support the referendum it adopted a rather reserved attitude toward the various proposals for regulatory legislation. Although the Social Democrats kept the door open for possible future cooperation in the passage of such legislation,[23] they did not participate as active partners in the interparty negotiations which undertook to hammer out a generally acceptable compromise. All parties, of course, took part in the meetings of the Reichstag's Legal Committee where the various bills were discussed in detail; but the hard work of drafting several different versions of a compromise bill was left to representatives from the middle parties. Rather characteristically, leaders of the SPD Reichstag delegation made arrangements so that they would be kept informed about the content of these discussions without accepting any responsibility for the outcome of the negotiations. Their tactics were quite obvious. They clearly expected that if the other parties wanted a definitive regulation of the properties question they would recognize Social Democratic aid as indispensable and then write a bill sufficiently rigorous to win SPD support.

Although the SPD did not participate in the interparty negotiations concerning the formulation of regulatory legislation, the other parties knew its most important demands. The Social Democratic press and speakers in the Legal Committee readily identified the "inadequacies" of various proposals while recommending new improvements.[24] The "wait-

[22] This was the opinion of the very well-informed Catholic editor, academician, and politician, Georg Schreiber, *Politisches Jahrbuch 1926*, p. 68. See, too, the editorial comments of the *Kölnische Zeitung*, 21 Feb. 1926 (Nr. 138) and Thoma, *Journal of Comparative Legislation and International Law*, 10: 58.

[23] Hermann Müller's remarks in the Reichstag. *Verhandlungen*, 388 (27 Jan. 1926): 5157–58 and Dr. Rosenfeld's comments to the Legal Committee, *Frankfurter Zeitung*, 5 Feb. 1926 (Nr. 94).

[24] For example, *Vorwärts*, 6 Feb. (Nr. 61), 27 Feb. (Nr. 98), 12 March (Nr. 119), and 24 April 1926 (Nr. 191), and the remarks by Dr. Rosenfeld at sessions of the Legal Committee, *Frankfurter Zeitung*, 19 Feb. (Nr. 132), 25 Feb. (Nr. 148), and 21 April 1926 (Nr. 293).

and-see" approach adopted by the SPD offered it several apparent advantages. Social Democrats were spared the necessity of playing a leading role in the interparty negotiations, one which otherwise would have been natural due to the party's size and the strong interest its leaders had expressed in blocking the excessive claims of the princes. Such a role would have been awkward as long as the party was supporting the referendum campaign. The Communists surely would have used the inevitable parliamentary compromises as grounds for subjecting the leaders of the SPD to renewed charges of betraying the interests of the people. The "wait-and-see" attitude also appeared to increase the SPD's bargaining position with the middle parties. The longer the SPD refused to commit itself, the more it could insist on important concessions. Crispien was later to defend the actions of the Reichstag delegation at a meeting of party functionaries in Berlin. "[W]e observed the old Social Democratic tactic of improving the law as much as possible without thereby committing ourselves on the final vote." [25]

Due to the calculated reserve of the SPD, the main work of establishing an acceptable common proposal fell upon members of the middle parties which were supporting the existing Luther (later Marx) government, with the addition of a representative from the small group of middle class splinter parties, the *Wirtschaftliche Vereinigung*.[26] The work of reaching a compromise was deliberately left *to the parties*; the cabinet itself avoided taking responsibility for the outcome of these negotiations as long as possible. Only at quite a late point (30 April 1926) was the compromise proposal declared a government bill. Since the parties actively engaged in these negotiations (DDP, Center, DVP, BVP, WV) did not control a potential majority in the Reichstag, their representatives obviously knew that any agreement they might reach would be tentative.[27] Even if they made a successful compromise among themselves and submitted a joint legislative proposal, they knew that they would have to find still further support

[25] *Vorwärts*, 7 July 1926 (Nr. 314).
[26] The *Wirtschaftliche Vereinigung* (WV) was a parliamentary association of the *Wirtschaftspartei*, the *Bayerischer Bauernbund*, and the *Deutsch-Hannoversche Partei* between 1924–28 in order to attain *Fraktion* status. Schumacher, *Bredt*, pp. 176–77.
[27] Consider Karl Anton Schulte's description of the difficult negotiations leading to the second version of the Compromise and his admonition that it ought to be accepted by the Reichstag without *essential* changes. "Das Kompromiss," *Germania*, 10 March 1926 (Nr. 116); Kahl, *Deutsche Juristen-Zeitung*, 31: 1058.

before their bill could pass. In order to win this support, significant new alterations in the proposal would probably be necessary, yet major changes almost certainly would be unacceptable to one or more of the original parties to the compromise. This awareness hindered the process of agreement even among the middle parties. The *Fraktionen* refused to give firm commitments to support the proposals worked out by their own representatives.[28]

Other difficulties impeded the efforts of the middle parties to arrive at a generally acceptable legislative solution. Even among the five participating parties views on how to handle the disputed claims varied widely. The balance of opinion among them, particularly during the first few months, was rather more favorable to the princes than in the Reichstag as a whole. Only the Democratic Party stood firmly for strong curbs on the princes' claims. Although the other middle parties gradually adopted positions that took at least some account of the popular protests against a strictly judicial determination of the princes' claims, they did so slowly and, in the case of the BVP and DVP, very reluctantly. Furthermore, the composition of the small interparty negotiating committee that carried on the bulk of the discussions formulating the various versions of the Compromise Bill showed a noticeable predominance of conservative views.[29] The views of the left were decidedly underrepresented; here, too, we see a significant consequence of the SPD's actions.

Under these circumstances it proved difficult to resolve a number of disputed points, especially whether the arbitration court should be composed entirely of trained jurists or should have a strong lay element, the guidelines that would be set for the determination of contested claims, whether to allow re-examination of previously settled cases, etc. The first so-called "Compromise Bill," actually a totally new bill substituted for the original DDP proposal, later underwent major revision and reappeared in three ever-expanded versions without finding support from enough parties to ensure its passage. The middle parties could not even agree on whether they should look more to the left or to the right for the votes

[28] See below, p. 170.
[29] The members were Schulte and Wegmann for the Center; Wunderlich, Kempkes and Kahl for the DVP; Pfleger for the BVP; Hampe for the WV; and von Richthofen and Brodauf for the DDP. (Only the two Democrats favored very far-reaching legislation.) Schulte, *Politisches Jahrbuch 1926*, p. 495, note 1.

they needed.[30] The question of where and how to obtain additional support remained unresolved until finally all efforts to get a law through the Reichstag were abandoned. The following pages will describe in some detail the various proposals, counter-proposals, and amendments made during these interparty negotiations, not so much for their own sake but as indications of defensive behavior by the parties in an increasingly tense situation.

* * * *

The first serious consideration of possible parliamentary action took place in January and February. The parties restated their general views, confidential discussions were begun, and to all appearances the gradual process of mutual adjustment of differences seemed to be working. However, by the end of February the initiative and referendum campaign began to worry the leaders of a number of parties. Immediate political considerations infringed more and more on the legislative process.

The Reichstag's Legal Committee began its hearings on the royal properties question on 7 January.[31] The bills which the DDP and KPD had introduced before Christmas served as the starting point for the Committee's discussions, but the Committee interpreted its responsibilities broadly.[32] Of course, the various bills were examined closely, but the Committee also devoted much time to a full investigation of the various disputed claims and, through the work of some of its members, played an important part in the formulation of new legislative proposals. Between 7 January and 26 June 1926, forty-four sessions of the full Committee were held for the discussion of matters relating to the royal properties ques-

[30] Cf. the pointed, but justified query by the DNVP's representative in the Legal Committee, Dr. Hanemann, whether the middle parties intended to rely on the SPD or on the DNVP to get their bill accepted. *Frankfurter Zeitung*, 22 April 1926 (Nr. 295).
[31] The *Frankfurter Zeitung* published extensive reports of the Committee's deliberations. Most other papers reported only highlights. The protocols of this important committee's sessions are in the Politisches Archiv of the foreign office in Bonn and were utilized by Schüren, p. 300.
[32] The accounts by Wilhelm Kahl, "Das Fürstendrama," *Deutsche Juristen-Zeitung*, 31 (Nr. 15, 1 Aug. 1926): 1057–63, and Karl Anton Schulte, "Die Auseinandersetzung mit den ehemals regierenden Fürsten," *Politisches Jahrbuch 1926*, pp. 489–531, discuss the activities of the Legal Committee as it attempted to cope with the substantive problems of the proposed legislation. Kahl was chairman of the Legal Committee; Schulte chaired the meetings of the representatives from the middle parties who tried to work out the details of the Compromise Bill.

tion.[33] In addition, there were over a hundred smaller meetings to prepare proposals for the consideration of the larger body or to resolve differences.[34]

During January the Committee occupied itself with various preliminary matters; it did not take up any of the legislative proposals at once.[35] It heard statements from each of the state governments regarding the settlements that had been concluded and those cases which still were unresolved. It also heard their opinions on the desirability of national legislation. Most state governments informed the Committee that they regarded the settlements they had already concluded as final and therefore saw no need for national legislation, at least not for their own states.[36] Thuringia, Prussia, Mecklenburg-Strelitz, Hesse-Darmstadt, and Lippe-Detmold favored a national law to relieve them from certain difficulties.[37] Bavaria, true to its particularist heritage, rejected any consideration of a *Reich* law, claiming that such a law would violate the constitutionally guaranteed rights of the individual states.[38] Indeed, for some time the Bavarian government refused to acknowledge the competence of the Legal Committee to investigate the settlements.[39] Toward the end of January the Committee discussed and recommended passage of a bill which temporarily suspended all court cases while new legislation was under consideration (the *Sperrgesetz*).[40] These pre-

[33] *Frankfurter Zeitung*, 27 June 1926 (Nr. 471).
[34] Karl Anton Schulte, *Was geschieht mit dem Fürsten-Vermögen?* (M. Gladbach, 1926), p. 13.
[35] The Committee met ten times between 7 January and 2 February 1926, before turning to the discussion of the specific legislative proposals themselves.
[36] See, for instance, the statement by the government of Saxony. *Frankfurter Zeitung*, 14 Jan. 1926 (Nr. 34). The author of the confidential memorandum in the DDP Papers observed that in some cases official statements by the state governments (for example, Württemberg and Brunswick) that national legislation was not necessary reflected the views of the right coalitions then in power rather than the actual interests of the inhabitants of the states involved. DDP Papers, reel 38, folder 759, p. 5.
[37] *Frankfurter Zeitung*, 8 Jan. (Nr. 19), 9 Jan. (Nr. 21), 13 Jan. (Nr. 31), 20 Jan. (Nr. 51), 27 Jan. 1926 (Nr. 69).
[38] The Bavarian *Staatsrat*, Dr. Quark, informed the Committee: "The regulation of the relations between the states and their former princely houses . . . is a matter for the states [to decide]. Regulation of this question through *national legislation* would therefore constitute a *severe interference* in the rights of the states and must be emphatically rejected by Bavaria" (emphasis in original). Ibid., 13 Jan. 1926 (Nr. 31). On the Bavarian settlement with the Wittelsbachs, Kurt Sendtner, *Rupprecht von Wittelsbach, Kronprinz von Bayern* (Munich, 1954), pp. 465–72; Schüren, pp. 287–88.
[39] *Frankfurter Zeitung*, 22 Jan. 1926 (Nrs. 56 and 57).
[40] See above, Chapter III, note 29. Only the DNVP and BVP objected to the *Sperrgesetz* in the Committee debate. Ibid., 27 Jan. 1926 (Nr. 69).

liminary sessions of the Legal Committee undoubtedly served a useful purpose, yet essentially the Committee was marking time until the middle parties were ready to submit their Compromise Bill.[41]

The DDP proposal to empower each state legislature to regulate the property settlement with its former ruling house in a definitive manner, excluding any recourse to the courts, had not found much acceptance by mid-January. The parties on the right rejected it on principle,[42] but even parties which recognized the urgent need for some kind of regulation had doubts about the formulation of the DDP bill.[43] Leaving the decision to the state legislatures would not have guaranteed a speedy conclusion to the controversy as partisan disputes simply would have been transferred to the level of state politics. Where states were governed by a right coalition, the claims of the princes might still have been favored at the expense of the public. In any case, no uniform treatment of similar problems (*Aufwertung*, for example) could result if each state legislature was authorized to pass whatever laws it considered appropriate. Some parties thought it improper to allow the state governments and legislatures to make the final decision in disputes whose outcome so directly interested them. Since the DVP and Center Party insisted that contested claims must be decided by some kind of court,[44] and the SPD,

---

[41] One touch of scandal enlivened the hearings. During the report on the situation in Thuringia it was revealed that Dr. Everling, one of the DNVP's representatives on the Committee, was also legal adviser to the duke of Altenburg. Representatives for several other parties (KPD, SPD, DDP and Center) thought that this involved a conflict of interest and declared that he should resign from the Committee. He defended his participation by stating that on the Committee he represented only "his *legal principles* which, to be sure, were diametrically opposed to bills that aimed at robbing the princely houses." Although his Nationalist colleagues expressly approved his continued presence on the Committee, when the possibility developed that formal steps would be taken to exclude him he announced that he had resigned his position as legal adviser to the duke "without pressure *(Anregung)* from any side." Ibid., 9 Jan. (Nr. 21), 10 Jan. (Nr. 24) and 12 Jan. 1926 (Nr. 29). Later Dr. Rosenfeld charged that representatives of the DNVP had met with the former crown prince to work out plans for the defense of Hohenzollern interests. The Nationalist members of the Legal Committee gave an evasive reply. Ibid., 10 Feb. 1926 (Nr. 107).

[42] Statements made by Barth and Lohmann for the DNVP, ibid., 10 Feb. (Nr. 107) and 13 Feb. 1926 (Nr. 116); by Wunderlich for the DVP, ibid., 12 Feb. 1926 (Nr. 113); and by Frick for the *Völkische*, ibid., 18 Feb. 1926 (Nr. 129).

[43] Various reservations about the original DDP bill are mentioned in the "Vertraulich" memorandum, DDP Papers, reel 38, folder 759, pp. 9–10, and by Schulte, *Was geschieht mit dem Fürsten-Vermögen?*, p. 9. Likewise see Schulte's article "Die vermögensrechtliche Auseinandersetzung mit den ehemalige Fürstenhäusern," *Deutsche Juristen-Zeitung*, 31 (Nr. 2, 15 Jan. 1926): 109–15.

[44] The "Vertraulich" memorandum, p. 10.

on whose aid the Democrats had been counting,[45] had agreed
to join with the KPD in supporting the referendum, the leaders of the DDP found themselves sponsoring a bill which had
no prospects. Rather reluctantly they agreed to join with
representatives of the other middle parties in trying to work
out a new proposal.[46]

Informal meetings for the exchange of views among members of different parties in the Reichstag which presumably
started about the time the first bills were introduced early in
December resumed after the Christmas holidays. Most crucial
negotiations, however, were carried out on a more organized
basis by specially selected representatives of the middle parties.[47] These men were experts, they themselves sat on the
Legal Committee, and in most cases they possessed considerable influence in their own parties even though they were
not empowered to make binding commitments.[48] The first
formal meeting was held on 15 January. The negotiating
committee early established contact with a qualified representative of the SPD (Otto Landsberg) in the hope that the
Social Democrats could be drawn into the interparty negotiations.[49] Although it proved impossible to persuade the
Social Democrats to join the talks,[50] they were kept informed
of all major developments. Later, the DNVP was granted the
same courtesy.[51]

Despite the fact that Chancellor Luther declared that the
speedy enactment of national legislation was a necessity and
that "the national government wished to spare the German
people the disorder *(Unruhe)* of a referendum," [52] he made
no effort to construct a workable compromise. He permitted
the attendance of undersecretaries from the ministries of
interior and justice at the meetings of the middle party rep-

[45] Ibid., p. 9; Koch-Weser's explanation to the DDP *Parteiausschuss* 10 March 1926,
DDP Papers, reel 37, folder 731, p. 3.

[46] "That such a solution can only be made by compromise is, of course, undeniable." The "Vertraulich" memorandum, p. 8.

[47] Schulte, *Politisches Jahrbuch 1926*, p. 495.

[48] See the statements made by Schulte to the Legal Committee, *Frankfurter Zeitung*,
10 Feb. (Nr. 107), 13 March (Nr. 192), and 21 April 1926 (Nr. 293).

[49] Bundesarchiv. "Auseinandersetzung," Bd. 1, RK 39326.

[50] Some early contacts notwithstanding. See below, pp. 162–65.

[51] Schulte, "Die Auseinandersetzung mit den Fürstenhäusern," *Germania*, 2 Feb.
1929 (Nr. 54).

[52] Reichstag. *Verhandlungen*, 388 (26 Jan. 1926): 5146. Thälmann immediately
yelled, "Impertinence to call the referendum 'a disorder'!" Idem. Hermann Müller
also criticized the chancellor's choice of words. Ibid., p. 5157.

resentatives, but restricted their participation to the giving of technical (sachliche) advice.[53] The cabinet confirmed this policy.[54] The high governmental officials present at the negotiating sessions were not empowered to discuss political questions; even their observations regarding legal technicalities were to be considered personal, not of an official character. Only when the parties were clearly at an impasse did Luther begin to expand the role of governmental participation.[55]

By 2 February 1926, discussions had advanced sufficiently for the middle parties to submit a compromise bill to the Legal Committee.[56] The proposal attempted to specify uniform and impartial procedures for regulating the property settlements and thus avoid the defects of the Democratic Party's bill. As far as possible the sponsors of the Compromise Bill wanted to maintain the principle that the disputes were of a legal nature and that they must be resolved by juridical methods.[57] Any openly avowed handling of them as political questions was rejected. Nevertheless, it was recognized that the formal legal claims of the princes could not be considered in a vacuum, since the altered structure of government and

[53] Bundesarchiv. "Auseinandersetzung." Bd. 1, RK39326. Staatssekretär Curt Joel represented the ministry of justice, Erich Zweigert, the ministry of interior.

[54] At the meeting 15 Feb. 1926. Kabinettsprotokolle, reel 1837, frames D767659–61.

[55] At the height of the Flag Crisis, the Frankfurter Zeitung wrote that Luther "had maneuvered Germany into another serious governmental crisis by his entirely intentional unpolitical 'objectivity.'" It then continued with a direct reference to his handling of the properties question. "The only tactic Herr Dr. Luther appears to know is to let the parties flounder in order then in a moment of general exhaustion and bewilderment to step onstage as a deus ex machina. This overly clever tactic can be employed for some time, but its [usefulness] wears out. In a truly serious crisis it can fail disastrously." 7 May 1926 (Nr. 338). The Center Party leader, Wilhelm Marx, also criticized Luther's inactivity. Hugo Stehkämper, ed., Der Nachlass des Reichskanzlers Wilhelm Marx, Mitteilungen aus dem Stadtarchiv von Köln, Vols. 52–55 (Cologne, 1968), 3: 12–13. Luther merely mentions "the politically very thorny problem of the princely settlements" in his memoirs, giving no indication of his own policies. Politiker ohne Partei, p. 417.

[56] Frankfurter Zeitung, 2 Feb. 1926 (Nr. 87) printed the text of the Compromise. See, too, its earlier reports on the progress of the interparty negotiations, 16 Jan. (Nr. 42), 17 Jan. (Nr. 44), 22 Jan. (Nr. 57) and 24 Jan. 1926 (Nr. 63).

[57] According to Wilhelm Kahl the technical problems which made the drafting of the different versions of the Compromise Bill difficult were "the creation of new rights; the fashioning of new norms capable of application to numerous entirely different sets of conditions...; the discovery of unconventional methods for adjusting [concepts] of law and equity; and the often hopeless attempt to take into account a pressing political situation without surrendering inalienable legal principles." Deutsche Juristen-Zeitung, 31: 1058.

the material conditions of the post-war era must be taken into account.[58] The new proposal put emphasis on the concept of equity *(Billigkeit)* rather than the more rigid provisions of private law.[59]

The Compromise Bill proposed to establish a special arbitration court *(Sondergericht)* with exclusive competence over all disputes between the former ruling families and the state governments not already settled in one form or another. The court was to be composed of experienced jurists named by the president of the *Reichsgericht*. In reaching its decisions the special court was to follow certain specific guidelines *(Richtlinien)*, rather than simply apply previously existing laws. The guidelines permitted the court to determine whether specific pieces of property had been acquired by acts of sovereignty, rather than through the procedures of private law. The court was authorized to take a number of different considerations into account in determining whether, and how much, compensation should be granted to the former rulers for property passing into the hands of the states. The division of contested properties was supposed to take the financial needs and resources of the particular state into account, but the former ruling families were to be guaranteed a "würdige Lebenshaltung." All *Aufwertung* settlements would have to follow the same general standards which applied to ordinary citizens. The use of any payments the former ruling families received was to be restricted to private or charitable purposes—an attempt to prevent the princes from subsidizing antirepublican groups.

Basically, this first Compromise Bill was a very moderate piece of legislation.[60] Although it would have blocked some of the more excessive princely claims, it disregarded current public opinion. In particular, this proposal failed to recognize

---

[58] See, for instance, the comments by Hampe, speaking for the *Wirtschaftliche Vereinigung*. Reichstag. *Verhandlungen*, 388 (27 Jan. 1926): 5188. His views were more moderate than they had been in early December. This change was undoubtedly due to the strong feelings the issue aroused among his party's middle-class following.

[59] *Kölnische Zeitung*, 3 Feb. 1926 (Nr. 88).

[60] The bill seems to have been primarily the work of the representatives for the Center, DVP and WV: it bore Schulte's name. The part played by the DDP's representatives in the formulation of the first Compromise Bill must have been rather small. At any rate, leading Democratic politicians and newspapers began demanding far-reaching amendments as soon as the draft was published. The DDP Reichstag delegation did not bind itself to the specific text of the first Compromise Bill. *Frankfurter Zeitung*, 3 Feb. 1926 (Nr. 89); *Vossische Zeitung*, 3 Feb. 1926 (Nr. 29).

the intense general distrust of professional jurists in whose hands its authors still intended to leave all final decisions.[61]

During February the Legal Committee turned its attention to the three proposed laws then before it.[62] The original KPD proposal for complete confiscation was killed in committee after a little discussion.[63] Occasionally a speaker referred to the DDP bill, but no action was taken on it. The center of attention was the Compromise Bill. Although only the KPD categorically rejected the Compromise,[64] nearly all of the parties expressed reservations of some kind. Possible amendments were suggested, particularly by those who wanted more restrictions on the claims of the princes. However, the changes that would have satisfied the left angered the right. Only a few days after the Compromise Bill had been introduced, the undersecretary of interior reported that its prospects were "extraordinarily doubtful."[65]

For the next five months the parties argued publicly and privately over suggested improvements.[66] As time went on some parties agreed to alter important features of the Compromise, but the most critical amendments remained at issue until the final version of the bill was withdrawn and the Reichstag abandoned its efforts to legislate on this problem. The parliamentary balance between left and right was too close to encourage clear decisions. The protracted, inconclusive debate over possible amendments sharpened divisions within important parties, divisions already fostered by the

[61] *Frankfurter Zeitung*, 3 Feb. (Nr. 88), and reporting a resolution by the Hamburg DDP, 25 Feb. 1926 (Nr. 150). Otto Landsberg, "Das Fürstenkompromiss," *Vorwärts*, 6 Feb. 1929 (Nr. 61) and Paul Löbe, "Das Kompromiss für die Fürsten," *Volkswacht* (Breslau), 5 Feb. 1926, reprinted in Alfred Friedmann, *Kompromissantrag "Schulte u. Gen." und Volksbegehren* [Berlin, 1926], a pamphlet defending the compromise.

[62] A debate on general principles lasted 2–18 Feb.; after 19 Feb. the Committee turned to a discussion of the Compromise Bill section by section.

[63] This was its Reichstag bill, *Drucksache* Nr. 1539, not to be confused with the initiative and referendum measure. Only the KPD and SPD voted for it. *Frankfurter Zeitung*, 20 Feb. 1926 (Nr. 135).

[64] *Rote Fahne*, 3 Feb. 1926, called it the "law for the hindering of the confiscation of the princes." Also see Neubauer's article, ibid., 9 Feb. 1926, and his statements in the Legal Committee, *Frankfurter Zeitung*, 18 Feb. 1926 (Nr. 129).

[65] Zweigert's report to *Staatssekretär* Pünder, 5 Feb. 1926. Bundesarchiv. "Auseinandersetzung," Bd. 1, RK507.

[66] A survey of the points most at issue as of the first of March is included in the *Kabinettsprotokolle*, frames D767919–23. Dr. Pfleger, who reported the final version of the Compromise Bill out from committee to the full body of the Reichstag, presented a lengthy account of the major problems and the proposed ways of handling them, unfortunately without discussing the political aspects of the proposals. Reichstag. *Verhandlungen*, 390 (29 June 1926): 7664–69.

initiative and referendum movement. Under these circumstances party positions regarding the Compromise Bill tended to fluctuate with the flow of political events. Old demands were never entirely dropped and, if the situation appeared favorable, they were easily resumed. In the end there was no final resolution of differences.

Speakers for the non-Communist left (SPD, DDP, left Center) generally agreed in their identification of the main defects in the Compromise Bill and demanded changes, with a certain variance in detail, in three key sections of the proposal. First of all, they recognized the need to alter the composition of the arbitration court. The Social Democrats would have preferred to create a special court composed entirely of individuals named by the Reichstag; [67] the other two parties were willing to balance the influence of trained jurists by the addition of some laymen.[68] The section establishing the guidelines for the court was also marked for significant alterations and tightening of language. A full description of all the amendments or additions recommended is not necessary here; essentially these changes were designed to improve the position of the state governments vis-à-vis the former ruling families in the division of property. For example, there were proposals to extend the categories of property which could be transferred to the state without compensation, or for only a nominal sum.[69] The wording of important passages, e.g. "würdige Lebenshaltung," was thought much too ambiguous.[70] In some cases, the legislators wrote new provisions

[67] Rosenfeld's remarks in the Legal Committee, *Frankfurter Zeitung,* 5 Feb. (Nr. 94) and 19 Feb. 1926 (Nr. 132). This was almost surely a bargaining point, rather than a demand the SPD actually expected the middle parties to accept.

[68] The "Vertraulich" memorandum, DDP Papers, reel 38, folder 759, pp. 11–12. *Frankfurter Zeitung,* 27 Feb. 1926 (Nr. 155); ibid., 4 March 1926 (Nr. 168), reporting an amendment introduced by the Center Party which would have named four laymen to the nine-member special court; *Tremonia,* 25 Feb. 1926.

[69] The SPD urged four far-ranging changes which in substance would have amounted to virtual confiscation: all properties which a ruling house had acquired according to the forms of public law *(völkerrechtlichen-staatsrechtlichen . . . Titeln),* all properties acquired by the forms of private law if the public position of the ruler played a decisive role in their acquisition, and all objects of historical, cultural or educational value were to be transferred to the states without compensation. Moreover, agricultural or forest lands the income of which was essential to a state government were also to be transferred to them. Rosenfeld's statement to the Legal Committee, *Frankfurter Zeitung,* 25 Feb. 1926 (Nr. 148).

[70] *Frankfurter Zeitung,* 3 Feb. 1926 (Nr. 88).

specifically to meet the needs of a particular state.[71] The third crucial change, which the SPD insisted on, and the other parties supported without going as far in their own demands, would have extended the competence of the court to permit it to re-examine cases that had already been settled (*Rückwirkung*).[72] This was a particularly controversial suggestion.[73] In general the right (DNVP, DVP, BVP)[74] viewed the attempts to write such changes into the Compromise Bill as unacceptable and tried in various ways to prevent major concessions to the left. Indeed, the DNVP even undertook to strengthen the strictly juristic composition of the arbitration court rather than to dilute it.[75]

In addition to strongly opposing the alterations in the Compromise wanted by the left, representatives for the right parties attempted to prevent any action in the Reichstag, much preferring to delay consideration of regulative legislation until after the referendum.[76] Karl Trucksaess, the DVP's business manager, reported to Stresemann on 27 April 1926 that Baron von Brandenstein of the *Hofkammervereinigung* had been in "constant communication" with the party's members on the Legal Committee.[77] In addition, various conservative dignitaries sought to influence the Reich chancellor directly. Luther met, at least twice, with Friedrich Boden who rep-

[71] Despite partisan exaggeration Friedrich Everling, a DNVP pamphleteer, remarked with a certain element of truth: "Behind the thin veneer of the separate paragraphs . . . an informed reader could perceive a palace or an estate they wanted to have. The law with the long name is becoming more and more a law by the Prussian finance ministry for the confiscation of [the property of] the Hohenzollerns." *Fürstenenteignung, Reich und Preussen*. (Berlin, 1926), p. 16. Even the Democratic Party's expert, von Richthofen, observed that since the law was really intended for those states that wanted to use it, special attention was naturally given their views. *Frankfurter Zeitung*, 24 March 1926 (Nr. 222).

[72] Von Richthofen's report to the DDP *Parteiausschuss*, 10 March 1926. DDP Papers, reel 37, folder 731, p. 1.

[73] See the reports of the discussions in the Legal Committee, *Frankfurter Zeitung*, 10 Feb. (Nr. 107), 13 Feb. (Nr. 116), 19 Feb. (Nr. 132), 26 Feb. (Nr. 151), 19 March (Nr. 208), and 23 April 1926 (Nr. 298).

[74] Some elements in the Center Party shared the concern of parties further to the right that the problem be handled primarily as a set of legal questions. The original position taken by the party revealed a strong preoccupation with the need to guard established legal rights, qualified only through the application of some concepts of equity.

[75] *Frankfurter Zeitung*, 13 Feb. (Nr. 116), 22 April 1926 (Nr. 295); *Vossische Zeitung*, 20 Feb. 1926 (Nr. 44).

[76] *Frankfurter Zeitung*, 13 March (Nr. 193), 17 April 1926 (Nr. 284).

[77] Bundesarchiv. Deutsches Volkspartei. A. Reichsgeschäftsstelle. R4511/20, pp. 63–71.

resented the interests of the former rulers, and also received a delegation from the *Hofkammervereinigung* as well as communications from Herr von Berg, the Hohenzollerns' agent.[78]

It was recognized from the start that there was little hope for the Compromise Bill unless the Social Democrats could be persuaded to take an interest in its passage. The cabinet discussed this problem on 1 February, the day before the Compromise was submitted to the Legal Committee, in connection with a request from the minister of interior, Dr. Külz, for permission to set the dates for the initiative *(Volksbegehren)*.[79] The chancellor once again stated his desire to spare the people the need for a popular vote, and remarked that although the situation was very unclear, perhaps help could be obtained from the SPD for passing a law in the Reichstag. If this was at all possible, he added, it would "not serve our purposes to [obligate] the SPD to fix its [position] regarding the initiative right now." [80] Külz replied that no more than three weeks could be allowed for testing this possibility, otherwise, "one gave too much time for agitation." After the minister of justice, Marx, reported on the progress of the Compromise Bill, and Undersecretary Robert Weismann, the representative of the Prussian government at meetings of the Reich cabinet and confidential agent for Otto Braun,[81] declared that discussions with the SPD would not be "unrewarding" *(aussichtslos)*, Luther recommended against setting the dates for the initiative at present. It would just make the "retreat" more difficult for the SPD, he said.

Despite the fact that the published reaction of Social Democratic spokesmen to the first draft of the Compromise was rather cool,[82] there are reasons for believing that the party's leadership was indeed preparing to reach an understanding with the Compromise parties, though probably without intending a complete "retreat" from the initiative and referendum campaign. On the evening of 3 February—that is,

[78] Max von Stockhausen, *Sechs Jahre Reichskanzlei* (Bonn, 1954), p. 206, diary entry 24 Feb. 1926; Bundesarchiv. "Auseinandersetzung," Bd. 1, RK1795, zu RK2973, RK2836, RK2993.
[79] *Kabinettsprotokolle* (1 Feb. 1926), reel 1837, frames D767401–2. Also see the report from the minister of interior dated 30 Jan. 1926, prepared for this meeting of cabinet members, ibid., frames D767457–58.
[80] Idem.
[81] Brecht, *Aus nächster Nahe*, pp. 327–28; Schulze, pp. 377–81.
[82] *Germania*, 6 Feb. 1926 (Nr. 62), complained that *Vorwärts's* comments on the Compromise Bill were "rather too patronizing" *(ziemlich gnädige)*.

one day after the middle parties introduced their Compromise Bill—*Vorwärts* published sensational revelations of "Communist Stab-in-the-Back-Tactics."[83] On the basis of a secret information bulletin intended for circulation within the Berlin regional KPD which had come into the hands of Social Democrats, *Vorwärts* showed that the Communists' real intention was to gain influence among previously non-Communist masses through the activities associated with the referendum campaign, United Front committees, etc.[84] In a tone of great indignation, *Vorwärts* editorially denounced the Communists for not being sincerely interested in the confiscation of the royal properties as such.[85] The article was immediately republished as a special leaflet for mass distribution.[86]

During the next few days the same warning of Communist "sabotage" was repeated in a variety of ways. The leaders of at least one of the SPD's regional organizations (Württemberg) announced that they had been compelled to abandon all cooperative actions with the KPD in making arrangements for the initiative.[87] On 4 February, the Free Trade Unions' Executive Board issued a statement attacking the Communists' attempt to form United Front committees. "There is absolutely no possibility of the KPD working together with us honestly; the past has taught us that sufficiently well. . . .

[83] 3 Feb. 1926 (Nr. 56).

[84] "Rundschreiben Nr. 12 der Politischen Abteilung der Kommunistischen Bezirksleitung Berlin-Brandenburg." This directive said, in part: ". . . We have an opportunity for the first time in . . . years to show the validity of the Leninist principle that the task of a revolutionary party is to guide, to organize, and to lead ten or a hundred times as many people as it has members. . . . [The task of the party is] to bring the still chaotic masses who are interested in the confiscation of the princes' properties into an organizational relationship. The *Action Committees* in the administrative districts shall serve this purpose. . . . For us the question of the confiscation of the princes' properties involves more far-reaching goals, so that the balloting has significance only as a propagandistic action and as a thermometer of our strength. Our comrades must . . . pay careful attention to this."

[85] The immediate response of *Germania* to these revelations was also interesting. It hoped that the SPD would now be encouraged to re-examine its position "and to consider if it would not be doing more good by participating in the *parliamentary solution* of the conflict." 4 Feb. 1926 (Nr. 57), emphasis in the original.

[86] "Sonderabdruck aus Nr. 56/57 vom 3. und 4. Februar."

[87] "Instead of supplying information about the initiative and referendum the Communist speakers [tried to] arouse suspicions about the Social Democratic Party, indulged in the strongest kind of accusations against its leaders, and demanded that the action be extended to the confiscation of all private property and to the purely Communistic goal of a workers' and peasants' government." *Frankfurter Zeitung,* 4 Feb. 1926 (Nr. 92), relaying a report from the *Schwäbische Tagwacht.* See, too, Alwin Saenger, "Die Abfindung der ehemaligen deutschen Fürsten," *Sozialistische Monatshefte,* 63 (8 Feb. 1926): 69–73.

Whoever cooperates with these committees abandons the trade union unity of the ADGB." [88] Two days later, the SPD Executive Board described the United Front committees as a weapon which the KPD was trying to use to destroy the organization of the SPD and the trade unions. It, too, insisted, "Every joint action is to be averted. Appeals, advertisements, meetings, demonstrations are to be sponsored by our party alone . . . [Our meetings] should not become forums for the Communists." [89]

The Social Democratic leaders certainly had grounds for warning against Communist United Front appeals; however, the timing and nature of these concentrated attacks plainly suggest a deliberate effort to prepare their followers for a new shift in alignments. The revelation of the Communists' real aims was scarcely startling. *Rote Fahne* replied that there was nothing secret about the KPD's reason for participating in the referendum campaign and that the goals of the United Front movement had been openly discussed in the Communist press.[90]

While criticism of the KPD's behavior was still going on, *Vorwärts* published its first somewhat sympathetic account of the Compromise Bill in an article by Otto Landsberg.[91] He wrote that it would be tactically unwise to stake everything on a single card.

> From this point of view it can only suit us if a change in legislation protects the German people from becoming the victim of an unfavorable legal position in case the referendum . . . contrary to our expectations turns out against us and thus favors the princes.[92]

In another article *Vorwärts*'s editors admitted that the SPD was making efforts "to improve and sharpen" the Compromise Bill.[93]

[88] *Vorwärts*, 4 Feb. 1926 (Nr. 57). The union leaders observed that although the ADGB had played a role as mediator between the SPD and KPD to help them find a way to co-sponsor the initiative and referendum, "the further execution of the action is an affair for the *parties*, not the trade unions" (emphasis in original).

[89] Ibid., 6 Feb. 1926 (Nr. 61). Similarly, 8 Feb. (Nr. 64), 11 Feb. (Nr. 70) and 16 Feb. 1926 (Nr. 78).

[90] *Rote Fahne*, 4 Feb. 1926. See, too, the statement by the KPD Central Committee, ibid., 6 Feb. 1926.

[91] *Vorwärts*, 6 Feb. 1926 (Nr. 61).

[92] Idem. See, too, the statement issued by the *Sozialdemokratische Pressedienst*, quoted by the *Vossische Zeitung*, 6 Feb. 1926 (Nr. 32).

[93] 8 Feb. 1926 (Nr. 64).

The contacts between the SPD and the middle parties appear to have reached a semi-official stage.[94] Now it was *Rote Fahne*'s opportunity for a sharp attack. It identified Landsberg as the spokesman for a group of right-wing SPD leaders who wanted to spoil the confiscation campaign, and asked with special emphasis: "Shall a group of middle-class (*verbürgerlichten*) Social Democratic leaders now succeed in breaking the common front and helping the princes in their theft of millions?"[95] *Vorwärts* was unable to deny that discussions between representatives of the SPD and the middle parties had taken place; all it could do was try to minimize their significance.[96] Such meetings, it said, were "natural" (*selbstverständlich*) in the course of legislative work, and in any case were "not binding"[97]—as though any of the interparty discussions over the Compromise at this point were binding! Landsberg soon wrote an article defending himself, but now adopted a rather more cautious attitude toward the Compromise and stated explicitly that the fight for the initiative and referendum would be continued.[98] These rather embarrassed explanations were clearly intended to pacify angry SPD members who wanted unqualified support of the confiscation proposal.

In mid-February, the government acceded to insistent requests from Communists and Social Democrats that the ministry of interior cease delaying the official announcement of the dates for the initiative.[99] Once the dates (March 4–17) were made public, the parties sponsoring the initiative intensified their preparatory activities in order to ensure its success. The contacts between the SPD and the middle parties for the purpose of improving the Compromise grew rather

[94] *Frankfurter Zeitung*, 13 Feb. 1926 (Nr. 117); *Germania*, 13 Feb. 1926 (Nr. 73).
[95] *Rote Fahne*, 13 Feb. 1926.
[96] *Vorwärts*, 13 Feb. (Nrs. 73 and 74), 16 Feb. 1926 (Nr. 78).
[97] Ibid., 13 Feb. (Nr. 73).
[98] Ibid., 18 Feb. 1926 (Nr. 82). Thereafter Landsberg stepped somewhat into the background, allowing his colleague Dr. Rosenfeld to present the party's views most of the time. For example, the next main article in *Vorwärts* concerning the shaping of the Compromise Bill was by Rosenfeld, 27 Feb. 1926 (Nr. 98). See, also, the prominent part Rosenfeld took in the Legal Committee's deliberations. *Frankfurter Zeitung*, 18 Feb. (Nr. 129), 19 Feb. (Nr. 132), 24 Feb. (Nr. 146), and 25 Feb. 1926 (Nr. 148).
[99] By 10 Feb. Dr. Külz felt obliged to ask for the cabinet's authorization to start the initiative proceedings—not the "three weeks' time" he had thought available for delay on 1 Feb. The cabinet agreed to his request on 15 Feb. and the official announcement followed on the next day. Bundesarchiv. "Auseinandersetzung," RK1036, zu RK1255.

less close.[100] If the Social Democratic leaders had wanted to come to an understanding with the middle parties in early February, their plans had miscarried. Social Democratic spokesmen still argued that steps taken to strengthen the Compromise Bill as a "safeguard" *(Notlösung)*, in case the confiscation campaign failed, were consistent with full support of the initiative and referendum.[101] Nevertheless, as long as the SPD publicly maintained that the success of the popular movement was its primary aim, its parliamentarians' attempts to gain support for major changes in the Compromise were handicapped. It is arguable that a shift to the left in the balance of political forces in the Legal Committee and the Reichstag was possible at this time, as the steadily mounting public reaction against the princes began to affect the posture of some of the middle parties, but only decisive, fully committed parliamentary leadership by the Social Democrats could have brought about such a shift.[102] With the SPD maintaining a foot in both camps, that was impossible.

While the Legal Committee continued its formal consideration of the Compromise Bill, the real work of devising a more generally acceptable version remained in the hands of the middle parties. The representatives of the DDP regarded themselves as "mediators" between the SPD and the other middle parties.[103] In any case, they knew that unless major alterations were made in the bill large numbers of rebellious Democratic Party voters would sign the initiative petitions.[104] It was the end of the month before the representatives for

[100] Schulte, *Politisches Jahrbuch 1926,* p. 502, states that both the SPD and DNVP had shown some willingness to accept the first Compromise Bill, but that the initiative campaign ruined these chances for agreement.

[101] *Vorwärts,* 17 Feb. 1926 (Nr. 79). The next issue (Nr. 80) publicized Dr. Rosenfeld's statement in the Legal Committee that the SPD's activities in the Committee and in the initiative and referendum campaign had nothing to do with each other. A month later he repeated the same claim: ". . . In no case will our agreement to the Compromise alter our position on the initiative and referendum, even in the slightest. The initiative and referendum will run their course independent of the Reichstag negotiations." *Frankfurter Zeitung,* 12 March 1926, quoting an article in *Vorwärts.*

[102] The *Frankfurter Zeitung,* for instance, urged the SPD to push actively for improvements in the Compromise Bill. 6 Feb. 1926 (Nr. 98).

[103] The "Vertraulich" memorandum, DDP Papers, reel 38, folder 759, pp. 14–15; remarks by von Richthofen in the Legal Committee, *Frankfurter Zeitung,* 25 Feb. 1926 (Nr. 148); ibid., 27 Feb. 1926 (Nr. 155).

[104] According to a note in the Marx *Nachlass* both the DDP and Center showed a willingness to accept new modifications in the Compromise Bill because of their voters' attraction to the radical confiscation proposal. Stürmer, p. 156. Also see the *Frankfurter Zeitung's* comments on the DDP's attitude, 24 March 1926 (Nr. 222).

the Center Party moved far from their original position.[105] In the meantime, the negotiations among the middle parties made very little headway, in part due to the DVP.[106] The reserve maintained by the government, its unwillingness to express any opinion on the substance of the Compromise Bill, added to the general indecisiveness.[107] This further hindered the representatives of the middle parties from reaching an agreement since they naturally wanted to know what changes were acceptable to the cabinet. It soon became obvious that the government would have to supply "a certain direction" to the negotiations.[108]

Luther was still unwilling to take responsibility for drafting a specific proposal and securing the necessary parliamentary support for it. However, he did agree to meet with the leaders of the coalition parties to help them reach an understanding.[109] Between 22 February and 5 March, the negotiators for the middle parties held a series of intensive discussions to prepare for the meeting with the chancellor. Despite the direct participation of the ministers of justice and interior in some of these talks, the deadlock continued.[110] Only some changes regarding relatively minor issues were accepted.

The approaching date for the beginning of the initiative (4 March) increased the urgency for an agreement.[111] Without

[105] See below, Chapter VI, pp. 188–89.

[106] A report on the progress of the interparty negotiations as of 19 February noted that representative Wunderlich of the People's Party had complained that the Democrats were trying to push the bill so far to the left that the DVP could hardly go along with it. Bundesarchiv, "Auseinandersetzung," Bd. 1, RK1180. Also see interior minister Külz's summary of the discussions he and justice minister Marx had had with the representatives of the middle parties. Ibid., Bd. 1, RK1596. Külz himself took the position that the arbitration court had to be composed primarily of trained jurists.

[107] The cabinet decided 15 Feb. 1926 to take no position on the Compromise Bill until the Legal Committee had completed its first reading of the bill. *Kabinettsprotokolle*, reel 1837, frames D767659–61.

[108] Bundesarchiv. "Auseinandersetzung," Bd. 1, zu RK1498. The phrase stems from a recommendation made by interior minister Külz at a cabinet meeting 22 Feb. 1926. Similar requests had also been made by Undersecretary Joel from the justice ministry and by Dr. Kahl, chairman of the Legal Committee. Ibid., RK1180 and RK1328.

[109] Luther said he would talk with the leaders of the coalition parties first and then meet with the heads of the other parties. The second set of meetings never took place. *Kabinettsprotokolle*, reel 1837, frames D767773–74.

[110] Bundesarchiv. "Auseinandersetzung," Bd. 1, RK1596, RK1917; *Frankfurter Zeitung*, 4 March 1926 (Nr. 167); Karl Anton Schulte, "Das Kompromiss," *Germania*, 10 March 1926 (Nr. 116).

[111] All the middle parties agreed that speedy handling of the bill was mandatory. Bundesarchiv. "Auseinandersetzung," Bd. 1, RK1596.

it, there was a good chance that not all of the parties supporting the governing coalition would adopt a position opposing the initiative.[112] For some time, strong pressures had
been building up within the Democratic Party to support the
initiative, or at least not oppose it.[113] Even the Center Party's
Reichstag delegation, although issuing a statement urging its
voters not to sign the petitions, saw fit to have its representatives in the Legal Committee submit an amendment adding
laymen to the special court in an attempt to quiet discontent
over the Compromise Bill.[114] The differences among the middle parties appeared to be polarizing rather than diminishing.

Although Luther was preparing to leave Berlin for talks at
Geneva, he scheduled a meeting with the leaders of the middle parties just before his departure on 5 March.[115] The chief
points of disagreement once again underwent review. Ernst
Scholz, the head of the DVP Reichstag delegation, argued
that the bill should be drafted so the DNVP could accept it
as readily as the SPD and said it would be better to pass the
bill with the DNVP's help than to keep making changes to
get the support of the SPD.[116] The spokesmen for the Center
and Democratic parties countered that the help of the SPD
was necessary for final passage. Nevertheless, the pressure

[112] Chancellor Luther stressed the importance of all the government parties agreeing on a mutually acceptable proposal. Ibid., RK1917. A letter dated 9 March 1926,
from the national office of the DVP to a party official in Dresden blamed the slow
pace of the Reichstag's actions on the absence of any government sponsored bill.
The recent more active participation of representatives of the government in the
interparty discussions was explained by its concern lest "any of the governing parties
declare for the initiative." Bundesarchiv. Deutsche Volkspartei. A. Reichsgeschäftsstelle. Volksbegehren auf entschädigungslose Enteignung der Fürstenhäuser am 20
Juni 1926, Bd. 1: Schriftwechsel. R4511/20, pp. 23–25.

[113] On 1 March the DDP's Reichstag delegation heard a report from its chief
representative on the Legal Committee, von Richthofen, who stated that despite
some improvements the Compromise was still unacceptable to the party. The delegation decided to wait a few more days before announcing its views on the initiative
in order to see if any important changes would be made in the Compromise.
Frankfurter Zeitung, 2 March 1926 (Nr. 162).

[114] Germania, 3 March 1926 (Nr. 103); Frankfurter Zeitung, 3 March 1926 (Nr. 166).
A few days later, after a new revision of the bill had been worked out, Schulte called
for its speedy passage "in order to save the German people from further agitation
and great excitement. . . . Hands away from the initiative and hands away from the
referendum. This must be the slogan of all fair-minded men, especially now that a
legislative solution is in the works. . . ." Germania, 10 March 1926 (Nr. 116).

[115] He scheduled the meeting with the party leaders after a conference with key
cabinet members. Bundesarchiv. "Auseinandersetzung," Bd. 1, RK1917.

[116] Ibid., Bd. 1, RK1918. The DVP Fraktion reportedly believed the SPD would
accept the compromise "without a fuss" after the referendum was defeated. Dörr,
p. 240.

of circumstances moved the party leaders toward a tentative accord.[117] That evening after Luther's departure the negotiations continued. Basic agreement was obtained on the formulation of a revised version of the Compromise, as well as an understanding that in the future only jointly supported amendments would be introduced by any of the governing parties.[118] The leaders of the DDP, fearful of losing all possibility of influencing the other parties if they openly aided the initiative movement,[119] accepted a joint agreement to oppose the signing of initiative petitions.[120]

After editing by the ministry of justice, the revised Compromise Bill was ready for submission to the Legal Committee on 12 March.[121] The new bill made several concessions to the demands of the left, without abandoning the principles of the original bill. The authors of the Compromise defined their legislative intent more precisely than they had done in the earlier version; the new bill contained twenty-four paragraphs instead of thirteen. The special court was now to be composed of four laymen and four professional jurists, all appointed by the president of the Supreme Court (*Reichsgericht*), serving as chairman.[122] The guidelines were improved

---

[117] Bundesarchiv. "Auseinandersetzung," Bd. 1, RK1918.

[118] Idem; *Frankfurter Zeitung,* 6 March (Nrs. 173 and 174) and 7 March 1926 (Nr. 176). This interfractional agreement was not limited to the properties question. It established ground rules regarding the relation of the governing parties and the government which lasted for some time. Sturmer, pp. 146–47, 292–93; Haungs, pp. 169–70.

[119] Koch-Weser's remarks to the DDP *Parteiausschuss,* 10 March 1926. DDP Papers, reel 37, folder 731, p. 5. Representatives of the DVP had demanded to know why they should be asked to support the Compromise when part of the DDP was supporting the initiative. Idem.

[120] Bundesarchiv. "Auseinandersetzung," Bd. 1, RK1918. The leaders of the DDP issued a formal statement: "The negotiations by the governing parties . . . have reached a result which makes it possible for the Democratic Reichstag delegation to give its agreement to the Compromise Bill. The leadership of the Democratic Party now expects that friends of the party will not participate in the initiative, which because of the uncertainty of its outcome and doubts regarding its formulation was only to be recommended if an acceptable parliamentary ruling was not attained. . . . Considering what was attainable, the Democratic Party's Reichstag delegation has unanimously accepted the basis of the Compromise." *Frankfurter Zeitung,* 7 March 1926 (Nr. 176). The *Frankfurter Zeitung* made clear that it did not approve of this decision. Indeed, the party leaders hurriedly called a meeting of the party's advisory council to confirm their action.

[121] *Frankfurter Zeitung,* 10 March (Nr. 184), 13 March (Nr. 193). The text of the bill was published 11 March 1926 (Nr. 186).

[122] Dr. Marx informed the Legal Committee that the lay members of the court would be chosen on the basis of broadly defined suitability; they would not need to have legal training. Ibid., 7 March (Nr. 176).

in several respects. The court was to divide the contested property into three categories: 1) properties gained by the princes in their capacity as sovereigns were to become state property, 2) properties acquired exclusively by some *Privat-rechtstitel* were to remain private property, 3) all properties not clearly included in one or the other of these categories were to be divided between the state government and the former ruling family according to a specific set of rules. Compensation for certain types of property that were to be transferred to the states was now restricted where previously it had been permitted.[123] Revision of settlements made after 1918 *(Rückwirking)* was authorized only if both the state government and the royal family requested it—a severe restriction on the provision's possible effectiveness.[124] Members of the former ruling families were now to be insured an "angemessene Lebenshaltung" rather than a "würdige" one.[125]

Hopes that the agreement of 5 March would open the way for rapid parliamentary action on the revised bill proved illusory. The acceptance of the agreement did not even bind the middle parties to support it as it stood. They simply recognized a "fundamental consensus over the main principles of the draft," [126] which, in fact, left them far apart on some important details. Members of the People's Party's Reichstag delegation refused to compel some dissidents to accept the new changes by ordering *Fraktionszwang*.[127] A spokesman for the DVP questioned, "as a jurist," certain

[123] Sections 5 and 6 declared that Civil List payments, *Kronfideikomissrente*, etc., insofar as they were not intrinsically private in character were to expire without need for compensation and that the states did not have to pay for the acquisition of palaces, theaters, museums and similar properties if they had been open to the public before 1918. *Frankfurter Zeitung*, 11 March 1926 (Nr. 186).

[124] Ibid., 8 March 1926 (Nr. 179); von Richthofen's report to the Advisory Committee 10 March 1926, DDP Papers, reel 37, p. 1. Revision of divisions of property between ruling families and the governments of the states they ruled that had been made before 1918 was not allowed despite the protests of the DDP and SPD.

[125] According to section 8 of the new bill, consideration of the number of members as well as continuing obligations to maintain certain monuments were to be taken into account in determining the amount of the "suitable" income allotted to a former ruler. *Frankfurter Zeitung*, 11 March 1926 (Nr. 186).

[126] Statement by Schulte in the Legal Committee, *Frankfurter Zeitung*, 13 March 1926 (Nr. 192).

[127] Ibid., 11 March 1926 (Nr. 187). The DVP members who opposed the bill were led by the prominent former minister, Dr. Rudolf Heinze. It is worth noting that Heinze had actively sought the merger of the DNVP, DVP and rightist elements from other parties in 1919, but Stresemann had blocked the development of these plans. Turner, pp. 32–33.

sections of the revised bill when it was submitted to the Legal Committee.[128] Newspaper reports suggested the Bavarian People's Party also was unhappy with the announced revisions.[129]

Despite the government's efforts to foster agreement on the basis of the revised Compromise Bill, Justice Minister Marx was forced to inform the Legal Committee that the cabinet had yet made no decision to sponsor the bill. It had not even reached a judgment on whether the proposed law represented a constitutional change. With key members of the government still in Geneva, the rest of the cabinet could not undertake to decide these weighty issues.[130] Thus, within a week's time, it became clear that no speedy passage of the bill through the Reichstag would result from the 5 March agreement. Party leaders and other policy-makers intended— whether saying so or not—to wait for the results of the initiative before committing themselves to a particular piece of legislation.

Most parliamentary negotiations take place quietly, without great public attention, but after mid-February the various party leadership bodies and the Reichstag *Fraktionen* discovered that the spreading discontent over the scandal of the royal properties settlements could not safely be ignored. Attendance at mass meetings and demonstrations organized by the sponsors of the initiative movement confirmed that the slogan, "Not a penny for the princes!" was very popular. [131] Even middle-class newspapers admitted the genuine mass basis for the demonstrations, although they sometimes tried to discount the significance of such widespread complaints.[132]

The fact that active, vocal discontent was expressed by nearly all social classes, not merely among the proletarians, was more impressive and much more politically significant than the sheer size of the movement itself.[133] Effective as the

[128] Dr. Wunderlich, *Frankfurter Zeitung*, 13 March 1926 (Nr. 192). On the other hand, the *Kölnische Zeitung* was urging acceptance of the bill as a "lesser evil." 11 March 1926 (Nr. 186).
[129] *Frankfurter Zeitung*, 11 March 1926 (Nr. 187); *Vossische Zeitung*, 10 March (Nr. 59) and 12 March 1926 (Nr. 61). Also, see Cohnstaedt's remarks at the DDP *Parteiausschuss* meeting 10 March 1926, DDP Papers, reel 37, folder 731, p. 12.
[130] *Frankfurter Zeitung*, 13 March 1926 (Nr. 192).
[131] *Rote Fahne*, 27 Jan., 24 and 30 March 1926. *Frankfurter Zeitung*, 1 Feb. (Nr. 83) and 3 Feb. 1926 (Nr. 89). The *Reichsbanner* meeting in Hamburg 20–21 February 1926, was much larger than expected. *Das Reichsbanner*, 1 March 1926.
[132] *Germania*, 28 Jan., 1926 (Nr. 45); *Frankfurter Zeitung*, 28 Jan. 1926 (Nr. 73).
[133] Leber, pp. 46–47.

propaganda of the Marxist parties was, it would be too simple to ascribe the growth of public alarm to this alone. Even as presented by the "respectable" press, revelations of the very generous living standard existing settlements allowed the former ruling families, to say nothing of the extensive claims still pending, aroused many people who never thought of listening to the "Reds." Millions of ordinary people, angry over their own losses in the war and inflation,[134] and suffering from the immediate hardships of a winter of high unemployment, refused to subscribe to the view that the German princes deserved continued "fidelity and gratitude." [135] Indeed, the defenders of the princes' rights must have created new opponents by their crude insults of majority opinion:

> Unorganized masses are . . . incapable of making serious decisions . . . . Let us say openly: the worst failings in character from which the German people suffer are envy and greed and you [sponsors of the initiative] are counting on these two weaknesses of character. With their help . . . you are seeking to upset the people and set them in motion.[136]

The growth of discontent beyond anticipated bounds was revealed in a number of ways besides the crowded demonstrations. The editor of a Catholic newspaper in Dortmund commented on the flood of bitter letters the paper had received.[137] A Berlin paper with rightist connections reportedly declined to print an article defending the princes' claims out of fear of losing too many subscribers.[138] Questions from throughout the country forced the surprised headquarters of the German People's Party to explain why it had maintained silence regarding the initiative—the leaders of the party had thought there would be no need to warn their voters against

---

[134] Professor Krüger, a leader of the Democrats in Thuringia, justified his abandonment of more moderate views on the grounds that ". . .the *inflation* brought the *confiscation* [of properties owned] *by widest circles of the people*. . ." (emphasis in original). *Frankfurter Zeitung,* 11 Jan. 1926 (Nr. 26).

[135] From the formal statement of the DNVP Reichstag delegation, *Deutsche Allgemeine Zeitung,* 5 March 1926 (Nr. 105–106).

[136] Von Freytagh-Loringhoven (DNVP). Reichstag. *Verhandlungen,* 389 (6 March 1926): 6023. The Court Preacher at Potsdam reportedly stated that "whoever is not true to the king is a scoundrel *(ein Lump)!" Frankfurter Zeitung,* 28 Jan. 1926 (Nr. 73).

[137] *Tremonia,* 25 Feb. 1926.

[138] *Vorwärts,* 4 June 1926 (Nr. 258). Bundesarchiv. Deutsche Volkspartei, R4511/20, pp. 23–25. The paper was not identified by name but was termed "right of the DVP."

participating in it![139] The most significant indicator of an unusual degree of popular engagement, however, was the outbreak of open dissension inside the Democratic and Catholic Center parties.[140]

Ever since the SPD's sudden decision to campaign for total confiscation, the Democratic Party's policy-makers found themselves facing a dilemma that the leaders of some of the other parties were to encounter later, that is, they had to establish an official policy while fully aware that any decision they made would fail to satisfy some, or perhaps many, of their followers. Once it was clear that the original DDP bill had no chance of passing, some Democratic leaders seem to have grasped after a straw—the thought of somehow organizing an alternative referendum for the expropriation of the princes' properties in exchange for reasonable compensation.[141] Whether members of the DDP with basically different sympathies would have held together in such an undertaking is a matter for speculation; the reality of politics did not give the party that choice. The party's leaders had to decide whether to back the existing initiative proposal despite the fact that most Democrats did not approve of total confiscation without compensation, or to oppose it and continue the probably vain task of improving the Compromise Bill which, as it stood, appeared inadequate and unacceptable to many party members.

The reader is already aware of the DDP leaders' actual decision to oppose the signing of the initiative petitions and the critical role consideration for the views of the party's coalition partners played in this decision. The strong pressures against this choice and the immediate reaction to it remain to be described.

Throughout February, the DDP leaders deliberately

[139] Idem. Also, see the letter from *General-Sekretär* Dieckmann in Dresden, 4 March 1926. Bundesarchiv. Deutsche Volkspartei, R4511/20, pp. 13–17. Somewhat earlier the regular DVP information bulletin, *"rote Mitteilungen,"* Nr. 4 (20 Feb. 1926), indicated that the party leadership thought it was "inopportune" *(unzweckmässig)* for the party to publicize its opposition to the initiative and referendum on the grounds that it would only provide the left with further reasons for agitation. Ibid., R4511/21, p. 305.

[140] We shall only discuss the problems faced by the Democrats here; the description of the Center Party's difficulties is reserved for the next chapter.

[141] *Frankfurter Zeitung,* 22 Feb. 1926 (Nr. 141), reporting a resolution from the *Demokratische Beamtenausschuss;* comments by Koch-Weser (p. 3), Falk (p. 13) and Hustaedt (p. 15) at the 10 March 1926 meeting of the DDP *Parteiausschuss,* DDP Papers, reel 37, folder 731.

avoided any statement regarding the initiative in the belief that a manifestation of great public concern would help them obtain what they wanted in the Reichstag.[142] In the meantime—particularly after the dates for the signing of the petitions were announced on 16 February—a number of local party organizations, newspapers, and other affiliated groups called for the support of the initiative and referendum movement,[143] usually with the qualifying phrase "if the Reichstag does not produce an acceptable solution." [144] The Compromise Bill, in both its original and revised form, was too weak for these Democrats.[145] Since neither the *Parteivorstand* nor the Reichstag *Fraktion*, the bodies responsible for establishing policy binding on the party nationwide, had yet declared against the initiative, it was perfectly proper for local meetings of Democrats to pass resolutions and for influential individuals to state their opinions regarding such an important domestic issue.

Questions of party discipline and unity grew critical only when the Reichstag *Fraktion* announced its acceptance of the newly revised Compromise Bill and directed party members not to sign the initiative petitions. This was on 6 March, two days after the beginning of the initiative! The late timing made rational persuasion impossible; acceptance of the directive depended solely on the authority of the national leaders of the party.[146] It immediately became clear that the heads of the Democratic Party had expected a greater sacrifice of personal opinion than many of their followers were willing

[142] Idem, the remarks by Koch-Weser, pp. 3–4.

[143] Resolutions by the Pomeranian DDP, *Frankfurter Zeitung*, 9 Feb. 1926 (Nr. 106); by the Hamburg *Jungdemokraten*, ibid., 20 Feb. 1926 (Nr. 136); by a meeting of the Hamburg DDP, ibid., 25 Feb. 1926 (Nr. 150); by the DDP *Landesvorstand* in Hesse, ibid., 1 March 1926 (Nr. 160); and by the DDP local organization in Spandau, ibid., 3 March 1926 (Nr. 166).

[144] This phrase is not a literal quotation but represents the essence of a number of slightly differing statements.

[145] In addition to the groups cited above, objections were reported from the party organizations in Zwickau, Berlin, Wiesbaden and Cologne, *Frankfurter Zeitung*, 17 Feb. (Nr. 128), 4 March, (Nr. 169) and 7 March (Nr. 176). See, too, the *Frankfurter Zeitung*'s own editorial, 7 March 1926 (Nr. 177).

[146] At the *Parteiausschuss* meeting, 10 March 1926, one of the sympathizers with the dissidents, Dr. Richard Frankfurter, commented, "Our party leadership and the policies of the *Fraktion* are taking the wrong path. There is fear that the feelings of the people might flood into the *Fraktion*'s quarters." He complained that the party Advisory Committee had been convened at such a late date that it now could not do anything else but support the *Fraktion*. DDP Papers, reel 37, folder 731, p. 14. Similar criticism was also expressed at a meeting of Berlin party supporters, *Frankfurter Zeitung*, 14 March 1926 (Nr. 195).

to make. The leaders of the DDP in Hamburg and Hesse recommended signing the initiative petitions; other regional organizations hotly debated the same action.[147] The great left-liberal press, in particular the *Frankfurter Zeitung,* printed the declaration by the national leaders, but continued to campaign for the initiative with undiminished energy.[148] Even after the Advisory Committee confirmed the Reichstag delegation's decision, the *Frankfurter Zeitung* asserted, "For members of the German Democratic Party who want to think and act [according to their own judgment], the resolution by their Party Advisory Committee puts absolutely no obstacle in their way." [149] To be sure, this newspaper was not a party organ, but it was intimately associated with the Democratic Party by editorial policy and the notable role its editors played in party circles.[150] Thus, the open disregard of a formal party commitment was painfully conspicuous. The announcement on 7 March that several prominent Democratic politicians had formed a "Citizens' Committee for the Success of the Initiative" gave conclusive proof that the leaders of the DDP had overestimated their own authority and influence.[151]

The party leaders called for a meeting of the Advisory

[147] Ibid., 7 March (Nr. 177) and 8 March (Nr. 179). Meetings of party leaders in Greater Thuringia and Württemberg discussed the position taken by the party's national leadership, ibid., 8 March (Nr. 178) and 9 March (Nr. 180). In both of these cases the presence of prominent members of the *Fraktion* (Gertrud Bäumer and Hermann Dietrich respectively) appears to have influenced the participants to accept the policy which the *Fraktion* had announced.

[148] Ibid., 7 March (Nr. 177) and 8 March 1926 (Nr. 179).

[149] Ibid., 12 March 1926 (Nr. 191).

[150] Modris Eksteins, *The Limits of Reason: The German Democratic Press and the Collapse of Weimar Democracy* (London, 1975), pp. 93–96, 122–30; Schneider, pp. 237–44.

[151] The *Frankfurter Zeitung* printed an appeal from this *Staatsbürgerliche Ausschuss zur Förderung des Volksbegehrens* on its front page, 7 March 1926 (Nr. 177). The appeal called for support of the initiative on the grounds that the Compromise Bill, even as revised, did not meet the needs of the public. Much of the appeal attempted to allay fears that the initiative measure would endanger all property rights. ". . . It will not 'confiscate' private property in the usual sense, but will declare *pieces of property whose ownership is contested* to be the property of the state" (emphasis in original). The signers of the appeal stated that precisely because they believed in private property but at the same time regarded themselves "as conscious defenders of the interests of the state against an outdated feudal mentality," they had formed this committee. The appeal ended with the slogan, "Public prosperity before princely privilege! State properties for the states!" It was signed by the attorney Dr. Berndt (Stettin), the editor Dr. Cohnstaedt (Frankfurt a.M.), *Oberbürgermeister* Dr. Dullo (Berlin-Wilmersdorf), *Landtag* member Professor Julius Gressler (Barmen), a judge, Dr. Grossmann (Berlin), *Landtag* member Erich Hermann (Breslau), Senior Cantor Ludwig Schmal (Berlin), editor Wilhelm Nowack (Berlin), and the editor and member of the *Landtag,* Otto Nuschke.

Committee at the same time they announced their policy regarding the initiative, knowing full well that their decision would be contested. The Advisory Committee met a few days later (10 March) and confirmed, as such bodies almost invariably do, the action taken by the party leaders.[152] Fortunately, a protocol of the discussion at the meeting has survived, for it reveals that the participants, while arguing over different tactics, had already begun to perceive the disruptive effect of the controversy.

Erich Koch-Weser [153] began his remarks by declaring he had not seen such "a picture . . . of defective solidarity" since he had taken over the party chairmanship.[154] He returned to this theme at the end of his main speech. "The joy of leading a small party stops the moment he ceases to hold the party united behind him." [155] The Social Democrats were to blame for the DDP's difficulties; they had seen fit "to radicalize themselves" and preferred "a propagandistic success to a success for the republic." [156] Some men in the party seemed to think the DDP should always second whatever the SPD did, he said; but the party would die if it ceased to follow an independent policy.

He described in some detail the alternatives available to the DDP during the past weeks and explained the considerations which had led the leaders to make the choice they did.

> It was very useful that an increasingly determined attitude spread throughout the country, but every propaganda effort *(Agitation)* must come to an end when it gets to a matter of harvesting the practical results that one wanted to attain through the propaganda.[157]

"What did the opponents within the party want?" he asked. They could not have obtained any more concessions regarding the compromise, and to favor the initiative openly would have antagonized the other middle-class parties. "If we take part in making the Compromise, then we must . . . show that

[152] *Frankfurter Zeitung,* 11 March 1926 (Nr. 187).

[153] There is an excellent brief character sketch of Koch-Weser in Schulz, 1: 249–51. See, too, Attila Chanady, "Erich Koch-Weser and the Weimar Republic," *Canadian Journal of History,* 7 (Nr. 1, April, 1972): 51–63.

[154] DDP Papers, reel 37, folder 731, pp. 1–2.

[155] Ibid., p. 7.

[156] Ibid., p. 2.

[157] Ibid., p. 4.

we are a party that understands how to keep and carry out [its promises]." [158] Later Koch reiterated that the dispute was over tactics and claimed that the tactics followed so far had proved right. He ended by urging the Advisory Committee to "offer the country a picture of close solidarity." [159] Several other speakers argued along the same lines, insisting that commitments made by the party leaders could not be disavowed.[160]

The spokesmen for the opposition, Otto Nuschke, Dr. Grossmann, Conrad Berndt, Dr. Cohnstaedt, and Peter Stubmann, protested that their actions had been entirely loyal, that they had no desire to discredit Koch-Weser, or the leaders of the Reichstag delegation.[161] "There can be absolutely no talk of a party split." [162] They, too, stressed tactics: only more pressure on the Reichstag would force necessary improvements in the Compromise.[163] They agreed that the DDP could not with propriety issue orders for its voters to support the initiative, but they wanted the party to leave each individual member free to make the decision himself.[164] Their resolution to this effect obtained only thirteen votes, however, while ninety were cast for the alternative motion approving the decisions taken by the party leaders.[165]

The support that the DDP's leaders received from the Advisory Committee was a formal, but empty triumph. It is doubtful if more than a handful of Democrats who already intended to sign the petitions were deterred by their party's

[158] Ibid., p. 6. When one of the opponents of the officially announced policy cited the example of opposition to the Dawes Plan within the DNVP the previous year, Koch curtly replied that the DNVP's behavior should scarcely serve as a model, p. 10.

[159] Ibid., p. 17.

[160] Ibid., Hoepker-Aschoff, pp. 8–10; Grzimek, p. 12; Bernard Falk, p. 13; Theodor Vogelstein, p. 14.

[161] They affirmed their confidence in Koch's leadership and offered a resolution to that effect. Ibid., Nuschke, p. 8; Grossmann's resolution, p. 17. Nuschke did reject, however, Koch's insinuation that his group was working for the Social Democrats. "Just as many maintain contact with the right [a probable reference to the *Liberale Vereinigung*] so there must also be people among us who keep up ties with the left" (p. 8).

[162] Ibid., Grossmann, p. 13.

[163] Ibid., Nuschke, p. 8; Berndt, p. 11; interestingly enough von Richthofen, who, of course, supported the Reichstag delegation's decision, nonetheless called the initiative "the indispensible precondition" for passage of a good Compromise Bill. Ibid., pp. 15–16.

[164] Ibid., Cohnstaedt, pp. 11–12; Stubmann, pp. 13–14; Meyer, p. 15.

[165] Ibid., p. 17. After this vote a speaker for the minority moved unanimous approval of the majority resolution.

official disapprobation. In fact, the resolution did not even silence all dissident voices in the press and local party organizations.[166] The unity of the party was only superficially maintained. It would face still harder tests during the forthcoming referendum.

Tensions between party leaders and their followers were not a disorder peculiar to the larger parties. Some small parties also encountered trouble because of growing popular support for the initiative measure. In 1925–26, the National Socialists were still near the borderline between a sect and a true party.[167] Nevertheless, the problem that was to plague the party until the Blood Purge of 1934, namely, disagreement between Hitler, who so often followed opportunistic policies, and elements in the party that wanted a firm commitment to radical social changes, revealed itself in a brief, sharp conflict over the NSDAP's support or rejection of the "Marxist" confiscation proposal.

Toward the end of January, 1926, Gregor Strasser—probably in a move to challenge Hitler's control of the party, at least outside of Bavaria—arranged a meeting of important party members from northern Germany at Hanover.[168] Without Hitler's approval Strasser had recently distributed the

[166] A meeting of DDP *Vertrauensmänner* in Coblenz voted on 14 March to leave the decision up to the individual voter, *Frankfurter Zeiting*, 18 March 1926 (Nr. 205). Dr. Grossman, one of the organizers of the citizens' committee which opposed the announced party policy, stated at a meeting in Berlin that he would support confiscation without compensation if the Reichstag did not accept the Compromise Bill, ibid., 17 March 1927 (Nr. 204). Even the *Parteiausschuss* meeting which confirmed the Reichstag delegation's decision to abstain from the initiative thought it wise to censure rightist obstruction of that initiative. Ibid., 11 March 1926 (Nr. 187).

[167] Through association with the *Deutschvölkische Freiheitspartei* the National Socialists were just able to attain the status of a recognized *Fraktion* in the Reichstag. In the Berlin municipal elections October 1925, the list of candidates submitted by the recently established branch of the NSDAP received only 137 votes and ended in last place. Martin Brozat, "Die Anfänge der Berliner NSDAP 1926/27," *Vierteljahrshefte für Zeitgeschichte*, 8 (Nr. 1, Jan. 1960): 86, note 4. Even in Bavaria the party obtained only 5 percent of the votes in the December 1924 elections. Bracher, *Deutschland zwischen Demokratie und Diktatur*, p. 68.

[168] The older versions of what happened at the Hanover and Bamberg meetings— Otto Strasser, *Hitler and I* (Boston, 1940), pp. 83–89, and Konrad Heiden, *Der Fuehrer* (Boston, 1944), pp. 284–88—have been corrected in many particulars by recent research: Joseph Goebbels, *Das Tagebuch 1925/26*, ed. Helmut Heiber, *Schriftenreihe der Vierteljahrshefte für Zeitgeschichte*, 1 (Stuttgart, 1960): 55–56, 60–61; Ernest K. Bramsted, *Goebbels and National Socialist Propaganda 1925–1945* (East Lansing, 1965), pp. 10–12; Jeremy Noakes, "Conflict and Development in the NSDAP 1924–27," *Journal of Contemporary History*, 1 (Nr. 4, Oct., 1966): 3–36; Dietrich Orlow, "The Conversion of Myths into Political Power: The Case of the Nazi Party 1925–1926," *American Historical Review*, 72 (Nr. 3, April, 1967): 906–24; and going farthest in a revisionary assessment of the actions of the northern Nazis: Joseph Nyomarkay, *Charisma and Factionalism in the Nazi Party* (Minneapolis, 1967), especially pp. 74–89.

draft of a new party program which proposed major changes in the economic and political structure of Germany, including the partial nationalization of industry and the division of the great landed estates.[169] A desire to substitute a "national" socialism for the "alien" Marxist principles of the older workers' parties underlay his thinking. Confiscation of the princes' properties fit in with the ideas of the Strasser circle, but was not favored by Hitler. His personal representative at the Hanover meeting, the ineffectual Gottfried Feder, mustered only a single supporter during the discussion.[170] Even though the confiscation measure was sponsored by the "Reds," the meeting resolved to support it.[171] In order to stress the distinctness of the NSDAP's partisan standpoint, and probably to make the decision more palatable for those Nazis who opposed the attack on the princes' properties, the party's Reichstag members were instructed to seek an amendment calling for the expropriation of "Bank-und Börsenfürsten," all Eastern European Jews who had entered Germany since 1914, and war and inflation profiteers.[172]

Hitler moved rapidly to prevent Strasser from gaining general support for his position within the party and to rescind the Hanover decision, presumably because backing a radical measure at this time would have endangered his own efforts to obtain substantial financial support from right-wing industrialists and other wealthy persons.[173] He called a special meeting at Bamberg on 14 February, and saw to it that numerous loyal followers from Bavaria were in attendance.[174]

[169] Orlow, p. 920; Strasser, pp. 81–83.

[170] David Schoenbaum, *Hitler's Social Revolution* (Garden City, 1967), p. 23.

[171] Noakes, p. 26, informs us that one of the participants at the meeting recalled that "this question was extremely embarrassing for everybody and they would much rather have avoided taking a position on it."

[172] Idem. Dr. Wilhelm Frick introduced corresponding motions at meetings of the Legal Committee. *Frankfurter Zeitung*, 27 Jan. (Nr. 69) and 25 March 1926 (Nr. 224). In addition, see Frick's account of the party's parliamentary activities, "Die Nationalsozialisten im Reichstag 1925/26," *Nationalsozialistisches Jahrbuch 1927*, p. 127.

[173] Within a year, Hitler composed a carefully adjusted version of his basic ideas for distribution to selected industrialists. Henry Ashby Turner, Jr., "Hitler's Secret Pamphlet for Industrialists, 1927," *Journal of Modern History*, 40 (Nr. 3, Sept. 1968): 348–74. According to Heiden, pp. 287–88, Hitler received substantial sums from the divorced wife of the duke of Sachsen-Anhalt and from the duke of Saxe-Coburg-Gotha. After the Nazis came to power in Thuringia, they concluded a settlement with their *Parteigenosse*, the duke of Saxe-Coburg-Gotha, on terms which were very much in his favor. Witzmann, pp. 144–45, 184.

[174] Orlow, pp. 920–22. Despite Otto Strasser's assertion that Hitler arranged the meeting at a time and place inconvenient for leaders from north Germany, records of the meeting show that many of Gregor Strasser's supporters were present. Noakes, p. 29.

In a lengthy speech he expounded his views on foreign policy, Bolshevism, and domestic questions. When Hitler insisted that the property of the former rulers deserved the same protection as that of all other Germans, his vocabulary did not differ from that of spokesmen for the more traditional right.[175] Goebbels, who was then one of Strasser's aides, confided his immediate reaction to his diary:

> Hitler speaks for two hours. I am staggered. Is that Hitler? A reactionary? Amazingly awkward and uncertain of himself. . . . The princes' settlements! Rights must remain rights. Even for the princes. Question of private property not to be shaken! (sic!) Dreadful! I no longer believe unqualifiedly in Hitler: this is a terrible thing: my inner security is gone.[176]

Nevertheless, Hitler easily dominated the Bamberg meeting; Goebbels and Strasser scarcely ventured to say a word.[177] The decisions of the Hanover meeting that had not met with Hitler's approval were overruled.[178] Hitler proclaimed that the original NSDAP program of 1920 was sacrosanct and persuaded Strasser to withdraw the draft program he had circulated among party leaders.[179] During the next few months the party headquarters in Munich tightened its control over the activities of local and regional units of the party.[180] Discipline, not autonomy, was to govern the internal structure of the NSDAP. The party's role throughout the remainder of the properties controversy was inconspicuous.

Unlikely as it may seem Bavaria offered a noteworthy case of the followers of a non-Marxist party sympathizing in substantial numbers with the proposal to seize the lands and wealth of the former ruling families. Most Bavarians remained

---

[175] Noakes, p. 30.

[176] Goebbels, *Tagebuch*, p. 60.

[177] Otto Strasser claimed that Goebbels betrayed Gregor Strasser by siding with Hitler at the Bamberg meeting. Goebbels's own diary entry belies this assertion. There is no doubt, however, that Hitler won Goebbels over by mid-April, ibid., p. 72.

[178] On 17 Feb. Dr. Frick informed the Legal Committee that his *Fraktion* opposed both the DDP bill and the confiscation proposal. *Frankfurter Zeitung*, 18 Feb. 1926 (Nr. 129). By May even Gregor Strasser opposed the referendum on the grounds that it was a machination of plutocratic profiteers. Schoenbaum, p. 24.

[179] Orlow, p. 922; Noakes, p. 31. An important assembly of party members declared the 1920 program *"unabänderlich"* in May 1926. Bracher, *Die Auflösung*, p. 108.

[180] Orlow, pp. 922–23. The appearance of a pamphlet attacking the Hohenzollerns occasioned an order that in the future all literature issued by regional party organizations must first be approved by party headquarters in Munich. Noakes, pp. 31–32.

monarchists at heart throughout the Weimar years.[181] The dominant Bavarian People's Party (BVP) imprinted a markedly conservative character on the Munich government.[182] Nevertheless, the Bavarian Peasants' League (*Bauernbund*), scarcely a quarter the size of the BVP, maintained a distinct democratic character relatively uninfluenced by the surrounding political climate.[183] Even as a strictly Bavarian party the *Bauernbund's* strength was narrowly circumscribed. Its appeal was limited to the peasantry and inhabitants of country towns in certain areas of Lower and Upper Bavaria and Swabia.[184] However, it did more than organize and represent the interests of a particular social-economic group; over the course of time it had developed a genuine political tradition.

The Peasants' League was an outgrowth of the agrarian discontent of the early 1890s. Unlike the movement in northern Germany, where through the *Bund der Landwirte* the small peasants were led to identify their interests with those of the large landowners and thus were brought into the conservative camp, the Peasants' League maintained an independent course of its own. It associated more with the political left than with the right in Bavarian politics. A strong strain of anticlericalism made the Catholic Center Party (later the BVP) its chief rival.[185] During the revolution of 1918/19 the *Bauernbund* had cooperated with the Eisner regime; indeed, it had been entrusted with the major responsibility of organizing peasants' councils.[186] After Kurt Eisner's murder, it joined a left coalition headed by the Majority Social Democrat, Johannes Hoffmann. However, when the short episode of rev-

[181] Heinz Gollwitzer, "Bayern 1918–1933," *Vierteljahrshefte für Zeitgeschichte*, 3 (Nr. 4, Oct., 1955): 384–85.

[182] Karl Buchheim, *Geschichte der christlichen Parteien in Deutschland* (Munich, 1953), pp. 345–74, provides an excellent brief account of the BVP. For fuller detail, Klaus Schönhoven, *Die Bayerische Volkspartei, 1924–1932, Beiträge zur Geschichte des Parlamentarismus und der politischen Parteien*, 46 (Düsseldorf, 1972).

The BVP rejected the initiative and referendum without hesitation. Minister-President Held, in a speech in Munich 1 March 1926, stated he would undertake to "maintain order and legality by all the means available to the state . . . [and] rejected all radical agitation among the peasantry. . . ." *Frankfurter Zeitung*, 2 March 1926 (Nr. 164). He kept his word. The Bavarian authorities repeatedly harassed the backers of the initiative movement. Ibid., 10 Feb. (Nr. 108), 26 Feb. (Nr. 153), 3 March (Nr. 166) and 9 March 1926 (Nr. 180). Schüren, pp. 118, 128.

[183] After 1923 its full name was the *Bayerische Bauern- und Mittelstandsbund.*

[184] Meinrad Hagmann, *Der Weg ins Verhängnis* (Munich, 1946), pp. 27*–28*.

[185] Buchheim, p. 306; Molt, p. 135.

[186] Allan Mitchell, *Revolution in Bavaria 1918–1919* (Princeton, 1965), pp. 119–20, 156–58, 180, and passim.

olutionary politics in Bavaria ended, leaders of the League found it possible to accept the much more conservative middle-class governments that followed.[187]

At the start of the initiative proceedings in March 1926, the leaders of the Peasants' League, like the heads of the other parties belonging to the current governing coalition in Bavaria, issued a statement opposing the initiative.[188] The minister for the national government residing in Munich, von Haniel, reported that many *Bauernbund* supporters were dissatisfied with the overly moderate policies their leaders had been following and that they were likely to support confiscation.[189] A meeting of *Vertrauensmänner* in the Cham district approved of the initiative nearly unanimously, "since the small peasants, the leaseholders, workers, and shopkeepers *(Kleinbürger)* have likewise lost their money." [190] The *Landauer Volksblatt* said that "the will of the people, not the party leaders should decide." [191] The level of participation in the initiative for Bavaria as a whole was very low, but relatively higher figures were reported in some of the areas where the Peasants' League was most strongly rooted.[192] When the referendum vote in June approached, the League's leaders saw how hopeless it would be to issue another statement directly counter to the sentiments of their followers. Like the heads of the Democratic Party, they chose to let their party members decide how to vote without official instructions.[193]

Dissident voters in the parties of the right and right center tended to be isolated individuals, unorganized and unable to find spokesmen for their views in party councils. The leaders

[187] The Bavarian minister of agriculture was named by the BBB nearly continuously throughout the Weimar era. *Ursachen und Folgen,* 7: 682–83.

[188] *Frankfurter Zeitung,* 4 March 1926 (Nr. 168).

[189] In a report dated 4 March 1926. Bundesarchiv. "Auseinandersetzung," Bd. 1, RK1799.

[190] *Vorwärts,* 4 March 1926 (Nr. 106).

[191] Quoted in the *Frankfurter Zeitung,* 9 March 1926 (Nr. 181).

[192] Most notably the districts Landau, Regen, Straubing and Bogen in Lower Bavaria, Traunstein and Weilheim in Upper Bavaria, and Günzburg, Illertissen and Mindelheim in Swabia. On the other hand, many districts where the BBB regularly did well reported the same low figures for participation in the initiative as areas where the BVP dominated. In the case of the Markt-Oberdorf district in Swabia, only 74 people out of nearly 16,000 registered voters ventured to sign the lists. Such low participation suggests the existence of strong administrative and other political pressures against participation.

[193] The report by von Haniel, 8 June 1926. Bundesarchiv. "Auseinandersetzung," Bd. 2, RK 4587; *Frankfurter Zeitung,* 8 June (Nr. 419) and 17 June 1926 (Nr. 442).

of the DNVP acted as though only a misunderstanding would cause their followers to sign the lists.

> This time the slogan is "Stay at home!" No one should let himself be misled by warnings from Socialist officials *(Behorden)* and party agitators. Signing the . . . lists for a referendum is not a civic and national duty like participation in elections. . . . It is obvious that every decent and law-abiding German will stay away from these lists.[194]

Friedrich von Berg-Markienen as marshal of the German nobility (he was also the legal representative for the Hohenzollern family) issued a proclamation:

> The German nobles stand faithfully by their princes. . . . They demand that . . . possessions sanctified by hundreds of years of tradition not be usurped through *any kind of seizure* born out of envy and incitement and . . . in violation of law and the constitution. . . . Every voter for the confiscation of the princes' properties participates in an unpardonable crime. Through such a robbery of its princes our people will rob themselves of their honorable name.[195]

The unruffled front of opposition to the initiative maintained by the DNVP and DVP should not cause one to assume that they had no dissident followers, however.[196] Only after the unexpectedly great success of the initiative did the parties and patriotic organizations that had joined forces for Hindenburg's election combine to combat the referendum.[197]

Twelve and a half million people (over 30 percent of the qualified voters) signed the initiative petitions between 4–17 March 1926.[198] The results surprised everyone. Four million signatures had been needed. During the campaign *Rote Fahne* had set a goal of "at least" eight to ten million, but quite

---

[194] *Deutsche Allgemeine Zeitung*, 5 March 1926 (Nrs. 105–106). On the other hand, the local association of the DNVP in the election district Potsdam I was concerned enough to order that "information personnel" be stationed at the registration offices in order to "enlighten unknowing or undecided voters on the true purpose of the initiative." This and other examples of questionable practices by the right were cited by the Social Democratic speaker, Arthur Crispien. Reichstag. *Verhandlungen*, 389 (6 March 1926): 6021.

[195] *Frankfurter Zeitung*, 1 March 1926 (Nr. 160), emphasis in original.

[196] Ibid., 5 March 1926 (Nr. 171).

[197] See below, Chapter VII, pp. 239–40.

[198] The official results were 12,523,929. *Frankfurter Zeitung*, 15 April 1926 (Nr. 276).

clearly had not thought such a total was likely.[199] The Social
Democrats reported that the turnout was twice as large as
had been expected.[200] The *Frankfurter Zeitung* noted that "not
even in their wildest dreams had people foreseen [such re-
sults] a few weeks earlier." [201]

Impressive though the level of support for the initiative
was, it varied greatly throughout the country. In some rural
areas and small towns participation was insignificant.[202] Ten
out of thirty-five of the principal election districts reported
fewer people supporting the initiative than had voted for the
Marxist parties in the last Reichstag elections—all of them
were agricultural regions.[203] The KPD and SPD had always
had limited success in establishing contact with the rural
population. Occasional week-end sorties of campaigners into
the countryside could not duplicate the effect which the systematic distribution of propaganda materials, newspaper
publicity, and repeated mass demonstrations had on the urban population.[204] The opponents of the initiative movement

[199] In a communique from the *Sekretariat* of the Berlin regional organization, *Rote
Fahne*, 23 Feb. 1926. After the initiative campaign was over, however, Max Engel
admitted that only optimists had expected that many signatures, ibid., 19 March
1926.

[200] *Jahrbuch . . . 1926*, p. 114.

[201] 25 March 1926 (Nr. 225).

[202] The following are only samples: 772 out of 11,900 qualified voters signed the
lists in the town of Rosenheim in Bavaria, 304 out of 4,400 in Landsberg, and only
34 out of not quite 3,200 in Donauwörth; participation in predominantly agricultural
or forested areas was also frequently very low: 546 out of over 16,000 voters in
the Aichach district, 439 out of 15,700 in the Garmisch area, 133 out of 11,200 in
the Wertingen area, and 834 out of over 24,000 in the district around Passau. Some
parts of Pomerania reported similar minimal returns: the *Kreise* Bublitz (930 out of
12,600), Greifenberg (957 out of 26,000), Schivelbein (953 out of 13,600), and the
Landkreise Köslin (946 out of nearly 18,000) and Stolp (1,653 out of over 47,000).
Most of the *Stadtkreise* in Pomerania reported noticeably higher participation than
the surrounding countryside. Further to the west, the town of Buckeburg in tiny
Schaumburg-Lippe reported only 180 signatures from 3,800 registered voters. However, interest in the properties dispute in this former principality was overshadowed
by an almost simultaneous plebiscite whether or not to merge with the state of
Prussia. Severing, 2: 89. Further low figures of this general order could be cited
from any of the election districts mentioned in the next footnote in addition to
those of Breslau, Oppeln, and Coblenz-Trier.

[203] They were: East Prussia (with a participation equal to 75.7 percent of the
combined KPD-SPD-USPD vote in Dec. 1924), Frankfurt/0. (89.6 percent), Pomerania (74.3 percent), Magdeburg (94.7 percent), Weser-Ems (98.1 percent), East
Hanover (92.8 percent), Upper Bavaria-Swabia (74.3 percent), Lower Bavaria (62.9
percent), Franconia (82.8 percent), and Mecklenburg (86.4 percent). Sozialdemokratische Partei Deutschlands. *Referentenmaterial zur Fürstenabfindung* (Berlin, 1926),
p. 8.

[204] *Rote Fahne*, 14 Feb. 1926, and a message from the KPD Central Committee
outlining work still to be done, ibid., 1 April 1926. Kasper, *Wissenschaftliche Zeitschrift
der Universität Rostock*, 17 (Nr. 2/3, 1968); 173–80, documents certain local successes
of the KPD in associating resentment against the princes' claims with basic agrarian
discontent.

played upon the traditional conservatism of many peasants by the spread of false or misleading information.[205] Fear of reprisals from local employers or creditors undoubtedly intimidated many otherwise sympathetic rural laborers and small peasants.[206]

The bulk of support came from urban, industrialized areas.[207] No one was surprised by the strong turnout in traditionally "Red" centers such as Berlin, Hamburg, and Saxony.[208] However, the extent to which Catholic workers ignored their own party's recommendations was very striking. Figures for the Cologne-Aachen district were over half again as large as the combined KPD-SPD-USPD vote in December 1924; Coblenz-Trier, Düsseldorf-East, and Oppeln showed a similar trend.[209] The results in Baden (184.8 percent of the combined left vote) were even more impressive, especially when one considers that the inhabitants felt little hostility to their former ruling house.[210] Elsewhere, as in many of the Berlin-Potsdam districts, it was clear that Protestant middle-class voters also favored the initiative proposal.[211] Clearly the directives issued by party leaders had had only limited ef-

---

[205] Harry Graf Kessler noted in his diary that he spent an evening talking with peasants at an inn in the *Frankenwald*. The newspapers they had seen said they should not sign the lists because that would mean giving the princes money. They were amazed when he explained the true situation to them. *Tagebücher 1918–1937*, pp. 464–65. The *Landbund* in Thuringia reportedly suggested that people signing the lists would have to bear the cost of the proceedings if the initiative did not succeed. *Frankfurter Zeitung*, 12 March 1926 (Nr. 190).

[206] Von Haniel reported on the results in Bavaria, 26 March 1926. He explained that the relatively low level of participation was due to 1) the fact most Bavarians considered the problem settled as far as they were concerned; 2) the Wittelsbachs were still popular; 3) the strongly expressed hostility of church and state authorities caused fear that any open disregard of their views would harm one's business. Bundesarchiv. "Auseinandersetzung," Bd. 1, RK2439.

[207] The *Vossische Zeitung* calculated that the signatures collected in twenty *Grossstädte* were sufficient to meet the legally required minimum. 19 March 1926 (Nr. 67).

[208] Even so, the high level of participation in Hamburg, for instance, indicated that numerous middle-class voters must have supported the initiative. *Frankfurter Zeitung*, 18 March 1926 (Nr. 206).

[209] Cologne-Aachen (158.3 percent), Coblenz-Trier (144.2 percent), Düsseldorf-East (143.5 percent), Oppeln (144.1 percent). SPD. *Referentenmaterial zur Fürstenabfindung*, p. 8.

[210] Idem; Köhler, pp. 110–11.

[211] The districts Berlin-Mitte, Tiergarten, Wedding, Prenzlauer Berg, Friedrichshain, Kreuzberg, Neu-Kölln, Tempelhof, Treptow, Köpenick, Spandau, Lichtenberg, Weissensee, Pankow, and Reinickendorf all reported larger numbers of people signing the lists than voted for the SPD, KPD, USPD, DDP and Center parties in the December 1924 Reichstag elections. Some of the increase probably came from previously indifferent or inactive left voters, but numerous DVP and DNVP voters must also have signed the lists. Contemporary newspaper reports confirm this assumption, see the series of articles in *Vorwärts* entitled, "Aus der Woche des Volksbegehrens," 14 March (Nr. 123), 15 March (Nr. 124), and 17 March 1926 (Nr. 127).

fectiveness on voters determined to express their indignation and grievances in a simple, direct way. Many politicians must have wondered whether this indignation would continue undiminished until the forthcoming referendum.

The KPD and the SPD were pleased by the success of the initiative, especially because it had appealed so strongly to social groups that normally rejected any association with the working class.[212] Each unhesitatingly interpreted the outcome as a partisan victory.[213] The parties at the other end of the political spectrum tried to pretend that "isolated right voters played only an extremely insignificant part" in the over-all results.[214] However, the attempted demonstration that this was so rested on some rather crude statistical manipulations. The Center Party was neither happy with the results, nor able to ignore them. *Germania* wrote, "These are things which give [cause] for thought." [215]

[212] *Vorwärts,* 18 March 1926 (Nr. 130); *Rote Fahne,* 18 March 1926.

[213] Max Engel, "Nach unserem grossen Erfolg," *Rote Fahne,* 19 March 1926; also an article, ibid., 21 March 1926, attacking the left-wing Socialist *Leipziger Volkszeitung* for claiming the initiative was a success for the SPD; *Jahrbuch der Deutschen Sozialdemokratie . . . 1926,* pp. 7–8.

[214] *Berliner Lokal-Anzeiger,* 15 April 1926. It claimed that an examination of the final statistics showed that virtually all nonworking class participation had come from the Center and Democratic Party voters. The *Kölnische Zeitung,* a DVP paper, asserted that the results of the initiative were not especially significant and that most of the middle-class voters who supported it were "big-city Democrats." 19 March 1926 (Nr. 208).

[215] *Germania,* 18 March 1926 (Nr. 129). Marx noted that 25–30 percent of the signatures came from middle-class voters. Stehkämper, 3: 12.

VI: *"The Center Party Must Remain the Center Party."*

There was little that was strictly new in the debate that the initiative and referendum movement generated in the Center Party. An issue which posed alternatives such as "republic *versus* monarchy" or "social justice *versus* preservation of established property rights" was almost bound to foster dissension among the Center Party's followers.[1] Moreover, since the Center had actively participated in a coalition throughout most of 1925 the dominant tone of which was set by the conservative German Nationalists, strong tensions had been created between the convinced republicans and more traditional elements within the party.

The leaders of the Center Party clearly had not anticipated any challenge from their followers when the properties question first began to attract public attention. They seem to have intended to leave the policy decisions, whether concerning the Reichstag legislation or participation in the initiative proceedings, to the appropriate party experts. The rest of the party was expected to accept these decisions passively and

---

[1] Although the following discussion emphasizes the antagonistic elements inside the Center Party, the reader should not overlook the strong ties of loyalty (as well as the realistic assessment that a Catholic splinter movement had very limited chances of prospering) which bound even such outspoken rivals as Wirth and Stegerwald to the party. Morsey, *Die Deutsche Zentrumpartei 1917–1923*, pp. 428–29.

obediently. Consider, for example, the formulation of the party's position regarding the regulatory legislation: for some time after other papers were full of news about the princes' property claims, *Germania* treated the subject cautiously, and certainly gave no premature revelation of what the party's own policies would be.[2] The first major articles appeared after the middle parties had substantively agreed on the first version of the Compromise.[3] They were a series of dry, authoritative accounts written by Karl Anton Schulte, the jurist who was the party's chief negotiator in the Reichstag.[4] Some smaller regional newspapers discussed the property settlements very critically;[5] but *Germania*, conscious of its role as party organ, refused to acknowledge that any Catholics quarreled with the policies established by the Center's Reichstag delegation. Only when public opinion in one of the great regional bases of the Center's power, Cologne, was strong enough to induce the local party organization to criticize some of the main features of the Compromise Bill did the national party begin to modify its position.[6] To avert the multiplication of similar resolutions,[7] the Center Party's Reichstag delegation moved to incorporate some of the Co-

[2] The first indication came late in January. *Germania,* 27 Jan. 1926 (Nr. 43).

[3] Ibid., 30 Jan. (Nr. 49), 2 Feb. (Nr. 54), 4 Feb. (Nr. 59), 11 Feb. (Nr. 70), 26 Feb. (Nr. 95), and 10 March 1926 (Nr. 116).

[4] In his first article Schulte expressed his regret that so much propagandistic talk was being injected into the discussion. He urged "reserve and full objectivity."

[5] Particularly the *Badische Beobachter.* See *Frankfurter Zeitung,* 10 March 1926 (Nr. 183). Unfortunately I was not able to consult files of this paper. However, *Tremonia,* the Center paper for the Dortmund area, was noticeably more sympathetic toward popular demands than *Germania* although it respected officially announced party policy.

[6] A meeting of local party leaders in Cologne approved—after a "lively" discussion—a resolution opposing the initiative and referendum as formulated by the KPD and SPD. But at the same time they urged the passage of a law that would establish an arbitration court, the members of which would be named by the Reichstag and with a majority of laymen. All *Aufwertung* claims would have to be settled according to the same rates that applied to ordinary citizens. The court would also be empowered to reexamine existing settlements to determine if they met the general guidelines established in the new law. *Kölnische Volkszeitung,* 23 Feb. 1926 (Nr. 143); *Germania,* 24 Feb. 1926 (Nr. 91); *Frankfurter Zeitung,* 25 Feb. 1926 (Nr. 148). In his article summarizing the entire course of the controversy, Schulte mentioned that there was disagreement over the composition of the special court, but he did not acknowledge that dissident elements within the Center Party were among those which insisted that laymen be on the court as well as professional jurists. *Politisches Jahrbuch 1926,* p. 496.

[7] The Center Party in Bochum and the *Arbeitgemeinschaft der Arbeiterzentrumswähler Westdeutschland* adopted the Cologne demands. *Frankfurter Zeitung,* 3 March (Nr. 166) and 4 March 1926 (Nr. 168); *Tremonia,* 25 Feb. 1926. Also see the letters warning Marx of the state of public opinion, Stehkämper, 3: 15–19.

logne demands into the Compromise Bill and, thereafter, grudgingly recognized that popular feelings should be taken more into account.

The rejection of any participation in the Communist-Socialist-sponsored confiscation campaign had seemed entirely self-evident to the Center Party's policy-makers.[8] The confiscation proposal was contrary to all law, Schulte had written; its enactment was beneath the dignity of the German nation. "It would mean the robbery of the princely houses and totally deprive them of their rights."[9] Isolated voices to the contrary were ignored until the signing of the initiative petitions actually started. But as reports of the heavy participation in urban areas with a large Catholic population accumulated,[10] it became more and more impossible to deny that Center Party followers were supporting the initiative. Alarm broke out in high quarters of the party as the drive for signatures entered its last week. Urgent appeals to the party followers were issued and two new themes entered official utterances— a stress on party discipline and a sudden emphasis on the highest Christian principles.

On 4 March, *Germania* denied that any Center Party members favored the initiative.[11] There were some differences over the Reichstag bill, it said, but "full unity" prevailed in rejecting confiscation. By 9 March, the paper was forced to concede that some members sympathized with the initiative, either out of indignation "which can be explained psychologically because of the . . . general impoverishment," or for tactical reasons. "Only thus can the voices *in our ranks* which speak in favor of the initiative be explained." *Germania* called upon Center Party followers not to be misled by "moods of the moment." This was a matter of principle; confiscation violated the Christian concept of property.[12]

[8] See the statement issued by the Reichstag delegation, *Germania*, 3 March 1926 (Nr. 103).

[9] Ibid., 30 Jan. 1926 (Nr. 49).

[10] For example, the *Frankfurter Zeitung* reported strong support for the initiative developing in the Breslau area, 11 March (Nr. 188) and 17 March 1926 (Nr. 204). Some Catholic *Arbeitervereine* openly urged participation despite the Reichstag delegation's decision. After the initiative was over *Germania* revealed that it had received "mountains of mail" every day attacking the party's official policy. 18 March 1926 (Nr. 129).

[11] 4 March 1926 (Nr. 106).

[12] 9 March 1926 (Nr. 114), emphasis in original. Marx later wrote, *"Shameful as it is, it has to be admitted that wide circles of Center Party members had lost confidence in their party and were more receptive to selfish motives than able to recognize that even in this question law and justice had to be decisive."* Stehkämper, 3: 11–12, emphasis in original.

Earlier, spokesmen for the Center Party had employed legal and constitutional arguments against confiscation. Now, as some groups within the party dared challenge the Reichstag delegation's proclamation,[13] higher sanctions were remembered. The Bishop of Passau, Dr. Sigismund Freiherr Felix von Ow-Felldorf, condemned the initiative in his diocesan newsletter as a violation of the Seventh Commandment.[14] The initiative, he said, was only the first step toward a general assault on all property. If it was successful, an attack on the property of the church and private citizens would follow. He forbade all believing Catholics to sign the initiative petitions and urged them to retract their names if they had signed unwittingly.[15] Other church dignitaries—although not all— gave similar warnings.[16]

A meeting of Center Party members in the greater Berlin area, 12 March, questioned the party's opposition to the initiative after hearing a report by the Reichstag delegate, Richard Schönborn.[17] The meeting accepted a resolution that called the policy statement by the Reichstag delegation an "attack on the rights guaranteed to every citizen in the Weimar Constitution" and exhorted the voters to support the initiative as the "only effective means" of obtaining satisfactory legislation.[18] Such open defiance outraged the heads of the party. *Germania* at first tried to avoid publishing a report of the meeting. Only when other papers commented on this

[13] For example, the Catholic *Arbeiterverein* in Hanau, *Frankfurter Zeitung,* 9 March 1926 (Nr. 181), and the Center Party in München-Gladbach, *Germania,* 9 March 1926 (Nr. 114).

[14] *Frankfurter Zeitung,* 12 March 1926 (Nr. 190); *Germania,* 14 March 1926 (Nr. 123); Schüren, pp. 129–30.

[15] Names once entered on the petitions could not be legally withdrawn. When questioned in the Legal Committee about the bishop's statement the minister of justice, Dr. Marx, observed, "The fact that the bishop of Passau has spoken of such a pastoral right simply proves that he has spoken only as an ecclesiastical authority *(Oberhirt)* and not as a politician and statesman. (Much laughter)." *Frankfurter Zeitung,* 25 March 1926 (Nr. 224).

[16] For example, Bishop von Keppler of Rottenberg, ibid., 16 March 1926 (Nr. 199) and Bishop Schreiber of Meissen, Stehkämper, 3: 16. Bishop Antonius of Regensburg, however, replied to an inquiry whether signing the lists violated a commandment of God or the Church, that "with all actions much depends on the conscience. The judgment [of conscience], however, is made by God." *Frankfurter Zeitung,* 18 April 1926, reprinting a story from the *Regensburger Echo.*

[17] He reported he had spoken against the prohibition of participation in the initiative, but had been the only member of the Reichstag delegation to do so. He preferred to leave the decision up to the individual voter. *Germania,* 14 March 1926 (Nr. 123).

[18] Idem.

omission did it print the story,[19] but simultaneously sought to argue that the meeting did not truly represent the views of the membership of the Berlin Center Party.[20]

The day after the Berlin meeting, which it was still ignoring, *Germania* published an article entitled "The Center Party Must Remain the Center Party."[21] It deserves extensive quotation. The reasons the Reichstag delegation ordered party voters not to sign the lists were "obvious" (*selbstverständlich*). It was surprising that some Center Party people, and worse yet, a Catholic newspaper, the *Badische Beobachter*, had approved of confiscation without compensation. For a party paper to declare openly that the Center Party's politicians should recognize the mood of the people and act accordingly was highly unusual, and it raised, *Germania* said, an issue of deep significance. "Above all, this is a sign that our party is not an entirely sound organism in which all the parts gladly and in a disciplined manner follow the directives of its thinking brain."

The Center Party, the editorial writer continued, differed from other parties:

We profit from religious values and insights (*Erkenntnissen*) which are of supernatural origin. First of all, we ought to know for certain that the norms which the church as an interpreter of the Divine Will lays down for the individual and for society are applicable to all temporal circumstances. . . . Neither as Catholics nor as Center Party members were we born yesterday; we have a past, a tradition. This fact is left out of consideration . . . by those in our ranks who bring questions (*Problematik*) . . . *where none should be.*

Young Catholics, in particular, lacked a proper sense of tradition, *Germania*'s writer said.[22] The war and its aftermath had caused much confusion. As a result, ". . . we are still a long way from being a party with inner solidarity and infused by *one* spirit. To create this is the object of an active, undisputed

[19] *Frankfurter Zeitung*, 14 March 1926 (Nr. 196).
[20] *Germania* claimed that it was not a regular meeting of the party *Vertrauensmänner*, but only a general meeting heavily packed with young people from the *Windthorstbund* and, therefore, the resolutions lacked any binding character. *Germania*, 14 March (Nr. 123) and 18 March 1926 (Nr. 129). Some of the participants at the meeting did not let this assertion go unchallenged. *Frankfurter Zeitung*, 16 March 1926 (Nr. 201).
[21] *Germania*, 13 March 1926 (Nr. 122). Emphasis in the following quotations is as in the original.
[22] The *Windthorstbund* was not directly named.

leadership which demands unqualified adherence from the party."[23]

Germania was surely right when it identified the loosening hold of tradition on Center Party voters as a reason for party disunity.[24] However, the leaders for whom the newspaper spoke were scarcely willing to admit that the collapse of traditional "moral" forces was part of an irreversible secular trend. They instinctively reached for higher sanctions when their own authority was being defied. After the initiative was over, they endeavored to investigate the reasons for the "unbelievable" lack of discipline among the Catholic voters and to re-establish firm control.[25] These investigations concentrated on some of the surface features of the recent discontent; however, the roots of the Center's troubles in 1926 ran deep.[26]

The Center's historical function as the defender of Germany's Catholic population gave it a social and economic inclusiveness unequaled by any other party.[27] The *Frankfurter*

[23] The *Kölnische Volkszeitung* likewise published an editorial entitled "Come to Your Senses" which defended the policy laid down by the Reichstag delegation. It appeared only a day before the end of the initiative proceedings, however. 16 March 1926 (Nr. 198).

[24] Morsey, *Die Deutsche Zentrumspartei*, pp. 607–21.

[25] See below, pp. 214–16.

[26] The *Frankfurter Zeitung*, 17 March 1926 (Nr. 203), published a letter from an unnamed Center Party member who observed, "there is universal agreement . . . among members of the Center Party as well as among the Democrats that the necessary contact between a member of parliament and the voters is missing because of the large election districts and the fixed list [system of nominating Reichstag candidates]." The divergent views over the properties dispute demonstrated how necessary it was for the Reichstag delegates to keep in touch with public opinion. The writer went on to assert that "the association of Catholics with groups desiring greater freedom *(freiheitlichen Elementen)* has never been harmful—just the reverse!"

[27] Sigmund Neumann's brief appraisal of the Center Party in *Die Parteien der Weimarer Republik*, pp. 41–48, is still a good starting point. It can be supplemented by Bracher, *Die Auflösung*, pp. 89–93 and passim; and for a broader historical range by Buchheim, *Geschichte der christlichen Parteien in Deutschland*, pp. 296–344, or Heinrich Lutz, *Demokratie im Zwielicht* (Munich, 1963). The account of the Weimar period in the old standard history of the Center Party is rather scanty: Karl Bachem, *Vorgeschichte, Geschichte und Politik der Deutschen Zentrumspartei*, Vol. 8 (Cologne, 1931).

In recent years there has been very active investigation of the party's history during Weimar. Overviews are given by Peter Haungs, "Die Zentrumspartei in der Weimarer Republik," *Civitas: Jahrbuch für Christliche Gesellschaftsordnung*, 6 (1967): 252–85; Josef Becker, "Die deutsche Zentrumspartei 1918–1933. Grundprobleme ihrer Entwicklung," *Aus Politik und Zeitgeschichte* (issue B11/68, 13 March 1968), pp. 3–15; and Kurt Töpner, "Der deutsche Katholizismus zwischen 1918 und 1933," in Hans Joachim Schoeps, ed., *Zeitgeist in Wandel* (Stuttgart, 1968), 2: 176–202. The most important narrative to date is Rudolf Morsey, *Die Deutsche Zentrumspartei 1917–1923;* valuable in its own right is Klaus Epstein's review article of this book, "The

Zentrum Party in the Weimar Republic," *Journal of Modern History*, 39 (Nr. 2, June, 1967): 160–63. Morsey has also edited the records of the meetings at the Center's Reichstag delegation and its Executive Board for the years 1926–33. These records are of fundamental importance, but, especially for the year 1926, are often disappointing because of the extremely summary form in which policy discussions were recorded in the minutes. *Die Protokolle der Reichstagsfraktion und des Fraktionsvorstands der Deutschen Zentrumspartei 1926–1933, Veröffentlichungen der Kommission für Zeitgeschichte bei der Katholischen Akademie in Bayern* in association with the *Kommission für Geschichte des Parlamentarismus und der politischen Parteien*, Series A, Vol. 9 (Mainz, 1969).

Johannes Schauff, *Die deutschen Katholiken und die Zentrumspartei* (Cologne, 1928), provides an analysis of the voting behavior of Catholics both inside and out of the Center Party. For an examination of their role in a particularly significant election, John K. Zeender, "German Catholics and the Presidential Election of 1925," *Journal of Modern History*, 35 (Nr. 4, Dec., 1963): 366–81. The dissertation by Helga Grebing, *Zentrum und katholische Arbeiterschaft 1918–1935* (Free University of Berlin, 1953), explores the tensions in the relationship among party leaders and the desires of the organized Catholic workers. Her later articles, "Zentrumspartei und politischer Katholizmus," *Colloquium*, 11 (Nr. 2, 1957): 6–8, and "Die Konservativen und Christlichen seit 1918," *Politische Studien*, 9 (Nr. 99, July, 1958): 482–91, make only limited use of her detailed findings; however, her survey, *Geschichte der deutschen Arbeiterbewegung*, is useful. Early efforts to widen the appeal of the party to new social groups are described by John K. Zeender, "German Catholics and the Concept of an Interconfessional Party 1900–1922," *Journal of Central European Affairs*, 23 (Nr. 4, Jan., 1964): 424–39. See, too, the recent studies by Zeender, *The German Center Party, 1890–1906, Transactions of the American Philosophical Society*, N.S., Vol. 66, Part I (Philadelphia, 1976) and Ronald J. Ross, *Beleaguered Tower: The Dilemma of Political Catholicism in Wilhelmine Germany* (Notre Dame, 1976).

A number of active Center Party politicians submitted contributions explaining the party's work during the first ten years of the Republic for the semi-official volume, Karl Anton Schulte (ed.), *Nationale Arbeit. Das Zentrum und sein Wirken in der deutschen Republik* (Berlin and Leipzig, 1929). Friedrich Dessauer's booklet, *Das Zentrum* (Berlin, 1931), concentrated its attention on party principles rather than on its activities.

Rudolf Morsey in *Das Ende der Parteien*, p. 282, has commented on the noticeable reluctance of Center Party figures to write memoirs. Joseph Joos, *Am Räderwerk der Zeit* (Augsburg, 1951), and Georg Schreiber, *Zwischen Demokratie und Diktatur* (Regensburg and Münster, 1949), are both rather slight. Much more informative is Heinrich Köhler, *Lebenserinnerungen des Politiker und Staatsmannes, 1878–1949*, edited with a useful introduction by Josef Becker (Stuttgart, 1964). Hugo Stehkämper has prepared an invaluable guide with extensive quotations to the papers of former Chancellor Marx. *Der Nachlass des Reichskanzlers Wilhelm Marx* (4 vols.; Cologne, 1968). Heinrich Brüning, *Memoiren, 1918–1934* (Stuttgart, 1970), concentrates primarily on his chancellorship.

Klaus Epstein, *Matthias Erzberger and the Dilemma of German Democracy* (Princeton, 1959), is virtually the only significant work in English on this phase of the Center Party's history. The collection of short biographies, edited by Rudolf Morsey, *Zeitgeschichte in Lebensbildern: Aus dem deutschen Katholizismus des 20. Jahrhunderts* (Mainz, 1973), is very useful. Joseph Wirth, who attempted to continue the party's commitment to republican politics which Erzberger had begun, is the subject of two good articles: Karl Griewank, "Dr. Wirth und die Krisen der Weimarer Republik," *Wissenschaftliche Zeitschrift der Friedrich-Schiller-Universität Jena. Gesellschafts und Sprachwissenschaftliche Reihe*. 1 (Nr. 1, 1951/52): 1–10, and Josef Becker, "Joseph Wirth und die Krise des Zentrums während des IV. Kabinettes Marx (1927–1928)," *Zeitschrift für die Geschichte des Oberrheins*, 109 (Nr. 2, 1961): 362–482. On Wirth's main rival: Josef Deutz, *Adam Stegerwald. Gewerkschaftler, Politiker, Minister 1874–1945* (Co-

Zeitung once wrote that "the Center Party is a small Reichstag by itself."[28] It encompassed nearly all social classes, ranging from peasants and industrial workers on the one hand, across broad segments of the middle class, to church dignitaries and aristocratic landowners on the other. Except where political issues touched on fundamental religious concerns, no single set of political or social values governed the reactions of the different groups belonging to the Center Party.[29] For a long time the heads of the party had been able to rely on strong customary acceptance of their authority to maintain unity. Usually, however, they tempered their exercise of decisive control by undertaking the widest possible accommodation of divergent interests.[30] The practice of calculated compromise that usually worked well within the party was extended to relations with other parties as well:

logne, 1952), and Helmut J. Schorr, *Adam Stegerwald. Gewerkschaftler und Politiker der ersten deutschen Republik* (Recklinghausen, 1966). Paul Weymar's officially approved biography of *Konrad Adenauer* (Munich, 1955) contains some information on his activities during the Weimar Republic, particularly pp. 129–43, on his attempt to form a Great Coalition government in 1926. Also consult Fritz Stern, "Adenauer and a Crisis in Weimar Democracy," *Political Science Quarterly,* 73 (Nr. 1, March, 1958): 1–27. Oswald Wachtling, *Joseph Joos: Journalist, Arbeiterführer, Zentrumspolitiker. Politische Biographie, 1878–1933, Veröffentlichungen der Kommission für Zeitgeschichte,* Series B, Vol. 16 (Mainz, 1974). Theodor Eschenburg, "Carl Sonnenschein," in *Die Improvisierte Demokratie,* pp. 110–42, gives a sympathetic portrait of a priest with a strong concern for remedying social evils. Arthur Wynen, *Ludwig Kaas: Aus seinem Leben und Wirken* (Trier, 1953), is inadequate.

The activities of the Center Party in the end phase of the Republic have attracted much interest. Morsey contributed a major chapter, "Die Deutsche Zentrumspartei," to the collective work, *Das Ende der Parteien,* pp. 281–453, and rewrote his conclusions in more popular form, "The Center Party between the Fronts," in *The Path to Dictatorship,* pp. 68–88. Werner Conze, "Brünings Politik unter dem Druck der Grossen Krise," *Historische Zeitschrift,* 199 (Nr. 3, 1964): 529–50, and Josef Becker, "Heinrich Brüning in den Krisenjahren der Weimarer Republik," *Geschichte in Wissenschaft und Unterricht,* 17 (Nr. 4, April, 1966): 201–19, give rather different assessments of Brüning's policies. All of these articles establish lines of continuity between the policies of the Center in the 1920s and the years 1930–33.

[28] 10 Jan. 1925 (Nr. 26). Similarly, Bracher, *Die Auflösung,* p. 92.

[29] Joos emphasized the inclusiveness of the Center's commitments. "Religion *and* love of our country, fatherland *and* humanity, Germany *and* Europe, centralism *and* federalism, power *and* law." Quoted by Neumann, p. 47, emphasis as in original.

[30] Consider the following characterization of the party's long-time leader, Constantin Fehrenbach, who died early in 1926. "A sense for political realities and limits was characteristic of Fehrenbach's entire political career. He constantly strived for inner unity across divisions, for the *Volksgemeinschaft.* In his efforts to resolve frictions in his own camp or to come to an understanding with other parties his nature—always abhorring a fight—was . . . almost too understanding and . . . too ready for compromise, so [his policies] lacked consistency and determination." Hermann Sacher quoted by Morsey, *Die Deutsche Zentrumspartei 1917–1923,* p. 336, note 10. Similarly, on Trimborn, ibid., p. 574.

The Center Party was the party of the Catholics but not the Catholic Party. It represented the interests of the Catholic Church, but outside this sphere it followed policies determined by tactical or substantive considerations . . . which other groups could credibly be expected to support. Thus, it was a reliable coalition partner—the word "reliable" is not meant to suggest any moral quality but is simply a political observation: it was calculable, one knew where one was and could rely on its readiness to make compromises.[31]

In 1924, Wilhelm Marx endeavored to elevate the spirit of compromise into national purpose by attempting to form a political *Volksgemeinschaft*, reaching from the Social Democrats to the Nationalists. The undertaking failed, but the fact that it was attempted by a Center Party leader is itself significant.[32]

Because neither a left nor a right coalition in the Reichstag was possible without the Center Party, it was rather freer than the other parties to determine its political alignments as it saw fit.[33] The "traditional elasticity"[34] of its relations with other parties gave the Center a freedom to maneuver which enabled it to avoid being trapped into supporting partisan aims incompatible with its own interests.[35] The leaders of the Center regarded a coalition with other parties as a kind of

[31] Otto Heinrich von der Gablentz, *Politische Parteien als Ausdruck gesellschaftlicher Kräfte* (Berlin, 1952), p. 15.

[32] Stürmer, pp. 73–78, emphasizes that the effort to form a nearly all-inclusive *Volksgemeinschaft* coalition was intended at least as much to assuage conflicts inside the Center Party as to find a stable government for Germany. See, too, Lutz, pp. 102–4; Braun, pp. 151 and 166–67; and Westarp, *Am Grabe der Parteiherrschaft*, p. 67.

[33] See Stegerwald's defense at the 1928 party convention of the course the party had taken in recent years, reprinted in *Ursachen und Folgen*, 7: 333–34. To be sure, like other politicians conscious of criticism from within their own ranks, he emphasized *how little* freedom of choice the party had had. "In any case, the Center Party is much more restricted in its choice whether or not it will participate in a government than all the other parties. The main questions facing the Center Party . . . are whether it will occupy a more or a less exposed position in a government, whether it will take responsibility for departments of great or of lesser [importance]" (p. 334). Similarly the Prussian *Landtag* member, Friedrich Grebe, wrote, "We are a born minority. Cooperation with other parties is thus an *enduring necessity.*" *Germania*, 15 Sept. 1925 (Nr. 430), emphasis in original. Other statements often stressed the Center's "duty" to participate in governments. Morsey, *Die Deutsche Zentrumspartei 1917–1923*, p. 312, note 7. Such statements obviously play down the extent to which the Center was able to influence the character of the coalitions it joined.

[34] Bachem, 8: 257, quoted by Morsey, *Die Deutsche Zentrumspartei 1917–1923*, p. 172.

[35] Morsey, in *Das Ende der Parteien*, pp. 412–13.

"working agreement," not a "community of ideas."[36] Such adaptability did not please its sometime partners.[37] Although occasionally the Center's leaders acted indecisively, in general their "middle-of-the-road" policies (*Politik der Mitte*) were the results of conscious purpose.[38] Perhaps more than anything else, the reluctance of the Center leaders to abandon the Weimar Coalition in Prussia at a time when they supported right and middle-party coalitions at the national level illustrates how deliberately they wanted to avoid "clear battlefronts."[39]

Not all Center Party adherents shared their leaders' preference for treating political alignments as a question of tactics. Three different groupings—reactionary, interdenominational, and republican—sought to identify the party with a distinct political commitment and replace the fluctuating associations of the past by a firm alliance with like-minded forces in other parties. These groupings never became strong enough to justify calling them factions.[40] The intermittent shifts of national politics, the skill of the party leaders in devising compromises, and the strong attachment of the bulk of the party to middle-of-the-road policies tended to dissipate sectarian obstinacy.[41] Nevertheless, these groupings worried party leaders, primarily because they were the chief sources of intra-party criticism of official actions. Furthermore, party leaders sensed that if any of these groupings

[36] According to Marx at the *Parteitag*, Nov. 1925. *Germania*, 16 Nov. 1925 (Nr. 537). His words were "nur *Arbeitsgemeinschaften*, kein *Ideengemeinschaften*."

[37] A Nationalist writer later claimed that the Center obtained its dominant position in German politics in the mid-twenties only "by managing constantly to play the right and the left off against one another." Axel von Freytagh-Loringhoven, *Deutschnationale Volkspartei* (Berlin, 1931), p. 31. Chancellor Marx's political adaptability was attacked in almost identical terms by SPD and DVP critics: Georg Decker, "Lehren des Volksentscheids," *Die Gesellschaft* (1926, Part 2): 195, and Deutsche Volkspartei, *Wahlhandbuch 1928* (Berlin, 1928), pp. 119–20.

[38] Stürmer, pp. 262-64, 274; Haungs, pp. 71, 254–56; Lutz, p. 90.

[39] Proponents of a particular direction did not always recognize that the Center's leaders wanted to avoid the polarization of German politics. For instance, the *Frankfurter Zeitung*, 10 Jan. 1925 (Nr. 26). On the Center's divergent policies regarding coalition in the Reich and the Prussian governments, Neumann, pp. 45–46; Schulze, pp. 517–18.

[40] For example, the sharp rivalry between Wirth and Stegerwald diminished after 1926. They actually joined to oppose the formation of the right-oriented fourth Marx government and the high pay raises for government officials which Finance Minister Köhler introduced in 1927. Schorr, pp. 103–8, 116-27; Köhler, pp. 255–65.

[41] Zeender, *Journal of Central European Affairs*, 23: 438; Stürmer, p. 274.

successfully realized its goals, the traditional character of the Center Party and probably its further existence would be endangered.

The most conservative elements in the pre-war Center had been embittered by the party's rapid acceptance of the revolution as "an accomplished fact."[42] Some followed the example of the historian Martin Spahn and transferred their allegiance to the DNVP which, for its part, gladly encouraged such political conversions.[43] Others remained associated with the Center Party, but devoted much energy to attacks on prominent party leaders for betraying "Catholic" principles.[44] Mostly landed aristocrats or intellectuals, these men scorned cooperation with the "irreligious" socialists.[45] They did not disguise their monarchist sympathies and tended to oppose all social changes, unless they turned back toward the hierarchical order of a pre-industrial world.

During the mid-twenties, Franz von Papen played a prominent part among the defenders of "Christian-Conservative thinking." He wrote occasional articles on the importance of "moral principles" in politics, vaguely identifying "justice and love" as the necessary basis for all political action.[46] At the same time, he argued for "authoritarian leadership in parties aware of their responsibility."

> The examination of how suitable [a political program] is for the present time . . . is a matter for the appropriate bodies *(Instanzen)* and party conventions. The determination of tactics, however, is the responsibility of authoritarian leadership. This leadership can never rest with the masses. That is the first, most essential point—indeed, the presupposition of the Christian-Conservative idea.[47]

---

[42] Morsey, *Die Deutsche Zentrumspartei 1917–1923*, p. 83.

[43] Ibid., pp. 312–15, 352, 404; Buchheim, p. 329. Spahn's joining of the DNVP was especially disturbing because his father had long been one of the most prominent of Center leaders.

[44] Morsey, *Die Deutsche Zentrumspartei 1917–1923*, pp. 172–76, 236–42.

[45] The Weimar Coalition was called "a political mixed marriage with heresy," ibid., p. 172. The expression of such rightist sentiments had started even before 1918, very largely in reaction to the Center's support of Prussian electoral reform. Zeender, *Journal of Central European Affairs*, 23: 429–30.

[46] "Der christlich-konservative Gedanke," *Germania*, 6 Sept. 1925 (Nr. 416). Papen's statement of principles in his *Memoirs* (London, 1952), pp. 90–97, indicates a highly unrealistic and superficial understanding of modern life. See the perceptive appraisal by Theodor Eschenburg, "Franz von Papen," *Vierteljahrshefte für Zeitgeschichte*, 1 (Nr. 2, April, 1953): 152–69; Bracher, *Die Auflösung*, pp. 518–19.

[47] *Germania*, 6 Sept. 1925 (Nr. 416).

Yet neither such a theoretical affirmation of the party leaders' responsibility for making binding decisions, nor his own position as a member of the Prussian *Landtag* delegation and as the major stockholder in the *Germania* publishing company, prevented von Papen from following an independent course when it suited his purposes.[48] Early in 1925, von Papen and a few friends defied party discipline in order to vote with the parties of the right against the formation of a Weimar Coalition in Prussia, a government which Wilhelm Marx was scheduled to head.[49] A few months later, he campaigned openly for Hindenburg's election, once again rejecting Marx because he was the joint candidate of the republican parties.[50] Even in his memoirs, written after the Second World War, von Papen blamed the Center Party for failing "to break with the Socialists in order to rescue the right-wing parties from the torpidity of endless opposition."[51]

Reactionary Catholics like Papen exercised very limited influence directly within the Center Party.[52] Nonetheless, they could capitalize on their wealth, social position, and extensive contacts when they wanted to make their views known.[53] Particularly useful were their connections with powerful Catholic associations and important members of the church hierarchy. Many of the higher clergy were themselves very conservative. Before the elections to the Weimar National Assembly the Prussian bishops warned believing Catholics against "Christianity-hating socialism."[54] A few years later, Cardinal Faulhaber publicly declared that the revolution of 1918 was due

[48] He tells with great pride of his independent course as a member of the Prussian *Landtag*. *Memoirs*, pp. 100, 106–10. On his relations with the *Germania* editorial staff, ibid., pp. 111–13. But now see Herbert Gottward, "Franz von Papen und die 'Germania.' Ein Beitrag zur Geschichte des politischen Katholizismus und der Zentrumspresse in der Weimarer Republik," *Jahrbuch für Geschichte*, 6 (1972): 539–604, and Jürgen A. Bach, *Franz von Papen in der Weimarer Republik. Aktivitäten in Politik und Presse, 1918–1932* (Düsseldorf, 1977).

[49] *Memoirs*, p. 106; Eyck, 1: 428–29.

[50] *Memoirs*, pp. 107–8.

[51] Ibid., p. 106.

[52] Papen, himself, admits that he was "an outsider." Ibid., p. 108. One of the first consequences of the revolution had been the vanishing of aristocrats from prominent positions in the party delegations. Morsey, *Die Deutsche Zentrumspartei 1917–1923*, p. 154.

[53] Eschenburg, *Vierteljahrshefte für Zeitgeschichte*, 1: 156.

[54] Morsey, *Die Deutsche Zentrumspartei 1917–1923*, p. 134; a similar appeal for the election of candidates who stood for "order, religion and morality" during the 1921 Prussian *Landtag* elections is mentioned by Zeender, *Journal of Central European Affairs*, 23: 437, note 52.

to "perjury and high treason," and thus would forever "carry the mark of Cain."[55] In 1925, the cardinal archbishop of Breslau cautioned Catholic youth against joining the *Reichsbanner*.[56] Although the hierarchy no longer exercised the same degree of influence in Center Party affairs it once had done, party leaders scarcely dared to ignore the views of the prelates.

Although out-and-out reaction found relatively little support among the Center Party's voters, party leaders knew that more moderate shadings of conservative and monarchist opinions were widely accepted. Hence, great care was taken in the composition of statements of general principles. Ambiguity or outright omission of significant words helped avoid arousing unwanted controversy. The Center's "Guidelines" of 1922, for example, stated that the party was committed to "the Christian conception of the state," that it was a "constitutional party" which accepted the "state [established] by the German People" *(deutschen Volksstaat)*. However, there was no mention of the words "republic" or "democracy."[57] By 1925–26, the party openly admitted its acceptance of the Republic and the Weimar Constitution, but with subtle qualifying phrases calculated to allay dissatisfaction among its right wing.[58] Even so, a flurry of complaints came into *Germania*'s editorial offices when the paper printed a front page

[55] In a speech at the *Katholikentag* in 1922. Morsey, *Die Deutsche Zentrumspartei 1917–1923*, p. 476. It is noteworthy that Chancellor Wirth had been criticized for interjecting politics at a non-partisan occasion when he praised the recently murdered Erzberger at the *Katholikentag* the previous year. Ibid., pp. 401–2. Lutz, pp. 82–83, 95–100.

[56] Becker, *Zeitschrift für die Geschichte des Oberrheins*, 109: 390, note 129.

[57] *Ursachen und Folgen*, 7: 325–27; Morsey, *Die Deutsche Zentrumspartei 1917–1923*, pp. 437–42. Party leaders prided themselves on their clever choice of the word *Volksstaat*, ibid., p. 440.

[58] A resolution passed at the 1925 party convention stated: "The Center Party is in its basic character a constitutional party. Its principles . . . regarding the state and authority enable it to approve every form of government in which these principles find realization. . . . The Center Party affirms [its allegiance] to the German Republic as it is established in the Weimar Constitution and considers both its protection and its infusion with the Christian spirit as [a party] duty. . . ." Bachem, 8: 339.

The party's Advisory Committee restated this commitment 3 October 1926: "[The Center Party] considers itself and its members obligated to strengthen and fortify the German Republic internally. The indispensible foundation stones of the German Republic, as of every state, are and will remain Christian morality and order, a sound family life, family, occupational and national unity, and the strictest social justice. The German Republic requires this, in truth, conservative spirit. This is the goal of the Center's policies, not a Republic shaped by materialistic or individualistic [values]." *Ursachen und Folgen*, 7: 328.

illustration of a young man carrying the black-red-gold banner of the Republic in the issue announcing the opening of the 1925 party convention.[59] Regard for the views of supporters who did not wholeheartedly accept the Republic was not the sole motivation for the Center leaders' concessions to conservative opinion; the desire to establish a basis for closer collaboration with the Bavarian People's Party and, perhaps, the eventual reunification of the two parties, also acted as a strong inducement.[60]

It is not easy to characterize the views of the second major tendency within the Center Party, the Brauns-Stegerwald grouping, by one word or phrase. Its own spokesmen felt this difficulty. They strung together a number of different adjectives to identify their aims, i.e., "German, Christian, democratic, social."[61] Even so, these words required further explication to give them a specific meaning. For example, they wanted an "organic" democracy, not formalistic "western" democracy.[62] Heinrich Brauns and Adam Stegerwald articulated the views of organized Catholic workers who, out of religious conviction, rejected Marxian socialism, a rejection that was reinforced by a history of bitter fights with the Free Trade Unions.[63] They thought of themselves as patriotic Germans and wanted to cooperate with "sound" national elements across confessional and class lines.[64] Committed republicans both inside and outside the Center Party labelled this group "reactionary."[65] However, a strong commitment to modern social legislation as well as the fact that the group had few ties with the old ruling classes point to the inadequacy of any such categorization. Traditional values were important to the leaders of this group, yet did not set unalterable limits to their thinking. During the first years of the Republic they urged the creation of a new interdenominational party in the hope that Catholics and Protestants could overcome their differences within the bounds of a single, strong "moderate"

[59] *Germania,* 15 Nov. 1925 (Nr. 536) and the remarks of its editor, Dr. Spiecker, at the convention. Ibid., 17 Nov. 1925 (Nr. 538).

[60] Zeender, *Journal of Modern History,* 35: 379; Buchheim, p. 368; Lutz, pp. 104–9.

[61] Schorr, p. 70.

[62] Morsey, *Die Deutsche Zentrumspartei 1917–1923,* p. 371.

[63] Schorr, pp. 67–69; Buchheim, pp. 412–13; Lutz, p. 106.

[64] "The Christian workers' movement is called upon to work toward the formation of a united national sentiment *(Gedankens)* in Germany." Schorr, p. 68, quoting a speech by Stegerwald 25 April 1920.

[65] Ibid., pp. 81–87.

party.[66] This goal was, in fact, premature in the early twenties. The bulk of the Center Party held tenaciously to its traditional identity. The creation of such an interdenominational party came about only after 1945.

On most matters Brauns and Stegerwald enjoyed distinct advantages for making their views known at the highest levels of the party. Heinrich Brauns was named minister of labor in the Fehrenbach government of 1920 because of his years of experience in Catholic educational and social welfare activities.[67] His expertise, combined with the inability of other parties to agree on a replacement equally acceptable to the left and the right, enabled him to maintain that post until 1928 despite numerous changes of cabinets. This exceptional continuity of service gave Brauns great weight in cabinet meetings and Center Party councils alike.[68]

Adam Stegerwald's political career grew out of his achievements as an organizer and leader of the Christian Trade Unions.[69] He obtained office a number of times, but unlike Brauns, saw his tenure of ministerial positions suffer the usual vicissitudes of Weimar politics.[70] Even when out of office, his name remained among those regularly mentioned whenever a cabinet was being formed. As spokesman for one of the most powerful and best organized interest groups associated with the Center Party, and as a ranking member of the *Parteivorstand*, he could expect a careful hearing on nearly all matters of domestic policy.[71] When Wilhelm Marx became seriously ill in 1928, Stegerwald functioned as *de facto* party

[66] Buchheim, pp. 412–13.

[67] Morsey, *Die Deutsche Zentrumspartei 1917–1923*, pp. 95, 332–33, 620; Köhler, pp. 220–21; Hubert Mockenhaupt, "Heinrich Brauns (1868–1939)," in Morsey, ed., *Zeitgeschichte in Lebensbildern*, pp. 148–59. Mockenhaupt has also edited a collection of his articles and speeches. Heinrich Brauns, *Katholische Sozialpolitik im 20. Jahrhundert: Ausgewählte Aufsätze und Reden, Veröffentlichungen der Kommission für Zeitgeschichte*, Series A, Vol. 19 (Mainz, 1976).

[68] Haungs, pp. 259–60.

[69] Schorr, pp. 24–62; Köhler, pp. 223–24; Rudolf Morsey, "Adam Stegerwald (1874–1945)," in *Zeitgeschichte in Lebensbildern*, pp. 206–19; Ellen L. Evans, "Adam Stegerwald and the Role of the Christian Trade Unions in the Weimar Republic," *Catholic Historical Review*, 59 (Nr. 4, Jan., 1974): 602–26.

[70] He was Prussian minister for welfare, 1919–21, Prussian minister-president, 1921, national minister of transport, 1929–30, and minister of labor, 1930–32. He rejected a second appointment as Prussian minister of welfare late in 1921 and was mentioned as a possible chancellor in 1923 and 1927. Schorr, pp. 62–67, 80–81, 106, 151–246.

[71] Throughout the twenties Stegerwald was regularly re-elected as one of the party's vice-presidents and thus was automatically a member of the *Parteivorstand*. Morsey, *Die Deutsche Zentrumspartei 1917–1923*, p. 587.

chairman and head of the Reichstag delegation.[72] Overconfidently, he expected that the party convention would confirm his succession to these positions.[73] Many delegates to the convention, however, thought he was too closely identified with the interests of the trade unionists and disliked his abrasive manner. They turned instead to the less controversial cleric, Ludwig Kaas.[74] Although Stegerwald failed to realize his highest ambitions, his career within the Center Party was very successful in all ordinary senses of the word.

The singular contrast between Brauns's and Stegerwald's effective relations with the other members of the party leadership on matters of day-to-day politics and the complete lack of success they had in their efforts to persuade the party to transform itself should be emphasized. The creation of a new party—particularly one intended to bridge the major religious denominations—would have been difficult under any circumstances. Yet the methods Brauns and Stegerwald employed were almost certainly too timid to achieve their goals. They concentrated on propagating their ideas through speeches and articles, but did relatively little to force the project ahead against the will of existing policy-making bodies within the party.

Until recently the extent of Brauns's involvement in projects for establishing a new interdenominational party in the early twenties has been insufficiently recognized.[75] In part, this is because Brauns preferred to argue his case confidentially through established party channels. The revolution was only a few days old when Brauns submitted a memorandum to the leaders of the Center Party in the Rhineland urging the abandonment of the old party identity in order to create a new party capable of competing with the Social Democrats for the support of the masses.[76] Similar recommendations were made by other individuals associated with the *Volksverein*.

[72] Schorr, p. 134.
[73] Schorr, pp. 132–33, reports that Stegerwald wrote out a few lines of thanks to the convention for electing him party chairman, but never had the opportunity to deliver the speech. The note still remains in the Stegerwald Archive.
[74] Ibid., pp. 128–51; Morsey, in *Das Ende der Parteien*, pp. 285–91; and the letter from Karl Bachem to Richard Müller (Fulda), ibid., p. 419.
[75] Morsey, *Die Deutsche Zentrumspartei 1917–1923*, p. 370.
[76] Ibid., pp. 95–96; Zeender, *Journal of Central European Affairs*, 23: 432–33. Both Zeender (pp. 424–33) and Morsey (pp. 33–41) emphasize that the debate over interconfessionality versus pure or "integral" Catholicism started well before the beginning of the First World War—in the period of the *Zentrumsstreit* and *Gewerksschaftsstreit*. Also, see Schorr, pp. 38–49.

Although the idea of creating a new party was discussed, the bulk of the party's leaders refused to accept the idea that the old Center Party was unsuited for the new time.[77] If they felt any doubts whether the further existence of the Center Party was justified, the attacks of the new Prussian minister of culture, Adolf Hoffmann, on the established forms of religious instruction in the schools rapidly swept away any uncertainty. Under circumstances that to many Catholics seemed reminiscent of the *Kulturkampf* the party rallied loyally to its "old banner."[78] A few relatively minor gestures of accommodation were made to the idea of a more broadly based popular party. In some areas the Center Party added the words "Christian People's Party" or "Free German People's Party" to its name on election placards,[79] while party officials from time to time expressed an interest in winning the support of Protestants.[80]

Stegerwald showed rather more flair than Brauns for attracting publicity for his efforts to encourage the formation of a truly new party. His appeal at Essen 21 November 1920, for "remodeling the German party system" was designed to receive maximum attention.[81] The ideas he expressed in this speech have been widely regarded as a major forerunner of the present Christian Democratic Union.[82] "We demand a Christian state," he said. "The state [must] remain attuned to the Christian traditions of our culture and not define its task by ignoring the living forces of Christianity. . . ."[83] He

---

[77] Morsey, *Die Deutsche Zentrumspartei 1917–1923*, pp. 96–109.

[78] Ibid., pp. 110–17, 133–42, 607–10.

[79] Ibid., pp. 98–99, 103, 108–9. But in 1920 the eminent party leader and historian Karl Bachem refused the request of the editors of the *Handbuch der Politik* that he write an article on the "Christliche Volkspartei." With some indignation he wrote, "Why do you want to drop the article on the 'Zentrum'? The Center Party still exists . . . without any interruption in its historical continuity. . . . To be sure, it is correct that the supporters of the Center Party in *Berlin* fought the election campaign as the Christian People's Party. However, this change of 'firm' in Berlin was very premature, did not correspond at all with the intentions of the whole Center Party, and in no way sets the standard—for the Berlin Center Party is not yet that of Germany." Ibid., p. 290, note 34.

[80] Ibid., pp. 101, 108, 132, 134, 368, 473; on the vain efforts to attract more Protestants into the Center Party, Buchheim, pp. 332–35.

[81] Schorr, p. 71; Zeender, *Journal of Central European Affairs*, 23: 435–37.

[82] Schorr, p. 310; Leo Schwering, *Frühgeschichte der Christlich-Demokratischen Union* (Recklinghausen, 1963), p. 50. The extent of Heinrich Brüning's involvement in the formulation of this speech has been much discussed. Ibid., p. 51; Morsey, *Die Deutsche Zentrumspartei 1917–1923*, p. 370, note 5.

[83] Schorr, pp. 69–70, 302. According to Morsey, *Die Deutsche Zentrumspartei 1917–1923*, p. 365, Brauns argued before the party's Advisory Committee that continued political cooperation with the Social Democrats was "extremely hazardous."

argued that the fragmentation of political opinion endangered these and other crucial values while at the same time it robbed Germany's foreign and domestic policies of the strength of continuity. He saw the establishment of a party joining "patriotic, Christian, popular (volkstümlich) and truly social elements from all . . . classes," [84] and thus potentially able to counterbalance the SPD as a major step toward a more stable and healthy political system. He proposed various measures to prepare the ground for such a party—most notably by the establishment of a special newspaper.[85] He suggested that the membership of the Christian Trade Unions might serve as a base from which the new party could expand since Catholics and Protestants were already successfully cooperating in these unions.[86]

Despite a brief flush of newspaper interst in Stegerwald's speech his proposal was given a "first class burial." [87] Stegerwald may have thought that the political situation was so fluid his speech itself would unleash a rush of acceptance for the new party.[88] Preparatory discussions had been limited to his colleagues in the Christian Trade Unions and the Center Party. The unionists promised him wholehearted support but the party leadership turned a deaf ear.

Professor Morsey's researches have disclosed that Stegerwald's Essen speech did not come as the surprise to the Center's leadership which many contemporaries assumed it had been.[89] With Brauns's support, Stegerwald presented his ideas at meetings of the Center's Reichstag delegation and Advisory Committee about a month before the Essen speech, but was unable to convince these policy-making groups that a new interdenominational party was feasible.[90] The Advisory

---

[84] Schorr, p. 70. On another occasion he spoke of the need "to draw many of our best people out of their political apathy and their hostility toward the party system." Ibid., p. 67.

[85] Ibid., p. 71. The paper, Der Deutsche, began publication in April 1921. Ibid., p. 74. The other preliminary steps Stegerwald recommended included the foundation of a "People's Bank" and the formation of a parliamentary action committee.

[86] Schorr, p. 70; Morsey, Die Deutsche Zentrumspartei 1917–1923, p. 366.

[87] Schwering, p. 50.

[88] Morsey, Die Deutsche Zentrumspartei 1917–1923, pp. 372, 374–5; Schorr, pp. 77–78.

[89] Morsey, Die Deutsche Zentrumspartei 1917–1923, pp. 363–69.

[90] Stegerwald and Brauns presented their ideas to the Reichstag delegation on 18 Oct. and to the party Advisory Committee 30–31 Oct. 1920. On the latter occasion Brauns urged "Let's not be petty, the time [for forming a new party] has never been more favorable." Ibid., p. 366.

Committee sidetracked the crucial issue by resolving to "enlarge" the party's following and by appointing a committee to prepare a new party program.[91] Stegerwald delivered his famous public address fully aware that his proposals did not have the backing of the Center's leadership, yet he did not venture to confront them with an accomplished fact.[92] Much to the disappointment of some of his associates he failed to announce the formation of the new party despite his eloquent description of the need for such a step. Neither did he fight relentlessly for its creation thereafter.[93] He seems to have thought that either a process of consolidation among the various parties would take place voluntarily, or that some kind of drastic revision of the constitution would occur.[94] He continued to write and speak in favor of his project, modifying it as time went along.[95] However, he rejected the risks involved in an open break with the Center's leaders, probably the only way that a genuine new party could have been brought into existence.

As time went on, Stegerwald appears to have abandoned hope for any rapid changes of the German party system.[96] He and Brauns accepted whatever course of policy the party leadership established even though they made it clear that they preferred ties with the other middle-class parties rather than close association with the Social Democrats.[97] In 1922 Stegerwald advocated bringing the Center, DVP, BVP, and

[91] Stegerwald was, to be sure, named to this committee. Ibid., pp. 368, 376; Zeender, *Journal of Central European Affairs*, 23: 437; Schorr, p. 75.

[92] Morsey, *Die Deutsche Zentrumspartei 1917–1923*, p. 375.

[93] Ibid., p. 371.

[94] "If every party hard-neckedly sticks to its name, party tradition and its previous party program, then one does not need to be a prophet to . . . predict that in a short time a new formation of the party system will be brought about from the outside, without the consent of the parties." From a speech to the *Parteitag* of the Prussian Center Party, 12 Dec. 1920, quoted by Schorr, p. 72. In a speech at Coesfeld, 20 Oct. 1926, he formulated the alternatives somewhat differently. "For Germany in the foreseeable future there is only an either/or choice: *either several parties find their way into a coalition of some duration or a modification of the system of government toward that of the Americans or the Swiss must come about*" (i.e., creation of a strong, independent president or appointment of the cabinet for a fixed period of time), *Germania*, 21 Oct. 1926 (Nr. 490), emphasis in original.

[95] Morsey, *Die Deutsche Zentrumspartei 1917–1923*, pp. 376–78.

[96] Ibid., pp. 407–8.

[97] Ibid., pp. 469–70, 610–11. At the 1925 party convention Brauns argued against any explicit commitment to republican principles on the grounds that Christian values constituted the foundation of the Center's beliefs. Consequently, he said, the party should tolerate divergent political attitudes, including acceptance of constitutional monarchy. *Germania*, 17 Nov. 1925 (Nr. 538).

the Democrats into a close parliamentary alliance *(Arbeitsge-meinschaft)* to counteract the merger of the SPD and USPD.[98] In 1924 he urged the inclusion of the DNVP in the national government:

> The parliamentary system has the advantage that it educates the citizen for responsibility. For this reason I would have liked to have seen the Nationalists enter the government if it had been possible. Then their propagandistic chattering against the government and the governing parties would have finally had to stop.[99]

When the right coalition was formed in 1925, many observers considered it proof of Stegerwald's growing influence on the Center Party's policy. Generally he relied on tactical arguments to justify cooperation with the right. Like a number of other Center leaders, he stated that it was important for the party to maintain its freedom of action; it, therefore, had to be careful to avoid any one-sided identification with a particular political direction.[100] But for all of Stegerwald's stress on problems of tactics, few observers regarded his statements as impartial policy recommendations. If for no other reasons, his vigorous, persistent criticism of the group of committed republicans around Joseph Wirth made that impossible.[101]

After the death of Matthias Erzberger, Joseph Wirth emerged as the leader of that segment of the Center Party which defended the Republic out of deep conviction, not just for reasons of expediency.[102] Through a strong avowal of

[98] Schorr, p. 77.

[99] From an article published 2 Dec. 1924, quoted by Schorr, p. 89. Two years later he still justified his past efforts "to burden the right with responsibility for the state." There was no real danger in this policy, he said, because "German politics since the revolution have been [dictated] 75 percent by necessity and no party, whether right or left-oriented, was in the position to substantially change this." Ibid., p. 307.

[100] Schorr, pp. 90–91; "[The party] must consider step by step *what it itself wants,* independent of right and left." *Germania,* 21 Oct. 1926 (Nr. 490), emphasis in original.

[101] Morsey, *Die Deutsche Zentrumspartei 1917–1923,* p. 428. In 1923 Stegerwald wrote, "Above all I am a determined opponent of formal democracy. Whoever believes that in the present situation in Germany he needs only the majority of those people who voted in the Reichstag elections behind him in order to restore a powerless state from . . . collapse . . . to its [rightful] place in the world is a political child." Schorr, p. 80.

[102] Morsey, *Die Deutsche Zentrumspartei 1917–1923,* esp. pp. 386–92, 418–430, 457–67, 490–96; Thomas A. Knapp, "Joseph Wirth (1879–1956)," in Morsey, ed., *Zeitgeschichte in Lebensbildern,* pp. 160–73.

republicanism, he hoped for a permanent reorientation of the Center Party toward the left.[103] Under very difficult conditions he served as chancellor from May 1921 until November 1922. He undertook unpopular commitments in foreign affairs necessary to implement the "Fulfillment" policy; and, in order to have as strong a hand as possible, as well as for greater domestic stability, he sought the closest possible cooperation with the Social Democrats.[104]

From the first, Wirth's words and actions displeased many of the more conservative Center Party members.[105] However, Wirth established an unrivaled popularity with the masses of the electorate by relying on his own political initiative, his youth, and skill as an orator. Even Heinrich Köhler—no friendly witness—admitted that anyone who heard Joseph Wirth at his best never forgot the experience.[106] Unfortunately, he lacked a securely organized base of power within the party itself. A temperamental dislike of any kind of bureaucratic routine combined with his unusually rapid rise to national prominence had prevented him from building a *Hausmacht*.[107] Although he had good friends such as Joseph Joos or Heinrich Imbusch among the leaders of the Catholic Worker's Association,[108] ready contact with certain newspapers,[109] and many ardent admirers in the *Windthorstbund*, the Catholic youth organization,[110] this kind of support carried relatively little weight in key party councils.[111] Even his ties with the Center Party in Baden where he started his career were weak and often troubled.[112]

[103] He went so far as to identify patriotism with support of the Republic: "Whoever loves his country follows the banner of the German Republic." Ibid., p. 391. On another occasion he said that if it came to a battle between the proletariat and the middle classes he would stand on the side of the proletariat. Ibid., p. 405.

[104] Rosenberg, pp. 377–80, 393–94.

[105] Morsey, *Die Deutsche Zentrumspartei 1917–1923*, pp. 405, 411–12, 425; Stehkämper, 3: 305–7.

[106] Köhler, pp. 172–73.

[107] Morsey, *Die Deutsche Zentrumspartei 1917–1923*, pp. 387, 492; Köhler, p. 171; Brecht, *Aus Nächster Nähe*, p. 344; Becker, *Zeitschrift für die Geschichte des Oberrheins*, 109: 362–65.

[108] Ibid., pp. 366–67.

[109] Especially the *Rhein-Mainische Volkszeitung* among the Center newspapers, Buchheim, p. 338. The strong backing given him by the Democratic (and largely Jewish-owned!) Berlin press did not necessarily strengthen his position with many Centerists. Köhler, p. 182.

[110] Morsey, *Die Deutsche Zentrumspartei 1917–1923*, pp. 387, 593–94.

[111] Morsey, in *Das Ende der Parteien*, pp. 415–16.

[112] However, the head of the Baden *Zentrum*, Dr. Josef Schofer, repeatedly defended Wirth when his actions outraged many party members. Becker, *Zeitschrift für die Geschichte des Oberrheins*, 109: 365–66.

Despite the fact that the Social Democrats forced Wirth's resignation as chancellor late in 1922 by abruptly refusing to join a Great Coalition government that he was attempting to form,[113] his conviction that a left course was the only proper one for the Center Party seems never to have wavered.[114] Time and again Wirth and his friends appealed to "all those . . . who are not willing to let their religious, social, and political convictions be lost in some kind of reactionary party merger." [115] Such statements naturally produced bitter exchanges with Stegerwald.[116] In 1924 Wirth helped found the *Reichsbanner*. He spoke regularly at its meetings, and took pride in stressing his connections with this republican organization when other Center Party figures later quietly dropped their membership.[117] Nothing he did could prevent the Center's leadership from returning to its time-honored "middle-of-the-road policy"—a slogan used in the mid-twenties to justify coalitions with the right. When the newly-formed first Luther cabinet sought the approval of the Reichstag in January 1925, Wirth and Imbusch ignored party discipline to vote against the formation of a *Bürgerblock* government.[118]

Wirth's relations to the Center's Reichstag delegation worsened during the spring and summer of 1925 as the party proceeded to cooperate with its middle-class allies in the passage of a series of tax and tariff measures which benefited great industrial and agricultural interests at the expense of the workers and other consumers.[119] In mid-August, at the end of the Reichstag session, Wirth wrote Constantin Fehrenbach, the chairman of the *Fraktion,* "True to the demo-

[113] Morsey, *Die Deutsche Zentrumspartei 1917–1923,* pp. 487–88; Heiber, p. 116. A year earlier the unwillingness of the DDP and DVP had prevented the formation of a Great Coalition government. Lothar Albertin, "Die Verantwortung der liberalen Parteien für das Scheitern der Grossen Koalition im Herbst 1921," *Historische Zeitschrift,* 205 (Nr. 3, Dec. 1967): 566–627.
[114] Griewank, *Wissenschaftliche Zeitschrift der Friedrich-Schiller Universität Jena,* 1: 7–8.
[115] Schorr, p. 82.
[116] Morsey, *Die Deutsche Zentrumspartei 1917–1923,* pp. 428–29.
[117] Becker, *Zeitschrift für die Geschichte des Oberrheins,* 109: 367.
[118] Ten other members of the *Fraktion* absented themselves and three abstained during the vote. Becker, *Zeitschrift für die Geschichte des Oberrheins,* 109: 368–69; Max von Stockhausen, *Sechs Jahre Reichskanzlei* (Bonn, 1954), p. 145, diary entry for 22 Jan. 1925.
[119] Heiber, pp. 166–67; Alexander Gerschenkron, *Bread and Democracy in Germany* (Berkeley, 1943), pp. 113–20; Becker, *Zeitschrift für die Geschichte des Oberrheins,* 109: 368. For a statement of the Catholic workers' dissatisfaction with these laws see the unsigned article, "Arbeiter in Zentrum," *Kölnische Volkszeitung,* 10 Nov. 1925 (Nr. 834).

cratic . . . line I have taken in the German Reichstag, I wish to inform . . . [you] that I will henceforth [occupy a seat] *outside the delegation* of the Center Party [and] will regard myself as a representative of the *social* and *republican* Center." [120] Although Wirth did nothing to encourage others to follow his example and, indeed, took pains to emphasize that he still remained in the party despite his resignation from the *Fraktion*, [121] his step could not help attracting attention. The smoldering intra-party controversy burst into a blaze which lasted for the rest of the year.

Wirth insisted that he had not acted rashly.[122] He feared that the legislative record of the Reichstag delegation in recent months was indicative of a basic alteration in the Center's commitments. By resigning from the Reichstag delegation and thus calling attention to party values, he hoped to bring about a revival of the "old spirit of the Center" with its dedication to the "norms of *Christian democracy*." [123]

Dr. Karl Spiecker, former press secretary for the first two Marx cabinets and a man with unusually good connections with the other republican parties,[124] strongly seconded Wirth's attack on the Reichstag delegation in mid-September at a meeting of active party members in the Berlin area: "Does our Center Party still work toward the formation of a new Germany, or are we giving aid to those forces that want a restoration of the old Germany?" [125] He continued, "For us

[120] *Germania,* 24 Aug. 1925 (Nr. 393), emphasis in original; Stehkämper, 3: 306–8, 312–15.

[121] In a letter to *Germania,* 1 Sept. 1925 (Nr. 406), Wirth emphasized that he had grown up in the Center Party and always would remain a *Zentrumsmann.*

[122] Idem. Fehrenbach had already revealed that Wirth threatened to resign "three or four times" during the past year. Ibid., 25 Aug. 1925 (Nr. 395).

[123] Ibid., 1 Sept. 1925 (Nr. 406), emphasis in original. Later, at the party convention in November all sides tried to play down their differences. Wirth placed less emphasis on the dispute over principles but argued that the party's policies had been the result of false tactics. In particular, the party's leadership had mistakenly believed that it was possible to carry out foreign policy with the aid of the left while passing major tax legislation in conjunction with the right. "That was the great mistake in our policy during the past half-year. Through its taking a *position against the left*—whether intended or not does not matter—it forced those elements which are willing to accept a [common] line with us on foreign affairs into a hostile *(staatsfeindliche)* position in domestic policy." Ibid., 17 Nov. 1925 (Nr. 538), emphasis in original.

[124] Becker, *Zeitschrift für die Geschichte des Oberrheins,* 109: 364.

[125] *Germania,* 12 Sept. 1925 (Nr. 427). Compare Friedrich Dessauer's opinion: *"The Reichstag delegation no longer fights so fervently for the new forms and for the Republic as earlier when it sided with the left in support of the Republic and saved it. On the contrary, it is undertaking a rapprochement with the forces on the right which were previously so very hostile and is making concessions of form and substance to them."* Rhein-Mainische Volkszeitung, 28 Sept. 1925 (Nr. 224), emphasis in original.

the *Republic* is not 'a,' but 'the' form of state." [126] Many of the party's following had been growing dissatisfied for some time, but the Reichstag delegation had failed to perceive it.

> . . . [T]he crisis into which we in the Center have fallen is a crisis in confidence; . . . the bond between the voters and the men elected into the Reichstag has increasingly loosened, contact has disappeared, confidence has grown ever thinner and the satisfaction of party membership *(Parteifreudigkeit)* ever weaker. [127]

Other parties, he said, might be able to adopt any tactics that seemed likely to give them parliamentary advantages, but for the Center to follow "just tactics" without considering the feelings of its voters "meant death." [128] Following Spiecker's address, the meeting resolved that the Reichstag delegation should see to it "that the German Republic continues to maintain its genuine democratic character. In particular, reactionary efforts in the field of social [policy] must receive a decisive rejection from the Center Party's delegation in the Reichstag, in true adherence to the fine old Center tradition [and do so] more clearly than in past months. . . ." [129] Like a number of similar resolutions from other cities, that of the Berlin party members called for a reconciliation between Wirth and the Reichstag delegation, and denounced the *Bürgerblock* government.[130]

Spokesmen for the Reichstag delegation replied to such criticism by asserting that the party's policies in the past months had been set by circumstances, that no alternative to

[126] *Frankfurter Zeitung,* 14 Sept. 1925 (Nr. 684).

[127] *Germania,* 12 Sept. 1925 (Nr. 427). A correspondent "aus der nordischen Diaspora" wrote: "Unfortunately the prevalent view among wide circles of the electorate today is that burdens are always dumped on *them alone.* . . . One cannot resist the impression that a much too *authoritarian position* which [thinks] the electorate simply ought to accept whatever was decided 'higher up' has been adopted by the Reichstag delegation." Ibid., 1 Sept. 1925 (Nr. 407).

[128] *Germania,* 12 Sept. 1925 (Nr. 427). A more specific warning was made by Willy Elfes, a speaker at a meeting of the *Verband der Katholischen Arbeitervereine Westdeutschlands* in October. "The Catholic workers consider themselves part of the Center Party; they gladly declare that the party is dear to their hearts. However, the party must be on its guard not to lose its followers among the workers. Truly, the workers are not demanding too much. They want the right to feel at home in the party . . . Dr. Wirth is a popular politician with the workers. Whoever . . . renounces Wirth, simultaneously renounces 90% of the Catholic working people." *Rhein-Mainische Volkszeitung,* 5 Nov. 1925 (Nr. 256).

[129] *Frankfurter Zeitung,* 14 Sept. 1925 (Nr. 684).

[130] Düsseldorf, Elberfeld and Franfkurt a.M. were among the local party units which openly criticized the Reichstag delegation, idem; *Germania,* 1 Sept. (Nr. 407) and 20 Sept. 1925 (Nr. 440).

passing the tax and tariff legislation in conjunction with the right had existed. Fehrenbach wrote:

> The Reichstag delegation entered into cooperation with the right when the Luther cabinet was formed and *had to do it* after the elections had strengthened their ranks and after the German People's Party withdrew its support from the previous parliamentary grouping *(Arbeitsgemeinschaft)*. To have remained . . . simply in an oppositional minority when the greatest legislative tasks awaited solution would have contradicted the whole tradition of the Center Party which has always aimed only at the national interest. . . .[131]

He also stressed the importance of maintaining the Center's historic freedom of choice between right and left.

Substantially the same arguments were made by Johannes Giesberts in an effort to bridge the intra-party differences. Admitting that important groups of Center Party voters, "especially the urban and industrial population," distrusted the Reichstag delegation, he nevertheless suggested that such critics failed to recognize the pivotal role the Center was playing in the Reichstag, adding that many of its accomplishments should not "be shouted about" in public. "The parties of the right have had to make in association with the Center Party the same policies the Great Coalition that Wirth wanted would have made." He joined a chorus of voices calling on the party to regain its "old unity and solidarity." [132]

The most emotional defense of the Reichstag delegation came from Josef Andre, a trade union official who clearly felt that the charges against the *Fraktion* were unfair. He scarcely veiled his hostility toward Wirth. He wrote that a member of the Reichstag

> who works like a bee for his delegation on a committee—or on several committees—cannot . . . speak every day about the party program or about true . . . democracy or write articles concerning fine republican principles and make spendid programmatic addresses at all sorts of conferences. He has to study dry government bills, work on motions, take part in all kinds of preliminary conferences, read letters and petitions in order to do his part in the committee meetings themselves.

[131] *Germania*, 25 Aug. 1925 (Nr. 395), emphasis in original. Similarly Stegerwald, ibid., 1 Oct. 1925 (Nr. 459) and Marx and Fehrenbach, again, at the 1925 party convention, ibid., 16 Nov. 1925 (Nr. 537).

[132] Ibid., 13 Oct. 1925 (Nr. 478). Even Joos defended the *Fraktion* without denying his sympathy for Wirth. Ibid., 13 Sept. 1925 (Nr. 428).

There were plenty of hard working members of the Center's Reichstag delegation who fulfilled their obligations, he said, even if the authors of the recent resolutions did not realize it.

> But it is remarkable that those representatives who have fulfilled their duties most conscientiously are now suddenly supposed to be less worthy of trust, less devoted to the constitution, less democratic and republican in spirit than those colleagues who for some reason or other were frequently missing from the Reichstag . . . working on a new program or caught up in the search for new ideas.[133]

The decision of the German Nationalists to break with the first Luther government helped the Center Party out of "the worst crisis since the party was formed." [134] The party press speedily adopted many of the arguments of Wirth's supporters and denounced the Nationalists for their irresponsibility and "party egotism." [135] Even Stegerwald admitted that a Great Coalition should now be the objective of Center policies.[136]

A spirit of reconciliation dominated the party convention when it met in mid-November 1925.[137] Wirth received a friendly hearing from the assembled party regulars, in part because he himself adopted a generally moderate tone.[138] Nevertheless, Wirth and Stegerwald exchanged sharp words on the second day of the meeting.[139] Wirth accused his rival of having close ties to the right; Stegerwald countered that his ties were not as close as Wirth's associations with the left. Chairman Marx tried to establish an official position which would free the party from the destructive impact of either a fixed left or right orientation. "The Center *has a character of*

---

[133] Ibid., 20 Sept. 1925 (Nr. 440).

[134] Ibid., 13 Oct. 1925 (Nr. 478). A month later Fehrenbach said, "A difficult time lies behind us. I venture to say that, despite all its difficulties, for the Center Party the period of the *Kulturkampf* was *not such a serious and difficult period* considered politically, *as the last few years.*" Ibid., 16 Nov. 1925 (Nr. 537), emphasis in original.

[135] *Germania,* 24 Oct. (Nr. 499), 27 Oct. (Nr. 502), 1 and 15 Nov. 1925 (Nr. 536).

[136] Ibid., 18 Nov. 1925 (Nr. 540).

[137] *Germania* wrote, "The Center Party has been freed from a dangerous squeeze by the course of developments" and called upon the convention "to 'stabilize like a rock of bronze' the character of the party as a party of the middle . . . that observes a clear limit concerning tactics as well as on matters of principle." 10 Nov. 1925 (Nr. 527).

[138] Ibid., 17 Nov. 1925 (Nr. 538).

[139] Ibid., 18 Nov. 1925 (Nr. 540); Schorr, pp. 98–99; Lutz, pp. 105–7.

its own (ist etwas Eigenes)," he said.[140] Such a phrase could mask, but could not overcome the existence of real differences.

By the end of the convention Wirth indicated his willingness to resume his membership in the Reichstag delegation.[141] Nevertheless, he had already issued a warning:

In the coming months the Christian and Catholic republicans will be knocking at the doors of the party. (Representative Joos: "They are already in!") That is right, but not there where it is important to have them. Not in the Reichstag delegation and on those policy bodies *(politischen Kommissionen)* where the decisions are really made. I am not going to lead anyone out of the Center's camp! *But take care that you do not drive millions into the arms of radicalism or lethargy through false tactics!* [142]

The echo of these words must have run through the minds of the leaders of the Center Party in the spring of 1926 as, to their astonishment, masses of Catholic voters supported the Communist and Socialist initiative proposal.

During the initiative and referendum campaign Wirth avoided speaking out directly on the royal properties issue, although some of his close associates did so.[143] Wirth preferred to stress the necessity of sustained cooperation among the republican parties. In February he told a *Reichsbanner* meeting, "The Republic today is not going to be overthrown by reactionary forces. But it can be undermined . . . if we republicans do not understand each other." [144] Supporters of all three republican parties needed to improve their sense of engagement in a common task. Regarding the Center Party, he said, with prophetic truth, that he was afraid of those men who always said that they acted the way the "facts of the situation" dictated. Tomorrow or the next day he

[140] *Germania,* 16 Nov. 1925 (Nr. 537), emphasis in original.

[141] Ibid., 18 Nov. 1925 (Nr. 540). It was July 1926, however, before Wirth actually rejoined the *Fraktion.* Becker, *Zeitschrift für die Geschichte des Oberrheins,* 109: 369.

[142] *Germania,* 18 Nov. 1925, emphasis in original.

[143] Wirth felt obligated to remain silent because of the part he had played in dealing with the ruling house in Baden in 1918. Stehkämper, 3: 308. In April a Catholic nobleman writing in the Nationalist journal, *Eiserne Blätter,* charged that Center Party voters who signed the initiative petitions had been misled by the "Wirth press" which "deliberately and consciously has aimed at erasing the barriers between the Christian-National conservatism of the old Center and anti-Christian international socialism." 8 (Nr. 17, 25 April 1926): 286. For a rather different interpretation of the same phenomena, see Wilhelm Sollmann's article, "Tatchristen und Wortchristen," *Vorwärts,* 26 March 1926 (Nr. 143).

[144] *Frankfurter Zeitung,* 27 Feb. 1926 (Nr. 144).

wondered if they would not find that the "facts" necessitated reactionary choices. He called his speech "a warning to republicans." "Ability in the handling of secondary matters ought not to cause [us] to overlook the most important concerns." [145]

In the weeks immediately after the initiative the leaders of the Center Party tried to refurbish their damaged authority. Numerous articles in the press and a special meeting of the party's Advisory Committee on 28 March attempted to diagnose what had gone wrong. The question of why so many party followers had ignored the decisions of the leadership stimulated a variety of responses. Some analysts identified certain groups that had been most receptive to the appeal of confiscation—the inflation-sufferers, for example.[146] Such people, it was agreed, had acted under the influence of understandable, but misguided emotions which caused "a certain loss of political reflection and a weakening of Center Party principles." [147] These people must be warned that confiscation of the princes' properties would bring no noticeable improvement in their own condition, while it might well have dangerous consequences for other social groups. Presumably other voters had acted out of tactical considerations in the desire to put greater pressure on the Reichstag. However sincere their motives, it was said, these individuals ignored the basic fact of party effectiveness, possible only if all its members stood solidly behind a single, unified command.[148] Lapses of this kind were particularly distressing since the Center Party's voters had formerly been unique in their "relatively constant solidarity and high sense of discipline." [149]

The Center press did not challenge the decisions the party leaders had made, rather it commented on the specific conditions that hindered the "proper" reception of these deci-

---

[145] Idem. A few days later he repeated these same thoughts and asked that the Center "not follow a policy of the pendulum or fly wheel." Ibid., 8 March 1926 (Nr. 179).

[146] For example, the speech by the director of the *Volksverein für das katholische Deutschland*, Dr. Hohn, at the meeting of the Center Party's Advisory Committee, 28 March. *Germania*, 29 March 1926 (Nr. 148); *Tremonia*, 25 March 1926; *Kölnische Volkszeitung*, 31 March 1926 (Nr. 239).

[147] Dr. Hohn, *Germania*, 29 March 1926 (Nr. 148).

[148] Idem.

[149] An unsigned article titled "Volksbegehren und Parteiautorität," *Germania*, 21 March 1926 (Nr. 135). The writer added that there was no reason to fear that the dissidents would break with the party, but their behavior had expressed a lack of confidence in the leadership.

sions. The Compromise Bill, it was said, had not made sufficient progress in the Reichstag so as to appear as a meaningful alternative to the initiative proposal.[150] Moreover, official party policy had been announced at much too late a date to influence many members' decisions.[151] *Germania* wished that a definitive statement of policy had been made at the beginning of the controversy.

> This case has shown very clearly that the principle of *"compromise"* which is so much talked about, that is, the method of bridging divergent opinions *after they have been formed,* could not develop any authoritative power of suggestion. In such cases political gains can be made only [if they are] developed by a clear initiative coming from leaders aware of their own responsibility.[152]

Above all, commentators saw the need for closer contact between the Reichstag delegation and ordinary party followers throughout the country. Policy-makers' decisions would be accepted if party members felt that their views were heard and respected.[153] The recent symptoms of distrust could be overcome by the revival of a true sense of intimacy and unity within the party.[154] The clear implication of such appeals for greater harmony between the leaders and the led was that an improved relationship would enable the party's leaders to set policy more effectively, not necessarily that the heads of the party should adopt the views of their followers.[155] Party Chairman Marx protested that "the old relation between *the*

---

[150] *Kölnische Volkszeitung,* 31 March 1926 (Nr. 239).

[151] *Germania,* 29 March 1926 (Nr. 148).

[152] Ibid., 21 March 1926 (Nr. 135), emphasis in original.

[153] Idem; *Tremonia,* 25 March 1926.

[154] *Germania* called for "grösseren Unmittelbarkeit" between voters and party leaders. 21 March 1926 (Nr. 135).

[155] A few voices did interpret the call for greater contact in a genuinely democratic sense. For example, the *Kölnische Volkszeitung* wrote, "In general one might wish that the Reichstag delegation would . . . keep voters throughout the country . . . better informed concerning its work and the main lines of its policies . . . even with respect to legislative discussions or negotiations—than it has in the past. . . ." 14 April 1926 (Nr. 274).
The parish priest Roser, a party district chairman in Baden, expressed himself even more bluntly in a private letter to Wilhelm Marx. He accused the party leadership of having withdrawn into a position of "splendid isolation" from their own voters and that this was the reason why Catholic voters "went to the townhalls and signed their names in disregard of the [party's] announced policy." Becker, *Zeitschrift für die Geschichte des Oberrheins,* 109: 371, note 41. Other private letters criticizing the conduct of the Reichstag delegation in 1925–26 are cited in Stehkämper, 3: 261, 318–19, 324.

people and their political leaders has been destroyed." [156] Another
member of the party's Advisory Committee stressed that it
was "an undesirable situation when important groups of voters deviated so sharply *from the official opinion of the [Reichstag]
delegation* in such a significant political demonstration." [157]

On 28 March, the Advisory Committee unanimously approved the decisions that the Reichstag delegation had made
and confirmed its right to issue policy directives binding on
the party as a whole.[158] Two weeks later (13 April) representatives of the Center Party in the Rhineland—the area where
the greatest breach of discipline had occurred—met and after
a lengthy discussion reaffirmed the decisions made by the
Reichstag delegation and the Advisory Committee.[159] Dissidents at this meeting were not entirely muffled, however.[160]
The resolution approving the party's official policy passed
by "a great majority," but not unanimously! Moreover, the
meeting addressed a "pressing" appeal to the Reichstag delegation, urging that in future consideration of the Compromise Bill they ". . . take the general impoverishment of the
people into account more than had been done previously." [161]

From March onward the Center Party's parliamentarians
did, indeed, show somewhat greater willingness to consider
amendments to the Compromise Bill to meet some of the
popular demands. Henceforth they seemed much more interested in winning Social Democratic support, whereas earlier they had held a position very close to that of the DVP.[162]
But as so often is the case, timing played a decisive role in
the outcome of events. The Center Party's growing willingness to consider legislation that would have permitted major
challenges to "the established legal rights" of the former
rulers came too late. At one point the Social Democratic

[156] *Germania*, 29 March 1926 (Nr. 148), emphasis in original.

[157] Dr. Hohn, idem, emphasis in original. On the other hand, Friedrich Dessauer
wrote, "I have told the party's Executive Board and repeat it publicly: *the Center's
voters did not make the mistake, the leadership did.*" *Rhein-Mainische Volkszeitung*, 14 May
1926 (Nr. 110), emphasis in original.

[158] *Germania*, 29 March 1926 (Nr. 148); *Frankfurter Zeitung*, 29 March 1926 (Nr.
235).

[159] *Germania*, 14 and 15 April 1926 (Nrs. 171 and 173); *Kölnische Volkszeitung*, 14
April 1926 (Nr. 274).

[160] *Germania*, 15 April 1926 (Nr. 173), took pains to emphasize that all viewpoints
were heard and that no kind of *Versammlungsregie* had been applied.

[161] Ibid., 14 April 1926 (Nr. 171).

[162] *Frankfurter Zeitung*, 22 March 1926 (Nr. 217), reporting an article in the *Schlesische
Volkszeitung; Tremonia*, 30 March 1926; *Germania*, 23 April 1926 (Nr. 187).

parliamentarians, by and large eminently practical men, had been on the verge of aiding in the passage of effective regulatory legislation.[163] A more accommodating attitude by the Center's representatives at an early point in the interparty negotiations might have encouraged the Social Democratic leaders to support a suitably worded version of the Compromise Bill despite the clamor they were certain to face in their own party. After the great success of the initiative and, in succeeding months, as public support continued to mount for the drastic solution of total confiscation, the spokesmen for the SPD felt entitled to demand more far-ranging changes in the proposed legislation. The chief negotiators for the Center felt some of the same pressure and were dismayed that a "factual" discussion of the problem was increasingly impossible.[164]

[163] See above, Chapter V, p. 165. Also see the articles by Alwin Saenger, "Die Abfindung der ehemaligen deutschen Fürsten," *Sozialistische Monatshefte,* 63 (8 Feb. 1926). 69–73, and Otto Landsberg, "Grundsätzliches zur Fürstenabfindung," *Die Justiz,* 1 (Nr. 4, April 1926): 363–67.

[164] Joseph Joos, "Zentrumswähler im Volksentscheid," *Germania,* 22 June 1926 (Nr. 282). Schulte, *Was geschieht mit dem Fürstenvermogen?* pp. 11–13.

VII: From the Initiative to the Referendum, March—June, 1926: Chances for Parliamentary Action Fade.

The first effect of the successful outcome of the initiative was to encourage the efforts of the middle parties to obtain speedy Reichstag action on the proposed regulatory legislation in order to reduce popular interest in the much more radical referendum proposal. However, as the Center and Democratic parties tried to gain acceptance of some fairly far-ranging amendments to the original Compromise Bill in order to pacify their own discontented followers and win the eventual support of the Social Democrats, they encountered resistance from their partners, the DVP and BVP, who showed no great willingness to make major concessions at the expense of the former ruling families. Thus, the process of negotiation among the governing middle parties was prolonged until May, by which time the approach of the referendum drew attention away from the parliamentary arena to the great debate in progress for the popular vote. By early June it was clear that no regulatory legislation would be passed before the referendum was over.

Immediately after the initiative, the press of the Democratic, Center, and People's parties called upon the Reichstag to pass acceptable regulatory legislation before 20 June. The *Kölnische Zeitung* said, "It is the job of the middle parties to formulate their compromise proposal and to accelerate their

work in order to curb the inclination of the voting masses to
find a radical solution over the head of the Reichstag."[1]
Throughout the last half of March and still more intensively
in April, key representatives for these parties conferred with
members of the government and with other parties in an
effort to work out the terms of a bill which could obtain the
support of a majority in the Reichstag.

It was clear that Social Democratic aid was indispensable;
it was also clear that the SPD considered far-reaching demands justified in light of the surprising success of the initiative movement. While the Social Democrats insisted on
substantial alterations in the existing Compromise Bill, their
spokesmen emphasized that their willingness to discuss improvements in the Reichstag legislation did not represent a
commitment to support such legislation under any circumstances.[2] Nevertheless, middle-class politicians still hoped to
discover some way of tying the SPD's leaders to a parliamentary compromise so that in the end the party would drop
its agitation for the referendum.[3]

Other unforeseen difficulties must be overcome. On 20
March, government and party leaders met and decided to
speed up the Legal Committee's work so that its report and
the finished bill could be presented to the Reichstag directly
after the forthcoming Easter holidays.[4] But to everyone's
surprise, Dr. Hoepker-Aschoff, the Prussian finance minister,
announced that the newest version of the Compromise Bill

[1] *Kölnische Zeitung*, 18 March 1926 (Nr. 207). The next day it wrote that if voters
continued to be strongly influenced by their emotions the referendum might pass.
That would mean "the *undermining the chief legal and moral pillars of . . . the state.*"
Ibid., 19 March 1926 (Nr. 208), emphasis in original. The *Frankfurter Zeitung* called
upon the Reichstag "to work fast and well." 25 March (Nr. 226) and 30 March 1926
(Nr. 239); *Vossische Zeitung*, 16 March 1926 (Nr. 64). *Germania*, likewise, urged the
Reichstag to act so that dissatisfied voters could see there was some alternative to
full confiscation. Otherwise the situation could "lead to the most serious internal
political complications and the most undesirable political constellations." 18 March
(Nr. 129) and similarly, 19 March 1926 (Nr. 132). See, too, the discussion in the
Center Party Reichstag *Fraktion*, 18 March 1926. Morsey, *Protokolle*, pp. 21–22.
[2] Two days after the conclusion of the initiative the SPD's representative on the
Legal Committee enumerated a great many improvements his party considered the
Compromise Bill needed. He indicated that favorable consideration of these amend-
ments would be crucial if the SPD were to accept the bill. *Vorwärts*, 19 March 1926
(Nr. 132); *Frankfurter Zeitung*, 20 March 1926 (Nr. 212).
[3] *Kölnische Zeitung*, 19 March (Nr. 208) and 25 April 1926 (Nr. 305). According to
Stürmer, p. 157, representatives for the SPD had accepted part of the Compromise
Bill by the end of March and it was expected that they would give their consent to
the whole bill by the time it came to a vote.
[4] *Frankfurter Zeitung*, 21 March 1926 (Nr. 215).

weakened the position of the Prussian state vis-à-vis the Hohen-zollerns rather than improving it.[5] Since the purpose of the proposed law was to aid states such as Prussia, the bill's sponsors had to take Dr. Hoepker-Aschoff's criticisms into account, even though this meant a new delay in submitting the bill to the Reichstag.[6] A month was consumed in nego-tiations before the Prussian government agreed that the Com-promise Bill, as further revised, offered a tolerable solution.

The new delays provoked complaints that the national gov-ernment failed to show sufficient interest in the needed leg-islation.[7] Even by the end of March the cabinet had not yet determined whether the Compromise Bill touched on con-stitutional issues—no mere legal technicality since all cal-culations of the bill's possibilities in the Reichstag depended on knowing whether a two-thirds or just a simple majority was necessary.[8] The cabinet justified its inaction on the grounds that it was waiting until the final draft of the bill was available.[9] Nonetheless the government gradually ac-cepted some responsibility for the progress of critical ne-gotiations. On 25 March 1926, the cabinet ordered the ministry of justice to participate more actively in the for-mulation of the new law. "The bill must be expedited by all means." [10]

[5] He observed that according to the *Vergleich* concluded in October 1925 the Hohenzollern family had renounced the *Kronfideikommissrente* and *Krondonation* and had agreed to the transfer of certain historic buildings to the state without claiming compensation. However Section 5 of the Compromise appeared to permit such transfers of property or the cessation of old rights without any compensation only insofar as no *Privatrechtstitel* of the former ruling family were involved, a situation which in some cases at least arguably existed in Prussia. *Vossische Zeitung*, 24 March 1926 (Nr. 71); *Frankfurter Zeitung*, 24 March 1926 (Nr. 222). The government of Hesse later expressed similar worries. Ibid., 21 April 1926 (Nr. 292).

[6] Bundesarchiv. "Auseinandersetzung," Bd. 1, RK2122; von Richthofen's remarks in the Legal Committee, *Frankfurter Zeitung*, 24 March 1926 (Nr. 222).

[7] Complaints by the representatives Wunderlich, Landsberg, and Kahl in the Legal Committee, *Frankfurter Zeitung*, 24 March 1926 (Nr. 222) and Justice Minister Marx's report to the cabinet 25 March 1926. The Committee requested "eine positive Mit-arbeit," he said. *Kabinettsprotokolle*, reel 1838, frame D768153.

[8] Idem. In part the delay was due to differing opinions by Justice Minister Marx and Interior Minister Külz regarding the bill's constitutionality. Further on this subject, Bundesarchiv. "Auseinandersetzung," Bd. 1, RK2985; *Frankfurter Zeitung*, 21 April (Nr. 293) and 23 April 1926 (Nr. 297).

[9] Marx's statement to the Legal Committee, *Frankfurter Zeitung*, 25 March 1926 (Nr. 224).

[10] Bundesarchiv. "Auseinandersetzung," Bd. 1, RK2800. The admonition was repeated by Interior Minister Külz at a meeting of cabinet members 15 April 1926. *Kabinettsprotokolle*, reel 1838, frame D768463.

While the Reichstag observed Easter recess during the first two weeks of April, officials in the ministry of justice worked on a new version of the Compromise Bill.[11] There were no major changes. The composition of the court remained as it had been in the previous version; however, rather more specific instructions on how the court should treat particular types of problems were given, and the court's authority was slightly enlarged. Improvements were made in the wording of the bill, in particular, by giving a more precise definition of property "acquired by private means." The vagueness of the earlier definition had been one of the Prussian government's strongest reasons for objecting to the Compromise Bill.

Once the Reichstag reassembled, representatives for the coalition of middle parties and members of the government met and, on 15 April, agreed to submit the newest draft to the Legal Committee.[12] The commitment of the middle parties to the Compromise remained tentative; they were free to submit new amendments if they chose, and were not bound to support the bill under all circumstances.[13] This was a grave tactical weakness. Even more fatal was the fact that no one had been able to discover a way for securing a firm majority for the regulatory legislation in the Reichstag. Some politicians continued to expect last minute aid from the Social Democrats.[14] They thought that the SPD would not care to risk going without any legislation at all, if, as was likely, the referendum measure failed. In the meantime, the bill's sponsors attempted to get the bill through committee by use of "changing majorities," that is, by accepting the support of

[11] *Frankfurter Zeitung*, 14 April 1926 (Nr. 274); the text of the new version was printed, ibid., 17 April 1926 (Nr. 283). One result of these alterations would have been the reclassification of the crown prince's Oels estate as property of the state. *Vossische Zeitung*, 18 April 1926 (Nr. 93).

[12] *Kabinettsprotokolle*, reel 1838, frames D768464-65. The DDP made its approval contingent on the bill being acceptable to the Prussian government.

[13] *Frankfurter Zeitung*, 17 April 1926 (Nr. 282); statement by Schulte in the Legal Committee, ibid., 21 April 1926 (Nr. 293). On the other hand, Dr. Külz informed the Committee that the bill, as then phrased, was acceptable to the government. Idem.

[14] Dr. Külz at a meeting of cabinet members 15 April 1926. *Kabinettsprotokolle*, reel 1838, frame D768463; editorial comment by the *Kölnische Zeitung*, 17 April 1926 (Nr. 285) and *Frankfurter Zeitung*, 21 April 1926 (Nr. 294). *Vorwärts*'s initial reaction to the newest proposal was quite negative: its editors complained that the initiative movement did not seem to have made "any special impact" on the middle-class parties, 17 April 1926 (Nr. 179).

the DNVP for the passage of some sections of the bill and the support of the SPD for other parts of it.[15]

The new proposal was no sooner launched when it ran aground. The Legal Committee began voting on the bill 21 April, although the political situation remained unclear. Speakers for the DNVP warned that any aid from their side would depend on the sponsors' willingness to change the court back into a body of trained jurists.[16] The Social Democrats, likewise, made their support contingent on the acceptance of one of their most keenly desired amendments, one which would have extended the competence of the court to permit it to review previously concluded property settlements, even if they had been made before 1918.[17] On 22 April, when this suggested change was rejected, the SPD voted against a key section of the bill and thus ensured its defeat.[18] The Committee immediately adjourned in order to permit new interparty discussions. "A catastrophe has just struck in the Legal Committee," a confidential report from the Reichstag noted. "Excitement is great." [19]

High level discussions were already in progress, involving the sponsors of the Compromise, members of the national government, and important Prussian officials.[20] With the parties deadlocked in the Legal Committee, attention now focused on these meetings. If Prussia's demands could be satisfied, perhaps agreement with the Social Democrats would follow quite rapidly. As the *Frankfurter Zeitung* observed:

> Drawing the Prussian minister-president and finance minister into the conference could give an opportunity to learn in authoritative form whether the Prussian government will accept the Compromise proposal . . . and, in so doing, provide a point of departure for negotiations with the Social Democrats to create a majority.[21]

[15] *Frankfurter Zeitung*, 23 April 1926 (Nr. 300).

[16] Statements by Everling and Hannemann, *Frankfurter Zeitung*, 21 April (Nr. 293) and 22 April 1926 (Nr. 295).

[17] Ibid., 23 April 1926 (Nr. 298).

[18] Idem. The Social Democrats voted against Section Two of the bill along with the Communists and the representative for the *Völkische Freiheitspartei*. The DVP, DDP, Center, and WV voted for it; the DNVP abstained and the BVP's representative was absent.

[19] *Radlauer-Bericht aus dem Reichstage* (22 April 1926). Bundesarchiv. "Auseinandersetzung," Bd. 1, unnumbered.

[20] Bundesarchiv. "Auseinandersetzung," Bd. 1, RK3179; *Frankfurter Zeitung*, 23 April 1926 (Nrs. 298 and 299).

[21] Ibid., 23 April 1926 (Nr. 298).

A lengthy meeting of the principal negotiators took place 23 April 1926, with Chancellor Luther and Minister-President Braun in attendance. Some concessions to the wishes of the Prussian government were made.[22] The state would be permitted to acquire certain museum collections at their *Ertragswert* (virtually nothing) and would obtain favorable opportunities for purchasing some real estate allotted to the former ruling family. On the other hand, the Prussian government abandoned its request that the court be given far-reaching powers to revise already settled cases. Luther had previously made it clear that he would not accept any reopening of property settlements concluded before 1918.[23] As a result of the agreements reached at this meeting, the Prussian finance minister was authorized to declare the Compromise "acceptable." [24] In addition, Otto Braun consented to act as an intermediary with the Social Democratic Reichstag delegation but refused to guarantee that they would accept the Compromise.[25]

Braun conferred first with the SPD's members on the Legal Committee and then joined with them in another meeting with the bill's chief sponsors.[26] No conclusive understanding was reached, but the Social Democrats did undertake to permit the Legal Committee to resume its work.[27] Max von Stockhausen, a young official in the chancellor's office, noted in his diary 23 April: "Many difficulties regarding the Compromise. . . . Negotiations with the Social Democrats. People think results will be seen tomorrow." [28] However, the stumbling blocks of the court's composition and its authority to revise already-settled cases still remained. The Social Dem-

[22] Bundesarchiv. "Auseinandersetzung," Bd. 1, RK3259; *Frankfurter Zeitung,* 24 April 1926 (Nrs. 301 and 302).

[23] He very clearly defined his views concerning *Rückwirkung* at meetings with other cabinet ministers and representatives of the governing parties on 15 and 16 April. *Kabinettsprotokolle,* reel 1838, frames D768462 and D768464. There is no reason to think he altered his opinion in the next few days.

[24] Hoepker-Aschoff's statement to the Legal Committee, *Frankfurter Zeitung,* 25 April 1926 (Nr. 304).

[25] Bundesarchiv. "Auseinandersetzung," Bd. 1, RK3259 and RK3336.

[26] *Frankfurter Zeitung,* 24 April 1926 (Nr. 302). Braun makes no mention of his role in these important negotiations in his memoirs despite an assertion that he would relate what happened "in so far as I was an active participant." *Von Weimar zu Hitler,* pp. 214–15. Schulze, too, does not comment on Braun's activities in this respect, pp. 508–9.

[27] By agreeing to abstain as a rule during the voting while the Committee continued with the reading of the bill section by section. *Frankfurter Zeitung,* 25 April 1926 (Nr. 305).

[28] *Sechs Jahre Reichskanzlei,* p. 214.

ocratic Reichstag delegation announced that "it could not appraise the Compromise simply from the point of view of Prussia" and that it would still insist on further modifications in the bill.[29] The Legal Committee continued its deliberations for a few more days, but, since partisan standpoints showed no further sign of shifting, observers reported on 28 April that discussions had "completely stalled." [30] The speeches in the Committee sounded as though they were delivered "at a graveside." [31]

The deadlock over the Compromise heightened the worries of the middle parties. Even the *Kölnische Zeitung* declared that to go into the referendum without any action by the Reichstag was "catastrophic politics." [32] Furthermore, it called upon the DNVP to abandon its rigid objections:

> The Compromise must be brought about. . . . Due to our unfortunate party divisions this is not possible unless the parties [demonstrate] far-reaching self-denial and sacrifice, but the sacrifice must be made in the interest of the state as a whole. It follows from the nature of the issue that the German Nationalists will have to concede the most. First of all, because this corresponds to . . . the prevailing state of public opinion and, secondly, because only if the Social Democrats are able to vote for the Compromise Bill as a block does there exist any hope that the referendum can still be avoided. . . .[33]

The Democratic and Center press also left no doubt that their parties were ready to join with the Social Democrats in order to see the bill through the Reichstag.[34] However, despite all efforts at persuasion, the SPD remained firm in its refusal to support the Compromise.

[29] *Vorwärts*, 24 April 1926 (Nr. 191).

[30] *Frankfurter Zeitung*, 29 April 1926 (Nr. 314).

[31] Idem.

[32] 25 April 1926 (Nr. 305). This was despite the fact that prominent DVP politicians were privately urging delay in the hope that an emasculated bill could be passed after the referendum failed. A report by *Regierungsrat* Wienstein, 29 April 1926. Bundesarchiv. "Auseinandersetzung," Bd. 1, RK3337; *Frankfurter Zeitung*, 20 April (Nr. 291) and 29 April 1926 (Nr. 315). The official DVP information leaflet, "rote Mitteilungen," Nr. 9 (30 April 1926), stated that passage of the Compromise before the referendum was desirable, but not likely. Bundesarchiv. *Deutsches Volkspartei*, R4511/21.

[33] *Kölnische Zeitung*, 25 April 1926 (Nr. 305). Nonetheless, Count Westarp announced that his party would not "abandon its principles because of the whip of the referendum." A speech to a meeting of DNVP members in the Potsdam area, reported in the *Frankfurter Zeitung*, 26 April 1926 (Nr. 307).

[34] *Germania*, 23 April (Nr. 187), 29 April 1926 (Nr. 197); *Frankfurter Zeitung*, 28 April 1926 (Nr. 313).

The reason is not hard to determine. On 24 April, the national government, in accord with its legal obligations, submitted the initiative-sponsored measure for full confiscation to the Reichstag.[35] It would have been daring, indeed, if the leaders of the Social Democratic Party had repudiated the initiative proposal just as parliamentary and public attention was focused on it. It would have given the KPD a cheap propaganda victory and, almost surely, would have had serious consequences inside the party. From this point on, *Vorwärts* adopted a cliché-ridden, but determined tone: "Your Compromise for the princes has miscarried. . . . The fight for the referendum begins. The people have the floor: for justice against the princes, for the protection of the highest principles of legality against reactionary and monarchistic forces." [36]

In the last days of April it became obvious that action on the Compromise Bill was going to be delayed a long time. The Democratic and Center parties made frantic efforts to give their dissatisfied voters some alternative to total confiscation.[37] Both parties proposed substitute amendments to the initiative measure.[38] The Democrats reverted to their original view that confiscation should be permitted, but the individual state governments would set the terms and would be empowered to grant the former ruling families financial settlements.[39] Their efforts to persuade other delegations to try this approach proved vain.[40] The Center sought support for an abridged version of the last Compromise Bill which stressed general principles, leaving the details to be worked

[35] *Frankfurter Zeitung,* 25 April 1926 (Nr. 305); *Kabinettsprotokolle,* reel 1838, frame D768544; Reichstag, *Drucksache* (3. Wahlperiod), Nr. 2229.

[36] 25 April (Nr. 193); on 30 April (Nr. 202) it headlined "The Referendum–The Only Solution," and 7 May 1926 (Nr. 212) ran a cartoon entitled, "Away with the Compromises."

[37] *Frankfurter Zeitung,* 29 April 1926 (Nr. 315); *Germania,* 29 April 1926 (Nr. 197); Morsey, *Protokolle,* pp. 27–29.

[38] Reichstag, *Drucksache* (3. Wahlperiod), Nrs. 2234 and 2236. If the Reichstag had accepted either of these substitute measures, both the alternative proposal and the SPD-KPD measure would have had to have been submitted to the people in the referendum.

[39] Statement by von Richthofen, Reichstag. *Verhandlungen,* 390 (28 April 1926): 6915–16.

[40] *Frankfurter Zeitung,* 5 May 1926 (Nr. 330) on the vote in the Legal Committee; ibid., 7 May 1926 (Nr. 337) on the vote in the Reichstag itself. Only the *Wirtschaftliche Vereinigung* gave its support to the DDP. Bredt, Reichstag. *Verhandlungen,* 390 (6 May 1926): 7041–42.

out after the referendum.[41] The Center's purpose was simple. *Germania* wrote that the party "intended to create a platform for its own use during the referendum and give the other parties of the middle an opportunity for joining it on this platform, too." It was essential that the middle party voters demonstrate that they had independent views; that there were three sides, not just two, on the properties question.[42] Such statements echoed one of the Center's favorite catchwords—that it followed a distinct policy of its own, independent of either left or right. The party's leaders, concerned with holding their regular voters in line, totally misjudged the possibility for creating a third option at this late stage of the controversy. Only the equally desperate Democrats and the *Wirtschaftliche Vereinigung* were willing to back the Center's motion.[43]

At long last, on 30 April, the Luther cabinet decided to take over responsibility for the Compromise and, after making a few minor modifications, reintroduce it as a government-sponsored bill.[44] "The Reichstag has failed," Minister of Interior Külz stated. "Now the government must introduce a Compromise proposal Prussia will accept." [45] Luther and the other cabinet members agreed. Later in the day, the cabinet reaffirmed its decision, even though the Center's Reichstag delegation—still trying to win support for its alternative referendum proposal—sent word that a government bill was

---

[41] It is noteworthy that this draft bill indicated that laymen should play a leading *(massgebend)* role in the special court. *Germania*, 29 April 1926 (Nr. 197).

[42] "The goal must be that the referendum fails without doing a service for the monarchists and without leaving everything as it was before." Ibid., 7 May 1926 (Nr. 211).

[43] *Frankfurter Zeitung*, 5 May 1926 (Nr. 330); 7 May 1926 (Nr. 337).

[44] Schulte, in *Politisches Jahrbuch 1926*, pp. 507–9, 518. A meeting of the representatives of the governing parties had expressed the desire that the government assume responsibility for the bill. Bundesarchiv. "Auseinandersetzung," Bd. 1, zu RK3498.

[45] Idem. The prominent expert on constitutional law, Otto Koellreutter, wrote an article entitled "Parliamentary Bankruptcy" for the *Deutsche Allgemeine Zeitung*, 4 May 1926 (Nrs. 202–203). He blamed a declining sense of responsibility within the parliamentary system and lack of leadership from the government for the failure to pass suitable legislation. He then commented on the inappropriateness of a referendum in a large nation: "A mass of over 40 million voters . . . sinks irremediably under the influence of unrestrained and irresponsible demagogy. . . . Someone must finally have the courage to say plainly that democracy is *not* the rule of the masses, that the masses can never rule, and can participate in the state only to a very limited extent."

"undesirable" at that time.[46] Luther now wanted fast action.[47] The new bill was speedily readied and on 3 May the government presented it to the *Reichsrat*.[48] It is an open question whether Chancellor Luther could have forced this bill through the Reichstag before 20 June, thereby taking some wind out of the sails of the referendum.[49]

Almost immediately the Flag Crisis intervened. Luther's arbitrary and politically tactless handling of this question forced his resignation. The chancellor expressly favored legislative regulation of the princes' property settlements in order to avoid "the disorder" of a referendum.[50] Yet with remarkable insensitivity to the state of public opinion, Luther asked President von Hindenburg to authorize German consular stations to fly the old black-white-red colors of the Empire alongside the black-red-gold banner of the Republic.[51] The ensuing controversy over the Flag Decree at once disrupted domestic politics, widening the division between republican and antirepublican forces. In the end, Luther resigned and a short, unwanted cabinet crisis occurred.

The first news of the Flag Decree produced immediate protests from the three republican parties, the *Reichsbanner*, and similar organizations.[52] *Germania* asked how the cabinet could think of "stirring up [this] wasp nest . . . at the present critical time without an especially pressing reason."[53]

[46] Bundesarchiv. "Auseinandersetzung," Bd. 1, RK3629; Morsey, *Protokolle,* p. 31. *Germania,* 1 May 1926 (Nr. 201), doubted if the government bill would have more success than the previous Compromise. "It comes late—but hopefully not too late." *Vossische Zeitung* also took a rather pessimistic view, largely because of the DVP's attitude. 1 May 1926 (Nr. 104).

[47] Bundesarchiv. "Auseinandersetzung," Bd. 1, zu RK3498.

[48] *Frankfurter Zeitung,* 4 May 1926 (Nr. 328).

[49] This was the *Frankfurter Zeitung*'s opinion, 1 May 1926 (Nr. 321).

[50] See above, Chapter V, pp. 156, 162.

[51] More accurately, diplomatic missions and consular stations in seaports were instructed to display the merchant marine flag as well as the regular national flag. The marine flag was black-white-red with an insert of black-red-gold in the upper left-hand corner. The Decree was issued 5 May 1926. Eyck, 2: 92–94; Schneider, pp. 89–93; Andreas Dorpalen, *Hindenburg and the Weimar Republic* (Princeton, 1964), pp. 104–6; Fritz Stern, "Adenauer and a Crisis in Weimar Democracy," *Political Science Quarterly,* 73 (Nr. 1, March 1958): 1–27. Luther admitted that the responsibility for seeking the Flag Decree was his own. *Politiker ohne Partei,* pp. 417–18.

[52] *Vorwärts,* 5 May 1926 (Nr. 208); *Frankfurter Zeitung,* 5 May (Nr. 331), 6 May (Nr. 334) and regularly thereafter until Luther's resignation on 12 May 1926; *Vossische Zeitung,* 7 May (Nr. 109), 9 May (Nr. 111) and 12 May 1926 (Nr. 113).

[53] Quoted in a survey of press reactions by the *Frankfurter Zeitung,* 5 May 1926 (Nr. 332). Cf. the discussion in the Center Party's Reichstag delegation, 4 and 5 May, Morsey, *Protokolle,* pp. 32–33.

Leading Democratic and Center Party politicians tried to get the government to rescind, or at least delay, the order.[54] They disapproved of the content of the decree, but Luther's clumsy handling of such a sensitive question angered them even more. He had not taken the trouble to inform the leaders of the coalition parties of his intentions until the decree was ready for President Hindenburg's signature.[55] Koch-Weser protested, "We have emphasized often enough that we are glad to leave the leadership [in the hands] of the government, but 'to lead' does not mean to sally forth alone, and without consultation." [56]

The cabinet had not foreseen "how much excitement . . . would be caused by the new regulation." [57] For a week, Luther tried to find some way of appeasing his critics

[54] Comments by Külz and Brauns at a cabinet meeting on the morning of 5 May 1926. *Kabinettsprotokolle*, reel 1839, frames D768743–44; *Frankfurter Zeitung*, 6 May 1926 (Nr. 333). The Social Democrats speedily indicated that they would submit a motion questioning the government's action. Stern, *Political Science Quarterly*, 73: 7; the text of the motion was printed by *Vorwärts*, 7 May 1926 (Nr. 212).

[55] Even the DVP's press service, the *Nationalliberale Korrespondenz*, stated that "much discontent would have been avoided if the government had not limited itself to the unanimous agreement of the parties' men in the cabinet, but had sought close contact with the *Fraktionen*. . . ." It approved of the Flag Decree, however. *Frankfurter Zeitung*, 6 May 1926 (Nr. 335). Johann Giesberts (Center) called Luther's failure to inform the parliamentarians an affront to the parties. Reichstag. *Verhandlungen*, 390 (11 May 1926): 7169. The Social Democrat, Rudolf Breitscheid, joined these critics. "We can not . . . escape the impression that it is the practice of the government . . . to push the parliament more and more into the background and to treat it, intentionally or unintentionally, with contempt. . . . The government justifies its action [by pointing to] its . . . right to issue administrative orders. True enough, but such an action contradicts the spirit of democratic parliamentary life. . . . [I] would have thought . . . that Chancellor Luther above all had reason to communicate with the parties before [issuing such an order]. He presides at the head of a minority government and he knows as well as we do that it is . . . doubly necessary for him to be sure of the agreement of at least the parties supporting his government before he undertakes such a step. It was not done." Ibid., p. 7155. Stürmer (p. 96, note 51) cites a passage from the original manuscript of Luther's memoirs which clearly indicates that he hoped to find a way to rule without being troubled by the Reichstag more than a few weeks out of the year. See too, Haungs's characterization of Luther as chancellor, pp. 106–8, 110–12.

[56] *Frankfurter Zeitung*, 9 May 1926 (Nr. 343). He elaborated on the same point a few days later. "In this case the action of the chancellor runs counter to the agreement expressly concluded between him and the [governing] parties that [he would] hear the views of the parties before [acting] on important matters. . . . Moreover, the chancellor required the ministers to [treat the whole matter] as a confidential one, thus making it impossible for them to acquaint their parties . . . in time." Reichstag. *Verhandlungen*, 390 (12 May 1926): 7195.

[57] Thus Interior Minister Külz explained the cabinet's unanimous vote approving the decree. At a meeting of the DDP Executive Board, 10 May 1926. DDP Papers, reel 37, folder 730. Luther himself thought the issue concerned only a "bagatelle." Braun, p. 190.

without retracting the decree. He offered to make some minor changes, but they were rejected as insufficient.[58] A carefully composed letter from President Hindenburg, published by prearrangement, failed to mollify the discontented republicans.[59] Luther's best chance for survival depended on the fear of the coalition parties that highly undesirable consequences would follow the collapse of the government. Germany's foreign affairs as well as the confused state of its domestic politics made even an ordinary cabinet crisis unwise; worse yet, some politicians feared that Hindenburg might decide to dissolve the Reichstag in the event of a vote of no confidence.[60] New elections would have been disastrous for the middle parties just then. Others speculated that the president himself might resign if the Reichstag repudiated the Flag Decree.[61]

For a short time it seemed that these unwanted alternatives could still be avoided. The leaders of the Center Party were willing to give the Luther government a second chance; [62] much depended, therefore, on the Democrats. Some prominent members of the DDP, including Interior Minister Külz, thought it imprudent for the party to abandon a position of influence in the existing cabinet over a question of "senti-

[58] Stern, *Political Science Quarterly*, 73: 6, 10. The Democrats would have abandoned their support of a motion of no confidence if Luther had suspended the decree. Koch-Weser at the DDP Executive Board meeting 10 May 1926. DDP Papers, reel 37, folder 730, p. 14. But Luther was willing to delay putting the order into effect only for the time needed to inform the most remote diplomatic posts. *Frankfurter Zeitung*, 12 May 1926 (Nrs. 349 and 350).

[59] Hubatsch, pp. 235–36. The *Frankfurter Zeitung* stated that "it worsens the situation instead of easing it." 11 May 1926 (Nr. 346). Even the right was annoyed; the conciliatory tone of the letter was considered unnecessary. Dorpalen, p. 106.

[60] The different possibilities were exhaustively discussed at the DDP *Vorstand* meeting, 10 May 1926 (DDP Papers, reel 37, folder 730) and at a cabinet meeting the same day (*Kabinettsprotokolle*, reel 1839, frames D768784–90).

[61] Stern thinks that this was not a very serious possibility; he suggests the threat was just a means of intimidating the opponents of the Flag Decree and reminds us that Hindenburg had regularly threatened to resign in order to get his way during the war. *Political Science Quarterly*, 73: 9. A similar view was expressed by Georg Bernhard, editor-in-chief of the *Vossische Zeitung*, at the DDP *Vorstand* meeting 10 May 1926. DDP Papers, reel 37, folder 730, p. 6. *Vorwärts*, 9 May 1926 (Nr. 216), did not take these threats seriously either.

[62] Heinrich Brauns stated at a cabinet meeting on 10 May that Hindenburg's letter provided a basis which "permits the cabinet crisis to be avoided and [it] must be avoided." *Kabinettsprotokolle*, reel 1839, frame D768785; also Marx's statement, Morsey, *Protokolle*, p. 36. The Democratic minister Külz reported to his party colleagues that the Center wanted to reach an understanding on the Flag Decree and felt that the Democrats were trying to force its hand. DDP Papers, reel 37, folder 730, p. 4.

ment." [63] Party Chairman Koch-Weser, however, looked upon Luther's recent deeds as only the last in a series of basically unacceptable acts, attributable, he said, to Luther's "rightist subconscious." [64] After considerable debate, he convinced the party's Executive Board and Reichstag delegation to maintain a firm stand.[65] "We will lose our organized members if we have to tell them that we retreated on this question for the sake of Germany's welfare. And without the organized members we would never be able to fight an election campaign." [66] On 12 May 1926, the Reichstag rejected Communist and Social Democratic motions of no confidence; then it accepted a less sweeping Democratic motion condemning Chancellor Luther's conduct of the affair.[67] Luther resigned at once.

No one wanted a long crisis.[68] But, given the strained state of domestic politics, what kind of coalition could be formed? Fundamentally the political situation had not altered much since the prolonged crisis at the beginning of the year, although feelings were now running higher because of the referendum campaign and the Flag Decree. The DNVP's continued hostility toward Stresemann's foreign policy made a right coalition impossible.[69] There was little attraction in reviving the minority coalition of the middle, since its inherent

[63] DDP Papers, reel 37, folder 730, p. 13.

[64] Ibid., p. 2. See, too, his comments at the *Vorstand* meeting 20 May 1926, ibid., p. 2, and at the *Parteiausschuss* meeting 28 Nov. 1926, ibid., reel 38, folder 760, p. 2. Stephan, pp. 322–25; Schneider, pp. 89–93.

[65] *Frankfurter Zeitung*, 11 May 1926 (Nr. 347); Koch's report to the party Executive Board 20 May 1926. DDP Papers, reel 37, folder 730. The decision apparently was not an easy one. The Communist representative Walter Stoecker claimed that a member of the DDP had told him that if he had to say what his party would do he would go out in the *Tiergarten*, pick a daisy and start plucking: "Will we give in? Will we stand firm? . . ." Reichstag. *Verhandlungen,* 390 (11 May 1926): 7180.

[66]*Vorstand* meeting, 10 May 1926, DDP Papers, reel 37, folder 730, p. 14. Not all members of the *Vorstand* shared Koch-Weser's preference for a left orientation. Georg Gothein argued that "by going along with the Social Democrats we have lost so many supporters it is now time we attract voters to us again from the right by different tactics." Ibid., p. 6.

[67] *Frankfurter Zeitung*, 13 May 1926 (Nrs. 352 and 353). The DNVP played a crucial role in the overthrow of Chancellor Luther. Its representatives abstained during the voting on the DDP's motion; if they had voted against it he would have been saved.

[68] Haungs, pp. 109–16.

[69] *Frankfurter Zeitung*, 13 May 1926 (Nr. 353); *Kölnische Zeitung*, 9 May 1926 (Nr. 343). In a speech two weeks later Stresemann emphasized that the DVP and Center could not cooperate with the DNVP because of its attitude on foreign affairs. *Frankfurter Zeitung*, 30 May 1926 (Nr. 395).

weaknesses had been so clearly exposed.[70] The most plausible solutions (a Weimar or a Great Coalition) necessitated the SPD's entry into the government.[71]

At the height of the flag dispute Koch-Weser explicitly admonished the Social Democrats:

> . . . [E]veryone that joins the fight now and [thus] causes a governmental crisis also has an obligation to contribute positively toward ending the crisis. Only if the Social Democrats fully acknowledge this obligation can this crisis be overcome without harm to the Republic.[72]

The SPD responded by admitting that such a responsibility existed in principle,[73] and the Reichstag delegation authorized discussions with other parties.[74] Yet certain passages in

[70] " . . . [A] solution which only avoids decisions, which always reserves for itself the choice of going right or left, is no solution. The five-month-long experiment with this combination of the middle does not encourage [a desire] to repeat it." Ibid., 13 May 1926 (Nr. 353). "Politische Umschau," *Deutsche Stimmen,* 38 (Nr. 10, 10 May 1926): 225–26.

[71] Several participants at the DDP *Vorstand* meeting, 10 May 1926, mentioned the possibility of a Weimar Coalition, e.g., Gustav Stolper and Hermann Fischer, DDP Papers, reel 37, folder 730, pp. 8, 12. Koch-Weser stated that "the Social Democrats consider themselves obligated to enter the government." Ibid., p. 14. *Vorwärts* clearly preferred a Weimar Coalition, 9 May (Nr. 216) and 14 May 1926 (Nr. 255). Dr. Ferdinand Friedensburg wrote an article entitled, "The Psychological Moment!" for the *Vossische Zeitung,* 15 May 1926 (Nr. 116), calling for a Great Coalition government. Among other things, he said, "the developments of recent days show how dangerous it is for the largest party in the Reichstag not to be participating in the government."

[72] *Frankfurter Zeitung,* 9 May 1926 (Nr. 343). A few days later he was even more pointed. "I might add that if we were certain that the Social Democrats would always be as ready to stand on our side during the formation of a new government as they are at cooperating to overthrow a government, then the danger of causing a crisis would be less . . . than it is today. (Representative Müller, Franken: Do you want to find the majority for it Herr Koch? We are willing!) In January the majority was there. I believe I can say . . . that in January you did not recognize the difficulties that would result from participating as a silent partner in a coalition led by an 'unpolitical' chancellor with rightist sympathies. These difficulties are now recognized by all sides." Reichstag. *Verhandlungen,* 390 (12 May 1926): 7192.

[73] "The parties must not simply overthrow a government and leave it to the president to name a new one. . . . Overthrowing governments for purely negative reasons does not lead to the parliamentary system but rather opens the way for personal government [by the president] and the rule of the bureaucracy. . . . *Thus the Social Democrats cannot withdraw into the role of an interested spectator in case of a governmental crisis.* They have never done that during the Republic. They have borne in more than one coalition government the burden of shared responsibility, which is perhaps even harder to bear than the burden of sole responsibility. . . . However they have never understood their readiness [to cooperate] as . . . an obligation [to work with] every party and help form a government under any conditions." *Vorwärts,* 9 May 1926 (Nr. 216), emphasis in original.

[74] Ibid., 11 May 1926 (Nr. 218).

Vorwärts editorials showed that the Social Democrats' readiness to assume responsibility was by no means unequivocal. *Vorwärts* observed that "due to the current tensions, difficulties in creating a governing coalition with the Social Democrats are unusually great" and asked the middle parties to prove their willingness to accept a new political orientation by making some concessions. Then the editorial writer continued:

> [A stable republican government] can be attained in either of two ways: if the Social Democratic Party participates in the new government *or if it otherwise obtains a position that permits it to watch how things develop and exercise a certain [amount of] influence on them.*[75]

On this occasion the hesitations of the Social Democrats were not too important. Spokesmen for the People's Party made it clear that they would refuse any ties with the SPD as long as the royal properties question was before the public, while the Center Party's leaders did not want to join with the Social Democrats unless they had the DVP as a supporting counterbalance on the right.[76]

Attention rapidly focused on discovering the right individual for the chancellorship. Hindenburg gave Otto Gessler, the *Reichswehr* minister, the first opportunity to sound out the different parties.[77] When he found no satisfactory support for his own candidacy, Konrad Adenauer was summoned from Cologne. Adenauer was reluctant to leave the security of his position as mayor for the transitory status as head of the national government. He wanted the backing of a firm majority, but when exploratory discussions showed that there was no chance of establishing a Great Coalition, he refused to undertake efforts to form a government on some other basis.[78]

---

[75] Ibid., 13 May 1926 (Nr. 222), italics added.

[76] Stern, *Political Science Quarterly*, 73: 18–20; *Frankfurter Zeitung*, 13 May 1926 (Nr. 353); Morsey, *Protokolle*, p. 38.

[77] The SPD had strong objections to Gessler. He might have won at least some initial support from the DNVP, but such aid was unacceptable in the eyes of the Center and DDP. *Frankfurter Zeitung*, 14 May (Nrs. 355 and 356) and 15 May 1926 (Nr. 357); Schreiber, *Politisches Jahrbuch 1926*, p. 64.

[78] Stern, *Political Science Quarterly*, 73: 14, 16–20; Paul Weymar, *Konrad Adenauer* (Munich, 1955), pp. 129–43; Adenauer's press release explaining why he had abandoned his attempt to form a government, *Frankfurter Zeitung*, 16 May 1926 (Nr. 360); *Germania*, 22 May 1926 (Nr. 234). Much new detail is given by Hugo Stehkämper, "Konrad Adenauer und das Reichskanzleramt während der Weimarer Zeit," in *Konrad Adenauer, Oberbürgermeister von Köln. Festgabe der Stadt Köln zum 100. Geburtstag ihres Ehrenburgers am 5. Januar 1976* (Cologne, 1976), pp. 405–31.

At this point, President Hindenburg took matters into his own hands. He wrote the minister of justice, Marx, urging him to take over the chancellorship and to retain the rest of the previous cabinet.[79] This was speedily done. To allay misgivings on the left the two principal members of the coalition, the DVP and Center Party, issued a joint declaration.

> It is agreed that the foreign and domestic situation requires the rapid creation of a government that is supported by a majority in the Reichstag. Other parties that recognize the validity of existing international agreements and offer security for the continuation of our previous foreign policy can be considered for the creation of the majority.[80]

On the other hand, no attempt was made to rescind the Flag Decree.[81] Indeed, the political situation was so tenuous parliamentary leaders thought it best to avoid a conventional vote of confidence. The Reichstag simply "took cognizance" of the new chancellor's statement and then proceeded with the business of the day.[82] *Faute de mieux,* a minority government once again guided Germany's affairs.

Most observers saw the third Marx government as a temporary expedient, needed to bridge a few weeks until a Great Coalition could be arranged later in the summer.[83] The cabinet decided not to fill two vacant cabinet posts until after 20 June in order to ease its future reorganization.[84] The ever

---

[79] "The present situation of the nation can not tolerate a . . . long governmental crisis" (from Hindenburg's letter to Marx, *Frankfurter Zeitung,* 16 May 1926 [Nr. 360]).

[80] Ibid., 17 May 1926 (Nr. 361). Ambassador D'Abernon's cable to Foreign Minister Chamberlain reporting the end of the cabinet crisis interpreted both this resolution and the failure of Adenauer's candidacy as signs that the Locarno agreements were finding increasing acceptance. *Documents on British Foreign Policy 1919–1939,* Series 1A, Vol. 1, Nr. 526.

[81] Dorpalen, p. 106; at a meeting of the DDP Executive Board 20 May 1926, Koch-Weser said "it was entirely understandable" that there could be no retraction of the decree. DDP Papers, reel 37, folder 730, p. 1.

[82] Reichstag, *Verhandlungen,* 390 (19 May 1926): 7337–39; *Frankfurter Zeitung,* 20 May 1926 (Nr. 371).

[83] *Germania,* 14 May (Nr. 221) and 1 June 1926 (Nr. 249) when it said, "We hope that June 20th unblocks the road to the Great Coalition." *Kölnische Volkszeitung,* 6 June 1926 (Nr. 409); Schreiber, *Politisches Jahrbuch 1926,* p. 67; *Vorwärts,* 16 May 1926 (Nr. 227); letter from the DDP national office to local party officials, 19 May 1926. DDP Papers, reel 38, folder 759, p. 6; *Vossische Zeitung,* 16 May (Nr. 117) and 18 May 1926 (Nr. 118).

[84] *Kabinettsprotokolle* (31 May 1926), reel 1839, frames D769010–12.

prudent Marx waited a couple of months before moving into the chancellor's residence.[85]

Just as the Flag Crisis was developing, the initiative-sponsored bill went before the Reichstag for formal debate.[86] The national government took pains to prevent any possible suspicion that by submitting the confiscation proposal it in some way approved of it.

> Confiscation of the entire wealth of the princes without compensation along the lines set forth in this bill runs contrary to the principles on which any act of legislation must be based in a state that respects the rule of law. It is not possible for the national government to see in the content of the bill a useful basis on which the states and the former ruling houses can come to terms. [The government] speaks most decidedly against the acceptance of the bill. . . .[87]

The Reichstag debate itself scarcely requires recapitulation.[88] Party positions were already well established. Only the Communists and the Social Democrats approved of confiscation.[89] All the other parties rejected the proposal; most, in strong and emphatic terms.[90]

---

[85] On 9 August 1926, Stresemann noted, "The prospects for the creation of a Great Coalition have lessened markedly in the last few weeks. The present cabinet may well last longer than people prophesied when it was formed. In this connection it is interesting that Dr. Marx is now occupying the chancellor's residence. More and more the government appears to be consolidating itself." *Nachlass*, reel 3146, frame H162205. A good short account of Marx's career is Hugo Stehkämper, "Wilhelm Marx (1863–1946)," in Morsey, ed., *Zeitgeschichte in Lebensbildern*, pp. 174–205.

[86] The first reading was held 28–30 April; the second and third readings, with much less debate, on 6 May 1926.

[87] In a formal statement accompanying the bill. Reichstag. *Drucksache* (3. Wahlperiode), Nr. 2229.

[88] See below, pp. 264–72, for a discussion of the arguments pro and con that prevailed throughout the entire controversy.

[89] For the KPD, Neubauer and Rosenberg. Reichstag. *Verhandlungen*, 390 (28 April 1926): 6907–12 and (30 April): 6946–51; for the SPD, Rosenfeld and Saenger, ibid., (28 April): 6896–6904 and (29 April): 6935–41.

[90] Count Westarp (DNVP) termed the initiative "an initiative of injustice and force." Ibid., p. 6904. Dr. Külz also considered direct popular legislation wrong in this case although he used much more moderate language than Count Westarp. He thought it best in a parliamentary system to use parliamentary means for solving such a question. Ibid., pp. 6917–18. Dr. Wunderlich spoke for the DVP (pp. 6906–07) and Schulte for the Center (pp. 6918–20).

The Democratic Party's spokesman, Baron von Richthofen, used much of his time to blame various other parties for the failure to arrive at a satisfactory solution, ibid., pp. 6912–16. So, too, the comment by his colleague, Dr. Haas (Baden) on a later occasion (19 May 1926): "It is not our fault if [a legislative ruling] was frustrated and conflict in domestic politics has been intensified at a time when the German people need, above all, internal peace." Ibid., p. 7337.

There were indications, however, that the issue was dividing political forces in a way that no longer corresponded to the superficial polarization of the working-class parties on the one side and the *bürgerliche* parties on the other. Observers noted that the People's Party sided with the Nationalists rather than with its coalition partners on a significant procedural question.[91] This provoked the Democratic leader, Koch-Weser, to accuse the DVP of "desperado politics." [92]

The spokesman for the Center Party, Karl Anton Schulte—no doubt still smarting over the complete failure of the Compromise on which he had worked tirelessly—made an angry attack on the confiscation proposal. Not only would it be a "heavy blow against legally established rights," he said,

> But also an offense against justice in a higher sense and against equity. It . . . is not in accord with the Christian conception of protection of property rights (shouts of approval and disagreement) and cannot be combined with moral or ethical values at all. (More shouting.) [93]

He then proceeded to denounce the sections of the confiscation proposal which specified social uses for various types of property. "This part is likely to excite the covetousness of broad masses of the people." [94] At this point, he was interrupted and it took some time before he could complete his statement. A few days later, the Center's Reichstag delegation sent one of its vice-chairmen, Herr von Guerard, to replace Schulte as its chief negotiator, ostensibly because interparty discussions no longer related primarily to legal questions. But *Vorwärts* observed that Schulte had been replaced because of the way he had discredited himself in the eyes of many Center voters by insulting the masses.[95]

The second and third reading of the proposal for full confiscation took place on 6 May.[96] The voting went as expected

---

[91] On a Center Party motion to send the confiscation proposal and its amendments to the Legal Committee. The purpose of this motion was to permit time for further interparty negotiations on a possible alternative to the referendum. *Frankfurter Zeitung*, 1 May 1926 (Nr. 321); *Germania*, 1 May 1926 (Nr. 201).

[92] Reichstag. *Verhandlungen*, 390 (30 April 1926): 6962.

[93] Ibid., (28 April 1926): 6918.

[94] Idem.

[95] 3 May 1926 (Nr. 204). For the discussion in the Center *Fraktion* see Morsey, *Protokolle*, pp. 29–30.

[96] The most noteworthy aspect of the debate was a lengthy speech by Scheidemann. With deliberate intent he attacked the former emperor, continuing until the representatives for the DNVP left the chamber. The issue was "the existence or non-existence of the Republic," he said (p. 7035). Reichstag. *Verhandlungen*, 390 (6 May 1926): 7029–37.

with only its sponsors voting for it; the result was 141 for, 236 against.[97] However, 7 members of the Democratic Party's delegation (more than one-fifth of the delegation) left the floor of the house rather than consent to party discipline and vote against the bill.[98]

Luther had decided that the government would sponsor legislation to regulate the property settlements just before the flag dispute pushed all other issues aside. By the time the new Marx government was able to attend to legislative business, it was practically too late for the Reichstag to act. Marx was named chancellor on 17 May, the same day the date for the referendum (20 June 1926) was officially announced.[99] The last weeks of the referendum campaign monopolized the attention of the parties; most of them saw little point in debating the pros and cons of regulatory legislation again until the referendum was over.[100]

The Democrats' alarm that masses of their followers would vote for confiscation unless some meaningful alternative was forthcoming now reached into the cabinet. Dr. Külz, the minister of interior, urgently requested that action on the government bill be completed in the short time remaining before the referendum. "The danger of a success for the Social Democrats and the Communists . . . is now greater than ever." [101] He believed that adoption of the regulatory legislation was still possible if the government altered its opinion

[97] Ibid., pp. 7045, 7047–50; *Frankfurter Zeitung*, 7 May 1926 (Nr. 337).

[98] Idem. They were Ludwig Bergstraesser, then an archivist at the *Reichsarchiv;* Alfred Brodauf, a judge in Chemnitz and a leading member of the *Republikanische Reichsbund;* Adolf Korell, a pastor in Hesse; and four representatives closely identified with the Hirsch-Duncker unions: Ernst Lemmer, Heinrich Rönneburg, Gustav Schneider, and Paul Ziegler. It is noteworthy that Anton Erkelenz submitted to *Fraktionszwang* on this occasion although he later announced his support of the referendum. See below, pp. 251–52.

[99] Ibid., 18 May 1926 (Nr. 363); *Rote Fahne*, 18 May 1926.

[100] *Frankfurter Zeitung*, 22 May 1926 (Nr. 376).

[101] *Kabinettsprotokolle* (7 June 1926), reel 1839, frame D769106. Weismann pointed out that the Prussian government also "saw the danger of the referendum succeeding as very great." Ibid., frame D769107. Külz told a reporter shortly before the referendum that "one should turn to the people for a decision by means of new [Reichstag] elections or through a vote on the law only if it proves impossible to reach a solution in the Reichstag. . . . And then [one could] spare the people . . . the enormous excitement and the deepening of differences that are inevitably associated with such a referendum" *Frankfurter Zeitung*, 19 June 1926 (Nr. 449). Armin Behrendt mentions Külz's opposition to the initiative and referendum but does not discuss his attempt to further the passage of regulatory legislation, *Wilhelm Külz: Aus dem Leben eines Suchenden* (Berlin, 1968), pp. 78–79.

that a two-thirds majority was necessary.[102] The bill, as it stood, violated certain provisions of the Constitution and, therefore, required acceptance by at least two-thirds of the Reichstag in order to avoid a challenge by the courts.[103] However, he argued that questions about the bill's constitutionality could be removed without much difficulty by adding a preamble to the draft bill that specified the grounds for the legislation.[104] Then, passage by a simple majority in the Reichstag would suffice.[105] The cabinet tentatively accepted Külz's proposal and started discussions with party leaders to see if it would find general acceptance.[106] Support of the Social Democrats for this maneuver was essential.[107] Before there was a chance to persuade them, however, a letter from Hindenburg attacking the referendum appeared in the press.[108] Angered, the Social Democrats turned with redoubled energy to fight for the referendum. The last slim possibility for Reichstag action before 20 June vanished.

Chancellor Marx insisted that at least the first reading of the government's bill should be completed.[109] It was sent to the Reichstag on 1 June and rather perfunctorily discussed on 10 June. The speakers preferred to expound their views on the more pressing question of the referendum.[110] Marx

[102] See Külz's letter, dated 3 June 1926, presenting his arguments for consideration by the chancellor and other cabinet members. *Kabinettsprotokolle,* frames D769110–11. He had already brought up the subject at the first meeting of the new cabinet, 17 May 1926. Ibid., frame D768807. Similar arguments had appeared even earlier in the Democratic press, see, Erich Eyck, "Verfassungsändernd?" *Vossische Zeitung,* 20 April 1926 (Nr. 94) and Dr. Fritz Poetzsch, "Die Verfassungsfrage im Fürstenkompromiss," ibid., 24 April 1926 (Nr. 98).

[103] In particular, Article 153, section 2, which established the general principle that confiscation was legitimate only if it served specific purposes of public benefit and did not simply enrich the state. *Kabinettsprotokolle,* reel 1839, frame D768110.

[104] His suggestion read, "Since the legal relationships between the former ruling princely houses and the states have been destroyed by the revolution of the year 1918 and since . . . the legal principles and the purposes [originally] established for the use of the properties . . . of the former princely houses have also been robbed of their foundation, the following is directed to re-establish ordered legal relationships. . . ." Ibid., frame D769111. He added that the courts could scarcely fail to find this purpose in accord with the "general welfare."

[105] He calculated that a majority could be found if the middle parties, including the *Wirtschaftspartei,* voted for the bill, the SPD abstained and some members of the DNVP absented themselves from the floor of the house. Ibid., frame D769107.

[106] Bundesarchiv. "Auseinandersetzung," Bd. 2, zu RK4713.

[107] *Frankfurter Zeitung,* 8 June (Nr. 418) and 9 June 1926 (Nr. 421).

[108] See below, pp. 244–46.

[109] *Kabinettsprotokolle,* reel 1839, frame D769106.

[110] And on the seemliness of the Hindenburg letter. Von Guerard spoke for the governing coalition, Hermann Müller for the SPD, Dr. Barth for the DNVP, and Neubauer for the KPD. Reichstag. *Verhandlungen,* 390 (10 June 1926): 7422–32.

tried to still the fears of those who thought that attempts to get satisfactory regulatory legislation would be abandoned if the referendum failed. The government saw in the present bill an acceptable solution, he said, and would not alter its views later.[111] Indeed, the chancellor threatened "to draw the necessary conclusions" [112] if the Reichstag failed to pass a suitable law—a somewhat vaguely phrased threat to resign or to dissolve the Reichstag if that was necessary.

One of the most remarkable features of the dispute over the princes' property settlements was the way it excited groups of voters usually indifferent to routine political controversies and, almost at once, polarized public opinion. These features became even more marked as the referendum campaign progressed into its final month. Yet it is also worth noting how persistently most of the political parties strove to guard their distinctive identities in a situation that forced them, willy-nilly, into one of two camps. As the referendum approached the parties issued, in addition to masses of propaganda material intended for general circulation, a variety of specific instructions directing their own followers how to behave on voting day.[113] On examination, these different instructions, and in the case of the Democratic and Center parties, the difficulties party leaders encountered in getting their decisions accepted, show that the division of the parties into those which supported the referendum (only the KPD and SPD) and those which rejected it (all the others) is valid only as the simplest kind of description. Some nuances in the announced positions of the parties opposing the referendum reflected, as at the time of the initiative, the existence of internal discord. On the other hand, almost all the parties

[111] Ibid., pp. 7421–22.
In his statement to the Reichstag, Marx explicitly termed the referendum proposal unacceptable and contrary to the principles of a *Rechtsstaat.* Just before voting day both Marx and Interior Minister Külz gave interviews to the Wolff news agency in which they re-emphasized their disapproval of the confiscation proposal. Ibid., 18 June (Nr. 446) and 19 June 1926 (Nr. 449). The cabinet approved these remarks prior to the interviews. *Kabinettsprotokolle* (17 June 1926), reel 1839, frames D769281–82.
[112] Reichstag. *Verhandlungen,* 390 (10 June 1926): 7422. The *Frankfurter Zeitung* thought Marx's statement rather weak, but observed, "With us a statesman can live a long time just because of his weakness." 11 June 1926 (Nr. 427). The *Vossische Zeitung* later commented on the strange omission of any official *Begründung* for this law, contrasting this with the very full statement that accompanied the initiative proposal when it had to be submitted to the Reichstag. 30 June 1926 (Nr. 155).
[113] Schulte, *Was geschieht mit dem Fürsten-Vermögen?,* pp. 44–48, reprints all the statements by the major parties opposed to the referendum.

showed an unmistakable distrust of any close association with other parties which could encourage a weakening of voter identification. Even when temporarily engaged in a common undertaking, they preferred to conduct parallel rather than joint operations and to differentiate their positions in other ways.

Of all the parties, those of the right and right center, in conjunction with some nationalist organizations, demonstrated the most effective cooperation. The success of a similar grouping, the so-called *Reichsblock*, in the Hindenburg election the preceding year, encouraged renewed collaboration,[114] particularly after the surprising results of the KPD-SPD sponsored initiative movement bared the need for much more intensive propagandistic activity on the part of the right.[115]

On 15 April 1926, the head of the *Hofkammervereinigung*, Baron von Brandenstein, quietly brought representatives of the DNVP, DVP, the *Wirtschaftspartei*, the *Deutschvölkische Freiheitsbewegung*, and the *Vereinigte Vaterländische Verbände* together.[116] They decided to form a "Working Committee" to fight the referendum. After some discussion it was agreed that the committee should avoid attracting attention as much as possible. It would raise funds, supply propaganda materials, and coordinate activities undertaken by the participating groups, but each of the parties was to conduct its own propaganda and decide for itself what use it would make of the committee's services. Because of the range of parties participating in the committee it was agreed that it was necessary to avoid any open defense of the monarchy or partisan criticism of the various proposals to regulate the property settlements since such topics were potentially divisive. Unanimity was to be maintained by making the main theme of all arguments against the referendum "the defense against

[114] Dorpalen, pp. 65–81; Schüren, pp. 171–72, 177–83.

[115] An appeal for funds sent out by the *Vereinigte Vaterländische Verbände* directly after the initiative emphasized that "the counter-propaganda during the initiative has not worked, otherwise the number who signed would not have reached such a frightening total." A letter to *Geheimrat* von Priesdorff from Count von der Goltz's secretary, 26 March 1926. Bundesarchiv. Deutsche Volkspartei. Reichsgeschäftsstelle. R4511/20, pp. 29–31.

[116] Letters from Karl Trucksaess to Dr. Scholz, the head of the DVP's Reichstag delegation, 19 April 1926. Ibid., pp. 55–56, and to Stresemann, 27 April 1926, ibid., pp. 63–71; in addition to the groups mentioned in the text, Dörr lists the *Landbund, Stahlhelm, Jungdeutschen Orden, Tannenbergbund,* and the *Deutsche Industriellenvereinigung* as participating in the Committee (p. 234, note 55); Karl, p. 39.

Bolshevik plans to destroy private property." [117] This was successfully done.

The relationship of the People's Party to the Working Committee was somewhat delicate. Consideration for the Democratic and Center parties, its partners in the governing coalition, made any publicized association with the oppositional parties on the right rather embarrassing, as well as tactically unwise. "If we now by ourselves joined a bloc with the parties of the right, we would give the Center and the Democrats . . . a pretext to go their own way and, thus, harm our common interest." [118] Most members of the People's Party probably felt quite at home defending the property rights of the princes and, by extension, those of the middle class, in collaboration with the Nationalists. [119] Yet, Stresemann, as party chairman and foreign minister, could not afford to ignore the potential danger of such ties. [120]

The *Bundesarchiv* contains a very interesting exchange of letters between Stresemann and Karl Trucksaess, the party's business manager on this subject. On his own authority, Trucksaess had responded to communications from the sponsors of the Working Committee, had attended its organizational meeting, and then had made arrangements for the continued participation of the DVP in the committee's activities. [121] Stresemann was not informed of these developments; indeed he seems to have first learned of them as the result of a news conference that the committee sponsored on 21 April 1926. [122] He demanded an explanation from Trucksaess:

[117] In addition to the letters cited in the preceding note, see the undated statement announcing the formation of the Committee, Bundesarchiv. Deutsche Volkspartei. Reichsgeschäftsstelle. R4511/20, pp. 3–6.

[118] A letter from Trucksaess to the local DVP in Brandenburg a. H., 4 May 1926. Ibid., pp. 87–88.

[119] But not all. Some local units of the party appear to have disapproved of the idea of cooperating with the right. Ibid., pp. 11, 89.

[120] See Turner's discussion, pp. 224–26, of Stresemann's angry reaction to Karl Jarres's proposal in July 1926 that the DVP and DNVP cooperate parliamentarily. He also warned the party office against contacts with rightist Catholics out of consideration for the views of the Center. Stresemann, *Vermächtnis*, 2: 401.

[121] In a letter dated 13 April 1926, Trucksaess informed the *Vereinigung Deutscher Hofkammern* that his business office was responsible for all matters regarding propaganda. The Reichstag delegation, he said, was to be consulted only regarding the legislation currently under consideration in the Legal Committee. Bundesarchiv. Deutsche Volkspartei. Reichsgeschäftsstelle. R4511/20, p. 53.

[122] On 19 April 1926, Trucksaess informed Dr. Scholz that the Working Committee had been organized and asked him to represent the DVP at its news conference. Ibid., pp. 55–56. There is no indication that he also notified Stresemann. Scholz was well-known for favoring a right-orientation for the DVP.

The question of the states' disputes with their [former] princes requires the most cautious handling if important interests . . . are not to suffer. In my capacity as party chairman I therefore urgently request that you do not take on any obligations concerning participation in any committee before the party Executive Board has established a clear policy on this matter. Furthermore, because of several inquiries that I have received, I request that you confirm that the German People's Party has not already made commitments of this sort. . . .[123]

Trucksaess's reply was a masterpiece of evasion.[124] Unable to deny the existence of ties with the right, he minimized their significance. The agreements concerned "only purely technical matters" and did not bind the party in any way politically, he said. Indeed, he claimed that he persuaded the representatives of the other parties to organize an inconspicuous committee rather than follow the example of the highly publicized *Reichsblock* which the Nationalists wanted to renew. He gave a number of different reasons to justify his decision to associate the DVP with the parties of the right: requests from various parts of the country that the party take a more active role in combatting leftist agitation, the knowledge that "politically neutral groups (landowners, industrialists, bankers)" were ready to finance propaganda against the referendum, and "rather fierce *(stürmischen)* urgings from the right." Throughout the letter Trucksaess implied that it had not seemed necessary to consult his party chief (or that there was no time to do so) and that he had prevented undesirable consequences by acting as he had done.

After Stresemann's sharp reprimand to Trucksaess, the DVP's association with the right became somewhat more circumspect, but was not terminated.[125] The party drew heavily

[123] Ibid., p. 59; an excerpt is printed in Stresemann, *Vermächtnis*, 2: 402.

[124] All the quotations in this paragraph are from his letter to Stresemann, 27 April 1926. Bundesarchiv. Deutsche Volkspartei. Reichsgeschäftsstelle. R4511/20, pp. 63–71. Typical of the kind of innocuous coloration Trucksaess tried to give his explanation of what had happened is his identification of the instigator of the Working Committee, Herr von Brandenstein, as head of the *Reichsgrundbesitzerverband* whereas in the letter to Scholz, cited above note 122, he matter-of-factly described him as spokesman for the *Hofkammervereinigung*.

[125] See the letter from Count von der Goltz to Admiral Brüninghaus, 27 April 1926, complaining about the changed attitude of the DVP's representative at the Committee's meeting that day and Trucksaess's explanation of the party's policy to Brüninghaus. Ibid., pp. 73–74. Throughout May and early June, Trucksaess was regularly notified of the meetings of the Committee and presumably attended. Ibid., pp. 83, 97, 99, 101. Unfortunately the DVP materials at the Bundesarchiv do not contain transcripts of these meetings.

on the committee's stocks of leaflets, posters, and prepared
newspaper articles for circulation against the referendum.[126]
Even a glance at the materials the DVP prepared itself, or at
the articles in the *Kölnische Zeitung,* will show how faithfully
the People's Party kept its promise to maintain a common
line against the referendum along with its partners in the
committee. A DVP appeal foresaw a series of drastic consequences:

> The acceptance of the law proposed in the referendum will have
> the following catastrophic effects:
>
> *Resignation of the president* and the *national government,* dissolution
> of the *Reichstag,* a *state crisis,* political chaos.
>
> A *radical left government* with a corresponding Reichstag and pres-
> ident.
>
> *Destruction* of all legal security and *order,* the collapse of the state's
> credit and that of industry . . . , catastrophic unemployment
> and limitless suffering, *economic chaos, Bolshevism.*
>
> Whoever wants to avoid these dangers must reject the referen-
> dum through abstention! [127]

This appeal can be compared with an equivalent passage from
one of the Working Committee's a most widely distributed
pamphlets:

> Since Cain killed Abel there is hidden in every one of us a little
> bit of Cain that won't let us rest if our brother is better off [than]
> we are. This *Cain in us* is the ally of *Bolshevism.*
>
> They plan to use step by step the envy of part of the people to
> destroy the other parts. The plan is:

---

[126] The Bundesarchiv possesses a sizable folder of materials used by the DVP
during the campaign. Deutsche Volkspartei. Reichsgeschäftsstelle. Volksbegehren
auf entschädigungslose Enteignung der Fürstenhäuser am 20 Juni 1926. Bd. 2.
Propaganda- und Informationsmaterial, R4511/21. Among the most intriguing
items are a series of newspaper articles entitled "Der Volksentscheid und der
Beamte," etc. intended for use by the provincial press. There are also three separate
sets of short articles written appropriately to appeal to Center Party readers, to
Nationalists, and to a more republican-inclined audience. Ibid., pp. 3–11. Also of
value are the photographs of posters against the referendum in the Müller und
Graef Collection at the Hoover Library.

[127] *Kölnische Zeitung,* 19 June 1926 (Nr. 448), emphasis in original. Similarly, 6 June
(Nr. 414), 8 June (Nrs. 418 and 419), 12 June (Nr. 431), 17 June (Nr. 442) and 18
June 1926 (Nr. 445). See, too, the leaflet declaring "We don't want to help the
Bolsheviks do their business!" Bundesarchiv. Flugblatt Aufruf der DVP, ZS81–42/
2, and an appeal published in the *Freiburger Zeitung,* "Stay home on June 20th.
Moscow has ordered confiscation!" Quoted in the *Frankfurter Zeitung,* 19 June 1926
(Nr. 448).

first *everyone* shall help against the *princes;* then the *peasants* shall help against the *big landowners;* then the *workers* shall help against the *peasants;* then the *renters* shall help against the *house owners;* then those who have nothing shall help against *people with means (Rentner);*

then those *whose existence has been destroyed* shall help against *everyone* who still has a *living.* With each confiscation the number of those whose existence has been destroyed will grow and thereby [increase] the *army of Bolshevism.*

That is permanent destruction without [making it possible for] even a single decent worker to climb upwards. [It is] a triumph for *Schadenfreude,* for vileness and envy—other than that, nothing.[128]

The tone of the DVP's appeal was a little less vulgar—after all, the party's writers knew they were addressing a "respectable" class of voters—but the scare technique was, as agreed, the same.[129]

The most prominent opponents of the referendum did not limit their efforts to coordinating and financing the propagandistic activities of the parties of the right and right center.[130] They knew that President Hindenburg would have a crucial decision to make if the referendum measure passed even though they were certain he would not allow it to become law. However, they wanted him to announce his views before the constitutionally prescribed time in order to reduce the turnout on 20 June.[131] A number of old acquaintances

[128] *Volk! Entscheide! Material zum Volksentscheid nach amtlichen Quellen bearbeitet* (Berlin, 1926), p. 11, emphasis in original.

[129] Admiral Willi Brüninghaus appealed to the superior political sensitivities of the readers of the *Kölnische Zeitung* in an article entitled "Rechtsstaat oder Bolschewismus?" 16 June 1926. He wrote that he considered the referendum "a classic example that our people . . . still does not understand how to value and to correctly apply the rights the constitution gives them."

Dr. Wunderlich, as head of the DVP in Saxony, ordered a close watch of the polls during the referendum, a tactic the Nationalists had also adopted in order to intimidate potential voters. He justified the order by saying it was "in the interest of party discipline" *Vossische Zeitung,* 22 June 1926 (Nr. 148).

[130] *Vorwärts* reprinted a circular from Ernst von Borsig, head of the German Employers Association, requesting that its members contribute at least twenty pfennige per employee to the fight against the referendum. 11 June 1926 (Nr. 271). An adjutant of the former crown prince wrote Walter von Molo, the author of the bestseller, *Fridericus Rex,* asking him to allow the use of his name opposing the referendum. He not only refused, but informed the republican press of the incident. *Vossische Zeitung,* 11 June 1926 (Nr. 139).

[131] Dorpalen, pp. 107–8. Count Westarp at a regional meeting of the DNVP in Osnabrück, 5 June 1926, stated, "It is not enough to defeat the referendum measure. [Our] goal must be to significantly reduce the twelve and one-half million of the

warned him of the danger of passivity. Among them was the former crown prince:

> I have gained the impression from the most varied observations that we are on the eve of a second revolution. . . . The party of the leftists (including the Democrats) are working systematically to bring [it] about. In part unconsciously, but in the largest part entirely aware [of what they are doing], the main instigators of this movement are of a purely Bolshevist makeup. The rabble-rousing against our Hohenzollern house, against the judiciary, against landed property, and ultimately all property is just the . . . first spade-work for the Bolshevization of Germany.[132]

Actually, Hindenburg needed no prompting.[133] In March he had written to Dr. Marx outlining his strong reservations against the Compromise Bill on constitutional grounds.[134] Yet for him to speak out publicly before the vote on the referendum would have itself been an act of doubtful constitutionality.

Otto Meissner devised a way for the president to satisfy his monarchist friends.[135] Hindenburg's campaign manager in 1925, Friedrich Wilhelm von Loebell, had already written, warning him that the Communists and Socialists were misrepresenting the reasons for his silence.[136] On 22 May, Hin-

---

initiative and thereby deliver the parties of revolution . . . a clearly recognizable defeat," quoted by Schreiber, *Politisches Jahrbuch 1926*, p. 70, note 3.

[132] An unsigned carbon of a letter dated 14 May 1926 among the Hans von Seeckt papers, reel 22, item 162. Also see the interviews granted to representatives of the Hearst press by Prince August Wilhelm and the former kaiser. *San Francisco Examiner,* 14 June 1926, p. 5, and 18 June 1926, p. 6. The kaiser stated that it was the "menace to the state which alarm[ed] him far more than the possibility of personal loss."

The belief that the left would soon attempt an uprising seems to have been prevalent in rightist circles. Several prominent men including Heinrich Class, of the Pan-German League, and Alfred Hugenberg discussed the possible need to establish a dictatorship with the backing of the military and suspending the Reichstag indefinitely. The Prussian police learned of these discussions, reacted somewhat hastily, and created quite a sensation by searching a number of homes of leading rightists without, however, finding evidence of any truly serious plot. *Frankfurter Zeitung,* 12 May (Nr. 351), 13 May (Nr. 352), 15 May (Nr. 357), 18 May (Nr. 363) and 29 May 1926 (Nr. 391); *Kabinettsprotokolle* (4 June 1926), reel 1839, frames D769072–74; Braun, pp. 195–97; Severing, 2: 87–89.

[133] Reportedly he told his family the night before the referendum, "I will not put . . . my name on a document that is a disgrace for Germany. . . . If the referendum tomorrow goes against me [sic!], I will leave Berlin at once," quoted by Lucas, p. 46.

[134] Hubatsch, pp. 232–33. Also see his objections in 1929 to a law limiting the claims of the *Standesherren.* Bundesarchiv. "Auseinandersetzung," Bd. 4, RK4455.

[135] Dorpalen, p. 108; Haungs, p. 203; Schüren, pp. 172–77.

[136] Hubatsch, pp. 236–37.

denburg replied to this letter.[137] He said his position did not permit him to comment on the political aspects of the issue or take part in a public demonstration as Loebell had urged. However, he was glad to express his "personal views" on the moral and legal questions raised by the proposed confiscation. As one who "had spent his life in the service of the kings of Prussia and German emperors," he regarded the referendum movement as "coarse ingratitude" as well as "a great injustice." If it succeeded, it would "incite the instincts of the masses" to further attacks on property and by undermining "respect for the law and for legally established property rights" do incalculable damage to the life of the nation.

Hindenburg was surely aware that Loebell intended to print this "private" communication in his right-wing periodical, *Deutschen-Spiegel.*[138] As so often in his long career, Hindenburg's strict sense of correctness did not prevent him from bowing to the convenience of the moment. In this connection it seems appropriate to mention that his belief in the sanctity of property rights had not always been as strong as he let it appear in 1926. In July 1918, he composed a memorandum in order to justify the high command's desire to annex extensive territories along Germany's eastern frontiers:

> Scruples . . . against the required confiscation of Polish private property in the border areas can be dispelled. The modern conception of law (*Rechtsbewusstsein*) regarding personal freedom and property has changed. Extensive . . . interference in private life and in property rights, unheard of even a few years ago, is accepted today as an unquestioned right of the state. With growing recognition of the need for an especially secure frontier defense as a result of the experiences of this war, modern legal thinking will adjust itself to this challenge.[139]

In other words, legal relativism was welcome if used against the Poles!

In order to maximize the effect of Hindenburg's warning, Loebell intended to publish the letter just a few days before the referendum, but *Vorwärts* obtained a copy of the document

[137] Ibid., pp. 237–39. All the quotations in this paragraph are from this letter.
[138] Some scholars have doubted whether Hindenburg knew what use Loebell would make of the letter, Dörr, p. 238; Lucas, p. 47. However, recent researches make it clear that he did. Dorpalen, p. 108; Haungs, p. 203; and Stehkämper, 3: 13.
[139] "Denkschrift über den Polnischen Grenzstreifen," in Hubatsch, p. 177.

from a sympathetic printer in Loebell's plant and, on 6 June 1926, exposed the whole maneuver.[140] The parties on the left immediately decried such a misuse of the prestige of the president.[141] The cabinet had to defend the right of the president to express his private opinions, but did so with some embarrassment since it had not received any advance notice of the letter or its contents.[142] Since the new cabinet was hardly three weeks old, and none of the republican parties wanted to provoke a grave crisis, the questioning of the constitutionality of Hindenburg's action was not pushed too hard.[143] The Reichstag rejected a Communist resolution of no confidence; during the vote the Social Democrats abstained.[144] On the whole, the attempt to draw Hindenburg into the fight against the referendum does not appear to have aided the right. The exposure of the arranged character of his public intervention perhaps even caused some undecided voters to support the confiscation measure.[145] The creation of a solid front of "middle-class" parties against the "socialists" that rightist leaders hoped for was not helped, either.[146] In fact, for a time the republican parties drew closer together.[147]

The most successful achievement produced by the Working Committee's coordination of the opposition of the parties of the right and right center to the referendum was the agreement to order all their voters to abstain during the voting, rather than to vote "no." As we explained earlier, general

[140] *Deutschen-Spiegel*, 7 June 1926; *Vorwärts*, 6 June 1926 (Nr. 262); *Frankfurter Zeitung*, 7 June 1926 (Nr. 415).

[141] "Hands off the President!" *Germania* editorialized, 7 June 1926 (Nr. 265); *Frankfurter Zeitung*, 8 June 1926 (Nr. 419).

[142] Ibid., 9 June 1926 (Nr. 420); Bundesarchiv. "Auseinandersetzung," Bd. 2, RK4598; *Kabinettsprotokolle*, reel 1839, frames D769139–43. Chancellor Marx defended Hindenburg in the Reichstag. *Verhandlungen*, 390 (10 June 1926): 7425–26.

[143] See the statements by Müller, v. Guerard and Koch-Weser, ibid., 7423–25, 7433.

[144] Knowing very well that the SPD would not support the KPD motion, Neubauer called the Social Democrats "the stable boys (*Steigbügelhalter*) of reaction" and ended by saying, "We are not afraid of the [forthcoming] struggle, but we demand a clear decision from the Social Democrats, a clear commitment, and the dropping of all double-dealing. Now is the time to repulse the power of the reactionaries by the power of the proletariat!" Ibid., pp. 7431–32. The vote took place the next day. Ibid., 11 June 1926: 7457. *Rote Fahne*, 11 June 1926.

[145] Friedrich Stampfer claimed this was so. Stampfer, p. 447. The *Frankfurter Zeitung* reported that the *Schlesischer Bauernbund* decided to allow its members to vote as they pleased after the publication of the letter to Loebell. 14 June 1926 (Nr. 435).

[146] Dorpalen, p. 109; *Kölnische Zeitung*, 6 June 1926 (Nr. 414).

[147] *Germania*, 7 June 1926 (Nr. 257), wrote that on this issue the Center Party drew a clear line between the Weimar Coalition and the *Reichsblock*.

abstention from voting by one clearly defined portion of the electorate made possible the intimidation—the left called it "Wahlterror"—of other segments of the population.[148] This was particularly effective in small towns and rural areas where individual voters were known and could be identified if they went to the polling place.[149] Moreover, it ensured that regular voters for the parties which ordered abstention did not privately ignore their leaders' directives in the seclusion of the voting booth. Unfortunately the available source materials do not clarify when the decision was made, but it appears that some kind of understanding regarding tactics was reached by the middle of May. The Nationalists, the People's Party, the Bavarian People's Party, the National Socialists, the *Deutsch-Hannoverische Partei,* the *Wirtschaftspartei,* and *Liberale Vereinigung* [150] all issued similar directives to their followers.[151] It hardly seems probable that all these parties reached their decisions independently and without prior consultation.

Usually the Center Party profited by being able to choose whether it would associate with the parties on its left or on its right. But for the vote on the referendum its leaders defined a policy distinctly its own. They soon discovered that the freedom of a middle position also had its disadvantages.

On the one hand, large segments of the Center Party did not want to further the aims of the monarchists who were working for the failure of referendum with the expectation that no further legislation would then be attempted. The Center still hoped for regulation of the settlements, and thought that the former ruling families should be required to make some sacrifices corresponding to the general impoverishment of the German people since the war. On the other hand, most Catholics believed in the sanctity of estab-

[148] See above, Chapter V, p. 144.

[149] The *Landbund* in Thuringia ordered, "The watchword for our members runs: 'No true *Landbündler* will participate in the voting!' We definitely hope that the members will act accordingly. However in order to know for the future who is with us and who is against us, we request [you] to identify who participates in the voting," quoted by Fritsch, *Wissenschaftliche Zeitschrift der Universität Jena,* 19: 385.

[150] An association of right-wing Democrats and some members of the People's Party who hoped to find a way of overcoming the division of the German liberals. Turner, pp. 253–54; Eugen Schiffer, *Ein Leben für den Liberalismus* (Berlin, 1951), p. 235; *Frankfurter Zeitung,* 2 Feb. 1926 (Nr. 87); and the sharp debate over its merits in the DDP *Vorstand* meeting, 6 Nov. 1926. DDP Papers, reel 37, folder 730.

[151] *Frankfurter Zeitung,* 21 May (Nr. 374), 30 May (Nr. 395), 4 June (Nr. 407), and 5 June 1926 (Nr. 411); *Deutsche Mittelstands-Zeitung,* 1 June 1926 (Nr. 6); Dörr, p. 533.

lished property rights. Few accepted the principle of confiscation without compensation, even if they left the political implications of the KPD-SPD undertaking momentarily aside. For these reasons, the Center Party's Executive Board officially announced that it expected all party members "not to vote for the referendum measure," but did not explicitly order them to abstain.[152]

Because of the difficulties experienced during the initiative campaign, the party leadership did not content itself by merely indicating the policy that lower levels of the party were to follow. Speakers able to explain why the party had adopted its official position attended meetings of the Center's regional organizations and encouraged them to concur with the national policy.[153] The press was flooded with exhortatory articles. Pains were taken to ensure uniform handling of the key issues [154] and prevent known indiscipline among party followers from becoming too evident.[155] Despite all, the *Rhein-Mainische Volkszeitung* printed articles urging voters to accept the referendum proposal "as a lesser evil" and suggested that no party policy ought to have been issued, but that the decision should have been left to the conscience of each individual.[156] The Dortmund paper *Tremonia*, which had

[152] Resolution of the *Reichsparteivorstand*, 19 May 1926. *Germania*, 20 May 1926 (Nr. 230); *Frankfurter Zeitung*, 20 May 1926 (Nrs. 370 and 371); Morsey, *Protokolle*, p. 44, note 7.

[153] For example, Karl Anton Schulte and Dr. Johannes Linneborn were the principal speakers at an assembly of party members in Westphalia. *Kölnische Volkszeitung*, 19 June 1926 (Nr. 444). The Cologne party organization ratified the national policy by a vote of 171 to 5, but added that it did so because of Dr. Marx's promise to see that a satisfactory regulatory law was passed. "Center Party supporters should have *confidence* in the chancellor, who is also their highly esteemed party leader, that he . . . *will keep his word.*" Ibid., 12 June 1926 (Nr. 427), emphasis in original. Stehkämper, 3: 20.

[154] The *Augustinus-Verein*, the Catholic press organization, seconded the decision of the party leadership. Ibid., 6 June (Nr. 409) and 9 June 1926 (Nr. 416); *Frankfurter Zeitung*, 5 June 1926 (Nr. 411). The *Kölnische Volkszeitung*, 14 June (Nr. 431) momentarily argued for voter abstention but returned to the official party policy the next day, 15 June 1926 (Nr. 434).

[155] The local party leadership at Höchst a. M. issued a statement that party followers were free to decide for themselves how to vote. *Rhein-Mainische Volkszeitung*, 12 June 1926 (Nr. 133); *Frankfurter Zeitung*, 16 June 1926 (Nr. 441). The head of the *Verband christlich-evangelischer Arbeitnehmer* wrote Chancellor Marx on 21 May 1926, explaining that numerous congregations had lost their property as a result of the legislation ending the inflation. He said for that reason many good Christians now thought that "if the government confiscated the property of the churches, then we want [to see the property] of the princes confiscated." Bundesarchiv. "Auseinandersetzung," Bd. 2, RK432226.

[156] 14 May (Nr. 110), 20 May (Nr. 115) and 2 June 1926 (Nr. 125); Stehkämper, 3: 13.

earlier modified its views to bring them into accord with the national party policy, sharply attacked the blatant impropriety of a Reichstag member, Friedrich Dessauer, publishing views contrary to those decided upon by the party leaders.

> It would be desirable if the reins were *pulled somewhat tighter* in the *Fraktion* so that this kind of escapade does not happen again in the future. It is not the *first* [such] romp that parliamentarians have taken in the last few months. . . . How would the *Fraktion* react if one of the larger Center journals should sometime intentionally and *knowingly* violate its specific directives? [157]

Once again, as during the initiative, the Catholic bishops took upon themselves the responsibility of announcing the congruence between God's Word and the party's *Parole*.[158] On 1 June 1926, they issued a statement declaring the referendum proposal contrary to Christian moral principles and directed that it be read from all pulpits the following Sunday.[159] Episcopal admonitions such as these may have been effective with the most devout Center Party supporters, among women, or in rural areas where critical attitudes toward the church hierarchy had not yet infiltrated, but they appear to have been widely ignored in the heavily industrialized areas.[160] In Berlin, a number of young Catholics, mostly from the Windthorst League and apparently with ties to the Kuczynski Committee, formed a "National Committee of Catholic Youth to Protect the Seventh Commandment Against the Princes."[161] On the last Sunday before the vote

[157] 28 May 1926 (Nr. 143), emphasis in original, and again on 14 June 1926 (Nr. 160). The conduct of Dessauer and the *Rhein-Mainische Volkszeitung* were discussed in the Reichstag *Fraktion*. Morsey, *Protokolle*, pp. 50 and 54.

[158] Schüren (pp. 210–11) has found evidence that authorities in the Vatican were contacted by opponents of the referendum and then directed the German bishops to issue a formal statement.

[159] *Germania*, 6 June 1926 (Nr. 256); Stehkämper, 3: 13. Reportedly "sounds of protest" (*Unmutsstimmen*) were heard in the churches in various localities when the bishops' statement was read. Hildegard Pleyer, *Politische Werbung in der Weimarer Republik* (dissertation, University of Münster, 1960), p. 115. The *Frankfurter Zeitung* printed an article from an unidentified Catholic criticizing the bishops' stand. The writer observed that they had not protested the "confiscation" of the life-savings of ordinary people by the *Aufwertung* legislation. 13 June 1926 (Nr. 432). A Catholic judge in Berlin, Dr. Robert Scholz, wrote a letter protesting against the churchmen mixing in politics. As a jurist he argued it was wrong to call the confiscation of the princes' properties "theft." *Vossische Zeitung*, 19 June 1926 (Nr. 146).

[160] Contrast the "yes" vote in Münster (15.3 percent of the voters) or in the Coblenz-Trier district (17.8 percent) with that of Cologne (39.2 percent). The national average was 36.4 percent. See the more detailed analysis below, Chapter VIII, pp. 278–82.

[161] *Frankfurter Zeitung*, 11 June 1926 (Nr. 427). A small Catholic splinter party, the *Christliche-soziale Reichspartei*, also favored confiscation. Ibid., 18 June 1926 (Nr. 447);

on the referendum, members of this committee distributed leaflets to churchgoers attacking the bishops' statements.[162] Such "incredible" [163] conduct brought immediate reprimands and a flurry of newspaper articles from party spokesmen. A major party paper responded by printing the message in bigger letters:

> SHALL THE SEVENTH COMMANDMENT BE REPEALED BY A REFERENDUM? NO! NO CHRISTIAN WILL VOTE FOR CONFISCATION WITHOUT COMPENSATION.[164]

During the last days, as it became more and more apparent that the parties on the right had directed their followers to abstain in order to be able to intimidate the other voters, some of the Center's leaders began to worry that their own policy was being misunderstood. On 17 June 1926, the Berlin regional *Vorstand* ordered its voters to go to the polls and vote "no." Abstention would "cause suspicions that the Center was aiding those circles that combined distinct political objectives with their propaganda against the referendum." [165] *Germania* adopted the same recommendation in its final editorial. It stressed once again that perennial theme—the

---

Karl, pp. 14, 29, 44–45. On Vitus Heller and the *Christliche-soziale Reichspartei* generally, Grebing, *Geschichte der deutschen Arbeiterbewegung*, p. 204; Thomas Knapp, "The Red and the Black: Catholic Socialists in the Weimar Republic," *Catholic Historical Review*, 61 (Nr. 3, July, 1975): 386–408.

[162] Kuczynski gives an illustration of the leaflet between pp. 112–13.

[163] *Kölnische Volkszeitung*, 12 June 1926 (Nr. 427).

The headquarters of the *Windthorstbund* disassociated itself from any responsibility for this committee, calling it an action by individual members and not of the organizations they claimed to speak for. *Germania*, 11 June 1926 (Nr. 265); *Frankfurter Zeitung*, 12 June 1926 (Nr. 430); Stehkämper, 3: 14; Morsey, *Protokolle*, pp. 47–48. The leadership of the party in the Berlin region ordered disciplinary actions against two of the ring-leaders, Erwin Niffka and Hans Grundel. *Germania*, 15 June 1926 (Nr. 271). Niffka was active in the *Reichsbanner*. Rohe, p. 68 and passim. I have not been able to identify Grundel.

Friedrich Muckermann S.J. wrote that those who favored the referendum had forgotten "the ethical, moral, and religious majesty of the law." *Germania*, 15 June (Nr. 270). Similarly, 15 June (Nr. 271), 17 June (Nrs. 274 and 275) and 18 June 1926 (Nr. 277) and Schulte, *Was geschieht mit dem Fürsten-Vermögen?*, p. 30. Protestant churchmen also spoke out against the referendum. Schüren, pp. 210–14; *Frankfurter Zeitung*, 23 May (Nr. 379), 26 May (Nr. 383), 11 June 1926 (Nr. 428). But their views do not seem to have attracted as much attention as those of the Catholic bishops. Furthermore some concerned Protestant clergymen argued that the referendum involved only political issues, not moral ones. Ibid., 17 June 1926 (Nr. 443).

[164] In block letters on the front page of the *Kölnische Volkszeitung*, 18 June 1926 (Nr. 443).

[165] *Germania*, 17 June 1926 (Nr. 274); *Vorwärts*, 17 June 1926 (Nr. 281).

independence of the Center Party from both the right and the left.[166]

The Democratic Party also went its own way, more from necessity than by choice. It alone of all the parties "decline[d] to issue a directive." [167] The announcement of a more definite official line, whether favorable or unfavorable to the referendum, would have caused very serious party defections. Bernard Falk openly admitted in the Prussian *Landtag* that "there are surely very few on our party's Executive Board who do not hold the same position that my friend Hoepker-Aschoff and I believe in, [rejection of the confiscation proposal]. But we know, unfortunately, that our supporters throughout the country would refuse to follow us . . . if we tried to make [them] uphold our position." [168]

The leaders of the DDP recognized that their followers differed over current social and economic priorities because, although some segments of the German middle classes had remained prosperous despite the war and inflation, many had been ruined. The official statement tried to do justice to both sides:

> Men disabled in the war, Germans living in foreign countries, refugees, savers, purchasers of war loans, mortgage holders, creditors, owners of foreign securities, and . . . all the others hurt by the war . . . have lost nearly everything. The party Executive Board considers it an *injustice* to leave great wealth in the hands of the princes, wealth they were able to acquire only [because] they were rulers. . . .

The Democratic Party, they said, still wanted to see suitable legislation passed; it was the fault of other parties that the Reichstag failed to act.

> On the other hand, the party cannot offer its help for [a proposal to] confiscate without compensation, since it regards private property as the foundation of a productive economy, and as an institution guaranteed by the constitution. . . .[169]

[166] 20 June 1926 (Nr. 280); also see the statement "Against Loebell and against Rosenfeld," 16 June 1926 (Nr. 273).
[167] From the official statement issued by the DDP Executive Board, 20 May 1926. *Frankfurter Zeitung*, 21 May 1926 (Nr. 373).
[168] Prussia. Landtag. *Sitzungsberichte*, 8 (2 June 1926) (2. Wahlperiode): 12230. Also Anton Erkelenz's remark at the *Vorstand* meeting on 20 May 1926. "We can compose resolutions any way we want, [but] great parts of our electorate have already made up their minds in favor of confiscation." DDP Papers, reel 37, folder 730, p. 4, and Ludwig Haas's remarks to the leaders of the DDP in Bavaria. *Frankfurter Zeitung*, 28 June 1926 (Nr. 472).
[169] Ibid., 21 May 1926 (Nr. 373).

As a result of this conflict of views, the party leaders decided to allow each individual voter to choose for himself what he wanted to do.[170]

This decision satisfied neither those members who were most determined to support the referendum, nor those most opposed to it. On 3 June Koch-Weser noted in his diary that it was an "almost insoluble task to hold the two halves of the *Fraktion* and party together." [171] The special "Citizens' Committee" that had already backed the initiative [172] renewed its efforts to influence the voters.[173]

> The German people has given itself the right to decide for itself major questions of law and politics by the constitutional form of a direct popular vote. Our voting on June 20th should be *free* . . . , uninfluenced by authorities whoever they may be. . . . We will vote "yes" on June 20th.[174]

A lengthy list of signatures from throughout most of Germany was appended to a subsequent appeal.[175] The day before the voting took place, Anton Erkelenz, spokesman for the working-class and white-collar supporters of the party, publicly

[170] The *Vorstand* emphasized that this policy applied to all local and regional organizations as well. Idem. A letter from the party's national office, 26 May 1926, explained, "If electoral district or local groups start to issue orders directly *favoring* the referendum there will be no way to stop other party organizations from issuing orders *against* the referendum. And then a very mixed picture would develop that would cause the party harm in every direction." This letter's contents were marked "not for publication." DDP Papers, reel 38, folder 759, emphasis in original.

[171] Quoted by Haungs, p. 57.

[172] See above, Chapter V, p. 175.

[173] The organizers of the Committee were listed as Otto Nuschke, Julius Gressler, Erich Herrmann, all three members of the Prussian *Landtag*, Dr. Grossmann, a judge at the *Kammergericht* in Berlin, and three individuals I have not been able to identify, Koenke, Gwack and Grete Ilm. *Frankfurter Zeitung*, 9 June 1926 (Nr. 421). Dr. Grossmann was an active member of the *Republikanischer Richterbund*. Because of this association and his sharp attacks on the courts' handling of the princes' claims he was expelled from the *Preussischer Richterverein*. *Vossische Zeitung*, 7 May (Nr. 109), 4 July (Nr. 159) and 7 July 1926 (Nr. 161).

[174] *Frankfurter Zeitung*, 9 June 1926 (Nr. 421). With deliberate purpose, the authors of this appeal reminded the public that the president had not spoken out "when the inflation and *Aufwertung* legislation confiscated millions from our best and most decent fellow citizens. . . ." Many ruined mortgage holders, small savers, etc. had voted for Hindenburg in the expectation that he would aid them. They were bitterly disappointed when he did nothing. Wheeler-Bennett, pp. 303–4; Otto Pirlet, *Der politische Kampf um die Aufwertungsgesetzgebung nach dem 1. Weltkrieg* (dissertation, University of Cologne, 1959), p. 108; also see the open letter to Hindenburg published in the *Frankfurter Zeitung*, 16 June 1926 (Nr. 441).

[175] Ibid., 16 June (Nr. 440). A special appeal to women voters was also issued. Ibid., 19 June 1926.

declared that he intended to vote "yes." [176] The Reichstag could always give the former rulers some sort of "donation" to keep them from being impoverished if the referendum passed, he said, but if it failed, the Reichstag probably would never act on the proposed regulatory legislation.[177]

As in the Center Party, fear that unfair methods used by the right to discourage potential voters from going to the polls might succeed caused various local groups or individuals to urge all Democrats to vote, even if they intended to vote "no." [178] The influential big-city newspapers usually friendly toward the DDP recognized why the party leaders had had to handle the issue with great caution; however, their own editorial policy clearly favored the referendum.[179]

The confirmed opponents of confiscation were headed by Hjalmar Schacht, one of the original founders of the DDP and, since 1923, the head of the *Reichsbank*. Unable to attend the meeting of the party's Executive Board when it met to decide what directions to give the Democratic voters, he wrote a letter that was read at the meeting.[180] In it he urged the party leaders not to release the voters and recommended, instead, a firm stand against confiscation. Only the rather elderly Georg Gothein—who had connections with the mining industry—shared Schacht's views.[181] On 13 June 1926,

---

[176] Ibid., 19 June 1926 (Nr. 449). Other recommendations that DDP voters cast "yes" votes were reported from some of the local organizations. Ibid., 23 May (Nr. 379), 3 June (Nr. 406) and 9 June 1926 (Nr. 422).

[177] Interestingly enough, *Vorwärts* had also mentioned the possibility of granting the former rulers a pension if any of them were left truly without a penny. 30 May 1926 (Nr. 250).

[178] Statements by the party organizations in Hesse, Württemberg and Bavaria and by Dr. Cohnstaedt, a member of the *Vorstand*, and by the retired general, Berthold von Deimling. *Frankfurter Zeitung*, 6 June (Nr. 414), 7 June (Nr. 415), 19 June (Nr. 448), 18 June (Nr. 445) and 13 June 1926 (Nr. 433). In some cases these statements constituted transparent evasions of official party policy. Any voter reading them surely understood that he should vote "yes" if he went to the polls.

[179] Ibid., 26 May (Nr. 384), 11 June (Nr. 428), and 20 June 1926 (Nr. 452); *Berliner Tageblatt* (Wochen-Ausgabe), 17 June 1926. The *Vossische Zeitung* held closely to the official party policy of taking no stand, but it repeatedly emphasized that it was every citizen's duty to vote and devoted much space to the rebuttal of rightist propaganda. 4 June (Nr. 133), 10 June (Nr. 138), 16 June (Nr. 143), 17 June (Nr. 144) and 18 June 1926 (Nr. 145).

[180] Schacht's letter to Koch-Weser explaining the grounds for his resignation, *Frankfurter Zeitung*, 15 June 1926 (Nr. 437); the *Vorstand* meeting, 20 May 1926. DDP Papers, reel 37, folder 730.

[181] Idem. Ludwig Haas gave different reasons for opposing confiscation, i.e., certain promises he and others had made to the former ruling family in Baden. The DDP Executive Board accepted the resolution that left the choice up to the

Schacht, with some publicity, announced his resignation from the Democratic party. From his youth, he declared, he had believed in private property as the most valuable of social institutions. If he "remained passive" while the party carried out a course of action he had tried to prevent, he feared he would lose "the moral basis for my future action. . . ."[182] The well-known writer on political subjects, Paul Rohrbach, also left the party, although in his case anger over the conduct of the pacifists like Ludwig Quidde played a part in addition to disapproval of the party's stand regarding the referendum.[183] Worried party leaders ordered local organizations to report on the number of resignations they had received and the reasons for them.[184]

To offer some counterweight against the "Citizens' Committee" favoring the referendum, a number of the DDP's prominent adherents, including Friedrich Meinecke, Hans Delbrück, and Count Montgelas, published an appeal defending private property. Interestingly enough, instead of suggesting a "no" vote, they urged that voters abstain.[185] Thus, in a badly divided condition, the Democratic Party waited out the results of the first great national referendum as best it could.[186]

During this period the *Reichsbanner* likewise found itself in an awkward position. Since the start of the controversy its units had taken a prominent part in many demonstrations

individual voter by a vote of 18 to 2. Later Gothein wrote an article attacking this decision which appeared in the *Hamburger Fremdenblatt*, quoted at length by the *Kölnische Zeitung*, 15 June 1926 (Nr. 436).

[182] *Frankfurter Zeitung*, 15 June 1926 (Nr. 437). In his memoirs Schacht commented that he resigned because "the Party attacked the fundamental law of property ownership." *My First Seventy-Six Years* (London, 1955), p. 154.

[183] *Vossische Zeitung*, 24 June 1926 (Nr. 150); *Frankfurter Zeitung*, 24 June 1926 (Nr. 462); *Der Deutsche Gedanke*, 3 (Nr. 10, 26 May 1926): 578, and (Nr. 12, 25 June 1926): 710–19.

[184] A letter from the national office, 26 June 1926. DDP Papers, reel 38, folder 759.

[185] *Frankfurter Zeitung*, 20 June 1926 (Nr. 451). The appeal was signed by Delbrück, Gothein, Junck, Meinecke, Graf Montgelas, Rohrbach, and Schliepmann. The *Vossische Zeitung*, 18 June 1926 (Nr. 145), reported that Otto Fischbeck, Graf Bernstorff, Oskar Meyer, Julius Kopsch, and Gottfried Schurig signed a similar declaration for the *Liberale Vereinigung*. See, too, the *Liberale Vereinigung* poster opposing confiscation in the Müller und Graef Collection at the Hoover Library.

[186] Consider the worried tone in the private letters of Helene Lange to Emmy Beckmann in Helene Lange, *Was ich hier geliebt. Briefe* (Tübingen, 1957), p. 276 (a letter dated 9 June 1926), and Eduard Hamm to Otto Gessler in Otto Gessler, *Reichswehrpolitik in der Weimarer Zeit* (Stuttgart, 1958), p. 501 (20 June 1926).

against the princes' claims.[187] Its own membership seemed invigorated by the chance to defend the Republic against monarchism.[188] Yet as time went on, difficulties developed. Despite strict orders to the contrary, some local units showed a readiness to join in Communist-led demonstrations.[189] But more serious than these scattered violations of organizational discipline was the growing dissatisfaction of many Center Party leaders over the *Reichsbanner*'s subordination, as they saw it, to the service of the Social Democratic Party.[190] With a human unwillingness to examine their own mistakes, the Center's leaders blamed much of the indiscipline in their own ranks on the influence of the *Reichsbanner*.[191] Officials of that organization were well aware of the need for great tact in the handling of political questions and, at least ostensibly, they tried to define a sphere of activity for the *Reichsbanner* without running afoul of "party matters." [192] In mid-May, Otto Hörsing, the organization's founder, advised an assembly of *Reichsbanner* delegates from throughout the country that the organization was not free to propagandize openly for the referendum, because unanimity among the three republican parties did not exist.[193] A new organizational statute was issued at the end of this meeting.[194] A non-controversial statement of purpose emphasizing the defense of the Re-

[187] *Frankfurter Zeitung*, 15 Dec. 1925 (Nr. 931), 17 Jan. (Nr. 44), 28 Jan. 1926 (Nr. 73); *Das Reichsbanner*, 15 Jan. (Nr. 2), supplement for Brunswick, and 1 Feb. 1926 (Nr. 3), supplements for the districts Dortmund, Düsseldorf and Cologne, for eastern Westphalia and Lippe, and for Magdeburg; Rohe, p. 296, note 1.

[188] Attendance at the convention at Hamburg was much higher than anticipated. Ibid., 1 March 1926 (Nr. 5). The Flag Decree reinforced these feelings. *Frankfurter Zeitung*, 6 May 1926 (Nr. 334).

[189] Ibid., 28 Jan. 1926 (Nr. 74); Fritsch, *Wissenschaftliche Zeitschrift der Universität Jena*, 19: 378–81; Knoch, *Wissenschaftliche Zeitschrift der Technischen Hochschule Magdeburg*, 10: 419–20, 424; Karl, p. 47; Kuczynski, p. 90; also see the appeal that the *Rote Frontkämpferbund* directed to the members of the *Reichsbanner*, illustrated in Kuczynski, between pp. 112–13.

[190] Rohe, pp. 279–303; Roger Philip Chickering, "The Reichsbanner and the Weimar Republic, 1924–1926," *Journal of Modern History*, 40 (Nr. 4, Dec. 1968): 528–30. Chickering stops his survey of the development of the *Reichsbanner* just prior to the initiative and referendum of 1926 even though a discussion of the organization's activities in the campaign would have been relevant to the problem he emphasizes throughout, namely the difficulties of cooperation of the predominantly Social Democratic membership with Center and Democratic Party colleagues.

[191] Rohe, pp. 289, 296.

[192] *Das Reichsbanner*, 15 Jan. (Nr. 2), supplement for the district Hamburg, Bremen and northern Hanover; 1 Feb. 1926 (Nr. 3), supplement for the districts Baden and the Palatinate. Rohe, pp. 329–30.

[193] Rohe, p. 86, note 2.

[194] Reprinted in *Ursachen und Folgen*, 7: 427–29.

public concluded with the clear admonition that "the discussion of party politics and religious questions . . . [was] prohibited."[195] This was surely a gesture of appeasement to those who disapproved of the partisan involvement of individual *Reichsbanner* troops, especially the Center Party's leaders.

On the second of June, the *Reichsbanner* issued a formal statement regarding the referendum:

> There is within the *Reichsbanner* only one opinion: the demands of the former German princes are *unjustified* and must be *rejected*. . . . Differences of opinion exist over the way to go about this. Expecially in the Center Party there are doubts concerning the proposal favored by the Social Democrats. . . . However, it is the . . . right and duty of the *Reichsbanner* . . . *to counter monarchist propaganda* and to clarify the [true nature of] the princes' demands. Then every German citizen can decide according to his own conscience whether to vote "yes" or "no" on June 20th.[196]

The bulk of its members almost certainly would have preferred a stronger stand; the requirements of interparty cooperation among the chief supporters of the Republic seemed to demand a rather weak evasion.

According to the propagandists for the right, the "Reds" were making plans to use the referendum as the first step toward a general assault on all forms of property.[197] A closer examination of the actual relations between the KPD and SPD might have dispelled these anxieties. The leaders of the working class parties recognized that the referendum was primarily a demonstrative gesture, reflecting political convictions and resentments. Even though there was little chance that the proposal would pass, each party wanted to display the energy and discipline of its organization to its best advantage and, thus, take the lion's share of credit for mobi-

---

[195] Ibid., p. 428. The original *Bundessatzungen* did not contain any such prohibition and even the stated purpose of the organization was quite brief. *Das Reichsbanner*, 15 April 1924 (Nr. 1). Rohe, p. 74, points out that the organizational statute grew more and more elaborate each time it was revised.

[196] *Frankfurter Zeitung*, 3 June 1926 (Nr. 405), emphasis in original.

[197] A report on rumors the rightists were spreading in rural areas said that the "Reds" would start with the princes but finally rob everyone "who has a cow, a bed, or a chair to call his own." *Frankfurter Zeitung*, 16 June 1926 (Nr. 439). Hindenburg had been told that the Communists were marking the houses of monarchists in preparation for violent demonstrations toward the end of May on Red Front Fighter Day. Braun, p. 200. Actually the demonstrations that day, although large, were quite orderly. *Frankfurter Zeitung*, 27 May 1926 (Nr. 385).

lization of voters during the campaign, whatever the outcome might be.[198]

The Communists used a variety of pretexts to try to widen the field of joint action, on the whole, with little success.[199] The Social Democratic leaders perceived that the Communists' true intent was to gain effective contact with regular Social Democratic and trade union members, and then do everything possible to undermine the authority of the SPD and ADGB leadership. These leaders, in self-defense, prohibited their followers from making any ties with the KPD that went beyond the strictly limited terms of the January, 1926, agreement.[200] It is clear that the two parties' temporary commitment to further the confiscation measure did nothing to erase their customary rivalry.

The activities of the Social Democratic Party on behalf of the referendum were well-prepared and elaborate.[201] Speakers, demonstrations, posters and leaflets, special newspaper articles, door-to-door canvassing were provided on a large scale.[202] But in all this there was little that was remarkable; the SPD's efforts were organized very much as in an ordinary election campaign.[203] If one reads the directives regularly published in *Rote Fahne*, on the other hand, it is clear that

[198] *Rote Fahne*, 1 April and 22 June 1926; *Jahrbuch der Deutschen Sozialdemokratie . . . 1926*, pp. 7–8; *Vorwärts*, 17 Feb. 1926 (Nr. 79); Rosenfeld, Reichstag. *Verhandlungen*, 390 (28 April 1926): 6897.

[199] An official report admitted as much. "And if it was not possible to extend these contacts [in United Front groups] and broaden the activity unleashed as a result of the propaganda [against the princes] into an active struggle for wider-reaching demands of the party, that is no reason to condemn these contacts. . . . It must be a stimulus for us to strengthen these contacts and fill the weapon [thus] created with a revolutionary fighting spirit." *Bericht der Bezirksleitung der KPD Berlin-Brandenburg-Lausitz*, p. 14.

[200] See above, Chapter IV, pp. 137–38; Knoch, *Wissenschaftliche Zeitschrift der Technischen Hochschule Magdeburg*, 10: 422; Fritsch, *Wissenschaftliche Zeitschrift der Universität Jena*, 19: 389.

[201] Although the party carried the main weight of the active campaigning, the trade unions also expressed their formal support of the referendum. *Vorwärts*, 4 June (Nr. 259) and 17 June 1926 (Nr. 280).

[202] See the report by Franz Künstler, the leader of the party organization in Berlin, ibid., 24 June 1926 (Nr. 293). He claimed that the Communists had been forced to concentrate on street demonstrations because they lacked the manpower to carry out widespread house-to-house campaigning the way the SPD did. Habedank, on the other hand, asserts that the SPD organization did very little, but bases his argument on the SPD's refusal to join forces with the KPD to get out the vote (p. 42).

[203] Perhaps the only concession to the special character of the referendum situation was a certain easing up of direct attacks on the KPD in the pages of *Vorwärts* during the period of the signing of the initiative petitions and the last weeks before the referendum itself. The *Rote Fahne* by and large did not return this courtesy.

the freshly installed leadership of the Communist Party did not think of the campaign in terms of electoral success.[204] For them it was an important trial run, a training mission for the party, in properly executed United Front tactics.

The United Front policy was, in part, designed to lessen old tensions between rank-and-file Social Democrats and their Communist fellow workers. Bitterness existed in many localities and the leaders of the KPD knew that it, as well as the resistance of the SPD and ADGB officials, had to be overcome if joint action were to be anything more than a slogan.[205] Throughout the referendum campaign, much of the Communist propaganda was directed at the non-Communist workers, trying to convince them of the sincerity of the KPD and persuade them to act on their own, to force their leaders to adopt more militant stands, and above all, to join in locally organized United Front Committees.[206] With great pride *Rote Fahne* enumerated the formation of such groups, but this did not disguise the fact that most such United Front Committees were formed in small, relatively insignificant places.[207] No lasting breakthrough to the masses of organized voters outside the ranks of the KPD occurred, the intense efforts of the Communists notwithstanding.[208]

---

[204] An article in *Rote Fahne*, 15 June 1926, stressed the importance of forming United Front committees in the factories. It then observed "that the referendum is not being carried on just as a single campaign for votes, but in fact [it is] a political conflict between the reactionaries and the working class." See, too, the directives from *Agitprop*, ibid., 19 March and 20 May 1926.

[205] Philipp Dengel's report in *Bericht über die Verhandlungen des XI. Parteitags der Kommunistischen Partei Deutschlands* (Berlin, 1927), pp. 35–36. The SPD rejected a KPD proposal that squads of men from both parties do campaign work together on the grounds that the men would probably get into fights with each other. *Rote Fahne*, 27 May 1926.

[206] See, in particular, the special appeals of 12 and 19 June 1926.

[207] Brief listings appeared in *Rote Fahne* from January on, usually accompanied by urgings for still further action. When Social Democratic and trade union members in Essen and Königsberg forced their local organizations to participate together with the KPD in protest demonstrations against the government at the time of the Hindenburg letter, *Rote Fahne* called upon the Berlin workers to follow this "inspiring example." 11 June 1926. *Geschichte der deutschen Arbeiterbewegung*, 4: 112.

[208] Communists were inclined to magnify the significance of their threat to the SPD, e.g., Wilhelm Florin, Reichstag. *Verhandlungen*, 390 (30 June 1926): 7727–28, and D. Manuilski, "Zur Tagung der Erweiterten Exekutive," *Die Kommunistische Internationale*, 7 (Nr. 2, Feb. 1926 "issued in March"): 117. There is no doubt that these efforts worried the SPD leaders, but it appears, even from some contemporary Communist reports, that they were generally able to block unwanted developments. *Rote Fahne*, 6 June and 13 July 1926; *Bericht der Bezirksleitung der KPD Berlin-Brandenburg-Lausitz*, p. 26. However, the *Jahrbuch der Deutschen Sozialdemokratie . . . 1926*, p. 7, was somewhat smug in its claim that "despite all their efforts the Communists

Building new ties with non-Communist workers and other sympathetic individuals was only part of the KPD's work "from below." Its own party members must be instructed in proper methods and objectives. Work for the referendum campaign was expected from every member, but not just any kind of work was good enough.[209] The heads of *Agitprop* and *Orgbüro* gave careful guidance and criticized the performance of assigned tasks as the campaign progressed.[210] Party members were not to satisfy themselves merely by talking against the princes' claims or distributing propaganda in their own residential areas. The center of each member's activities, it was stressed, must be in the factories.[211] That was where the party wanted to shift its most intensive work for reasons that had nothing to do with the possible confiscation of the former rulers' properties.[212] For much the same reason, party members were reminded that in any discussion of the issue they should tie it to other more important Communist demands and never handle it as a goal important for its own sake.[213]

The application of the United Front policy "from above" rested on the conclusion and subsequent implementation of a formal ageement between the KPD's leaders on the one hand and the heads of the SPD and ADGB on the other. Both sides observed the fixed terms of agreement, but beyond that went their separate ways. The temporary collaboration with the SPD on the referendum campaign by no means restrained the KPD from "unmasking" its reformist rivals as enemies of the working class. Almost every Communist speech or article contained some reference to the "hypocrisy" or "treason" of the Social Democratic Party's leaders:

> The alliance of the SPD with the monarchist Marx government is a deliberate blow against the proletarian United Front and causes severe dangers for the proletariat. . . . Since the SPD's leaders continue to support the class enemy, the workers must

---

did not succeed in forming the United Front committees that they intended to use as destructive cells against the Social Democratic Party in any locality, yes, scarcely in any factory worth mentioning throughout the nation."

[209] *Rote Fahne*, 20 May, 10 and 19 June 1926.

[210] Detailed instructions: ibid., 20 May, 1, 4, and 6 June 1926; systematic criticism of recent work done: 19 March and 13 July 1926.

[211] Ibid., 19 March, 1 April, 6 June, and especially 15 June 1926.

[212] See above, Chapter III, p. 78.

[213] *Rote Fahne*, 19 March, 20 May, and Thälmann's front page article, 20 June 1926.

with redoubled zeal join in the "Red front" from the bottom up, so that [these] hostile blows can be parried.[214]

Not satisfied with waiting for the Social Democratic leaders to compromise themselves, Communist policy-makers sought out occasions to submit new bids for cooperation to the SPD and ADGB leaders, fully expecting the refusals that came almost automatically in reply. Then, denunciations written in phrases of still greater indignation seemed warranted, e.g., "The Social Democratic leadership stands on the other side of the barricades." [215]

The efforts of the KPD's leaders to enlarge the scope of the working-class alliance had the character of a carefully performed exercise. They declared that the success of the referendum demanded more intensive cooperation than the original January agreement allowed for; they wanted to see the formation of teams to get out the vote composed of members from both parties, and in the last stage of the campaign renewed their pleas for huge joint street demonstrations.[216] The SPD refused to consider these suggestions.[217]

Rather more interesting were the attempts made by the KPD to transfer the public involvement that was so strongly aroused over the properties question to other issues of the day where the leadership of the Communist Party could be even more obviously displayed.[218] A week after the conclusion of the initiative proceedings, the Communists organized demonstrations on a self-proclaimed "Day for the Unemployed." [219] At about the same time (March 1926), they began suggesting that all the working-class organizations in Berlin hold a joint demonstration on the first of May—"as at the time of the Rathenau murder or during May 1923." The Social Democrats evaded the invitation by declaring that it

[214] Ibid., 20 May 1926. The previous day the SPD had allowed the new Marx government to take office. For a sample of similar attacks, ibid., 18 March, 26 March, 5, 7, and 18 June 1926.

[215] Ibid., 12 June 1926. The main article, 1 May 1926, asked the Social Democratic workers whether they wanted to side "with the Weimar Coalition or with the Communist Party?"

[216] Ibid., 27 May, 5, 10 June 1926.

[217] The parties held separate demonstrations. The KPD on Sunday, 13 June and the SPD on Monday, 14 June. Ibid., 15 June 1926; *Vorwärts*, 13 June (Nr. 274), 14 June (Nr. 274a), and 15 June 1926 (Nr. 276).

[218] *Rote Fahne*, 12 June 1926, said that United Front activities were to be carried out "under the Red Flag and for the solutions [offered by] the KDP!"

[219] Ibid., 21 and 24 March 1926; *Frankfurter Zeitung*, 24 March 1926 (Nr. 223).

was the responsibility of the trade unions to decide whether or not to announce a joint work stoppage. The ADGB devoted two meetings to the discussion of this matter, but in the end replied, as the SPD had surely foreseen, that "experiences in the past" forced them to reject the KPD's bid.[220] *Rote Fahne* badgered the unions and the SPD for the next month, attacking the reformist attitudes dominant in their midst and encouraging the rank-and-file membership to compel their leaders to reverse this decision.[221]

For a brief moment during the British General Strike (3–12 May 1926), the leaders of the KPD dropped their cautious probing of the SPD's and ADGB's hold on their followers and, in accord with advice from the Comintern, told the workers of Germany to prepare for "struggles outside the confines of parliament."[222] Since the controversy over the Flag Decree was then at its height, the KPD may well have hoped that masses of unattached workers and Social Democrats would rally in support of a decisive course of action. On 6 May 1926, Thälmann published a letter to the ADGB calling for a sympathy strike and a series of other measures in behalf of the English miners. Another article in the same issue of *Rote Fahne* informed the whole working class that "the officials of the ADGB will only accept the proposals of the KPD if they are *forced* to do so by the workers."[223] The ADGB prudently rejected the KPD's demands. The Miners' Union had already warned its members:

> Wait . . . for the results of the discussions [going on among] the appropriate organizations—reject [all] interference by outsiders (*Unberufener*) concerning this question, and do not let yourselves be swept into irresponsible acts by anyone.[224]

[220] *Rote Fahne,* 18 and 28 March 1926.

[221] *Rote Fahne* objected not only to the unions' refusal to agree to joint demonstrations but also to their official statement which spoke of the need "to maintain a democratic republic in our fatherland." 10 April 1926. Further on this theme, 12, 13, 17, 28, and 29 April and 1 May 1926.

[222] A. J. P. Taylor, *English History, 1914–1945* (New York and Oxford, 1965), pp. 239–49. *Rote Fahne,* 13 May 1926 and the earlier assessments of the situation by the Comintern, 4 and 7 May 1926.

[223] He called for rapid action to demonstrate international solidarity. Steps were to be taken to prevent *any* coal from being exported—not just to England—and even reparations deliveries should be stopped. Contributions from all ADGB members were to be collected to help the English workers and, at the same time, steps were to be taken to win improved conditions for the German workers. He called for an immediate strike of the mining, railway, transport, and metal-working unions. *Rote Fahne,* 6 May 1926.

[224] Printed with a sharply critical commentary, ibid., 5 May 1926.

In response, the KPD's Central Committee adopted a tone befitting a truly revolutionary party. It reminded its followers of "the lessons of the past, of 1920 and 1923!" and concluded an appeal with the words *"Es lebe der Kampf!"* [225] This defiant stance lasted only a little over a week, for when Luther resigned and simultaneously the General Strike in England began to collapse, and KPD returned to slogans that suited the "Period of Temporary Stabilization of Capitalism." [226]

On the sixth of June, *Agitprop* listed "Ten Commandments" [*sic!*] for every party worker in Berlin:

1. Thou shalt perform *Agitprop* work immediately after your shift ends from June 13th to 20th.
2. Thou shalt persuade your factory crew to form a United Front Committee by [distributing] revolutionary United Front propaganda.
3. Thou shalt not wait for orders from above, but prove your own initiative.
4. Thou shalt defer private affairs until after June 20th.
5. Thou shalt win at least two helpers for electioneering from the circles of sympathizers.
6. Thou shalt win 100 votes for the referendum.
7. Thou shalt sell 100 "Referendum Marks" at 10 pfennig each.
8. Thou shalt sell leaflets, account for [your sales] promptly, and promote the *Rote Fahne.*
9. Thou shalt recruit new members.
10. Thou shalt insure that the party [retains] the leadership of the movement and associate this campaign with the other demands of the party.[227]

As this recitation of "Commandments" makes plain, the party worked hard during the campaign for the realization of certain limited, practical objectives while avoiding the kind of unrealistic revolutionary posturing its own "Ultra-left" recommended.[228] In the last days before the vote on the refer-

[225] Ibid., 8 May 1926.
[226] Reports of both these developments, ibid., 13 May 1926.
[227] Ibid., 6 June 1926.
[228] Cf. the emphasis given to gaining new subscribers for the party's newspapers. Ibid., 19 March, 1 April, and 16 June 1926; *Bericht über die Verhandlungen des XI. Parteitags der Kommunistischen Partei Deutschlands,* p. 36.
    The "Ultra-left" considered the referendum just a "parliamentary-democratic" voting gesture and said the party should have organized the masses for an open confrontation with the bourgeoisie, perhaps in the form of a twenty-four hour protest

endum, the Communists were already giving prominence to a new United Front slogan that called for a "Congress of Laboring People" to be held later in the year.[229]

The KPD's leadership viewed United Front tactics not only as a means to promote greater proletarian unity, but also as a way to multiply internal tensions among the middle classes and to establish contacts with organizations or individuals that had previously maintained a certain distance from the KPD.[230] In this respect the Kuczynski Committee supplemented the activities of the Communist Party in an important way.[231] It supervised the production of numerous pamphlets, leaflets, and posters; it supplied speakers and sponsored some demonstrations of its own; it made a movie, *"Keinen Pfennig den Fürsten"*; and, in general, supplied information to, and coordinated the activities of many different groups favoring confiscation.[232] To do so it recruited the services of many different left intellectuals.[233] We have already mentioned how it encouraged some fringe groups to protest the Center's official policy; [234] it also had ties with some members

---

strike. See the sharp criticism of these views, *Rote Fahne,* 15 and 16 April, 6 and 7 July 1926; Knoch, *Wissenschaftliche Zeitschrift der Technischen Hochschule Magdeburg,* 10: 421.

[229] *Rote Fahne,* 12 and 20 June 1926. The "Congress of Laboring People" was finally held early in December. It was not a great success. Ibid., 1–7 Dec. 1926; Flechtheim, pp. 138–39; *Geschichte der deutschen Arbeiterbewegung,* 4: 126–27.

[230] See Thälmann's remarks, *Rote Fahne,* 27 Feb. and 20 June 1926.

[231] See the instructions, ibid., 1 May 1926, ordering all party members to collect funds for the Kuczynski Committee and to do so in places the party ordinarily found unreceptive; Kuczynski, p. 91.

[232] Ibid., pp. 98–100 and passim; *Vossische Zeitung,* 20 June 1926 (Nr. 147); *Vorwärts,* 12 June (Nr. 272) and 13 June 1926 (Nr. 274).

[233] Sometimes only after a certain initial resistance. At first Hellmut von Gerlach, despite his sharp opposition to the princes' claims, refused to cooperate with the Kuczynski Committee because of its Communist ties. However, the argument that the former rulers were likely to use the monies they would receive to subsidize militarist and counter-revolutionary activities finally induced him to support full confiscation. Ruth Greuner, *Wandlungen eines Aufrechten. Lebensbild Hellmut von Gerlachs* (Berlin, 1965), pp. 173–74. Ludwig Quidde also had questioned the confiscation of private property. Habedank, pp. 29–31, 33, 36.

A number of prominent artists and intellectuals signed a statement favoring participation in the initiative, distributed by the Kuczynski Committee 5 March 1926. Among them were Johannes R. Becher, Albert Einstein, Manfred Georg, George Grosz, Wilhelm Herzog, Kurt Hiller, Siegfried Jacobsohn, Alfred Kerr, Kurt Kersten, Kurt Kläber, Käthe Kollwitz, Paul Loebe [!], Siegfried Marck, Leonard Nelson, Paul Oestreich, Max Pechstein, Lothar Persius, Erwin Piscator, Bruno Schönlank, Helene Stoecker, Kurt Tucholsky, and Heinrich Zille. Karl, pp. 84–85.

[234] See above, p. 249.

of other parties.[235] In general, the functions of the Kuczynski Committee paralleled those of the "Working Committee" for the parties on the right, except that it did not fear the open glare of publicity.

In the course of the discussion thus far there has been occasion to quote a variety of different statements concerning the handling of the princes' claims to large property settlements and, especially, the radical proposal to confiscate the entirety of their possessions. It would be repetitious to summarize here the arguments that the different parties and groups used to justify the positions they adopted.[236] However, before turning to an examination of the results of the referendum of 20 June 1926, it may be worthwhile to describe the sharp divisions of public opinion that were reflected in the statements for or against the referendum.

As the controversy attracted more and more attention, the complicated legal and technical aspects of the problem largely disappeared from sight. Conflicting general principles, often reduced to emotionally charged symbols, came to the forefront.[237] This was to some extent the result of propagandistic simplification. Yet the propaganda itself expressed numerous deep feelings of resentment, some of more or less recent origin, others much older; it did not create them out of whole cloth.

Those who suffered most from the effects of the inflation ranked prominently among the irate and disaffected. Ranging from members of old prosperous and respectable classes to simple laborers who had somehow saved a small nest egg, they were in no way a homogenous group, yet they all knew

---

[235] The *Jungdemokraten* in Berlin and some other localities openly declared their support of confiscation and attacked the weakness of the DDP's official policy. *Frankfurter Zeitung*, 3 June 1926 (Nr. 406); *Rote Fahne*, 11 June 1926. A channel of communication between the Committee and at least portions of the Democratic Party presumably existed through Ludwig Quidde and other members of the *Liga für Menschenrechte*. The circle of writers associated with *Die Weltbühne* actively supported the Kuczynski Committee's activities. Deak, pp. 159–61. I have not found clear evidence that establishes a tie between the left-Socialists Kurt Rosenfeld and Heinrich Stroebel and the Kuczynski group. It seems a safe assumption that the critics of the official Social Democratic leadership maintained at least informal contacts with members of the Committee. Deak, pp. 266, 271–72; Reichstag. *Verhandlungen*, 385: 2029 and 2039.

[236] Günther gives a good summary of the various parties' views, pp. 84–100.

[237] "As the campaign between 'monarchists' and 'anti-monarchists' unfolded, every scandal, every symbol, every event, during the years of the civil war was revived— the Fehme affairs, the flag question." Ruth Fischer, p. 523. Likewise, Georg Decker, "Lehren des Volksentscheids," *Die Gesellschaft* (1926, Nr. 2), pp. 199–200, but with a different explanation of what the referendum symbolized.

the bitterness of an irretrievable, largely incomprehensible loss. Moreover, they felt betrayed by the politicians on the right.

> Millions of combat veterans and their dependents have [had their property] *confiscated* by the *Aufwertung* laws, very largely without any compensation. . . . The same parties [that passed the *Aufwertung* legislation] now have lined up with a gigantic expenditure of moral outrage and unconstitutional terror [to protect] the property of the princes. You have . . . refused to apply the same Christian and ethical principles to the property of the people as to that of the princes.[238]

The gross inequity of such a situation seemed to justify drastic measures. One group called for "an eye for an eye, a tooth for a tooth."[239] Many had not forgotten their traditional loyalties, but neither had they forgotten the patriotic appeals that had persuaded them to buy what were now worthless war bonds.[240] For some, the princes seemed to have joined the ranks of the unscrupulous profiteers who secured great wealth despite the ruin of millions of other people.[241]

In many respects it is difficult to distinguish those whose lives had been ruined by the war from those who suffered

[238] From the open letter from the *Sparer-Bund, Hypothekengläubiger-und Sparerschutzverband für das Deutsche Reich* to Count Westarp, *Frankfurter Zeitung*, 17 June 1926 (Nr. 444). This was in reply to a formal statement by Westarp a few days earlier in which he had denied that there was any connection between the *Aufwertung* question and the referendum campaign. *Korrespondenz der Deutschnationalen Volkspartei*, Nr. 59 (12 June 1926), quoted by Dörr, pp. 534–35; further details in Schüren, pp. 189–97.

[239] Dörr, p. 237.

[240] See the statement by the *Hypothekengläubiger-und Sparer-Schutzverbands, Ortsgruppe Rastenburg*, *Frankfurter Zeitung*, 1 March 1926 (Nr. 160). The *Landesverband Westfalen des Sparerbundes* declared that if the national government did not permit it to begin initiative proceedings on a more favorable *Aufwertung* law, it would urge its members to vote for the confiscation of the princes' properties. Bundesarchiv. "Auseinandersetzung," Bd. 2, RK4732. Also see the KPD propaganda leaflet reproducing a picture of Hindenburg from a war bond appeal and asking if his promises had been kept. Bundesarchiv. Flugschriften, ZS81–65/13. *Rote Fahne*, 11 June 1926.

[241] "Possessors of savings . . . have been ruthlessly abandoned; their possessions must go to pay for the costs of the war. Owners of land and [other] real assets, however, have retained their property. The princes, [like the other great landowners], are joining the ranks of dishonest debtors . . ." from the letter to Westarp, quoted above, note 238. "Now the big capitalists who control the economy are fighting our claims with the money they have stolen from us. Our vote for the referendum is a necessary act of *self-defense*." From a speech by Professor Köhler to a meeting of the *Reichsarbeitsgemeinschaft der Aufwertungsgeschädigten und Mieterorganisation*, *Frankfurter Zeitung*, 16 June 1926 (Nr. 441), emphasis in original. On the tensions and resentments of the traditional middle classes see Bracher, *Die Auflösung*, pp. 158–65 and Heinrich August Winkler, *Mittelstand, Demokratie und Nationalsozialismus* (Cologne, 1972).

from inflation. After 1923, most German economic experts regarded a cautious budgetary policy as essential in order to maintain the stability of the currency, and at the same time deprive the Allies of a possible excuse for demanding higher reparations payments.[242] The social result was misery for many disabled veterans, widows, and others trying to live on entirely inadequate pensions. Here, too, the sums of money many former rulers and their dependents were receiving seemed unjustifiable.[243] One of the most frequent demands was that the princes should share the general impoverishment of the people.[244]

One could list many other segments of the German population that were victims of circumstances or felt unfairly treated by existing laws and, thus, became adherents of the referendum campaign.[245] But the anger of the unemployed, the trade unionists, the lower ranks of the civil service, or whatever the group might be, cannot be fully explained by their own particular grievances. Old class hostilities still remained alive. The propaganda of the left encouraged their expression.[246] One did not need the eyes of George Grosz

[242] Köhler, pp. 27*–38*, 241–64; Luther, *Politiker ohne Partei*, pp. 214–25, 251–74 and passim; and Finance Minister Reinhold's speech on the budget, *Schulthess 1926*, pp. 37–41.

In this connection it is worth noting that the German embassy in Washington forwarded unfavorable editorials in the *Baltimore Sun* and *Washington Post* to the foreign office in Berlin. On 6 Nov. 1925, the *Post* wrote, "If Prussia has agreed to deliver this to the kaiser, the rest of Germany ought to interfere. Germany should take all the Hohenzollern property and use it for payments under the Dawes Plan. . . ." German Foreign Office Records, reel 2281, frame E137213.

[243] Consider the following letter received by the KPD Reichstag delegation from the widow of a scholar. "I am a war widow with a pension of 50 marks since I have been declared unemployable. The local authorities give me an additional 29 marks a month! Worst of all, if I still had some income of my own, my pension would be cut. How can anyone exist on such means in these dear times. If the state has taken our husbands, then the state has the duty first of all to compensate us. Did any princes fall in the war? Do they suffer the same need as we?" *Rote Fahne*, 23 Dec. 1925. Members of invalid veterans' groups frequently participated in rallies against the princes' claims. For instance, *Frankfurter Zeitung*, 17 Jan. (Nr. 44) and 1 Feb. 1926 (Nr. 83); *Rote Fahne*, 19 Jan. 1926.

[244] For instance, Brodauf (DDP), Reichstag. *Verhandlungen*, 388 (3 Dec. 1925): 4757, or the resolution of the Rhineland Center Party, *Germania*, 14 April 1926 (Nr. 171). Also the cartoons in *Vorwärts*, 30 May (Nr. 250), and 12 June 1926 (Nr. 273).

[245] To cite only one of many contemporary observers who did so, Schulte, *Was geschieht mit dem Fürsten-Vermögen?*, pp. 14–15.

[246] For example a poster depicting a crowned princeling and his mistress being supported by the masses, Müller und Graef Collection, Hoover Library. Or the jingle quoted by Ruth Fischer, p. 524, "SPD und KPD ziehen jetzt an einem Strick/ Das bricht den Fürsten das Genick."

or Käthe Kollwitz to recognize the senseless brutality of traditional class distinctions.[247] Even the old champion of wom-
en's rights, Helene Lange, admitted to a friend that she felt
rather uneasy about the success of the initiative campaign,
but then continued, "As much as I am for justice [according
to the law], things are going so miserably for their 'subjects,'
it cannot harm the princes . . . to work. The old ones could
get an old-age pension—we don't always get that." [248]

It was easy to remember William II's belligerent words and
promises, or the unashamed annexationism many of the German princes engaged in during the war. Many people, highly
conscious of their own losses, did not hesitate "to ascribe
the disastrous war and [Germany's] collapse to the false policies of the ruling houses, especially the Hohenzollerns" and
believed that confiscation was "a just punishment." [249] To be
sure, statements such as Dr. Rosenfeld's "the princes . . .
plunged the German people into the war" led to denials and
countercharges by the right,[250] but the left could always out-
trump the monarchists by an allusion to the "deserter" at
Doorn.[251]

> If only [the princes] did not forget the modesty and humility of
> their *worthy* ancestors when making their claims. [They should]
> remember that in the same situation Frederick the Great would
> have ended his life on the battlefields of 1918, not at all as they
> [are doing], in palaces surrounded by court marshals, chamber-

---

[247] Both supported the work of the Kuczynski Committee. Habedank, p. 37. One
of Grosz's cartoons opposing the princes' settlements is reproduced in F. A. Krummacher and Albert Wucher, eds., *Die Weimarer Republik. Ihre Geschichte in Texten, Bildern
und Dokumenten* (Munich, 1965), p. 222. Istvan Deak, *Weimar Germany's Left-Wing
Intellectuals* (Berkeley and Los Angeles, 1968), p. 159. Beth Irwin Lewis, *George Grosz.
Art and Politics in the Weimar Republic* (Madison, 1971).

[248] A letter to Emmy Beckmann, 19 March 1926, in *Was ich hier geliebt*, pp. 270–
71. The SPD Reichstag delegation retrospectively claimed that as Socialists they
supported the idea of confiscation in accord with the principle "He who does not
work, shall not eat." *Jahrbuch der deutschen Sozialdemokratie . . 1926*, pp. 115–16.

[249] Schulte, *Was geschieht mit dem Fürsten-Vermögen?*, p. 15. The recent conclusion
of the Locarno Agreements and Germany's prospective entry into the League of
Nations had helped revive a general discussion of "war-guilt." Heiber, p. 178.

[250] Reichstag. *Verhandlungen*, 390 (28 April 1926): 6899; Saenger, ibid., (29 April
1926), pp. 6937–40; *Frankfurter Zeitung*, 11 March 1926; Arnold Freymuth, *Fürstenenteignung—Volksrecht* (Berlin, 1926), p. 19. Two examples of Nationalist counter-
attacks: Westarp, Reichstag. *Verhandlungen*, 390 (28 April 1926): 6904–6; and v.
Lindeiner-Wildau, ibid., 391 (9 Nov. 1926): 7989–90.

[251] Sollmann's remarks at a *Reichsbanner* meeting, *Frankfurter Zeitung*, 28 Jan. 1926
(Nr. 73); *Rote Fahne*, 19 Jan. 1926. Rightist circles in Germany were privately very
critical of the way the Kaiser had acted. Ilsemann, 2: 10 (diary entry 4 Feb. 1924)
and passim.

lains, and squads of servants, haggling and fighting with their people. . . .[252]

Pamphleteers dug back into history in order to recapitulate the failings or "crimes" of the princes.[253] Otto Wels, for instance, reminded an audience in Frankfurt a.M. that the Hessian princes had grown rich from the sale of mercenaries and then observed, even more pointedly, that "a big share of the princes' properties came from . . . monastic estates that the rulers took from the *Catholic Church* without [giving it] any compensation at the time of the Reformation." [254] In Bavaria supporters of the referendum put up posters saying, "Bavarians! Not a penny for the Prussian princes! Vote 'yes.' " [255] The warning query, "Republic or Monarchy?" served as political cement for nearly all of these complaints.[256] From the start, speakers favoring rigorous treatment of the princes' claims had emphasized that this was a political question, not strictly a legal one.[257] Moreover, many politicians who knew that there were reasons to be worried about the direction German public life seemed to be taking looked upon the referendum campaign as a demonstration of support for the Republic and hoped for the reversal of the recent sucesses that the right had had in domestic politics.

The opponents of confiscation often seemed inclined to blame the mass discontent on propagandistic incitement and showed little real comprehension of the problems and feelings of the supporters of the referendum. Dr. Kahl, for instance, soberly argued that the existing social deprivation stood "in no causal connection" with the existence of the

[252] Wilhelm Kiefer, "Das Problem der Fürstenabfindung," *Frankfurter Zeitung,* 17 March 1926 (Nr. 202), emphasis in original.
[253] Heinrich Grasshoff, *Fünf Jahrhunderte Fürstenraub* (Berlin, 1926) and *Das wahre Gesicht der Hohenzollern* (Berlin, 1926). Both these pamphlets were written for the Kuczynski Committee.
[254] *Frankfurter Zeitung,* 6 March 1926 (Nr. 174), emphasis in original; similar charges, ibid., 4 Dec. 1925 (Nr. 904) and 7 March 1926 (Nr. 176) and the cartoon in *Vorwärts,* 5 March 1926 (Nr. 107), labeling the princes "parasites by the Grace of God."
[255] *Kölnische Zeitung,* 19 June 1926 (Nr. 450); Schulte, *Was geschieht mit dem Fürsten-Vermögen?,* p. 15.
[256] To cite only one example, Scheidemann's speech. Reichstag. *Verhandlungen,* 390 (6 May 1926): 7035.
[257] *Vorwärts,* 1 Dec. 1925 (Nr. 566); *Frankfurter Zeitung,* 4 Dec. 1925 (Nr. 903); Adam Röder, "Die Hohenzollern-Abfindung," *Tremonia,* 2 Jan. 1926; Hermann Dietrich (DDP), Reichstag. *Verhandlungen,* 388 (2 Dec. 1925): 4718; Rosenberg (KPD), ibid., 390 (30 April 1926): 6946–51.

princes' claims.[258] Like many other Center politicians, Karl Anton Schulte believed that idealistic appeals emphasizing self-denial would help party followers make a "proper" decision.

> For the first time the German people shall act as legislator.... A *serious obligation* accompanies this *important right*. *Free of any constraint* the German people ... will make a *just decision, uninfluenced* by the need and misery of the moment; *free* from resentments and anger; borne by a noble feeling of responsibility, by the desire for self-respect and [honor in the eyes] of coming generations; worthy of their great past, their high culture, and their place among the nations of the world.[259]

Both Kahl and Schulte were sincere men, and undoubtedly voiced the opinions held by many respectable middle-class people who were worried about the violation of basic legal principles and the unforeseeable consequences of a successful referendum. All too often, however, the legal and moral arguments made against any restriction of the rights of the princes were rigid, biased, and almost unbelievably cynical.[260] This was particularly true of the monarchists' use of the doctrine that all citizens were equal in the eyes of the law to defend the outmoded property rights of the former ruling houses. The *Deutsche Tageszeitung* wrote of "the rights of cit-

---

[258] Ibid., (3 Dec. 1925), p. 4749. Also see the leaflet warning invalids and other economically dispossessed people that they would not benefit from the confiscation. Bundesarchiv. Deutsche Volkspartei, RK4511/21. Stegerwald wrote that there was "a great deal of confusion of questions relating to the princes' claims and *Aufwertung* that properly have nothing to do with each other," quoted by Decker, *Die Gesellschaft* (1926, Nr. 2), p. 200. The Bavarian People's Party stated, "Through the confiscation of the princes' properties not a single war invalid will receive a penny more, no one who is unemployed [obtain] a better chance to get a job, no one [who lost his] savings will receive a higher *Aufwertung*," quoted by Günther, p. 91.

[259] *Was geschieht mit dem Fürsten-Vermögen?*, p. 2, emphasis in original.

[260] Consider, for instance, the statement issued by the *Kirchensenat der evangelischen Kirche der altpreussischen Union:* "For us this is not a matter of parties or politics— the Evangelical Church stands above the parties and refrains from taking any political position—but, for us it is simply a matter dealing with concerns of the Christian conscience and the Word of God. These concerns appear to us, in this instance as in so many ways in our public life [today], most seriously endangered.... Many people, embittered by their own impoverishment and disappointed in their hopes in the state, have lost their feeling for right and justice. Fidelity and faith will be shattered and the foundations of an orderly system of government will be undermined if entire properties are taken away from individual citizens (*Volksgenossen*) without any compensation. Evangelical Christians! Let us maintain a clear vision, stout courage and a good conscience amidst a great confusion of spirits! Let us hold to the holy commandments of God in [a spirit of] truth and justice!" *Frankfurter Zeitung*, 26 May 1926 (Nr. 383).

izens who had the misfortune also to be princes[!]." [261]
Spokesmen for the right repeatedly assumed the shrill tones
of moral censors: "In frivolous exploitation of the difficulties
of the present time, you [the SPD and KPD] . . . have recourse
to the lower instincts in your fight for confiscation . . . you
employ hate, folly, envy, dissatisfaction, and greed." [262] The
Nationalist publicist, Friedrich Everling, declared that "envy
is the dominant democratic characteristic. He who is inferior
always wants equality." [263]

People who held opinions such as these either could not
comprehend that traditional morality and unquestioning respect for the law had been shaken by conditions that had
little or nothing to do with the abolition of the monarchy in
Germany, or refused to admit this was so.[264] They kept alive
hopes that they would be able to undo the changes made
since 1918.

> Yet, this downright distorted Prussia under the leadership of
> Braun, Severing, and Höpker-Aschoff is still for us *our Prussia,*
> *our Prussia,* in which forces live that are now only slumbering but
> which will one day again awake and in an hour when the present
> time will seem like a bad dream.[265]

[261] Quoted in a survey of press opinions by *Frankfurter Zeitung,* 3 Feb. 1926 (Nr.
90); the statement by Georg Barth for the DNVP in the Legal Committee, ibid., 10
Feb. 1926 (Nr. 107); Dr. Wunderlich (DVP), Reichstag. *Verhandlungen,* 390 (28 April
1926): 6909; the statement presented to Chancellor Luther by the representative
of the *Hofkammervereinigung* emphasized that the former rulers should not be treated
as "second class citizens." Bundesarchiv. "Auseinandersetzung," Bd. 1, zu RK2973.

[262] Westarp, Reichstag. *Verhandlungen,* 390 (28 April 1926): 6906. The opponents
of the referendum in Mecklenburg ran newspaper notices that only "scoundrels,
thieves and people without honor" would go to the ballot boxes. *Frankfurter Zeitung,*
21 June 1926 (Nr. 453). Even Stresemann spoke of the campaign's appeal "to the
very crudest instincts." Since he was speaking after the defeat of the referendum,
however, he went on to praise "the sound sense of the people" for rejecting these
appeals. These comments were made in a speech to the *Verein Deutscher Studenten* 6
July 1926. Stresemann *Nachlass,* reel 3146, frame H161951.

[263] *Recht oder Raub in der Republik?* (Berlin, 1926), p. 10. A similar statement by
the former kaiser was lampooned in *Vorwärts,* 25 Feb. 1926 (Nr. 93). After the results
of the initiative were known, Duke Bernhard of Saxe-Meiningen lamented in a private
letter, 29 March 1926, to his old friend General von Gossler that the German people
no longer constituted a true nation (*Volk*), "if it is possible that nearly every third
adult has a criminal soul, is a thief at least in thought." Bundesarchiv, H08–34/7.

[264] Valuable on this wide-ranging subject are: Albrecht Mendelssohn-Bartholdy,
The War and German Society (New Haven, 1937); Otto Baumgarten et al., *Geistige und
sittliche Wirkungen des Krieges in Deutschland* (Stuttgart, 1927), pp. 1–88; and Hans
Ostwald, *Sittengeschichte der Inflation* (Berlin, 1931).

[265] Hans-Joachim von Rohr, member of the DNVP and a leader of the Pomeranian
Landbund. Prussia. Landtag. *Sitzungsberichte* 8 (2 June 1926): 12199, emphasis in
original.

Self-righteousness of this kind did not feel the need to observe the standards of decency so persistently demanded
from others.[266] One of the most widely distributed pamphlets
issued by the rightist "Working Committee" pretended to
know that

> the leader of the Committee for the Confiscation of the Princes'
> Properties is the Galician Jew Kuszcinski [sic]. The chief whip is
> *Scheidemann,* who, *already anticipating* [*its results*], has furnished his
> house in Cassel with the Kaiser's furniture. . . . The leader of the
> movement in *Silesia,* an apprentice barber, has been convicted
> once before because he confused "mine" and "thine"—etc.,
> etc. . . .[267]

It is not surprising that an issue which first began to attract
public attention because of a series of court decisions was
constantly discussed in terms of rights and justice. Yet it is
remarkable how many of the same words such as "justice,"
"theft," and "greed" were used by both sides, although with
special connotations or with very different sets of references.

For the defenders of the princes, justice was the determination of legal rights through the interpretation of existing
laws, no matter how these legal arrangements may have come
into being. Moreover they insisted that recognized legal experts in the administrative departments and judiciary should
interpret these rights, irrespective of the fact that class prej-
udice was deeply entrenched in these bodies. In a higher
sense conservatives equated justice with morality, divine law,
and an undying recognition of the past services of the German
rulers.[268] The backers of the referendum, and many who could
not accept the referendum proposal because of its extreme
formulation, refused to recognize justice as the rigid application of legal paragraphs, often very much out of date. They
believed in justice in the sense of equity; it was necessary to

---

[266] On the ability of Nationalists to view anyone who thought differently than they
did as a traitor and excuse any crime, including political murder, if done for reasons
they approved, see Stresemann, *Vermächtnis,* 2: 315–16, 321–22; Severing, 1: 327–
28.

[267] *Volk! Entscheid!,* p. 15. Similarly a leaflet, Bundesarchiv. Deutsche Volkspartei,
R4511/21, and a poster contrasting swilling socialists with a destitute family. Müller
und Graef Collection, Hoover Library. In fairness it must be said that the left was
not always very truthful in its propaganda either.

[268] The DNVP distributed posters bearing the portraits of the Great Elector,
Frederick the Great and the Emperor William I, accompanied by the question, "Is
this the thanks for our efforts?" Georg Bernhard questioned editorially the appro-
priateness of such appeals to gratitude and rather maliciously wondered how these
Hohenzollerns would have judged the behavior of William II. *Vossische Zeitung,* 20
June 1926 (Nr. 147).

determine what was fair considering Germany's changed political and economic conditions.[269] The princes must share the suffering of the German people, they said. When propagandists emphasized the blunders and ruthlessness of past rulers the concept of equity sometimes transmuted itself into retributive justice. Those who favored strict controls or confiscation tried to convince the public that the princes deserved no special consideration, and, above all, that their behavior had seldom been characterized by unswerving devotion to high moral principles.[270]

When conservatives claimed that a radical questioning of the legal titles of the princes' estates would set a precedent for future challenges of other people's rights, the left countered, appropriately enough, that many of the princes' claims rested on antiquated forms of possession that had nothing in common with middle class property rights. If conservatives argued that seizure of the properties of the former rulers was simply theft, the left answered that the methods many princes had used to acquire their wealth in the past, e.g. the dispossession of peasant landholders (Bauernlegen), the seizure of church lands, were essentially the same as theft. The opponents of the referendum denounced the greed of the masses with almost religious zeal, but the other side distributed posters showing a hammer labeled "The Referendum" slamming down on grasping royal hands.[271]

The last days before the referendum saw a flurry of propagandistic activities of all kinds. Given such excited conditions, it is hardly surprising that some groups tried to deceive the voters by last minute tricks.[272] On 20 June 1926, voting on the first German nationwide referendum took place in a generally orderly fashion although in some localities the police had prepared for possible violence.[273]

[269] These thoughts were often reduced to slogans such as "Rights of the people over rights of the princes" or "The welfare of people must prevail over princely selfishness." Frankfurter Zeitung, 1 Feb. (Nr. 83) and 20 Feb. 1926 (Nr. 136).

[270] Hence the great prominence given the scandal regarding the mistresses of the last grand duke of Mecklenburg-Strelitz. Ibid., 14 Jan. 1926 (Nr. 34), or the treatment accorded to the defeated north German princes in 1866. Ibid., 2 Feb. 1926 (Nr. 86).

[271] Müller und Graef Collection, Hoover Library. Similarly, Social Democratic and Communist leaflets at the Bundesarchiv, Z581–30/55, ZS81–65/13.

[272] According to a report in Vorwärts, 19 June 1926 (Nr. 284), the Nationalists printed up handbills that looked like ballots with the "no" circle marked and the heading, "Not a penny for the princes, therefore 'No.' "

[273] Frankfurter Zeitung, 21 June 1926 (Nr. 453); Vossische Zeitung, 22 June 1926 (Nr. 148).

VIII: The Failure of the Referendum and Its Aftermath

Somewhat over fifteen and one-half million people participated in the referendum; almost fourteen and one-half million of them (36.4 percent of the qualified voters) favored confiscation.[1] Taking into consideration the policy of abstention adopted by the middle-class parties of the right, this was by usual election standards an impressive turnout. Over a third more "yes" votes were cast in the referendum than the working class parties had garnered in the last Reichstag election of December 1924.[2] A slightly larger number of voters had sufficed to elect Hindenburg president the preceding year. The radical KPD-SPD referendum proposal attracted the support of more people than later, under very changed circumstances, would vote for the NSDAP in the landslide elections of 1932.[3] Nonetheless, the referendum's backers fell far short of obtaining the 19,892,975 votes

[1] The final detailed results are recorded in: Germany. Statistisches Reichsamt. *Statistik des Deutschen Reichs.* Vol. 332: *Volksbegehren und Volksentscheid "Enteignung der Fürstenvermögen,"* (Berlin, 1926). See Table III.

[2] 135.2 percent; in absolute numbers 14,455,181 compared with 10,688,969. *Wirtschaft und Statistik,* 6: (Nr. 12, July 1926): 403–4.

[3] Hindenburg obtained 14,655,641 votes. The candidates of the KPD and SPD in the first round, Thälmann and Braun, together received under 10 million votes (Thälmann: 1,871,815; Braun: 7,802,497). In July 1932 the National Socialists received 13,745,781 votes (37.3 percent of the votes cast).

273

TABLE III

Results of the Initiative and Referendum

a. number of voters who signed the initiative petitions
b. percent of qualified voters
c. number of qualified voters (*ortsanwesenden Stimmberechtigten*)
d. participation in referendum
e. percent participation
f. invalid votes
g. percent invalid votes
h. "Yes" votes
i. percent "Yes" votes
j. "No" votes
k. percent "No" votes

Election District	a	b	c	d	e	f	g	h	i	j	k
Germany as a whole	12523750	31.8	39737724	15599890	39.3	558995	1.4	14455181	36.4	585714	1.5
1. East Prussia	166078	12.6	1306623	279372	21.4	5042	0.4	264576	20.2	9754	0.7
2. Berlin	864362	58.9	1489145	1018896	68.4	45165	3.0	942654	63.3	31077	2.1
3. Potsdam II	514067	43.5	1208588	636647	52.7	25251	2.1	589712	48.8	21684	1.8
4. Potsdam I	479491	40.8	1203081	614526	51.1	25691	2.1	566822	47.1	22013	1.8
5. Frankfurt/O.	244600	23.5	1037722	323941	31.2	12989	1.3	297532	28.7	13420	1.3
6. Pomerania	204715	17.8	1149356	286862	25.0	5781	0.5	269406	23.4	11675	1.0
7. Breslau	383561	32.0	1201485	421194	35.1	13457	1.1	383226	31.9	24511	2.0
8. Liegnitz	267415	34.8	770684	287903	37.4	11339	1.5	263149	34.1	13415	1.7
9. Oppeln	153038	19.3	794260	210730	26.5	4895	0.6	193855	24.4	11980	1.5
10. Magdeburg	377452	35.4	1065874	493672	46.3	23164	2.2	453811	42.6	16697	1.6
11. Merseburg	307266	34.3	891752	378123	42.4	14319	1.6	351232	39.4	12572	1.4
12. Thuringia	561530	39.8	1421220	638497	44.9	31077	2.2	582502	41.0	24918	1.8
13. Schleswig-Holstein	296073	29.4	1014076	382701	37.7	15976	1.6	353005	34.8	13720	1.4

14. Weser-Ems	201228	22.3	909894	279327	30.7	12486	1.4	255941	28.1	10900	1.2
15. East Hanover	152647	23.4	657353	199731	30.4	9820	1.5	180403	27.4	9508	1.4
16. South Hanover-Brunswick	441067	35.1	1264248	532084	42.1	28156	2.2	479895	38.0	24033	1.9
17. Westphalia North	358081	26.8	1357974	483227	35.6	17557	1.3	448079	33.0	17591	1.3
18. Westphalia South	580807	35.2	1641512	777206	47.3	26224	1.6	727725	44.3	23257	1.4
19. Hesse-Nassau	538098	34.2	1592789	682980	42.9	23232	1.5	635511	39.9	24237	1.5
20. Cologne-Aachen	366540	27.1	1363813	495705	36.3	9077	0.7	465923	34.2	20705	1.5
21. Coblenz-Trier	118723	15.8	757484	145100	19.2	2969	0.4	134988	17.8	7143	0.9
22. Düsseldorf-East	533996	39.0	1400185	620609	44.3	16913	1.2	585496	41.8	18200	1.3
23. Düsseldorf-West	259427	24.6	1066823	379664	35.6	7203	0.7	359833	33.7	12628	1.2
24. Upper Bavaria-Swabia	209071	13.6	1550050	334607	21.6	4118	0.3	319886	20.6	10603	0.7
25. Lower Bavaria	61822	7.9	779440	102963	13.2	1571	0.2	97303	12.5	4089	0.5
26. Franconia	321760	20.6	1570382	441406	28.1	10243	0.7	416666	26.5	14487	0.9
27. The Palatinate	158892	28.2	565876	195407	34.5	3879	0.7	185113	32.7	6415	1.1
28. Dresden-Bautzen	545864	44.4	1250638	607193	48.6	30056	2.4	551569	44.1	25568	2.0
29. Leipzig	418047	48.4	869996	499025	57.4	23960	2.8	452574	52.0	22491	2.6
30. Chemnitz-Zwickau	577155	49.4	1191033	598265	50.2	34443	2.9	541011	45.4	22811	1.9
31. Württemberg	478034	29.3	1654043	591236	35.7	8514	0.5	563544	34.1	19178	1.2
32. Baden	500238	34.7	1441789	584472	40.5	12309	0.9	548417	38.0	23746	1.6
33. Hesse-Darmstadt	325609	37.5	871728	374728	43.0	10156	1.2	348954	40.0	15618	1.8
34. Hamburg	395836	47.4	851890	489695	57.5	22462	2.6	449142	52.7	18091	2.1
35. Mecklenburg	161160	28.1	574918	212196	36.9	9501	1.7	195726	34.0	6969	1.2

needed for passage. There is little doubt that the legal requirement that this referendum must obtain a majority of all qualified voters impeded the legitimate expression of the popular will.[4]

Voter participation in the referendum varied markedly from region to region, following quite closely the pattern of the results of the initiative. Berlin far outpaced the rest of the nation: an impressive 68.4 percent of its voters went to the polls, while 63.3 percent voted "yes."[5] More than half of the eligible voters participated in the Berlin suburbs and in the traditional "Red" districts in Saxony and Hamburg.[6] At the other extreme, only 13.2 percent of the voters in Lower Bavaria ventured to the polls.[7] Yet even there the turnout fully equaled the combined left-wing vote (KPD-SPD-USPD) in December 1924, and constituted a great increase over the initiative results in March.[8] Only two of the large voting districts reported fewer "yes" votes than the parties of the left had obtained in 1924. They were the Junker strongholds of East Prussia and Pomerania, rural aras where intimidation of the voters was very feasible.[9] In some communities the

[4] Georg Decker argued that if the election had been conducted without intimidation of voters there would have been a "strong majority for the confiscation law." "Lehren des Volksentscheid," *Die Gesellschaft* (1926, Part 2), p. 199. Others observed that since only about thirty million voters normally participated in national elections, the fourteen and a half million "yes" votes reflected the opinion of very nearly half of Germany's politically active citizens. *Germania*, 21 June 1926 (Nr. 281). Könnemann, *Wissenschaftliche Zeitschrift der Universität Halle-Wittenberg*, 7: 557.

[5] Over half again as many "yes" votes were given as the combined left obtained in Dec. 1924 (158.9 percent). *Vorwärts* wrote, "If Berlin were the nation, the princes would be packing today. . . ." 21 June 1926 (Nr. 286a).

[6] In Hamburg 57.5 percent, Leipzig 57.4 percent, Potsdam II 52.7 percent, Potsdam I 51.1 percent and Chemnitz-Zwickau 50.2 percent of the eligible voters participated in the referendum. The "yes" vote was respectively: 52.7 percent, 52.0 percent, 48.8 percent, 47.1 percent, and 45.4 percent. These figures are for the *Wahlkreise;* the vote in the cities proper was slightly higher.

[7] 12.5 percent voted "yes."

[8] Even the low total of 97,303 "yes" votes out of 779,440 registered voters represented a 57.9 percent increase over the results of the initiative. In other parts of Bavaria the "yes" vote was somewhat higher: 20.6 percent in Upper Bavaria-Swabia, 26.5 percent in Franconia, and 32.7 percent in the Palatinate. A third of the voters in Munich cast "yes" votes. Ambassador von Haniel reported to the national government that an increase over the initiative results of this order, especially in Munich, had not been expected. Bundesarchiv. "Auseinandersetzung," Bd. 2, RK4965.

[9] 20.2 percent of the eligible voters in East Prussia and 23.4 percent in Pomerania voted "yes." The results equalled only 90.7 percent and 97.6 percent respectively of the combined left vote in December 1924. The *Berliner Tageblatt* compiled a list of 219 villages and landed estates in Pomerania where not a single vote was cast, according to a report in *Vorwärts*, 25 June 1926 (Nr. 295).

votes were counted separately for men and women. In both Protestant and Catholic regions fewer women participated than men and fewer voted "yes."[10]

If one calculated the results to reflect the performance in each federal state instead of by election district, the three Hanseatic cities—Hamburg, Lübeck, and Bremen—and the Protestant territories of central Germany—Saxony, Anhalt, Thuringia, and Hesse—headed the list, all with 40 percent or more "yes" votes.[11] Bavaria and the tiny backwater of Waldeck reported the lowest returns. In Prussia the heavy vote in Berlin and the industrialized areas was diluted by the returns from the countryside. Prussia's total of 36.6 percent "yes" votes was virtually the same as the national average.

The greatest interest in and support for the referendum came from the big cities. Of the forty-seven cities with a population over one hundred thousand, only eight reported results under the national average.[12] And, of them, only the

TABLE IV
Percentage of "Yes" Votes by States

National Average 36.4

Hamburg 52.7	Lippe 35.0
Lübeck 46.9	Württemberg 34.1
Saxony 46.7	Schaumburg-Lippe 33.5
Anhalt 45.7	Mecklenburg-Schwerin 32.2
Bremen 45.1	Mecklenburg-Strelitz 28.1
Thuringia 42.8	Oldenburg 24.4
Hesse 40.0	Bavaria 22.8
Brunswick 38.7	Waldeck 16.6
Baden 38.0	
Prussia 36.6	

Statistik des Deutschen Reichs, 332: 27-28

[10] In Berlin-Spandau 62.6 percent of the men voted "yes" and 56.1 percent of the women; in Cologne the figures were 46.5 percent and 32.9 percent. In the town of Weimar 36.5 percent of the men voted "yes" compared with 25.5 percent of the women. In the rural area of Moosburg in Upper Bavaria the figures were 18.4 percent and 6.5 percent respectively. *Statistik des Deutschen Reichs*, 332: 29–32.

[11] See Table IV.

[12] The eight were: Wiesbaden 35.9 percent "yes" votes, Plauen 34.2 percent, Aachen 34.0 percent, Munich 33.3 percent, Düsseldorf 33.1 percent, München-Gladbach 32.1 percent, Mulheim a. Ruhr 31.9 percent, and Münster 15.3 percent. The returns for Aachen, Munich, Düsseldorf, and München-Gladbach were actually relatively high if one considers that their population was largely Catholic. At first

Catholic episcopal center of Münster turned in an exceptionally low share of "yes" votes (15.3 percent). Although three of the fourteen major election districts with a predominantly urban composition reported slightly lower percentages of "yes" votes than the national average, all three were in Catholic parts of western Germany.[13] On the other hand, returns from all but five of the twenty-one predominantly agricultural election districts were below, often substantially below, the national average.[14] All five exceptions: Potsdam 1, Magdeburg, Hesse-Darmstadt, Hesse-Nassau and Baden were areas of mixed economy in which well-established support for the working class parties existed.[15]

TABLE V
Predominantly Urban Election Districts

(Percentage of eligible voters who cast "Yes" votes)

Over National Average (36.4)		Under National Average	
Berlin	63.3	Cologne-Aachen (C)	34.2
Hamburg	52.7	Düsseldorf-West (C)	33.7
Leipzig	52.0	Westphalia-North (C)	33.0
Potsdam II	48.8		
Chemnitz-Zwickau	45.4		
Westphalia South (C)	44.3		
Dresden-Bautzen	44.1		
Düsseldorf-East (C)	41.8		
Thuringia	41.0		
Merseburg	39.4		
South-Hanover-Brunswick	38.0		

(C) more than half the population Catholic

Bracher, *Die Auflösung*, pp. 647ff. and *Statistik des Deutschen Reichs*, 332: 6-7.

glance the results in Plauen seem unusually low in comparison with other cities in Saxony such as Leipzig with a 54.9 percent "yes" vote, Chemnitz 46.9 percent, and Dresden 45.6 percent. However, the middle-class Protestant parties were strong in Plauen. Hindenburg had obtained nearly two-thirds of the vote in 1925 (38,742 out of 61,124). Thus, the 25,480 "yes" votes cast in the referendum (34.2 percent) constituted a respectable showing (113.6 percent of the left vote in 1924).
[13] They were Cologne-Aachen (34.2 percent), Düsseldorf-West (33.7 percent), and Westphalia-North (33.0 percent). See Table V.
[14] See Table VI.
[15] The SPD's and the KPD's shares of the vote in the Dec. 1924 Reichstag election were:

TABLE VI
Predominantly Rural Election Districts
(Percentage of eligible voters who cast "Yes" votes)

Over National Average (36.4)		Under National Average	
Potsdam I	47.1	Schleswig-Holstein	34.8
Magdeburg	42.6	Liegnitz	34.1
Hesse-Darmstadt	40.0	Württemberg (C)	34.1
Hesse-Nassau	39.9	Mecklenburg	34.0
Baden (C)	38.0	The Palatinate (C)	32.7
		Breslau (C)	31.9
		Frankfurt/O	28.7
		Weser-Ems	28.1
		East Hanover	27.4
		Franconia (C)	26.5
		Oppeln (C)	24.4
		Pomerania	23.4
		Upper Bavaria-Swabia (C)	20.6
		East Prussia	20.2
		Coblenz-Trier (C)	17.8
		Lower Bavaria (C)	12.5

(C) more than half the population Catholic

Bracher, *Die Auflösung*, pp. 647ff. and *Statistik des Deutschen Reichs*, 332: 6-7.

Many Catholics simply ignored the instructions of their clergy and party leaders.[16] In Baden, 38 percent of the voters (548,417) marked their ballots "yes"; in the stronghold of the Center Party in the Rhineland, the Cologne-Aachen district, the figures were 34.2 percent and 465,923. The full significance of such returns becomes clearer if one calculates the "yes" vote in relation to the strength of the workers' parties in these districts. In both Baden and Cologne-Aachen twice as many people voted for confiscation as voted for the KPD, SPD, or USPD in the December 1924 Reichstag elec-

	SPD	KPD
Potsdam I	30.3%	12.1%
Magdeburg	39.2%	5.2%
Hesse-Darmstadt	35.6%	5.4%
Hesse-Nassau	31.7%	5.4%
Baden	19.9%	6.5%

See the tables in *Das Ende der Parteien*, pp. 777–78.

[16] *Germania* did not attempt to deny that this had happened, 21 June 1926 (Nr. 281). Friedrich Grebe undertook a careful analysis of the official results. Ibid., 14 July 1926 (Nr. 321). Schüren, pp. 229–31.

tions. Some of the increase undoubtedly came from left-wing voters who had not voted in 1924, from Democratic Party members, and even from followers of the other Protestant middle-class parties, or previously inactive voters who were stirred to go to the polls by the special nature of the issues involved. Admitting all this, it is clear that thousands of normal Center Party voters defied official party policy to vote "yes." The trend is apparent in nearly all regions of traditional Center Party predominance. For the nation as a whole the "yes" vote equaled 135.2 percent of the combined left vote in the last Reichstag election. Of the fifteen major election districts with levels above this national average, *nine* were Catholic Center areas.[17]

TABLE VII

The "Yes" Vote as a Percentage of the Combined Left Vote (KPD-SPD-USPD) in the December, 1924, Reichstag Election

National Average (135.2%)

Cologne-Aachen (C)	209.0	Leipzig	127.7
Baden (C)	202.9	Dresden-Bautzen	125.5
Oppeln (C)	189.0	Thuringia	125.5
Düsseldorf-West (C)	174.3	Weser-Ems	124.4
Württemberg (C)	167.3	Schleswig-Holstein	122.4
Potsdam II	167.1	Chemnitz-Zwickau	121.0
Coblenz-Trier (C)	163.5	The Palatinate	120.5
Berlin	158.9	Liegnitz	118.1
Düsseldorf-East	158.0	South Hanover-Brunswick	116.7
Hamburg	152.1	Merseburg	116.1
Westphalia-South (C)	150.4	Magdeburg	114.0
Westphalia-North (C)	145.0	Breslau (C)	113.9
Potsdam I	144.9	Upper Bavaria-Swabia (C)	113.8
Hesse-Nassau	143.3	Frankfurt/O	109.0
Hesse-Darmstadt	135.8	East Hanover	109.0
		Franconia (C)	109.0
		Mecklenburg	104.9
		Lower Bavaria (C)	100.4
		Pomerania	97.6
		East Prussia	90.7

(C) more than half the population Catholic

Wirtschaft und Statistik, 6: Nr. 12 (July, 1926), 403-4.

---

[17] See Table VII.

Examination of local returns confirms even more vividly than the composite results that there was substantial Catholic support for the referendum. Consider the following sampling of cities in the Rhineland and Ruhr:

	No. of "Yes" Votes	Percentage of all Eligible Voters	Percentage of Combined KPD-SPD-USPD Vote in December 1924
Aachen	35,974	34.0%	225.4%
Cologne	189,582	39.2%	210.9%
Essen	126,583	39.8%	164.5%
Krefeld	37,538	41.1%	250.5%
München-Gladbach	23,709	32.1%	226.8%
Gelsenkirchen	57,753	46.9%	164.7%

The "yes" vote was considerably lower in rural areas and the smaller towns than in industrialized centers, yet in many cases the low "yes" vote would have been much lower if all normal Center Party supporters had obeyed party instructions:

	No. of "Yes" Votes	Percentage of all Eligible Voters	Percentage of Combined KPD-SPD-USPD Vote in December 1924
Lkr. Bonn	14,652	29.5%	181.2%
Kr. Julich	6,218	20.9%	214.9%
Kr. Cleve	9,593	22.7%	216.3%
Kr. Grevenbroich	7,661	23.9%	171.8%
Kr. Borken	4,136	15.3%	423.8%
Lkr. Münster	5,098	17.8%	284.6%

In some parts of Baden where the KPD's and SPD's supporters scarcely counted, strong backing for the referendum was reported:

A.B. Engen	6,402	48.8%	441.5%
A.B. Messkirch	2,657	30.4%	643.3%
A.B. Pfullendorf	1,539	34.5%	501.3%
A.B. Überlingen	7,924	44.1%	667.6%
A.B. Tauberbischofsheim	6,310	27.3%	566.4%

The preceding samples do not pretend to describe the full pattern of voting in all Center Party districts. The bulk of the Catholic voters obeyed the admonitions of their leaders. We have emphasized evidence of disregard for party discipline because of the great worry (and surprise!) it caused the Center's leadership.

By contrast, the Bavarian People's Party succeeded in exercising much greater control over the behavior of its followers and other would-be voters for the confiscation proposal. In the Markt-Oberdorf area of Swabia only 227 out of 15,785 eligible voters participated in the referendum. This gave it the lowest level (1.4 percent) of participation in the nation (1.3 percent "yes" votes). More than half the districts in Lower Bavaria and Upper Bavaria-Swabia reported that under 15 percent of their voters went to the polls. Party loyalty and the conservative, monarchist sentiments of most rural Bavarians were not the only reasons for such a low turnout. The special position the BVP enjoyed in Bavarian politics allowed it to apply the machinery of state and local government to control the circulation of propaganda or demonstrations favoring the referendum. Through the *Bauerverein* and other economic or patriotic groups it was possible to organize strong social pressures against participation. Such forms of intimidation, however, were most effective in areas where the population was small. The larger cities reported figures considerably higher than most of the countryside.

	"Yes" Vote	Percentage of Eligible Voters	Percentage of Left Vote December 1924
Munich	146,166	33.3%	119.4%
Augsburg	39,120	37.6%	124.6%
Regensburg	10,733	22.2%	112.3%

Opponents of the confiscation measure in rural Protestant areas of Germany were also quite successful in discouraging probable supporters of the referendum from going to the polls. In Pomerania, for instance, where the German Nationalists were by far the strongest party and could rely on the

Landbund as an important organizational supplement, many rural laborers who normally voted Social Democratic or Communist apparently feared to vote:

	"Yes" Vote	Percentage of Eligible Voters	Percentage of Left Vote December 1924
Kr. Anklam	4,804	22.6%	88.4%
Kr. Greifenberg	2,072	8.0%	58.7%
Kr. Kammin	3,188	11.6%	64.5%
Lkr. Köslin	2,164	12.0%	69.8%

Yet, in some towns figures surpassing the last left vote were reported:

	"Yes" Vote	Percentage of Eligible Voters	Percentage of Left Vote December 1924
Stkr. Stettin	81,957	45.3%	142.0%
Stkr. Kolberg	6,922	35.0%	152.1%
Stkr. Köslin	6,523	37.7%	114.3%

Given the character of the province the low returns from the rural districts predominated.

Whatever the success of the Nationalists and the other middle-class parties in maintaining the discipline of their own followers and intimidating other voters in the agricultural districts, many city dwellers chose to follow their own conscience. Consider the following predominantly middle-class districts of Berlin:

	"Yes" Vote	Percentage of Eligible Voters	Percentage of Left Vote
Berlin Mitte	127,561	56.7%	174.4%
Tiergarten	111,215	49.5%	165.4%
Charlottenburg	119,844	45.5%	179.5%
Schöneberg	76,261	41.5%	177.4%

However, it was not merely metropolitan centers like Berlin and Hamburg that reported such results. A number of small or medium-sized towns gave similar evidence of middle-class support for the referendum:

	"Yes" Vote	Percentage of Eligible Voters	Percentage of Left Vote
Wilhelmsburg (In East Hanover)	15,161	72.1%	162.5%
Grünberg (In the Liegnitz district)	9,251	56.0%	154.6%
Eberswalde (R.B. Potsdam)	8,861	46.1%	161.3%
Wurzen (Near Leipzig)	6,698	54.6%	132.6%
Wiesbaden	27,783	35.9%	150.6%

Table VIII lists the districts where a majority of all eligible voters approved the KPD-SPD proposal.

*　　*　　*　　*

The reaction of the major parties to the results of the referendum followed predictable lines. The Nationalists and the People's Party generally chose to ignore the fact that substantial numbers of middle-class people had voted for confiscation or they tried to pretend that all who did so were supporters of the Democratic and Center Parties.[18] The DNVP and DVP press credited everyone who did not go to the polls with the right's own political values: "Thus souls are divided. Two great camps face one another: the camp of about 25 million decent people opposed to the camp of about 15 million robbers, thieves, liars and—nitwits *(Dummköpfe)*."[19] They did not bother to subtract from their self-satisfied calculations, the ill, the indifferent, or the intimidated.[20]

[18] The Center Reichstag representative Andre wrote a rebuttal of such appraisals, *Germania*, 29 June 1926 (Nr. 294). Schüren, pp. 232–35.

[19] *Korrespondenz der Deutschnationalen Volkspartei*, 22 June 1926 (Nr. 65), quoted by Andre, idem, emphasis in original. The *Kölnische Zeitung* wrote, "*An impressive majority of the German people, 25 million against 15, has broken the Communistic-Socialistic advance.*" 21 June 1926 (Nr. 453). The former kaiser shared such opinions. His first comment on hearing the results of the referendum was, "So there are 14 million greedy bastards *(Schweinehunde)* in Germany." On second thought however, he said, "*de facto*, the vote was not really over money, but a choice between monarchy and the Republic. The majority has decided for monarchy! We shall have to follow up on these lines in the future." Ilsemann, 2: 40.

[20] Somewhat as an exception, a writer in the journal, *Eiserne Blätter*, commented sadly on how many non-Marxist voters—especially in Berlin—failed to demonstrate proper loyalty to their former rulers. Gustav Roethe, "Bemerkungen über den Volksentscheid," *Eiserne Blätter*, 8 (Nr. 27, 4 July 1926): 451–56.

The elation of the right was duplicated on the left. The Communists called the results "a clear decision of the majority of the working people against Hindenburg, against the Marx government, and against the Reichstag."[21] They demanded the dissolution of the Reichstag and immediate new elections. The KPD Central Committee described "the lessons and conclusions" gained from the referendum: Democratic institutions had failed because of the entrenched power of the bourgeoisie and the use of "open brutal terror" to defeat the popular will. It said the fifteen million voters must be consolidated into a permanent united front in order to continue to fight for a Workers' and Peasants' government.[22] The chief villains were the Social Democratic leaders whose only purpose in joining the referendum campaign was "to throttle it."[23] The KPD attributed the demonstrative success of the referendum to its own activities.[24]

As was natural, the SPD denied such claims.[25] Now that the referendum was over, some Social Democrats were willing to say that Communist participation had lost, rather than gained, votes.[26] Even so, the fourteen and one-half million "yes" votes were interpreted as "a great moral victory."[27]

[21] From a statement by the Communist Reichstag delegation the day after the referendum. *Frankfurter Zeitung*, 22 June 1926 (Nr. 456).

[22] *Rote Fahne*, 22 June 1926. It quoted with approval a remark attributed to a Social Democratic member of the *Reichsbanner*. "Fifteen million—not a bad result. If every one of the fifteen million took up a truncheon, then the princes really would get nothing." The Communist representative Neubauer told the Legal Committee that "the solution of the dispute cannot take place in parliament. What was neglected by the first revolution must be made good by a second revolution outside the confines of parliament." *Frankfurter Zeitung*, 23 June 1926 (Nr. 458).

[23] The confiscation should have been done in 1918, *Rote Fahne* said, and would have been carried out "if such . . . cowards and servants of capitalism as Ebert, Scheidemann, and Südekum had not been leaders." 22 June 1926. Further attacks of this kind: ibid., 23, 24 and 25 June 1926, and by Neubauer, Reichstag. *Verhandlungen*, 390 (30 June 1926): 7707–8.

[24] See Thälmann's front page article, *Rote Fahne*, 20 June 1926.

[25] *Vorwärts*, 21 June 1926 (Nr. 287).

[26] Idem; a letter by Franz Künstler, ibid., 24 June 1926 (Nr. 293); Müller, Reichstag. *Verhandlungen*, 390 (29 June 1926): 7693. On 24 June, the Kuczynski Committee urged the Social Democratic and Free Trade Union leaders to continue the fight for confiscation by further public demonstrations in conjunction with the Communists. The SPD Executive Board saw no reason even to discuss the possibility of such joint action: "The Communist methods of agitation hurt the movement for confiscation of the princes' properties . . . very much. If the Communists had not conducted their agitation with so little sense of responsibility, it surely would have been possible to have gained several million more votes." *Frankfurter Zeitung*, 30 June 1926 (Nr. 478). The Kuczynski Committee continued its own efforts throughout the summer. Kuczynski, p. 113; Könnemann, *Wissenschaftliche Zeitschrift der Universität Halle-Wittenberg*, 7: 558–59; Schüren, pp. 262–64.

[27] *Jahrbuch der Deutschen Sozialdemokratie . . . 1926*, p. 7.

Vorwärts confidently assessed the referendum's results as "a considerable *strengthening of the position of the Social Democratic Party*" and reminded the middle-class parties of the discontent in their ranks.[28] In the days immediately after the referendum, the Social Democratic policy-makers believed that they were in a strong bargaining position. They expected the governing coalition to offer some new major concessions in order to satisfy the SPD's previously stated objections to the Compromise Bill.[29] When the Social Democratic leaders said that the fight would continue in the Reichstag,[30] they seem to have had no premonition that protests would flare up among their own followers the moment the Reichstag delegation abandoned the idea of total confiscation and began to move toward the acceptance of the Compromise.

The Democratic and Center Party press adopted a more sober tone than their competitors on the left and right, understandably so in light of these two parties' experiences during the campaign. The *Frankfurter Zeitung* tried to take a balanced view of the results:

> If one focuses one's attention on the proposed law submitted by the Social Democrats and the Communists for a vote [by the people], then the result is a failure and one cannot say that it was an undeserved failure.

> Yet if one seeks [to discover] the judgment of the people on the princes' claims, then it is a devasting judgment.[31]

Quite understandably, the Catholic press was preoccupied with the disobedience of so many Center voters. Joseph Joos wrote that "this regrettable fact ought neither to be denied nor in any way obfuscated." [32] Renewed discussion of the causes of the failure of party authority continued for some

---

[28] *Vorwärts*, 21 June 1926 (Nr. 287), emphasis in original. In the preceding issue (Nr. 286a), partisan optimism was so high the editors claimed that "in the first [national] referendum we reached a number of votes sufficient to fill over half of the Reichstag in a [regular] election!"

[29] Cf. the subsequent explanation, *Jahrbuch der Deutschen Sozialdemokratie . . . 1926*, p. 8.

[30] *Vorwärts*, 21 June 1926 (Nr. 286a).

[31] 21 June 1926 (Nr. 453). A few days later Koch-Weser admitted that the sponsors of the referendum had achieved a great success. "However," he continued, "speaking purely objectively you [the SPD] have obtained nothing as a result of the referendum insofar as the [Compromise] legislation is concerned." Reichstag. *Verhandlungen*, 390 (29 June 1926): 7681.

[32] *Germania*, 22 June 1926 (Nr. 282).

TABLE VIII: Districts with 50% or More "Yes" Votes

1. East Prussia

    None

2. Berlin

B-A 1. Berlin Mitte	56.7%
B-A 3. Wedding	74.3
B-A 4. Prenzlauer Berg	67.5
B-A 5. Friedrichshain (Teil)	69.8
B-A 6. Kreuzberg	60.4

3. Potsdam II

B-A 13. Tempelhof	54.1
B-A 14. Neukölln	72.2
B-A 15. Treptow (Teil)	64.5
B-A 16. Köpenick (Teil)	64.1
Kr. Teltow	51.8

4. Potsdam I

B-A 5. Friedrichshain (Teil)	71.5
B-A 8. Spandau (Teil)	58.9
B-A 15. Treptow (Teil)	73.7
B-A 16. Köpenick (Teil)	55.1
B-A 17. Lichtenberg	66.2
B-A 18. Weissensee	62.2
B-A 20. Reinickendorf	61.0
Stkr. Brandenburg a.d.H.	55.9
Kr. Niederbarmin	53.3
Stkr. Rathenow	61.7
Stkr. Wittenberge	52.0

5. Frankfurt a.d. Oder

Kr. Spremburg	56.3
Stkr. Forst	51.2

6. Pomerania

    None

7. Breslau

Stkr. Waldenburg	50.6
Lkr. Waldenburg	55.5

8. Liegnitz

Stkr. Grünberg	56.0

9. Oppeln

Kr. Tarnowitz	50.8

10. Magdeburg

Stkr. Burg	62.0
Kr. Calbe	52.8
Stkr. Magdeburg	52.4
Kr. Wanzleben	53.7
Kr. Bernburg	51.1

11. Merseburg

Lkr. Zeitz	56.5
Saalkreis	52.4

12. Thuringia

Lkr. Sonneberg	65.5
Kr. Schleusingen	55.0
Lkr. Altenburg	60.3
Lkr. Arnstadt	53.0
Stkr. Zella-Mehlis	50.4
Stkr. Jena	52.3
Stkr. Gera	55.1
Stkr. Altenberg	52.8

13. Schleswig-Holstein

Stkr. Altona	55.8
Stkr. Neumünster	50.8
Stkr. Wandsbek	53.0

14. Weser-Ems

Stadt Delmenhorst	50.2
Stadt Rüstingen	56.8

15. East Hanover

Stkr. Harburg	58.8
Stkr. Wilhelmsburg	72.1
Kr. Blumenthal	53.2

16. South Hanover-Brunswick

Stkr. Hannover	51.7
Lkr. Hannover	55.3

17. Westphalia-North

Stkr. Gladbeck	56.7
Lkr. Bielefeld	53.4

18. Westphalia-South

Stkr. Herne	52.7
Stkr. Hörde	64.3
Lkr. Hörde	57.4
Kr. Schwelm	51.3
Stkr. Dortmund	55.5
Lkr. Dortmund	56.2
Lkr. Bochum	51.9

19. Hesse-Nassau

Kr. Höchst	54.1
Lkr. Hanau	61.9
Stkr. Frankfurt a.M.	51.8
Lkr. Cassel	61.5

20. Cologne-Aachen

None

21. Coblenz-Trier

None

22. Düsseldorf-East

Stkr. Solingen	61.4
Ldkr. Solingen	53.9

23. Düsseldorf-West

Stkr. Hamborn	54.5

24. Upper Bavaria-Swabia

None

25. Lower Bavaria

None

26. Franconia

Neustadt b. Coburg	50.6

27. The Palatinate

Ludwigshafen	54.0
B-A Ludwigshafen	50.8

28. Dresden-Bautzen

Stadt Freital	67.3
Amtsh. Löbau	50.1
Amtsh. Zittau	55.7
Amtsh. Dresden	50.3

29. Leipzig		
	Stadt Leipzig	54.9
	Stadt Worzen	54.6
	Amtsh. Leipzig	62.7
30. Chemnitz-Zwickau		
	Stadt Glauchau	51.4
	Amtsh. Chemnitz	53.1
	Amtsh. Stollberg	50.8
	Amtsh. Zwickau	55.9
31. Württemberg		
	Ob.-Amt Esslingen	51.9
	Stuttgart Amt	55.2
	Göppingen	57.7
32. Baden		
	A.B. Säckingen	53.3
	A.B. Mannheim	54.9
33. Hesse-Darmstadt		
	Kr. Gross Gerau	51.2
	Kr. Offenbach	67.4
34. Hamburg		
	Stadt Hamburg	53.4
35. Mecklenburg		
	None	

Statistik des Deutschen Reichs, Vol. 332.

time in Center Party circles.[33] Democrats and Centrists alike agreed that parliamentary action was urgent now that the referendum had failed. The day after the referendum, the Center's Reichstag delegation issued a statement identifying the properties dispute as "the most important current political question." Speedy passage of appropriate legislation was mandatory, they said, in order "to calm the domestic scene and mend the disturbed respect for law among the people." [34]

[33] Ibid., 21 June (Nr. 281) and 29 June 1926 (Nr. 295); *Tremonia,* 24 June 1926. A meeting of the party's Advisory Committee was held on 4 July to examine the reasons why the voters had shown so little regard for party discipline. *Germania,* 5 July 1926 (Nr. 305).
[34] Ibid., 22 June 1926 (Nr. 282); Morsey, *Protokolle,* pp. 48–49. In calling for rapid legislative action the *Frankfurter Zeitung* denounced the conduct of the Social Democratic leaders, obviously expecting them to make speedy amends. "They recognized

In the early stages of the initiative and referendum campaign, the republican press had written in glowing terms about institutions which permitted the direct expression of the popular will.[35] Although some people began to call for new referenda the moment the first was over, other voices were also heard. The *Kölnische Zeitung* announced its opposition to such "constitutionally permitted opportunities for inciting the people." [36]

> Even if one is not an enthusiastic admirer of parliamentary forms, one can still consider them, when rationally controlled, as the best method of government, relatively speaking, or at any rate, the only kind feasible under existing conditions. Anyone who [holds these opinions] must hope that the initiative and referendum will be left standing unused in a corner as much as possible, rather than being employed as a weapon against the legislators in parliament. And if there appear to be no hopes of this, then it may be necessary to consider moving [such] dangerous equipment from the armory of the Constitution.[37]

Germania, too, questioned whether any party would benefit by further referenda.[38] Whatever meaning the parties put on the results of the referendum, or however they reinterpreted the results for their own partisan purposes, they still could not escape the necessities of the basic political situation in Germany. As the *Frankfurter Zeitung* put it, "In a word, we are once again ensnared in maneuvering for a majority." [39]

---

the defects of the [referendum] proposal, but they did not have the courage to reject the all too popular slogans stemming from their neighbors on the left. These 'leaders' of Germany's largest party do not lead; they run along behind the instincts of their followers. A somewhat improved, but in fact only a little more moderate, proposal would have attracted millions of non-socialist voters." 21 June 1926 (Nr. 454).

[35] See above, Chapter V, pp. 175, 184, and Chapter VII, p. 225.

[36] 20 June 1926 (Nr. 451).

[37] Idem. It seems to have been a DVP policy to attack the use of initiative and referendum proceedings. The *Kölnische Zeitung* elaborated on this theme 21 June 1926 (Nr. 454): "Even though a parliamentary body is not entirely free from influences of the moment . . . [by comparison] the masses completely lack a steady, clear and considered judgment on the subjects laid before them for direct decision. Particularly when economic questions [*materielle Dinge*] are involved, they fall victim to slogans and . . . demagogy much too easily. Anyone who favors a true democracy must eliminate competition between plebiscitary and parliamentary [forms of] legislation." On 6 July, Stresemann told a student group that it had been a mistake to entrust "a politically immature people" with powers "that should never have been given it." Stresemann *Nachlass,* reel 3146, frame H161951.

[38] *Germania,* 27 June 1926 (Nr. 292); more generally, Schiffers, pp. 253–58.

[39] 22 June (Nr. 456) and in a similar vein, 23 June 1926 (Nr. 460); *Vossische Zeitung,* 22 June 1926 (Nr. 148).

Intensive negotiations among the major parties began at once.[40] The Legal Committee, whose work had been paralyzed since the end of April, resumed its discussions of the Compromise Bill. Since the bill was now a government-sponsored measure, Chancellor Marx and other members of the cabinet played a very active part in these negotiations. Leaders of the Center Party were scarcely tempted to let things drift after the results of the referendum.

Heinrich Brauns wrote Otto Gessler during the course of the negotiations following the referendum.

> Important and difficult decisions will be made this week. The Center can scarcely depart from its [announced] position that "the passage of the law regulating the princes' settlements is essential using whatever means necessary." At any rate I am of that opinion. In the Rhineland and in Westphalia hundreds of thousands of Center Party followers have voted for the Social Democratic referendum. . . . [T]he law absolutely must be made with [the help of] the Social Democrats.[41]

Stimulated by the strong leadership now coming from Marx and by a general desire to eliminate a very troublesome issue from the domestic scene, the parties belonging to the governing coalition appear to have reconciled most of their previous differences. This enabled them to maintain a unified stance in their negotiations regarding the details of the Compromise Bill with the two "wing" parties outside the coalition, something they had not always done in the past.[42] There was no question now of formulating the bill to the liking of the Nationalists, even though some help from them was essential in order to secure passage of the bill by the two-thirds majority needed to ensure against any challenge of the bill's

---

[40] Time was short since the Reichstag was scheduled to recess for the summer the first week in July.

[41] Quoted by Ernst Deuerlein, "Heinrich Brauns—Schattenriss eines Sozialpolitikers," in Ferdinand A. Hermens and Theodor Schieder, eds. *Staat, Wirtschaft und Politik in der Weimarer Republik. Festschrift für Heinrich Brüning* (Berlin, 1967), p. 66.

[42] Earlier the representatives of the DVP had shown a willingness to support some changes desired by the DNVP, now they adopted a rather more conciliatory attitude toward the wishes of the left. See the statements by Dr. Wunderlich in the Legal Committee, *Frankfurter Zeitung*, 24 June (Nr. 461) and 25 June 1926 (Nr. 464), and by von Campe, Prussia. Landtag. *Sitzungsberichte*, 9 (5 July 1925): 13580. The *Wirtschaftspartei*, although not part of the governing coalition, accepted the government's view that passage of the bill was necessary to calm public opinion. *Deutsche Mittelstands-Zeitung*, 4 July 1926 (Nr. 7).

constitutionality.[43] The governing parties regarded aid from the Social Democrats as their best hope.[44] They knew that they would have to make some concessions to gain the support of the Social Democratic Reichstag delegation for the Compromise, but did not intend to rewrite the law drastically on its behalf.[45] The negotiators for the middle-party coalition obviously expected that in the end the leaders of the SPD would act responsibly and persuade their followers that the Compromise, even if less rigorous than they thought desirable, was better than no national regulatory legislation at all. Thus, Chancellor Marx and other chief negotiators were prepared for hard bargaining over the exact terms on which the SPD would support the government bill.

Between 22 and 26 June, the Legal Committee moved ahead rapidly with its consideration of the latest version of the Compromise Bill, its proceedings obviously expedited by the private interparty discussions that went on simultaneously. To save time, debate was limited to specific details of the bill or proposed amendments.[46] Some changes recommended by the SPD were accepted. They were, most notably, the elimination of any right of the former rulers to claim compensation for Civil List, *Kronfideikommissrente,* and other similar payments they had once received; [47] the empowering of the special court to reexamine the settlements made since

[43] *Frankfurter Zeitung,* 24 June 1926 (Nr. 462); Brauns wrote Gessler (in the letter cited above, note 41) that it would be necessary for "ten to twenty representatives from the right to absent themselves" during the voting so the law could pass with the required majority.

At a cabinet meeting on 22 June Dr. Külz recommended consideration of his earlier proposal to alter the constitutional character of the bill by an appropriately worded preamble so that the bill could be passed by a simple majority. *Kabinetts-protokolle,* reel 1839, frame D769295. Such a decision would have been popular in the DDP. Anton Erkelenz advocated this course in an article in the *Vossische Zeitung,* 22 June 1926 (Nr. 148). However, the chancellor replied to a question in the Legal Committee the next day that the cabinet had not changed its position and that there were no plans to add such a preamble. *Frankfurter Zeitung,* 24 June 1926 (Nr. 461).

[44] Ibid., 23 June (Nr. 459), 29 June (Nr. 475) and 30 June (Nr. 477); Schulte in *Politisches Jahrbuch 1926,* p. 525. The records of the discussions in the cabinet of the political aspects of the issue are disappointingly sparse, e.g. *Kabinettsprotokolle,* reel 1839, frames D769294–95.

[45] *Kölnische Zeitung,* 26 June 1926 (Nr. 469).

[46] *Frankfurter Zeitung,* 23 June 1926 (Nr. 458).

[47] Ibid., 25 June 1926 (Nr. 464). In this case, the DVP's representative broke ranks from the other governmental parties in order to vote with the right against this particular amendment, *Vossische Zeitung,* 25 June 1926 (Nr. 151). The BVP reportedly had reservations about other parts of the bill as well. Ibid., 23 June 1926 (Nr. 149).

1918 to determine if they corresponded to the terms of the new law; [48] and the limitation of the guarantee that members of the former ruling houses would be assured "a suitable standard of living" to the then-living members of the princely houses.[49] Other, more far-reaching Social Democratic demands, such as authorization for the court to revise arrangements concluded *before* the revolution, or restricting the composition of the court to laymen named by the Reichstag, did not find support.[50]

The rapid completion of the Committee's discussions was a hopeful sign, but a close look at the pattern of voting in the Committee showed that there was still no assurance the bill would succeed once it was before the Reichstag as a whole. Only a minority of the representatives in the Legal Committee actually voted for the bill as it was read section by section. The usual voting pattern was eleven votes "for" (from the middle parties), three votes "against" (from the KPD), and twelve abstentions (the SPD, DNVP, and *Völkische* representatives).[51] This alignment had to be changed if the bill was to obtain approval from the full house.[52]

Interparty negotiations were still in progress when the government bill came up for its second reading in the Reichstag on 29 June.[53] The leaders of the Social Democratic Party were very nearly ready to support the bill; they seem to have recognized that few further amendments were obtainable and were concentrating their attention on other objects of negotiation. Chancellor Marx informed the cabinet that key members of the SPD's Reichstag delegation desired to have the names of the men being considered for the special arbitration court cleared with them before any formal appointments were made.[54] Furthermore, the SPD leaders were

[48] *Frankfurter Zeitung,* 24 June 1926 (Nr. 461).

[49] Ibid., 26 June 1926 (Nr. 467). Another SPD amendment proposing that the members of the former ruling families be encouraged to adopt a "bürgerliche Beruf" was not accepted.

[50] Ibid., 24 June 1926 (Nr. 461). Rosenfeld and Landsberg made strong appeals for revision of settlements concluded *before* 1918, citing certain questionable acts by Prussia's Frederick William IV. They told the Committee that "this question is of decisive importance for the Social Democrats." Idem.

[51] Ibid., 24–27 June 1926.

[52] At the conclusion of the Committee's deliberations the DNVP's representative Barth made a point of stating that the DNVP had abstained during key Committee votes only to avoid obstructing deliberations; he implied that his party might well act differently when the final vote came. Ibid., 27 June 1926 (Nr. 470).

[53] Ibid., 29 June (Nr. 475) and 30 June 1926 (Nr. 477).

[54] Bundesarchiv. "Auseinandersetzung," Bd. 2, zu RK5220 and zu RK5262.

insisting that their party's support of the government bill depended on the middle parties' acceptance of a low tariff on grain, another important measure just then before the Reichstag.[55] In order to ensure the DNVP's compliance with the government's decision to pass the regulatory legislation with the aid of the SPD, Marx wanted to obtain a dissolution order from President Hindenburg and believed that he would grant him this request.[56] At the high point of the confidential negotiations Marx declared his readiness to inform Hermann Müller that the cabinet would either insist on dissolution or resign if the bulk of the Social Democrats cooperated with the government parties and the bill then failed due to the obstinacy of the DNVP.[57]

Nevertheless, the agreement of the Social Democrats that had seemed nearly assured failed to materialize. On the evening of 1 July 1926, the SPD's Reichstag delegation decided to ignore the advice of its leaders as well as a resolution from the Prussian *Landtag* delegation favoring acceptance and voted 73-38 against accepting the government's bill.[58] The next day, the spokesman for the SPD charged that the middle parties were at fault for showing too little interest in the amendments wanted by the SPD.[59] No one was deceived by these claims; it was only too apparent that the Social Dem-

[55] Brauns to Gessler, quoted by Deuerlein in *Staat, Wirtschaft und Politik in der Weimarer Republik*, p. 67.

[56] On 25 June Marx informed the cabinet that he had the impression from talking with the president that he "would not shrink away from" dissolving the Reichstag if that was necessary. *Kabinettsprotokolle*, reel 1839, frame D769333. Brauns, however, was not so sure that Hindenburg would actually do this. The letter to Gessler, op. cit., p. 66. On the basis of information in the Westarp papers, Dörr, p. 243 and note 81, says that Hindenburg intended neither to sign the government bill into law if it passed through the Reichstag nor grant a dissolution order if it failed. Dörr also suggests that the stiff opposition that the DNVP put up against the bill had been arranged by Westarp with the tacit approval of the president in order to spare him the embarrassment of another governmental crisis. On the other hand, it must be mentioned that there were strong pressures on the DNVP's parliamentary leaders attempting to persuade them not to block the bill's passage. The *Landbund*, in particular, hoped that the demonstration of an accommodating attitude on this issue might smooth the way for the reentry of the DNVP into the government. Ibid., pp. 241–42; Chickering, *Journal of Modern History*, 39: 77; Dorpalen, pp. 109–10.

[57] *Kabinettsprotokolle*, reel 1840, frames D769452–53. The implication of such a promise quite clearly was that the Center, if forced to do so, would force the dissolution of the Reichstag in conjunction with the DDP and the SPD and form a Weimar Coalition after the new election. For its part, the *Frankfurter Zeitung* recommended such a course of action, 29 June 1926 (Nr. 476).

[58] *Vorwärts*, 2 July 1926 (Nr. 307); *Jahrbuch der Deutschen Sozialdemokratie . . . 1926*, pp. 8–9, 120; Schulze, p. 508 and note 158.

[59] Wels, Reichstag. *Verhandlungen*, 390 (2 July 1926): 7803–5.

ocrats did not want to take responsibility for the consequences of their own decision.[60]

Feelings had remained strong within the party that confiscation was the only desirable solution despite the defeat of the referendum. As it had become quite obvious that the party's parliamentary leaders intended to support the government's bill, a wave of opposition welled up, among the lesser party functionaries in particular.[61] Prominent left socialists such as Kurt Rosenfeld encouraged this opposition. He published an article in some of the regional SPD newspapers—Vorwärts refused to print it—in which he damned the numerous deficiencies of the Compromise Bill and criticized the party's leaders for being willing to cooperate with the Marx government.[62] The party organization in Chemnitz wired the Reichstag delegation that the bill was "entirely inadequate" and urged it to seek the dissolution of the Reichstag and new elections.[63] From outside the party, the Communists also did everything possible to discredit the Social Democratic leaders and increase the pressure on them.[64] The SPD's policy-makers had thought that they had

[60] See, for example, Germania, 2 July 1926 (Nr. 301) where it refuted the arguments Vorwärts had put forward to justify the party's decision.

[61] Theodor Wolff in a very critical editorial in the Berliner Tageblatt (Wochen-Ausgabe), 8 July 1926, noted that all the responsible SPD leaders had favored the acceptance of the bill but "the mass of lesser party officials, the political bowling cronies (Kegelbrüder), have triumphed." Carl von Ossietzky agreed that it had been resistance within the organization that forced the rejection of the bill, but he, unlike Wolff, was delighted by the result and only wondered why it had taken the party so long. "What would have been the result of [the SPD's] acceptance [of the bill]?" he asked. "Great discontent among the party's voters, damage to the party organizations, heated debate between the left and the right (possible extension of the Saxon Conflict to the whole party), and defections to the Communists." Die Weltbühne, 22 (Nr. 27, 6 July 1926): 3.

[62] Rote Fahne reprinted most of it, 30 June 1926. It is rather characteristic of official SPD efforts to sweep intra-party conflicts under the rug that Friedrich Stampfer never mentioned any of these differences in his account, Die vierzehn Jahre der ersten Deutschen Republik, pp. 443–48.

[63] Rote Fahne, 30 June 1926. On 6 July the party workers in Berlin approved the Fraktion's decision and urged continued opposition should the bill be re-introduced in the fall. Vorwärts, 7 July 1926 (Nr. 314). Vorwärts did not mention any meetings before the Reichstag delegation made its decision to reject the bill, but the functionaries in Berlin undoubtedly had found ways for making their views known.

[64] Rote Fahne, 26, 27 June and 1, 2 July 1926; Neubauer's attacks on the SPD's leaders. Reichstag. Verhandlungen, 390 (30 June 1926): 7707–8. The Communists took advantage of the aroused state of public feeling by organizing a recruiting week right after the referendum was over. Bericht der Bezirksleitung der KPD Berlin-Brandenburg-Lausitz, p. 23; Rote Fahne, 25 June 1926. If the Berliner Lokal-Anzeiger's report, 1 July 1925, is correct, Communists successfully ousted the Social Democratic leaders of the Berlin local of the Metal Workers Union.

eliminated dissension inside the party by joining the Communists to support the initiative and referendum movement.
They now found themselves confronted with the same dissension, or worse.

The SPD's leaders were plainly embarrassed. Stresemann
noted in his diary that on the day after the momentous decision by the SPD Reichstag delegation, Undersecretary Weismann, almost certainly acting at Otto Braun's instigation,
informed the national government that:

> In the fall the Social Democratic Party would be ready to accept
> the law "as it stands". . . . The reason for the defeat of the lead-
> ership was simply . . . that they had not had time *to assume a new
> posture*. Their followers still had the speeches in mind that they
> had given favoring confiscation without compensation. . . . How-
> ever, today (the day after the vote of the *Fraktion*) the outcry
> (*Katzenjammer*) was so great, they would gladly undo everything,
> if it were only possible.[65]

Stresemann added that the first concrete result of the SPD's
decision was a higher tariff on grain. Earlier there had been
considerable support for its efforts to keep the duty relatively
low, but after the SPD turned down the law regulating the
property settlements, "no one felt obligated any longer to
take its views into consideration." [66]

For a moment, Marx considered submitting the cabinet's
resignation since he had previously promised that the government would "draw the necessary conclusions" if the bill
failed.[67] But most members of the cabinet, including Brauns,
Külz and Stresemann, considered the cabinet's resignation
under such circumstances a politically senseless gesture.[68]
Because of existing divisions among the parties and the impossibility of either the SPD or the DNVP entering the government at that time another minority government of the
middle parties would have been necessary. Hindenburg, too,
did not want to see a new cabinet crisis, and agreed to issue

---

[65] *Vermächtnis*, 2: 406, emphasis in original.

[66] Ibid., p. 407.

[67] *Kabinettsprotokolle* (2 July 1926), reel 1840, frame D769454. Although Marx
stressed that the resignation would be the correct thing to do by accepted rules of
parliamentary government, his chief reason for wanting to resign "as a gesture"
was almost surely to remove any grounds for criticism from Center Party followers
who had trusted in his promise that a suitable law would be passed. This was the
opinion of the *Vossische Zeitung*, 3 July 1926 (Nr. 158).

[68] *Kabinettsprotokolle*, reel 1840, frames D769454–55.

a public statement approving the continuation of the Marx government in office.[69]

On 2 July 1926, the Reichstag debated the bill to regulate the princes' settlements. After representatives for the SPD and the DNVP announced their refusal to support the government proposal,[70] the chancellor withdrew the bill rather than let it be defeated on the final vote.[71] The work of the parliamentarians had been for naught.[72] Except for an extension of the *Sperrgesetz* that prohibited the regular courts from issuing any new decisions regarding the princely claims, the situation returned to what it had been the preceding year before the conclusion of the Prussian-Hohenzollern *Vergleich*.[73] Only the right [74] and the extreme left [75] looked upon such inconclusive results with pleasure.

The decision of the SPD Reichstag *Fraktion,* in particular, the party's resumption of partisan slogans irrelevant to the needs of practical politics, drew sharp criticism from all the middle-class parties. *Vossische Zeitung* called the decision to reject the government proposal "an act of stupidity of truly gigantic proportions." [76] *Germania* labeled it "the victory of irrationality." [77] The *Kölnische Zeitung* stated that the SPD had

[69] Ibid., frame D769457; Dorpalen, p. 110. On the other hand he refused to strengthen Marx's bargaining position for the passage of the government's bill by granting him authority to dissolve the Reichstag if necessary. Haungs, pp. 203–4, 284.

[70] Wels, Reichstag. *Verhandlungen,* 390: 7803–5; Westarp, ibid., pp. 7805–9.

[71] Ibid., pp. 7809–10; Stehkämper, 3: 14.

[72] Even before the collapse of all hopes for the bill, the *Vossische Zeitung* complained that neither the legislators nor the cabinet seemed to understand the absolute urgency of passing the bill. It objected to the "wheeling and dealing" *(Compromisselns und Kuhhandeln)* that was being used in the attempt to find a large enough majority. "The Reichstag is very nearly on the point of wasting away most of the last scraps of respect and confidence [it still enjoys] with the people." 30 June 1926 (Nr. 155).

[73] Ibid., 3 July 1926 (Nr. 158).

[74] Anticipating the bill's failure the *Berliner Lokal-Anzeiger,* 1 July 1926, wrote that "the empty working of the parliamentary machinery continues to clatter along. Yesterday [we] saw exactly the same scene as the day before yesterday: four or five short partisan speeches and a series of votes. . . . [Everything was] just as monotonous, just as tedious, just as inconsequential as on Tuesday. . . . [As different sections of the bill were accepted by the vote of different majorities], laughter spread through the House. A *Völkische* member shouts, '[How about this] heading? "Monkey-business" [*Affentheater*].' He is not entirely wrong, that wild man."

[75] *Rote Fahne,* 2 and 3 July 1926; Deak, p. 160.

[76] 3 July 1926 (Nr. 158). Theodor Wolff likewise wrote, "If we had to pick out the finest recent example of political stupidity, we might have some difficulty. But just now after the latest events, the Social Democrats appear to stand in the very front row of competitors." *Berliner Tageblatt* (Wochen-Ausgabe), 8 July 1926.

[77] It continued, "All rational considerations favored acceptance of the law. . . . However, Messrs. Levi and Rosenfeld are running things at the moment. The shriek

discredited parliamentary procedures as well as direct democracy by its conduct in recent weeks.[78]

It was not merely that the Social Democrats had chosen to ignore the obvious need for regulatory legislation in order to help the state governments (especially Prussia) escape from very unfavorable legal positions vis-à-vis their former ruling families.[79] The regulation of the property settlements had been expected to open the way for the creation of a more stable majority government on the basis of the Great Coalition.[80] The Social Democrats were fully aware of this when they voted against the government bill; there had been numerous warnings that they must demonstrate their political reliability by constructive support of this legislation.[81] The Reichstag *Fraktion*'s vote was rightly interpreted as yet another rejection of the Great Coalition:

> Once again forces in the Social Democratic Reichstag delegation who do not make their political decisions on the basis of sober judgment, but rather [give decisive] consideration to Communist competition in [mass] agitation have won the upper hand. The damage that has been caused by this decision will be hard to repair. Not only has the question of the princes' settlements reached an impasse, the expected clear determination of the future course of German domestic policy has been completely spoiled. Everything is going to stay as it has been.[82]

Thus, some of the closest allies of the Social Democrats in the Democratic and Center parties found themselves forced to adopt critical attitudes not greatly differing from those taken by men who had never been sympathetic toward a left

---

of propaganda from the street drowns out the voice of . . . political reflection." 2 July 1926 (Nr. 300).

[78] 2 July 1926 (Nr. 485).

[79] At a cabinet meeting on 2 July, Brauns advocated dropping the government bill. Since the SPD had chosen to let the bill fail, he said, it would not hurt to make the Prussian government bear the consequences. *Kabinettsprotokolle*, reel 1840, frame D769455.

[80] See above, Chapter VII, pp. 231–34.

[81] For instance, *Germania* had written that "the party that causes the failure of the proposed law simultaneously takes on a heavy responsibility." 29 June 1926 (Nr. 294); *Berliner Tageblatt* (Wochen-Ausgabe), 17 June 1926; *Vossische Zeitung*, 2 July 1926 (Nr. 157); as well as remarks by Koch-Weser at a meeting of Democratic women, *Frankfurter Zeitung*, 29 June 1926 (Nr. 474), and in the Reichstag. *Verhandlungen*, 390 (29 June 1926): 7681.

[82] *Rhein-Mainische Volkszeitung*, 3 July 1926 (Nr. 150). Also the formal statement issued by the DDP Executive Board, quoted above, Chapter I, p. 12. Similar conclusions were drawn by *Tremonia*, 5 July 1926 (Nr. 181); *Kölnische Volkszeitung*, 2 July 1926 (Nr. 481); *Vossische Zeitung*, 3 July 1926 (Nr. 158) and 4 July 1926 (Nr. 159).

orientation.[83] Unquestionably, the SPD's behavior on this issue reinforced the old belief that it preferred the freedom of irresponsible agitation to the constraints required by collaboration in a multi-party coalition.[84]

As all immediate chances for consolidating a predominantly republican government faded, some elements in the DVP and DNVP tried once again to induce the Center, and to some extent even the Democrats, to reexamine their political alignments. The *Kölnische Zeitung* wondered whether "the Center and the Democrats [did] not now see that serious *cooperation with the Social Democrats* is *impossible* after their display of purely partisan tactics today." [85] Such bids were not followed by any immediate regrouping of political forces in Germany. Working-class Catholics, manifestly distrustful of their party leaders' policies regarding the former rulers' properties, would scarcely have tolerated the Center's conclusion of a sudden new alliance with the right. *Germania* candidly admitted as much just after the referendum:

> To follow the beckonings of the right in the present situation would be the worst possible way . . . to strengthen party authority and give our whole political existence a firm footing again. We will not cure the symptoms of illness in our midst with the *Bürgerblock.* . . . [86]

In the course of the summer and fall, the parties on the right continued their blandishments and eventually, in January 1927, persuaded the Center to enter a right coalition in which the DNVP played a prominent role.[87] The Center was not ready to take such a step in the summer of 1926, however. Prudence and necessity dictated a reaffirmation of the "Politik der Mitte." [88] Indeed, all the major parties appear to have

[83] For instance, compare the articles by Andre and Joos in *Germania*, 4 July (Nr. 304) and 6 July 1926 (Nr. 306).

[84] Ibid., 3 July 1926 (Nr. 303); Schulte in *Politisches Jahrbuch 1926*, p. 527.

[85] 2 July 1926 (Nr. 485), emphasis in original. On 10 July 1926 (Nr. 505), this DVP paper suggested that the formation of a new government in Prussia was clearly desirable since the Social Democrats had so pointedly demonstrated their preference for irresponsible agitation.

[86] 22 June 1926 (Nr. 282).

[87] Turner, pp. 224–30; Becker, *Zeitschrift für die Geschichte des Oberrheins*, 109: 371–73; Stürmer, pp. 182–90, 200–25.

[88] Stegerwald told the Center's Advisory Committee on 4 July 1926 that a Great Coalition would have been the best choice at that time, but as long as the Social Democrats were so poorly led there was no chance of it. Thus the Center had to stick to its middle course, he said. *Germania*, 5 July 1926 (Nr. 305). Similar editorial opinion, ibid., 8 July (Nr. 310) and 11 July 1926 (Nr. 316).

more or less agreed to leave the question of the enlargement of the existing coalition or the organization of an entirely new government in abeyance while the Reichstag went on a long summer vacation.[89]

Within a few weeks of the collapse of the Compromise Bill, the legal representatives for the Hohenzollern family resumed negotiations with the Prussian government. On 4 July, Herr von Berg suggested further negotiations to the Prussian authorities. He asserted that the royal house had tried hard in the past to reach a mutually acceptable settlement, and that it had already agreed to abandon its claims to a great part of the property in question. They were giving up "83 percent of the total," he said. Berg urged the resumption of talks "in order to remove [this] cause of discord in our public life once and for all," and recommended using the *Vergleich* of October 1925, as the basis for the new round of negotiations.[90] Otto Braun replied for the Prussian government on 21 July.[91] He denied Berg's claim that the royal family had tried to be accommodating in the past. There could be no longer any question, he said, of working out a new agreement along the lines of the proposed settlement of 1925: "Only negotiations that take into account the results of the Reichstag's discussions . . . can be considered in the light of the present state of affairs. The Prussian government is ready [to enter into] such negotiations." [92]

By the end of August, serious talks over the details of the settlement were under way. There seems to have been a widespread desire to get the matter settled as quickly and quietly as possible. Early in September Chancellor Marx received a report on the progress of the Prussian-Hohenzollern

[89] Except the KPD that tried desperately to force a vote of no confidence against the Marx government, Reichstag. *Verhandlungen,* 390 (2 July 1926): 7834–35, and also against the Weimar Coalition government in Prussia. Prussia. Landtag. *Sitzungsberichte,* 9 (5 July 1926): 13589, 13879. Heinrich Brauns had foreseen that basic political decisions would be deferred until the fall even when the SPD was still considering what position it would take on the Compromise Bill. See his letter to Gessler, quoted in *Staat, Wirtschaft und Politik in der Weimarer Republik,* p. 67; likewise a letter from Marx to Pünder, 27 July 1926, quoted by Stürmer, p. 162.

[90] *Vorwärts* published the text of the letter, 6 July 1926 (Nr. 312).

[91] *Vorwärts,* 23 July 1926 (Nr. 342). The paper did not make any editorial comment on Braun's willingness to negotiate.

[92] Idem. In response to a resolution made by the DVP, Braun stated early in July that the Prussian government wanted the matter settled as rapidly as possible. Prussia. Landtag. *Sitzungsberichte,* 9 (5 July 1926): 13575, 13579–80, 13583–84. The Prussian cabinet authorized formal discussions on 13 August 1926. Bundesarchiv. "Auseinandersetzung," Bd. 2, RK6725.

discussions.[93] The observer for the chancellor's office reported that the Prussian government's demands were reasonable; as things stood there was no reason for the national government to intervene, but some pressure might have to be applied later to encourage the Hohenzollerns to moderate their claims. Above all, the report concluded (and one can assume Marx concurred) that it was essential to keep the matter from coming up again in the Reichstag.

Hindenburg, likewise, wanted the issue resolved by the two principal parties to the dispute, and wanted them to do so as rapidly as possible. He apparently feared that if the Reichstag took up the subject again it might pass legislation very restrictive of the princes' rights, which he could not accept.[94] If at all possible he wanted to avoid a political crisis in which he would feel obligated to refuse to sign important legislation. On his own initiative, the president urged von Berg not to push the royal family's claims too far,[95] and also encouraged Marx to use his influence with the Prussian justice minister, Am Zehnhoff, a Center Party man, in favor of a speedy settlement.[96]

The toughest problems were practical ones; how much agricultural and forest property would remain in the possession of the Hohenzollern family and how much compensation should they receive for various properties taken over by the state.[97] The royal family no longer attached so much weight to a strictly accurate distribution of the contested properties in accordance with established legal and historical rights.[98] For its part, the Prussian government feared the expiration of the *Sperrgesetz,* or other unfavorable developments, if it allowed these direct negotiations to lapse.[99] Accordingly, after some very hard bargaining, both sides accepted a new,

[93] Ibid., RK6438.

[94] A note by Pünder, dated 8 Sept. 1926, recording a report by Meissner on Hindenburg's views and actions. Ibid., RK6991.

[95] Idem.

[96] Idem; Dorpalen, pp. 110–11; Schüren, pp. 252–55.

[97] Bundesarchiv. "Auseinandersetzung," Bd. 2, RK7177.

[98] Dr. Offermann, who had been sent as an observer by the chancellor's office, reported that in the negotiations "the former ruling house is, to all appearances, putting particular weight on obtaining as much money as possible in cash." Bundesarchiv. "Auseinandersetzung," Bd. 2, zu RK6991. One reason for this may well have been because bankers who previously had granted generous loans now started requesting repayment, rather to the surprise of leading members of the royal family. Ilsemann, 2: 42.

[99] *Vorwärts,* 13 Oct. 1926 (Nr. 482); *Jahrbuch der Deutschen Sozialdemokratie . . . 1926,* p. 9.

considerably amended version of the October 1925 *Vergleich*.[100] Probably neither the Prussian government nor the Hohenzollern family was wholly satisfied with the final agreement, yet both sides could console themselves with the thought that they had fared better than they might have done under other circumstances.[101]

The Hohenzollern family received almost two-thirds of the contested agricultural and forest lands, worth an estimated 37.4 million marks; a number of palaces, villas, and other buildings, primarily for residential purposes, valued at 59.9 million marks; as well as further real estate of various kinds worth 10.3 million.[102] The family agreed to permit the state to take over the historically important Bellevue and Babelsberg palaces in Berlin and Potsdam, which had earlier been recognized as private possessions, in return for a somewhat larger amount of landed property.[103] The former royal house abandoned all its claims for compensation for the old *Kronfideikommissrente*.[104] However, it did secure 15 million marks in cash compensation for private properties (furnishings, equipment, parcels of land adjacent to unquestioned state properties, etc.) transferred to the state. In addition, the royal family received one million marks as the result of the division of certain securities to which both the state and the family had some claim.[105]

These terms were noticeably less generous than those that had been written into the proposed settlement of 1925. The

[100] Prussia. Landtag. *Drucksache*, (2. Wahlperiode 1925/26), Nr. 4160, contains the text of the agreement originally concluded between the Prussian state and the Hohenzollern family 12 October 1925 with the alterations formally accepted on 6 October 1926 as well as an official explanation of the reasons for the conclusion of the settlement.

[101] Schüren, pp. 255–56.

[102] Prussia. Landtag. *Drucksache*, (2. Wahlperiode 1925/26), pp. 5381–94; *Vossische Zeitung*, 7 October 1926 (Nr. 240); Günther, pp. 149–50, 160–62, 166–68, 173–74.

[103] Babelsberg almost certainly would have been recognized as the property of the Prussian state without any compensation for the royal family if the Compromise Bill had become law. Bellevue, on the other hand, was unquestionably private and the Prussian government gave the Hohenzollerns 50,000 *Morgen* of land in order to acquire it. Hoepker-Aschoff considered this trade a good one. Schulte in *Politisches Jahrbuch 1926*, pp. 528–29.

[104] Prussia. Landtag. *Drucksache*. Nr. 4160, p. 5379.

[105] Schulte in *Politisches Jahrbuch 1926*, p. 491. Before the war the administrators of the *Kronfideikommissfonds* had amassed a large sum of capital invested in various forms of securities. In 1918 these capital holdings were valued at 88.58 million; the inflation, however, wiped out nearly all of this fortune. By 1926 what was left was worth only 1.3 million. This was divided according to a formula that gave the royal family 1 million and the state .3 million.

304 CRISIS OF THE WEIMAR REPUBLIC

Hohenzollerns received around ten percent less land, less real estate, and only one-half as much cash compensation as they would have gained if the 1925 settlement had been ratified.[106] On the other hand, the former royal family still had reason to be pleased with the final settlement. If the Reichstag had passed the last version of the Compromise Bill, the Hohenzollern family would have received even less.[107] Indeed, annoyed middle-class critics of the SPD did not hesitate to point out that, but for their unwise rejection of the Compromise, the state of Prussia would have obtained a clear title to substantially more land and other properties that now stayed in the hands of the Hohenzollern family or went to the state only in return for some kind of compensation.[108] Under the terms of the Compromise, Prussia would have paid only an estimated six or seven million in cash instead of the fifteen million in the 1926 settlement.[109]

The Prussian government was aware that in many ways the new settlement was deficient from the state's point of view; however, the cabinet felt constrained to accept it. Finance Minister Hoepker-Aschoff explained the situation to the *Landtag*. If the Prussian government did not act, the whole question was certain to come up again when the Reichstag reconvened. ". . .[T]hat would spark the division of the German people again and would increase the differences among the parties and cause yet another crisis in national politics." [110] While all this was going on, Hoepker-Aschoff added, the Prussian government still could not be sure that its claims would receive a favorable handling. Inaction might lead to a steady deterioration of Prussia's position vis-à-vis the royal family, especially if the regular courts were permitted to resume hearing contested cases and the previous pattern of adverse judgments continued. The Prussian government believed that it had to accept the 1926 negotiated settlement "in order to prevent worse from happening." [111]

[106] Günther, cited above note 102, gives a detailed breakdown of the differences between the 1925 and 1926 settlements.

[107] Schulte, in *Politisches Jahrbuch 1926*, pp. 518–20, 528–29. In particular, the Leopold line, a side branch of the family, would have lost the very valuable Flatow-Krojanke estates. As it was, this branch of the family retained the bulk of these lands but relinquished certain other holdings to the state.

[108] *Vossische Zeitung*, 7 Oct. 1926 (Nr. 240).

[109] Idem; Schulte in *Politisches Jahrbuch 1926*, p. 528.

[110] Prussia. Landtag. *Sitzungsberichte*, 10 (11 Oct. 1926): 14262.

[111] *Jahrbuch der Deutschen Sozialdemokratie... 1926*, pp. 9, 372–73. Professor Dorpalen (p. 111) interprets the phrase "to avoid worse consequences," in a political

As soon as the terms of the settlement had been agreed upon, the Prussian government laid the text of the agreement before the *Landtag* for immediate ratification. It was debated on 11 and 12 October 1926. Ratification was certain from the start. All the middle-class parties from the DDP to the DNVP were prepared to vote for the settlement.[112] The Communists opposed this "surprise move by the princes' flunkies," [113] but despite the use of all kinds of parliamentary obstruction, they were unable to block passage of the settlement.[114]

Once again the Social Democrats faced a difficult and unpleasant decision. The votes of the SPD *Landtag* delegation were not essential for the ratification of the settlement. Many members of the delegation disliked the terms of the settlement and wanted to vote against it; it was even less popular with the organized party workers throughout the country.[115] Yet political expediency and good sense spoke for the acceptance of the settlement. The Prussian government had decided that, under the circumstances, the best solution for the whole question was the new settlement.[116] It would have been very embarrassing for the SPD's *Landtag* delegation to repudiate the Prussian government's decision, considering the dominant role Social Democratic ministers played in it.[117] Moreover, it must be remembered that only three months earlier, the *Landtag* delegation itself had urged the Social Democrats in the Reichstag to support the Compromise Bill out of concern for the interests of the Prussian state.[118] To vote against the settlement as a demonstrative gesture might

---

sense, i.e., that the Prussian government wanted to avoid a grave political crisis in which President Hindenburg might have resigned. This possibility did exist and the Prussian government was undoubtedly aware of it, but Dorpalen seems to overlook the fact that the phrase was regularly used in contexts referring to the probable adverse financial and legal consequences for the Prussian state if it did not conclude a definitive settlement quite rapidly.

[112] *Jahrbuch der Deutschen Sozialdemokratie . . . 1926,* pp. 9–10.

[113] *Rote Fahne,* 6 Oct. 1926.

[114] See below, pp. 307–309.

[115] See the comments by Wilke (Stettin) at the party's convention the next year. *Sozialdemokratischer Parteitag 1927,* p. 79.

[116] *Vorwärts,* 6 Oct. (Nrs. 470 and 471) and 7 Oct. 1926 (Nr. 472).

[117] Koch-Weser later told his party's Advisory Committee that the settlement gave the Prussian government much more than the Socialists had thought possible to obtain in 1920. The *Parteiausschuss* meeting 28 Nov. 1926. DDP Papers, reel 38, folder 760, p. 3. The leaders of the SPD *Landtag* delegation admitted as much. *Vorwärts,* 7 Oct. 1926 (Nr. 472).

[118] See above, p. 295.

have been popular within the party, but the direct consequence of such a vote in which the SPD sided with the Communists against all the middle-class parties almost certainly
would have been the collapse of the existing Weimar Coalition in Prussia.[119]

Soon after the conclusion of the negotiations between the
representatives for the Hohenzollern family and the Prussian
government, the Social Democratic members of the *Landtag*
met to decide what they would do.[120] Otto Braun and the
national Executive Board recommended acceptance of the
settlement. The *Landtag* delegates let it be known that they
could not give their direct consent to a settlement that left
properties worth more than a hundred million marks in the
hands of the former royal family.[121] Nevertheless, they agreed
to do nothing that might interfere with the acceptance of the
settlement. A clear majority of the delegation authorized Otto
Braun to sign the settlement after the *Landtag* ratified it, but
at the same time decided that the delegation itself would
abstain during the vote on ratification.[122] Thus, as we have
seen previously on more than one occasion, an important
Social Democratic policy-making body preferred a calculated
half-measure over a clear, forthright decision.

If the SPD's *Landtag* delegates believed they had found a
way to avoid trouble with the party's coalition partners and
their own followers, they soon discovered that such hopes
were mistaken. Their decision to abstain was greeted with
some annoyance by the SPD's allies in Prussia. For instance,
Tremonia, the Center paper in Dortmund, wrote that *"the
largest party in the government was openly confessing its own cow-
ardice"* in refusing to vote for the settlement.[123] Pressure from
the radical left outside the party was also very strong,[124] but

[119] *Jahrbuch der Deutschen Sozialdemokratie... 1926,* p. 10; an appeal from the Executive Board "To the Party" printed in *Vorwärts,* 13 Oct. 1926 (Nr. 482).

[120] The most detailed report of the *Fraktion*'s deliberations was made by representative Heilmann to a meeting of party functionaries on 26 October. *Vorwärts,* 27
Oct. 1926 (Nr. 506).

[121] Ibid., 7 Oct. 1926 (Nr. 472).

[122] Ibid., 27 Oct. 1926 (Nr. 506). Heilmann defined his party's position as follows:
"Not because we are in any way in agreement with the terms of the settlement...
but simply because the Prussian government considers the settlement the only way
to prevent still greater damage to the state's finances, we do not intend to interfere
with its passage." Prussia. Landtag. *Sitzungsberichte,* 10 (11 Oct. 1926): 14284.

[123] 8 Oct. 1926 (Nr. 276), emphasis in original; *Vossische Zeitung,* 14 Oct. 1926 (Nr.
246).

[124] The unattached left intellectuals who wrote for the *Weltbühne* were extremely
angry over the new settlement. Arthur Seehof in an article entitled "15,000,000=0?"

more seriously, dissatisfied groups inside the SPD did not hesitate to challenge the apparent course of party policy. A conference of party and trade union functionaries in the Greater Berlin area *unanimously* passed a resolution on 11 October, calling on the *Landtag* delegation to "do all in its power to prevent the acceptance" of the settlement. The delegation reexamined its earlier decision to abstain after learning of this resolution.[125] Leading left-wing Social Democrats took advantage of the militant mood of the organized party workers to press for a clear rejection of the settlement. The fact that a special recruiting week had already been scheduled to start just a few days after the vote in the *Landtag* undoubtedly encouraged many Social Democrats to rebel against what appeared to them an unsuitable compromise of party principles.[126] Braun confessed in his memoirs that he had had "to employ his entire [store of] authority, even to the point of threatening to resign" in order to prevent the delegation from making a clearly irresponsible decision.[127] In order to minimize discontent, the leaders of the *Landtag* delegation notified members absolutely opposed to the settlement that they could absent themselves from the floor of the house, if they so chose. Only a few did so.[128]

The *Landtag* approved the settlement on 12 October 1926.[129] There was little actual debate during the two sessions devoted to the question. The Communist delegation, following the leadership of Wilhelm Pieck, raised a series of points

called upon "the Kuczynski-Committee, Communists, and Republicans [to] take the lead! the Social Democratic workers will follow." *Weltbühne*, 22 (Nr. 42, 19 Oct. 1926): 607. Also, "Morus" (i.e., Richard Lewinsohn), "Hohenzollern-Beute," ibid., (Nr. 41, 12 Oct. 1926): 577–81, and the issues throughout November and December in which the editors tried to encourage a new initiative and referendum movement. Schiffers, pp. 214–15.

[125] *Vorwärts*, 12 Oct. (Nr. 480) and 27 Oct. 1926 (Nr. 506).

[126] In a special statement published in *Vorwärts*, 13 Oct. 1926 (Nr. 482), the SPD's Executive Board urged all members to keep the recruiting week in mind and warned that the Communists would do all in their power to disrupt it. The Executive Board made a point of emphasizing that "there have always been differences of opinion [within the party] over parliamentary tactics and there always will be. [These differences] have never hindered the powerful growth of the Social Democratic Party. *They have never kept any comrade from fulfilling his duty toward the party*" (emphasis in original). Also see the preface to the pamphlet, *Referenten- und Diskussionsmaterial zur Sozialdemokratischen Werbewoche (16.–24. Oktober, 1926)*.

[127] Braun, p. 216; and more generally on the difficulties of his position, ibid., pp. 139–40, 184–85; Schulze, pp. 508–9.

[128] Heilmann's report, *Vorwärts*, 27 Oct. 1926 (Nr. 506).

[129] *Vossische Zeitung*, 13 Oct. 1926 (Nr. 245); *Kölnische Zeitung*, 13 Oct. (Nr. 764) and 16 Oct. 1926 (Nr. 771).

of order in an attempt to delay consideration of the settlement.[130] When these parliamentary maneuvers failed, the delegation tried, in vain, to force votes of no confidence against the responsible ministers. The Communists then resorted to still more disruptive methods. They shouted down speakers, packed the gallery with noisy sympathizers, threw objects at the rostrum, and despite the ejection of many of their members, forced the presiding officers to suspend debate a number of times to restore order. Their verbal assaults were directed at least as much against the Social Democratic Party as the Hohenzollern family and the settlement.[131] Indeed, one Communist and a Social Democrat began a fist fight on the floor of the house.[132] The deliberate obstruction reached its high point immediately prior to the voting. The stenographic account is remarkably vivid:

> Vice President Garnich:—"We come now to the vote." (Noise, whistling and catcalls from the Communists. "Let order be restored!"—a shout from the Communists directed at the parliamentary reporter Metzenthin: "You rat *(Lump)*, haven't you denounced enough people yet?!")
>
> —"I eject the delegate Kollwitz from the hall." (Renewed noise and yelling from the Communists: "Finks!" A Communist delegate throws some parliamentary papers at Vice-President Garnich; Shouts: "Out, out!"—Delegate Jendrosch physically threatens the reporter Metzenthin—Shouts from the right: "Police!"—The presiding officer gavels for order—The Communist delegates force their way up to the rostrum; some of them try to climb up on the podium. A Communist delegate . . . throws the files containing the [printed] order of the day at the presiding officer. The parliamentary reporters and Vice-President Garnich leave their seats. . . .)[133]

It was nearly an hour before the assembly was able to resume its business.

After the vote, Pieck justified the KPD's tactics. ". . .[B]y our obstruction we have accomplished [what we set out to prove]. We made you use open force . . . and thereby publicly

---

[130] Prussia. Landtag. *Sitzungsberichte,* 10 (11 and 12 Oct. 1926): 14255–60, 14266–70, 14283–88, 14399–404.

[131] Bartels, ibid., pp. 14270–80, 14312–19; and the unsigned article in *Vorwärts* replying to these attacks, 12 Oct. 1926 (Nr. 480).

[132] *Vossische Zeitung,* 13 Oct. 1926 (Nr. 245).

[133] Prussia. Landtag. *Sitzungsberichte,* 10 (12 Oct. 1926): 14400.

reveal that any outrage against the minority is acceptable [if it enables you to give] the Hohenzollerns this gift." [134]

The disorderly behavior of the Communist *Landtag* delegation had the full approval of the KPD's leadership; by contrast many rank-and-file Social Democrats, bitterly angry over the settlement, felt compelled to demonstrate their indignation against the decisions made by their own party in various ways short of violence. Some tore up their membership cards and joined the KPD.[135] Many more cancelled their subscriptions to *Vorwärts*.[136] Others, many of them minor functionaries who normally played an indispensable part as links between the party's political leadership and the ordinary workers in the factories and residential districts, refused to cooperate during what had been intended to be a major recruiting campaign. The recruiting week was a failure.[137] The official report by the party organization in Berlin subsequently admitted that "in almost all sections there were vigorous disputes. Rarely has the party had to face such a trial," but then the report reached an optimistic conclusion: ". . . it is a sign of the party's inner strength that it survived this test so surprisingly well." [138]

Otto Braun told the delegates at the 1927 party convention that he had stated during the height of the intra-party controversy that the excitement of the rank-and-file was the result

[134] Ibid., p. 14404. Likewise, his article, "Unser Obstruktions-Kampf gegen den Hohenzollernblock," *Rote Fahne*, 17 Oct. 1926.

[135] Ibid., 16 Oct. 1926. On 19 Oct. *Rote Fahne* reported that a man who had been a member of the SPD since 1884 came to the KPD headquarters in Essen to change his party membership.

[136] *Vorwärts* sent out form letters to angry subscribers stating that differences of opinion had always existed in the party but that "earlier it had always been unthinkable that [anyone] would cancel his subscription to the party organ out of anger over tactical questions relating to Social Democratic policy!" reprinted in *Rote Fahne*, 14 Nov. 1926.

[137] On the eve of the recruiting week, *Vorwärts* exhorted, "Now it is necessary *to learn from the mistakes of the past* and to seek practical successes by practical routes. [Hard] work and energy are needed, not [intra-party] fighting and scandal." 15 Oct. 1926 (Nr. 487), emphasis in original. Rosenfeld, Hildebrandt and Geiger all claimed that the Hohenzollern settlement had had disastrous effects on recruitment. See the discussion at the Berlin functionaries' conference on 26 Oct. Ibid., 27 Oct. 1926 (Nr. 506). *Rote Fahne* quoted with pleasure from a confidential SPD report: "The most urgent appeals and requests to responsible functionaries for their cooperation in organizing the recruiting work were without effect, so much so, one wondered if *these were really party members one was dealing with.*" 16 Oct. 1926, emphasis in original.

[138] Bezirksverband Berlin der SPD. *Jahresbericht 1925/1926* (Berlin, 1927), pp. 10–13.

CRISIS OF THE WEIMAR REPUBLIC

310

of a temporary mood and "in two or three weeks no one will even be talking about the settlement." [139] He claimed he had been right. However, his assertion, if not exactly false, was certainly an overstatement. Two weeks after the ratification of the Hohenzollern settlement, the Social Democratic functionaries in Berlin were still in no mood to condone the decisions of the *Landtag* delegation and the party leaders. After an active discussion in which left socialists such as Rosenfeld, Hoffmann, Künstler, and Hildebrandt expressed their opinions very bluntly, the functionaries passed a resolution declaring that "the abstention of the *Landtag* delegation ran contrary to the views of the great majority of the Berlin party members" and regretted that the delegation had taken such a stand.[140]

The fact that the party leaders avoided calling a national party convention in 1926 also tends to belie Braun's assertion that the discontent inside the party was not very serious.[141] At any rate, tempers exploded when the issue came up at the 1927 convention. Kurt Rosenfeld questioned the way the matter had been handled in order to illustrate the inadequacy of the party's existing policies which he thought much more favorable to compromise than to the class struggle. He declared that it had been a great joy to work during the initiative and referendum campaign because "the entire proletariat rallied together." [142] The acceptance of the Hohenzollern settlement by the Prussian government destroyed this spirit; indeed, he said, "it was felt as a betrayal *(Dolchstoss)* of the front that had worked together against the princes." [143] This decision cost the party the gains it had made among Center Party followers and other discontented groups through its activities in support of the referendum. "We should learn the lesson that there are battles that one must carry through

---

[139] *Sozialdemokratischer Parteitag 1927*, p. 74.

[140] Hildebrandt stated that "the princely settlement should have been stopped even at the cost of withdrawing our party from the government." Künstler and Hoffmann criticized *Vorwärts* for editorial decisions that discriminated against those who advocated a firm line against the settlement. *Vorwärts*, 27 Oct. 1926 (Nr. 506).

[141] Hunt, *German Social Democracy*, p. 47. Interestingly enough, the leaders of the Center Party likewise decided against holding a national party convention in 1926, "for a number of important reasons." *Germania*, 1 Nov. 1926 (Nr. 509).

[142] *Sozialdemokratischer Parteitag 1927*, p. 62.

[143] Ibid., p. 63. Wilke (Stettin) stated that the party membership had become very excited over the issue and did not settle down right after the settlement was concluded. Ibid., p. 79.

to the end without compromise." [144] Otto Braun resolutely defended what had been done: "For me, the Hohenzollern settlement is finished [business]." [145] He charged that Rosenfeld himself was not free from inconsistency on the question of the former royal properties, and from that point the debate degenerated as each man, with undisguised animosity, accused the other of falsely reporting discussions in the Prussian Provisional Government in 1918–19.[146]

It can scarcely be doubted that great discontent existed at various levels of the Social Democratic Party after the conclusion of the Prussian-Hohenzollern settlement. Rosenfeld and other prominent left-wing socialists not only expressed this discontent, but tried to organize and channel it against the established party leadership. Their strong advocacy of the initiative and referendum campaign and, after the failure of the referendum, their refusal to abandon the uncompromising demand for total confiscation must be viewed as part of their persistent efforts to bring about a redirection of party policies.[147] Their rigid adherence to the idea of confiscation was almost certainly determined as much by tactical considerations as was the desire of Otto Braun and the party's Executive Board to accept a negotiated settlement once both the referendum and the Compromise Bill had failed. The actions of Rosenfeld and his friends throughout this controversy aimed at driving a wedge between the SPD and the middle-class parties. In this respect they were not entirely unsuccessful, although they failed to wrest control of the party away from the dominant reformist leadership. In a general sense, Otto Braun was correct in saying that most of the dissatisfaction in 1926 was only a temporary mood. No serious defections occurred as a result of the anger over the Hohenzollern settlement; the old, recognized leaders retained control of the party (although not without some finessing); and the left-wing socialist opposition remained as a vocal minority inside the party until 1931.

Throughout the twenties, many critics charged that the Social Democratic leadership stifled intra-party democracy

[144] Ibid., p. 63. Rosenfeld also complained that as a representative from Thuringia he knew how the conclusion of the Prussian settlement left that small state in very grave difficulties.
[145] Ibid., p. 75.
[146] Ibid., pp. 74–75, 94–98, 98–100, 101. See above, Chapter II, p. 41.
[147] See above, Chapter IV, pp. 105–111, 125–29.

through manipulation and heavy reliance on party discipline, and were so successful at this that they felt free to pursue their chosen policies in open disregard of the sentiments of their followers. Similar charges can still be encountered in recent historical studies. Yet, the actual behavior of the SPD's leaders during the controversy over the princes' properties suggests that such charges are not entirely valid. Time and again during the course of the controversy, the SPD's policy-makers wavered, even though most of them knew that ultimately the party would have to accept some kind of a moderate solution. The party leaders were eager to avoid unpopular decisions that would expose them to outbursts of criticism within the party, and above all were unwilling to do anything that might precipitate a new party split. Perhaps it might be argued that the Social Democratic leadership paid too much, not too little, attention to the opinions of more radical elements inside the party.

Although the left socialists were unable to force the party leaders to adopt a policy fully consistent with the doctrines of "class struggle," their pressure, reinforced by a ground swell of public opinion and the cleverly developed tactics of the KPD, unquestionably encouraged the party leadership to seek a solution through half-measures. Between October, 1925, and October, 1926, the responsible policy-making bodies of the Social Democratic Party decided against participation in a Great Coalition government, but agreed to give minority governments of the middle the support (toleration) necessary to permit them to function; they accepted the Communist bid to sponsor the referendum, yet kept open the possibility of accepting "suitable" Reichstag legislation; party experts examined the main features of the Compromise Bill very closely and suggested numerous amendments, but avoided commitments to supply the parliamentary help needed to ensure the passage of the bill; and, in the end, the *Landtag* delegation decided to permit the ratification of the Hohenzollern settlement, but refused to vote for it. Reliance on complicated half-measures had become a regular habit with the party's leaders. Yet, through the overuse of such tactics, they gained a reputation for doubtful reliability with many politicians among the middle parties.

In November 1926, the question of the princely settlements

briefly emerged in the Reichstag once again.[148] A Catholic
trade unionist, Joseph Ersing, compared the behavior of the
Social Democratic *Landtag* delegation with the divided vote
of the DNVP's Reichstag delegation on the Dawes Plan.[149]
Eduard Bernstein exclaimed, "That was entirely different!"
Ersing then retorted: "Different in your opinion. In our opinion, political parties have to have the courage to take the
appropriate steps if they acknowledge the necessities of politics." He said the Social Democrats should have recognized
that complete confiscation was impossible, and should have
avoided causing so much confusion among the German people: "I believe that even you will come to realize that . . . it
is . . . possible to pose as the champion of the people *(Volks-
triumphator)* for several weeks or even months, but that in the
long run you cannot conduct successful politics that way." [150]
A few months later, Stresemann explained to a correspondent
why it had not been possible to form a Great Coalition. "It
does not do any good to have the Social Democratic General
Staff on one's side if at a decisive moment the Officer Corps
revolts." [151]

In January 1927, the *Frankfurter Zeitung,* long an advocate
of the Great Coalition, castigated the apparent aimlessness
of the SPD's actions during the newest cabinet crisis. It reflected,

> It seems unbelievable that the Social Democrats have had no
> definite goal. But unfortunately that is just what we have learned

---

[148] Primarily as a result of KPD attempts to force a discussion of some especially
controversial aspects of the Prussian settlement. Reichstag. *Drucksache.* Nr. 2589,
and *Verhandlungen,* 391 (3 Nov. 1926): 7871–72.

[149] Ibid. (10 Nov. 1926), p. 8005.

[150] Idem. Karl Anton Schulte observed that *"on this question the Social Democrats
showed an uncertainty without equal and revealed an unusual lack of responsible political insight
and clarity concerning objectives"* in *Politisches Jahrbuch 1926,* p. 530, emphasis in original.
Heinrich Köhler was later to state that he favored "drawing the DNVP into the
government" in 1927 because of the SPD's refusal to act responsibly. "In recent
years it had become steadily clearer to me that the Social Democrats lacked the
most important requirements for leading the state. The statement made by their
party chairman Wels that 'It is better to make mistakes with the masses, than govern
against the will of the masses,' shocked me. That was not based on any serious
consideration of the state's needs; it meant a so-called kind of governing according
to concerns of the moment. Moreover, the national Center Party needed to be freed
from an ideological dependence on the left. It had to retain the possibility of forming
majorities on either side." Köhler, pp. 191–92.

[151] Quoted by Becker, *Geschichte in Wissenschaft und Unterricht,* 17: 211.

to expect for over a year now. During this entire period, the Social Democrats have, in reality, had no policy. They are without leadership, without direction, fluctuating between actual opportunism and radicalism that exists in mock actions but not in reality. Thus, in practice, they exclude themselves [from responsibility]. The end result is . . . a fateful weakening of the entire left. And this weakening of the entire left is no longer just a matter of concern for the Social Democrats. . . .[152]

The advantage of hindsight gives us added reasons for admiring this editorial writer's perception. The indecisiveness of the SPD during the mid-twenties did, in fact, contribute to the steady undermining of the republican left in Germany.[153] To be sure, the SPD repeatedly proclaimed its belief in the Republic. Its official representatives participated in innumerable ceremonial observances in sincere, if usually rather uninspired, demonstrations of this belief. Yet, the persistence of pre-war "oppositional" attitudes at nearly all levels of the party, and the uncertainty of the leaders when confronted by a conflict between their own judgment as practical politicians experienced in dealing with other parties, and their sense of loyalty to the special values, the ideals, and the unity of the party as a social movement, weakened the ability of the SPD to take actions that would not merely have "defended" but effectively strengthened republican values and institutions.

After all, the Social Democratic Party was the largest party in Germany throughout the 1920s. When it refused to offer leadership on domestic issues at the national level, its sometime allies among the middle-class parties were unlikely to do so. On nearly every occasion when foreign affairs were not involved, the People's Party's Reichstag and Prussian Landtag delegations manifested a clear preference for alliance with "responsible" Nationalists. The Democratic Party was too weak to command much respect or compel cooperation.

[152] 6 Jan. 1927, quoted by Schreiber, in Politisches Jahrbuch 1927/28, p. 81, note 2. Erich Koch-Weser, who as much as anyone had tried to draw the Social Democrats into open cooperation with the republican middle parties, did not soon forget how the SPD had behaved during the controversy over the princely property settlements. See his remarks to the DDP Executive Board, 12 Feb. 1927. Demokratischer Zeitungsdienst, 13 Feb. 1927, in the DDP Papers, reel 37, folder 730, and to the party's Advisory Committee, 29 April 1928. Democratischer Zeitungsdienst, 30 April 1928; Chanady, Historical Studies. Australia and New Zealand, 12: 493, 498.
[153] See the critical assessments of the SPD's behavior by Stürmer, pp. 161–62, and Eyck, 2: 91–93.

The Center Party, although much stronger than the DDP, was unlikely to sponsor major new legislation outside its realm of special concerns regarding school and religious affairs. Alarmed by clear indications of increasingly serious differences among the very mixed social and economic groups that traditionally supported the party, the Center's leaders, in their own way not unlike the leaders of the SPD, tried to satisfy all sides by a middle-of-the-road policy scarcely designed to encourage innovation. It is true that many leading Social Democrats advocated active, open participation in the national government, but they *did not insist* on it. The leaders of the SPD settled all too readily for arrangements that permitted them to make their party's influence felt "behind the scenes" and let them respond to policies and legislative proposals made by others, rather than trying to establish policy themselves. This caution was more than a method of tactics; it was rooted in attitudes so basic and pervasive they were accepted as self-evident, and not usually even articulated.

Social Democratic policy-makers quite clearly believed that time itself worked toward the solution of problems. They showed a strong preference for deferring action on complicated political questions. They apparently thought that many problems would resolve themselves gradually, that is, that administrative actions, or piecemeal legislation at the state level could substitute for a single, uniform but inevitably much more controversial decision by the national government or legislature.[154] The belief that Germany's political life was still "temporarily" unsettled as a result of the lost war likewise encouraged the postponement of action on many serious domestic problems. It appears to have been a generally held assumption that sooner or later public opinion would calm down, party relationships stabilize and, thus, permit the serious, constructive handling of questions that could be discussed at present only for propagandistic effect, if at all. In the meantime, many politicians thought it best to let sleeping dogs lie. Such attitudes were by no means limited to the politicians of any one party, but widespread acceptance of these attitudes by Social Democrats greatly curtailed the party's ability to match its basic commitment to change with

[154] Anthony Glees, "Albert C. Grzesinski and the Politics of Prussia, 1926–1930," *English Historical Review*, 89 (Nr. 353, Oct. 1974): 814–34.

imaginative actions that went beyond the level of election-eering propaganda.

The belief that time was on their side prevented the leaders of the Social Democratic Party (and others) from recognizing what we now see only too well, namely, that many domestic problems were growing more complicated as time passed and less capable of resolution within a democratic framework. Moreover, the Social Democratic Party seems to have found it very difficult to understand the crucial importance of *timing* in making major decisions. By proceeding cautiously, by adopting temporary positions primarily to satisfy potential critics within the party and only later, after much tacking, announcing a definite, final course, the SPD leaders allowed opportunities to slip away at an early stage of events that could never be regained later. The party simply did not have the same freedom of choice at a late stage of a controversy, nor could its decisions then affect the decisions of other parties with the same impact as they might have done earlier.

Passage of time allowed other parties a chance to seize the political initiative and formulate the scope of the subsequent controversy according to their own partisan interests or, at the very least, saw them adopt fixed "official" positions that, once announced, were very hard to alter. Yet, on occasion after occasion, the decisions actually taken by the Social Democratic leadership express an inherent belief that there were advantages to be gained from delay, and show little or no recognition that a cautious approach also involved serious risks.

A wider conception of political leadership might have recognized that the SPD's effectiveness could have been enhanced in other ways than merely through attempts to maintain the unity, strength, and appeal of the party itself. The Communists regularly accused the Social Democratic leadership of "betraying" the proletariat; yet surely men such as Erich Koch-Weser or Joseph Wirth, who wanted to cooperate with the SPD in the mid-twenties, had rather stronger grounds for feeling "betrayed" by the SPD's sudden reversals of policy and persistent unwillingness to accept responsibility than did the leaders of the KPD.[155] An appropriately for-

---

[155] Wirth wrote an open letter to Professor Lujo Brentano defending his belief in the need for cooperation by the republican parties but at the same time attacking the propagandistic attitudes so prevalent in the SPD. *Tremonia*, 25 Sept. 1926 (Nr. 263).

mulated policy, consistently applied, might well have expanded the effective influence of the SPD by strengthening the republican elements within the Democratic and Center parties.

The SPD's participation in the initiative and referendum campaign of 1926 is a case in point. Social Democratic policymakers considered whether or not a referendum was feasible in the fall of 1925, but for various "weighty" reasons they decided to keep the idea in reserve while they waited to see what kind of legislation the other parties in the Reichstag were willing to enact. The Communists, however, did not wait until the Reichstag had "failed." As soon as they ascertained that there was unusually great public indignation over the princes' claims, they arranged to start initiative proceedings deliberately formulated to suit their own partisan purposes and embarrass or enrage all other parties. The leaders of the SPD soon felt compelled to accept the Communist bid to co-sponsor the initiative and referendum even though this meant a major reversal of previous policy and ran counter to their sustained efforts to maintain at least tacit cooperation with the parties of the middle. With little or no preparation, they suddenly committed themselves to fight publicly for a proposal that they neither had helped formulate, nor truly approved. There is no need to summarize the rest of the details. For some time, the Social Democrats believed that they still possessed freedom of action, but once they had surrendered the advantages of timing, the free choice of their own partners, and the formulation of at least the rough outlines of an eventual solution for the controversy, they had lost their most valuable options. Ultimately, they were forced to make some very unpalatable choices. They certainly never regained a chance for offering distinctive leadership on this issue.

However, what if the Social Democratic Party had made certain other decisions? Historical conjecture can be dangerous, but it is necessary if we are to judge whether any alternatives existed other than the course actually taken.[156] What would have happened if the Social Democrats had an-

---

[156] Conjecture regarding possible alternatives to the actual outcome of the revolution of 1918/19 has been characteristic of the recent historical literature on the *Räte*. Wolfgang J. Mommsen, "Die deutsche Revolution, 1918–1920. Politische Revolution und soziale Protestbewegung," *Geschichte und Gesellschaft*, 4 (Nr. 3, 1978): 362–91.

nounced that they were going to sponsor an initiative and referendum in November or early December 1925, on a proposal to confiscate the former rulers' properties, while granting a moderate compensation? Such a proposal would have been in accord with many previous statements by Social Democratic spokesmen regarding the proper solution of this complicated issue. At the same time, this would have been a very suitable occasion for inaugurating the use of the as yet untried democratic institution of direct legislation by the people.

The Democrats would have surely supported such an initiative and referendum. The leaders of the Center might have hesitated for a time, but the intensity of popular feeling in all but the most traditionally conservative segments of the party would probably have caused them to give their approval. The parties of the right and right center would not have liked the proposed confiscation, even though it allowed for compensation, but they would have been hard put to prevent large numbers of their regular followers, still resentful over the effects of the war and the inflation, from voting for such a referendum. It was easy for the defenders of the princes to argue that the actual SPD-KPD referendum proposal was the first step toward Bolshevism and would endanger all rights of property; this argument would have been much less convincing if the proposal had permitted a moderate compensation. The parties of the right and right center might have found it difficult to maintain a common policy of opposition to such a referendum.

On the other hand, by sponsoring such a proposal, the SPD would have exposed itself to intensely harsh and bitter criticism from the KPD and from some of its own party followers. The Communists might well have tried to start an alternative initiative and referendum for total confiscation without compensation. Yet, even when supplemented by groups such as the Kuczynski Committee, the KPD's financial and organizational resources were limited; it might not have been able to sustain an elaborate campaign. In any case, if the SPD and its Weimar Coalition allies had announced the start of initiative proceedings on a moderate proposal, any subsequent Communist efforts to sponsor a separate initiative and referendum would have worsened its reputation, already established during the Hindenburg election, for spoiling the chances for a victory for the republican left by narrow and shortsighted partisanship.

The most serious trouble for the Social Democratic leadership would have come from the persistent left-wing critics within the party. This faction's consistent rejection of close ties with the middle-class parties would have led them to condemn the party leaders' actions. There would have been serious debate within the party; the left socialists surely would have attempted to stimulate resistance by appeals to the "working class" values of the party's organized members. In some key districts, they might even have been able to obtain resolutions critical of announced party policy. However, in such a situation the party leadership did not have to be paralyzed by fear of a ruinous intra-party conflict. Although many rank-and-file Social Democrats were uncertain whether they approved of collaboration with middle-class parties "in principle," the success of the *Reichsbanner* reveals that many of these same men were perfectly willing to work with members of the two other Weimar Coalition parties when such collaboration took a visibly practical form. It seems a safe conjecture to say that an initiative and referendum campaign presented as a joint republican cause would have been accepted by the bulk of the Social Democrats.

Rather than retreating in the face of criticism from inside the party, the leaders of the SPD should have been willing to explain at length, if necessary, the reasons for the decisions they made. An open defense of their actual judgment that cooperation with the middle-class republican parties was essential, and that some kind of moderate compensation for the princes was justifiable, should have been attempted. Certainly it would have been more forthright, and, probably more effective, than what the Social Democratic parliamentarians actually did, namely, to say one thing for popular effect while simultaneously pursuing quite a different set of objectives when negotiating with the other parties. There was undeniably a certain lack of openness, of candor, in the practice of the Social Democratic leaders. This deviousness was not the result of "hypocrisy," nor had the SPD's policy-makers become "bourgeois" in their thinking and attitudes. On the one hand, they themselves felt great loyalty to the party and to the basic values of the working class. Yet, they also knew full well that the realities of politics in Germany in the 1920s required many compromises. The party leaders feared that their followers' natural response would be to reject any compromise as inherently unsatisfactory. They also doubted the rank-and-file's capacity to understand the technical aspects involved in most legislation. Distrusting their followers' ability to make informed judgments, the Social Democratic leaders fell into the more or less devious habits we have described. Basically, they seem to have assumed that their followers' opinions were, for all intents and purposes, fixed. As a result, they underestimated their own ability to create the support they needed. Moreover, doubts regarding the continued loyalty of the organized party members made the SPD's leaders timid and unsure in their formulation of policy. Yet, in fact, even during the crisis years of 1930–33, the bulk of the Social Democratic voters remained true to the party. The SPD suffered some decline, but did not disintegrate in the way the DDP and DVP did.[157] Given the advantage of hindsight, it seems apparent that the Social Democratic leaders could have relied on the deep organizational loyalty of their followers more than they did. Instead, they feared to subject it to tests that involved some risk.

In a variety of respects, not alone because of the emergence of the controversy over the princes' property claims, the late fall of 1925 was an excellent occasion for collaboration among the republican parties. Yet the possibilities that existed were not turned to advantage for the same reasons that the SPD had rejected the formation of a Great Coalition government during the Christmas crisis of 1925–26: hesitation to do anything that might disrupt party unity and a belief that a more favorable moment would come. A larger and more positive conception of political leadership might have recognized that the party itself could have been strengthened by decisive actions that also strengthened its own most dependable allies.

In the preceding pages we have employed conjecture to describe a possible alternative to the course of action actually taken in 1925–26 and, thereby, sought to emphasize the intangible elements of timing, judgment, and habit that prevented the SPD from exploiting more effectively the aroused state of public opinion during the properties controversy. Contrasting the actual referendum with a hypothetical alternative also serves to remind us that political relationships were really rather fluid in the mid-1920s. Political leaders knew that the instability in the relations of the major parties

---

[157] Milatz in *Das Ende der Parteien*, pp. 746–47, 769, 776–77, 786–87, 792.

with one another influenced and, in turn, was influenced by the balance of interest groups and ideological groupings inside each party. Fearful of inadvertently unleashing a sudden shift of party ties, they tended to act cautiously, sounding their way before advancing. More imagination might have enabled them to take advantage of this fluidity to improve their overall political position as well as that of the Republic.

A clear reaffirmation of republican goals was needed in 1925–26. Every cabinet crisis, every piece of major legislation that was blocked in the Reichstag, or had to be enacted by use of the Emergency Powers of the president,[158] furthered the growing decline of confidence in republican institutions. In particular, a clear demonstration of positive, purposeful action was needed, rather than routine exhortations. To be convincing, such actions must be undertaken by the political parties. Associations of well-intentioned individuals like Joseph Wirth and his collaborators on the journal, *Deutsche Republik*, which was founded the fall of 1926, were no adequate substitute.[159] Over and above the need to strengthen confidence in democratic institutions, it was necessary for the republican parties to prove that they were capable of instigating constructive reforms that large numbers of Germans, regardless of party affiliation, would accept as desirable. Given the distribution of party strength in the Reichstag this was not easy for them to do. The three Weimar parties, plus the DVP, cooperated regularly on matters relating to foreign affairs, but they themselves considered this an unavoidable duty and knew full well that they gained no wide public respect for doing so. The SPD, DDP, and Center almost always could agree on opposing "arbitrary" governmental actions reminiscent of pre-1918 conditions—the Flag Decree or the Seeckt affair, for instance—but there was nothing new in this. The sponsoring of the first nationwide referendum in German history on a proposal calculated to mobilize the

---

[158] In this connection it may be worth mentioning that the well-known legal scholar Walter Jellinek suggested the use of Article 48 to enact the government's bill should it fail to obtain the needed two-thirds majority in the Reichstag. *Vossische Zeitung*, 29 June 1926 (Nr. 154). Ernst Eckstein promptly rejected this idea as unrealistic, but also insisted it was wrong in principle. "We should not declare parliamentary techniques bankrupt at every occasion and call for an Article 48-dictatorship just because we still have not fully mastered parliamentary techniques." Ibid., 2 July 1926 (Nr. 157).

[159] Becker, *Zeitschrift für die Geschichte des Oberrheins*, 109: 369–71; Buchheim, pp. 338–39; and Köhler, pp. 182–86.

support of a large proportion of the politically active citizens would have been an important practical demonstration of republican cooperation and leadership.[160] The use of the plebiscitary procedures allowed by the constitution did not necessarily need to acerbate the latent conflict between such forms and the functioning of parliamentary institutions. The success of such a referendum—or even its failure, if the "yes" votes exceeded the sponsoring parties' usual election turnout—would have encouraged further parliamentary and election cooperation by the three republican parties.

We have so far focused our attention on the indecisive or unclear way in which the Social Democratic leaders responded at times when confronted with major policy choices. Concentration on the decisions of one party aids clarity of exposition, yet the special emphasis given the decisions of the SPD can also be justified on the grounds that as the largest of all the parties there was a natural expectation that it should give a sense of direction to national politics. When the SPD renounced opportunities for offering badly needed leadership, the weaker parties of the middle, or an "unpolitical" chancellor such as Hans Luther, were unlikely to do so.

Yet it would be wrong to single out the Social Democratic leaders for blame. They were by no means the only politicians who were hesitant, overcautious, and fearful of provoking discord among their followers. Indeed, if their conduct had not been so typical of the way in which the leaders of nearly all the parties in Germany acted when forced to make unpleasant choices, it would hardly have been worthwhile to examine their behavior in such detail.[161]

In particular, we have had occasion to see how uncertainly Center and Democratic leaders acted when their officially announced policies failed to find automatic acceptance. We have also described what pains these party leaders took to

---

[160] After the failure of the referendum von Ossietzky wrote in *Die Weltbühne* criticizing the choice of "the foolish word 'confiscation.' A political success was needed, not a demonstration. If only the Kuczynski Committee had found a better formulation, the referendum would have passed with a majority of five or perhaps even ten million. The great storm is over; German everyday [life] is back again," quoted by Könnemann, *Wissenschaftliche Zeitschrift der Universität Halle-Wittenberg*, 7: 557. Könnemann, however, does not agree that a compromise formula would have guaranteed a victory.

[161] See Haungs's conclusions regarding the failure of the parties to establish true parliamentary government, pp. 285–94.

stress their parties' distinctive, separate identities. In both parties, and especially in the Center, there would have been much resistance to any close or prolonged cooperation with the SPD. Yet, the gradual shift toward the right inside the Center that became evident in 1928–29 with the election of Ludwig Kaas as party chairman and Heinrich Brüning as head of the Reichstag delegation was still tentative in 1925–26.[162] An impressive demonstration of republican solidarity might have restored general credibility to the policies advocated by Wirth and his friends.

Whether or not this conjecture is valid, it is quite certain that the actual failure of the Compromise Bill was due to the inability of the major parties to establish a clearly defined orientation either to the right or the left in German domestic politics. Reliance on "changing majorities" was entirely inadequate. If anything, this policy impeded rather than encouraged parliamentary compromise.

One thing is undeniably clear. The parties of the right and right center on the one hand, and the Communists on the other, showed much greater resourcefulness throughout the properties controversy than did the three main republican parties. This is particularly true of their responses to the new and untried institution of the initiative and referendum.

The reaction of the DNVP and those parties and organizations that accepted its leadership on this issue was remarkably clear and consistent. From the start, they found ways of enveloping their support of the princes' claims in widely acceptable slogans regarding the sanctity of property rights and the need to defend moral values. They never wavered in their opposition to confiscation, or in their denunciation of the abuse of initiative and referendum proceedings. Yet their response was by no means the blind "Bolshevik scare" reaction that one might assume it was from reading many of the speeches or the pamphlets issued during the course of the campaign. As soon as the results of the initiative showed the extent of popular dissatisfaction with the princes' claims, the parties and other organizations on the right and right-of-center realized that it was essential to abandon separate party stances in order to combat the referendum proposal effectively. Their previously successful cooperation during the presidential elections of 1925

[162] Morsey in *The Path to Dictatorship*, pp. 70–71.

undoubtedly facilitated this renewed merger of forces. By contrast, the Democrats and the Center Party seem to have never quite recognized that it was virtually impossible to maintain distinct party positions in a referendum situation. Right down until the final weeks before the referendum, these two parties kept trying to devise alternatives that would free them from having to choose either of the undesirable alternatives offered by the referendum. The Nationalists and the other groups that coordinated their policies through the "Working Committee" showed particular shrewdness in utilizing the legal requirements for the conduct of a referendum to ensure the ineffectiveness of a democratic institution potentially very dangerous to their vested interests. The order that their followers abstain rather than vote "no" made possible various forms of electoral intimidation and thus substantially reduced the total "yes" vote.

The defeat of the referendum of 20 June and the subsequent failure of the Reichstag to pass any regulatory legislation must have given the supporters of the princes much satisfaction, even if mixed with some disappointment. The tactics of the Nationalists and their allies had succeeded in protecting the former ruling families from the loss of their property,[163] but the defeat of the referendum was no victory for monarchism. Almost half of the politically active Germans had voted "yes," without regard for the "immortal services" of their princes; nor had they worried that they thereby broke old ties of "loyalty." We can agree with Manfred Dörr that

the action by the left caused great damage to the idea of monarchism and forced the party [the DNVP] to face up to the fact that the restoration of a monarchical form of government was no longer possible by legal means, [a fact previously] never admitted by many Nationalists.[164]

At the opposite end of the political spectrum, the Communists showed equally great adaptability and cleverness throughout the properties controversy, especially in exploiting the untried institution of the initiative and referendum very much to their own advantage. From the start, the KPD's

---

[163] Not long after the conclusion of the Hohenzollern settlement Herr von Berg resigned as the legal representative for the Hohenzollern family. The press speculated that the former kaiser had been displeased with the terms of the settlement, but the true cause was von Berg's distrust of another of the kaiser's financial advisers. *Vorwärts,* 10 Dec. (Nr. 581) and 21 Dec. 1926 (Nr. 599); Ilsemann, 2: 42.

[164] Dörr, p. 240, and similar observations by Ilsemann, 2: 42, and Fischer, p. 523.

leaders made clear their stand regarding both the referendum proposal and the Reichstag legislation. Thereafter, they never deviated. To be sure, this consistency was possible because the Communist leaders were not greatly concerned with finding a solution for the difficult problems raised by the properties dispute. They never really disguised the fact that their chief interests in heightening the controversy were distinctly partisan: the successful application of United Front tactics, the discrediting of the Social Democratic leadership and parliamentary practices, and the strengthening of the KPD organizationally. Even so, the policies they established were much clearer, and surely much more comprehensible to their followers, than the two-fold course of action adopted by the Social Democratic policy-makers.

As we have already emphasized, the Communists must be credited with having recognized the fundamental difference between the use of forms of direct democracy on the one hand and parliamentary processes on the other. By being the first to start initiative proceedings and formulating the measure that was to go before the public in accord with its own views, the KPD obtained tactical advantages that lasted throughout the remainder of the referendum campaign, far surpassing its actual parliamentary strength or firm popular backing. All the other parties were forced to react as best they could, with the resultant embarrassment and difficulties we have described.

In the past, United Front tactics had been the cause of some of the most bitterly debated controversies within the German Communist Party. However, the leadership of the KPD, only recently placed in charge of the party, knew that it had to prove its competence and reliability through the successful employment of these tactics. United Front appeals concerning most standard issues (unemployment, for example) had only limited, unspectacular results. The German Communist leaders were fortunate that the controversy over the princes' property settlements emerged so opportunely in the late fall of 1925.

The way the issue stirred up deep feelings which ran across an unusually wide range of German society made it particularly well suited for a United Front campaign. The leaders of the KPD recognized this exceptional opportunity for what it was, perhaps not quite as instantaneously as some East German historians imply, but certainly far more rapidly than

326   CRISIS OF THE WEIMAR REPUBLIC

the leaders of any other party did. In February, Ernst Thälmann was able to inform the ECCI:

The campaign against the princes' settlements does not depend
only on Social Democratic and Communist party members; it is
becoming a serious peoples' movement. The significance of the
campaign is as follows: it is taking place under proletarian he-
gemony, it strengthens antimonarchistic tendencies, it increases
the divisions within the bourgeoisie, it is loosening the ties between the middle-class parties and *the Social Democratic Party,* it is
improving the class basis of the proletariat and permits contacts
with various previously inaccessible segments of the population.[165]

The campaign, in fact, was a great success, even if some
particular goals—such as consolidating the millions who supported the referendum into a firm block that would support
many other far-ranging Communist demands—failed to be
accomplished.[166]

Above all, the success of the campaign against the princes'
claims helped to confirm the authority of the Thälmann-led
Central Committee. Stalin himself praised the tactics chosen
by the German Communist leaders.[167] It surely is not coin-
cidental that important "intra-party discussions" took place
shortly after the initiative and then again after the vote on
the referendum. The pages of *Rote Fahne* at the time were
filled with abstruse theoretical arguments and polemic
against the opponents of the now dominant tendency in the
KPD.[168] The "Ultra-left" leaders, Karl Korsch and Ernst
Schwarz, were expelled from the party on 30 April 1926;
Ruth Fischer and Hugo Urbahns were reprimanded a few
days after the referendum.[169] Moreover, the party leadership
arranged important district and regional meetings in areas
such as Berlin where opposition to the ECCI Open Letter
had once been strong, and in most cases now obtained sub-

[165] *Rote Fahne,* 27 Feb. 1926, emphasis in original. Also an article by the important
Comintern official, Dimitri Manuilski, "Zur Tagung der Erweiterten Exekutive," *Die
Kommunistische Internationale,* 7 (Nr. 2, Feb. 1926, "issued in March"): 120.
[166] *Rote Fahne,* 20 June 1926; Schüren, pp. 260–67, 275–77.
[167] Stalin, *Works,* 8: 118.
[168] *Rote Fahne,* 30 March, 2–23 April, 15 June, 3–15 July 1926.
[169] Ibid., 4 May, 4 and 11 July 1926; Bahne, *Vierteljahrshefte für Zeitgeschichte,* 9:
366–67, 371–73. The final elimination of the Ultra-left opposition was accomplished
in stages over the next year and a half, Weber, *Die Wandlung,* 1: 137–85.

stantial majorities ratifying the new policies.[170] Although not necessarily the most obvious consequence of the initiative and referendum movement, the effective consolidation of the Thälmann Central Committee's control over the KPD may have been one of its most important results.

The three parties most strongly committed to the support of the Republic performed far less effectively than either the anti-democratic, basically monarchistic right or the equally anti-democratic Communist left. They failed first and foremost to understand the importance of political cooperation. Even in the definition of their separate party policies, they showed much indecision and unclarity. The leaders of these key parties expected the final resolution of the controversy to take place in the Reichstag; they all acted—whether they supported or opposed the referendum proceedings—as though the referendum campaign was a kind of interlude, or even sideshow, to the "true" legislative process. Few of them seem to have realized how much the initiative and referendum movement would disrupt "normal" politics. They did not trust the constructive potential of this new institution and, thus, never tried to use it to pass seriously needed legislation when they had a good opportunity to do so.

The leaders of the Center Party wanted to maintain a consistent policy of opposition to the confiscation proposal, but found it increasingly difficult to persuade all of their followers that this policy was correct. Astonished by the degree of resistance they encountered, they responded by insisting on discipline, unity, and the acceptance of their authority. They were very reluctant to admit how seriously they had misjudged the views of large segments of their party followers during the first months of the controversy and preferred to admonish their "mistaken" followers about high moral and religious principles.

---

[170] Thälmann spoke to a meeting of party workers on June 29th; after his speech a resolution accepting the policies set by the Central Committee in accord with the ECCI's letter was approved by an impressive majority—only 35 out of some 800 members present opposed the resolution. *Rote Fahne*, 1 July 1926. A *Bezirksparteitag* was held in Berlin 3 and 4 July 1926. Reportedly a solid four-fifths of the delegates now supported the Central Committee. All resolutions suggested by the Ultra-left were rejected. Ibid., 6 July 1926. Fritsch, *Wissenschaftliche Zeitschrift der Universität Jena*, 19: 383–84, 390, discusses the consolidation of the new party leadership in Thuringia.

The DDP faced a somewhat different dilemma. Once the initiative and referendum movement was under way, the leaders of the Democratic Party found themselves with very little power to control the kinds of decisions forced upon them. The DDP was too weak to compel the other parties to consider its proposals as seriously as their merits deserved, and it became more and more apparent as time went on that the DDP could not even insist that its own party followers stand together. Most Democratic voters made up their own minds whether or not to support the initiative and referendum. However, the decision the party leadership finally made against issuing official orders regarding the referendum was not because it believed that each voter should be left free to make his decision as his own judgment and conscience dictated. It was simply the only practical way to prevent the party from splitting wide open. The Social Democratic *Landtag* delegation's conduct during the final vote on the Prussian-Hohenzollern settlement displayed the same weakness.

We have already described the way in which the Social Democratic Party responded with too little resourcefulness on an occasion which offered possibilities for a positive republican achievement. Once the SPD's leaders, through their own hesitation, allowed the Communists to define the terms of the initiative and referendum proposal, they found themselves trapped in a situation where their political judgment recommended one course of action, whereas their great concern over threats to party unity demanded a very different kind of behavior. They tried to master the situation by cosponsoring the referendum and at the same time working toward the improvement of the parliamentary legislation proposed by the middle parties. This attempt to straddle two horses failed. The SPD's behavior after the referendum had failed was particularly awkward; it certainly did nothing to increase the party's reputation for reliability.

If one examines the decisions made by the three Weimar parties during the course of the controversy over the former rulers' properties, it becomes obvious that the leaders of these parties never quite understood how a referendum campaign differed from a regular election on the one hand, or voting in a parliamentary body on the other. To a certain extent, party leaders tended to see the referendum as a demonstration of partisan appeal, coherence, and discipline; yet, at the same time, they seem to have expected rank-and-file

voters to obey official instructions with the same recognition
of tactical necessities and virtually automatic dependability
that could be demanded from members of a parliamentary
Fraktion. Count Montgelas commented,

> There are tactics in the political contest between party organi-
> zations and there have to be tactics. However, they are . . . the
> concern of the leaders. . . . Ordinary people [*das Volk*] are unable
> to have any interest in tactics—and have none. Whoever has
> spoken recently with people out of all walks of life and professions
> knows that in this case the people are not at all heeding the
> different directives regarding tactics.[171]

There is little doubt that the progress of the initiative and
referendum campaign interfered with the ability of the parties
to reach a legislative solution in the Reichstag. The tempo
of interparty negotiation and compromise was, to all intents
and purposes, set and also distorted by the pace of the referendum movement. Direct legislation by the people might
have been a useful means of reaching a solution to the properties question if the Reichstag had failed to produce satisfactory legislation because of obdurate party differences. Or,
better yet, a suitably formulated initiative and referendum
movement might have been substituted for parliamentary
action from the start. The course actually followed, i.e., that
of conducting an initiative and referendum campaign while
parliamentary action on the same problem was simultaneously in process, was ill-considered and almost inherently
doomed to failure. It is difficult to estimate precisely what
effect the failure of both the referendum campaign and the
extended Reichstag deliberations had on public opinion.
However, there can be little doubt that these striking failures
furthered the steadily growing distrust of democratic processes.[172]

Certainly, the first use of the nationwide initiative and referendum proceedings in 1926 set a deleterious precedent for
the remaining years of the Weimar Republic.[173] Due to lack

---

[171] *Vossische Zeitung,* 18 June 1926 (Nr. 145).

[172] In 1934 former Chancellor Marx wrote, "The idea of parliamentarianism had
again suffered damage: *the events of the year 1926 were the best encouragement for the
events of 1933!*" Stehkämper, 3: 14, emphasis in original.

[173] Schiffers would qualify this generally held judgment by pointing to the way it
encouraged various groups and associations to attempt to achieve their goals by
direct legislation (pp. 13–14, 223–31, 259–61). Schüren, too, argues that the *Fürstenenteignung* referendum was not altogether harmful (pp. 280–82). However, the
fact remains that there was not a single successful initiative and referendum on the
national level.

of daring and imagination, the republican parties made no efforts to use these forms of direct legislation for constructive purposes. They left them to be abused by the parties of the extreme left and right that had no desire to strengthen the Republic. These parties employed the initiative and referendum provisions of the constitution for deliberately destructive and demagogic aims, as, for instance, in the KPD's initiative against the construction of the battle cruiser "A" in 1928, the Nationalist and National Socialist sponsored referendum against the Young Plan in 1929, and the effort by the "National Opposition," supported by the KPD, to force the dissolution of the Prussian *Landtag* in 1931. The resultant discrediting of these methods of direct democracy when employed on a national scale is well-known. Even so, there is some irony in this unedifying outcome of institutions originally described as an "educational assignment" (*erzieherische Arbeit*) by which "political sense will be planted in the people and grow." [174]

[174] Koch-Weser, Germany. *Verhandlungen der verfassungsgebenden Deutschen Nationalversammlung*, 336: 307.

Bibliography

UNPUBLISHED DOCUMENTS
Bundesarchiv Koblenz
    Reichskanzlei. Akten betreffend vermögensrechtliche Auseinandersetzung mit
    den früher regierenden Fürstenhäusern. Alte Reichskanzlei. *Kais. Haus* 2. Bände
    1–4. (Cited as Bundesarchiv. "Auseinandersetzung").
    Deutsche Volkspartei. A. Reichsgeschäftsstelle. Volksbegehren auf entschädi-
    gungslose Enteignung der Fürstenhäuser am 20. Juni 1926. Bd. 1: Schriftwech-
    sel. R4511/20, Bd. 2: Propaganda-und Informationsmaterial R4511/21.
Bundesarchiv-Militärarchiv
    Nachlass Konrad von Gossler. Briefe des Herzogs Bernhard von Sachsen-Mei-
    ningen an General von Gossler 1918–1926. H 08-34/7.
The Hoover Library, Stanford University, Palo Alto
    Microfilm Collection. Special Collection. NSDAP Hauptarchiv. Reels 36–39:
    records of the Deutsche Demokratische Partei. (Cited as DDP Papers). The
    documents themselves are now in the Bundesarchiv.
    Hans von Seeckt Papers (microfilm).
    The Müller and Graef Collection (posters).
University of California Library, Berkeley
    Germany. Auswartiges Amt. Politisches Archiv. Nachlass Stresemann (micro-
    film).
    Germany. Alte Reichskanzlei. Kabinettsprotokolle (microfilm).
NEWSPAPERS
Berliner Lokal-Anzeiger
Berliner Tageblatt (Wochen-Ausgabe)
Deutsche Allgemeine Zeitung
Deutsche Mittelstandszeitung
Frankfurter Zeitung
Die Freiheit
Germania
Kölnische Zeitung

Kölnische Volkszeitung
Das Reichsbanner
Rhein-Mainische Volkszeitung
Rote Fahne
Tremonia
Vorwärts
Vossische Zeitung

REFERENCE WORKS

Anschütz, Gerhard. *Die Verfassung des Deutschen Reichs von 11. August 1919.* 14th ed. 1933. Reprint. Bad Homburg: 1968.

Bitter, *Handwörterbuch der Preussischen Verwaltung.* Ed. by Bill Drews and Franz Hoffmann. 3rd ed. Berlin & Leipzig: 1928.

Diederich, Nils, Neidhard Fuchs, Irene Kullack & Horst W. Schmollinger. *Wahlstatistik in Deutschland. Bibliographie der deutschen Wahlstatistik, 1848–1975.* Munich: 1976.

Fricke, Dieter, ed. *Die bürgerlichen Parteien in Deutschland. Handbuch der Geschichte der bürgerlichen Parteien und anderer bürgerlicher Interessenorganisationen vom Vormärz bis zum Jahre 1945.* 2 vols. Berlin: 1968–70.

Hagmann, Meinrad. *Der Weg ins Verhängnis.* Munich: 1946.

Handwörterbuch der Rechtswissenschaft. Ed. by Fritz Stier-Somlo and Alexander Elster. 8 vols. Berlin & Leipzig: 1926–37.

Handwörterbuch der Staatswissenschaften. 3rd ed., 7 vols. Jena: 1909–11. 4th ed., 8 vols. plus supplement. Jena: 1923–28.

Harms, Bernhard, ed. *Volk und Reich der Deutschen.* 2 vols. Berlin: 1929.

Herre, Paul. *Politisches Handwörterbuch.* 2 vols. Leipzig: 1923.

Horkenbach, Cuno, ed. *Das Deutsche Reich von 1918 bis Heute.* Berlin: 1929.

Institut für Marxismus-Leninismus beim Zentralkomitee der SED. *Geschichte der deutschen Arbeiterbewegung. Chronik.* Vol. 2. Berlin: 1966.

Müller-Jabusch, Maximilian. *Politischer Almanach 1925.* Berlin & Leipzig: 1925.

Osterroth, Franz. *Biographisches Lexikon des Sozialismus.* Vol. 1: *Verstorbene Persönlichkeiten.* Hanover: 1960.

——— & Dieter Schuster. *Chronik der deutschen Sozialdemokratie.* Hanover: 1963.

Reichstags-Handbuch. 3. Wahlperiode, 1924. Berlin: 1925.

Schreiber, Georg, ed. *Politisches Jahrbuch 1925, 1926,* and *1927/28.* München-Gladbach: 1925–28.

Schulthess' Europäischer Geschichtskalender. 1918–1926. Munich: 1919–27.

Schumacher, Martin. *Wahlen und Abstimmungen, 1918–1933: Eine Bibliographie zur Statistik und Analyse der politischen Wahlen in der Weimarer Republik. Bibliographien zur Geschichte des Parlamentarismus und der politischen Parteien,* Nr. 7. Düsseldorf: 1976.

Stachura, Peter D. *The Weimar Era and Hitler, 1918–1933. A Critical Bibliography.* Oxford: 1977.

Ullmann, Hans-Peter. *Bibliographie zur Geschichte der deutschen Parteien und Interessenverbände.* Göttingen: 1978.

Wörterbuch des Deutschen Staats- und Verwaltungsrechts. 2nd ed., 3 vols. Tübingen: 1911–14.

DOCUMENTARY COLLECTIONS AND OFFICIAL PUBLICATIONS

Allgemeiner Deutscher Gewerkschaftsbund. *Jahrbuch 1925.* Berlin: 1926.

———. *Protokoll der Verhandlungen des 12. Kongresses der Gewerkschaften Deutschlands.* Berlin: 1925.

Burdick, Charles B. and Ralph H. Lutz, eds. *The Political Institutions of the German Revolution 1918–1919.* Stanford: 1966.

Degras, Jane, ed. *The Communist International 1919–1943. Documents.* 3 vols. London: 1956–65.

Generalverwaltung des Preussischen Königshauses. *Vermögensauseinandersetzung mit den Hohenzollern. Der Vertrag vom 12. Oktober 1925.* Berlin: 1925.

Germany. *Reichs-Gesetzblatt 1921.*
Germany. Reichstag. *Verhandlungen.*
Germany. Reichstag. *Drucksache.*
Germany. Statistisches Reichsamt. *Statistisches Jahrbuch für das Deutsche Reich 1926* and *1927.*
Germany. Statistisches Reichsamt. *Statistik des Deutschen Reiches.* Vols. 315, 321, 332.
Kommunistische Partei Deutschlands. *Bericht über die Verhandlungen 10. Parteitags der Kommunistischen Partei Deutschlands Berlin vom 12. bis. 17. Juli 1925.* Berlin: 1926.
————. *Bericht über die Verhandlungen 11. Parteitags der Kommunistischen Partei Deutschlands Essen vom 2. bis 7. März 1927.* Berlin: 1927.
————. *Bericht der Bezirksleitung der KPD. Berlin-Brandenburg-Lausitz über die Tätigkeit der Organisation vom 15. November 1925 bis 31. Mai 1926.* Berlin: 1926.
Krummacher, F. A. and Albert Wucher, eds. *Die Weimarer Republik. Ihre Geschichte in Texten, Bildern und Dokumenten.* Munich: 1965.
Marx-Engels-Lenin-Stalin-Institut beim Zentralkomitee der SED, eds. *Zur Geschichte der Kommunistischen Partei Deutschlands.* Berlin: 1954.
Medlicott, W. N., et al. eds. *Documents on British Foreign Policy, 1919–1939.* Series 1A, Vol. 1. London: 1966.
Michaelis, Herbert and Ernst Schraepler, eds. *Ursachen und Folgen. Vom deutschen Zusammenbruch 1918 und 1945 bis zur staatlichen Neuordnung Deutschlands in der Gegenwart.* 26 vols. Vols. 3–8. Berlin: 1959.
Morsey, Rudolf, ed. *Die Protokolle der Reichstagsfraktion und des Fraktionsvorstands der deutschen Zentrumspartei, 1926–1933. Veröffentlichungen der Kommission für Zeitgeschichte bei der Katholischen Akademie in Bayern* in cooperation with the *Kommission für Geschichte des Parlamentarismus und der Politischen Parteien.* Series A: *Quellen,* Vol. 9. Mainz: 1969.
Nationalsozialistisches Jahrbuch 1927, n.p. n.d.
Prussia. Landtag. *Sitzungsberichte.*
Prussia. Landtag. *Drucksache.*
Prussia. *Preussische Gesetzsammlung. 1918.*
Prussia. *Preussische Gesetzsammlung. 1926.*
Schulze, Hagen, ed. *Anpassung oder Widerstand? Aus den Akten des Parteivorstands der deutschen Sozialdemokratie 1932/33. Archiv für Sozialgeschichte.* Beiheft 4. Bonn-Bad Godesberg: 1975.
Sozialdemokratische Partei Deutschlands. *Sozialdemokratischer Parteitag 1925 in Heidelberg. Protokoll.* Berlin: 1925.
————. *Sozialdemokratischer Parteitag 1927 in Kiel. Protokoll.* Berlin: 1927.
————. *Jahrbuch der deutschen Sozialdemokratie für das Jahr 1926.* Berlin: 1927.
————. *Jahrbuch der deutschen Sozialdemokratie für das Jahr 1927.* Berlin: 1928.
————. *Sozialdemokratische Parteikorrespondenz für die Jahre 1923 bis 1928 (Ergänzungsband).* Berlin: 1930.
————. *Bezirksverband Berlin. Jahresbericht 1925/1926.* Berlin: 1927.
Weber, Hermann, ed., *Der deutsche Kommunismus.* Cologne & Berlin: 1963.

PAMPHLETS AND OTHER CONTEMPORARY WRITINGS ON POLITICS
Allgemeiner deutscher Gewerkschaftsbund. *Ist ein Einheitsfront mit den Kommunisten möglich?* Berlin: 1922.
Bäumer, Gertrud. *Grundlagen demokratischer Politik.* Karlsruhe: 1928.
Calker, Fritz van. *Wesen und Sinn der politischen Parteien.* Tübingen: 1928.
Dessauer, Friedrich. *Das Zentrum.* Berlin: 1931.
Deutsche Demokratische Partei. *Schriftenreihe für politische Werbung.* Nr. 1: *Der Wahlkampf 1928.* Berlin: 1928.
Deutsche Demokratische Partei. *Die Deutsche Demokratische Partei: ihr Programm und ihre Organisation.* Berlin: n.d.
Deutsche Volkspartei. *Wahlhandbuch 1928.* Berlin: 1928.
Dix, Arthur. *Die deutschen Reichstagswahlen 1870–1930 und die Wandlungen der Volksgliederung.* Tübingen: 1930.

Erkelenz, Anton (ed.). *Zehn Jahre deutsche Republik: Ein Handbuch für republikanische Politik.* Berlin: 1928.

Everling, Friedrich. *Recht oder Raub in der Republik. Die Wahrheit über den Fürstenabfindung.* Neu-Finkenkrug: 1926.

———. *Republik oder Monarchie?* Berlin: 1924.

Fraenkel, Ernst. *Zur Soziologie der Klassenjustiz.* Berlin: 1927.

Freymuth, Arnold. *Fürstenenteignung—Volksrecht!* Berlin: 1926.

Freytagh-Loringhoven, Axel von. *Deutschnationale Volkspartei.* Berlin: 1931.

Frick, Wilhelm. *Die Nationalsozialisten im Reichstag 1924–28.* Munich: 1928.

Friedmann, Alfred. *Der Kompromissantrag "Schulte u. Gen." und Volksbegehren.* Berlin: 1926.

———. *Fürstenabfindung und Zuständigkeitsfrage: Ein Rechtsgutachten.* Berlin: 1926.

———. *Der Gesetzentwurf der Demokraten über die Fürsten "abfindung."* Berlin: 1925.

Grasshoff, Dr. Heinrich. *Das wahre Gesicht der Hohenzollern.* Berlin: 1926.

———. *Fünf Jahrhunderte Fürstenraub.* Berlin: 1926.

Heinig, Kurt. *Fürstenabfindung? Ein Lesebuch zum Volksentscheid.* Berlin: 1926.

Kaisenberg, Georg. *Der Weg der Volksgesetzgebung: Volksbegehren und Volksentscheid.* Berlin: 1926.

Kempkes, Adolf, ed. *Deutscher Aufbau: Nationalliberale Arbeit der Deutschen Volkspartei.* Berlin: 1927.

Koellreutter, Otto. *Die politischen Parteien im modernen Staate.* Breslau: 1926.

———. *Der deutsche Staat als Bundesstaat und als Parteienstaat.* Tübingen: 1927.

Kommunistische Partei Deutschlands. Zentralkomitee. Sekretariat. *Rundschreiben Nr. 1/26. Anweisungen für die Kampagne zur Fürstenenteignung, gegen die Erwerbslosigkeit.* Berlin: 1926.

Kommunistische Partei Deutschlands, Zentralkomitee. *Zum Fall Maslow.* Berlin: 1926.

Lambach, Walther. *Die Herrschaft der Fünfhundert.* Hamburg: 1926.

Marck, Siegfried. *Reformismus und Radikalismus in der deutschen Sozialdemokratie.* Berlin: 1927.

———. *Sozialdemokratie.* Berlin: 1931.

Marr, Heinz. *Klasse und Partei in der modernen Demokratie.* Frankfurt a. M.: 1925.

Meinecke, Friedrich. *Werke,* Vol. 2: *Politische Schriften und Reden,* ed. by Georg Kotowski. Darmstadt: 1958.

Nuschke, Otto. *Die Deutsche Demokratische Partei.* Berlin: 1928.

Preuss, Hugo. *Um die Reichsverfassung vom Weimar.* Berlin: 1924.

Rück, Fritz. *Reiche Fürsten, Arme Leute.* Berlin: 1926.

Saenger, Alwin. *Reichstagsabgeordneter Alwin Saenger gegen Grafen von Westarp: Rede zum Volksentscheid.* Berlin: 1926.

Scheidemann, Philipp. *Fürsten-Habgier: Die Forderungen der Fürsten an das notleidende Volk.* Cassel: 1926.

Schmidt, Georg, ed. *Für Volksbegehren, für Volksentscheid, für das Volk, gegen die Fürsten.* Berlin: 1926.

Schmitt, Carl. *Hugo Preuss, sein Staatsbegriff und seine Stellung in der deutschen Staatslehre.* Tübingen: 1930.

———. *Die geistgeschichtliche Lage des heutigen Parlamentarismus.* 2nd ed. Munich & Leipzig: 1926.

———. *Volksentscheid und Volksbegehren.* Berlin & Leipzig: 1927.

Schulte, Karl Anton, ed. *Nationale Arbeit: Das Zentrum in seinem Wirken in der Republik.* Essen: 1929.

———. *Was geschieht mit dem Fürstenvermogen?* München-Gladbach: 1926.

Schuster, Georg. *Der landesherrliche Grundbesitz in der Mark Brandenburg.* Berlin & Leipzig: 1925.

Sontag, Ernst. *Fürstenabfindungen in den letzten 500 Jahren.* Halle (Saale): 1926.

Sozialdemokratische Partei Deutschlands, Vorstand, ed. *Referenten- und Diskussionsmaterial zur Sozialdemokratischen Werbewoche (16.–24. Oktober 1926).* n.d., n.p.

———. *Referentenmaterial zur Fürstenabfindung.* Berlin: 1926.

Stein, Adolf (pseudonym: "A"). *Durch Volksentscheid zur neuen Revolution.* Berlin: 1926.

Triepel, Heinrich. *Wir müssen aus dem Turm heraus.* Berlin: 1925.
――――. *Die Staatsverfassung und die politischen Parteien.* 2nd ed. Berlin: 1930.
Troeltsch, Ernst. *Spektator-Briefe.* Tübingen: 1924.
Verdienste der Hohenzollern. n.d. n.p.
Die Vermögensverhaltnisse der früher regierenden Fürstenhäuser. Berlin: 1926.
Volk! Entscheide! Material zum Volksentscheid nach amtlichen Quellen bearbeitet. Berlin: 1926.
Weber, Max. *Gesammelte Politische Schriften.* 2nd enlarged edition, ed. by Johannes Winckelmann. Tübingen: 1958.
Weiss, Max, ed. *Politisches Handwörterbuch.* Berlin: 1928.
――――. *Der nationale Wille: Werden und Wirken der Deutschnationalen Volkspartei, 1918– 1928.* Essen: 1928.
Westarp, Graf. *Die Sendung der Deutschnationalen Volkspartei.* Berlin: 1927.

CONTEMPORARY JOURNAL ARTICLES
Best, Dr. Georg and Dr. Oscar Mügel. "Das Volksbegehren zur Aufwertung und Anleiheablösung," *Deutsche Juristen-Zeitung,* 31 (Nr. 14, 15 July 1926): 991–99.
"Brief eines erwerblos Arbeiters," *Eiserne Blätter: Wochenschrift für deutsche Politik und Kultur,* 8 (Nr. 32, 8 August 1926): 540–41.
Cremer, Dr. Karl. "Zur inneren Lage," *Deutsche Stimmen,* 38 (Nr. 6, 20 March 1926): 131–32.
Decker, Georg. "Krise des deutschen Parteisystems?" *Die Gesellschaft* (1926, Nr. 1): 1–16.
――――. "Lehren des Volksentscheids," *Die Gesellschaft,* (1926, Nr. 2): 193–204.
――――. "Die Reichstagswahlen," *Die Gesellschaft* (1928, Nr. 1): 481–84.
――――. "Wahlrechtsreform oder Reform der Politik?" *Die Gesellschaft* (1928, Nr. 2): 385–99.
――――. "Die Zentrumskrise," *Die Gesellschaft* (1925, Nr. 2): 410–28.
――――. "Zur Kritik der politischen Krisen," *Die Gesellschaft* (1929, Nr. 1): 1–13.
――――. "Zur Soziologie der Reichstagswahlen," *Die Gesellschaft* (1928, Nr. 2): 1–12.
"Die Liquidierung der Ultralinken in der KPD," *Die Kommunistische Internationale,* 7 (Nr. 3, March 1926): 237–45.
Enderle, August. "Die Partei und die Lage in den Gewerkschaften," *Die Internationale,* 8 (July 1925): 42–47.
Fischer, Kurt. "Die beginnende Herausbildung eines linken Flügels in der deutschen Arbeiterbewegung," *Die Kommunistische Internationale,* 7 (Nr. 2, February 1926): 199–208.
Gildemeister, Alfred. "Der Volksentscheid über die Fürstenabfindung," *Deutsche Stimmen,* 38 (Nr. 11, 5 June 1926): 257–61.
Gmelin, Hans. "Referendum," *Handbuch der Politik,* 3: 74–77. Berlin & Leipzig: 1921.
Gosnell, H. F. "The General Referendum on the Princes' Property," *American Political Science Review,* 21 (Nr. 1, Feb. 1927): 119–23.
Guttman, Bernhard. "Die nächste Phase der Republik," *Die Gesellschaft* (1926, Nr. 1): 306–15.
Hilferding, Rudolf. "Politische Probleme: Zum Aufruf Wirths und zur Rede Silverbergs," *Die Gesellschaft* (1926, Nr. 2): 289–302.
Hugenberg, Alfred. "Parteien und Parlamentarismus," *Eiserne Blätter: Wochenschrift für deutsche Politik und Kultur,* 8 (Nr. 3, 17 Jan. 1926): 45–48.
Jellinek, Walter. "Revolution und Reichsverfassung," *Jahrbuch des öffentlichen Rechts,* 9 (1920).
Kahl, Wilhelm. "Das Fürstendrama," *Deutsche Juristen-Zeitung,* 31 (Nr. 15, 1 Aug. 1926): 1057–63.
Koellreutter, Otto. "Die Auseinandersetzung mit den ehemaligen Fürstenhäusern," *Deutsche Juristen-Zeitung,* 31 (Nr. 2, 15 January 1926): 109–15.
Landsberg, Otto. "Grundsätzliches zur Fürstenabfindung," *Die Justiz,* 1 (Nr. 4, April 1926): 363–67.
Lania, Leo. "Eberts Erbe," *Weltbühne,* 21 (Nr. 18, 5 May 1925): 649.

Manuilski, Dimitri. "Zur Tagung der Erweiterten Exekutive," *Die Kommunistiche Internationale*, 7 (Nr. 2, February 1926): 105–21.
Maslow, Arkadi. "Ueber einige neuartige Umstände der Lage und ueber einige dementsprechend neuartige Aufgaben," *Die Internationale*, 7 (Nr. 7, July 1925).
Mendelssohn-Bartholdy, Albrecht. "The Political Dilemma in Germany," *Foreign Affairs*, 8 (Nr. 4, July 1930): 620–31.
Müller, Hermann. "Vom Deutschen Parlamentarismus," *Die Gesellschaft* (1926, Nr. 1): 289–305.
Munro, William B. "Initiative and Referendum," *Encyclopaedia of the Social Sciences*, 8 (New York, 1932): 51–52.
Neumann, Heinz. "Der neue Kurs der KPD," *Die Internationale*, 8 (September 1925).
Piatnitzki, Ossip. "Zur Zweiten Org-Beratung der KI—Sektionen," *Die Kommunistische Internationale*, 7 (Nr. 2, February 1926): 122–31.
Pollock, James K., Jr. "The German Party Systems," *American Political Science Review*, 23 (Nr. 4, November 1929): 859–91.
Remmele, Hermann. "Zur Beurteilung der Lage in Deutschland," *Die Kommunistische Internationale*, 7 (Nr. 7, July 1926): 600–5.
Roethe, Gustav. "Bemerkungen über den Volksentscheid," *Eiserne Blätter: Wochenschrift für deutsche Politik und Kultur*, 8 (Nr. 27, 4 July 1926): 451–56.
Rohrbach, Paul. "Die Fürstenenteignung," *Der Deutsche Gedanke*, 3 (Nr. 10, 26 May 1926): 578.
———. "Parteiismus," *Der deutsche Gedanke*, 3 (Nr. 3, 9 Feb. 1926): 134–38.
Saenger, Alwin. "Die Abfindung der ehemaligen deutschen Fürsten," *Sozialistische Monatshefte*, 63 (8 February 1926): 69–73.
Schlaffer, Joseph. "Lehren und Ergebnisse des Volksentscheidskampfes in Deutschland," *Die Kommunistische Internationale*, 7 (Nr. 8, August 1926): 783–800.
Schönbeck, Fritz. "Zur Vermögensauseinandersetzung zwischen dem preussischen Staat und dem Hause Hohenzollern," *Die Justiz*, 1 (Nr. 2, December 1925): 149–65.
Schulte, Karl Anton. "Fürstenenteignung oder Auseinandersetzung," *Der Zusammenschluss: Politische Monatsschrift zur Pflege der Deutsche Eintracht*, 1 (Nr. 2, May 1926): 31–40.
Severing, Carl. "Die beste Kritik," *Sozialistische Monatshefte*, 65 (19 September 1927): 697–701.
———. "Der 2. Wahlgang," *Sozialistische Monatshefte*, 62 (14 April 1925): 197–99.
———. "Kiel. Ein Nachwort zum Parteitag," *Die Gesellschaft* (1927, Nr. 2): 1–5.
Sorge, I. "Die Stellung der KPD zur Einheitsfronttaktik," *Die Kommunistische Internationale*, 7 (Nr. 1, January 1926): 64–78.
Thälmann, Ernst. "Zum 10. Parteitag," *Die Internationale*, 8 (July 1925).
Thoma, Richard. "The Referendum in Germany," *Journal of Comparative Legislation and International Law*, 3rd series, 10 (1928): 55–73.
———. "Zur Ideologie des Parlamentarismus und der Diktatur," *Archiv für Sozialwissenschaft und Sozialpolitik*, 53 (Nr. 1, 1924): 212–17.
Kaspar Hauser [Tucholsky, Kurt] "Dienstzeugnisse," *Weltbühne*, 21 (Nr. 23, 9 June 1925): 856–57.
Wunderlich, Johannes. "Aufwertung, Fürstenauseinandersetzung und Volksentscheid," *Deutsche Juristen-Zeitung*, 31 (Nr. 10, 15 May 1926): 701–5.
"Zwei Stimmen zur Fürstenabfindung," *Eiserne Blätter: Wochenschrift für deutsche Politik und Kultur*, 8 (Nr. 17, 25 April 1926): 235–37.

MEMOIRS, COLLECTIONS OF LETTERS, ETC.
Bismarck, Otto von. *Die gesammelten Werk*. Vol. X. Berlin: 1928.
Braun, Otto. *Von Weimar zu Hitler*. 2nd ed. New York: 1940.
Brauns, Heinrich. *Katholische Sozialpolitik im 20. Jahrhundert: Ausgewählte Aufsätze und Reden*. Ed. by Hubert Mockenhaupt. *Veröffentlichungen der Kommission für Zeitgeschichte*, Series A, Vol. 19. Mainz: 1976.
Brecht, Arnold. *Aus nächster Nähe: Lebenserinnerungen 1884–1927*. Stuttgart: 1966.

Brüning, Heinrich. *Memoiren, 1918–1934.* Stuttgart: 1970.

Kronprinzessen Cecile. *Erinnerungen an den Kronprinzen.* Biberach: 1952.

Curtis, Julius. *Sechs Jahre Minister der deutschen Republik.* Heidelberg: 1948.

D'Abernon, Viscount. *The Diary of an Ambassador.* Vol. III: *Dawes to Locarno 1924–1926.* New York: 1931.

Duderstadt, Henning. *Vom Reichsbanner zum Hakenkreuz.* Stuttgart: 1933.

Feder, Ernst. *Heute sprach ich mit . . . Tagebucher eines deutschen Publizisten, 1926–1933.* Stuttgart: 1971.

Fischer, Ruth. *Stalin and German Communism: A Study in the Origins of the State Party.* Cambridge: 1948.

Gessler, Otto. *Reichswehrpolitik in der Weimarer Zeit.* Stuttgart: 1958.

Goebbels, Joseph. *Das Tagebuch, 1925/26.* Ed. by Helmut Heiber. *Schriftenreihe der Vierteljahrshefte für Zeitgeschichte,* Nr. 1. Stuttgart: 1960.

Heuss, Theodor. *Erinnerungen 1905–1933.* Tübingen: 1963.

Holl, Karl and Adolf Wild, eds. *Ein Demokrat kommentiert Weimar: Die Berichte Hellmut von Gerlachs an die Carnegie-Friedensstiftung in New York, 1922–1930.* Bremen: 1973.

Hubatsch, Walther. *Hindenburg und der Staat.* Göttingen: 1966.

Ilsemann, Sigurd von. *Der Kaiser in Holland.* 2 vols. Munich: 1967–68.

Joos, Joseph. *Am Räderwerk der Zeit: Erinnerungen aus der katholischen und sozialen Bewegung und Politik.* Augsburg: 1951.

Keil, Wilhelm. *Erlebnisse eines Sozialdemokraten.* 2 vols. Stuttgart: 1947–48.

Kessler, Harry, Graf. *Tagebücher 1918–1937.* Frankfurt a.M.: 1961.

Köhler, Heinrich. *Lebenserinnerungen des Politikers und Staatsmannes, 1878–1949.* Ed. by Josef Becker. *Veröffentlichungen der Kommission für geschichtliche Landeskunde in Baden-Württemberg.* Series A: Quellen, Vol. 11. Stuttgart: 1964.

Lange, Helene. *Was ich hier geliebt. Briefe.* Ed. by Emmy Beckmann. Tübingen, 1957.

Leber, Julius. *Ein Mann geht seinen Weg: Schriften, Reden und Briefe.* Berlin: 1952.

Levi, Paul. *Zwischen Spartakus und Sozialdemokratie. Schriften, Aufsätze, Reden und Briefe.* Ed. by Charlotte Beradt. Frankfurt a.M.: 1969.

Löbe, Paul. *Erinnerungen eines Reichstagspräsidenten.* Berlin: 1949; enlarged 2nd edition: *Der Weg war lang.* Berlin: 1954.

Luther, Hans. *Politiker ohne Partei: Erinnerungen.* Stuttgart: 1960.

———. *Weimar und Bonn.* Munich: 1951.

Meissner, Otto. *Staatssekretär unter Ebert, Hindenburg, Hitler.* Hamburg: 1950.

Oehme, Walter. *Damals in der Reichskanzlei.* Berlin (East): 1958.

Papen, Franz von. *Memoirs.* London: 1952.

———. *Vom Scheitern einer Demokratie.* Mainz: 1968.

Potthoff, Heinrich, ed. *Friedrich v. Berg als Chef des Geheimen Zivilkabinetts, 1918: Erinnerungen aus seinem Nachlass. Quellen zur Geschichte des Parlamentarismus und der politischen Parteien.* Series I, Vol. 7. Düsseldorf: 1971.

Rabenau, Friedrich von, ed. *Seeckt: Aus seinen Leben, 1918–1936.* Leipzig: 1940.

Radbruch, Gustav. *Der innerer Weg: Aufriss meines Lebens.* Stuttgart: 1951.

Rheinbaben, Werner Freiherr von. *Viermal Deutschland.* Berlin: 1954.

Schacht, Hjalmar. *My First Seventy-Six Years.* London: 1955.

Schiffer, Eugen. *Ein Leben für den Liberalismus.* Berlin-Grunewald: 1951.

Schmidt-Hannover, Otto. *Umdenken oder Anarchie: Männer, Schicksale, Lehren.* Göttingen: 1959.

Schumacher, Martin, ed. *Erinnerungen und Dokumente von Joh. Victor Bredt, 1914 bis 1933. Quellen zur Geschichte des Parlamentarismus und der politischen Parteien.* Series III, Vol. 1. Düsseldorf: 1970.

Schreiber, Georg. *Zwischen Demokratie und Diktatur: Persönliche Erinnerungen an die Politik und Kultur des Reiches von 1919–1944.* Regensberg-Münster: 1949.

Schwerin von Krosigk, Lutz. *Es geschah in Deutschland: Menschenbilder unseres Jahrhunderts.* Tübingen: 1951.

Schlange-Schöningen, Hans. *Am Tage danach.* Hamburg: 1946.

Severing, Carl. *Mein Lebensweg.* 2 vols. Cologne: 1950.

Stalin, J. V. *Works.* Vols. 7 and 8. Moscow: 1954.

Stampfer, Friedrich. *Erfahrungen und Erkenntnisse. Aufzeichnungen aus meinem Leben.* Cologne: 1957.

Stehkämper, Hugo, ed. *Der Nachlass des Reichskanzlers Wilhelm Marx. Mitteilungen aus dem Stadtarchiv von Köln,* Vols. 52–55. Cologne, 1968.

Stockhausen, Max von. *Sechs Jahre Reichskanzlei.* Bonn: 1954.

Strasser, Otto. *Hitler and I.* Boston: 1940.

Stresemann, Gustav. *Vermächtnis.* 3 vols. Berlin: 1932–33.

Westarp, Kuno Graf. *Am Grabe der Parteiherrschaft: Bilanz des deutschen Parlamentarismus von 1918–1932.* Berlin: 1932.

Witzmann, Georg. *Thüringen von 1918–1933. Erinnerungen eines Politikers.* Meissenheim am Glan: 1958.

BIOGRAPHIES

Adolph, Hans J. L. *Otto Wels und die Politik der Deutschen Sozialdemokratie, 1894–1939. Veröffentlichungen der Historischen Kommission zu Berlin,* Vol. 33. Berlin: 1971.

Behrendt, Armin. *Wilhelm Külz—Aus dem Leben eines Suchenden.* Berlin (East): 1968.

Beradt, Charlotte. *Paul Levi. Ein demokratischer Sozialist in der Weimarer Republik.* Frankfurt a. M.: 1969.

Besson, Waldemar. *Friedrich Ebert. Verdienst und Grenze.* Göttingen: 1963.

Bredel, Willi. *Ernst Thälmann. Ein Beitrag zu einem politischen Lebensbild.* Berlin (East): 1948.

Deutz, Josef. *Adam Stegerwald. Gewerkschaftler, Politiker, Minister, 1874–1945.* Cologne: 1952.

Dorpalen, Andreas. *Hindenburg and the Weimar Republic.* Princeton: 1964.

Epstein, Klaus. *Matthias Erzberger and the Dilemma of German Democracy.* Princeton, 1959.

Eyck, Erich. *Bismarck. Leben und Werk.* 3 vols. Erlenbach-Zürich: 1941–44.

Görlitz, Walter. *Hindenburg.* Bonn: 1953.

Gross, Babette. *Willi Münzenberg. Schriftenreihe der Vierteljahrshefte für Zeitgeschichte,* Vol. 14/15. Stuttgart: 1967.

Heer, Hannes. *Ernst Thälmann in Selbstzeugnissen und Bilddokumenten.* Reinbek bei Hamburg: 1975.

Heiden, Konrad. *Der Fuehrer.* Boston: 1944.

Herre, Paul. *Kronprinz Wilhelm: Seine Rolle in der deutschen Politik.* Munich: 1954.

Koser, Reinhold. *Geschichte Friedrich des Grossen.* 4 vols. 1921–25. Reprint. Darmstadt: 1963.

Kuczynski, Jürgen. *René Kuczynski. Ein fortschrittlicher Wissenschaftler in der ersten Hälfte des 20. Jahrhunderts.* Berlin (East): 1957.

Lewis, Beth Irwin. *George Grosz. Art and Politics in the Weimar Republic.* Madison: 1971.

Morsey, Rudolf, ed. *Zeitgeschichte in Lebensbildern: Aus dem deutschen Katholizismus des 20. Jahrhunderts.* Mainz: 1973.

Schorr, Helmut J. *Adam Stegerwald. Gewerkschaftler und Politiker der ersten deutschen Republik.* Recklinghausen: 1967.

Schwarz, Gotthart. *Theodor Wolff und das 'Berliner Tageblatt.' Eine liberale Stimme in der deutschen Politik, 1906–1933. Tübinger Studien zur Geschichte und Politik,* Vol. 25. Tübingen: 1968.

Sendtner, Kurt. *Rupprecht von Wittelsbach, Kronprinz von Bayern.* Munich: 1954.

Stehkämper, Hugo, ed. *Konrad Adenauer, Oberbürgermeister von Köln. Festgabe der Stadt Köln zum 100. Geburtstag ihres Ehrenburgers am 5. Januar 1976.* Cologne: 1976.

Turner, Henry Ashby, Jr. *Stresemann and the Politics of the Weimar Republic.* Princeton: 1963.

Wachtling, Oswald. *Joseph Joos: Journalist, Arbeiterführer, Zentrumspolitiker. Politische Biographie, 1878–1933. Veröffentlichungen der Kommission für Zeitgeschichte.* Series B, Vol. 16. Mainz: 1974.

Weymar, Paul. *Konrad Adenauer.* Munich: 1955.

Wheeler-Bennett, John W. *Wooden Titan: Hindenburg in Twenty Years of German History, 1914–1934.* 1936. Reprint. London: 1963.

Wynen, Arthur. *Ludwig Kaas: Aus seinem Leben und Wirken.* Trier: 1953.

SECONDARY WORKS

Abendroth, Wolfgang. *Aufstieg und Krise der deutschen Sozialdemokratie.* Frankfurt a. M.: 1964.

Albertin, Lothar. *Liberalismus und Demokratie am Anfang der Weimarer Republik. Eine vergleichende Analyse der Deutschen Demokratischen Partei und der Deutschen Volkspartei. Beiträge zur Geschichte des Parlamentarismus und der politischen Parteien,* Vol. 45. Düsseldorf: 1972.

Angress, Werner T. *Stillborn Revolution. The Communist Bid for Power, 1921–1923.* Princeton: 1963.

Bach, Jürgen A. *Franz von Papen in der Weimarer Republik. Aktivitäten in Politik und Presse, 1918–1932.* Düsseldorf: 1977.

Bachem, Karl. *Vorgeschichte, Geschichte und Politik der Deutschen Zentrumspartei.* Vol. VIII. Cologne: 1931.

Baumgarten, Otto, et al. *Geistige und sittliche Wirkungen des Krieges in Deutschland.* Stuttgart: 1927.

Bergsträsser, Ludwig. *Die Entwicklung des Parlamentarismus in Deutschland.* Laupheim/Württemberg: 1954.

———. *Geschichte der politischen Parteien in Deutschland.* 11th ed. Munich: 1965.

Berlau, A. Joseph. *The German Social Democratic Party, 1914–1921. Columbia University. Faculty of Political Science. Studies in History, Economics and Public Law,* Vol. 557. New York: 1949.

Besson, Waldemar, Siegfried Lenz and Gerd Klepzig. *Jahr und Jahrgang 1926.* Hamburg, 1966.

Blaich, Fritz. *Die Wirtschaftskrise 1925/26 und die Reichsregierung: Von der Erwerbslosenfürsorge zur Konjunkturpolitik.* Kallmünz: 1977.

Bracher, Karl Dietrich. *Die Auflösung der Weimarer Republik.* 3rd ed. Villingen/Schwarzwald: 1960.

———. *Deutschland zwischen Demokratie und Diktatur.* Bern and Munich: 1964.

Bramsted, Ernest K. *Goebbels and National Socialist Propaganda, 1925–1945.* East Lansing: 1965.

Braunthal, Julius. *History of the International.* 2 vols. New York: 1967.

Bresciani-Turroni, Constantino. *The Economics of Inflation.* London: 1937.

Brunet, René. *The New German Constitution.* New York: 1922.

Buchheim, Karl. *Geschichte der christlichen Parteien in Deutschland.* Munich: 1953.

Carr, Edward Hallett. *The Interregnum, 1923–1924.* London: 1954.

———. *Socialism in One Country, 1924–1926.* Vol. III, Part 1. London: 1964.

Carsten, F. L. *The Reichswehr and Politics, 1918 to 1933.* Oxford: 1966.

Dahrendorf, Ralf. *Society and Democracy in Germany.* Garden City: 1967.

Deak, Istvan. *Weimar Germany's Left-Wing Intellectuals.* Berkeley and California: 1968.

Dederke, Karlheinz. *Reich und Republik. Deutschland, 1917–1933.* 2nd ed. Stuttgart: 1973.

Demeter, Karl. *Das Deutsche Offizierkorps in Gesellschaft und Staat, 1650–1945.* Frankfurt a. M.: 1964.

Drechsler, Hanno. *Die Sozialistische Arbeiterpartei Deutschlands. Marburger Abhandlungen zur Politische Wissenschaft,* Vol. 2. Meisenheim: 1964.

Dünow, Hermann. *Der Rote Frontkämpferbund.* Berlin: 1958.

Duverger, Maurice. *Political Parties: Their Organization and Activity in the Modern State.* 2nd ed., revised. London: 1959.

Ehni, Hans-Peter. *Bollwerk Preussen? Preussen-Regierung, Reich-Länder-Problem und Sozialdemokratie, 1928–1932. Schriftenreihe des Forschungsinstituts der Friedrich-Ebert-Stiftung,* Vol. 111. Bonn & Bad-Godesberg: 1975.

Eimers, Enno. *Das Verhältnis von Preussen und Reich in den ersten Jahren der Weimarer Republik (1918–1923).* Berlin: 1969.

Eksteins, Modris. *The Limits of Reason: The German Democratic Press and the Collapse of Weimar Democracy.* London: 1975.

Eschenburg, Theodor. *Die improvisierte Demokratie der Weimarer Republik. Gesammelte Aufsätze zur Weimarer Republik.* Munich: 1963.

Eyck, Erich. *Geschichte der Weimarer Republik.* 2 vols. Erlenbach-Zürich: 1954–56.

Finer, Herman. *Theory and Practice of Modern Government.* 1st ed., 2 vols. New York: 1932, revised ed. 1949.

Flechtheim, Ossip K. *Die Kommunistische Partei Deutschlands in der Weimarer Republik.* Offenbach/M.: 1948.

Fraenkel, Ernst. *Deutschland und die westlichen Demokratien.* 2nd ed. Stuttgart: 1964.

Friedrich, Carl J. *Constitutional Government and Democracy.* Boston: 1946.

Fromme, Friedrich Karl. *Von der Weimarer Verfassung zum Bonner Grundgesetz.* Tübingen: 1960.

Fülberth, Georg and Jürgen Harrer. *Die deutsche Sozialdemokratie, 1890–1933.* Vol. 1 of *Arbeiterbewegung und SPD.* Darmstadt: 1974.

Gablentz, Otto Heinrich von der. *Politische Parteien als Ausdruck gesellschaftlicher Kräfte.* Berlin: 1952.

Gay, Peter. *Weimar Culture: The Outsider as Insider.* New York: 1968.

Germany. Parteienrechtskommission. *Rechtliche Ordnung des Parteiwesens. Probleme eines Parteiengesetzes.* 2nd ed. Frankfurt a. M.: 1958.

Glum, Friedrich. *Das parlamentarische Regierungssystem in Deutschland, Grossbritannien und Frankreich.* Munich & Berlin: 1950.

Gordon, Harold, J., Jr. *The Reichswehr and the German Republic, 1919–1926.* Princeton: 1957.

Grebing, Helga. *Geschichte der deutschen Arbeiterbewegung.* Munich: 1966.

Habedank, Heinz. *Der Feind steht rechts.* Berlin: 1965.

Haungs, Peter. *Reichspräsident und parlamentarische Kabinettsregierung. Politische Forschungen,* Vol. 9. Cologne & Opladen, 1968.

Haussherr, Hans. *Verwaltungseinheit und Ressorttrennung vom Ende des 17. bis zum Beginn des 19. Jahrhunderts.* Berlin: 1953.

Headlam-Morley, Agnes. *The New Democratic Constitutions of Europe.* London: 1928.

Heiber, Helmut. *Die Republik von Weimar.* Munich: 1966.

Hermens, Ferdinand A. and Theodor Schieder, eds. *Staat, Wirtschaft und Politik in der Weimarer Republik: Festschrift für Heinrich Brüning.* Berlin: 1967.

Hertzmann, Lewis. *DNVP: Right-Wing Opposition in the Weimar Republic.* Lincoln: 1963.

Heydte, Friedrich August Freiherr von der and Karl Sacherl. *Soziologie der deutschen Parteien.* Munich: 1955.

Hintze, Otto. *Regierung und Verwaltung.* 2nd ed. Göttingen: 1967.

———. *Staat und Verfassung.* 2nd ed. Göttingen: 1962.

Hirsch-Weber, Wolfgang. *Gewerkschaften in der Politik: Von der Massenstreikdebatte zum Kampf um das Mitbestimmungsrecht.* Cologne & Opladen: 1959.

Hunt, Richard N. *German Social Democracy, 1919–1933.* New Haven: 1964.

Institut für Marxismus-Leninismus beim Zentralkomitee der SED. *Geschichte der deutschen Arbeiterbewegung.* Vol. IV: *Von 1924 bis Januar 1933.* Berlin: 1966.

Karl, Heinz. *Der deutsche Arbeiterklasse in Kampf um die Enteignung der Fürsten (1925/1926). Institut für Marxismus-Leninismus beim ZK der SED: Beiträge zur Geschichte und Theorie der Arbeiterbewegung,* Vol. 20. Berlin: 1957.

Kaufmann, Walter H. *Monarchism in the Weimar Republic.* New York: 1953.

Kehr, Eckart. *Der Primat der Innenpolitik.* Ed. by Hans-Ulrich Wehler. Berlin: 1965.

Key, V. O., Jr. *Politics, Parties, and Pressure Groups.* 4th ed. New York: 1958.

Kolb, Eberhard. *Die Arbeiterräte in der deutschen Innenpolitik, 1918–1919. Beiträge zur Geschichte des Parlamentarismus und der politischen Parteien,* Vol. 23. Düsseldorf: 1962.

Kolb, Eberhard. *Vom Kaiserreich zur Weimarer Republik.* Cologne: 1972.

Kornhauser, William. *The Politics of Mass Society.* Glencoe: 1959.

Koszyk, Kurt. *Geschichte der deutschen Presse.* Vol. III: *Deutsche Presse, 1914–1945. Abhandlungen und Materialien zur Publizistik,* Vol. 7. Berlin: 1972.

————. *Zwischen Kaiserreich und Diktatur. Die sozialdemokratische Presse von 1914 bis 1933. Deutsche Presseforschung*, Vol. 1. Heidelberg: 1958.

Kruck, Alfred. *Geschichte des Alldeutschen Verbandes, 1890–1939*. Wiesbaden: 1954.

Krummacher, F. A., ed. *Fünfzig Jahre deutsche Republik. Entstehung—Scheitern—Neubeginn*. Frankfurt a. M.: 1969.

Landauer, Carl. *European Socialism. A History of Ideas and Movements*. 2 vols. Berkeley: 1959.

Leibholz, Gerhard. *Strukturprobleme der modernen Demokratie*. 3rd ed. Karlsruhe: 1967.

Leites, Nathan. *On the Game of Politics in France*. Stanford: 1959.

Lidtke, Vernon L. *The Outlawed Party, 1878–1890*. Princeton: 1966.

Liebe, Werner. *Die Deutschnationale Volkspartei, 1918–1924. Beiträge zur Geschichte des Parlamentarismus und der politischen Parteien*, Vol. 8. Düsseldorf: 1956.

Lipset, Seymour Martin. *Political Man: The Social Bases of Politics*. New York: 1960.

Lowell, A. L. *Public Opinion and Popular Government*. New York: 1926.

Lucas, Friedrich J. *Hindenburg als Reichspräsident. Bonner Historische Forschungen*, Vol. 14. Bonn: 1959.

Lutz, Heinrich. *Demokratie in Zwielicht. Der Weg der deutschen Katholiken aus dem Kaiserreich in die Republik, 1914–1925*. Munich: 1963.

Maier, Charles. *Recasting Bourgeois Europe: Stabilization in France, Germany, and Italy in the Decade after World War I*. Princeton: 1975.

Mattern, Johannes. *Principles of the Constitutional Jurisprudence of the German National Republic*. Baltimore: 1928.

Matthias, Erich and Rudolf Morsey, eds. *Das Ende der Parteien 1933*. Düsseldorf: 1960.

McKenzie, R. T. *British Political Parties: the Distribution of Power within the Conservative and Labour Parties*. 2nd ed. New York & London: 1963.

Mendelssohn-Bartholdy, Albrecht. *The War and German Society*. New Haven: 1937.

Michels, Robert. *Political Parties: A Sociological Study of the Oligarchical Tendencies of Modern Democracy*. Glencoe: 1949.

————. *Umschichtungen in der herrschenden Klassen nach dem Kriege*. Stuttgart & Berlin: 1934.

Milatz, Alfred. *Wähler und Wahlen in der Weimarer Republik. Schriftenreihe der Bundeszentrale für politische Bildung*, Vol. 66. Bonn: 1965.

Miller, Susanne. *Die Bürde der Macht. Die deutsche Sozialdemokratie, 1918–1920. Beiträge zur Geschichte des Parlamentarismus und der politischen Parteien*, Vol. 63. Düsseldorf: 1978.

————. *Burgfrieden und Klassenkampf. Die deutsche Sozialdemokratie im Ersten Weltkrieg. Beiträge zur Geschichte des Parlamentarismus und der politischen Parteien*, Vol. 53. Düsseldorf: 1974.

Mitchell, Allan. *Revolution in Bavaria, 1918–1919*. Princeton: 1965.

Molt, Peter. *Der Reichstag vor der improvisierten Revolution. Politische Forschungen*, Vol. 4. Cologne & Opladen: 1963.

Mommsen, Hans, Dietmar Petzina and Bernd Weisbrod, eds. *Industrielles System und politische Entwicklung in der Weimarer Republik*. Düsseldorf: 1974.

Mommsen, Hans, ed. *Sozialdemokratie zwischen Klassenbewegung und Volkspartei*. Frankfurt a. M.: 1974.

Morgan, David W. *The Socialist Left and the German Revolution. A History of the German Independent Social Democratic Party, 1917–1922*. Ithaca: 1975.

Morsey, Rudolf. *Die Deutsche Zentrumspartei, 1917–1923. Beiträge zur Geschichte des Parlamentarismus und der politischen Parteien*, Vol. 32. Düsseldorf: 1966.

Neumann, Sigmund. *Die Parteien der Weimarer Republik*. Stuttgart: 1965. Reprint of *Die politischen Parteien in Deutschland*. Berlin: 1932.

Nicholls, Anthony and Erich Matthias, eds. *German Democracy and the Triumph of Hitler*. New York: 1971.

Nicholls, Anthony. *Weimar and the Rise of Hitler*. New York: 1968.

Nipperdey, Thomas. *Die Organisation der deutschen Parteien vor 1918. Beiträge zur Geschichte des Parlamentarismus und der politischen Parteien*, Vol. 18. Düsseldorf: 1961.

Nollau, Gunther. *International Communism and World Revolution*. New York: 1961.

Nyomarkay, Joseph. *Charisma and Factionalism in the Nazi Party*. Minneapolis: 1967.

Oppenheimer, Heinrich. *The Constitution of the German Republic*. London: 1923.

Ostwald, Hans. *Sittengeschichte der Inflation*. Berlin: 1931.

Pinson, Koppel S. *Modern Germany*. New York: 1954.

Potthoff, Heinrich. *Die Sozialdemokratie von den Anfängen bis 1945*. Vol. 1 of *Kleine Geschichte der SPD*. Bonn & Bad Godesberg: 1974.

Prager, Eugen. *Geschichte der U.S.P.D.* 2nd ed. Berlin: 1922.

Pritzkoleit, Kurt. *Die neuen Herren*. Vienna: 1955.

Ritter, Gerhard. *Staatskunst und Kriegshandwerk*. Vol. 2. Munich: 1960.

Ritter, Gerhard A. *Die Arbeiterbewegung im Wilhelminischen Reich. Studien zur Europäischen Geschichte aus dem Friedrich-Meinecke-Institut der Freien Universität Berlin*, Vol. 3. Berlin: 1959.

———. *Deutscher und britischer Parlamentarismus. Ein verfassungsgeschichtlicher Vergleich. Recht und Staat in Geschichte und Gegenwart*. Vol. 242/243. Tübingen: 1962.

———, ed. *Gesellschaft, Parlament und Regierung: Zur Geschichte des Parlamentarismus in Deutschland*. Düsseldorf: 1974.

Rohe, Karl. *Das Reichsbanner Schwarz-Rot-Gold. Beiträge zur Geschichte des Parlamentarismus und der politischen Parteien*, Vol. 34. Düsseldorf: 1966.

Rosenberg, Arthur. *Entstehung und Geschichte der Weimarer Republik*. Frankfurt a. M.: 1955.

Ross, Ronald J. *Beleaguered Tower: The Dilemma of Political Catholicism in Wilhelmine Germany*. Notre Dame: 1976.

Roth, Guenther. *The Social Democrats in Imperial Germany*. Totowa: 1963.

Rürup, Reinhard. *Probleme der Revolution in Deutschland. Institut für europäische Geschichte. Mainz. Vorträge*, Nr. 50. Wiesbaden: 1968.

Ryder, A. J. *The German Revolution in 1918*. Cambridge: 1967.

Schattschneider, E. E. *Party Government*. New York: 1942.

———. *The Semisovereign People*. New York: 1960.

Schauff, Johannes. *Die deutschen Katholiken und die Zentrumspartei*. Cologne: 1928. Reprinted as *Das Wahlverhalten der deutschen Katholiken im Kaiserreich und in der Weimarer Republik*. Edited by Rudolf Morsey. *Veröffentlichungen der Kommission für Zeitgeschichte*. Series A, Vol. 18. Mainz: 1975.

Schieder, Theodor. *Staat und Gesellschaft im Wandel unserer Zeit*. Munich: 1958.

Schiffers, Reinhard. *Elemente direkter Demokratie im Weimarer Regierungssystem. Beiträge zur Geschichte des Parlamentarismus und der politischen Parteien*, Vol. 40. Düsseldorf: 1971.

Schmoller, Gustav. *Umrisse und Untersuchungen zur Verfassungs-, Verwaltungs- und Wirtschaftsgeschichte*. Leipzig: 1898.

Schneider, Werner. *Die Deutsche Demokratische Partei in der Weimarer Republik, 1924–1930*. Munich: 1978.

Schoenbaum, David. *Hitler's Social Revolution*. Garden City: 1967.

Schönhoven, Klaus, *Die Bayerische Volkspartei, 1924–1932. Beiträge zur Geschichte des Parlamentarismus und der politischen Parteien*, Vol. 46. Düsseldorf: 1972.

Schorske, Carl. *German Social Democracy, 1905–1917*. Cambridge, Mass.: 1955.

Schüren, Ulrich. *Der Volksentscheid zur Fürstenenteignung 1926. Beiträge zur Geschichte des Parlamentarismus und der politischen Parteien*, Vol. 64. Düsseldorf: 1978.

Schulz, Gerhard. *Zwischen Demokratie und Diktatur. Verfassungspolitik und Reichsreform in der Weimarer Republik*. Vol. 1. Berlin: 1963.

Schulze, Hagen. *Otto Braun oder Preussens demokratische Sendung. Eine Biographie*. Berlin: 1977.

Schumacher, Martin. *Mittelstandsfront und Republik. Die Wirtschaftspartei—Reichspartei des deutschen Mittelstandes, 1919–1933. Beiträge zur Geschichte des Parlamentarismus und der politischen Parteien*. Vol. 44. Düsseldorf: 1972.

Schuster, Kurt G. P. *Der Rote Frontkämpferbund, 1924–1929. Beiträge zur Geschichte des Parlamentarismus und der politischen Parteien*, Vol. 55. Düsseldorf: 1975.

Schustereit, Hartmut. *Linksliberalismus und Sozialdemokratie in der Weimarer Republik.* Düsseldorf: 1975.

Schwend, Karl. *Bayern zwischen Monarchie und Diktatur.* Munich: 1954.

Schwering, Leo. *Frühgeschichte der Christlich-Demokratischen Union.* Recklinghausen: 1963.

Sheehan, James J. *German Liberalism in the Nineteenth Century.* Chicago: 1978.

Sontheimer, Kurt. *Antidemokratisches Denken in der Weimarer Republik.* Munich: 1962.

Spiro, Herbert J. *Government by Constitution.* New York: 1959.

Stampfer, Friedrich. *Die vierzehn Jahre der ersten Deutschen Republik.* Karlsbad: 1936.

Stephan, Werner. *Aufstieg und Verfall des Linksliberalismus, 1918–1933. Geschichte der Deutschen Demokratischen Partei.* Göttingen: 1973.

Stürmer, Michael. *Koalition und Opposition in der Weimarer Republik, 1924–1928. Beiträge zur Geschichte des Parlamentarismus und der politischen Parteien,* Vol. 36. Düsseldorf: 1967.

Thimme, Annelise. *Flucht in den Mythos. Die Deutschnationale Volkspartei und die Niederlage von 1918.* Göttingen: 1969.

Thimme, Roland. *Stresemann und die Deutsche Volkspartei, 1923–1925. Historische Studien,* Vol. 382. Lübeck & Hamburg: 1961.

Thoma, Richard. *Über Wesen und Erscheinungsformen der modernen Demokratie.* Bonn: 1948.

Timm, Helga. *Die deutsche Sozialpolitik und der Bruch der Grossen Koalition im März 1930. Beiträge zur Geschichte des Parlamentarismus und der politischen Parteien,* Vol. 1. Düsseldorf: 1952.

Tormin, Walter. *Geschichte der deutschen Parteien seit 1848.* 2nd ed. Stuttgart: 1967.

———. *Zwischen Rätediktatur und sozialer Demokratie. Die Geschichte der Rätebewegung in der deutschen Revolution 1918/19. Beiträge zur Geschichte des Parlamentarismus und der politischen Parteien,* Vol. 4. Düsseldorf: 1954.

Varain, Heinz Joseph. *Freie Gewerkschaften, Sozialdemokratie und Staat. Die Politik der Generalkommission unter der Führung Carl Legiens (1890–1920). Beiträge zur Geschichte des Parlamentarismus und der politischen Parteien,* Vol. 9. Düsseldorf: 1956.

Vietzke, Siegfried and Heinz Wohlgemuth. *Deutschland und die deutsche Arbeiterbewegung in der Zeit der Weimarer Republik, 1919–1933.* Berlin (East): 1966.

Wacker, Wolfgang. *Der Bau des Panzerschiffes "A" und der Reichstag. Tübingen Studien zur Geschichte und Politik,* Vol. 11. Tübingen: 1959.

Waldman, Eric. *The Spartacist Uprising of 1919.* Milwaukee: 1958.

Weber, Hermann. *Die Wandlung des deutschen Kommunismus. Die Stalinisierung der KPD, 1924–1929.* 2 vols. Frankfurt a. M.: 1969.

Winkler, Heinrich August. *Mittelstand, Demokratie und Nationalsozialismus. Die politische Entwicklung von Handwerk und Kleinhandel in der Weimarer Republik.* Cologne: 1972.

Wright, J. R. C. *"Above Parties": The Political Attitudes of the German Protestant Church Leadership, 1918–1933.* London: 1974.

Zeender, John K. *The German Center Party, 1890–1906. Transactions of the American Philosophical Society.* N.S. Vol. 66, Part 1. Philadelphia: 1976.

DISSERTATIONS

Braunthal, Gerard. "The Politics of the German Free Trade Unions During the Weimar Period." Unpublished Ph. D. dissertation, Columbia University, 1954.

Dörr, Manfred. *Die Deutschnationale Volkspartei 1925–1928.* Dissertation, University of Marburg, 1964.

Gengler, Ludwig Franz. *Die deutschen Monarchisten 1919 bis 1925.* Dissertation, University of Erlangen, 1932.

Grebing, Helga. "Zentrum und katholische Arbeiterschaft 1918–1925." Unpublished Ph. D. dissertation, Free University of Berlin, 1953.

Günther, Theodor. *Das Problem der Vermögensauseinandersetzung mit den ehemaligen Fürstenhäusern.* Dissertation, University of Leipzig, 1928.
Pirlet, Otto. *Der politische Kampf um die Aufwertungsgesetzgebung nach dem Ersten Weltkrieg.* Dissertation, University of Cologne, 1959.
Pleyer, Hildegard. *Politische Werbung in der Weimarer Republik.* Dissertation, University of Münster, 1960.
Wertheimer, Rudolf. *Der Einfluss des Reichspräsidenten auf die Gestaltung der Reichsregierung.* Inaugural dissertation, University of Heidelberg, 1929.

SCHOLARLY ARTICLES

Albertin, Lothar. "Die Verantwortung der liberalen Parteien für das Scheitern der Grossen Koalition im Herbst 1921," *Historische Zeitschrift,* 205 (Nr. 3, December 1967): 566–627.
Albertini, Rudolf von. "Regierung und Parlament in der Dritten Republik," *Historische Zeitschrift,* 188 (Nr. 1, August 1959): 17–48.
———. "Parteiorganisation und Parteibegriff in Frankreich, 1789–1940," *Historische Zeitschrift,* 193 (Nr. 3, December 1961): 529–600.
Angress, Werner T. "Pegasus and Insurrection: *Die Linkskurve* and its Heritage," *Central European History,* 1 (Nr. 1, March 1968): 35–55.
Arns, Günter, ed. "Erich Koch-Wesers Aufzeichnungen vom 13. Februar 1919," *Vierteljahrshefte für Zeitgeschichte,* 17 (Nr. 1, January 1969): 96–115.
Arns, Günter. "Friedrich Ebert als Reichspräsident," *Historische Zeitschrift.* Beiheft I: *Beiträge zur Geschichte der Weimarer Republik:* pp. 1–30. Munich: 1971.
———. "Die Linke in der SPD-Reichstagsfraktion im Herbst 1923," *Vierteljahrshefte für Zeitgeschichte,* 22 (Nr. 2, April 1974): 191–203.
Bahne, Siegfried. "Zwischen 'Luxemburgismus' und 'Stalinismus': Die 'ultralinke' Opposition in der KPD," *Vierteljahrshefte für Zeitgeschichte,* 9 (Nr. 4, October 1961): 359–83.
Becker, Josef. "Heinrich Brüning in den Krisenjahren der Weimarer Republik," *Geschichte in Wissenschaft und Unterricht,* 17 (Nr. 4, April 1966): 201–19.
———. "Joseph Wirth und die Krise des Zentrums während des IV. Kabinettes Marx (1927–1928)," *Zeitschrift für die Geschichte des Oberrheins,* 109 (Nr. 2, 1961): 362–482.
———. "Zur Politik der Wehrmachtsabteilung in der Regierungskrise 1926/27," *Vierteljahrshefte für Zeitgeschichte,* 14 (Nr. 1, January 1966), 69–78.
———. "Die deutsche Zentrumspartei, 1918–1933. Grundprobleme ihrer Entwicklung," *Aus Politik und Zeitgeschichte,* B11/68 (13 March 1968): 3–15.
Bendix, Reinhard. "Social Stratification and Political Power," *American Political Science Review,* 46 (Nr. 2, June 1952): 357–75.
Berndt, Roswitha. "Für und wider Preussen in der Weimarer Republik," *Wissenschaftliche Zeitschrift der Universität Halle-Wittenberg. Gesellschafts- und Sprachwissenschaftliche Reihe,* 25 (Nr. 1, 1976): 13–28.
———. "Rechtssozialdemokratische Koalitionspolitik in der Weimarer Republik," *Wissenschaftliche Zeitschrift der Universität Halle-Wittenberg. Gesellschafts- und Sprachwissenschaftliche Reihe,* 26 (Nr. 1, 1977): 43–52.
Besson, Waldemar. "Regierung und Opposition in der deutschen Politik," *Politische Vierteljahresschrift,* 3 (Nr. 3, September 1962): 225–41.
———. "Friedrich Meinecke und die Weimarer Republik," *Vierteljahrshefte für Zeitgeschichte,* 7 (Nr. 2, April 1959): 113–29.
———, ed. "Zur Frage der Staatsführung in der Weimarer Republik," *Vierteljahrshefte für Zeitgeschichte,* 7 (Nr. 1, January 1959): 85–111.
Biegert, Hans H. "Gewerkschaftspolitik in der Phase des Kapp-Lüttwitz-Putsches," in Hans Mommsen, et al., *Industrielles System und politische Entwicklung in der Weimarer Republik,* pp. 190–205. Düsseldorf: 1974.

Brozat, Martin, ed. "Die Anfänge der Berliner NSDAP 1926/27," *Vierteljahrshefte für Zeitgeschichte,* 8 (Nr. 1, January 1960): 85–118.

Buse, D. K. "Ebert and the German Crisis, 1917–1920," *Central European History,* 5 (Nr. 3, September 1972): 234–55.

Bussmann, Walter. "Politische Ideologien zwischen Monarchie und Weimarer Republik," *Historische Zeitschrift,* 190 (Nr. 1, 1960): 55–77.

Chanady, Attila. "Anton Erkelenz and Erich Koch-Weser," *Historical Studies: Australia and New Zealand,* 12 (Nr. 48, April 1967): 491–505.

————. "The Disintegration of the German National People's Party, 1924–1930," *Journal of Modern History,* 39 (Nr. 1, March 1967): 65–91.

————. "The Dissolution of the German Democratic Party in 1930," *American Historical Review,* 73 (Nr. 5, June 1968): 1433–53.

————. "Erich Koch-Weser and the Weimar Republic," *Canadian Journal of History,* 7 (Nr. 1, April 1972): 51–63.

Chickering, Roger Philip. "The Reichsbanner and the Weimar Republic, 1924–1926," *Journal of Modern History,* 40 (Nr. 4, December 1968): 524–34.

Conze, Werner. "Brünings Politik unter dem Druck der Grossen Krise," *Historische Zeitschrift,* 199 (Nr. 3, 1964): 529–50.

————. "Die Krise des Parteienstaates in Deutschland 1929/30," *Historische Zeitschrift,* 178 (1954): 47–83.

Craig, Gordon A. "Engagement and Neutrality in Weimar Germany," *Journal of Contemporary History,* 2 (Nr. 2, April 1967): 49–63.

Demeter, Karl. "Die Soziale Schichtung des deutschen Parlaments seit 1848, ein Spiegelbild der Strukturwandlung des Volkes," *Vierteljahrschrift für Sozial- und Wirtschaftsgeschichte,* 39 (Nr. 1, 1952): 1–29.

————. "Neues parteigeschichtliches Schrifttum," *Vierteljahrschrift für Sozial- und Wirtschaftsgeschichte,* 42 (Nr. 3, 1955): 246–54.

Diehl, Ernst. "Zum Kampf der KPD um die Einheitsfront der Arbeiterklasse," *Beiträge zur Geschichte der deutschen Arbeiterbewegung,* 7 (Nr. 1, 1965): 3–13.

Duverger, Maurice. "The Influence of the Electoral System on Political Life," *International Social Science Bulletin,* 3 (Nr. 2, Summer 1951): 314–52.

Ehni, Hans Peter. "Zum Parteienverhältnis in Preussen 1918–32. Ein Beitrag zur Funktion und Arbeitsweise der Weimarer Koalitionsparteien," *Archiv für Sozialgeschichte,* 11 (1971): 241–88.

"Einfluss der revolutionaren Arbeiterbewegung auf die deutsche Kunst in der Zeit von 1917–1933," *Wissenschaftliche Zeitschrift der Humboldt Universität zu Berlin. Gesellschafts- und Sprachwissenschaftliche Reihe,* 9 (Nr. 2, 1962): 157–231.

Epstein, Klaus. "The Zentrum Party in the Weimar Republic," *Journal of Modern History,* 39 (Nr. 2, June 1967): 160–63.

Erdmann, Karl Dietrich. "Die Geschichte der Weimarer Republik als Problem der Wissenschaft," *Vierteljahrshefte für Zeitgeschichte,* 3 (Nr. 1, January 1955): 1–19.

Ersil, Wilhelm & Ernst Laboor. "Die Parteidiskussion im September/Oktober 1925 und ihre Bedeutung für die marxistisch-leninistische Entwicklung der KPD," *Beiträge zur Geschichte der deutschen Arbeiterbewegung,* 8 (Nr. 4, 1966): 595–617.

Eschenburg, Theodor. "Franz von Papen," *Vierteljahrshefte für Zeitgeschichte,* 1 (Nr. 2, April 1953): 152–169.

Evans, Ellen L. "Adam Stegerwald and the Role of the Christian Trade Unions in the Weimar Republic," *Catholic Historical Review,* 59 (Nr. 4, Jan. 1974): 602–26.

————. "The Center Wages *Kulturpolitik:* Conflict in the Marx-Keudell Cabinet of 1927," *Central European History,* 2 (Nr. 2, June 1969): 139–58.

Facius, Friedrich. "Das Ende der kleinstaatlichen Monarchien Thüringens 1918: Ein Überblick," *Festschrift für Friedrich von Zahn.* Ed. by Walter Schlesinger. *Mitteldeutsche Forschungen,* Vol. 50/1: 50–64. Cologne: 1968.

Fieber, Hans-Joachim. "Die Bedeutung der Zentralausschusstagung der KPD vom 9. und 10. Mai 1925 für die Herausbildung einer marxistisch-leninistischen Führung," *Zeitschrift für Geschichtswissenschaft,* 15 (Nr. 7, 1967): 1212–26.

Frauendienst, Werner. "Demokratisierung des deutschen Konstitutionalismus in der Zeit Wilhelms II," *Zeitschrift für die gesamte Staatswissenschaft*, 113 (Nr. 4, 1957): 721–46.

Fritsch, Werner. "Die Massenbewegung der Werktätigen für die Enteignung der Fürsten 1925/26 in Thüringen," *Wissenschaftliche Zeitschrift der Friedrich-Schiller-Universität Jena. Gesellschafts- und Sprachwissenschaftliche Reihe*, 19 (Nr. 3, 1970): 375–93.

Friedlander, Henry Egon. "Conflict of Revolutionary Authority: Provisional Government vs. Berlin Soviet, November–December 1918," *International Review of Social History*, 7 (Nr. 2, 1962): 163–76.

Frye, Bruce B. "The German Democratic Party, 1918–1930," *Western Political Quarterly*, 16 (Nr. 1, March 1963): 167–79.

Gates, Robert A. "German Socialism and the Crisis of 1929–33," *Central European History*, 7 (Nr. 4, Dec. 1974): 332–59.

Glees, Anthony. "Albert C. Grzesinski and the Politics of Prussia, 1926–1930," *English Historical Review*, 89 (Nr. 353, Oct. 1974): 814–34.

Gollwitzer, Heinz. "Bayern 1918–1933." *Vierteljahrshefte für Zeitgeschichte*, 3 (Nr. 4 October 1955): 363–87.

Goriely, Georges. "Von der SPD oder: Masse und Ohnmacht," *Frankfurter Hefte*, 16 (April & May 1961): 225–34, 307–16.

Gottward, Herbert. "Franz von Papen und die 'Germania.' Ein Beitrag zur Geschichte des politischen Katholizismus und der Zentrumspresse in der Weimarer Republik," *Jahrbuch für Geschichte*, 6 (1972): 539–604.

Grebing, Helga. "Die Konservativen von 1848–1918," *Politische Studien*, 9 (June 1958): 403–12.

———. "Die Konservativen und Christlichen seit 1918," *Politische Studien*, 9 (July 1958): 482–91.

Greipl, Egon. "Von der Volksbetätigung zur Volksentscheidung. Direkte Demokratie in den Entwürfen zur Bamberger Verfassung," *Historisches Jahrbuch*, 93 (Nr. 2, 1973): 380–84.

Griewank, Karl. "Dr. Wirth und die Krisen der Weimarer Republik," *Wissenschaftliche Zeitschrift der Friedrich-Schiller-Universität Jena. Gesellschafts- und Sprachwissenschaftliche Reihe*, 1 (Nr. 1, 1951/52): 1–10.

Gross, Babette L. "The German Communists' United Front and Popular Front Ventures," in Milorad M. Drachkovitch & Branko Lazitch, eds. *The Comintern; Historical Highlights*, pp. 111–38. New York: 1966.

Gruber, Helmut. "Willi Münzenberg's German Communist Propaganda Empire, 1921–1933," *Journal of Modern History*, 38 (Nr. 3, September 1966): 278–97.

———. "Grundriss der Geschichte der deutschen Arbeiterbewegung," *Zeitschrift für Geschichtswissenschaft*, 10 (Nr. 6, 1962): 1338–1514.

Habedank, Heinz. "Die Aktionseinheit der Arbeiterparteien gegen die Fürstenabfindung 1926 und die freie Gewerkschaften," *Die Arbeit. Theoretische Zeitschrift des FDGB* (Nr. 10, 1966): 50–53.

Hartung, Fritz. "Studien zur Geschichte der Preussischen Verwaltung. Dritter Teil: Zur Geschichte des Beamtentums im 19. und 20. Jahrhundert," *Abhandlungen der Deutschen Akademie der Wissenschaften in Berlin. Philosophisch-historische Klasse.* Jahrgang 1945/46, Nr. 8.

Haungs, Peter. "Die Zentrumspartei in der Weimarer Republik," *Civitas: Jahrbuch für Christliche Gesellschaftsordnung*, 6 (1967): 252–85.

Hess, J. C. "Gab es eine Alternative? Zum Scheitern des Linksliberalismus in der Weimarer Republik," *Historische Zeitschrift*, 223 (Nr. 3, Dec. 1976): 638–54.

Hertzman, Lewis. "Conservative Nationalists under the Weimar Regime," *The Wiener Library Bulletin*, 14 (Nr. 3, 1960): 50–51.

———. "Gustav Stresemann: The Problem of Political Leadership in the Weimar Republic," *International Review of Social History*, 5 (Nr. 3, 1960): 361–77.

Hiller von Gaertringen, Friedrich Freiherr. "Zur Beurteilung des 'Monarchismus' in der Weimarer Republik," in *Tradition und Reform in der deutschen Politik. Gedenkschrift für Waldemar Besson*, pp. 138–86. Ed. by Gotthard Jasper. Frankfurt a. M.: 1976.

Holborn, Hajo. "Prussia and the Weimar Republic," *Social Research*, 23 (Nr. 3, Autumn 1956): 331–42.

Holl, Karl. "Konfessionalität, Konfessionalismus und demokratische Republik. Zu einigen Aspekten der Reichspräsidentenwahl von 1925," *Vierteljahrshefte für Zeitgeschichte*, 17 (Nr. 3, July 1969): 254–75.

Hunt, James C. "The Bourgeois Middle in German Politics, 1871–1933: Recent Literature," *Central European History*, 11 (Nr. 1, March 1978): 83–106.

Hunt, Richard. N. "Friedrich Ebert and the German Revolution of 1918," in Leonard Kreiger and Fritz Stern, eds. *The Responsibility of Power: Historical Essays in Honor of Hajo Holborn*, pp. 315–34. Garden City: 1967.

————. "Myths, Guilt and Shame in pre-Nazi Germany," *Virginia Quarterly Review*, 34 (Nr. 3, Summer 1958): 355–71.

Jones, Larry Eugene. " 'The Dying Middle': Weimar Germany and the Fragmentation of Bourgeois Politics," *Central European History*, 5 (Nr. 1, March 1972): 23–54.

————. "Gustav Stresemann and the Crisis of German Liberalism," *European Studies Review*, 4 (Nr. 2, April 1974): 141–63.

————. "Inflation, Revaluation and the Crisis of Middle-Class Politics. A Study of the Dissolution of the German Party System, 1923–28," *Central European History*, 12 (Nr. 2, June 1979): 143–68.

Kasper, Martin. "Oberlausitzer werktätige Bauern im Kampf gegen Fürstenabfindung, für den Reichskongress der Werktätigen," *Wissenschaftliche Zeitschrift der Universität Rostock. Gesellschafts- und Sprachwissenschaftliche Reihe*, 17 (Nr. 2/3, 1968): 173–80.

Kirchheimer, Otto. "The Waning of Opposition in Parliamentary Regimes," *Social Research*, 24 (Nr. 2, Summer 1957): 127–56.

Knapp, Thomas. "The Red and the Black: Catholic Socialists in the Weimar Republic," *Catholic Historical Review*, 61 (Nr. 3, July 1975): 386–408.

Knoch, Gerhard. "Der Kampf der Magdeburger Bezirksorganisation der KPD gegen die Fürstenabfindung 1926," *Wissenschaftliche Zeitschrift der Technischen Hochschule Magdeburg*, 10 (Nr. 4, 1966): 417–24.

Kölling, Mirjam. "Der Kampf der Kommunistischen Partei Deutschlands unter der Führung Ernst Thälmanns für die Einheitsfront in den ersten Jahren der relativen Stabilisierung (1924 bis 1927)," *Zeitschrift für Geschichtswissenschaft*, 2 (Nr. 1, 1954): 3–36.

Könnemann, Erwin. "Die Verhinderung der entschädigungslosen Enteignung der Fürsten 1925/26," *Wissenschaftliche Zeitschrift der Martin-Luther-Universität Halle-Wittenberg. Gesellschafts- und Sprachwissenschaftliche Reihe*, 7 (Nr. 3, 1957/58): 541–60.

Kollman, Eric C. "Reinterpreting Modern German History: The Weimar Republic," *Journal of Central European Affairs*, 21 (Nr. 4, Jan. 1962): 434–51.

Kotowski, Georg. "Parlamentarismus und Demokratie im Urteil Friedrich Meineckes," in *Zur Geschichte und Problematik der Demokratie. Festgabe für Hans Herzfeld*, pp. 187–203. Berlin: 1958.

Kunze, Bärbel, "Erich Matthias' Apologie der SPD-Entwicklung. Zur Historiographie über die Sozialdemokratie am Ende der Weimarer Republik," *Das Argument*, Nr. 63 (March 1971): 54–78.

Matthias, Erich. "German Social Democracy in the Weimar Republic," in Anthony Nicholls and Erich Matthias, eds. *German Democracy and the Triumph of Hitler*, pp. 47–57. New York: 1971.

————. "Der sozialistische Einfluss in der Weimarer Republik," *Politische Parteien in*

348   CRISIS OF THE WEIMAR REPUBLIC

Deutschland und Frankreich, 1918–1939, pp. 116–27. Ed. by Oswald Hauser. Wiesbaden: 1969.

Miller, Susanne. "Die Sozialdemokratie in der Spannung zwischen Oppositionstradition und Regierungsverantwortung in den Anfängen der Weimarer Republik," *Sozialdemokratie zwischen Klassenbewegung und Volkspartei,* pp. 84–97. Ed. by Hans Mommsen. Frankfurt a. M.: 1974.

———. "Die Entscheidung für das parlamentarische Demokratie," in *Fünfzig Jahre deutsche Republik. Entstehung—Scheitern—Neubeginn,* pp. 60–81. Ed. by F. A. Krummacher. Frankfurt a. M.: 1969.

Mommsen, Hans. "Die Sozialdemokratie in der Defensive. Der Immobilismus der SPD und der Aufstieg des Nationalsozialismus," *Sozialdemokratie zwischen Klassenbewegung und Volkspartei,* pp. 106–33. Ed. by Hans Mommsen. Frankfurt a. M.: 1974.

Mommsen, Wolfgang J. "Die deutsche Revolution, 1918–1920. Politische Revolution und soziale Protestbewegung," *Geschichte und Gesellschaft,* 4 (Nr. 3, 1978): 362–91.

Nettl, Peter. "The German Social Democratic Party, 1890–1914, as a Political Model," *Past and Present,* Nr. 30 (April, 1965): 65–95.

Neumann, Sigmund. "Political Parties, Germany," *Encyclopedia of the Social Sciences,* 11: 615–19. New York: 1933.

Niemann, Heinz. "Das Görlitzer Programm der SPD von 1921," *Zeitschrift für Geschichtswissenschaft,* 23 (Nr. 8, 1975): 908–19.

———. "Das Heidelberger Programm der SPD von 1925," *Zeitschrift für Geschichtswissenschaft,* 24 (Nr. 7, 1976): 786–94.

Nipperdey, Thomas. "Interessenverbände und Parteien in Deutschland vor dem Ersten Weltkrieg," *Politische Vierteljahresschrift,* 2 (Nr. 3, September 1961): 262–80.

———. "Die Organisation der bürgerlichen Parteien in Deutschland vor 1918," *Historische Zeitschrift,* 185 (June 1958): 550–602.

Noakes, Jeremy. "Conflict and Development in the NSDAP, 1924–1927," *Journal of Contemporary History,* 1 (Nr. 4, October 1966): 3–36.

Orlow, Dietrich. "The Conversion of Myths into Political Power: The Case of the Nazi Party, 1925–1926," *American Historical Review,* 72 (Nr. 3, April 1967): 906–24.

Pahl, Walther. "Gewerkschaften und Sozialdemokratie vor 1933," *Gewerkschaftliche Monatshefte,* 4 (December 1953): 720–24.

Phelps, Reginald H. "Aus den Seeckt-Dokumenten: I. Die Verabschiedung Seeckts 1926," *Deutsche Rundschau,* 78 (Nr. 9, September 1952): 881–92.

———. "Aus den Seeckt-Documenten. II: Seeckt und die Innenpolitik," *Deutsche Rundschau,* 78 (Nr. 10, October 1962): 1013–23.

Pies, Eberhard. "Sozialpolitik und Zentrum, 1924–1928. Zu den Bedingungen sozialpolitischer Theorie und Praxis der Deutschen Zentrumspartei in der Weimarer Republik," in *Industrielles System und politische Entwicklung in der Weimarer Republik,* pp. 259–70. Ed. by Hans Mommsen, Dietmar Petzina and Bernd Weisbrod. Düsseldorf: 1974.

Pikart, Eberhard. "Die Rolle der Parteien im deutschen konstitutionellen System vor 1914," *Zeitschrift für Politik,* 9, n.s. (Nr. 1, March 1962): 12–32.

Portner, Ernst. "Der Ansatz zur demokratischen Massenpartei im deutschen Linksliberalismus," *Vierteljahrshefte für Zeitgeschichte,* 13 (Nr. 2, April 1965): 150–61.

———. "Koch-Wesers Verfassungsentwurf," *Vierteljahrshefte für Zeitgeschichte,* 14 (Nr. 3, July 1966): 280–98.

Renzsch, Wolfgang. "Die 'direkte Gesetzgebung durch das Volk' im Eisenacher Programm," *Internationale Wissenschaftliche Korrespondenz zur Geschichte der deutschen Arbeiterbewegung,* 13 (Nr. 2, June 1977): 172–76.

Ritter, Gerhard. "Allgemeiner Charakter und geschichtliche Grundlagen des politischen Parteiwesens in Deutschland," in *Lebendige Vergangenheit*, pp. 55–83. Munich: 1958.

Ritter, Gerhard A. "Entwicklungsprobleme des deutschen Parlamentarismus," in *Gesellschaft, Parlament, und Regierung*, pp. 11–54. Ed. by Gerhard A. Ritter. Düsseldorf: 1974.

———. "Kontinuität und Umformung des deutschen Parteiensystems, 1918–1920," in *Entstehung und Wandel der modernen Gesellschaft. Festschrift für Hans Rosenberg zum 65. Geburtstag*, Ed. by Gerhard A. Ritter. Pp. 342–57. Berlin: 1970.

Rürup, Reinhard. "Entwurf einer demokratischen Republik? Entstehung und Grundlagen der Weimarer Verfassung," in *Fünfzig Jahre deutsche Republik. Entstehung—Scheitern—Neubeginn*, pp. 82–112. Ed. by F. A. Krummacher. Frankfurt a. M.: 1969.

Ruge, Wolfgang. "Arbeiten zur Rolle der Bourgeoisie in der Weimarer Republik," *Zeitschrift für Geschichtswissenschaft*. Sonderheft, 8 (1960): 344–57.

Schaefer, Friedrich. "Zur Frage des Wahlrechts in der Weimarer Republik," in *Staat, Wirtschaft und Politik in der Weimarer Republik. Festschrift für Heinrich Brüning*, pp. 119–40. Ed. by Ferdinand A. Hermens and Theodor Schieder. Berlin: 1967.

Schulze, Hagen. "Stabilität und Instabilität in der politischen Ordnung von Weimar," *Vierteljahrshefte für Zeitgeschichte*, 26 (Nr. 3, July 1978): 419–32.

Schwering, Leo. "Stegerwalds und Brünings Vorstellungen über Parteireform und Parteiensystem," in *Staat, Wirtschaft und Politik in der Weimarer Republik. Festschrift für Heinrich Brüning*, pp. 23–40. Ed. by Ferdinand A. Hermens and Theodor Schieder. Berlin: 1967.

Sheehan, James J. "Political Leadership in the German Reichstag, 1871–1918," *American Historical Review*, 74 (Nr. 2, December 1968): 511–28.

Sontheimer, Kurt. "Antidemokratisches Denken in der Weimarer Republik," *Vierteljahrshefte für Zeitgeschichte*, 5 (Nr. 1, January 1957): 42–62.

Southern, David B. "The Revaluation Question in the Weimar Republic," *Journal of Modern History*. On-Demand Supplement, 51 (Nr. 1, March 1979): D1029–53.

Stern, Fritz, "Adenauer and a Crisis in Weimar Democracy," *Political Science Quarterly*, 73 (Nr. 1, March 1958): 1–27.

Stehkämper, Hugo. "Konrad Adenauer und das Reichskanzleramt während der Weimarer Zeit," in *Konrad Adenauer. Oberbürgermeister von Köln. Festgabe der Stadt Köln zum 100. Geburtstag ihres Ehrenbürgers am 5. Januar 1976*, pp. 405–31. Ed. by Hugo Stehkämper. Cologne: 1976.

Stürmer, Michael. "Parliamentary Government in Weimar Germany, 1924–1928," in *German Democracy and the Triumph of Hitler*, pp. 59–77. Ed. by Anthony Nicholls and Erich Matthias. New York: 1971.

———. "Der unvollendete Parteienstaat—Zur Vorgeschichte des Präsidialregimes am Ende der Weimarer Republik," *Vierteljahrshefte für Zeitgeschichte*, 21 (Nr. 2, April 1973): 119–26.

Thimme, Anneliese. "Gustav Stresemann, Legende und Wirklichkeit," *Historische Zeitschrift*, 181 (Nr. 2, April 1956): 287–338.

Töpner, Kurt. "Der deutsche Katholizismus zwischen 1918 und 1933," in *Zeitgeist im Wandel*, 2: 176–202. Ed. by Hans Joachim Schoeps. 2 vols. Stuttgart: 1968.

Treviranus, Gottfried R. "Kuno Graf Westarp, 1864–1945," *Deutsche Rundschau*, 81 (Nr. 12, December 1955): 1263–65.

Turner, Henry Ashby Jr. "Hitler's Secret Pamphlet for Industrialists 1927," *Journal of Modern History*, 40 (Nr. 3, September 1968): 348–74.

Vierhaus, Rudolf. "Die politische Mitte in der Weimarer Republik," *Geschichte in Wissenschaft und Unterricht*, 15 (Nr. 3, March 1964): 133–49.

Wagner, Walter. "Der Feind von rechts. Politische Justiz in der Weimarer Republik," *Die Politische Meinung*, 6 (Nr. 58: March 1961): 50–63.

————. "Der Feind von links. Politische Justiz in der Weimarer Republik II," *Die Politische Meinung*, 6 (Nr. 60, May 1961): 48–61.

Weber, Hermann. "Zu den Beziehungen zwischen der KPD und der Kommunistischen Internationale," *Vierteljahrshefte für Zeitgeschichte*, 16 (Nr. 2, April 1968): 177–208.

Zeender, John K. "German Catholics and the Concept of an Interconfessional Party: 1900–1922," *Journal of Central European Affairs*, 23 (Nr. 4, January 1964): 424–39.

————. "The German Catholics and the Presidential Election of 1925," *Journal of Modern History*, 35 (Nr. 4, December 1963): 366–81.

INDEX

Grossmann, Dr., 175, n.151, 177, 178, n.166, 252, n.173
Grosz, George, 263, n.233, 266
Grundel, Hans, 250, n.163
Guérard, Theodor von, 235, 237, n.110

Haas, Ludwig, 234, n.90, 253, n.181
Haase, Hugo, 25
Haenisch, Conrad, 43
Hamm, Eduard, 254, n.186
Hampe, August, 152, n.29, 158, n.58
Haniel von Haimhausen, Edgar Karl Alfons, 182, 185, n.206, 276, n.8
Hanover, kingdom of, 30
Heilmann, Ernst, 132, 136, n.196, 306, n.120, n.122
Heine, Wolfgang, 44
Heinze, Rudolf, 170, n.127
Held, Heinrich, 118, n.108, 181, n.182
Heller, Vitus, 250, n.161
Hellpach, Willy, 118, n.108
Hermann, Erich, 175, n.151, 252, n.173
Herzog, Wilhelm, 262, n.233
Hesse: electorate of, 30; state of, 99, n.12, 154
Heuss, Theodor, 90, n.188, 116, n.97
Hildebrandt, 309, n.137, 310
Hildenbrand, Karl, 131, n.170
Hilferding, Rudolf, 107, n.53, 111, n.69, 129, n.160; on acceptance of governmental responsibility, 99, 114, 126
Hiller, Kurt, 263, n.233
Hindenburg, Paul von, 80, n.160, 85, n.168, 183, 256, n.197, 265, n.240, 285, 305, n.111; cabinet crisis and, 86, n.173, 130, n.167, 232–33, 297–98; and Compromise Bill, 244, 295; election of, 4, 118–19, 198, 239, 252, n.174, 273, 278, n.12, 318; and Flag Decree, 227–29; and Hohenzollern settlement, 302; and von Loebell letter, 237, n.110, 244–46; on Polish property rights, 245; referendum opposed by, 145, 243–46
Hirsch, Paul, 43
Hitler, Adolf, 178–80
Hoepker-Aschoff, Hermann, 48–49, 51, n.8, 251, 270; on Compromise Bill, 219–20, 223; on Hohenzollern settlement, 303, n.103, 304
Hörsing, Otto, 255
Hoffmann, Adolf, 41, 45, n.96, 131, n.171, 203, 310
Hoffmann, Johannes, 181
Hofkammer, 33, 46

Hofkammervereinigung, 161–62, 239, 270, n.261
Hohenzollern family, 12, 29–33, 36, n.57, 38–49, 62, 162, 180, n.180, 220, 244, 301–04, 308–09, 311; August Wilhelm, prince, 244, n.132; Friedrich Leopold, prince, 47, 304, n.107; Frederick William I, king, 32; Wilhelm crown prince, 47–48, 155, n.41, 221, n.11, 244; William I, king and emperor, 30, 271, n.268, William II, king and emperor, 22, 39–40, 45–46, 47, n.105, 88; criticism of, 39, 267–68, 270, n.263, 271, n.268; referendum condemned by, 244, n.132, 284, n.19
Hohn, Dr., 214, n.146, 216, n.157
Hugenberg, Alfred, 85, n.168, 244, n.132
Hunt, Richard N., 102, n.28, 107, n.51, 109–110

Imbusch, Heinrich, 207–208
Independent Social Democratic Party (USPD), 103, 107, 206; former members of, 110–11; and Hohenzollern properties, 41, 45; in 1918–19, 25–27, 135
Inflation, victims of, 36–37, 39, n.67, 55, 57–58, 62, 88, 172, 182, 189, 249, n.159, 251, 264–66, 269, n.258
Initiative and referendum: proposals for, 57–59; theory and practice of, x-xii, 15–17, 120, 141–46, 291, 328–30; battle cruiser "A" campaign, 61, 330; *Fürstenenteignung* campaign, 8, 10–13, 20–21, 55–63, 88–94, 131–141, 143–50, 162–68, 171–86, 187, 189–92, 213, 225–26, 234–91, 310–13, 317–30; results of initiative, 183–86; results of referendum, 273–84, 287–90; text of proposed law, 94, n.207

Jacobsohn, Siegfried, 263, n.233
Jarres, Karl, 118, n.108, 119, 240, n.120
Jellinek, Walter, 22, 321, n.158
Jendrosch, 308
Joel, Curt, 157, n.53, 167, n.108
Joos, Joseph, 18, n.47, 110, 194, n.29; and Joseph Wirth, 207, 211, n.132, 213; on results of referendum, 286
Junck, Johannes, 254, n.185
Jungdeutschen Orden, 239, n.116

Kaas, Ludwig, 202, 323
Kahl, Wilhelm, 152, n.29, 153, n.32, 167, n.108, 220, n.7, 268–69; on

358   CRISIS OF THE WEIMAR REPUBLIC

Regensburg, Bishop Antonius of, 190, n.16
Reichert, Jacob, 85, n.168
Reichsarbeitsgemeinschaft der Aufwertungs- geschädigten und Mieterorganisation, 265, n.241
Reichsbanner Schwarz-Rot-Gold, 122, n.124, 132, 171, n.131, 199, 227, 319; Catholics and, 199, 208, 213, 255–56; and referendum campaign, 56, n.35, 88, 254–56
Reichsblock, 239, 241, 246, n.147
Reichsrat, 227
Reichstag, debates in: 52–56, 230–31, 234–37, 246, 298; Legal Committee (*Rechtsausschuss*), 12, 55, 190, n.15, 219, 235, n.91; Compromise Bill considered by, 157–61, 166–71, 219, 221–24, 292–94; preliminary hearings held by, 153–56
Republic, support for: 1–3, 6–7, 227, 255–56, 321–22, 329–30; in Center Party, 199–200, 206, 208–10, 213–14, 321; initiative and referendum campaign tied to, 11, 13, 235, n.96, 255, 268, 284, n.19, 329–30; by SPD, 87, n.177, 108, 110, n.67, 113–14, 119–20, 231, 314–17
Republikanischer Anwaltsbund, 179, n.179
Republikanischer Reichsbund, 179, n.179
Reuss, 27
Revolution of 1918–19, 9, 22–28, 39–42, 103, 115, n.93, 181, 237, n.104, 317, n.156
Rhein-Mainische Volkszeitung, 207, n.109, 248, 249, n.157, 299
Richter, Ernst von, 46–48
Richthoven, Hartmann Freiherr von, 24, n.10, 147, n.19, 152, n.29, 234, n.90; on Compromise Bill, 39, n.68, 161, n.71, 168, n.113, 177, n.163; on DDP Bill, 51, n.7
Rönneburg, Heinrich, 236, n.98
Rohr, Hans-Joachim von, 270
Rohrbach, Paul, 254
Rosenberg, Arthur, 13, 71, n.114
Rosenfeld, Kurt, 37, n.61, 155, n.41, 165, n.98, 264, n.235, 267; on Compromise Bill, 166, n.101, 296; confiscation urged by, 25, 41; on initiative and referendum campaign, 166, n.101, 310–11; and left socialists, 108, 131, 296, 298, n.77, 309, n.137, 310–11
Roser, 215, n.155
Rote Fahne, 62–63, 79, 88, 183–84, 261, 296, n.62, 309, n.137; on KPD's role

in initiative and referendum campaign, 56, n.34, 60, 94, 164, 257–58, 260, n.218; SPD leaders criticized by, 165, 260, 285, n.23; Ultra-left criticized by, 74–75, 326
Rottenberg, bishop of, 190, n.16
Ruling families, former: legal rights and claims of, 20, 23–24, 28–33, 35–38, 175, n.151, 269–72; property settlements with, 9, 12, 22, n.2, 24, 28–29, 33–34, 49, 88, 154, 171–72, 179, n.173; *See also* Hohenzollern family

Saenger, Alwin, 24
Saxe-Coburg-Gotha. Duke Carl Eduard, 27–28, 35, 179, n.173; state of, 27–28
Saxe-Meiningen. Duke Bernhard, 36, n.57, 270, n.263
Saxony, state of, 34, 70, 104, 154, n.36, 185
Schacht, Hjalmar, 253–54
Schack, Graf, 144, n.12
Schaeffer, Hans, 37, n.61
Scheidemann, Philipp, 30, n.33, 37, 111, 120, 130, n.165, 271, 285, n.23; confiscation rejected by, 54; on initiative and referendum, 55, 235, n.96; on KPD, 129, n.160; on political responsibility, 112, n.77, 114, 125, n.140; cabinet, 42, n.82
Schiele, Martin, 5, n.13
Schiffers, Reinhard, xii, 329, n.173
Schlageter, Albert Leo, 65
Schleicher (trade unionist), 58, n.45
Schlesischer Bauernbund, 246, n.145
Schlieben, Hans von, 5, n.13
Schliepmann, 254, n.185
Schmalkaldic Forest, 30
Schmal, Ludwig, 175, n.151
Schmidt, Robert, 98, n.11
Schmitt, Carl, 108, n.56
Schneider, Gustav, 236, n.98
Schneller, Ernst, 55, 90, n.191
Schönborn, Richard, 190
Schönlank, Bruno, 263, n.233
Schofer, Josef, 207
Scholz, Ernst, 168, 240, n.122
Scholz, Robert, 249, n.159
Schreiber, Christian, bishop of Meissen, 190, n.16
Schüren, Ulrich, x–xiii, 329, n.173
Schulte, Karl Anton, 248, n.153, 313, n.150; and Compromise Bill, 151, n.27, 152, n.29, 153, n.32, 158, n.60,